Fully Updated as per
Latest NCERT Textbook

AF673495

NCERT SOLUTIONS

with Chapterwise **Study Notes**

MATHEMATICS 11th

Author

Vineet Kumar
Hewanti Kushwaha

arihant
SUCCESS AND NOTHING LESS

ARIHANT PRAKASHAN (Series), MEERUT

Administrative & Production Offices

Regd. Office

'Ramchhaya' 4577/15, Agarwal Road, Darya Ganj, New Delhi -110002
Tele: 011- 47630600, 43518550

Head Office

Kalindi, TP Nagar, Meerut (UP) - 250002
Tel: 0121-7156203, 7156204

Sales & Support Offices

Agra, Ahmedabad, Bengaluru, Bareilly, Chennai, Delhi, Guwahati, Hyderabad, Jaipur, Jhansi, Kolkata, Lucknow, Nagpur & Pune.

PRICE ₹375.00

PO No. : TXT-59-T070852-5-26

Published by Arihant Publications (India) Ltd.

For further information about the books published by Arihant, log on to www.arihantbooks.com or e-mail at info@arihantbooks.com

Follow us on

Preface

Feeling the immense importance and value of NCERT books, we are presenting this book, having the **NCERT Exercises Solutions**. For the overall benefit of the students we have made this book unique in such a way that it presents not only solutions but also detailed explanations. Through these detailed and through explanations, students can learn the concepts which will enhance their thinking and learning abilities.

We have introduced some Additional Features with the solutions which are given below:

- **Explanatory Solutions** Along with the solutions to questions we have given all the points that tell how to approach to solve a problem. Here we have tried to cover all those loopholes which may lead to confusion. All formulae and hints are discussed in full detail.
- Also included **Thinking Process** and **Mistake Alert** to understanding 'How to solve question' and points of mistakes.
- **Note** We have provided notes also to solutions in which special points are mentioned which are of great value for the students.

Apart from all those who helped in the compilation of this book a special note of thanks to all. With the hope that this book will be of great help to the students, we wish great success to our readers.

Vineet Kumar
Hewanti Kushwaha

Contents

Sets

CHAPTER 01

Important Points

01 Set A set is a well defined collection of objects (Like : Numbers, Persons, Rivers etc.). It is denoted by capital letters of English alphabets and the elements of a set are represented by small letters of English alphabets

Representations of sets

- **Roster form or Tabular form or Listing form** — In the roster form, all the elements of a set are listed, the elements are being separated by comma and are enclosed within brackets {} *e.g.*, The set of all even positive integers less than 7 in roster form as {2, 4, 6}.
- **Set-builder form or Rule method** — In set-builder form, all the elements of a set possess a single common property which is not possessed by any element outside the set, *e.g.*, $\{a, e, i, o, u\}$. If we denote this set by V, then $V = \{x : x \text{ is a vowel of English alphabet}\}$.

02 The empty set A set which does not contain any element is called the empty set or null set or the void set. The empty set is denoted by the symbol ϕ or {}.

03 Finite and infinite sets A set which consists of a definite number of elements is called finite, otherwise, the set is called infinite.

04 Equal sets Two sets A and B are said to be equal, if they have exactly the same elements and we write $A = B$. Otherwise, the sets are said to be unequal and we write $A \neq B$.

05 **Subsets** A set A is said to be a subset of set B, if every element of A is also an element of B. In other words, $A \subseteq B$ if whenever $a \in A$, then $a \in B$.

Note • The empty is a subset of each set.
• Each set is a subset of itself.

06 If $A' \subseteq B$ and $A \neq B$, then A is called a proper subset of B, written as $A \subset B$ and B is called super set of A.

07 **Subsets of set of real Numbers**

We known that every real number is either a rational or an irrational number and the set of real number is denoted by R.

There are many important subsets of R, N, Z, Q and T are the subsets of real numbers denoting the set of natural numbers, integers, rational numbers and irrational numbers respectively.

08 Intervals as subsets of R

(i) Open interval : $(a,b) = \{x : a < x < b\}$

(ii) Semi-open interval : $(a,b] = \{x : a < x \leq b\}$

(iii) Closed interval : $[a,b] = \{x : a \leq x \leq b\}$

(iv) Semi-closed interval : $[a, b) = \{x : a \leq x < b\}$
where $x \in R$.

09 **Universal set** A set that contains all sets in a given context, is called the universal set. It is usually denoted by U.

10 **Venn diagrams** Most of the relationship between two or more sets can be represented by means of diagrams which are known as Venn diagrams. In Venn diagram, the elements of the sets are written in their respective circles.

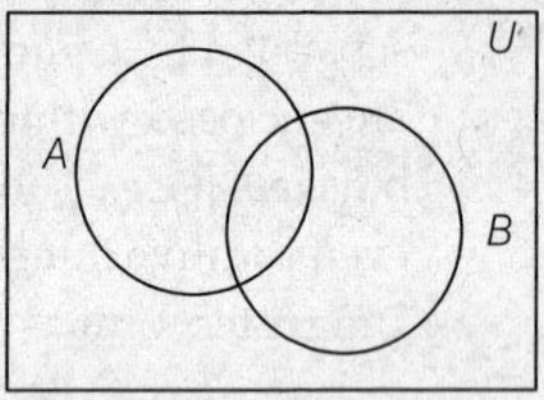

11 **Operations on Sets**

(i) **Union of sets** The union of two sets A and B is the set, which consists of all those elements which are either in A or in B or in both. In symbols, we write $A \cup B = \{x : x \in A \text{ or } x \in B\}$

Properties

(a) $A \cup B = B \cup A$ (Commutative law)

(b) $(A \cup B) \cup C = A \cup (B \cup C)$ (Associative law)

(c) $A \cup \phi = A$ (law of indentity element ϕ is the identity of U)

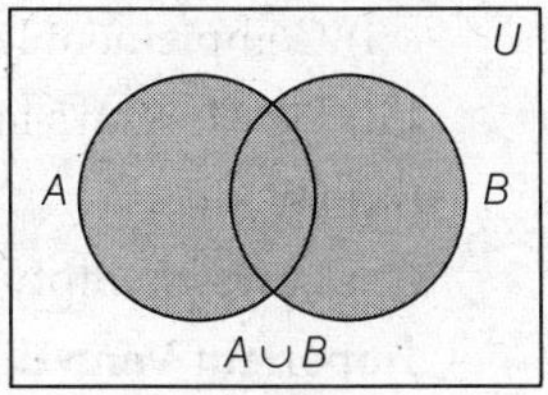

(d) $A \cup A = A$ (Idempotent law)

(e) $U \cup A = U$ (Law of union)

(ii) **Intersection of sets** The intersection of sets A and B is a set of all those elements which are common to both A and B.

In symbols, we write $A \cap B = \{x : x \in A \text{ and } x \in B\}$

Properties

(a) $A \cap B = B \cap A$ (Commutative law)

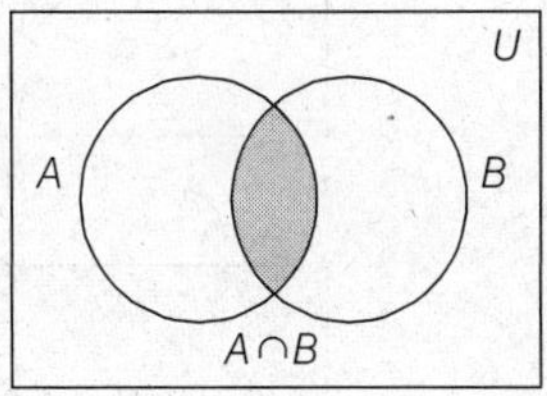

(b) $(A \cap B) \cap C = A \cap (B \cap C)$ (Associative law)

(c) $\phi \cap A = \phi, U \cap A = A$ (Law of ϕ and U)

(d) $A \cap A = A$ (Idempotent law)

(e) $A \cap (B \cup C) = (A \cap B) \cup (A \cap C)$ (Distributive law)

(iii) **Disjoint sets** Two sets A and B are called disjoint sets, if they have no common element *i.e.*, $A \cap B = \phi$

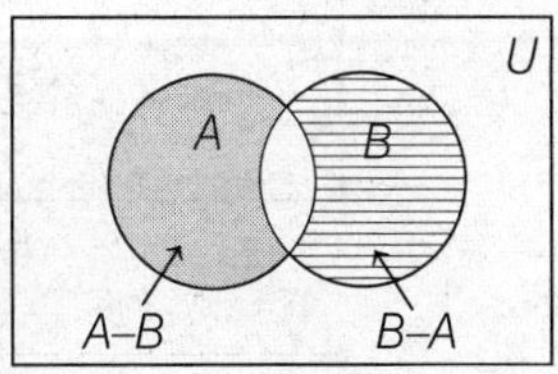

(iv) **Difference of set** The difference of the sets A and B in this order is the set of those elements which belong to A but not be B.

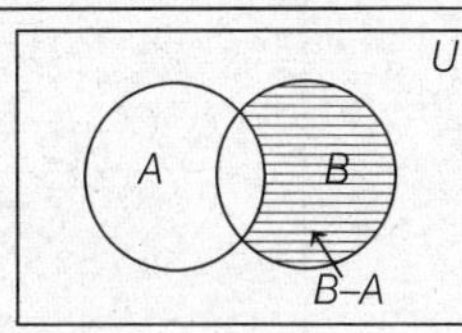

In symbols, we write

$$A - B = \{x : x \in A \text{ and } x \in B\}$$

$$B - A = \{x : x \in B \text{ and } x \in A\}$$

12 **Complement of a set** Let U be the universal set and A is a subset of U then, the complement of A is the set of all elements of U which are not the elements of A. It is represented by $\overline{A}$ or A'.

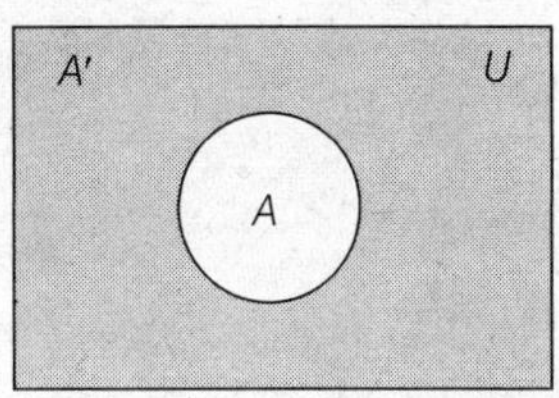

Hence, $A' = \{x : x \in U \text{ and } x \notin A\}$
$= U - A$

Properties

(i) Complement laws $A \cup A' = U$ and $A \cap A' = \phi$

(ii) De-Morgan's law $(A \cup B)' = A' \cap B'$ and $(A \cap B)' = A' \cup B'$

(iii) $(A')' = A$

(iv) Laws of empty set universal set $\phi' = U$ and $U' = \phi$

Important Venn diagrams

(1) 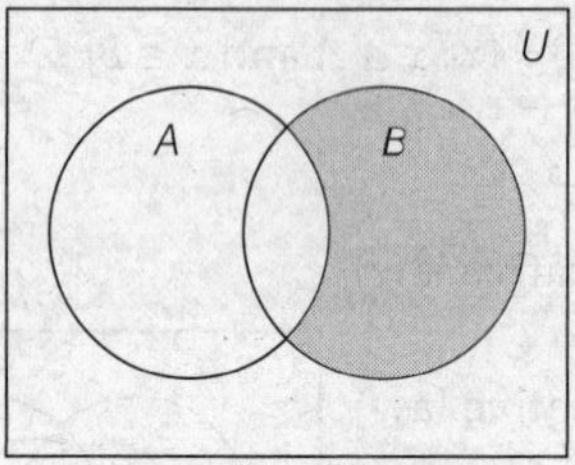

$(A' \cap B)$

(2) 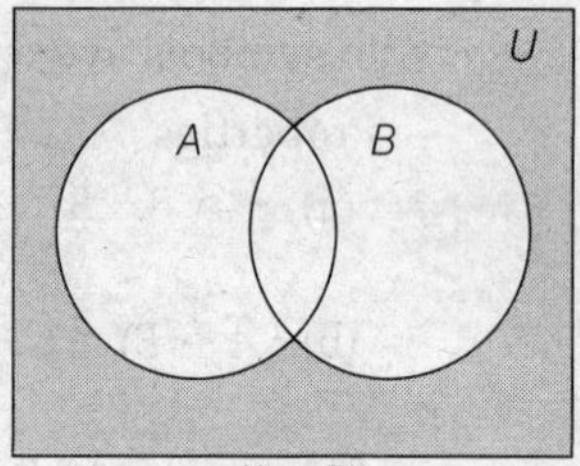

$(A \cup B)'$

(3) 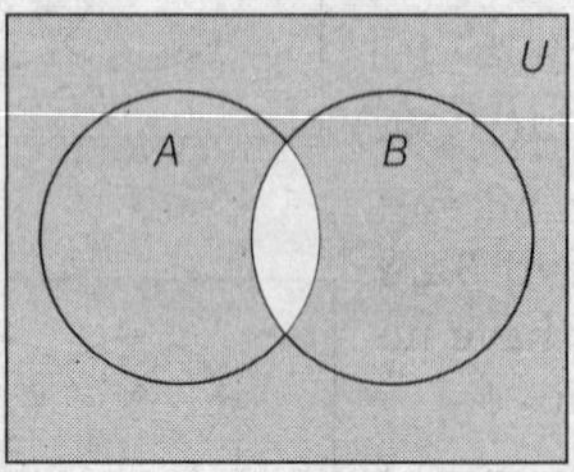

$(A \cap B)'$

(4) 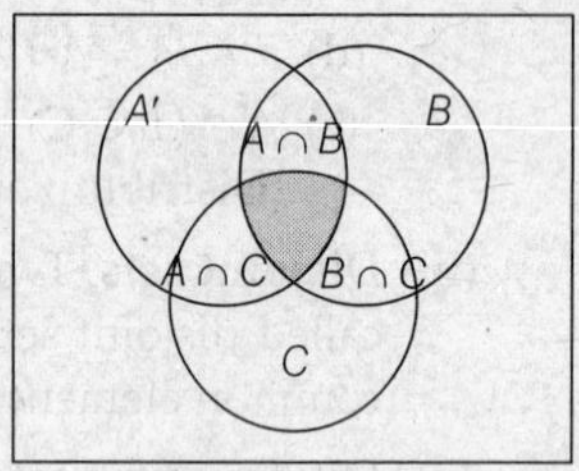

$A \cap B \cap C$

(5) 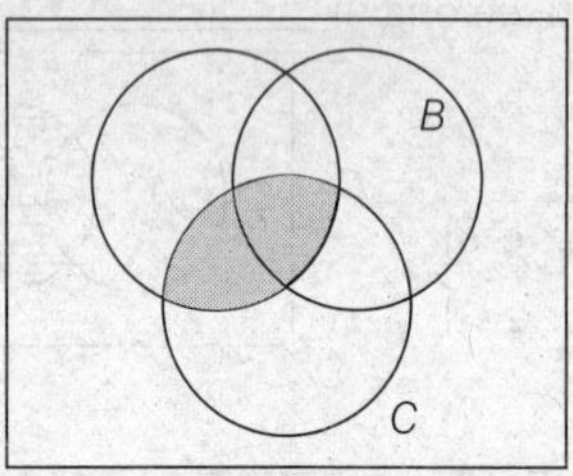

$A - (B - C)$

(6) 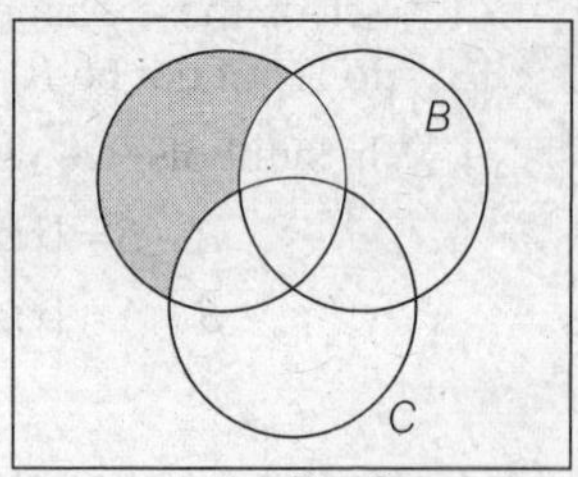

$(A - B) - C$

Exercise 1.1

Question 1 Which of the following are sets ? Justify your answer.

(i) The collection of all the months of a year beginning with the letter *J*.

(ii) The collection of ten most talented writers of India.

(iii) A team of eleven best cricket batsmen of the world.

(iv) The collection of all boys in your class.

(v) The collection of all natural numbers less than 100.

(vi) A collection of novels written by the writer Munshi Premchand.

(vii) The collection of all even integers.

(viii) The collection of questions in this chapter.

(ix) A collection of most dangerous animals of the world.

Sol. (i) We are sure that members of this collection are January, June and July.

So, this collection is well defined and hence, it is a set.

(ii) A writer may be most talented for one person and may not be for other.

So, this collection is not well defined. Hence, it is not a set.

(iii) A batsman may be best for one person and may not be, so for other.

So, this collection is not well defined. Hence, it is not a set.

(iv) We can make the collection of all boys in our class because they are class fellows.

So, this collection is well defined. Hence, it is a set.

(v) Here, members of the collection are 1, 2, 3, 4, ... 99.

So, this collection is well defined. Hence, it is a set.

(vi) Here, all the collections can be defined easily.

So, this collection is well defined. Hence, it is a set.

(vii) We can easily say that the members of this collection are 2, 4, 6, 8, …… .

So, this collection is well defined. Hence, it is a set.

(viii) The collection of questions in this chapter is well defined because one can definitely identify a question that belongs to this chapter.

So, it is a set.

(ix) The term most dangerous is not a clear term. An animal may be most dangerous to one person and may not be for the other.

So, it is not well defined. Hence, it is not a set.

Question 2 Let $A = \{1, 2, 3, 4, 5, 6\}$. Insert the appropriate symbol $\in$ or $\notin$ in the blank spaces

(i) 5 ...... A (ii) 8 ...... A (iii) 0 ...... A (iv) 4 ...... A
(v) 2 ...... A (vi) 10 ...... A

Sol. (i) $5 \in A$ (ii) $8 \notin A$ (iii) $0 \notin A$ (iv) $4 \in A$
(v) $2 \in A$ (vi) $10 \notin A$

Question 3 Write the following sets in roster form

(i) $A = \{x : x$ is an integer and $-3 \leq x < 7\}$
(ii) $B = \{x : x$ is a natural number less than $6\}$
(iii) $C = \{x : x$ is a two digit number such that the sum of its digits is $8\}$
(iv) $D = \{x : x$ is a prime number which is a divisor of $60\}$
(v) $E =$ The set of all letters in the word 'TRIGONOMETRY'
(vi) $F =$ The set of all letters in the word 'BETTER'.

A number that can be divided only by itself and 1 is called prime number.

Sol. (i) $A = \{x : x$ is an integer and $-3 \leq x < 7\}$. Then,
$A = \{-3, -2, -1, 0, 1, 2, 3, 4, 5, 6\}$
(ii) $B = \{1, 2, 3, 4, 5\}$
(iii) $C = \{17, 26, 35, 44, 53, 62, 71, 80\}$
(iv) $D = \{2, 3, 5\}$
(v) $E = \{T, R, I, G, O, N, M, E, Y\}$
(vi) $F = \{B, E, T, R\}$

Question 4 Write the following sets in set builder form

(i) $\{3, 6, 9, 12\}$ (ii) $\{2, 4, 8, 16, 32\}$ (iii) $\{5, 25, 125, 625\}$
(iv) $\{2, 4, 6, \ldots\}$ (v) $\{1, 4, 9 \ldots 100\}$

Sol. (i) Let $A = \{3, 6, 9, 12\}$
$\therefore A = \{x : x$ is a natural number that are multiple of 3 and $x < 15\}$

(ii) Let $B = \{2, 4, 8, 16, 32\}$ Here, we see that the elements of the given set one the powers of 2 (upto 5), so $B = \{x : x = 2^n, n \in N$ and $1 \leq n \leq 5\}$

(iii) Let $C = \{5, 25, 125, 625\}$ Here, we see that the elements of the given set are the powers of 5 (upto 4), so $C = \{x : x = 5^n, n \in N$ and $1 \leq n \leq 4\}$

(iv) Let $D = \{2, 4, 6, \ldots\}$ Here, we see that the elements of the set are even natural number, so $D = \{x : x$ is an even natural number$\}$

(v) Let $E = \{1, 4, 9, \ldots 10\}$ Here, we see that the elements of the set are the square of natural number $(1^2 = 1, 2^2 = 4, 3^2 = 9 \ \ldots)$, so $E = \{x : x = n^2, n \in N$ and $1 \leq n \leq 10\}$

Question 5 List all the elements of the following sets

(i) $A = \{x : x \text{ is an odd natural number}\}$

(ii) $B = \{x : x \text{ is an integer}, -\frac{1}{2} < x < \frac{9}{2}\}$

(iii) $C = \{x : x \text{ is an integer}, x^2 \leq 4\}$

(iv) $D = \{x : x \text{ is a letter in the word 'LOYAL'}\}$

(v) $E = \{x : x \text{ is a month of year not having 31 days}\}$

(vi) $F = \{x : x \text{ is a consonant in the English alphabet which precedes } k\}$

Sol. (i) A = Set of an odd natural number *i.e.* $\{1, 3, 5, 7, ...\}$

(ii) The integers lie in the range $-\frac{1}{2}$ and $\frac{9}{2}$ are 0, 1, 2, 3, 4 (integer means whole number no fraction).

$\therefore \; B = \{0, 1, 2, 3, 4\}$

(iii) The numbers whose square is ≤ 4 are $-2, -1, 0, 1, 2$

$(\because -2^2 = 4, -1^2 = 1, 0^2 = 0, 1^2 = 1, 2^2 = 4)$,

$\therefore C = \{-2, -1, 0, 1, 2\}$

Quick Solution

$$C = \{x : x \text{ is an integer}, x^2 \leq 4\}$$

$\because \quad x^2 \leq 4 \Rightarrow -2 \leq x \leq 2$

So, $\quad C = \{-2, -1, 0, 1, 2\}$

(iv) $D = \{L, O, Y, A\}$ [$\because$ Elements of the set are not repeated]

(v) E = {February, April, June, September, November}

(vi) $F = \{b, c, d, f, g, h, j\}$

Mistake Alert Students may mistakenly take $F = \{a, b, c, d, e, f, g, h, i, j\}$ instead of $F = \{b, c, d, f, g, h, j\}$

Question 6 Match each of the sets on the left in the roster form with the same set on the right described in the set builder form.

(i) {1, 2, 3, 6} (a) $\{x : x \text{ is a prime number and divisor of } 6\}$

(ii) {2, 3} (b) $\{x : x \text{ is an odd number less than } 10\}$

(iii) {M, A, T, H, E, I, C, S}

(c) $\{x : x \text{ is a natural number and divisor of } 6\}$

(iv) {1, 3, 5, 7, 9} (d) $\{x : x \text{ is a letter of the word MATHEMATICS}\}$

Sol. (i) The elements of {1, 2, 3, 6} set are natural number and divisors of 6.

(ii) The elements of set { 2, 3} are prime numbers and divisors of 6.

(iii) The elements of set {M, A, T, H, E, I , C, S} are the letters of the word MATHEMATICS.

(iv) The elements of set {1, 3, 5, 7, 9} are odd numbers less than 10.

Hence, (i) $\rightarrow$ (c) (ii) $\rightarrow$ (a) (iii) $\rightarrow$ (d) (iv) $\rightarrow$ (b)

Exercise 1.2

Question 1 Which of the following are examples of the null set?

(i) Set of odd natural numbers divisible by 2.
(ii) Set of even prime numbers.
(iii) $\{x : x \text{ is a natural number}, x < 5 \text{ and } x > 7\}$.
(iv) $\{y : y \text{ is a point common to any two parallel lines}\}$.

Sol. (i) There is no odd natural number divisible by 2, so there will be no element in this set, hence it is a null set.

(ii) There is only one even prime number which is 2 *i.e.,* there is a element in the set, so it is not a null set.

(iii) There is no natural number which is less than 5 and greater than 7 *i.e.,* there is no element in the set, so it is a null set.

(iv) Since, parallel lines never intersect each other, so they have no common point *i.e.,* no element in the set, so it is a null set.

Hence, (i), (iii) and (iv) are the examples of the null set.

Question 2 Which of the following sets are finite or infinite?

(i) The set of months of a year.
(ii) $\{1, 2, 3, \ldots\}$.
(iii) $\{1, 2, 3, \ldots 99, 100\}$.
(iv) The set of positive integers greater than 100.
(v) The set of prime numbers less than 99.

Sol. (i) The set of months of a year is a finite set because there are 12 months in a year.

(ii) $\{1, 2, 3, \ldots.\}$ is an infinite set because there are infinite natural numbers in it.

(iii) $\{1, 2, 3, \ldots 99, 100\}$ is a finite set because it contains first 100 natural numbers.

(iv) It is an infinite set because there are infinite numbers greater than 100 *i.e.,* 101, 102, 103 etc.,

(v) It is a finite set because there are 25 prime numbers less than 99 and that set is $\{2, 3, 4, 7, \ldots\ldots 97\}$.

Question 3 State whether each of the following set is finite or infinite :

(i) The set of lines which are parallel to the X-axis.
(ii) The set of letters in the English alphabet.
(iii) The set of numbers which are multiple of 5.
(iv) The set of animals living on the earth.
(v) The set of circles passing through the origin (0, 0).

Sol. (i) **Infinite** As infinite number of lines can be drawn parallel to X-axis.
(ii) **Finite** As there are 26 letters in the English alphabet.
(iii) **Infinite** As there are infinite multiples of 5 which are $\{5, 10, 15, 20, 25, \ldots\ldots\}$.
(iv) **Finite** As there are finite number of animals living on the earth.
(v) **Infinite** As infinite number of circles can be drawn passing through the origin.

Question 4 In the following, state whether $A = B$ or not

(i) $A = \{a, b, c, d\}$, $B = \{d, c, b, a\}$
(ii) $A = \{4, 8, 12, 16\}$, $B = \{8, 4, 16, 18\}$
(iii) $A = \{2, 4, 6, 8, 10\}$, $B = \{x : x$ is positive even integer and $x \le 10\}$
(iv) $A = \{x : x$ is a multiple of $10\}$
$B = \{10, 15, 20, 25, 30, \ldots\}$

◎ *Thinking Process* If $A = B$, then the elements of A and B must be equal and same.

Sol. (i) Here, all the elements of the sets A and B are same which are a, b, c and d. Thus, $A = B$.
(ii) Here, 12 is an element of A but not the element of B and 18 is an element of B but not the element of A. Thus, all the elements of the sets A and B are not same. Hence, $A \ne B$.
(iii) Here, $A = \{2, 4, 6, 8, 10\}$ and $B = \{x: x$ is positive even integer and $x \le 10\}$ $= \{2, 4, 6, 8, 10\}$ *i.e.,* So, all the elements of A and B are same.
Hence, $A = B$
(iv) Here, $A = \{x : x$ is a multiple of $10\}$ i.e.
$\{10, 20, 30, 40, \ldots\}$ and $B = \{10, 15, 20, 25, 30, \ldots\}$
Clearly, $A \ne B$ as all the elements of the sets A and B are not same.

Question 5 Are the following pair of sets equal? Give reasons.

(i) $A = \{2, 3\}$, $B = \{x : x$ is a solution of $x^2 + 5x + 6 = 0\}$
(ii) $A = \{x : x$ is a letter in the word FOLLOW$\}$
$B = \{y : y$ is a letter in the word WOLF$\}$.

Sol. (i) $A = \{2, 3\}$ and $B = \{x : x$ is a solution of $x^2 + 5x + 6 = 0\}$

First we find the solution of $x^2 + 5x + 6 = 0$

$\Rightarrow x^2 + 3x + 2x + 6 = 0 \Rightarrow x(x + 3) + 2(x + 3) = 0$

$\Rightarrow (x + 2)(x + 3) = 0 \Rightarrow x = -2, -3$

Therefore, $B = \{-2, -3\}$

The elements of A and B are not same, hence $A \neq B$.

(ii) Here, $A = \{x : x$ is a letter of the word FOLLOW$\} = \{F, O, L, W\}$

$B = \{y : y$ is a letter of the word WOLF$\} = \{W, O, L, F\}$

Since, every element of A is in B and every element of B is in A.

$\Rightarrow \quad A = B$

Question 6 From the sets of given below, select equal sets.

$A = \{2, 4, 8, 12\}$, $B = \{1, 2, 3, 4\}$, $C = \{4, 8, 12, 14\}$

$D = \{3, 1, 4, 2\}$, $E = \{-1, 1\}$, $F = \{0, a\}$

$G = \{1, -1\}$, $H = \{0, 1\}$

Sol. Here, elements of the sets B and D are same and that of E and G are same.

Hence, $B = D$ and $E = G$

Exercise 1.3

Question 1 Make correct statements by filling in the symbols $\subset$ or $\not\subset$ in the blank spaces

(i) $\{2, 3, 4\}$ ...... $\{1, 2, 3, 4, 5\}$

(ii) $\{a, b, c\}$ .... $\{b, c, d\}$

(iii) $\{x : x$ is a student of class XI of your school$\}$ ... $\{x : x$ is a student of your school$\}$.

(iv) $\{x : x$ is a circle in the plane$\}$... $\{x : x$ is a circle in the same plane with radius 1 unit$\}$

(v) $\{x : x$ is a triangle in a plane$\}$ ...$\{x : x$ is a rectangle in the plane$\}$

(vi) $\{x : x$ is an equilateral triangle in a plane$\}$ ......$\{x : x$ is a triangle in the same plane$\}$

(vii) $\{x : x$ is an even natural number$\}$ ...... $\{x : x$ is an integer$\}$.

◎ **Thinking Process** $A \subset B$ means that all the elements of set A are present in set B. $A \not\subset B$ means that all the elements of set A are not present in set B.

Sol. (i) $\{2, 3, 4\} \subset \{1, 2, 3, 4, 5\}$

[∵ all elements of Ist set are there in IInd set]

(ii) $\{a, b, c\} \not\subset \{b, c, d\}$

[∵ all elements of Ist set are not there in IInd set]

(iii) $\{x : x$ is a student of class XI of your school$\} \subset (x : x$ is a student of your school)

(∵ If a student is of class XI of your school, then surely he will be a student of your school)

(iv) $\{x : x$ is a circle in the plane$\} \not\subset (x : x$ is a circle in the same plane with radius 1 unit)

[∵ elements in the Ist set can be a circle of any radius, so its all element will not be there in the IInd set]

(v) $\{x : x$ is a triangle in a plane$\} \not\subset \{x : x$ is a rectangle in the plane$\}$

[∵ all elements of Ist set are not there in the IInd set]

(vi) $\{x : x$ is an equilateral triangle in a plane$\} \subset \{x : x$ is a triangle in the same plane$\}$

[∵ elements in the IInd set are triangles, so there will also be equilateral triangle, *i.e.*, all elements of Ist set are there in the IInd set].

(vii) $\{x : x$ is an even natural number$\} \subset \{x : x$ is an integer$\}$

[∵ all elements of Ist set will be there in the IInd set because integers have both even and odd natural number]

Question 2 Examine whether the following statements are true or false:

(i) $\{a, b\} \not\subset \{b, c, a\}$

(ii) $\{a, e\} \subset \{x : x$ is a vowel in the English alphabet$\}$

(iii) $\{1, 2, 3\} \subset \{1, 3, 5\}$

(iv) $\{a\} \subset \{a, b, c\}$

(v) $\{a\} \in \{a, b, c\}$

(vi) $\{x : x$ is an even natural number less than 6$\}$

$\subset \{x : x$ is a natural number which divides 36$\}$

Sol. (i) Since, the elements of set $\{a, b\}$ are also present in the set $\{b, c, a\}$. Hence, $\{a, b\} \not\subset \{b, c, a\}$ is false.

(ii) As vowels in the English alphabet are $\{a, e, i, o, u\}$, therefore $\{a, e\} \subset \{x : x$ is a vowel in English alphabet$\}$ is true.

(iii) $\{1, 2, 3\} \subset \{1, 3, 5\}$ is false because all the elements of the set $\{1, 2, 3\}$ do not belong to the set $\{1, 3, 5\}$.

(iv) $\{a\} \subset \{a, b, c\}$ is true as a is contained in the set $\{a, b, c\}$.

(v) It is false because $\{a\}$ is a subset of $\{a, b, c\}$ not an element.

(vi) $\{x : x$ is an even natural number less than 6$\} = \{2, 4\}$ and $\{x : x$ is a natural number which divides 36$\} = \{1, 2, 3, 4, 6, 9, 12, 18, 36\}$

$\Rightarrow$ Since, every element of set $\{2, 4\}$ is contained in the set $\{1, 2, 3, 4, 6, 12, 18, 36\}$, hence the given statement is true.

Question 3 Let $A = \{1, 2, \{3, 4\}, 5\}$. Which of the following statements are incorrect and why?

(i) $\{3, 4\} \subset A$ (ii) $\{3, 4\} \in A$ (iii) $\{\{3, 4\}\} \subset A$
(iv) $1 \in A$ (v) $1 \subset A$ (vi) $\{1, 2, 5\} \subset A$
(vii) $\{1, 2, 5\} \in A$ (viii) $\{1, 2, 3\} \subset A$ (ix) $\phi \in A$
(x) $\phi \subset A$ (xi) $\{\phi\} \subset A$

Sol. (i) It is incorrect because $\{3, 4\} \in A$ but $\{\{3, 4\}\} \subset A$ is correct. First of all, make it clear that the given set A has four elements 1, 2, {3, 4} and 5. Remember that {3, 4} is an element not a set.

(ii) $\{3, 4\} \in A$, it is a correct statement.

(iii) As we have discussed above, $\{\{3, 4\}\} \subset A$, it is a correct statement.

(iv) $1 \in A$, it is a correct statement.

(v) It is incorrect, as $1 \in A$.

(vi) $\{1, 2, 5\} \subset A$, it is a correct statement.

(vii) It is incorrect as $\{1, 2, 5\} \notin A$.

(viii) It is incorrect because 3 is not an element of A.

(ix) It is incorrect because $\phi \subset A$.

(x) $\phi \subset A$, it is a correct statement because ϕ is a subset of every set.

(xi) It is incorrect because ϕ is not an element of A.

Hence, (i) (v), (vii), (viii), (ix) and (xi) are the incorrect statements.

Mistake Alert Students may get confused between symbol '$\in$' and '$\subset$'. Symbol '$\in$' used for element of a set and '$\subset$' used for subset.

Question 4 Write down all the subsets of the following sets

(i) $\{a\}$ (ii) $\{a, b\}$ (iii) $\{1, 2, 3\}$ (iv) ϕ

Sol. (i) Subsets of $\{a\} = \phi, \{a\}$

(ii) Subsets of $\{a, b\} = \phi, \{a\}, \{b\}, \{a, b\}$

(iii) Subsets of $\{1, 2, 3\} = \phi, \{1\}, \{2\}, \{3\}, \{1, 2\}, \{1, 3\}, \{2, 3\}, \{1, 2, 3\}$

(iv) Subset of $\phi = \phi$

Note ϕ is a subset of all sets.

Question 5 Write the following as intervals

(i) $\{x : x \in R, -4 < x \leq 6\}$ (ii) $\{x : x \in R, -12 < x < -10\}$
(iii) $\{x : x \in R, 0 \leq x < 7\}$ (iv) $\{x : x \in R, 3 \leq x \leq 4\}$

Sol. Interval means a set having initial and final points.

(i) $(-4, 6]$ (ii) $(-12, -10)$ (iii) $[0, 7)$ (iv) $[3, 4]$

Question 6 Write the following intervals in set builder form

(i) $(-3,0)$ (ii) $[6,12]$

(iii) $(6,12]$ (iv) $[-23,5)$

Sol. We know that closed interval contains end points while open interval does not contain end points. Therefore,

(i) $(-3, 0) = \{x : x \in R, -3 < x < 0\}$ [$\because$ It is an open interval]

(ii) $[6, 12] = \{x : x \in R, 6 \le x \le 12\}$ [$\because$ It is a closed interval]

(iii) $(6, 12] = \{x : x \in R, 6 < x \le 12\}$ [$\because$ It is open from left and closed from right]

(iv) $[-23, 5) = \{x : x \in R, -23 \le x < 5\}$

[$\because$ It is closed from left and open from right]

Question 7 What universal set(s) would you propose for each of the following

(i) The set of right triangles.

(ii) The set of isosceles triangles.

Sol. The set U of all possible triangles is the universal set for each of the given sets.

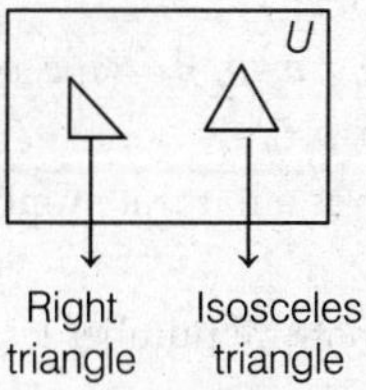

Question 8 Given, the sets $A = \{1, 3, 5\}$, $B = \{2, 4, 6\}$ and $C = \{0, 2, 4, 6, 8\}$, which of the following may be considered as universal set(s) for all three sets A, B and C?

(i) $\{0, 1, 2, 3, 4, 5, 6\}$

(ii) ϕ

(iii) $\{0, 1, 2, 3, 4, 5, 6, 7, 8, 9, 10\}$

(iv) $\{1, 2, 3, 4, 5, 6, 7, 8\}$

Sol. Universal set contains atleast all elements of A, B and C.

(i) Here, $8 \notin \{0, 1, 2, ,3, 4, 5, 6\}$, so we cannot consider it as a universal set.

(ii) ϕ cannot be considered as universal set.

(iii) $\{0, 1, 2, 3, 4, 5, 6, 7, 8, 9, 10\}$ is the universal set for the given sets A, B and C as all the elements of sets A, B and C are in set (iii).

(iv) Here, $0 \notin \{1, 2, 3, 4, 5, 6, 7, 8\}$, so we do not consider it as universal set.

Hence, the set (iii) is the universal set for given sets.

Exercise 1.4

Question 1 Find the union of each of the following pairs of sets

(i) $X = \{1, 3, 5\}, Y = \{1, 2, 3\}$

(ii) $A = \{a, e, i, o, u\}, B = \{a, b, c\}$

(iii) $A = \{x : x$ is a natural number and multiple of $3\}$
$B = \{x : x$ is a natural number less than $6\}$

(iv) $A = \{x : x$ is a natural number $1 < x \leq 6\}$
$B = \{x : x$ is a natural number $6 < x < 10\}$

(v) $A = \{1, 2, 3\}, B = \phi$

◎ ***Thinking Process*** Union of two sets is a set which has all elements of both sets.

Sol. (i) We know that union of two or more sets contains all the elements of the sets. We have, $X = \{1, 3, 5\}, Y = \{1, 2, 3\}$

$\therefore \quad X \cup Y = \{1, 2, 3, 5\}$

(ii) We have, $A = \{a, e, i, o, u\}, B = \{a, b, c\}$

$\therefore A \cup B = \{a, e, i, o, u, b, c\}$

(iii) We have, $A = \{x : x$ is a natural number and multiple of $3\}$

$\Rightarrow \quad A = \{3, 6, 9, 12, \ldots\}$

and $B = \{x : x$ is a natural number less than $6\}$

$= \{1, 2, 3, 4, 5\}$

$\therefore \ A \cup B = \{1, 2, 3, 4, 5, 6, 9, 12, 15\ldots\}$

(iv) We have, $A = \{x : x$ is a natural number and $1 < x \leq 6\}$

$\Rightarrow A = \{2, 3, 4, 5, 6\}$

$B = \{x : x$ is a natural number and $6 < x < 10\}$

$\Rightarrow B = \{7, 8, 9\}$

$\therefore \ A \cup B = \{2, 3, 4, 5, 6, 7, 8, 9\}$

(v) $A = \{1, 2, 3\}, B = \phi$

$\therefore \qquad A \cup B = \{1, 2, 3\}$

Question 2 Let $A = \{a, b\}$, $B = \{a, b, c\}$. Is $A \subset B$? What is $A \cup B$?

Sol. Since, every element of A is also an element of B, therefore $A \subset B$.

and $\qquad A \cup B = \{a, b, c\} = B$

Question 3 If A and B are two sets such that $A \subset B$, then what is $A \cup B$?

Sol. Since, A is a subset of B. Hence, every element of set A is contained in the set B. So, $A \cup B = B$.

Question 4 If $A=\{1,2,3,4\}$, $B=\{3,4,5,6\}$, $C=\{5,6,7,8\}$ and $D=\{7,8,9,10\}$; find

(i) $A\cup B$ (ii) $A\cup C$ (iii) $B\cup C$
(iv) $B\cup D$ (v) $A\cup B\cup C$ (vi) $A\cup B\cup D$
(vii) $B\cup C\cup D$.

Sol. (i) $A\cup B=\{1, 2, 3, 4\}\cup\{3, 4, 5, 6\}=\{1, 2, 3, 4, 5, 6\}$

(ii) $A\cup C=\{1, 2, 3, 4\}\cup\{5, 6, 7, 8\}=\{1, 2, 3, 4, 5, 6, 7, 8\}$

(iii) $B\cup C=\{3, 4, 5, 6\}\cup\{5, 6, 7, 8\}=\{3, 4, 5, 6, 7, 8\}$

(iv) $B\cup D=\{3, 4, 5, 6\}\cup\{7, 8, 9, 10\}=\{3, 4, 5, 6, 7, 8, 9, 10\}$

(v) $A\cup B\cup C=\{1, 2, 3, 4\}\cup\{3, 4, 5, 6\}\cup\{5, 6, 7, 8\}$
$=\{1, 2, 3, 4, 5, 6\}\cup\{5, 6, 7, 8\}=\{1, 2, 3, 4, 5, 6, 7, 8\}$

(vi) $A\cup B\cup D=\{1, 2, 3, 4\}\cup\{3, 4, 5, 6\}\cup\{7, 8, 9, 10\}$
$=\{1, 2, 3, 4, 5, 6\}\cup\{7, 8, 9, 10\}=\{1, 2, 3, 4, 5, 6, 7, 8, 9, 10\}$

(vii) $B\cup C\cup D=\{3, 4, 5, 6\}\cup\{5, 6, 7, 8\}\cup\{7, 8, 9, 10\}$
$=\{3, 4, 5, 6, 7, 8\}\cup\{7, 8, 9, 10\}=\{3, 4, 5, 6, 7, 8, 9, 10\}$

Question 5 Find the intersection of each pair of sets of question 1 above.

◎ ***Thinking Process*** For finding the intersection of two sets, we have to find the common elements in both the sets.

Sol. We know that the intersection of two or more sets is the set of common elements.

(i) $X\cap Y=\{1, 3, 5\}\cap\{1, 2, 3\}=\{1, 3\}$

(ii) $A\cap B=\{a, e, i, o, u\}\cap\{a, b, c\}=\{a\}$

(iii) $A\cap B=\{3, 6, 9, \ldots\}\cap\{1, 2, 3, 4, 5\}=\{3\}$

(iv) $A\cap B=\{2, 3, 4, 5, 6\}\cap\{7, 8, 9\}=\phi$

(v) $A\cap B=\{1, 2, 3\}\cap\phi=\phi$

Question 6 If $A=\{3,5,7,9,11\}$, $B=\{7,9,11,13\}$, $C=\{11,13,15\}$ and $D=\{15,17\}$; find

(i) $A\cap B$ (ii) $B\cap C$ (iii) $A\cap C\cap D$
(iv) $A\cap C$ (v) $B\cap D$ (vi) $A\cap(B\cup C)$
(vii) $A\cap D$ (viii) $A\cap(B\cup D)$ (ix) $(A\cap B)\cap(B\cup C)$
(x) $(A\cup D)\cap(B\cup C)$

Sol. (i) $A\cap B=\{3, 5, 7, 9, 11\}\cap\{7, 9, 11, 13\}=\{7, 9, 11\}$

(ii) $B\cap C=\{7, 9, 11, 13\}\cap\{11, 13, 15\}=\{11, 13\}$

(iii) $A\cap C\cap D=\{3, 5, 7, 9, 11\}\cap\{11, 13, 15\}\cap\{15, 17\}=\{11\}\cap\{15, 17\}=\phi$

(iv) $A\cap C=\{3, 5, 7, 9, 11\}\cap\{11, 13, 15\}=\{11\}$

(v) $B\cap D=\{7, 9, 11, 13)\cap\{15, 17\}=\phi$

(vi) $A \cap (B \cup C) = \{3, 5, 7, 9, 11\} \cap \{7, 9, 11, 13\} \cup \{11, 13, 15\}$

$= \{3, 5, 7, 9, 11\} \cap \{7, 9, 11, 13, 15\} = \{7, 9, 11\}$

(vii) $A \cap D = \{3, 5, 7, 9, 11\} \cap \{15, 17\} = \phi$

(viii) $A \cap (B \cup D) = \{3, 5, 7, 9, 11\} \cap \{7, 9, 11, 13\} \cup \{15, 17\}$

$= \{3, 5, 7, 9, 11\} \cap \{7, 9, 11, 13, 15, 17\} = \{7, 9, 11\}$

(ix) $(A \cap B) \cap (B \cup C) = \{3, 5, 7, 9, 11\} \cap \{7, 9, 11, 13\}$

$\cap \{7, 9, 11, 13\} \cup \{11, 13, 15\}$

$= \{7, 9, 11\} \cap \{7, 9, 11, 13, 15\} = \{7, 9, 11\}$

(x) $(A \cup D) \cap (B \cup C) = \{3, 5, 7, 9, 11\} \cup \{15, 17\}$

$\cap \{7, 9, 11, 13\} \cup \{11, 13, 15\}$

$= \{3, 5, 7, 9, 11, 15, 17\} \cap \{7, 9, 11, 13, 15\} = \{7, 9, 11, 15\}$

Question 7 If $A = \{x : x$ is a natural number$\}$,

$B = \{x : x$ is an even natural number$\}$,

$C = \{x : x$ an odd natural number$\}$ and

$D = \{x : x$ is a prime number$]$, find

(i) $A \cap B$ (ii) $A \cap C$ (iii) $A \cap D$

(iv) $B \cap C$ (v) $B \cap D$ (vi) $C \cap D$

Sol. A = Set of natural numbers = $\{1, 2, 3, 4, 5, ...\}$

B = Set of even natural numbers = $\{2, 4, 6, 8, 10, ...\}$

C = Set of odd natural numbers = $\{1, 3, 5, 7, 9, ...\}$

D = Set of prime numbers = $D = \{2, 3, 5, 7, 11, ...\}$

(i) $A \cap B = \{1, 2, 3, 4, 5....\} \cap \{2, 4, 6, 8, 10, ...\} = \{2, 4, 6, 8, 10, ...\} = B$

(ii) $A \cap C = \{1, 2, 3, 4, 5....\} \cap \{1, 3, 5, 7, 9, ...\} = \{1, 3, 5, 7, 9, ...\} = C$

(iii) $A \cap D = \{1, 2, 3, 4, 5, 6, 7, ...\} \cap \{2, 3, 5, 7, 11, ...\} = \{2, 3, 5, 7, ..\} = D$

(iv) $B \cap C = \{2, 4, 6, 8, 10....\} \cap \{1, 3, 5, 7, 9....\} = \phi$

(v) $B \cap D = \{2, 4, 6, 8, 10 ....\} \cap \{2, 3, 5, 7, 11.....\} = \{2\}$

(vi) $C \cap D = \{1, 3, 5, 7, 9, 11, ..\} \cap \{2, 3, 5, 7, 11..\} = \{3, 5, 7, 11..\} = \{x : x$ is an odd prime number$\}$

Question 8 Which of the following pairs of sets are disjoint?

(i) $\{1, 2, 3, 4\}$ and $\{x : x$ is a natural number and $4 \le x \le 6\}$

(ii) $\{a, e, i, o, u\}$ and $\{c, d, e, f\}$

(iii) $\{x : x$ is an even integer$\}$ and $\{x : x$ is an odd integer$\}$

◎ ***Thinking Process*** Two sets are disjoint when $A \cap B = \phi$, *i.e.*, null set (A set having no element).

Sol. (i) Let $A = \{1, 2, 3, 4\}$

and $B = \{x : x$ is a natural number and $4 \le x \le 6\} = \{4, 5, 6\}$ i.e. $A \cap B = \{4\}$

Therefore, the given sets are not disjoint.

(ii) $\{a, e, i, o, u\} \cap \{c, d, e, f\} = \{e\}$

Therefore, the given sets are not disjoint.

(iii) $\{x : x \text{ is an even integer}\} \cap \{x : x \text{ is an odd integer}\}$

$\{2, 4, 6, 8, 10 \ldots\} \cap \{1, 3, 5, 7, \ldots\} = \phi$

Hence, the given sets are disjoint.

Question 9 If $A = \{3, 6, 9, 12, 15, 18, 21\}$, $B = \{4, 8, 12, 16, 20\}$, $C = \{2, 4, 6, 8, 10, 12, 14, 16\}$ and $D = \{5, 10, 15, 20\}$, find

(i) $A - B$ (ii) $A - C$ (iii) $A - D$
(iv) $B - A$ (v) $C - A$ (vi) $D - A$
(vii) $B - C$ (viii) $B - D$ (ix) $C - B$
(x) $D - B$ (xi) $C - D$ (xii) $D - C$

Sol. (i) $A - B$ = { the elements which are in A but not in B}

$= \{3, 6, 9, 12, 15, 18, 21\} - \{4, 8, 12, 16, 20\} = \{3, 6, 9, 15, 18, 21\}$

(ii) $A - C$ = {the ele ments which are in A but not in C}

$= \{3, 6, 9, 12, 15, 18, 21\} - \{2, 4, 6, 8, 10, 12, 14, 16\}$

$= \{3, 9, 15, 18, 21\}$

(iii) $A - D$ = {the elements which are in A but not in D}

$= \{3, 6, 9, 12, 15, 18, 21\} - \{5, 10, 15, 20\} = \{3, 6, 9, 12, 18, 21\}$

(iv) $B - A$ = {the elements which are in B but not in A}

$= \{4, 8, 12, 16, 20\} - \{3, 6, 9, 12, 15, 18, 21\} = \{4, 8, 16, 20\}$

(v) $C - A$ = (the elements which are in C but not in A)

$= \{2, 4, 6, 8, 10, 12, 14, 16\} - \{3, 6, 9, 12, 15, 18, 21\}$

$= \{2, 4, 8, 10, 14, 16\}$

(vi) $D - A$ = {the elements which are in D but not in A}

$= \{5, 10, 15, 20\} - \{3, 6, 9, 12, 15, 18, 21\} = \{5, 10, 20\}$

(vii) $B - C$ = {the elements which are in B but not in C},

$= \{4, 8, 12, 16, 20\} - \{2, 4, 6, 8, 10, 12, 14, 16\} = \{20\}$

(viii) $B - D$ = {the elements which are in B but not in D}

$= \{4, 8, 12, 16, 20\} - \{5, 10, 15, 20\} = \{4, 8, 12, 16\}$

(ix) $C - B$ = {the elements which are in C but not in B}

$= \{2, 4, 6, 8, 10, 12, 14, 16\} - \{4, 8, 12, 16, 20\} = \{2, 6, 10, 14\}$

(x) $D - B$ = {the elements which are in D but not in B}

$= \{5, 10, 15, 20\} - \{4, 8, 12, 16, 20\} = \{5, 10, 15\}$

(xi) $C - D$ = {the elements which are in C but not in D}

$= \{2, 4, 6, 8, 10, 12, 14, 16\} - \{5, 10, 15, 20\} = \{2, 4, 6, 8, 12, 14, 16\}$

(xii) $D - C$ = {the elements which are in D but not in C}

$= \{5, 10, 15, 20\} - \{2, 4, 6, 8, 10, 12, 14, 16\} = \{5, 15, 20\}$

Mistake Alert Students may make mistakes while writing the set $A - B$ write the elements in the set $A - B$ that are in A but not in B. Sometimes students write the remaining elements of B in the set $A - B$.

Question 10 If $X = \{a, b, c, d\}$ and $Y = \{f, b, d, g\}$, find

(i) $X - Y$ (ii) $Y - X$ (iii) $X \cap Y$

Thinking Process Suppose, A and B are two sets, then $A - B$ is the set of all those elements which belongs to set A but not set B and $A \cap B$ is the set of all those elements which are common to both A and B.

Sol. (i) $X - Y$ = {the elements which are in X but not in Y}

$= \{a, b, c, d\} - \{f, b, d, g\} = \{a, c\}$

(ii) $Y - X$ = {the elements which are in Y but not in X}

$= \{f, b, d, g\} - \{a, b, c, d\} = \{f, g\}$

(iii) $X \cap Y$ = {the elements which are both in X and Y}

$= \{a, b, c, d\} \cap \{f, b, d, g\} = \{b, d\}$

Question 11 If R is the set of real numbers and Q is the set of rational numbers, then what is $R - Q$?

Sol. Since, set of real numbers contains a set of rational numbers and a set of irrational numbers.

$\therefore$ $R - Q$ = Set of irrational numbers.

Question 12 State whether each of the following statements is true or false. Justify your answer.

(i) $\{2, 3, 4, 5\}$ and $\{3, 6\}$ are disjoint sets.

(ii) $\{a, e, i, o, u\}$ and $\{a, b, c, d\}$ are disjoint sets.

(iii) $\{2, 6, 10, 14\}$ and $\{3, 7, 11, 15\}$ are disjoint sets.

(iv) $\{2, 6, 10\}$ and $\{3, 7, 11\}$ are disjoint sets.

Thinking Process If $A \cap B = \phi$, then sets A and B are said to be disjoint.

Sol. (i) $\{2, 3, 4, 5\} \cap \{3, 6\} = \{3\} \neq \phi$

So, the given sets are not disjoint and hence, given statement is false.

(ii) $\{a, e, i, o, u\} \cap \{a, b, c, d\} = \{a\} \neq \phi$

So, the given sets are not disjoint and hence, given statement is false.

(iii) $\{2, 6, 10, 14\} \cap \{3, 7, 11, 15\} = \phi$

So, the given sets are disjoint and hence, given statement is true.

(iv) $\{2, 6, 10\} \cap \{3, 7, 11\} = \phi$

So, the given sets are disjoint and hence, given statement is true.

Exercise 1.5

Question 1 Let $U = \{1, 2, 3, 4, 5, 6, 7, 8, 9\}$, $A = \{1, 2, 3, 4\}$, $B = \{2, 4, 6, 8\}$ and $C = \{3, 4, 5, 6\}$.

Find (i) A' (ii) B' (iii) $(A \cup C)'$
(iv) $(A \cup B)'$ (v) $(A')'$ (vi) $(B - C)'$

Thinking Process Complement of any set A (denoted A') $= U - A$ *i.e.*, the complement of a set A contains those elements which are in U but not in A.

Sol. (i) $A' = U - A =$ {the elements which are in U but not in A}
$= \{1, 2, 3, 4, 5, 6, 7, 8, 9\} - \{1, 2, 3, 4\} = \{5, 6, 7, 8, 9\}$

(ii) $B' = U - B =$ {the elements which are in U but not in B}
$= \{1, 2, 3, 4, 5, 6, 7, 8, 9\} - \{2, 4, 6, 8\} = \{1, 3, 5, 7, 9\}$

(iii) $(A \cup C)' = U - (A \cup C)$
$=$ {the elements which are in U but not in $(A \cup C)$}
$= \{1, 2, 3, 4, 5, 6, 7, 8, 9\} - \{1, 2, 3, 4, 5, 6\} = \{7, 8, 9\}$

(iv) $(A \cup B)' = U - (A \cup B)$
$=$ {the elements which are in U but not in $(A \cup B)$}
$= \{1, 2, 3, 4, 5, 6, 7, 8, 9\} - \{1, 2, 3, 4, 6, 8\} = \{5, 7, 9\}$

(v) $(A')' = A = \{1, 2, 3, 4\}$

(vi) $(B - C)' = U - (B - C)$
$=$ {the elements which are in U but not in $(B - C)$}
$= \{1, 2, 3, 4, 5, 6, 7, 8, 9\} - \{2, 8\} = \{1, 3, 4, 5, 6, 7, 9\}$

Question 2 If $U = \{a, b, c, d, e, f, g, h\}$, find the complements of the following sets

(i) $A = \{a, b, c\}$ (ii) $B = \{d, e, f, g\}$
(iii) $C = \{a, c, e, g\}$ (iv) $D = \{f, g, h, a\}$

Sol. (i) $A' = U - A =$ {the elements which are in U but not in A}
$= \{a, b, c, d, e, f, g, h\} - \{a, b, c\} = \{d, e, f, g, h\}$

(ii) $B' = U - B =$ {the elements which are in U but not in B}
$= \{a, b, c, d, e, f, g, h\} - \{d, e, f, g\} = \{a, b, c, h\}$

(iii) $C' = U - C =$ {the elements which are in U but not in C}
$= \{a, b, c, d, e, f, g, h\} - \{a, c, e, g\} = \{b, d, f, h\}$

(iv) $D' = U - D =$ {the elements which are in U but not in D}
$= \{a, b, c, d, e, f, g, h\} - \{f, g, h, a\} = \{b, c, d, e\}$

Question 3 Taking the set of natural numbers as the universal set, write down the complements of the following sets

(i) $\{x : x$ is an even natural number$\}$
(ii) $\{x : x$ is an odd natural number$\}$
(iii) $\{x : x$ is a positive multiple of 3$\}$
(iv) $\{x : x$ is a prime number$\}$
(v) $\{x : x$ is a natural number divisible by 3 and 5$\}$
(vi) $\{x : x$ is a perfect square$\}$
(vii) $\{x : x$ is a perfect cube$\}$
(viii) $\{x : x + 5 = 8\}$
(ix) $\{x : 2x + 5 = 9\}$
(x) $\{x : x \geq 7\}$
(xi) $\{x : x \in N$ and $2x + 1 > 10\}$

Sol. Given, U = A set of natural numbers = $\{1, 2, 3, 4, 5, 6, 7, 8 ....\}$

(i) Let $A = \{x : x$ is an even natural number$\}$
$= \{2, 4, 6, 8, 10, ...\}$
Now, complement of $A = A' = U - A$
$= \{1, 2, 3, 4, 5, 6, 7, 8, ...\} - \{2, 4, 6, 8, 10, ...\}$
$= \{1, 3, 5, 7, 9, ...\}$
$= \{x : x$ is an odd natural number$\}$

(ii) Let $A = \{x : x$ is an odd natural number$\}$
$= \{1, 3, 5, 7, 9, ...\}$
Now, complement of $A = A' = U - A$
$= \{1, 2, 3, 4, 5, 6, 7, 8, ...\} - \{1, 3, 5, 7, 9, ...\}$
$= \{2, 4, 6, 8, 10 ....\}$
$= \{x : x$ is an even natural number$\}$

(iii) Let $A = \{x : x$ is a positive multiple of 3$\}$
$= \{3, 6, 9, 12, 15, ...\}$
Now, complement of $A = A' = U - A$
$= \{1, 2, 3, 4, 5, 6, 7, 8, ...\} - \{3, 6, 9, 12, 15, ...\} = \{1, 2, 4, 5, ...\}$
$= \{x : x \in N$ and x is not a multiple of 3$\}$

(iv) Let $A = \{x : x$ is a prime number$\} = \{2, 3, 5, 7, 11, ...\}$
Therefore, complement of $A = A' = U - A$
$= \{1, 2, 3, 4, 5, 6, 7, 8, ...\} - \{2, 3, 5, 7, 11, ...\}$
$= \{1, 4, 6, 8 ...\}$
$= \{x : x$ is a positive composite number and $x = 1\}$

(v) Let $A = \{x : x$ is a natural number divisible by 3 and 5$\}$

$= \{15, 30, 45, 60, ...\}$

Therefore, complement of $A = A' = U - A$

$= \{1, 2, 3, 4, ...15, 16, ...30, 31 ....\} - \{15, 30, 45, 60, ..\}$

$= \{1, 2, 3, 4, ... 14, 16, 17, ... 29, ...\}$

$= \{x : x$ is a positive integer which is not divisible 15$\}$

(vi) Let $A = \{x : x$ is a perfect square$\}$

Therefore, complement of $A = A' = U - A$

$= \{x : x \in N$ and x is not a perfect square$\}$

(vii) Let $A = \{x : x$ is a perfect cube$\}$

Therefore, complement of $A = A' = U - A$

$= \{x : x \in N$ and x is not a perfect cube$\}$

(viii) Let $A = \{x : x + 5 = 8\} = \{x : x = 3\}$

Therefore, complement of $A = A' = U - A$

$= \{x : x \in N \text{ and } x \neq 3\}$

(ix) Let $A = \{x : 2x + 5 = 9\} \Rightarrow A = \{x : x = 2\}$

Therefore, complement of $A = A' = U - A = \{x : x \in N \text{ and } x \neq 2\}$

(x) Let $A = \{x : x \geq 7\}$

Therefore, complement of $A = A' = U - A = \{x : x \in N \text{ and } x < 7\}$

(xi) Let $A = \{x : x \in N \text{ and } 2x + 1 > 10\}$

$\Rightarrow \quad A = \{x : x \in N \text{ and } x > \frac{9}{2}\}$

Therefore, complement of $A = A' = U - A = \{x : x \in N \text{ and } x \leq \frac{9}{2}\}$

Mistake Alert Sometimes students get confused in natural numbers, odd natural numbers, even natural numbers and prime numbers.

Question 4 If $U = \{1, 2, 3, 4, 5, 6, 7, 8, 9\}$, $A = \{2, 4, 6, 8\}$ and $B = \{2, 3, 5, 7\}$. Verify that

(i) $(A \cup B)' = A' \cap B'$ (ii) $(A \cap B)' = A' \cup B'$

Sol. (i) $A \cup B = \{2, 4, 6, 8\} \cup \{2, 3, 5, 7\}$

$\Rightarrow \quad A \cup B = \{2, 3, 4, 5, 6, 7, 8\}$

$\Rightarrow (A \cup B)' = U - (A \cup B)$

$= \{$the elements which are in U but not in $(A \cup B)\}$

$= \{1, 2, 3, 4, 5, 6, 7, 8, 9\} - \{2, 3, 4, 5, 6, 7, 8\}$

$= \{1, 9\}$ ...(i)

Now, complememt of $A = A' = U - A$

$= \{$the elements which are in U but not in $A\}$

$= \{1, 2, 3, 4, 5, 6, 7, 8, 9\} - \{2, 4, 6, 8\} = \{1, 3, 5, 7, 9\}$

and, complement of $B = B' = U - B$

$= \{\text{the elements which are in } U \text{ but not in } B\}$

$= \{1, 2, 3, 4, 5, 6, 7, 8, 9\} - \{2, 3, 5, 7\}$

$= \{1, 4, 6, 8, 9\}$

$\Rightarrow \quad A' \cap B' = \{1, 3, 5, 7, 9\} \cap \{1, 4, 6, 8, 9\} = \{1, 9\}$ ...(ii)

From Eqs (i) and (ii), we get

$$(A \cup B)' = A' \cap B'$$

(ii) Now, $A \cap B = \{2, 4, 6, 8\} \cap \{2, 3, 5, 7\} = \{2\}$

$\therefore (A \cap B)' = U - (A \cap B)$

$= \{\text{the elements which are in } U \text{ but not in } (A \cap B)\}$

$= \{1, 2, 3, 4, 5, 6, 7, 8, 9\} - \{2\}$

$= \{1, 3, 4, 5, 6, 7, 8, 9\}$ ...(i)

Now, complement of $A = A' = \{1, 3, 5, 7, 9\}$

and complement of $B = B' = \{1, 4, 6, 8, 9\}$ as in part (i)

$\therefore \quad A' \cup B' = \{1, 3, 4, 5, 6, 7, 8, 9\}$ ...(ii)

From Eqs. (i) and (ii), we get

$$(A \cap B)' = A' \cup B'$$

Question 5 Draw appropriate Venn diagram for each of the following

(i) $(A \cup B)'$ (ii) $A' \cap B'$

(iii) $(A \cap B)'$ (iv) $A' \cup B'$

Sol. (i) $(A \cup B)' = U - (A \cup B) =$ Shaded area

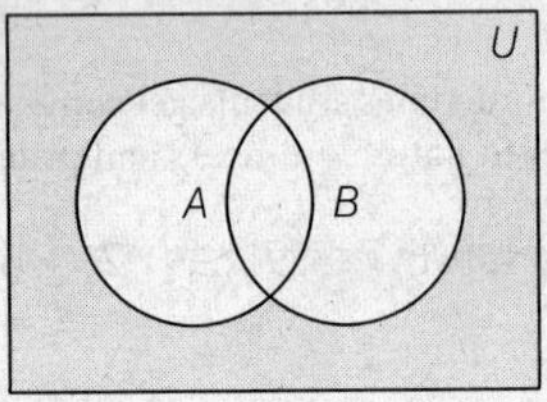

(ii) $A' \cap B' = (A \cup B)' =$ Shaded area (by de-Morgan's law)

(iii) $(A \cap B)' = U - (A \cap B) =$ Shaded area

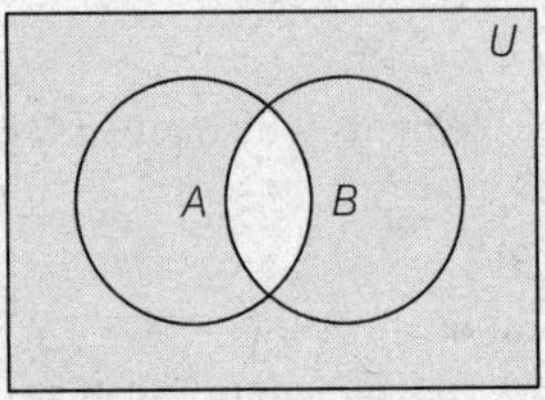

(iv) $A' \cup B' = (A \cap B)' =$ shaded area (By De-Morgan's law)

Question 6 Let U be the set of all triangles in a plane. If A is the set of all triangles with atleast one angle different from 60°, what is A' ?

Sol. A is the set of triangles in which no triangle is equilateral because one angle is different from 60° and we know that equilateral triangle has angle 60°.

$\therefore$ A' = Set of elements of U which are not in A = Set of equilateral triangles.

Question 7 Fill in the blanks to make each of the following a true statement

(i) $A \cup A' = ...$ (ii) $\phi' \cap A = ...$ (iii) $A \cap A' = ...$ (iv) $U' \cap A = ...$

Sol. (i) $A \cup A' = U$

Since, union of a set and its complement is equal to the universal set

(ii) $\phi' \cap A = U \cap A$ [$\because$ complement of null set is universal set]

$= A$ [intersection of any set A and universal set is equal to the set A]

(iii) $U \cap A' = \phi$

Since, intersection of a set and its complement is equal to the null set

(iv) $U' \cap A = \phi \cap A$ [$\because$ complement of a set is null set]

$= \phi$ [intersection of any set and null set is equal to the null set]

Miscellaneous Exercise

Question 1 Decide, among the following sets, which sets are subsets of one and another.

$A = \{x : x \in R \text{ and } x \text{ satisfy } x^2 - 8x + 12 = 0\}$

$B = \{2, 4, 6\}$, $C = \{2, 4, 6, 8, \dots\}$, $D = \{6\}$

◎ *Thinking Process* $A \subset B$, if every element of A is in B.

Sol. Given, $A = \{x : x \in R \text{ and } x \text{ satisfy } x^2 - 8x + 12 = 0\}$

$$\because \quad x^2 - 8x + 12 = 0$$
$$\Rightarrow \quad x - 6x - 2x + 12 = 0$$
$$\Rightarrow \quad x(x - 6) - 2(x - 6) = 0$$
$$\Rightarrow \quad (x - 2)(x - 6) = 0$$
$$\Rightarrow \quad x = 2, 6$$

$$A = \{6, 2\},$$
$$B = \{2, 4, 6\}$$
$$C = \{2, 4, 6, 8....\}$$
$$\text{and} \quad D = \{6\}$$

Clearly, every element of A is in B and C.

$\therefore$ $A \subset B$ and $A \subset C$

Again, every element of B is in C

$\therefore \quad B \subset C$

Also, every element of D is in A, B and C.

$\therefore \quad D \subset A, D \subset B$ and $D \subset C$.

Question 2 In each of the following, determine whether the statement is true or false. If it is true, prove it. If it is false, give an example.

(i) If $x \in A$ and $A \in B$, then $x \in B$.
(ii) If $A \subset B$ and $B \in C$, then $A \in C$.
(iii) If $A \subset B$ and $B \subset C$, then $A \subset C$.
(iv) If $A \not\subset B$ and $B \not\subset C$, then $A \not\subset C$.
(v) If $x \in A$ and $A \not\subset B$, then $x \in B$.
(vi) If $A \subset B$ and $x \notin B$, then $x \notin A$.

Sol. (i) **False**

Let $A = \{2\}$, $B = \{\{2\}, 3\}$

$\Rightarrow \quad 2 \in A$ and $A \in B$ but $2 \notin B$

So, $x \in A$ and $A \in B$ need not imply that $x \in B$.

(ii) **False**

Let $A = \{2\}$, $B = \{2, 3\}$ and $C = \{\{2,3\}, 4\}$

$\Rightarrow A \subset B$ and $B \in C$ but $A \notin C$

So, $A \subset B$ and $B \in C$ need not imply that $A \in C$.

(iii) **True**

Let $x \in A$, then

If $A \subset B \Rightarrow x \in B$ and if $B \subset C \Rightarrow x \in C$

$\Rightarrow x \in A \Rightarrow x \in C$

Hence, $A \subset C$

So, if $A \subset B$ and $B \subset C$, then $A \subset C$.

(iv) **False**

Let $A = \{1, 2\}$, $B = \{2, 3\}$ and $C = \{1, 2, 4\}$

$\Rightarrow \quad A \not\subset B$ and $B \not\subset C$ but $A \subset C$

Hence, $A \not\subset B$ and $B \not\subset C$ need not imply that $A \not\subset C$.

(v) **False**

Let $A = \{1, 2\}$ and $B = \{2, 3, 4, 5\}$

Clearly, $1 \in A$ and $A \not\subset B$ but $1 \notin B$.

Hence, $x \in A$ and $A \not\subset B$ need not imply that $x \in B$.

(vi) **True**

Let $A \subset B$, then if $x \in A \Rightarrow x \in B$ and if $x \notin B \Rightarrow x \notin A$

Question 3 Let A, B and C be the sets such that $A \cup B = A \cup C$ and $A \cap B = A \cap C$. Show that $B = C$.

Sol. Given, $A \cup B = A \cup C$

$\Rightarrow \quad (A \cup B) \cap C = (A \cup C) \cap C$

$\Rightarrow \quad (A \cap C) \cup (B \cap C) = C \quad [\because (A \cup C) \cap C = C]$

$\Rightarrow \quad (A \cap B) \cup (B \cap C) = C \quad [\because A \cap C = A \cap B, \text{give}] \quad \ldots\text{(i)}$

Again, $\quad A \cup B = A \cup C$

$\Rightarrow \quad (A \cup B) \cap B = (A \cup C) \cap B$

$\Rightarrow \quad B = [(A \cap B) \cup (C \cap B)] \quad [\because (A \cup B) \cap B = B]$

$\Rightarrow \quad B = (A \cap B) \cup (B \cap C) \quad \ldots\text{(ii)}$

From Eqs (i) and (ii), we get $B = C$

Question 4 Show that the following four conditions are equivalent:

(i) $A \subset B$ (ii) $A - B = \phi$
(iii) $A \cup B = B$ (iv) $A \cap B = A$

Sol. (i) $\Leftrightarrow$ (ii)

$A \subset B \Leftrightarrow$ all the elements of A are in B

$\Leftrightarrow A - B = \phi$

Hence, (i) $\Leftrightarrow$ (ii)

(ii) $\Leftrightarrow$ (iii)

Now, we have $A - B = \phi$

$\Leftrightarrow \quad A \subset B \Leftrightarrow A \cup B = B$

Hence, (ii) $\Leftrightarrow$ (iii)

(iii) $\Leftrightarrow$ (iv)

We have $A \cup B = B$

$\Leftrightarrow \quad A \subset B \Leftrightarrow A \cap B = A$

$\therefore$ (iii) $\Leftrightarrow$ (iv)

(iv) $\Leftrightarrow$ (i)

We have $A \cap B = A$

$\Leftrightarrow \quad A \subset B$

$\therefore$ (iv) $\Leftrightarrow$ (i)

Hence, (i) $\Leftrightarrow$ (ii) $\Leftrightarrow$ (iii) $\Leftrightarrow$ (iv)

Question 5 Show that if $A \subset B$, then $C - B \subset C - A$.

Sol. Let $x \in C - B$

$\Rightarrow \quad x \in C$ and $x \notin B$

$\Rightarrow \quad x \in C$ and $x \notin A$

$\Rightarrow \quad x \in C - A \quad (\because A \subset B)$

$\therefore \; C - B \subset C - A$

Question 6 Show that for any sets A and B, $A=(A\cap B)\cup(A-B)$ and $A\cup(B-A)=(A\cup B)$.

Sol. Now, $(A\cap B)\cup(A-B)$

$$=(A\cap B)\cup(A\cap B') \qquad [\because A-B=A\cap B']$$
$$=A\cap(B\cup B') \qquad [\because (A\cap B)\cup(A\cap B')=A\cap(B\cup B')]$$
$$=A\cap U \qquad [\because B\cup B'=U]$$
$$=A$$

Again, $A\cup(B-A)=A\cup(B\cap A')$ $\qquad (\because B-A=B\cap A')$

$$=(A\cup B)\cap(A\cup A')$$
$$[\because A\cup(B\cap A')=(A\cup B)\cap(A\cup A')]$$
$$=(A\cup B)\cap U \qquad (\because A\cup A'=U)$$
$$=A\cup B$$

Hence Proved.

Note $A-B=A\cap B'$.

Question 7 Using properties of sets, show that

(i) $A\cup(A\cap B)=A$ (ii) $A\cap(A\cup B)=A$

Sol. (i) $A\cup(A\cap B)=(A\cup A)\cap(A\cup B)=A\cap(A\cup B)=A$

(ii) $A\cap(A\cup B)=(A\cap A)\cup(A\cap B)=A\cup(A\cap B)=A$ **Hence Proved.**

Question 8 Show that $A\cap B=A\cap C$ need not imply $B=C$.

◎ ***Thinking Process*** To solve this type of problem, take some example which satisfy the given conditions.

Sol. Let $A=\{1, 2, 3, 4\}$, $B=\{3, 4, 5, 6\}$, $C=\{3, 4, 7, 8\}$

Then, $A\cap B=\{3, 4\}$ ...(i)

$A\cap C=\{3, 4\}$ ...(ii)

From Eqs. (i) and (ii), $A\cap B=A\cap C$ But $B\neq C$ **Hence Proved.**

Question 9 Let A and B be sets. If $A\cap X=B\cap X=\phi$ and $A\cup X=B\cup X$ for some set X, show that $A=B$.

◎ ***Thinking Process*** Use distributive law $A=A\cap(A\cup X)$, $B=B\cap(B\cup X)$ to show that $A=B$.

Sol. We know that two sets are equal when they are subsets of each other.

Now, we have

$$A\cup X=B\cup X \text{ for some set } X$$
$$\Rightarrow \quad A\cap(A\cup X)=A\cap(B\cup X)$$
$$\Rightarrow \quad A=(A\cap B)\cup(A\cap X)$$

[by distributive law and $A\cap(A\cup X)=A$]

$$\Rightarrow \quad A = (A \cap B) \cup \phi \qquad (\because A \cap X = \phi, \text{ Given})$$
$$\Rightarrow \quad A = A \cap B$$
$$\Rightarrow \quad A \subset B \qquad \ldots(i)$$

Again, $A \cup X = B \cup X$

or $B \cup X = A \cup X$

$$\Rightarrow \quad B \cap (B \cup X) = B \cap (A \cup X)$$
$$\Rightarrow \quad B = (B \cap A) \cup (B \cap X) \qquad \text{[by distributive law]}$$
$$\Rightarrow \quad B = (B \cap A) \cup \phi \qquad (\because B \cap X = \phi \text{ given})$$
$$\Rightarrow \quad B = (B \cap A)$$
$$\Rightarrow \quad B \subset A \qquad \ldots(ii)$$

From Eqs. (i) and (ii), we get $A = B$ **Hence Proved.**

Question 10 Find sets A, B and C such that $A \cap B$, $B \cap C$ and $A \cap C$ are non-empty sets and $(A \cap B) \cap C = \phi$.

Sol. Let $A = \{3, 4\}, B = \{4, 5\}, C = \{3, 5, 6\}$

Now, $A \cap B = \{3, 4\} \cap \{4, 5\} = \{4\} \neq \phi$,

$B \cap C = \{4, 5\} \cap \{3, 5, 6\} = \{5\} \neq \phi$,

$A \cap C = \{3, 4\} \cap \{3, 5, 6\} = \{3\} \neq \phi$

and $A \cap B \cap C = (A \cap B) \cap C = \{4\} \cap \{3, 5, 6\} = \phi$

Similarly, we can choose some other such type of sets also.

DIKSHA APP Questions

☐ Multiple Choice Questions

Q.1 Which of the following sets are null sets?

(a) $\{0\}$ (b) $\{\phi\}$

(c) $\{\}$ (d) Both (b) and (c)

Sol. (c) A null set is set that contains no elements. It is represented by the symbol $\{\}$ or ϕ.

Q.2 The members of the set $S = \{x : x$ is the square of an integer and $x < 100\}$ is

(a) $\{0, 2, 4, 5, 9, 58, 49, 56, 99, 12\}$

(b) $\{0, 1, 4, 9, 16, 25, 36, 49, 64, 81\}$

(c) $\{1, 4, 9, 16, 25, 36, 64, 81, 85, 99\}$

(d) $\{0, 1, 4, 9, 16, 25, 36, 49, 64, 121\}$

Sol. (b) Here, x is the square of an integer less than 100 and we know that integers are .... $-3,-2,-1,0,1,2,3$ ....

So, $S=\{0,1,4,9,16,25,36,49,64,81\}$

Mistake Alert Do not forget to include O in the set S.

Q.3 If A and B be any two sets, then $(A\cap B)'$ is equal to?

(a) $A'\cap B'$ (b) $A'\cup B'$
(c) $A\cap B$ (d) $A\cup B$

Sol. (b) By de-Morgan's law : $(A\cap B)'=A'\cup B'$

Q.4 Let A and B be subsets of set X. Then which of the following are true?

(a) $A-B=A\cup B$ (b) $A-B=A\cap B$
(c) $A-B=A'\cap B$ (d) $A-B=A\cap B'$

Sol. (d) If A and B are any two sets, then $A-B=A\cap B'$

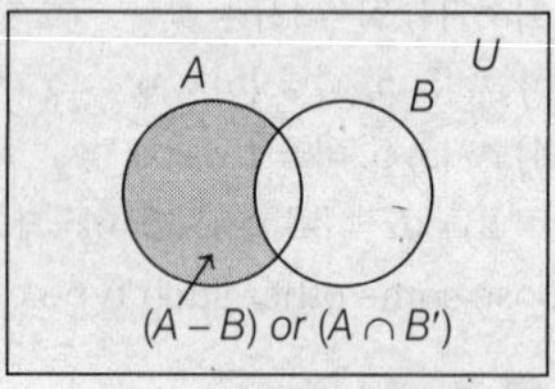

Q.5 If A and B are sets and $A\cup B=A\cap B$, then

(a) $A=\phi$ (b) $B=\phi$
(c) $A=B$ (d) None of these

Sol. (c) We have, $A\cup B=A\cap B$

Case I $A\neq B$

Let $A=\{a,b,c\}$ and $B=\{1,2,3\}$

LHS $=A\cup B=\{a,b,c,1,2,3\}$

RHS $=A\cap B=\phi$

$\therefore$ LHS $\neq$ RHS

Case II $A=B$

Let $A=\{1, 2, 3\}$ and $B=\{1, 2, 3\}$

LHS $=A\cup B=\{1, 2, 3\}$

RHS $=A\cap B=\{1, 2, 3\}$

$\therefore$ LHS $=$ RHS

So, if $A\cup B=A\cap B$, then $A=B$

Relations and Functions

CHAPTER 02

Important Points

01 Ordered pair If two elements are written in a specific order, then they form an ordered pair defined as (a, b). They are written in the brackets () and being separated by commas.

02 Cartesian product of sets Given two non-empty sets P and Q. The cartesian product $P \times Q$ is the set of all ordered pairs of elements from P to Q

i.e., $P \times Q = \{(p, q) : p \in P \text{ and } q \in Q\}$

Note (i) Number of elements in $(P \times Q)$ = Number of elements in P $\times$ Number of elements in Q

i.e., $n(P \times Q) = n(P) \times n(Q)$.

(ii) In general, $A \times B \neq B \times A$

(iii) If $A = \phi$ or $B = \phi$, then $A \times B = \phi$

(iv) If $(a,b) = (c,d) \Leftrightarrow a = c$ and $b = d$

(v) If A and B are non empty sets and at least one of them is infinite then $A \times B$ is also an infinite.

(vi) If $n(A) = p$ and $n(B) = q$, then $n(A \times B) = n(B \times A) = pq$.

(vii) $A \times A \times A = \{(a,b,c) : a. b, c \in A\}$
Here (a, b, c) is called an ordered triplet.

03 Relation A relation R from a non-empty set A to a non-empty set B is a subset of the cartesian product $A \times B$.

04 (i) The set of all first elements of the ordered pairs in a relation R from a set A to a set B is called the domain of the relation R.

(ii) The set of all second elements in a relation R from a set A to a set B is called the range of the relation R. The whole set B is called the co-domain of the relation R.

(iii) Range $\subset$ co-domain

(iv) A relation may be represented algebraically either by the roster method or by the set builder method.

(v) An arrow diagram is a visual presentation of a relation.

(vi) The total number of relations that can be defined from a set A to a set B is the number of possible subsets of $A \times B$. If $n(A) = p$ and $n(B) = q$, then number of relation from A to B is 2^{pq}.

Example

Consider the two sets $P = \{a, b, c\}$ and $Q = \{\text{Ali, Bhanu, Binoy, Chandra, Divya}\}$

$P \times Q = \{(a, \text{Ali}), (a, \text{Bhanu}), (a, \text{Binoy}), \ldots, (c, \text{Divya})\}$

Given $R = \{(x, y) : x$ is the first letter of the name $y, x \in P, y \in Q\}$.

i.e., $R = \{(a, \text{Ali}), (b, \text{Bhanu}), (b, \text{Binoy}), (c, \text{Chandra})\}$.

Arrow diagram for R

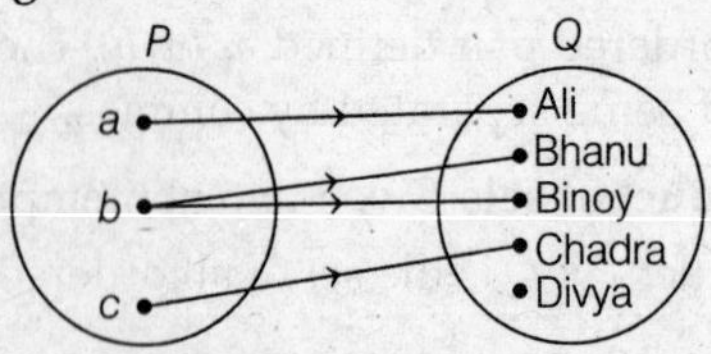

Domain of $R = \{a, b, c\}$

Range of $R = \{\text{Ali, Bhanu, Binoy, Chandra}\}$

Co-Domain of $R = Q$

Total number of relation from P to $Q = 2^{|P \times Q|} = 2^{|3 \times 5|} = 2^{15}$

Note A relation R from A to A is also stated as a relation on A.

05 Function A relation f from a set A to a set B is said to be a function if every element of set A has one and only one image in set B. The function f from A to B is denoted by $f : A \to B$

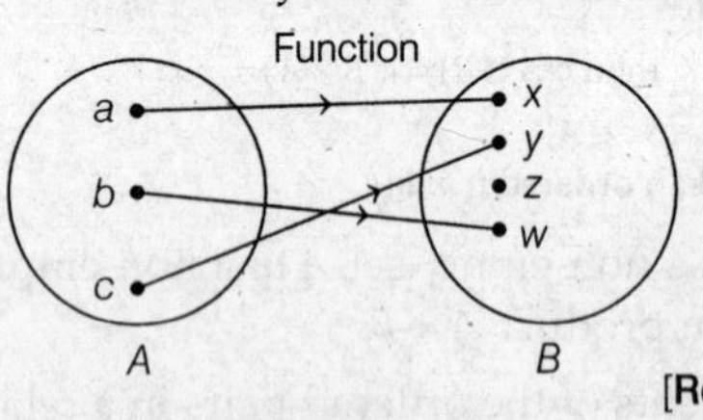

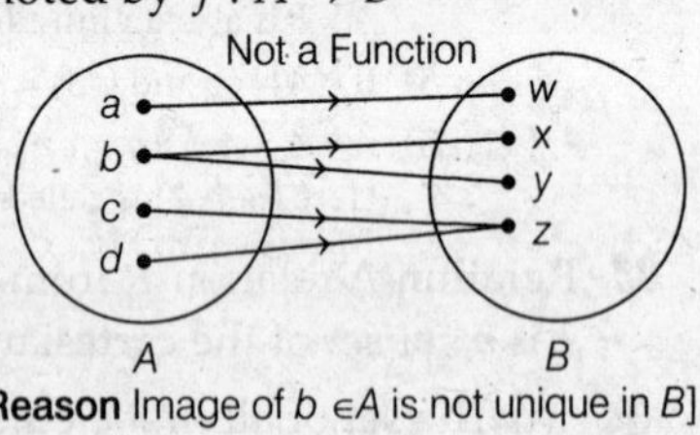

[Reason Image of $b \in A$ is not unique in B]

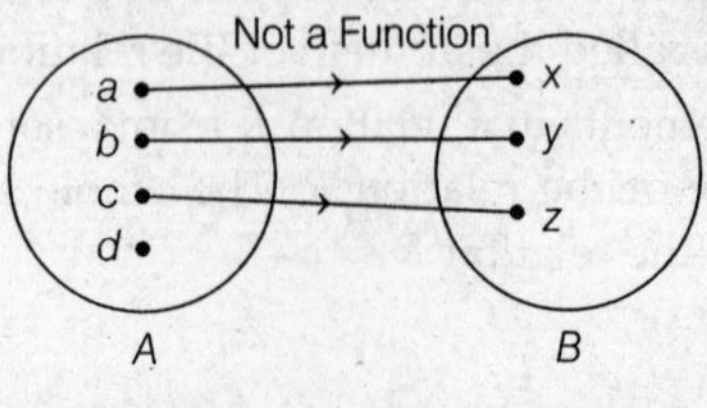

[Reason Image of $d \in A$ does not exist in B]

Note

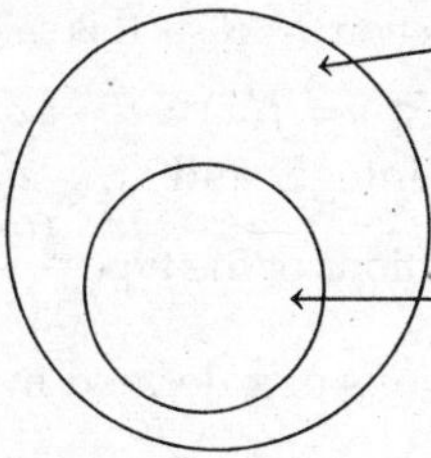

i.e., All functions are relations but not all relations are functions.

06 **Algebra of functions** For functions $f: X \rightarrow R$ and $g: X \rightarrow R$, we have

(i) $(f+g)(x)=f(x)+g(x), x \in X$ (Addition of two real functions)

(ii) $(f-g)(x)=f(x)-g(x), x \in X$
(Subtraction of a real function from another)

(iii) $(f \cdot g)(x)=f(x) \cdot g(x), x \in X$ (Multiplication of two real function)

(iv) $(kf)(x)=kf(x), x \in X$, where k is a real number. (Multiplication by a scalar)

(v) $\left(\frac{f}{g}\right)(x)=\frac{f(x)}{g(x)}, x \in X, g(x) \neq 0$ (Quotient of two real functions)

07 (i) A function which has either R or one of its subsets as its range, is called a real valued function. Further, if its domain is also either R or a subset of R, then it is called a real function.

(ii) In a function $f: A \rightarrow B$, A is the domain and B is the co-domain of f.

(iii) The range of the function is the set of images.

08 Some input fuctions

(i) **Constant function** Define the function $f: R \rightarrow R$ by $y=f(x)=c$, $x \in R$ where C is a constant and each $x \in R$. Here domain of f is R and its range is $\{c\}$.

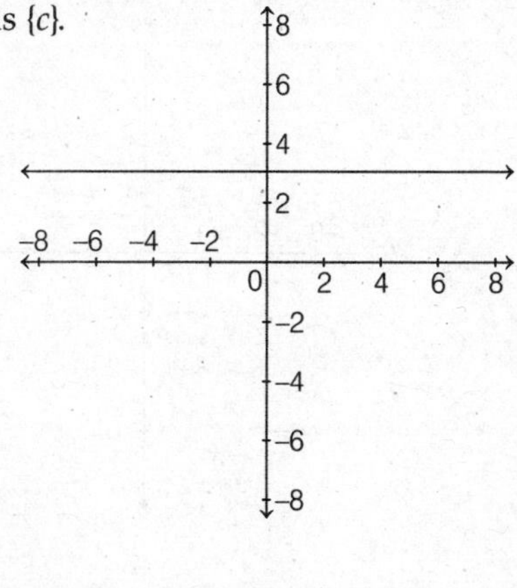

(ii) **Polynomial function** A function $f: R \to R$ is said to be polynomial function if for each x in R, $y = f(x) = a_0 + a_1 x + a_2 x^2 + \dots + a_n x^n$, where n is a non-negative integer and $a_0, a_1, a_2, \dots, a_n \in R$

(iii) **Rational functions** are functions of the type $\frac{f(x)}{g(x)}$, where $f(x)$ and $g(x)$ are polynomial functions of x defined in a domain, where $g(x) \neq 0$

09 **Modulus function** The function $f: R \to R$ defined by $f(x) = |x|$ for each $x \in R$ is called modulus function or absolute valued function. For each non-negative value of x, $f(x)$ is equal to x.

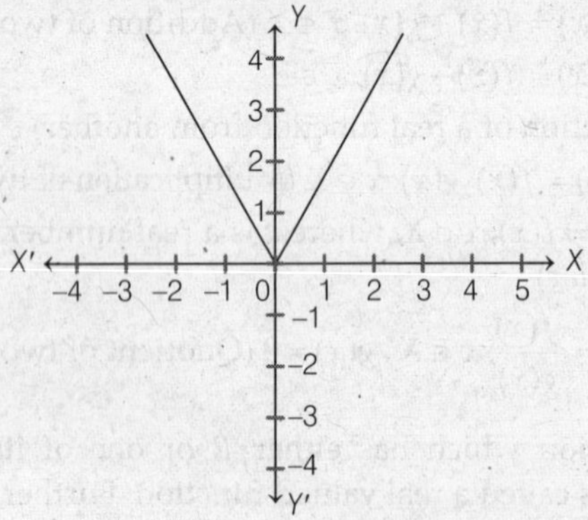

But for negative value of x, the value of $f(x)$ is positive, *i.e.*,

$$f(x) = \begin{cases} x, & x \geq 0 \\ -x, & x < 0 \end{cases}$$

10 **Greatest integer function** The function $f: R \to R$ defined by $f(x) = [x]$, $x \in R$ assumes the value of the greatest integer, less than or equal to x, such a function is called the greatest integer function.

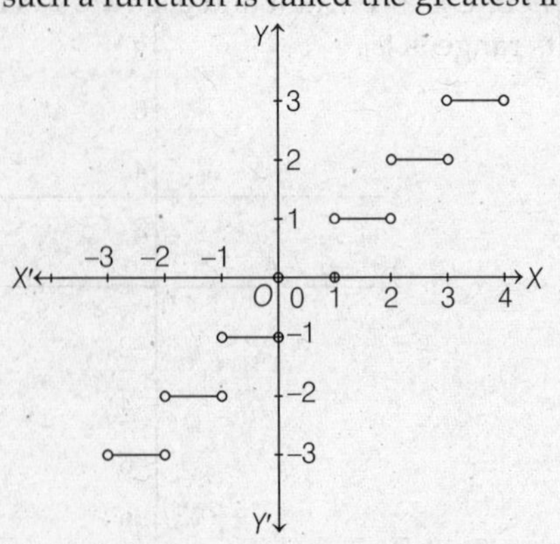

From the definition of $[x]$, we have

$$[x] = -1, \text{ for } -1 \le x < 0$$
$$[x] = 0, \text{ for } 0 \le x < 1$$
$$[x] = 1, \text{ for } 1 \le x < 2$$
$$[x] = 2, \text{ for } 2 \le x < 3 \text{ and so on.}$$

11 Signum function Let R be the set of real numbers, then the function $f : R \to R$ defined by

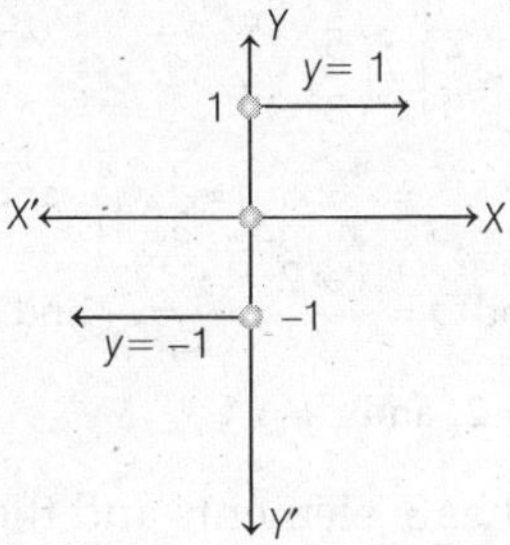

$$f(x) = \frac{|x|}{x} = \begin{cases} 1, & x > 0 \\ 0, & x = 0 \\ -1, & x < 0 \end{cases}$$ is known as signum function.

12 Identity function Let R be the set of real numbers. A real valued function f is defined as $f : R \to R$ by $y = f(x) = x$ for each value of $x \in R$. Such a function is called the identity function.

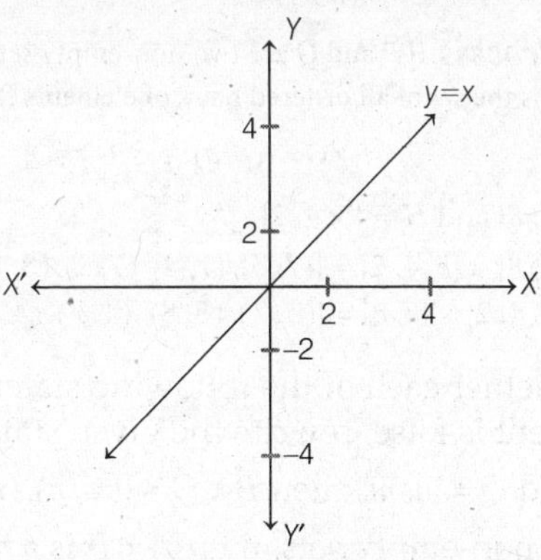

Exercise 2.1

Question 1 If $\left(\frac{x}{3}+1, y-\frac{2}{3}\right)=\left(\frac{5}{3}, \frac{1}{3}\right)$, find the values of x and y.

◎ *Thinking Process* Two ordered pairs (a, b) and (c, d) are equal if and only if $a=c$ and $b=d$.

Sol. Given, $\left(\frac{x}{3}+1, y-\frac{2}{3}\right)=\left(\frac{5}{3}, \frac{1}{3}\right)$

$$\Rightarrow \frac{x}{3}+1=\frac{5}{3} \text{ and } y-\frac{2}{3}=\frac{1}{3} \Rightarrow \frac{x}{3}=\frac{5}{3}-\frac{1}{1} \text{ and } y=\frac{1}{3}+\frac{2}{3}$$

$$\Rightarrow \frac{x}{3}=\frac{5-3}{3} \text{ and } y=\frac{1+2}{3} \Rightarrow \frac{x}{3}=\frac{2}{3} \text{ and } y=\frac{3}{3}$$

$$\Rightarrow x=2 \text{ and } y=1$$

Question 2 If the set A has 3 elements and the set $B=\{3, 4, 5\}$, then find the number of elements in $(A\times B)$.

◎ *Thinking Process* Here, we will use the formula $n(A\times B)=n(A)\times n(B)$ and simplify it.

Sol. Here, $n(A)=3$, $B=\{3, 4, 5\} \Rightarrow n(B)=3$

$$\therefore \quad n(A\times B)=n(A)\times n(B)=3\times 3=9$$

Question 3 If $G=\{7, 8\}$ and $H=\{5, 4, 2\}$, find $G\times H$ and $H\times G$.

◎ *Thinking Process* If P and Q are two non-empty sets, then cartesian product $P\times Q$ is the set of all ordered pairs of elements from P to Q *i.e.*,

$$P\times Q=\{(p, q): p\in P, q\in Q\}$$

Sol. Given, $G=\{7, 8\}$ and $H=\{5, 4, 2\}$

$$G\times H=\{7, 8\}\times\{5, 4, 2\}=\{(7, 5), (7, 4), (7, 2), (8, 5), (8, 4), (8, 2)\}$$

and $H\times G=\{5, 4, 2\}\times\{7, 8\}=\{(5, 7), (5, 8), (4, 7), (4, 8), (2, 7), (2, 8)\}$

Question 4 State whether each of the following statements are true or false. If the statement is false, rewrite the given statement correctly.

(i) If $P=\{m, n\}$ and $Q=\{n, m\}$, then $P\times Q=\{(m, n), (n, m)\}$.

(ii) If A and B are non-empty sets, then $A\times B$ is a non-empty set of ordered pairs (x, y) such that $x\in A$ and $y\in B$

(iii) If $A=\{1, 2\}$, $B=\{3, 4\}$, then $A\times(B\cap\phi)=\phi$.

Sol. (i) It is false, because if $P = \{m, n\}$ and $Q = \{n, m\}$, then

$$P \times Q = \{m, n\} \times \{n, m\} = \{(m, n), (m, m), (n, n), (n, m)\}$$

(ii) It is true, by defination of cartesian product.

(iii) It is true, because $B \cap \phi = \phi \Rightarrow A \times (B \cap \phi) = A \times \phi = \phi$

Question 5 If $A = \{-1, 1\}$, find $A \times A \times A$.

◎ *Thinking Process* $A \times A \times A = [(a, b, c) : a, b, c \in A]$

Sol. Given, $A = \{-1, 1\}$

$\Rightarrow$ $A \times A = \{-1, 1\} \times \{-1, 1\} = \{(-1, -1), (-1, 1), (1, -1), (1, 1)\}$

Again, $A \times A \times A = \{(-1, -1,)(-1, 1), (1, -1), (1, 1)\} \times \{-1, 1\}$

$= \{(-1, -1, -1), (-1, -1, 1), (-1, 1, -1), (-1, 1, 1)$

$(1, -1, -1), (1, -1, 1), (1, 1, -1), (1, 1, 1)\}$

Question 6 If $A \times B = \{(a, x), (a, y), (b, x), (b, y)\}$. Find A and B.

Sol. Since, $A \times B = \{(a, x), (a, y), (b, x), (b, y)\}$

From the given pairs, the first elements (a and b) come from set A and second elements (x and y) come from set B.

$\Rightarrow$ $A = \{a, b\}$ and $B = \{x, y\}$

Mistake Alert Elements are written only once don't repeat any element.

Question 7 Let $A = \{1, 2\}$, $B = \{1, 2, 3, 4\}$, $C = \{5, 6\}$ and $D = \{5, 6, 7, 8\}$. Verify that

(i) $A \times (B \cap C) = (A \times B) \cap (A \times C)$ (ii) $A \times C$ is a subset of $B \times D$.

Sol. (i) Given, $A = \{1, 2,\}$, $B = \{1, 2, 3, 4\}$, $C = \{5, 6\}$ and $D = \{5, 6, 7, 8\}$

$B \cap C = \{1, 2, 3, 4\} \cap \{5, 6\} = \phi$

$\therefore$ $A \times (B \cap C) = \{1, 2\} \times \phi = \phi$ ...(i)

Now, $A \times B = \{1, 2\} \times \{1, 2, 3, 4\}$

$= \{(1, 1), (1, 2), (1, 3), (1, 4), (2, 1), (2, 2), (2, 3), (2, 4)\}$

$A \times C = \{1, 2\} \times \{5, 6\} = \{(1, 5), (1, 6), (2, 5), (2, 6)\}$ ...(ii)

$\Rightarrow$ $(A \times B) \cap (A \times C)$

$= \{(1, 1), (1, 2), (1, 3), (1, 4), (2, 1), (2, 2)\}(2, 3), (2, 4)\}$

$\cap \{(1, 5), (1, 6), (2, 5), (2, 6)\}$

$= \phi$ ...(iii)

From Eqs. (i) and (iii), $A \times (B \cap C) = (A \times B) \cap (A \times C)$

(ii) $B \times D = \{1, 2, 3, 4\} \times \{5, 6, 7, 8\}$

$= \{(1, 5), (1, 6), (1, 7), (1, 8), (2, 5), (2, 6), (2, 7), (2, 8),$

$(3, 5), (3, 6), (3, 7), (3, 8), (4, 5), (4, 6), (4, 7), (4, 8)\}$ ...(iv)

From Eqs. (ii) and (iv), we see that all the elements of $A \times C$ are in $B \times D$.

Hence, $A \times C$ is a subset of $B \times D$.

Note If A is a non-empty set and B is an empty set, then $A \times B = \phi$.

Question 8 Let $A=\{1,2\}$ and $B=\{3,4\}$. Write $A\times B$. How many subsets will $A\times B$ have ? List them.

◎ *Thinking Process* If a set has n elements, then number of possible subsets $=2^n$

Sol. Given, $A = \{1, 2\}$ and $B = \{3, 4\}$

$\Rightarrow$ $A \times B = \{1, 2\} \times \{3, 4\}$

$A \times B = \{(1, 3), (1, 4), (2, 3), (2, 4)\}$

$\Rightarrow$ $n(A \times B) = 4$

$\Rightarrow$ Total subsets of $A \times B = 2^4 = 16$

Subsets of $A \times B$ are

ϕ, $\{(1, 3)\}$, $\{(1, 4)\}$, $\{(2, 3)\}$, $\{(2, 4)\}$, $\{(1, 3), (1, 4)\}$, $\{(1, 3), (2, 3)\}$,
$\{(1, 3), (2, 4)\}$, $\{(1, 4), (2, 3)\}$, $\{(1, 4), (2, 4)\}$, $\{(2, 3), (2, 4)\}$,
$\{(1, 3), (1, 4), (2, 3)\}$, $\{(1, 3), (1, 4), (2, 4)\}$,
$\{(1, 3), (2, 3), (2, 4)\}$, $\{(1, 4), (2, 3), (2, 4)\}$,
$\{(1, 3), (1, 4), (2, 3), (2, 4)\}$

Question 9 Let A and B be two sets such that $n(A)=3$ and $n(B)=2$. If $(x,1),(y,2),(z,1)$ are in $A\times B$, find A and B, where x, y, z are distinct elements.

Sol. Given,

$A\times B=\{(x,1),(y,2),(z,1)\}$

From the gives pairs, the first elements (x, y, z) come from set A and seoncd elements (1, 2) come from set B.

Here, $x, y, z \in A$ and $1, 2 \in B$

$\Rightarrow$ $A = \{x, y, z\}$ and $B = \{1, 2\}$

Question 10 The cartesian product $A\times A$ has 9 elements among which are found $(-1,0)$ and $(0,1)$. Find the set A and the remaining elements of $A\times A$.

Sol. Given, $(-1,0)\in A\times A$ and $(0,1)\in A\times A$

$\Rightarrow$ $A = \{-1, 0, 1\}$

$A \times A = \{-1, 0, 1\} \times \{-1, 0, 1\}$

$= \{(-1, -1), (-1, 0), (-1, 1), (0, -1), (0, 0), (0, 1),$
$(1, -1,), (1, 0), (1, 1)\}$

Hence, remaining elements are

$\{(-1, -1), (-1, 1), (0, -1), (0, 0), (1, -1), (1,0), (1, 1)\}$

Exercise 2.2

Question 1 Let $A = \{1, 2, 3, \ldots, 14\}$. Define a relation R from A to A by $R = \{(x, y) : 3x - y = 0, \text{ where } x, y \in A\}$.
Write down its domain, co-domain and range.

◎ *Thinking Process*

(i) Domain is the set of all first elements of the ordered pairs in a relation.
(ii) Range is the set of all second elements of the ordered pairs in a relation.
(iii) If R is a relation from a set A to a set B, then whole set B is called the co-domain of R. You should always remember that range $\subseteq$ co-domain.

Sol. (i) $R = \{(x, y) : 3x - y = 0, \text{ where, } x, y \in A\} = \{(1, 3), (2, 6), (3, 9), (4, 12)\}$

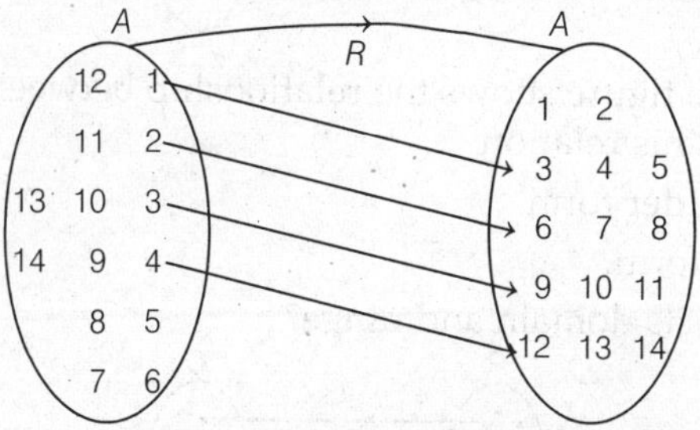

(ii) Domain = {1, 2, 3, 4}   (iii) Co-domain = {1, 2, 3, 4,...., 14}
(iv) Range = {3, 6, 9, 12}

Question 2 Define a relation R on the set N of natural numbers by $R = \{(x, y) : y = x + 5, x \text{ is a natural number less than } 4; x, y \in N\}$.
Depict this relationship using roster form. Write down the domain and the range.

Sol. Since, x is a natural number less than 4, *i.e.*, $x = 1, 2, 3$

(i) $R = \{(x, y) : y = x + 5, x \text{ is a natural number less than 4.}; x, y \in N\}$
$= \{(1, 6), (2, 7), (3, 8)\}$

The corresponding arrow diagram is shown in figure.

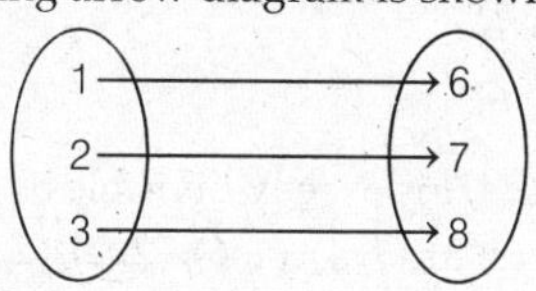

(ii) Domain = {1, 2, 3}
(iii) Range = {6, 7, 8}

Mistake Alert Students may get confuse to find the value of y.

Question 3 $A = \{1, 2, 3, 5\}$ and $B = \{4, 6, 9\}$. Define a relation R from A to B by $R = \{(x, y)$: the difference between x and y is odd; $x \in A, y \in B\}$. Write R in roster form.

◎ *Thinking Process* The difference between odd and one even number is always odd.

Sol. $R = \{(x, y)$: the difference between x and y is odd, $x \in A$, $y \in B\}$

$R = \{(1, 4), (1, 6), (2, 9), (3, 4), (3, 6), (5, 4), (5, 6)\}$

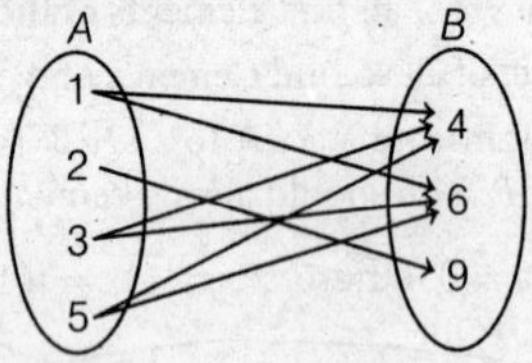

Question 4 The figure shows the relationship between the sets P and Q. Write this relation

(i) in set builder form.

(ii) in roster form.

What are its domain and range?

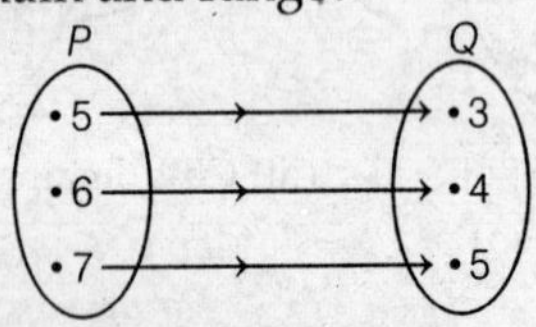

Sol. (i) In set builder form, $R = \{(x, y) : y = x - 2, x \in P$ and $y \in Q\}$

(ii) In roster form, $R = \{(5, 3), (6, 4), (7, 5)\}$

Here, domain = $\{5, 6, 7\}$ and range = $\{3, 4, 5\}$

Question 5 Let $A = \{1, 2, 3, 4, 6\}$. Let R be the relation on A defined by $\{(a, b): a, b \in A, b$ is exactly divisible by $a\}$.

(i) Write R in roster form.

(ii) Find the domain of R.

(iii) Find the range of R.

Sol. Given, $A = \{1, 2, 3, 4, 6\}$

(i) $R = \{(a, b) : a, b \in A, b$ is exactly divisible by $a\}$

$= \{(1, 1), (1, 2), (1, 3), (1, 4), (1, 6), (2, 2), (2, 4), (2, 6), (3, 3), (3, 6), (4, 4), (6, 6)\}$

(ii) Domian = $\{1, 2, 3, 4, 6\}$

(iii) Range = $\{1, 2, 3, 4, 6\}$

Question 6 Determine the domain and range of the relation R defined by $R = \{(x, x+5) : x \in \{0, 1, 2, 3, 4, 5\}\}$.

Sol. Given, $R = \{(x, x + 5) : x \in \{0, 1, 2, 3, 4, 5\}\}$ ...(i)

Putting $x = 0, 1, 2, 3, 4, 5$, we get

$\Rightarrow$ Domain $= \{0, 1, 2, 3, 4, 5\}$

After putting the value of x from Eq. (i), we get

$$y = x + 5 = 5, 6, 7, 8, 9, 10$$

$$\Rightarrow \quad \text{Range} = \{5, 6, 7, 8, 9, 10\}$$

Question 7 Write the relation $R = \{(x, x^3) : x$ is a prime number less than 10$\}$ in roster form.

Sol. Given, $R = \{(x, x^3) : x$ is a prime number less than 10$\}$

$\because$ Prime number less than 10 = 2, 3, 5, 7

$$\Rightarrow \quad R = \{(2, 2^3), (3, 3^3), (5, 5^3), (7, 7^3)\}$$

$$= \{(2, 8), (3, 27), (5, 125), (7, 343)\}$$

Mistake Alert Sometimes, students confuse between prime numbers and odd numbers.

Question 8 Let $A = \{x, y, z\}$ and $B = \{1, 2\}$. Find the number of relations from A to B.

Thinking Process If $n(A) = m$ and $n(B) = n$, then total number of relations from A to $B = 2^{mn}$.

Sol. Here, $A = \{x, y, z\}$ and $B = \{1, 2\}$

$\Rightarrow$ $n(A) = 3$, $n(B) = 2$

$\therefore$ Number of relations from A to $B = 2^{3 \times 2} = 2^6 = 64$

Question 9 Let R be the relation on Z defined by $R = \{(a, b) : a, b \in Z, a - b$ is an integer$\}$. Find the domain and range of R.

Sol. Given, $R = \{(a, b) : a, b \in Z, a - b$ is an integer$\}$

We know that if two numbers are integer, then their difference is also integer.

$$\text{Domain} = Z, \text{Range} = Z$$

Exercise 2.3

Question 1 Which of the following relations are functions? Give reasons. If it is a function, determine its domain and range.

(i) $\{(2,1),(5,1),(8,1),(11,1),(14,1),(17,1)\}$.

(ii) $\{(2,1),(4,2),(6,3),(8,4),(10,5),(12,6),(14,7)\}$.

(iii) $\{(1,3),(1,5),(2,5)\}$.

◎ *Thinking Process* Use arrow diagram to check easily whether given relation is a function or not. Using it, we can easily see that first component of the ordered pair is repeating or not and whether it has one image or more.

Sol. (i) Given, $R = \{(2, 1), (5, 1), (8, 1), (11, 1), (14, 1), (17, 1)\}$

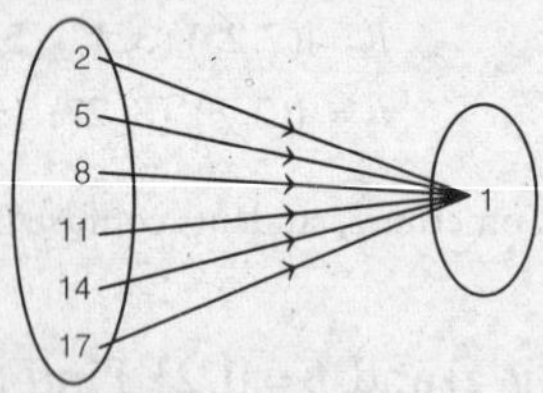

$\because$ It is clear from the above diagram that no two ordered pairs have the same first components.

Hence, this relation is a function.

Here, Domain = set of first components of the ordered pairs

$= \{2, 5, 8, 11, 14, 17\}$

Range = set of second components of the ordered pairs = $\{1\}$

(ii) Given, $R = \{(2, 1), (4, 2), (6, 3), (8, 4), (10, 5), (12, 6), (14, 7)\}$

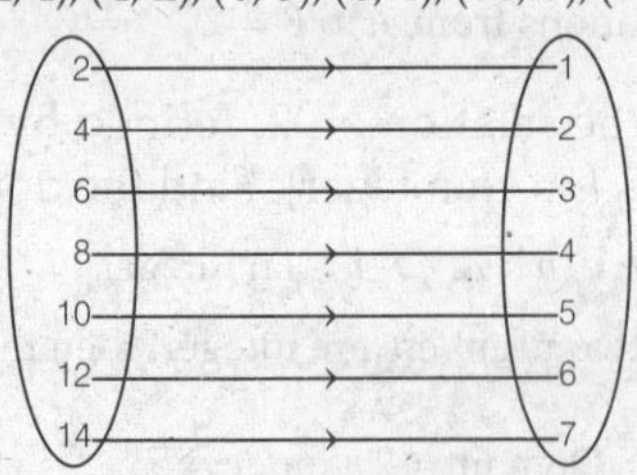

$\because$ No two ordered pairs have the same first components. Hence, this relation is a function.

Domain = set of first components of the ordered pairs

$= \{2, 4, 6, 8, 10, 12, 14\}$

Range = set of second components of the ordered pairs

$= \{1, 2, 3, 4, 5, 6, 7\}$

(iii) Given, $R = \{(1, 3), (1, 5), (2, 5)\}$

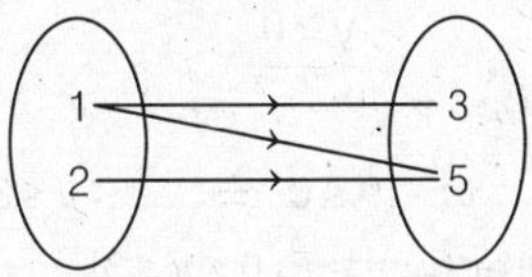

$\because$ Ordered pairs (1, 3) and (1, 5) have the first components same or we can say that the element '1' has two images 3 and 5. So, it is not a function.

Note In any two ordered pairs, if the first components same then it is not a function.

Question 2 Find the domain and range of the following real functions :

(i) $f(x) = -|x|$ (ii) $f(x) = \sqrt{9 - x^2}$

Sol. (i) $f(x) = -|x|$

We know that $|x|$ is defined as non-negative real number for every $x \in R$.

$\Rightarrow$ Domain $= R$

Now, $|x| \geq 0 \Rightarrow -|x| \leq 0$

i.e. $f(x) \leq 0$

$f(x) \in (-\infty, 0]$

Range of $f(x)$ is $R - (0, \infty)$ or $R^- \cup \{0\}$

Mistake Alert When multiply in any inequality with negative sign, reverse the sign of inequality. Sometimes students forget this.

(ii) $f(x) = \sqrt{9 - x^2}$

For function to be defined, $9 - x^2 \geq 0$

$\Rightarrow$ $x^2 - 9 \leq 0$ ...(i)

$\Rightarrow$ $\{x - (-3)\}(x - 3) \leq 0$

$\Rightarrow$ $-3 \leq x \leq 3$ {If $a < b$ and $(x - a)(x - b) \leq 0 \Rightarrow a \leq x \leq b$}

$\Rightarrow$ Domain $= [-3, 3] = \{x : x \in R \text{ and } -3 \leq x \leq 3\}$

Again for range,

Let $f(x) = y$, then $\Rightarrow y = \sqrt{9 - x^2}$

Squaring both sides, we get, $y^2 = 9 - x^2$

$\Rightarrow$ $x^2 = 9 - y^2$ ...(ii)

On putting the value of x^2 in Eq. (i), we get

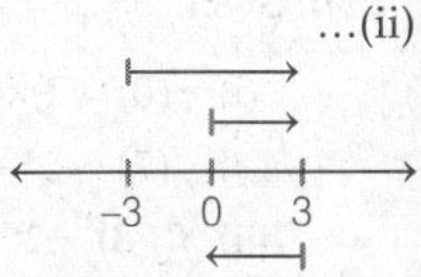

$\Rightarrow$ $9 - y^2 - 9 \leq 0$

$\Rightarrow$ $-y^2 \leq 0$

$\Rightarrow$ $y^2 \geq 0$

$-\infty < y < \infty$

But y cannot be negative $f(x)=\sqrt{9-x^2}$ cannot contain negative values

$\therefore \quad y \geq 0$

Also from Eq. (ii), $x = \sqrt{9 - y^2} \Rightarrow 9 - y^2 \geq 0 \quad (\because x^2 \geq 0)$

$\Rightarrow \quad y^2 - 9 \leq 0 \Rightarrow -3 \leq y \leq 3$

$\Rightarrow$ Range = $[0, 3]$ or $\{y : y \in R, 0 \leq y \leq 3\}$

Mistake Alert While finding the range or domain of a function, please be careful on squaring the function, sometimes it may give some extra values.

Quick Solution

$$f(x) = \sqrt{9 - x^2}$$

We know that f is not define for $9 - x^2 < 0$

That means

$$9 - x^2 \geq 0 \text{ for } f(x) = \sqrt{9 - x^2}$$

$\Rightarrow \quad x^2 - 9 \leq 0 \; \{\because a - b \geq 0 \Leftrightarrow b - a \leq 0\}$

$\Rightarrow \quad (x - (-3))\,(x - 3) \leq 0$

$\Rightarrow \quad -3 \leq x \leq 3$

Note If $a<b$ and $(x - a)(x-b) \leq 0 \Rightarrow a \leq x \leq b\}$

Again for range,

Let $\quad y = f(x) = \sqrt{9 - x^2}$

$\Rightarrow \quad y^2 = 9 - x^2, y \geq 0 \quad \ldots\text{(i)} \; \{\because \sqrt{9 - x^2} \geq 0\}$

$\Rightarrow \quad x^2 = 9 - y^2 \Rightarrow 9 - y^2 \geq 0 \; \{\because x^2 \geq 0 \text{ for all } x \in R\}$

$\Rightarrow \quad y^2 \leq 9 \Rightarrow |y| \leq 3 \Rightarrow -3 \leq y \leq 3$

from (i) $\quad y \geq 0 \Rightarrow 0 \leq y \leq 3$

$\therefore$ Range of $f = [0, 3]$

Question 3 A function f is defined by $f(x) = 2x - 5$, write down the values of

(i) $f(0)$ (ii) $f(7)$ (iii) $f(-3)$.

Sol. Given, $f(x) = 2x - 5$

(i) $f(0) = 2 \times 0 - 5 = 0 - 5 = -5$

(ii) $f(7) = 2 \times 7 - 5 = 14 - 5 = 9$

(iii) $f(-3) = 2(-3) - 5 = -6 - 5 = -11$

Question 4 The function 't' which maps temperature in degree Celsius into temperature in degree Fahrenheit is defined by $t(C)=\dfrac{9C}{5}+32$. Find

(i) $t(0)$ (ii) $t(28)$ (iii) $t(-10)$

(iv) The value of C, when $t(C)=212$.

Sol. Given, $t(C) = \dfrac{9C}{5} + 32$ ...(i)

(i) On putting C = 0 in Eq. (i), we get

$$t(0) = \frac{9 \times 0}{5} + 32 = 0 + 32 = 32$$

(ii) On putting C = 28 in Eq. (i), we get

$$t(28) = \frac{9 \times 28}{5} + 32 = \frac{252}{5} + \frac{32}{1} = \frac{252 + 160}{5} = \frac{412}{5}$$

(iii) On putting C = – 10 in Eq. (i), we get

$$t(-10) = \frac{9 \times (-10)}{5} + 32 = \frac{-9 \times 10}{5} + 32 = -9 \times 2 + 32$$

$$= -18 + 32 = 14$$

(iv) Now, putting $t(C) = 212$ in Eq. (i), we get

$$212 = \frac{9C}{5} + 32 \Rightarrow \frac{9C}{5} = 212 - 32$$

$$\Rightarrow \quad \frac{9C}{5} = 180 \Rightarrow C = \frac{5 \times 180}{9} \Rightarrow C = 5 \times 20 = 100$$

Question 5 Find the range of each of the following functions

(i) $f(x)=2-3x, x \in R, x>0$. (ii) $f(x)=x^2+2$, x is a real number.

(iii) $f(x)=x$, x is a real number.

Thinking Process For range put $f(x) = y$ and convert the function in the form of $x = f(y)$.

Sol. (i) Let $y = f(x) = 2 - 3x \Rightarrow y = 2 - 3x \Rightarrow 3x = 2 - y$

$$\Rightarrow \quad x = \frac{2-y}{3} \quad \text{...(i)}$$

Given, $x > 0$

On putting the value of x from Eq. (i), we get

$$\frac{2-y}{3} > 0 \Rightarrow 2 - y > 0$$

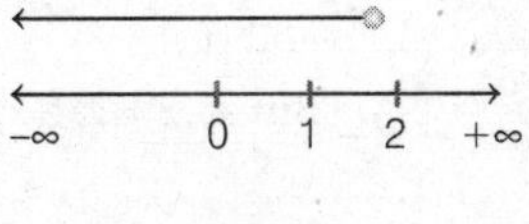

$$\Rightarrow \quad y - 2 < 0 \Rightarrow y < 2$$

$\therefore$ Range $(-\infty, 2) = \{y : y \in R \text{ and } y < 2\}$

(ii) Let $y = f(x) = x^2 + 2$

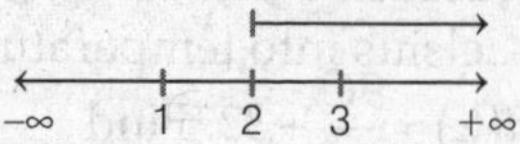

$\Rightarrow \quad y = x^2 + 2$

$\Rightarrow \quad x^2 = y - 2$

$\because \quad x^2 \geq 0$

$\Rightarrow \quad y - 2 \geq 0 \Rightarrow y \geq 2$

$\therefore$ Range = $[2, \infty)$ or $\{y : y \in R \text{ and } y \geq 2\}$

(iii) Let $y = f(x) = x$

$\Rightarrow \quad y = x \Rightarrow x = y$

$\because \quad x \in R$ (Given)

$\Rightarrow \quad y \in R$

$\therefore$ Range = $\{y : y \in R\}$

Miscellaneous Exercise

Question 1 The relation f is defined by $f(x) = \begin{cases} x^2, 0 \leq x \leq 3 \\ 3x, 3 \leq x \leq 10 \end{cases}$

The relation g is defined by $g(x) = \begin{cases} x^2, 0 \leq x \leq 2 \\ 3x, 2 \leq x \leq 10 \end{cases}$

Show that f is a function and g is not a function.

Sol. (a) Given, $f(x) = \begin{cases} x^2, & 0 \leq x \leq 3 \\ 3x, & 3 \leq x \leq 10 \end{cases}$

$\because \quad f(x) = x^2$ is well defined in $0 \leq x \leq 3$

and $\quad f(x) = 3x$ is also well defined in $3 \leq x \leq 10$

At $x = 3$, $f(x) = x^2 \Rightarrow f(3) = 3^2 = 9$

At $x = 3$, $f(x) = 3x \Rightarrow f(3) = 3 \times 3 = 9$

$\Rightarrow f(x)$ is defined at $x = 3$. Hence, f is a function.

(b) $g(x) = \begin{cases} x^2, & 0 \leq x \leq 2 \\ 3x, & 2 \leq x \leq 10 \end{cases}$

$\because \quad g(x) = x^2$ is well defined in $0 \leq x \leq 2$.

and $g(x) = 3x$ is also well defined in $2 \leq x \leq 10$

But at $x = 2$, $g(x) = x^2 \Rightarrow g(2) = 2^2 = 4$

At $x = 2$; $g(x) = 3x \Rightarrow g(2) = 3 \times 2 = 6$

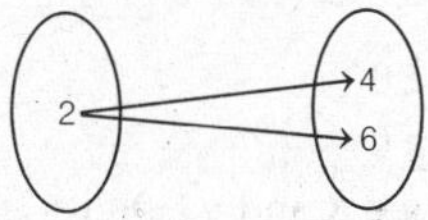

Therefore, $g(x)$ is not defined at $x = 2$. Hence, g is not a function.

Question 2 If $f(x) = x^2$, find $\frac{f(1.1) - f(1)}{1.1 - 1}$.

Sol. Given, $f(x) = x^2$

Putting $x = 1.1$, we get $f(1.1) = (1.1)^2 = 1.21$

Putting $x = 1$, we get $f(1) = 1^2 = 1$

$$\therefore \quad \frac{f(1.1) - f(1)}{1.1 - 1} = \frac{1.21 - 1}{1.1 - 1} = \frac{0.21}{0.1} = \frac{21}{10} = 2.1$$

Question 3 Find the domain of the function $f(x) = \frac{x^2 + 2x + 1}{x^2 - 8x + 12}$.

◎ ***Thinking Process*** If function is of the form $\frac{p(x)}{q(x)}$, then for these function to be defined put $q(x) \neq 0$.

Sol. We have $f(x) = \frac{x^2 + 2x + 1}{x^2 - 8x + 12}$

For function to be defined,

$$x^2 - 8x + 12 \neq 0 \Rightarrow x^2 - 6x - 2x + 12 \neq 0 \Rightarrow x(x - 6) - 2(x - 6) \neq 0$$

$$\Rightarrow \quad (x - 2)(x - 6) \neq 0 \Rightarrow x \neq 2 \text{ and } x \neq 6$$

Domain $= R - \{2, 6\}$

Question 4 Find the domain and the range of the real function f defined by $f(x) = \sqrt{x - 1}$.

Sol. Domain, $\because f(x) = \sqrt{x - 1}$

For function to be defined, the value inside the root should be non-negative

$$x - 1 \geq 0 \quad \ldots \text{(i)}$$

$$\Rightarrow \quad x \geq 1$$

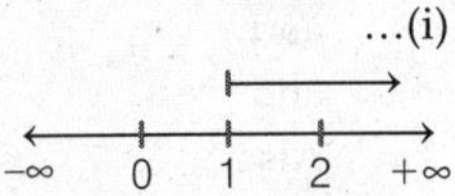

Domain $= [1, \infty)$

or $= \{x : x \in R \text{ and } x \geq 1\}$

Range, $f(x) = \sqrt{x - 1}$ or $y = \sqrt{x - 1}$

$$\Rightarrow \quad y^2 = x - 1 \Rightarrow x = y^2 + 1$$

Putting the value of x in Eq. (i), we get

$$\Rightarrow \quad y^2 + 1 - 1 \geq 0$$

$$\Rightarrow \quad -\infty < y < \infty$$

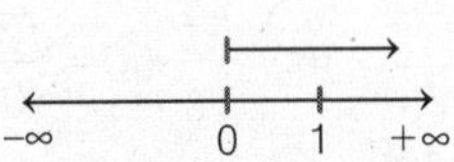

But y cannot be negative as the function $f(x)=\sqrt{x-1}$ cannot occur negative values

$$y^2 \geq 0$$

$$\therefore \quad y \geq 0$$

$\therefore$ Range = $[0, \infty)$ or $\{y : y \in R \text{ and } y \geq 0\}$

Question 5 Find the domain and the range of the real function f defined by $f(x) = |x-1|$.

Sol. We know that absolute or modulus functions are defined for all real values of x.

$\Rightarrow$ Domain = R

Now, $f(x) = |x - 1|$ can exist only non-negative values.

$\therefore$ Range = $\{y : y \geq 0\} = R^+ \cup \{0\}$ or $[0, \infty)$.

Question 6 Let $f = \left\{\left(x, \dfrac{x^2}{1+x^2}\right) : x \in R\right\}$ be a function from R to R. Determine the range of f.

Sol. Given, $f = \left\{\left(x, \dfrac{x^2}{1+x^2}\right) : x \in R\right\}$ and $f : R \to R$

Let $\quad y = \dfrac{x^2}{1+x^2}$

$\because$ $f(x)$ or y is non-negative for all values of x. *i.e.*, $y \geq 0$

and $\quad 1 + x^2 > x^2$

$\Rightarrow \quad 0 \leq y < 1$

$\therefore$ Range of $f = \{y : y \in R \text{ and } y \in [0, 1)\}$

Question 7 Let $f, g : R \to R$ be defined, respectively by $f(x) = x + 1, g(x) = 2x - 3$.
Find $f + g$, $f - g$ and $\dfrac{f}{g}$.

Sol. Given, $\quad f : R \to R$

and $\quad f(x) = x + 1$

and $\quad g : R \to R$

Also, $\quad g(x) = 2x - 3$

(a) $(f + g)(x) = f(x) + g(x) = x + 1 + 2x - 3 = 3x - 2$

(b) $(f - g)(x) = f(x) - g(x) = (x + 1) - (2x - 3) = x + 1 - 2x + 3 = 4 - x$

(c) $\left(\dfrac{f}{g}\right)(x) = \dfrac{f(x)}{g(x)} = \dfrac{x+1}{2x-3}$, where $2x - 3 \neq 0$ *i.e.*, $x \neq \dfrac{3}{2}$

Question 8 Let $f = \{(1,1),(2,3),(0,-1),(-1,-3)\}$ be a function from Z to Z defined by $f(x) = ax + b$ for some integers a and b. Determine a, b.

Sol. Given, $f = \{(1, 1), (2, 3), (0, -1), (-1, -3)\}$ and $f(x) = ax + b$

or $\quad y = ax + b \quad (\because y = f(x))$

At $\quad x = 1, y = 1$

$\Rightarrow \quad 1 = a + b \quad$ ...(i)

At $\quad x = 2, y = 3$

$\Rightarrow \quad 3 = 2a + b \quad$ ...(ii)

Subtracting Eq. (i) from Eq. (ii), we get

$$a = 2$$

On putting the value of a in Eq. (i), we get

$$b = 1 - 2 \Rightarrow b = -1$$

$\therefore$ Hence, $f(x) = ax + b = 2x - 1$

Question 9 Let R be a relation from N to N defined by $R = \{(a, b) : a, b \in N \text{ and } a = b^2\}$. Are the following true?

(i) $(a, a) \in R$, for all $a \in N$

(ii) $(a, b) \in R$ implies $(b, a) \in R$

(iii) $(a, b) \in R, (b, c) \in R$ implies $(a, c) \in R$. Justify your answer in each case.

Sol. Given, $R : N \to N$ defined by

$$R = \{(a, b) : a, b \in N \text{ and } a = b^2\}$$

(i) $(a, a) \in R$ for all $a \in N$

It is false, because $a = a^2$ is true only for $a = 1$ not for other natural number but given that $a \in N$.

(ii) $(a, b) \in R$ implies $(b, a) \in R$

It is false, because if $a = b^2$, then $b = a^2$ is not true.

For example, $4 = 2^2$, then $2 = 4^2$ is not true.

(iii) $(a, b) \in R$, $(b, c) \in R$ implies $(a, c) \in R$

It is false, because $a = b^2$ and $b = c^2 \Rightarrow a = (c^2)^2 = c^4 \Rightarrow a \neq c^2$

Question 10 Let $A = \{1, 2, 3, 4\}$, $B = \{1, 5, 9, 11, 15, 16\}$ and $f = \{(1, 5), (2, 9), (3, 1), (4, 5), (2, 11)\}$.

Are the following true?

(i) f is a relation from A to B.

(ii) f is a function from A to B.

Justify your answer in each case.

◎ ***Thinking Process*** If there are two orderd pairs with the same first component but different second components then given relation is not a function.

Sol. Given, $A = \{1, 2, 3, 4\}$, $B = \{1, 5, 9, 11, 15, 16\}$

and $$f = \{(1, 5), (2, 9), (3, 1), (4, 5), (2, 11)\}$$

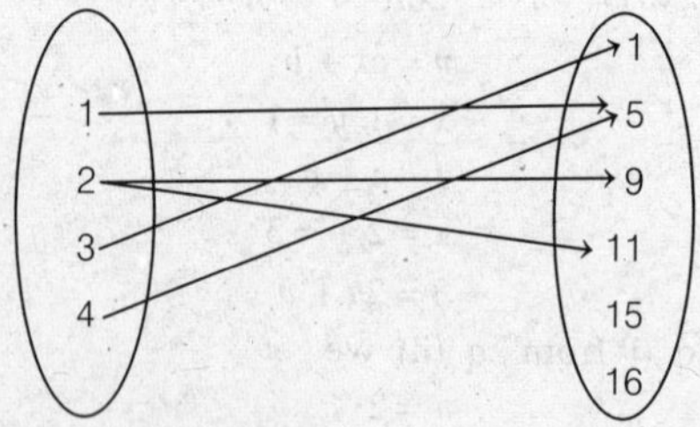

(i) $\because f$ is a subset of $A \times B$, hence it is a relation.

(ii) The ordered pair (2, 9) and (2, 11) have the first components same. Hence, f is not a function.

Question 11 Let f be the subset of $Z \times Z$ defined by $f = \{(ab, a + b) : a, b \in Z\}$. Is f a function from Z to Z ? Justify your answer.

Sol. Given $f = \{(ab, a + b) : a, b \in z\}$

Let we take $a = 0, b = 1$, then $ab = 0$ and $a + b = 0 + 1 = 1 \Rightarrow (0, 1) \in f$ and if we take $a = 0$ and $b = 2$, then $ab = 0$ and $a + b = 0 + 2 \Rightarrow (0, 2) \in f$. i.e. The first components of (0, 1) and (0, 2) are same.

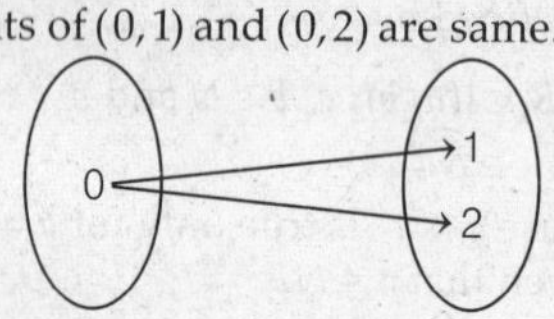

Hence, f is not a function.

Question 12 Let $A = \{9, 10, 11, 12, 13\}$ and let $f : A \to N$ defined by $f(n) =$ the highest prime factor of n. Find the range of f.

Sol. Given, $A = \{9, 10, 11, 12, 13\}$ and $f : A \to N$

We will find the highest prime factors of all the elements of the given set by factorizing them into prime factor.

For $n = 9$, $9 = 1 \times 3 \times 3$

$\Rightarrow$ Highest prime factor of 9 = 3

For $n = 10$, $10 = 1 \times 2 \times 5 \Rightarrow$ Highest prime factor of 10 = 5

For $n = 11$, $11 = 1 \times 11 \Rightarrow$ Highest prime factor of 11 = 11

For $n = 12$, $12 = 1 \times 2 \times 2 \times 3 \Rightarrow$ Highest prime factor of 12 = 3

For $n = 13$, $13 = 1 \times 13 \Rightarrow$ Highest prime factor of 13 = 13

$\therefore \quad f = \{(9, 3), (10, 5), (11, 11), (12, 3), (13, 13)\}$

$\Rightarrow \quad$ Range $= \{3, 5, 11, 13\}$ [$\because$ repetition is not allowed]

DIKSHA APP Questions

☐ Multiple Choice Questions

Q.1 Let $f(x)=\begin{cases}3-2x, & x<1\\ 3x+5, & 1\le x\le 2\\ 5x-2, & x>2\end{cases}$.

Then $2f(0)+f(3)=?$

(a) 17 (b) 19 (c) 24 (d) 31

Sol. (b) Given, $f(x)=\begin{cases}3-2x, & x<1\\ 3x+5, & 1\le x\le 2\\ 5x-2, & x>2\end{cases}$

For $x<1$

$$f(x)=3-2x$$

On putting $x=0$, we get

$$f(0)=3-2(0)=3$$

For $x>2$

$$f(x)=5x-2$$

On putting $x=3$, we get

$$f(3)=5(3)-2=13$$

$\because$ $2f(0)+f(3)=2(3)+13=19$

Q.2 Range of greatest integer function given by $f(x)=[x]$ is

(a) I or Z (b) N (c) W (d) R

Sol. (a) By defination of $[x]$, we get

$[x]=n$, where $n\le x<n+1$ and n is an integer

$\therefore$ Range of $[x]$ is the set of integers

i.e., Range of $[x]=I$ or Z

Note Defination of $f(n)=[x]$.

$[x]=n$, where $n\le x<n+1$ and $n\in I$ or Z and $x\in R$

Q.3 Let relation R is defined as $R=\{(x,x+2):x\in A\}$, where $A=\{0, 1, 2, 3\}$. Then range of the relation is.

(a) $\{2, 3\}$ (b) $\{4, 5\}$ (c) $\{2, 3, 4, 5\}$ (d) $\{0, 1, 2, 3\}$

◎ ***Thinking Process*** First, put the values of x and find y.

Sol. (c) Given $R = \{(x, x+2) : x \in A\}$ where

$A = \{0, 1, 2, 3\}$

Let $y = x + 2$

For $x \in A, y = 0 + 2 = 2$ {if $x = 0$}

$y = 1 + 2 = 3$ {if $x = 1$}

$y = 2 + 2 = 4$ {if $x = 2$}

$y = 3 + 2 = 5$ {if $x = 3$}

$\because$ $R = \{(0, 2), (1, 3), (2, 4), (3, 5)\}$

$\therefore$ Range of $R = \{2, 3, 4, 5\}$

Q.4 How many elements will be there in the cartesian product of A and B, if number of elements in A and B are 10 and 7 respectively?

(a) 3 (b) 17
(c) 70 (d) 10^7

Sol. (c) Given $n(A) = 10$, and $n(B) = 7$

we know $n(A \times B) = n(A) \times n(B)$

Then, number of elements in

$$A \times B = 10 \times 7 = 70$$

Q.5 If $n(A) = 5, n(B) = 4$ and $n(A \cap B) = 2$, then $n(A \times B) = ?$

(a) 6 (b) 10
(c) 12 (d) 20

Sol. (d) Given, $n(A) = 5, n(B) = 4$

by $n(A \times B) = n(A) \times n(B) = 5 \times 4 = 20$

Quick Solution

Let $A = \{1, 2, 3, 4, 5\}$

$B = \{3, 4, 6, 7\}$

Here, $(A \cap B) = \{3, 4\}$

Sets A and B satisfy all given conditions. In cartesian product of A and B we get 20 elements.

Q.6 If $R = \{(x, y) : x + 2y = 5\}$ is defined on set $A = \{1, 2, 3, 4, 5\}$, then the domain will be

(a) {1, 3} (b) {1, 2, 3} (c) {1, 2, 3, 4} (d) {1, 2, 3, 4, 5}

Sol. (a) Given, $R = \{(x, y) : x + 2y = 5\}$, where $A = \{1, 2, 3, 4, 5\}$

Here, $x + 2y = 5$

$\Rightarrow \quad y = \dfrac{5 - x}{2}$

We can put the value of $x = 1, 3$ only to get the value of y in A. So, when $x = 1$, get $y = 2$, and when $x = 3$ get $y = 1$.

Hence, domain is $\{1, 3\}$

☐ Subjective Type Questions

Q.1 Let $A = \{a, b, c\}$, $B = \{b, c, d\}$ and $C = \{b, d\}$ then find $(A - B) \times (B - C)$

Sol. Given $A = \{a, b, c\}$, $B = \{b, c, d\}$ and $C = \{b, d\}$, $A - B = \{a\}$, $B - C = \{c\}$

Now, $(A - B) \times (B - C) = \{(a, c)\}$

Q.2 Find the value of x for which, the functions $f(x) = 2x^2 - 2$ and $g(x) = 1 - x$ are equal.

Sol. Given $f(x) = 2x^2 - 2$ and $g(x) = 1 - x$ are equal

i.e. $2x^2 - 2 = 1 - x$

$\Rightarrow \quad 2x^2 + x - 3 = 0$

$\Rightarrow \quad 2x^2 + 3x - 2x - 3 = 0$

$\Rightarrow \quad (2x + 3)(x - 1) = 0$

Hence, $x = 1$ or $x = -\dfrac{3}{2}$

Q.3 If function $f = \{(1, 1), (0, -2), (3, 0), (2, 4)\}$ be a linear function defined by formula $f(x) = ax + b$. Then find 'a' and 'b'.

Sol. Given $f = \{(1, 1), (0, -2), (3, 0), (2, 4)\}$ and $f(x) = ax + b$.

$\because \quad (1, 1)$ and $(0, -2) \in f$

$\Rightarrow \quad f(1) = a(1) + b = 1$

$\Rightarrow \quad a + b = 1 \quad \ldots$ (i)

$\Rightarrow \quad f(0) = a(0) + b = -2$

$\Rightarrow \quad b = -2$

On putting $b = -2$ in Eq. (i), we get

$$a - 2 = 1 \Rightarrow a = 3$$

Hence, the values of $a = 3$ and $b = -2$

Q.4 Find the domain and range of the function $f(x)$ given below

$$f(x) = \frac{2x+3}{3x-2}$$

Sol. We have $f(x) = \dfrac{2x+3}{3x-2}$

We know that $f(x)$ is not define for $3x - 2 = 0$ or $x = \dfrac{2}{3}$.

So, $f(x)$ is defined every where in R except $\dfrac{2}{3}$

$\therefore$ Domain of $f = R - \left\{\dfrac{2}{3}\right\}$

Again for range

Let $\quad y = f(x) = \dfrac{2x+3}{3x-2}$

$\Rightarrow \quad (3x-2)\,y = 2x + 3$

$\Rightarrow 3x\,y - 2y - 2x - 3 = 0$

$\Rightarrow x(3y-2) - 2y - 3 = 0$

$\Rightarrow \quad x = \dfrac{2y+3}{3y-2}$

Since, x is not define for $3y - 2 = 0$ or $y = \dfrac{2}{3}$.

x is defined for $R - \left\{\dfrac{2}{3}\right\}$ or $y \in R - \left\{\dfrac{2}{3}\right\}$

$\Rightarrow$ Range of $f(x) = R - \left\{\dfrac{2}{3}\right\}$

Trigonometric Functions

CHAPTER 03

Important Points

01 The word 'Trigonometry' is derived from Greek words 'Trigon' and 'Metron' which means 'Measuring the sides of a triangle'.

02 An angle is a measure of rotation of a given ray about its initial point. The original ray is called the initial side and the final position of the ray after rotation is called the terminal side of the angle. The point of rotation is called the vertex.

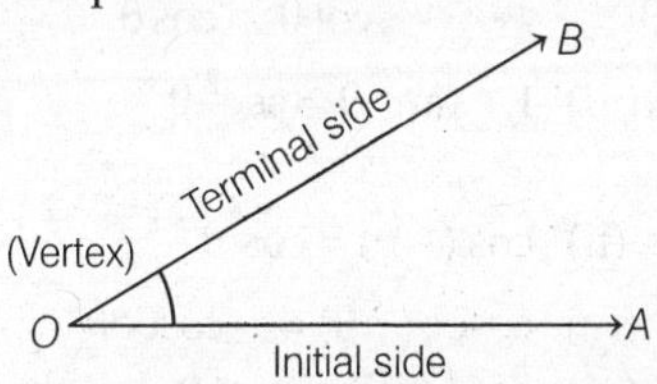

▲ (Positive angle anticlockwise sense)

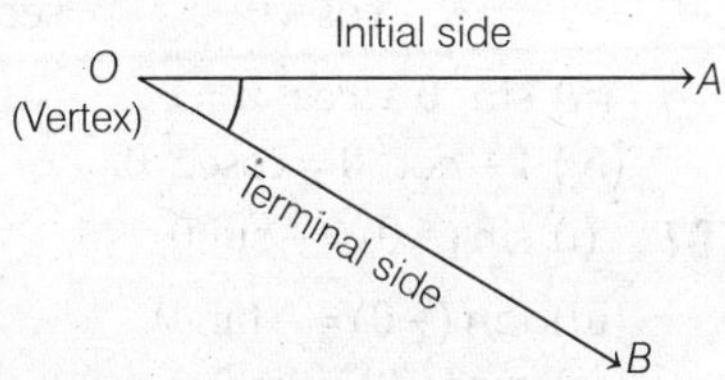

▲ (Negative angle clockwise sense)

03 Measurement of angle

- Sexagesimal system
  - 1 right angle = 90°
  - 1° (Degree) = 60′
  - 1′ (Minute) = 60″

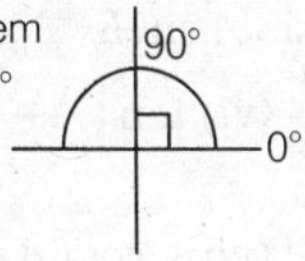

- Circular system
  - OP = Initial side
  - OQ = Terminal side
  - π rad $= \pi^c = 180°$
  - $1^c = \left(\frac{180}{\pi}\right)^\circ$ 57°16′ (approx)
  - $1^\circ = \left(\frac{\pi}{180}\right)^c$ 0.01746 rad (approx)

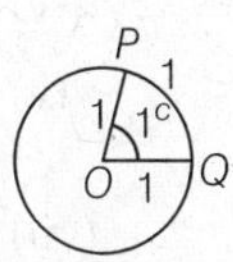

$$\text{Radian measure} = \frac{\pi}{180} \times \text{degree measure}$$

$$\text{Degree measure} = \frac{180}{\pi} \times \text{radian measure}$$

04 Quadrant system

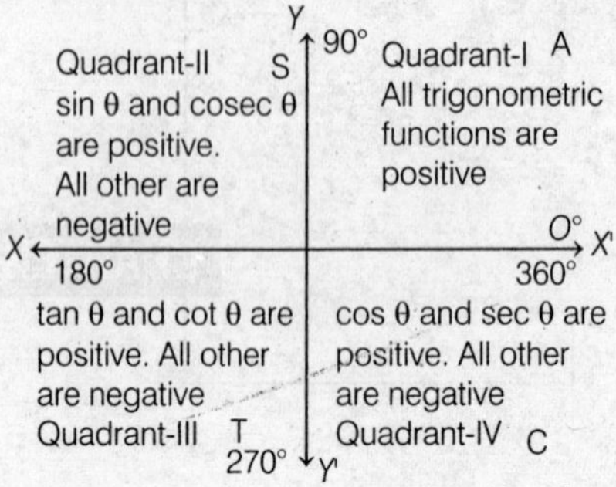

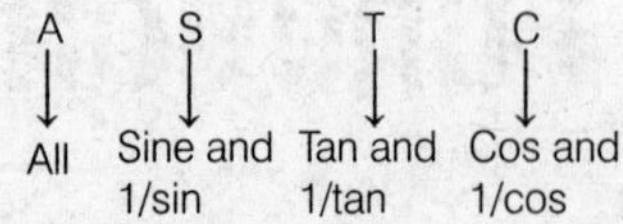

Remembering method
After School to Coaching

05 Relation between θ, l and r is $\theta = \frac{l}{r}$ or angle $= \frac{\text{arc}}{\text{radius}}$

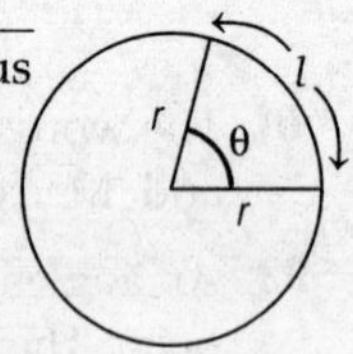

where, θ is the angle, r is radius and l is the length of arc.

Here, θ is always in radian.

06 Trigonometric Identies

(i) $\sin\theta = \frac{1}{\text{cosec}\theta}$, $\cos\theta = \frac{1}{\sec\theta}$ and $\tan\theta = \frac{1}{\cot\theta} = \frac{\sin\theta}{\cos\theta}$

(ii) $\sin^2\theta + \cos^2\theta = 1$ (iii) $1 + \tan^2\theta = \sec^2\theta$

(iv) $1 + \cot^2\theta = \text{cosec}^2\theta$

07 (i) $\sin(-\theta) = -\sin\theta$ (ii) $\cos(-\theta) = \cos\theta$

(iii) $\tan(-\theta) = -\tan\theta$ (iv) $\text{cosec}(-\theta) = -\text{cosec}\theta$

(v) $\sec(-\theta) = \sec\theta$ (vi) $\cot(-\theta) = -\cot\theta$

08 (i) $\sin(A+B) = \sin A \cos B + \cos A \sin B$

(ii) $\sin(A-B) = \sin A \cos B - \cos A \sin B$

(iii) $\cos(A+B) = \cos A \cos B - \sin A \sin B$

(iv) $\cos(A-B) = \cos A \cos B + \sin A \sin B$

(v) $\tan(A+B) = \frac{\tan A + \tan B}{1 - \tan A \tan B}$ (vi) $\tan(A-B) = \frac{\tan A - \tan B}{1 + \tan A \tan B}$

(vii) $\cot(A+B) = \frac{\cot A \cot B - 1}{\cot A + \cot B}$ (viii) $\cot(A-B) = \frac{\cot A \cot B + 1}{\cot B - \cot A}$

09 (i) $\sin^2 A - \sin^2 B = \cos^2 B - \cos^2 A = \sin(A+B)\sin(A-B)$

(ii) $\cos^2 A - \sin^2 B = \cos^2 B - \sin^2 A = \cos(A+B)\cos(A-B)$

(iii) $2\sin A \cos B = \sin(A+B) + \sin(A-B)$

(iv) $2\cos A \sin B = \sin(A+B) - \sin(A-B)$

(v) $2\cos A \cos B = \cos(A+B) + \cos(A-B)$

(vi) $2\sin A \sin B = \cos(A-B) - \cos(A+B)$

10 (i) $\sin C + \sin D = 2\sin\frac{C+D}{2}\cos\frac{C-D}{2}$

(ii) $\sin C - \sin D = 2\cos\frac{C+D}{2}\sin\frac{C-D}{2}$

(iii) $\cos C + \cos D = 2\cos\frac{C+D}{2}\cos\frac{C-D}{2}$

(iv) $\cos C - \cos D = 2\sin\frac{C+D}{2}\sin\frac{D-C}{2}$ (use if $D > C$)

$= -2\sin\frac{C+D}{2}\sin\frac{C-D}{2}$ (use if $C > D$)

11 (i) $\sin 2A = 2\sin A\cos A = \frac{2\tan A}{1+\tan^2 A}$

(ii) $\cos 2A = \cos^2 A - \sin^2 A = 1 - 2\sin^2 A$

$= 2\cos^2 A - 1 = \frac{1-\tan^2 A}{1+\tan^2 A}$

(iii) $\tan 2A = \frac{2\tan A}{1-\tan^2 A}$ (iv) $\sin 3A = 3\sin A - 4\sin^3 A$

(v) $\cos 3A = 4\cos^3 A - 3\cos A$ (vi) $\tan 3A = \frac{3\tan A - \tan^3 A}{1-3\tan^2 A}$

12 Some Standard Values of Trigonometric Ratios

Angle	0°	30°	45°	60°	90°	120°	135°	150°	180°
Sine	0	$\frac{1}{2}$	$\frac{1}{\sqrt{2}}$	$\frac{\sqrt{3}}{2}$	1	$\frac{\sqrt{3}}{2}$	$\frac{1}{\sqrt{2}}$	$\frac{1}{2}$	0
Cosine	1	$\frac{\sqrt{3}}{2}$	$\frac{1}{\sqrt{2}}$	$\frac{1}{2}$	0	$-\frac{1}{2}$	$-\frac{1}{\sqrt{2}}$	$-\frac{\sqrt{3}}{2}$	-1
Tangent	0	$\frac{1}{\sqrt{3}}$	1	$\sqrt{3}$	∞	$-\sqrt{3}$	-1	$-\frac{1}{\sqrt{3}}$	0
Cotangent	∞	$\sqrt{3}$	1	$\frac{1}{\sqrt{3}}$	0	$-\frac{1}{\sqrt{3}}$	-1	$-\sqrt{3}$	∞
Secant	1	$\frac{2}{\sqrt{3}}$	$\sqrt{2}$	2	∞	-2	$-\sqrt{2}$	$-\frac{2}{\sqrt{3}}$	-1
Cosecant	∞	2	$\sqrt{2}$	$\frac{2}{\sqrt{3}}$	1	$\frac{2}{\sqrt{3}}$	$\sqrt{2}$	2	∞

Note $\sin 18° = \frac{\sqrt{5}-1}{4}$, $\cos 18° = \frac{\sqrt{10+2\sqrt{5}}}{4}$, $\cos 36° = \frac{\sqrt{5}+1}{4}$

and $\sin 36° = \frac{\sqrt{10-2\sqrt{5}}}{4}$

13 Graph of trigonometric functions

(i) $y = \sin x$

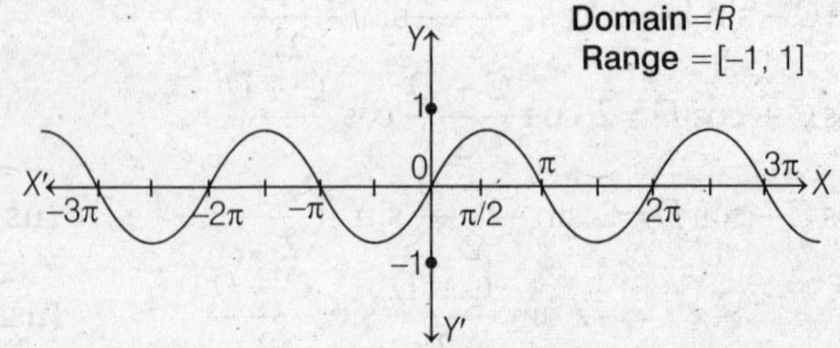

(ii) $y = \cos x$

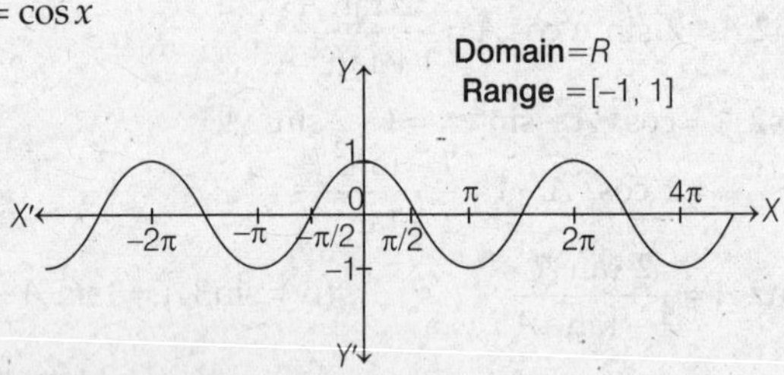

(iii) $y = \tan x$

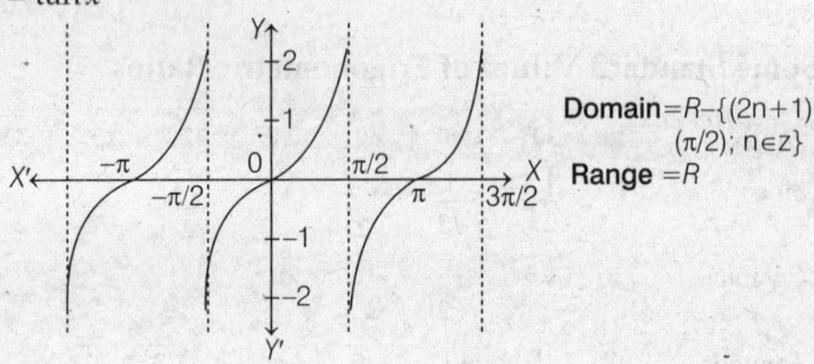

(iv) $y = \cot x$

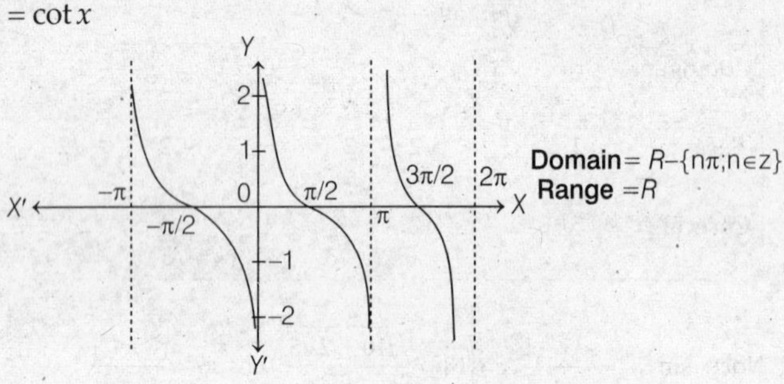

(v) $y = \sec x$

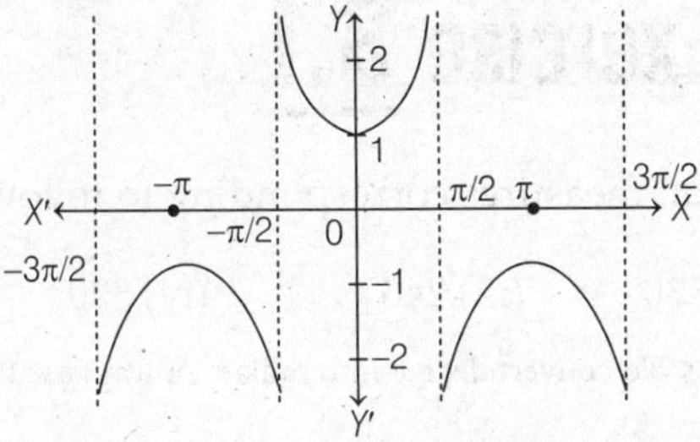

Domain= $R-\{(2n+1)\pi/2;\ n\in z\}$
Range $= R-(-1,1)$

(vi) $y = \text{cosec}x$

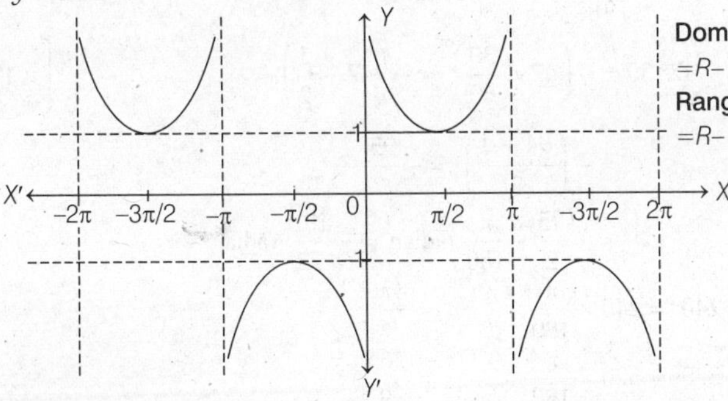

Domain $= R-\{n\pi; n\in z\}$
Range $= R-(-1,1)$

Where z is a set of all integers.

14 Some useful Results

(i) $\cos\left(\frac{\pi}{2}-x\right)=\sin x$ (ii) $\sin\left(\frac{\pi}{2}-x\right)=\cos x$

(iii) $\cos\left(\frac{\pi}{2}+x\right)=-\sin x$ (iv) $\sin\left(\frac{\pi}{2}+x\right)=\cos x$

(v) $\cos(\pi-x)=-\cos x$ (vi) $\sin(\pi-x)=\sin x$

(vii) $\cos(\pi+x)=-\cos x$ (viii) $\sin(\pi+x)=-\sin x$

(ix) $\cos\left(\frac{3\pi}{2}-x\right)=-\sin x$ (x) $\sin\left(\frac{3\pi}{2}-x\right)=-\cos x$

(xi) $\cos\left(\frac{3\pi}{2}+x\right)=\sin x$ (xii) $\sin\left(\frac{3\pi}{2}+x\right)=-\cos x$

(xiii) $\cos(2\pi-x)=\cos x$ (xiv) $\sin(2\pi-x)=-\sin x$

Note
- If we are adding or subtracting x in $\frac{\pi}{2}$ or $\frac{3\pi}{2}$ then change the trigonometric functions.
- If we are adding or subtracting x in π or 2π, then no change in Trigonometric functions.
- Positive and negative signs are take according to quadrant.

Exercise 3.1

Question 1 Find the radian measures corresponding to following degree measures

(i) $25°$ (ii) $-47°30'$ (iii) $240°$ (iv) $520°$

◎ **Thinking Process** To convert degree into radians, always use $1° = \frac{\pi}{180}$ rad

Sol. (i) $25° = 25 \times \frac{\pi}{180}$ rad $= \frac{5\pi}{36}$ radian $\left(\because 1° = \frac{\pi}{180} \text{ rad}\right)$

(ii) $-47°\,30' = -\left(47 + \frac{30}{60}\right)^\circ = -\left(47 + \frac{1}{2}\right)^\circ$ $\left[\because 1' = \left(\frac{1}{60}\right)^\circ\right]$

$= -\left(\frac{94+1}{2}\right)^\circ = -\frac{95°}{2}$

$= -\frac{95}{2} \times \frac{\pi}{180}$ radian $= -\frac{19\pi}{72}$ radian

(iii) $240° = 240 \times \frac{\pi}{180} = \frac{4\pi}{3}$

(iv) $520° = 520 \times \frac{\pi}{180} = \frac{26\pi}{9}$

Note In part (ii), remember that first convert the whole number in degree then, convert into the radian.

Question 2 Find the degree measures corresponding to the following radian measures $\left(\text{use } \pi = \frac{22}{7}\right)$:

(i) $\left(\frac{11}{16}\right)$ (ii) -4 (iii) $\frac{5\pi}{3}$ (iv) $\frac{7\pi}{6}$

◎ **Thinking Process** To convert radians into degree, always use $1^c = \left(\frac{180}{\pi}\right)^\circ$ and then put the value of $\pi = \frac{22}{7}$.

Sol. (i) $\left(\frac{11}{16}\right)^c = \left(\frac{11}{16} \times \frac{180}{\pi}\right)^\circ = \left(\frac{11}{8} \times \frac{90}{22} \times 7\right)^\circ = \left(\frac{45 \times 7}{8}\right)^\circ$ $\left[\because 1^c = \left(\frac{180}{\pi}\right)^\circ\right]$

$= \left(\frac{315}{8}\right)^\circ = 39° + \left(\frac{3}{8}\right)^\circ = 39° + \frac{3}{8} \times 60' = 39° + \left(\frac{45}{2}\right)'$ $(\because 1° = 60')$

$= 39° + 22' + \frac{1'}{2} = 39°\,22' + \frac{1 \times 60''}{2} = 39°\,22'\,30''$ $(\because 1' = 60'')$

(ii) $-4^c = -\left(4 \times \frac{180}{\pi}\right)^\circ = -\left(4 \times \frac{180}{22} \times 7\right)^\circ$

$$= \left(\frac{2 \times 1260}{11}\right)^\circ = -\left(\frac{2520}{11}\right)^\circ = -\left[229^\circ + \left(\frac{1}{11}\right)^\circ\right]$$

$$= -\left(229^\circ + \frac{1}{11} \times 60'\right) \qquad (\because 1^\circ = 60')$$

$$= -\left(229^\circ + 5' + \left(\frac{5}{11}\right)'\right)$$

$$= -\left(229^\circ\, 5' + \frac{5}{11} \times 60''\right) \qquad (\because 1' = 60'')$$

$$= -(229^\circ\, 5'\, 27'') \quad \text{(approx)}$$

(iii) $\left(\frac{5\pi}{3}\right) = \left(\frac{5\pi}{3} \times \frac{180}{\pi}\right)^\circ = 300^\circ \qquad \left[\because 1^c = \left(\frac{180}{\pi}\right)^\circ\right]$

(iv) $\left(\frac{7\pi}{6}\right) = \left(\frac{7\pi}{6} \times \frac{180}{\pi}\right)^\circ = 210^\circ$

Mistake Alert As in parts (i) and (ii), if division of numbers is in fraction, then it is compulsory to solve further to convert in minute and second and as in (ii) part negative sign indicates the clockwise direction only, while solving the problems it should be kept outside the brackets.

Question 3 A wheel makes 360 revolutions in one minute. Through how many radians does it turn in one second?

Sol. In 1 min, number of revolutions of wheel = 360

i.e., In 60 s, number of revolutions of wheel = 360

$\therefore$ In 1 s, number of revolutions of wheel = $\frac{360}{60} = 6$

In 1 revolution, angle = $360^\circ = 2\pi$

In 6 revolutions, angle = $2\pi \times 6 = 12\pi$ rad

Question 4 Find the degree measure of the angle subtended at the centre of a circle of radius 100 cm by an arc of length 22 cm. $\left(\text{Use } \pi = \frac{22}{7}\right)$

Thinking Process If a circle of radius r and an arc of length l subtends an angle θ radian at the centre, we use the formula

$$\theta = \frac{l}{r}$$

Sol. Here, $l = 22$ cm and $r = 100$ cm.

Using the formula $\theta = \frac{l}{r}$, we get

$$\theta = \frac{22}{100} = \frac{11}{50} \text{ rad} \qquad \left(\because \theta = \frac{l}{r}\right)$$

$$= \left(\frac{11}{50} \times \frac{180}{\pi}\right)^\circ = \left(\frac{11 \times 18 \times 7}{5 \times 22}\right)^\circ = \left(\frac{63}{5}\right)^\circ$$

$$= 12^\circ + \left(\frac{3}{5}\right)^\circ = 12^\circ + \frac{3}{5} \times 60' \qquad (\because 1^\circ = 60')$$

$$= 12^\circ 36'$$

Question 5 In a circle of diameter 40 cm, the length of a chord is 20 cm. Find the length of minor arc of the chord.

Sol. Given, diameter = 40 cm

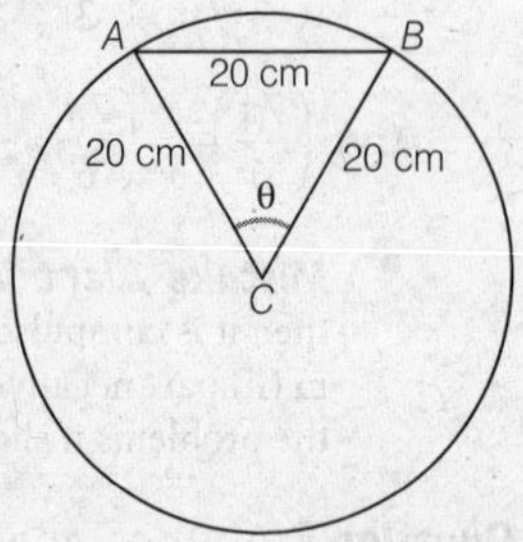

$\therefore$ Radius $CA = CB = \frac{\text{diameter}}{2} = \frac{40}{2} = 20$ cm

Also, chord $AB = 20$ cm

Now, we have all the three sides of Δ ABC equal so, it is an equilateral triangle.

$\therefore \theta = \angle ACB = 60^\circ = 60 \times \frac{\pi}{180}$ rad

Now, using the formula $\theta = \frac{l}{r}$

$$60 \times \frac{\pi}{180} = \frac{AB}{20} \Rightarrow AB = 60^\circ \times 20 \times \frac{\pi}{180^\circ} = \frac{20\pi}{3} \text{ cm}$$

Mistake Alert Always remember that in formula $\theta = \frac{l}{r}$, θ is measured in radian, so first convert the degree in radian whenever use this formula.

Question 6 If in two circles, arcs of the same length subtend angles of 60° and 75° at the centre, find the ratio of their radii.

Thinking Process Firstly, determine the radii of both circles by using the formula $\theta = \frac{l}{r}$ and then find their ratio.

Sol.

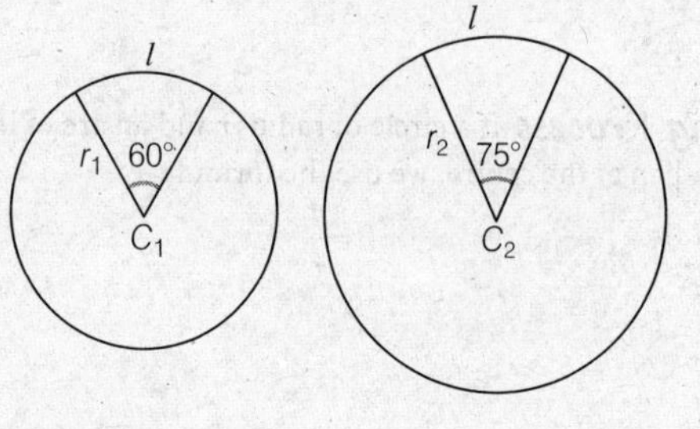

Using the formula $\theta = \frac{l}{r}$, we get

For first circle, $60 \times \frac{\pi}{180} = \frac{l}{r_1}$ ...(i)

And for second circle $75 \times \frac{\pi}{180} = \frac{l}{r_2}$ ...(ii)

On dividing Eq. (i) by Eq. (ii), we get

$$\frac{60 \times \frac{\pi}{180}}{75 \times \frac{\pi}{180}} = \frac{\frac{l}{r_1}}{\frac{l}{r_2}}$$

$$\Rightarrow \quad \frac{r_2}{r_1} = \frac{4}{5}$$

$$\Rightarrow \quad r_1 : r_2 = 5 : 4$$

Question 7 Find the angle in radian through which a pendulum swings if its length is 75 cm and the tip describes an arc of length

(a) 10 cm

(b) 15 cm

(c) 21 cm.

◎ ***Thinking Process*** Let r is length of pendulum and using the formula $\theta = \frac{l}{r}$,

Sol. (a) $\theta = \frac{10}{75} = \frac{2}{15}$ rad (b) $\theta = \frac{15}{75} = \frac{1}{5}$ rad (c) $\theta = \frac{21}{75} = \frac{7}{25}$ rad

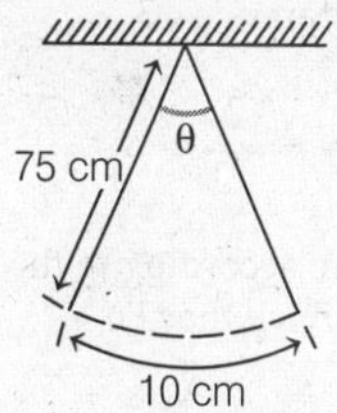

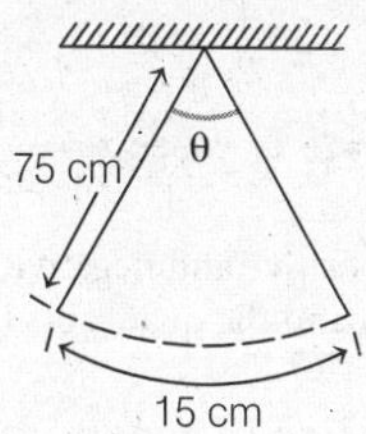

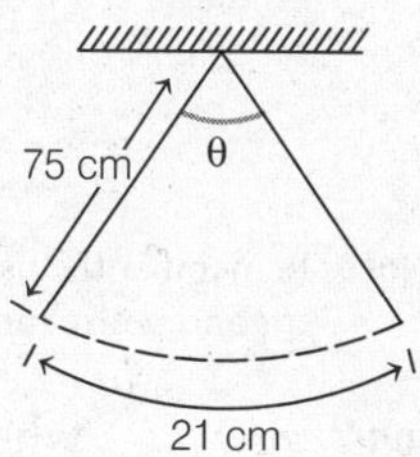

Exercise 3.2

Direction (Q. No. 1 to 5) *Find the values of other five trigonometric functions.*

Question 1 $\cos x = -\frac{1}{2}$, where x lies in third quadrant.

◎ ***Thinking Process*** To find the values of all trigonometric function, first of all, we should determine $\sin x$, by using $\sin^2 x + \cos^2 x = 1$. With the help of $\sin x$ and $\cos x$, we can determine the other trigonometric functions. After that we should apply the sign as per the quadrant system.

Sol. $\cos x = -\frac{1}{2}$

Given that x lies in third quadrant. *i.e.*, $\pi < x < \frac{3\pi}{2}$

We have, $\sin^2 x + \cos^2 x = 1 \Rightarrow \sin^2 x = 1 - \cos^2 x$

$$\Rightarrow \quad \sin^2 x = 1 - \left(-\frac{1}{2}\right)^2 \Rightarrow \sin^2 x = 1 - \frac{1}{4} = \frac{3}{4} \Rightarrow \sin x = \pm\frac{\sqrt{3}}{2}$$

$\because$ In third quadrant $\sin x$ is negative, so we will leave its positive value.

i.e., $\quad \sin x = -\frac{\sqrt{3}}{2}$

Now, $\quad \tan x = \frac{\sin x}{\cos x} = \frac{-\frac{\sqrt{3}}{2}}{-\frac{1}{2}} = \sqrt{3}, \ \cot x = \frac{1}{\tan x} = \frac{1}{\sqrt{3}}$

and $\quad \sec x = \frac{1}{\cos x} = -2, \ \operatorname{cosec} x = \frac{1}{\sin x} = -\frac{2}{\sqrt{3}}$

Note Remember the use of positive and negative sign, according to the trigonometric function and the quadrants in which they lie.

Question 2 $\sin x = \frac{3}{5}$, where x lies in second quadrant.

Sol. $\sin x = \frac{3}{5}$

Given that x lies in second quadrant.

i.e., $\quad \frac{\pi}{2} < x < \pi$

$$\therefore \sin^2 x + \cos^2 x = 1 \Rightarrow \cos^2 x = 1 - \sin^2 x = 1 - \left(\frac{3}{5}\right)^2 = 1 - \frac{9}{25} = \frac{25-9}{25} = \frac{16}{25}$$

$$\Rightarrow \qquad \cos x = \pm \frac{4}{5}$$

$\because$ In second quadrant, $\cos x$ is negative, so we will leave its positive value.

i.e., $\cos x = -\frac{4}{5} \Rightarrow \tan x = \frac{\sin x}{\cos x} = \frac{\frac{3}{5}}{-\frac{4}{5}} = -\frac{3}{4}$,

$$\cot x = \frac{1}{\tan x} = -\frac{4}{3}, \sec x = \frac{1}{\cos x} = -\frac{5}{4} \text{ and } \operatorname{cosec} x = \frac{1}{\sin x} = \frac{5}{3}$$

Question 3 $\cot x = \frac{3}{4}$, where x lies in third quadrant.

Sol. $\cot x = \frac{3}{4}$

Given that x lies in third quadrant.

i.e., $\pi < x < \frac{3\pi}{2} \Rightarrow \tan x = \frac{1}{\cot x} = \frac{4}{3}$

$\therefore \quad \sec^2 x = \tan^2 x + 1 = \frac{16}{9} + 1 \Rightarrow \sec^2 x = \frac{25}{9} \Rightarrow \sec x = \pm \frac{5}{3}$

$\because x$ lies in third quadrant, so we take only its negative value.

i.e., $\sec x = -\frac{5}{3} \Rightarrow \cos x = -\frac{3}{5}$

Now, $\tan x = \frac{\sin x}{\cos x} \Rightarrow \frac{4}{3} = \frac{\sin x}{-\frac{3}{5}} \Rightarrow \sin x = -\frac{4}{5}$ and $\operatorname{cosec} x = -\frac{5}{4}$

Question 4 $\sec x = \frac{13}{5}$, where x lies in fourth quadrant.

Sol. $\sec x = \frac{13}{5}$

Given that x lies in fourth quadrant.

i.e., $\frac{3\pi}{2} < x < 2\pi \Rightarrow \cos x = \frac{5}{13}$

Now, $\sin^2 x = 1 - \cos^2 x = 1 - \left(\frac{5}{13}\right)^2 = 1 - \frac{25}{169} = \frac{169 - 25}{169} = \frac{144}{169} = \left(\frac{12}{13}\right)^2$

$[\because \sin^2 x + \cos^2 x = 1]$

$$\Rightarrow \qquad \sin x = \pm \frac{12}{13}$$

Since, x lies in fourth quadrant, so we take only negative sign.

i.e., $\sin x = -\frac{12}{13}$

Now, $\tan x = \dfrac{\sin x}{\cos x} = \dfrac{-\left(\dfrac{12}{13}\right)}{\left(\dfrac{5}{13}\right)} = -\dfrac{12}{5}$

$\Rightarrow \quad \operatorname{cosec} x = \dfrac{1}{\sin x} = \dfrac{-13}{12}, \cot x = \dfrac{1}{\tan x} = -\dfrac{5}{12}$

Question 5 $\tan x = -\dfrac{5}{12}$, where x lies in second quadrant.

Sol. $\tan x = -\dfrac{5}{12}$

Given that x lies in second quadrant, *i.e.*, $\dfrac{\pi}{2} < x < \pi$

$\cot x = \dfrac{1}{\tan x} = -\dfrac{12}{5}$

Now, $\sec^2 x = 1 + \tan^2 x = 1 + \left(-\dfrac{5}{12}\right)^2 = 1 + \dfrac{25}{144} = \dfrac{169}{144}$

$\Rightarrow \quad \sec^2 x = \left(\dfrac{13}{12}\right)^2 \Rightarrow \sec x = \pm \dfrac{13}{12}$

$\because x$ lies in second quadrant, so we take negative sign.

$\therefore \quad \sec x = -\dfrac{13}{12} \Rightarrow \cos x = \dfrac{1}{\sec x} = \dfrac{-12}{13}$

Now, $\tan x = \dfrac{\sin x}{\cos x} \Rightarrow -\dfrac{5}{12} = \dfrac{\sin x}{-\dfrac{12}{13}} \Rightarrow \sin x = \dfrac{5}{13}$ and $\operatorname{cosec} x = \dfrac{1}{\sin x} = \dfrac{13}{5}$

Direction Find the value of the trigonometric functions in Q. Nos. 6 to 10.

Question 6 $\sin 765°$

◎ ***Thinking Process*** If the number is greater than 360°, then first try to convert it in the multiple of 360° to make it simple and then solve.

Sol. $\sin 765° = \sin (360 \times 2 + 45)° = \sin 45° = \dfrac{1}{\sqrt{2}}$ $\quad [\because \sin (2n\pi + \theta) = \sin\theta]$

Question 7 $\operatorname{cosec}(-1410°)$

Sol. $\operatorname{cosec}(-1410°) = -\operatorname{cosec}(1410°)$ $\quad [\because \operatorname{cosec}(-\theta) = -\operatorname{cosec}\theta]$

$= -\operatorname{cosec}(360 \times 4 - 30)°$

$= -(-\operatorname{cosec} 30°) = \operatorname{cosec} 30° = 2$ $[\because \operatorname{cosec}(2n\pi - \theta) = -\operatorname{cosec}\theta]$

Note Whenever a negative sign is given in the angle, then first take out negative sign from angle by using the to formula $\sin(-x) = -\sin x$ and $\cos(-x) = \cos x$, it will make your calculation easier.

Question 8 $\tan \frac{19\pi}{3}$

Sol. $\tan \frac{19\pi}{3} = \tan\left(\frac{18\pi + \pi}{3}\right) = \tan\left(6\pi + \frac{\pi}{3}\right) = \tan\left(2\pi \times 3 + \frac{\pi}{3}\right)$

$= \tan \frac{\pi}{3} = \sqrt{3}$ $[\because \tan(2n\pi + \theta) = \tan\theta]$

Question 9 $\sin\left(\frac{-11\pi}{3}\right)$

Sol. $\sin\left(\frac{-11\pi}{3}\right) = -\sin\left(\frac{11\pi}{3}\right) = -\sin\left(\frac{12\pi - \pi}{3}\right)$ $[\because \sin(-\theta) = -\sin\theta]$

$= -\sin\left(4\pi - \frac{\pi}{3}\right) = -\sin\left(2\pi \times 2 - \frac{\pi}{3}\right)$

$= -\left(-\sin\frac{\pi}{3}\right) = \sin\left(\frac{\pi}{3}\right) = \frac{\sqrt{3}}{2}$ $[\because \sin(2n\pi - \theta) = -\sin\theta]$

Question 10 $\cot\left(\frac{-15\pi}{4}\right)$

Sol. $\cot\left(-\frac{15\pi}{4}\right) = -\cot\left(\frac{15\pi}{4}\right) = -\cot\left(\frac{16\pi - \pi}{4}\right)$ $[\because \cot(-\theta) = -\cot\theta]$

$= -\cot\left(2\pi \times 2 - \frac{\pi}{4}\right)$

$= -\left(-\cot\frac{\pi}{4}\right) = \cot\frac{\pi}{4} = 1$ $[\because \cot(2n\pi - \theta) = -\cot\theta]$

Exercise 3.3

Question 1 Prove that $\sin^2\frac{\pi}{6} + \cos^2\frac{\pi}{3} - \tan^2\frac{\pi}{4} = -\frac{1}{2}$

Sol. We have, $\sin^2\frac{\pi}{6} + \cos^2\frac{\pi}{3} - \tan^2\frac{\pi}{4} = -\frac{1}{2}$

$\text{LHS} = \sin^2\frac{\pi}{6} + \cos^2\frac{\pi}{3} - \tan^2\frac{\pi}{4}$

$= \left(\frac{1}{2}\right)^2 + \left(\frac{1}{2}\right)^2 - (1)^2 = \frac{1}{4} + \frac{1}{4} - 1 = \frac{1}{2} - 1 = -\frac{1}{2} = \text{RHS}$

$\therefore$ LHS = RHS **Hence Proved.**

Mistake Alert $\sin^2\theta$ means $(\sin\theta)^2$, not $\sin\theta^2$

Question 2 Prove that $2\sin^2\frac{\pi}{6}+\text{cosec}^2\frac{7\pi}{6}\cos^2\frac{\pi}{3}=\frac{3}{2}$

◎ *Thinking Process* If the angle given in the questions is greater than $\frac{\pi}{2}$, then use the quadrant system to break that angle and simplify it.

Sol. We have, $2\sin^2\frac{\pi}{6}+\text{cosec}^2\frac{7\pi}{6}\cos^2\frac{\pi}{3}=\frac{3}{2}$

$$\text{LHS}=2\sin^2\frac{\pi}{6}+\text{cosec}^2\frac{7\pi}{6}\cos^2\frac{\pi}{3}=2\times\left(\frac{1}{2}\right)^2+\text{cosec}^2\left(\pi+\frac{\pi}{6}\right)\cos^2\frac{\pi}{3}$$

$$=2\times\frac{1}{4}+\text{cosec}^2\frac{\pi}{6}\cos^2\frac{\pi}{3}\qquad[\because \text{cosec}(\pi+\theta)=-\text{cosec}\,\theta]$$

$$=\frac{1}{2}+(2)^2\times\left(\frac{1}{2}\right)^2=\frac{1}{2}+1=\frac{3}{2}=\text{RHS}$$

$\therefore$ LHS = RHS **Hence Proved.**

Question 3 Prove that $\cot^2\frac{\pi}{6}+\text{cosec}\frac{5\pi}{6}+3\tan^2\frac{\pi}{6}=6$

Sol. We have, $\cot^2\frac{\pi}{6}+\text{cosec}\frac{5\pi}{6}+3\tan^2\frac{\pi}{6}=6$

$$\text{LHS}=\cot^2\frac{\pi}{6}+\text{cosec}\frac{5\pi}{6}+3\tan^2\frac{\pi}{6}$$

$$=(\sqrt{3})^2+\text{cosec}\left(\pi-\frac{\pi}{6}\right)+3\left(\frac{1}{\sqrt{3}}\right)^2$$

$$=3+\text{cosec}\frac{\pi}{6}+3\times\frac{1}{3}\qquad[\because \text{cosec}(\pi-\theta)=\text{cosec}\,\theta]$$

$$=3+2+1=6=\text{RHS}$$

$\therefore$ LHS = RHS **Hence Proved.**

Question 4 Prove that $2\sin^2\frac{3\pi}{4}+2\cos^2\frac{\pi}{4}+2\sec^2\frac{\pi}{3}=10$

Sol. $2\sin^2\frac{3\pi}{4}+2\cos^2\frac{\pi}{4}+2\sec^2\frac{\pi}{3}=10$

$$\text{LHS}=2\sin^2\frac{3\pi}{4}+2\cos^2\frac{\pi}{4}+2\sec^2\frac{\pi}{3}$$

$$=2\sin^2\left(\pi-\frac{\pi}{4}\right)+2\cos^2\frac{\pi}{4}+2\sec^2\frac{\pi}{3}$$

$$=2\sin^2\frac{\pi}{4}+2\times\left(\frac{1}{\sqrt{2}}\right)^2+2(2)^2\qquad[\because \sin(\pi-\theta)=\sin\theta]$$

$$=2\times\left(\frac{1}{\sqrt{2}}\right)^2+2\times\frac{1}{2}+2\times4=1+1+8=10=\text{RHS}$$

$\therefore$ LHS = RHS **Hence Proved.**

Question 5 Find the values of (i) $\sin 75°$ (ii) $\tan 15°$.

◎ **Thinking Process** Write $75° = 45° + 30°$ and $15° = 45° - 30°$ because values of 45° and 30° are well known. Then, use the formula of $\sin(A + B)$ and $\tan(A - B)$.

Sol. (i) $\sin 75° = \sin(45° + 30°)$

$$= \sin 45° \cos 30° + \cos 45° \sin 30°$$

$$[\because \sin(A + B) = \sin A \cos B + \cos A \sin B]$$

$$= \frac{1}{\sqrt{2}} \times \frac{\sqrt{3}}{2} + \frac{1}{\sqrt{2}} \times \frac{1}{2} = \frac{\sqrt{3} + 1}{2\sqrt{2}}$$

(ii) $\tan 15° = \tan(45° - 30°)$ $\left[\because \tan(A - B) = \dfrac{\tan A - \tan B}{1 + \tan A \tan B}\right]$

$$= \frac{\tan 45° - \tan 30°}{1 + \tan 45° \tan 30°} = \frac{1 - \frac{1}{\sqrt{3}}}{1 + \frac{1}{\sqrt{3}}} = \frac{\sqrt{3} - 1}{\sqrt{3} + 1}$$

$$= \frac{\sqrt{3} - 1}{\sqrt{3} + 1} \times \frac{\sqrt{3} - 1}{\sqrt{3} - 1} = \frac{(\sqrt{3} - 1)^2}{3 - 1}$$

$$= \frac{3 + 1 - 2\sqrt{3}}{2} = \frac{4 - 2\sqrt{3}}{2} = 2 - \sqrt{3}$$

Question 6 Prove that $\cos\left(\frac{\pi}{4} - x\right)\cos\left(\frac{\pi}{4} - y\right) - \sin\left(\frac{\pi}{4} - x\right)\sin\left(\frac{\pi}{4} - y\right)$ $= \sin(x + y)$

◎ **Thinking Process** Here, we will use the identity $\cos(A + B) = \cos A \cos B - \sin A \sin B$ to combine the LHS of given equation.

Sol. We have, $\cos\left(\frac{\pi}{4} - x\right)\cos\left(\frac{\pi}{4} - y\right) - \sin\left(\frac{\pi}{4} - x\right)\sin\left(\frac{\pi}{4} - y\right) = \sin(x + y)$

$\because$ LHS $= \cos\left(\frac{\pi}{4} - x\right)\cos\left(\frac{\pi}{4} - y\right) - \sin\left(\frac{\pi}{4} - x\right)\sin\left(\frac{\pi}{4} - y\right)$

Let $\frac{\pi}{4} - x = A$ and $\frac{\pi}{4} - y = B$

Then, LHS $= \cos A \cos B - \sin A \sin B = \cos(A + B)$

$$= \cos\left(\frac{\pi}{4} - x + \frac{\pi}{4} - y\right)$$

$$= \cos\left(\frac{\pi}{2} - x - y\right) = \cos\left[\frac{\pi}{2} - (x + y)\right] \quad \left[\because \cos\left(\frac{\pi}{2} - \theta\right) = \sin\theta\right]$$

$$= \sin(x + y) = \text{RHS}$$

$\therefore$ LHS = RHS **Hence Proved.**

Question 7 Prove that $\dfrac{\tan\left(\dfrac{\pi}{4}+x\right)}{\tan\left(\dfrac{\pi}{4}-x\right)}=\left(\dfrac{1+\tan x}{1-\tan x}\right)^2$.

◎ ***Thinking Process*** To expand LHS of given equation, we can use the identity $\tan(A+B)=\dfrac{\tan A+\tan B}{1-\tan A\tan B}$ considering $\dfrac{\pi}{4}$ as A and x as B.

Sol. We have, $\dfrac{\tan\left(\dfrac{\pi}{4}+x\right)}{\tan\left(\dfrac{\pi}{4}-x\right)}=\left(\dfrac{1+\tan x}{1-\tan x}\right)^2$

$$\text{LHS}=\frac{\tan\left(\frac{\pi}{4}+x\right)}{\tan\left(\frac{\pi}{4}-x\right)}=\frac{\tan\frac{\pi}{4}+\tan x}{1-\tan\frac{\pi}{4}\tan x}\times\frac{1+\tan\frac{\pi}{4}\tan x}{\tan\frac{\pi}{4}-\tan x}$$

$$\left(\because \tan(A+B)=\frac{\tan A+\tan B}{1-\tan A\tan B}\text{ and }\tan(A-B)=\frac{\tan A-\tan B}{1+\tan A\tan B}\right)$$

$$=\frac{1+\tan x}{1-\tan x}\times\frac{1+\tan x}{1-\tan x}=\left(\frac{1+\tan x}{1-\tan x}\right)^2=\text{RHS}$$

$\therefore$ LHS = RHS **Hence Proved.**

Question 8 Prove that $\dfrac{\cos(\pi+x)\cos(-x)}{\sin(\pi-x)\cos\left(\dfrac{\pi}{2}+x\right)}=\cot^2 x$.

Sol. $\dfrac{\cos(\pi+x)\cos(-x)}{\sin(\pi-x)\cos\left(\dfrac{\pi}{2}+x\right)}=\cot^2 x$

$$\text{LHS}=\frac{\cos(\pi+x)\cos(-x)}{\sin(\pi-x)\cos\left(\frac{\pi}{2}+x\right)}=\frac{(-\cos x)(\cos x)}{(\sin x)(-\sin x)}\quad\left(\begin{array}{c}\because\cos(\pi+\theta)=-\cos\theta\\ \cos(-\theta)=\cos\theta\\ \sin(\pi-\theta)=\sin\theta\\ \sin(-\theta)=-\sin\theta\end{array}\right)$$

$$=\frac{\cos^2 x}{\sin^2 x}=\cot^2 x=\text{RHS}$$

$\therefore$ LHS = RHS **Hence proved.**

Question 9 Prove that $\cos\left(\frac{3\pi}{2}+x\right)\cos(2\pi+x)\left[\cot\left(\frac{3\pi}{2}-x\right)+\cot(2\pi+x)\right]=1$

Sol. $\cos\left(\frac{3\pi}{2}+x\right)\cos(2\pi+x)\left[\cot\left(\frac{3\pi}{2}-x\right)+\cot(2\pi+x)\right]=1$

$$\text{LHS}=\cos\left(\frac{3\pi}{2}+x\right)\cos(2\pi+x)\left[\cot\left(\frac{3\pi}{2}-x\right)+\cot(2\pi+x)\right]$$

$$=(\sin x)(\cos x)[\tan x+\cot x]$$

$$=\sin x\cos x\left[\frac{\sin x}{\cos x}+\frac{\cos x}{\sin x}\right]\quad\left[\begin{array}{l}\because \cot\left(\frac{3\pi}{2}-\theta\right)=\tan\theta,\ \cos(2\pi+\theta)=\cos\theta\\ \cos\left(\frac{3\pi}{2}+\theta\right)=\sin\theta \text{ and } \cot(2\pi+\theta)=\cot\theta\end{array}\right]$$

$$=\sin x\cos x\left[\frac{\sin^2 x+\cos^2 x}{\cos x\sin x}\right]=1=\text{RHS}$$

$\therefore \text{LHS}=\text{RHS}$ **Hence Proved.**

Question 10 Prove that
$\sin(n+1)x\sin(n+2)x+\cos(n+1)x\cos(n+2)x=\cos x$

Sol. $\sin(n+1)x\sin(n+2)x+\cos(n+1)x\cos(n+2)x=\cos x$

$$\text{LHS}=\sin(n+1)x\sin(n+2)x+\cos(n+1)x\cos(n+2)x$$

$$=\cos[(n+2)x-(n+1)x]\quad[\cos(A-B)=\cos A\cos B+\sin A\sin B]$$

$$=\cos(nx+2x-nx-x)=\cos x=\text{RHS}$$

$\therefore \text{LHS}=\text{RHS}$ **Hence Proved.**

Question 11 Prove that $\cos\left(\frac{3\pi}{4}+x\right)-\cos\left(\frac{3\pi}{4}-x\right)=-\sqrt{2}\sin x$

◎ ***Thinking Process*** Here, we will use the formula
$\cos C-\cos D=-2\sin\left(\frac{C+D}{2}\right)\sin\left(\frac{C-D}{2}\right)$, to get the result easily.

Sol. $\cos\left(\frac{3\pi}{4}+x\right)-\cos\left(\frac{3\pi}{4}-x\right)=-\sqrt{2}\sin x$

$$\text{LHS}=\cos\left(\frac{3\pi}{4}\quad\right)\ \cos\left(\frac{3\pi}{4}-x\right)$$

$$=-2\sin\left(\frac{\frac{3\pi}{4}+x+\frac{3\pi}{4}-x}{2}\right)\sin\left(\frac{\frac{3\pi}{4}+x-\frac{3\pi}{4}+x}{2}\right)$$

$$= -2\sin\frac{3\pi}{4}\sin x = -2\sin\left(\pi - \frac{\pi}{4}\right)\sin x$$

$$= -2\sin\frac{\pi}{4}\sin x = -2 \times \frac{1}{\sqrt{2}}\sin x = -\sqrt{2}\sin x = \text{RHS} \quad [\because \sin(\pi - \theta) = \sin\theta]$$

$\therefore$ LHS = RHS **Hence Proved.**

Question 12 Prove that $\sin^2 6x - \sin^2 4x = \sin 2x \sin 10x$

Sol. $\sin^2 6x - \sin^2 4x = \sin 2x \sin 10x$

$$\text{LHS} = \sin^2 6x - \sin^2 4x = \sin(6x + 4x)\sin(6x - 4x)$$

$$[\because \sin^2 A - \sin^2 B = \sin(A + B)\sin(A - B)]$$

$$= \sin 10x \sin 2x = \text{RHS}$$

$\therefore$ LHS = RHS **Hence Proved.**

Question 13 Prove that $\cos^2 2x - \cos^2 6x = \sin 4x \sin 8x$.

◎ **Thinking Process** We will have to first convert in the form of $\sin^2 A - \sin^2 B$ by using the identity $\sin^2 A + \cos^2 A = 1$ and simplify it.

Sol. $\cos^2 2x - \cos^2 6x = \sin 4x \sin 8x$

$$\text{LHS} = \cos^2 2x - \cos^2 6x$$

$$= (1 - \sin^2 2x) - (1 - \sin^2 6x) \quad (\because \sin^2 A + \cos^2 A = 1)$$

$$= \sin^2 6x - \sin^2 2x$$

$$= \sin(6x + 2x)\sin(6x - 2x) \quad [\because \sin^2 A - \sin^2 B = \sin(A + B)\sin(A - B)]$$

$$= \sin 8x \sin 4x = \text{RHS}$$

$\therefore$ LHS = RHS **Hence Proved.**

Question 14 Prove that $\sin 2x + 2\sin 4x + \sin 6x = 4\cos^2 x \sin 4x$

◎ **Thinking Process** Here, we will use the formula $\sin A + \sin B = 2\sin\left(\frac{A + B}{2}\right)\cos\left(\frac{A - B}{2}\right)$.

Sol. $\sin 2x + 2\sin 4x + \sin 6x = 4\cos^2 x \sin 4x$

$$\text{LHS} = \sin 2x + 2\sin 4x + \sin 6x = \sin 6x + \sin 2x + 2\sin 4x$$

$$= 2\sin\frac{6x + 2x}{2}\cos\frac{6x - 2x}{2} + 2\sin 4x$$

$$\left[\because \sin A + \sin B = 2\sin\left(\frac{A + B}{2}\right)\cos\left(\frac{A - B}{2}\right)\right]$$

$$= 2\sin 4x \cos 2x + 2\sin 4x = 2\sin 4x(\cos 2x + 1)$$

$$= 2\sin 4x(2\cos^2 x - 1 + 1) = 2\sin 4x \, 2\cos^2 x = 4\cos^2 x \sin 4x = \text{RHS}$$

$\therefore$ LHS = RHS **Hence Proved.**

Question 15 Prove that $\cot 4x(\sin 5x+\sin 3x)=\cot x(\sin 5x-\sin 3x)$

Sol. Given, $\cot 4x(\sin 5x+\sin 3x)=\cot x(\sin 5x-\sin 3x)$

$$\text{LHS}=\cot 4x(\sin 5x+\sin 3x)$$

$$=\cot 4x\cdot 2\sin\frac{5x+3x}{2}\cos\frac{5x-3x}{2}$$

$$\left[\because \sin C+\sin D=2\sin\frac{C+D}{2}\cos\frac{C-D}{2}\right]$$

$$=\frac{\cos 4x}{\sin 4x}\times 2\sin 4x\cos x=2\cos 4x\cos x$$

$$\text{RHS}=\cot x(\sin 5x-\sin 3x)=\cot x\cdot 2\cos\frac{5x+3x}{2}\sin\frac{5x-3x}{2}$$

$$\left[\because \sin C-\sin D=2\cos\frac{C+D}{2}\sin\frac{C-D}{2}\right]$$

$$=\frac{\cos x}{\sin x}\times 2\cos 4x\sin x=2\cos 4x\cos x$$

$\therefore$ LHS = RHS **Hence Proved.**

Note Remember that $\sin 4x+\sin 3x\neq\sin 7x$.

Question 16 Prove that $\dfrac{\cos 9x-\cos 5x}{\sin 17x-\sin 3x}=-\dfrac{\sin 2x}{\cos 10x}$

◎ ***Thinking Process*** To prove this identity we will use the formulae

$$\cos C-\cos D=-2\sin\frac{C+D}{2}\sin\frac{C-D}{2}$$

$$\sin C-\sin D=2\cos\frac{C+D}{2}\sin\frac{C-D}{2}$$

Sol. Given, $\dfrac{\cos 9x-\cos 5x}{\sin 17x-\sin 3x}=-\dfrac{\sin 2x}{\cos 10x}$

$$\text{LHS}=\frac{\cos 9x-\cos 5x}{\sin 17x-\sin 3x}$$

$$=\frac{-2\sin\frac{9x+5x}{2}\sin\frac{9x-5x}{2}}{2\cos\frac{17x+3x}{2}\sin\frac{17x-3x}{2}} \quad \text{(by formulae)}$$

$$=\frac{-\sin 7x\sin 2x}{\cos 10x\sin 7x}=-\frac{\sin 2x}{\cos 10x}=\text{RHS}$$

$\therefore$ LHS = RHS **Hence Proved.**

Question 17 Prove that $\dfrac{\sin 5x + \sin 3x}{\cos 5x + \cos 3x} = \tan 4x$.

◎ *Thinking Process* Use the following formulae

$\sin C + \sin D = 2 \sin \dfrac{C+D}{2} \cos \dfrac{C-D}{2}$ and

$\cos C + \cos D = 2 \cos \dfrac{C+D}{2} \cos \dfrac{C-D}{2}$ to get the result.

Sol. Given, $\dfrac{\sin 5x + \sin 3x}{\cos 5x + \cos 3x} = \tan 4x$

$$\text{LHS} = \frac{\sin 5x + \sin 3x}{\cos 5x + \cos 3x} = \frac{2 \sin \dfrac{5x+3x}{2} \cos \dfrac{5x-3x}{2}}{2 \cos \dfrac{5x+3x}{2} \cos \dfrac{5x-3x}{2}} \quad \text{(by formulae)}$$

$$= \frac{\sin 4x \cos x}{\cos 4x \cos x} = \tan 4x = \text{RHS}$$

$\therefore$ LHS = RHS **Hence proved.**

Question 18 Prove that $\dfrac{\sin x - \sin y}{\cos x + \cos y} = \tan \dfrac{x-y}{2}$

Sol. Given, $\dfrac{\sin x - \sin y}{\cos x + \cos y} = \tan \dfrac{x-y}{2}$

$$\text{LHS} = \frac{\sin x - \sin y}{\cos x + \cos y} = \frac{2 \cos \dfrac{x+y}{2} \sin \dfrac{x-y}{2}}{2 \cos \dfrac{x+y}{2} \cos \dfrac{x-y}{2}} \quad \text{(by formulae)}$$

$$= \tan \frac{x-y}{2} = \text{RHS}$$

$\therefore$ LHS = RHS **Hence Proved.**

Question 19 Prove that $\dfrac{\sin x + \sin 3x}{\cos x + \cos 3x} = \tan 2x$

Sol. We have, $\dfrac{\sin x + \sin 3x}{\cos x + \cos 3x} = \tan 2x$

$$\text{LHS} = \frac{\sin x + \sin 3x}{\cos x + \cos 3x} = \frac{\sin 3x + \sin x}{\cos 3x + \cos x} = \frac{2 \sin \dfrac{3x+x}{2} \cos \dfrac{3x-x}{2}}{2 \cos \dfrac{3x+x}{2} \cos \dfrac{3x-x}{2}} \quad \text{(by formulae)}$$

$$= \frac{\sin 2x \cos x}{\cos 2x \cos x} = \tan 2x = \text{RHS}$$

$\therefore$ LHS = RHS **Hence Proved.**

Mistake Alert Take greater angle (*i.e.*, $3x$) as C and smaller angle (*i.e.*, x) as D to avoid the sign error.

Question 20 Prove that $\dfrac{\sin x-\sin 3x}{\sin^2 x-\cos^2 x}=2\sin x$

Thinking Process To simplify the LHS we should use the formulae

$$\sin C-\sin D=2\cos\frac{C+D}{2}\sin\frac{C-D}{2}$$

and $\cos^2 A-\sin^2 B=\cos(A+B)\cos(A-B)$

Sol. We have $\dfrac{\sin x-\sin 3x}{\sin^2 x-\cos^2 x}=2\sin x$

$$\text{LHS}=\frac{\sin x-\sin 3x}{\sin^2 x-\cos^2 x}=\frac{\sin 3x-\sin x}{\cos^2 x-\sin^2 x}=\frac{2\cos\frac{3x+x}{2}\sin\frac{3x-x}{2}}{\cos(x+x)\cos(x-x)}\text{ (by formulae)}$$

$$=\frac{2\cos 2x\sin x}{\cos 2x\cos 0}=2\sin x=\text{RHS}$$

$\therefore$ LHS = RHS **Hence Proved.**

Note Take the negative sign common in numerator as well as in denominator to make the term in standard formula.

Question 21 Prove that $\dfrac{\cos 4x+\cos 3x+\cos 2x}{\sin 4x+\sin 3x+\sin 2x}=\cot 3x$

Thinking Process To solve LHS part, we will make the pair of first and last terms in the numerator and denominator and then use the standard formulae to get the result. Here, we can't make the pair of first and second terms or second or third terms because after combining first and third term we get the angles $\frac{4x+2x}{2}=3x$, which we have already in second term so that we may solve it easily.

Sol. $\dfrac{\cos 4x+\cos 3x+\cos 2x}{\sin 4x+\sin 3x+\sin 2x}=\cot 3x$

$$\text{LHS}=\frac{\cos 4x+\cos 3x+\cos 2x}{\sin 4x+\sin 3x+\sin 2x}=\frac{(\cos 4x+\cos 2x)+\cos 3x}{(\sin 4x+\sin 2x)+\sin 3x}$$

$$=\frac{2\cos\frac{4x+2x}{2}\cos\frac{4x-2x}{2}+\cos 3x}{2\sin\frac{4x+2x}{2}\cos\frac{4x-2x}{2}+\sin 3x}\text{ (by formulae)}$$

$$=\frac{2\cos 3x\cos x+\cos 3x}{2\sin 3x\cos x+\sin 3x}=\frac{\cos 3x(2\cos x+1)}{\sin 3x(2\cos x+1)}=\cot 3x=\text{RHS}$$

$\therefore$ LHS = RHS **Hence proved.**

Question 22 $\cot x \cot 2x - \cot 2x \cot 3x - \cot 3x \cot x = 1$

◎ *Thinking Process* Here, we will write $3x = 2x + x$, then use the formula

$$\cot(A+B) = \frac{\cot A \cot B - 1}{\cot A + \cot B}$$ and simplify it.

Sol. We have, $\cot x \cot 2x - \cot 2x \cot 3x - \cot 3x \cot x = 1$

Now, $\cot 3x = \cot(2x + x) = \dfrac{\cot 2x \cot x - 1}{\cot 2x + \cot x}$ (by formulae)

$\Rightarrow \cot 3x \cot 2x + \cot 3x \cot x = \cot 2x \cot x - 1$

$\Rightarrow \cot x \cot 2x - \cot 2x \cot 3x - \cot 3x \cot x = 1$ **Hence Proved.**

Question 23 Prove that $\tan 4x = \dfrac{4\tan x(1-\tan^2 x)}{1-6\tan^2 x + \tan^4 x}$.

◎ *Thinking Process* To expand tan 4x, we will use the formula,

$\tan 2x = \dfrac{2\tan x}{1-\tan^2 x}$ two times and solve it.

Sol. We have, $\tan 4x = \dfrac{4\tan x(1-\tan^2 x)}{1-6\tan^2 x + \tan^4 x}$

$$\text{LHS} = \tan 4x = \tan 2(2x) = \frac{2\tan 2x}{1-\tan^2 2x} = \frac{2\dfrac{2\tan x}{1-\tan^2 x}}{1-\left(\dfrac{2\tan x}{1-\tan^2 x}\right)^2} \quad \text{(by formulae)}$$

$$= \frac{4\tan x}{1-\tan^2 x} \times \frac{(1-\tan^2 x)^2}{(1-\tan^2 x)^2 - 4\tan^2 x}$$

$$= \frac{4\tan x(1-\tan^2 x)}{1+\tan^4 x - 2\tan^2 x - 4\tan^2 x}$$

$$= \frac{4\tan x(1-\tan^2 x)}{1-6\tan^2 x + \tan^4 x} = \text{RHS}$$

$\therefore$ LHS = RHS **Hence Proved.**

Question 24 Prove that $\cos 4x = 1 - 8\sin^2 x \cos^2 x$.

◎ *Thinking Process* To expand cos 4x, firstly we will use the formula $\cos 2x = 1 - 2\sin^2 x$ and then further use $\sin 2x = 2\sin x \cos x$ to get the result.

Sol. We have, $\cos 4x = 1 - 8\sin^2 x \cos^2 x$

LHS $= \cos 4x = 1 - 2\sin^2 2x = 1 - 2(\sin 2x)^2$ (by formulae)

$= 1 - 2(2\sin x \cos x)^2 = 1 - 8\sin^2 x \cos^2 x = \text{RHS}$

$\therefore$ LHS = RHS **Hence Proved.**

Question 25 Prove that $\cos 6x = 32\cos^6 x - 48\cos^4 x + 18\cos^2 x - 1$.

Thinking Process To simplify cos 6x, firstly we will use the formula $\cos 2x = 2\cos^2 x - 1$ and then further use $\cos 3x = 4\cos^3 x - 3\cos x$

So We have, $\cos 6x = 32\cos^6 x - 48\cos^4 x + 18\cos^2 x - 1$

$$\text{LHS} = \cos 6x = \cos 2(3x) = 2\cos^2 3x - 1 = 2(\cos 3x)^2 - 1 \quad (\because \cos 2\theta = 2\cos^2\theta - 1)$$

$$= 2(4\cos^3 x - 3\cos x)^2 - 1 \quad (\because \cos 3\theta = 4\cos^3\theta - 3\cos\theta)$$

$$= 2(16\cos^6 x + 9\cos^2 x - 24\cos^4 x) - 1$$

$$= 32\cos^6 x - 48\cos^4 x + 18\cos^2 x - 1 = \text{RHS}$$

$\therefore$ LHS = RHS **Hence Proved.**

Miscellaneous Exercise

Direction (Q. Nos. 1 to 7) Prove the following.

Question 1 $2\cos\frac{\pi}{13}\cos\frac{9\pi}{13} + \cos\frac{3\pi}{13} + \cos\frac{5\pi}{13} = 0$

Thinking Process Here, in a first term we will use the formula $2\cos A\cos B = \cos(A+B) + \cos(A-B)$, then use

$$\cos C + \cos D = 2\cos\frac{C+D}{2}\cos\frac{C-D}{2}$$ and simplify it.

Sol. We have, $2\cos\frac{\pi}{13}\cos\frac{9\pi}{13} + \cos\frac{3\pi}{13} + \cos\frac{5\pi}{13} = 0$

$$\text{LHS} = 2\cos\frac{\pi}{13}\cos\frac{9\pi}{13} + \cos\frac{3\pi}{13} + \cos\frac{5\pi}{13}$$

$$= \cos\left(\frac{9\pi}{13} + \frac{\pi}{13}\right) + \cos\left(\frac{9\pi}{13} - \frac{\pi}{13}\right) + \cos\frac{5\pi}{13} + \cos\frac{3\pi}{13} \quad \text{(by formulae)}$$

$$= \cos\frac{10\pi}{13} + \cos\frac{8\pi}{13} + \cos\frac{5\pi}{13} + \cos\frac{3\pi}{13}$$

$$= \left(\cos\frac{10\pi}{13} + \cos\frac{3\pi}{13}\right) + \left(\cos\frac{8\pi}{13} + \cos\frac{5\pi}{13}\right)$$

$$= 2\cos\frac{\frac{10\pi}{13} + \frac{3\pi}{13}}{2}\cos\frac{\frac{10\pi}{13} - \frac{3\pi}{13}}{2} + 2\cos\frac{\frac{8\pi}{13} + \frac{5\pi}{13}}{2}\cos\frac{\frac{8\pi}{13} - \frac{5\pi}{13}}{2}$$

(by formulae)

$$= 2\cos\frac{\pi}{2}\cos\frac{7\pi}{26} + 2\cos\frac{\pi}{2}\cos\frac{3\pi}{26}$$

$$= 0 + 0 = 0 = \text{RHS} \quad \left(\because \cos\frac{\pi}{2} = 0\right)$$

$\therefore$ LHS = RHS **Hence Proved.**

Mistake Alert Remember that $\cos\frac{10\pi}{13}+\cos\frac{3\pi}{13}\neq\cos\frac{13\pi}{13}$.

Quick Solution

$$2\cos\frac{\pi}{13}\cos\frac{9\pi}{13}+\cos\frac{3\pi}{13}+\cos\frac{5\pi}{13}=0$$

$$\text{LHS}=2\cos\frac{\pi}{13}\cos\frac{9\pi}{13}+\cos\frac{3\pi}{13}+\cos\frac{5\pi}{13}$$

$$=\cos\left(\frac{9\pi}{13}+\frac{\pi}{13}\right)+\cos\left(\frac{9\pi}{13}-\frac{\pi}{13}\right)+\cos\frac{3\pi}{13}+\cos\frac{5\pi}{13}$$

$$=\cos\frac{10\pi}{13}+\cos\frac{8\pi}{13}+\cos\frac{3\pi}{13}+\cos\frac{5\pi}{13} \quad \text{\{by formula\}}$$

$$\cos\left(\pi-\frac{3\pi}{13}\right)+\cos\left(\pi-\frac{5\pi}{13}\right)+\cos\frac{3\pi}{13}+\cos\frac{5\pi}{13} \quad \{\because \cos(\pi-\theta)=-\cos)\}$$

$$=-\cos\frac{3\pi}{13}-\cos\frac{5\pi}{13}+\cos\frac{3\pi}{13}+\cos\frac{5\pi}{13}$$

Question 2 $(\sin 3x+\sin x)\sin x+(\cos 3x-\cos x)\cos x=0$

Sol. $\because$ LHS $=(\sin 3x+\sin x)\sin x+(\cos 3x-\cos x)\cos x$

$$=\left[2\sin\frac{3x+x}{2}\cos\frac{3x-x}{2}\right]\sin x+\left[-2\sin\frac{3x+x}{2}\sin\frac{3x-x}{2}\right]\cos x$$

(By formulae)

$$=2\sin 2x\cos x\sin x-2\sin 2x\sin x\cos x=0=\text{RHS}$$

$\therefore$ LHS = RHS **Hence Proved.**

Question 3 $(\cos x+\cos y)^2+(\sin x-\sin y)^2=4\cos^2\frac{x+y}{2}$

Sol. We have, $(\cos x+\cos y)^2+(\sin x-\sin y)^2=4\cos^2\frac{x+y}{2}$

$$\text{LHS}=(\cos x+\cos y)^2+(\sin x-\sin y)^2$$

$$=\left(2\cos\frac{x+y}{2}\cos\frac{x-y}{2}\right)^2+\left(2\cos\frac{x+y}{2}\sin\frac{x-y}{2}\right)^2 \quad \text{(by formulae)}$$

$$\left[\because \cos C+\cos D=2\cos\frac{C+D}{2}\cos\frac{C-D}{2}\right.$$

$$\left.\text{and } \sin C-\sin D=2\cos\frac{C+D}{2}\sin\frac{C-D}{2}\right]$$

$$=4\cos^2\frac{x+y}{2}\cos^2\frac{x-y}{2}+4\cos^2\frac{x+y}{2}\sin^2\frac{x-y}{2}$$

$$=4\cos^2\frac{x+y}{2}\left(\cos^2\frac{x-y}{2}+\sin^2\frac{x-y}{2}\right)=4\cos^2\frac{x+y}{2}=\text{RHS}$$

$(\because \cos^2 x+\sin^2 x=1)$

$\therefore$ LHS = RHS **Hence Proved.**

Question 4 $(\cos x - \cos y)^2 + (\sin x - \sin y)^2 = 4\sin^2 \frac{x-y}{2}$

Sol. $(\cos x - \cos y)^2 + (\sin x - \sin y)^2 = 4\sin^2 \frac{x-y}{2}$

$\because$ LHS $= (\cos x - \cos y)^2 + (\sin x - \sin y)^2$

$= \left(-2\sin\frac{x+y}{2}\sin\frac{x-y}{2}\right)^2 + \left(2\cos\frac{x+y}{2}\sin\frac{x-y}{2}\right)^2$ (By formulae)

$\left[\because \cos C - \cos D = -2\sin\frac{C+D}{2}\sin\frac{C-D}{2}\right.$

$\left.\text{and } \sin C - \sin D = 2\cos\frac{C+D}{2}\sin\frac{C-D}{2}\right]$

$= 4\sin^2\frac{x+y}{2}\sin^2\frac{x-y}{2} + 4\cos^2\frac{x+y}{2}\sin^2\frac{x-y}{2}$

$= 4\sin^2\frac{x-y}{2}\left(\sin^2\frac{x+y}{2} + \cos^2\frac{x+y}{2}\right)$

$= 4\sin^2\frac{x-y}{2} =$ RHS $\quad (\because \cos^2 x + \sin^2 x = 1)$

$\therefore$ LHS = RHS **Hence Proved.**

Mistake Alert It should be remembered that $\sin^2 A \neq \sin A^2$

i.e., $\left(\sin\frac{x+y}{2}\right)^2 \neq \sin\frac{(x+y)^2}{4}$

Question 5 $\sin x + \sin 3x + \sin 5x + \sin 7x = 4\cos x \cos 2x \sin 4x$

Thinking Process First, we will make the pair as $7x + x = 8x$, $5x + 3x = 8x$, to make the calculation easier and then, use the formulas

$\sin C + \sin D = 2\sin\frac{C+D}{2}\cos\frac{C-D}{2}$

and $\cos C + \cos D = 2\cos\frac{C+D}{2}\cos\frac{C-D}{2}$

Sol. We have, $\sin x + \sin 3x + \sin 5x + \sin 7x = 4\cos x\cos 2x \sin 4x$

LHS $= \sin x + \sin 3x + \sin 5x + \sin 7x = (\sin 7x + \sin x) + (\sin 5x + \sin 3x)$

$= 2\sin\frac{7x+x}{2}\cos\frac{7x-x}{2} + 2\sin\frac{5x+3x}{2}\cos\frac{5x-3x}{2}$ (by formulae)

$= 2\sin 4x\cos 3x + 2\sin 4x\cos x = 2\sin 4x(\cos 3x + \cos x)$

$= 2\sin 4x \cdot 2\cos\frac{3x+x}{2}\cos\frac{3x-x}{2}$ (by formulae)

$= 4\sin 4x\cos 2x\cos x =$ RHS

$\therefore$ LHS = RHS **Hence Proved.**

Mistake Alert Remember that $\sin 7x + \sin x \neq \sin 8x$.

Question 6 $\dfrac{(\sin 7x + \sin 5x) + (\sin 9x + \sin 3x)}{(\cos 7x + \cos 5x) + (\cos 9x + \cos 3x)} = \tan 6x$

Sol. We have, $\dfrac{(\sin 7x + \sin 5x) + (\sin 9x + \sin 3x)}{(\cos 7x + \cos 5x) + (\cos 9x + \cos 3x)} = \tan 6x$

$$\text{LHS} = \frac{(\sin 7x + \sin 5x) + (\sin 9x + \sin 3x)}{(\cos 7x + \cos 5x) + (\cos 9x + \cos 3x)}$$

$$= \frac{2\sin\frac{7x+5x}{2}\cos\frac{7x-5x}{2} + 2\sin\frac{9x+3x}{2}\cos\frac{9x-3x}{2}}{2\cos\frac{7x+5x}{2}\cos\frac{7x-5x}{2} + 2\cos\frac{9x+3x}{2}\cos\frac{9x-3x}{2}}$$

(By formulae)

$$\left[\because \sin C + \sin D = 2\sin\frac{C+D}{2}\cos\frac{C-D}{2}\right.$$
$$\left.\text{and } \cos C + \cos D = 2\cos\frac{C+D}{2}\cos\frac{C-D}{2}\right]$$

$$= \frac{2\sin 6x\cos x + 2\sin 6x\cos 3x}{2\cos 6x\cos x + 2\cos 6x\cos 3x}$$

$$= \frac{2\sin 6x(\cos x + \cos 3x)}{2\cos 6x(\cos x + \cos 3x)} = \tan 6x = \text{RHS}$$

$\therefore$ LHS = RHS **Hence Proved.**

Question 7 $\sin 3x + \sin 2x - \sin x = 4\sin x\cos\frac{x}{2}\cos\frac{3x}{2}$.

Sol. We have, $\sin 3x + \sin 2x - \sin x = 4\sin x\cos\frac{x}{2}\cos\frac{3x}{2}$

$$\text{LHS} = \sin 3x + \sin 2x - \sin x$$
$$= (\sin 3x - \sin x) + \sin 2x$$
$$= 2\cos\frac{3x+x}{2}\sin\frac{3x-x}{2} + \sin 2x$$

$$\left[\because \sin C - \sin D = 2\cos\frac{C+D}{2}\sin\frac{C-D}{2}\right]$$

$$= 2\cos 2x\sin x + 2\sin x\cos x \qquad (\because \sin 2x = 2\sin x\cos x)$$
$$= 2\sin x(\cos 2x + \cos x)$$
$$= 2\sin x\, 2\cos\frac{2x+x}{2}\cos\frac{2x-x}{2}$$

$$\left[\because \cos C + \cos D = 2\cos\frac{C+D}{2}\cos\frac{C-D}{2}\right]$$

$$= 4\sin x\cos\frac{3x}{2}\cos\frac{x}{2} = \text{RHS}$$

$\therefore$ LHS = RHS **Hence Proved.**

Direction (Q. No. 8 to 10) Find $\sin\frac{x}{2}, \cos\frac{x}{2}, \tan\frac{x}{2}$ in each of the following questions.

Question 8 $\tan x = -\frac{4}{3}$, where x is in second quadrant.

◎ ***Thinking Process*** Here, we have two methods of determining the values of $\sin\frac{x}{2}$, $\cos\frac{x}{2}$ and $\tan\frac{x}{2}$ either by using the identities $\sec^2 x - \tan^2 x = 1$ or $\tan 2x = \frac{2\tan x}{1-\tan^2 x}$ replacing x by $\frac{x}{2}$ and simplify it. After that apply the sign by using quadrant system.

Sol. Given, $\tan x = -\frac{4}{3}$, x lies in second quadrant.

i.e., $\frac{\pi}{2} < x < \pi \quad \because \tan x = \frac{2\tan\frac{x}{2}}{1-\tan^2\frac{x}{2}} = -\frac{4}{3}$

$\therefore\ 3\tan\frac{x}{2} = -2\left(1-\tan^2\frac{x}{2}\right) \Rightarrow 3\tan\frac{x}{2} = -2 + 2\tan^2\frac{x}{2}$

$\Rightarrow\quad 2\tan^2\frac{x}{2} - 3\tan\frac{x}{2} - 2 = 0 \Rightarrow 2\tan^2\frac{x}{2} - (4-1)\tan\frac{x}{2} - 2 = 0$

$\Rightarrow\quad 2\tan^2\frac{x}{2} - 4\tan\frac{x}{2} + \tan\frac{x}{2} - 2 = 0 \Rightarrow 2\tan^2\frac{x}{2} - (4-1)\tan\frac{x}{2} - 2 = 0$

$\Rightarrow 2\tan\frac{x}{2}\left(\tan\frac{x}{2} - 2\right) + 1\left(\tan\frac{x}{2} - 2\right) = 0 \Rightarrow \left(2\tan\frac{x}{2} + 1\right)\left(\tan\frac{x}{2} - 2\right) = 0$

$\Rightarrow \tan\frac{x}{2} = 2$ or $\tan\frac{x}{2} = -\frac{1}{2}$

$\because \frac{\pi}{2} < x < \pi \quad \Rightarrow \quad \frac{\pi}{4} < \frac{x}{2} < \frac{\pi}{2}$

i.e., $\frac{x}{2}$ lies in first quadrant.

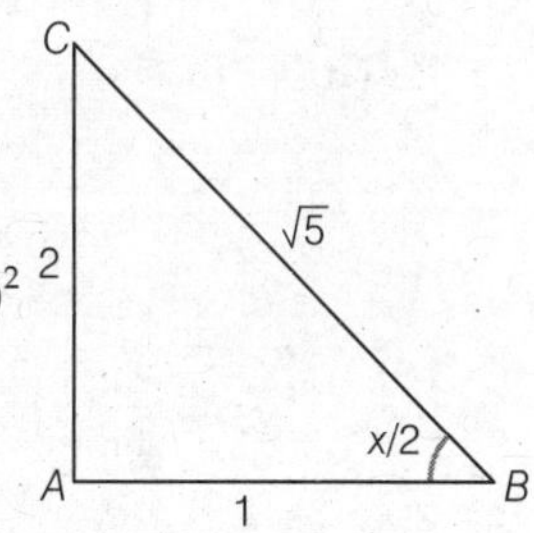

Therefore, $\tan\frac{x}{2} = 2 = \frac{2}{1} = \frac{\text{perpendicular}}{\text{base}} = \frac{AC}{AB}$

Using Pythagoras theorem, $(BC)^2 = (AC)^2 + (AB)^2$

$\Rightarrow \quad (BC)^2 = 4 + 1 = 5$

$\Rightarrow \quad BC = \sqrt{5}$

Now, $\sin\frac{x}{2} = \frac{\text{perpendicular}}{\text{hypotenuse}} = \frac{2}{\sqrt{5}} = \frac{2\sqrt{5}}{5}$

$\therefore \cos\frac{x}{2} = \frac{\text{base}}{\text{hypotenuse}} = \frac{1}{\sqrt{5}} = \frac{\sqrt{5}}{5}$

Mistake Alert Student are advised to use the positive and negative signs carefully according to the quadrant system.

Quick Solution

Given $\tan x = \frac{-4}{3}$ and x is in second quadrant.

i.e, $$\frac{\pi}{2} < x < \pi$$

$\Rightarrow$ $$\frac{\pi}{4} < \frac{x}{2} < \frac{\pi}{2}$$

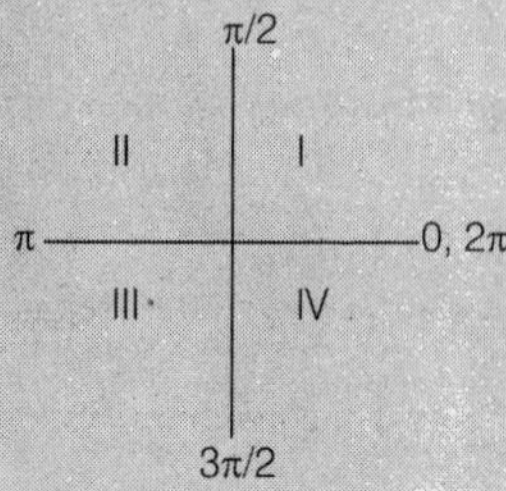

That means, $\frac{x}{2}$ lies in I quadrant

$\Rightarrow$ $\sin\frac{x}{2}$, $\cos\frac{x}{2}$ and $\tan\frac{x}{2}$ are positive.

Now, $$1 + \tan^2 x = \sec^2 x$$

$\Rightarrow$ $$\sec^2 x = 1 + \left(\frac{-4}{3}\right)^2 = \frac{25}{9} \Rightarrow \sec x = \pm\frac{5}{3}$$

We know that $\sec x$ is *–ve* in II Quadrant.

So, $$\sec x = \frac{-5}{3} \Rightarrow \cos x = \frac{-3}{5}$$

Now, $$\cos\frac{x}{2} = \pm\sqrt{\frac{1+\cos x}{2}} \qquad [\because \cos 2\theta = 2\cos^2\theta - 1]$$

$$= \sqrt{\frac{1+\left(\frac{-3}{5}\right)}{2}} \qquad \left[\because \cos\frac{x}{2} \text{ is positive}\right]$$

$$= \frac{1}{\sqrt{5}}$$

Again, $$\sin\frac{x}{2} = \pm\sqrt{\frac{1-\cos x}{2}} \qquad [\because \cos 2\theta = 1 - 2\sin^2\theta]$$

$$= \sqrt{\frac{1-\left(\frac{-3}{5}\right)}{2}} \qquad \left[\because \sin\frac{x}{2} \text{ is} + ve\right]$$

$$= \frac{2}{\sqrt{5}}$$

$$\tan\frac{x}{2} = \frac{\sin\frac{x}{2}}{\cos\frac{x}{2}} = \frac{2}{\sqrt{5}} \times \frac{\sqrt{5}}{1} = 2 \qquad \left[\because \tan\theta = \frac{\sin\theta}{2}\right]$$

$\therefore$ $$\sin\frac{x}{2} = \frac{2}{\sqrt{5}}, \cos\frac{x}{2} = \frac{1}{\sqrt{5}} \text{ and } \tan\frac{x}{2} = 2$$

i.e., $$\sin\frac{x}{2} = \frac{2\sqrt{5}}{5}, \cos\frac{x}{2} = \frac{\sqrt{5}}{5} \text{ and } \tan\frac{x}{2} = 2$$

Question 9 $\cos x = -\dfrac{1}{3}$, where x is in third quadrant.

Sol. Given, $\cos x = -\dfrac{1}{3}$, x is in third quadrant.

i.e., $$\pi < x < \frac{3\pi}{2}$$

($\because$ In third quadrant θ lies between π and $3\pi/2$)

From the formula $$\cos x = 2\cos^2\frac{x}{2} - 1$$

$$\Rightarrow \quad 2\cos^2\frac{x}{2} = 1 + \cos x = 1 - \frac{1}{3}$$

$$\Rightarrow \quad 2\cos^2\frac{x}{2} = \frac{2}{3}$$

$$\Rightarrow \quad \cos^2\frac{x}{2} = \frac{1}{3}$$

$$\Rightarrow \quad \cos\frac{x}{2} = \pm\frac{1}{\sqrt{3}}$$

Now, $$\pi < x < \frac{3\pi}{2} \Rightarrow \frac{\pi}{2} < \frac{x}{2} < \frac{3\pi}{4}$$

i.e., $\dfrac{x}{2}$ lies in second quadrant, therefore $\cos\dfrac{x}{2}$ will be negative

$$\Rightarrow \quad \cos\frac{x}{2} = -\frac{1}{\sqrt{3}} = -\frac{\sqrt{3}}{3}$$

Now, $\sin^2\dfrac{x}{2} = 1 - \cos^2\dfrac{x}{2}$

$$\sin^2\frac{x}{2} = 1 - \left(-\frac{1}{\sqrt{3}}\right)^2 = 1 - \frac{1}{3} = \frac{2}{3}$$

$$\Rightarrow \quad \sin\frac{x}{2} = \pm\sqrt{\frac{2}{3}}$$

$$\Rightarrow \quad \sin\frac{x}{2} = \sqrt{\frac{2}{3}} = \frac{\sqrt{6}}{3}$$ (As $\dfrac{x}{2}$ lies in second quadrant.)

$$\Rightarrow \quad \tan\frac{x}{2} = \frac{\sin\frac{x}{2}}{\cos\frac{x}{2}} = \frac{\sqrt{\frac{2}{3}}}{-\frac{1}{\sqrt{3}}} = -\sqrt{2}$$

Question 10 $\sin x = \frac{1}{4}$, where x is in second quadrant.

Sol. Given, $\sin x = \frac{1}{4}$, x is in second quadrant. *i.e.,* $\frac{\pi}{2} < x < \pi$

$$\because \quad \sin x = \frac{2\tan\frac{x}{2}}{1+\tan^2\frac{x}{2}} \therefore \frac{1}{4} = \frac{2\tan\frac{x}{2}}{1+\tan^2\frac{x}{2}}$$

$$\Rightarrow \quad 1+\tan^2\frac{x}{2} = 8\tan\frac{x}{2}$$

$$\Rightarrow \quad \tan^2\frac{x}{2} - 8\tan\frac{x}{2} + 1 = 0 \Rightarrow \tan\frac{x}{2} = \frac{8 \pm \sqrt{64-4}}{2} \quad \left[\because x = \frac{-b \pm \sqrt{b^2-4ac}}{2a}\right]$$

$$\Rightarrow \quad \tan\frac{x}{2} = \frac{8 \pm 2\sqrt{15}}{2} \Rightarrow \tan\frac{x}{2} = 4 \pm \sqrt{15}$$

$$\because \quad \frac{\pi}{2} < x < \pi \Rightarrow \frac{\pi}{4} < \frac{x}{2} < \frac{\pi}{2}$$

i.e., $\frac{x}{2}$ lies in Ist quadrant.

$$\Rightarrow \quad \tan\frac{x}{2} = 4 + \sqrt{15} \quad [\because \tan\theta \text{ is positive in Ist quardant}]$$

Now, $\sec^2\frac{x}{2} = 1 + \tan^2\frac{x}{2} = 1 + (4+\sqrt{15})^2 = 1 + 16 + 15 + 8\sqrt{15}$

$$\Rightarrow \quad \sec^2\frac{x}{2} = 32 + 8\sqrt{15} \Rightarrow \sec^2\frac{x}{2} = 8(4+\sqrt{15})$$

$$\Rightarrow \quad \cos^2\frac{x}{2} = \frac{1}{\sec^2\frac{x}{2}} = \frac{1}{8(4+\sqrt{15})} \times \frac{4-\sqrt{15}}{4-\sqrt{15}}$$

$$[\because (a+b)(a-b) = a^2 - b^2]$$

$$\Rightarrow \quad \cos^2\frac{x}{2} = \frac{(4-\sqrt{15})}{8} \times \frac{2}{2} \quad \text{[Multiply and divide by 2]}$$

$$\Rightarrow \quad \cos\frac{x}{2} = \frac{\sqrt{8-2\sqrt{15}}}{4}$$

Now, $\sin^2\frac{x}{2} = 1 - \cos^2\frac{x}{2} = 1 - \frac{8-2\sqrt{15}}{16}$

$$\sin^2\frac{x}{2} = \frac{16-8+2\sqrt{15}}{16} \Rightarrow \sin^2\frac{x}{2} = \frac{8+2\sqrt{15}}{16}$$

$$\Rightarrow \quad \sin\frac{x}{2} = \frac{\sqrt{8+2\sqrt{15}}}{4}$$

Quick Solution Given $\sin x = \frac{1}{4}$, x is in II quadrant.

i.e., $\frac{\pi}{2} < x < \pi \Rightarrow \frac{\pi}{4} < \frac{x}{2} < \frac{\pi}{2}$

$\Rightarrow$ $\frac{\pi}{2}$ lies in I quadrant $\Rightarrow \sin\frac{x}{2} > 0$, $\cos\frac{x}{2} > 0$ and $\tan\frac{x}{2} > 0$

Also, $\cos^2 x = 1 - \sin^2 x = 1 - \frac{1}{16} = \frac{15}{16} \Rightarrow \cos x = \pm\frac{\sqrt{15}}{4}$

$$\Rightarrow \quad \cos x = -\frac{\sqrt{15}}{4} \quad [\because \cos x \text{ is } -ve \text{ on II quadrant}]$$

Now,

$$\cos\frac{x}{2} = \pm\sqrt{\frac{1+\cos x}{2}} \quad \left[\because \cos\theta = 2\cos^2\frac{\theta}{2} - 1\right]$$

$$= \pm\sqrt{\frac{1-\frac{\sqrt{15}}{4}}{2}} = \pm\sqrt{\frac{8-2\sqrt{15}}{16}}$$

$$= \frac{\sqrt{8-2\sqrt{15}}}{4} \quad \left[\because \cos\frac{x}{2} > 0\right]$$

Now,

$$\sin\frac{x}{2} = \pm\sqrt{\frac{1-\cos x}{2}} = \pm\sqrt{\frac{1+\frac{\sqrt{15}}{4}}{2}} \quad \left[\because \cos\theta = 1 - 2\sin^2\frac{\theta}{2}\right]$$

$$= \pm\frac{\sqrt{8+2\sqrt{15}}}{4}$$

$$= \frac{\sqrt{8+2\sqrt{15}}}{4} \quad \left[\because \sin\frac{x}{2} > 0\right]$$

Now, $\because$

$$\tan\frac{x}{2} = \frac{\sin\frac{x}{2}}{\cos\frac{x}{2}} = \frac{\sqrt{8+2\sqrt{15}}}{4} \times \frac{4}{\sqrt{8-2\sqrt{15}}}$$

$$= \frac{\sqrt{4+\sqrt{15}}}{\sqrt{4-\sqrt{15}}} \times \frac{\sqrt{4-\sqrt{15}}}{\sqrt{4-\sqrt{15}}} = \frac{\sqrt{16-15}}{4-\sqrt{15}}$$

$$= \frac{1}{4-\sqrt{15}} \times \frac{4+\sqrt{15}}{4+\sqrt{15}} = \frac{4+\sqrt{15}}{1}$$

$$= 4 + \sqrt{15}$$

$\therefore$

$$\sin\frac{x}{2} = \frac{\sqrt{8+2\sqrt{15}}}{4}, \cos\frac{x}{2} = \frac{\sqrt{8-2\sqrt{15}}}{4}$$

and

$$\tan\frac{x}{2} = 4 + \sqrt{15}$$

DIKSHA APP Questions

Multiple Choice Questions

Q.1 The radius of the circle whose lengths is 15π cm makes an angle of $\frac{3\pi}{4}$ radian at the centre is

(a) 10 cm (b) 20 cm

(c) $11\frac{1}{4}$ cm (d) $22\frac{1}{2}$

Sol. (b) Let O be the centre and AB be the arc length of the circle.

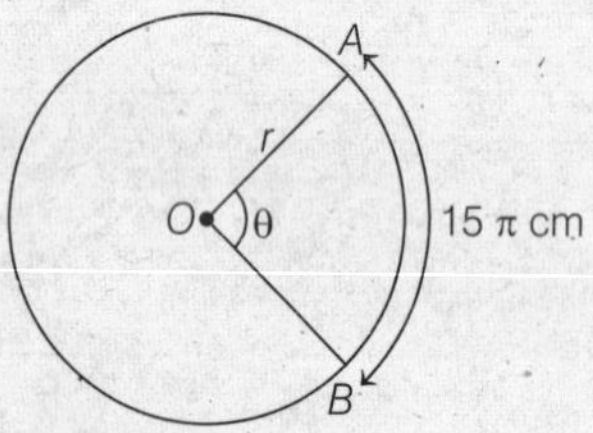

$$l = 15\pi \text{ cm}, \theta = \frac{3\pi}{4} \text{ radian}$$

$\because$ $$\theta = \frac{l}{r} \Rightarrow \frac{3\pi}{4} = \frac{15\pi}{r}$$

$\Rightarrow$ $$r = 20 \text{ cm}$$

Q.2 If $\tan\theta = \frac{1}{2}$ and $\tan\phi = \frac{1}{3}$, then the value of $\theta + \phi$ is

(a) $\frac{\pi}{6}$ (b) π (c) 0 (d) $\frac{\pi}{4}$

Sol. (d) Given, $\tan\theta = \frac{1}{2}$ and $\tan\phi = \frac{1}{3}$

$\because$ $$\tan(\theta + \phi) = \frac{\tan\theta + \tan\phi}{1 - \tan\theta\tan\phi}$$

$$\tan(\theta + \phi) = \frac{\frac{1}{2} + \frac{1}{3}}{1 - \left(\frac{1}{2}\right)\left(\frac{1}{3}\right)} = \frac{\left(\frac{5}{6}\right)}{\left(\frac{6-1}{6}\right)} = 1$$

$\Rightarrow$ $$\theta + \phi = \frac{\pi}{4}$$

Q.3 If $\cos x + \sqrt{3}\sin x = 2$, then the value of x is

(a) $\frac{\pi}{3}$ (b) $\frac{2\pi}{3}$ (c) $\frac{4\pi}{3}$ (d) $\frac{5\pi}{3}$

Sol. (a) Given, $\cos x + \sqrt{3}\sin x = 2$

i.e., $\frac{1}{2}\cos x + \frac{\sqrt{3}}{2}\sin x = 1$

$\because$ $\sin\frac{\pi}{6} = \frac{1}{2}$ and $\cos\frac{\pi}{6} = \frac{\sqrt{3}}{2}$,

$\therefore \sin\frac{\pi}{6}\cos x + \cos\frac{\pi}{6}\sin x = 1$

$\Rightarrow$ $\sin\left(\frac{\pi}{6} + x\right) = 1$ $[\because \sin A\cos B + \cos A\sin B = \sin(A + B)]$

$\Rightarrow$ $\sin\left(\frac{\pi}{6} + x\right) = \sin\frac{\pi}{2}$ $\left[\because \sin\frac{\pi}{2} = 1\right]$

$\Rightarrow$ $\frac{\pi}{6} + x = \frac{\pi}{2} \Rightarrow x = \frac{\pi}{2} - \frac{\pi}{6} \Rightarrow x = \frac{\pi}{3}$

Q.4 If $\cos x = \frac{-1}{2}$ and $0 < x < 2\pi$, then the solutions are

(a) $x = \frac{\pi}{3}, \frac{4\pi}{3}$ (b) $x = \frac{2\pi}{3}, \frac{4\pi}{3}$ (c) $x = \frac{2\pi}{3}, \frac{7\pi}{3}$ (d) $x = \frac{2\pi}{3}, \frac{5\pi}{3}$

Sol. (b) Given, $\cos x = \frac{-1}{2}$

$\because$ $\cos\frac{2\pi}{3} = -\frac{1}{2}$,

$\cos x = \cos\frac{2\pi}{3}$

$x = \frac{2\pi}{3}$ and $\cos\frac{4\pi}{3} = -\frac{1}{2}$

$\Rightarrow$ $\cos x = \cos\frac{4\pi}{3} \Rightarrow x = \frac{4\pi}{3}$

If $n = 0, \Rightarrow x = \pm\frac{2\pi}{3}$

$\Rightarrow$ $x = \frac{2\pi}{3}$ $[\because 0 < x < 2\pi]$

If $n = 1$,

$\Rightarrow$ $x = 2\pi \pm \frac{2\pi}{3} = 2\pi - \frac{2\pi}{3}$ $[\because 0 < x < 2\pi]$

$x = \frac{4\pi}{3}$

$\therefore$ $x = \frac{2\pi}{3}$ and $x = \frac{4\pi}{3}$

Q.5 If $\cos(A-B)=\frac{3}{5}$ and $\tan A\cdot\tan B=2$, then

(a) $\cos A\cos B=\frac{1}{5}$ (b) $\cos A\cos B=-\frac{1}{5}$

(c) $\sin A\sin B=\frac{1}{5}$ (d) $\sin A\sin B=\frac{-1}{5}$

Sol. (a) Given, $\cos(A-B)=\frac{3}{5}$ and $\tan A\cdot\tan B=2$

$\because$ $\cos(A-B)=\cos A\cos B+\sin A\sin B$

and $\tan A\tan B=\frac{\sin A\cdot\sin B}{\cos A\cdot\cos B}$,

$\therefore$ $\cos A\cos B+\sin A\sin B=\frac{3}{5}$ ... (i)

and $\frac{\sin A\sin B}{\cos A\cos B}=2$

i.e., $2\cos A\cos B-\sin A\sin B=0$ ... (ii)

On adding Eqs. (i) and (ii), we get

$$\cos A\cos B=\frac{1}{5} \text{ and } \sin A\sin B=\frac{2}{5}$$

Q.6 If $\tan x=x-\frac{1}{4x}$, then $\sec x-\tan x$ is

(a) $-2x,\frac{1}{2x}$ (b) $2x,-\frac{1}{2x}$ (c) $2x$ (d) $2x,\frac{1}{2x}$

Sol. (a) Given, $\tan x=x-\frac{1}{4x}$

$\because$ $1+\tan^2 x=\sec^2 x$,

$$\sec^2 x=1+\left(x-\frac{1}{4x}\right)^2=1+x^2+\frac{1}{16x^2}-\frac{1}{2}=x^2+\frac{1}{16x^2}+\frac{1}{2}$$

$$=x^2+\frac{1}{16x^2}+2(x)\left(\frac{1}{4x}\right)=\left(x+\frac{1}{4x}\right)^2$$

$$\sec x=\pm\left(x+\frac{1}{4x}\right)$$

If $\sec x=+\left(x+\frac{1}{4x}\right)\Rightarrow \sec x-\tan x=\left(x+\frac{1}{4x}\right)-\left(x-\frac{1}{4x}\right)=\frac{1}{2x}$

If $\sec x=-\left(x+\frac{1}{4x}\right)$

$\Rightarrow$ $\sec x-\tan x=-\left(x+\frac{1}{4x}\right)-\left(x-\frac{1}{4x}\right)=-2x$

$\therefore$ $\sec x-\tan x=-2x,\frac{1}{2x}$

☐ Subjective Type Questions

Q.1 If $\tan A = \dfrac{1-\cos B}{\sin B}$, then find the value of $\tan 2A$.

Sol. Given, $\tan A = \dfrac{1-\cos B}{\sin B}$

$\because$ $\cos 2x = 2\cos^2 x - 1 = 1 - 2\sin^2 x$

and $\sin 2x = 2\sin x \cdot \cos x,$

$$\tan A = \frac{1-\left(1-2\sin^2 \frac{B}{2}\right)}{2\sin \frac{B}{2} \cos \frac{B}{2}} = \frac{2\sin^2 \frac{B}{2}}{\alpha \sin \frac{\beta}{2} \cdot \cos \frac{B}{2}}$$

$$= \frac{\sin \frac{B}{2}}{\cos \frac{B}{2}} = \tan \frac{B}{2}$$

As we know that

$$\tan 2A = \frac{2\tan A}{1-\tan^2 A},$$

$$\tan 2A = \frac{2\tan \frac{B}{2}}{1-\tan^2 \frac{B}{2}} = \tan B$$

$\Rightarrow$ $\tan 2A = \tan B$

Q.2 If $\sin A = \dfrac{3}{5}$ and $\cos B = \dfrac{-12}{13}, 0 < A < \dfrac{\pi}{2}, \pi < B < \dfrac{3\pi}{2}$, then find $\cos(A+B)$.

Sol. Given, $\sin A = \dfrac{3}{5}$ and $0 < A < \dfrac{\pi}{2}$

$\because$ $\cos^2 A = 1 - \sin^2 A,$

$$\cos^2 A = 1 - \left(\frac{3}{5}\right)^2 = 1 - \frac{9}{25}$$

$$\cos^2 A = \frac{16}{25}$$

$\Rightarrow$ $\cos A = \pm \dfrac{4}{5}$

$\Rightarrow$ $\cos A = \dfrac{4}{5}$ $\quad \left[\because \cos A \text{ is + ve in} \left(0, \dfrac{\pi}{2}\right)\right]$

Again, given $\cos B = \dfrac{-12}{13}$, where $\pi < B < \dfrac{3\pi}{2}$

$\because$ $\sin^2 B = 1 - \cos^2 B, \sin^2 B = 1 - \left(\dfrac{-12}{13}\right)^2 = \dfrac{25}{169}$

$\Rightarrow \quad \sin B = \pm \dfrac{5}{13}$

$\Rightarrow \quad \sin B = \dfrac{-5}{13} \qquad \left[\because \sin B \text{ is } -\text{ve in } \left(\pi, \dfrac{3\pi}{2}\right)\right]$

Now,

$\because \quad \cos(A+B) = \cos A \cos B - \sin A \sin B$

$$= \left(\frac{4}{5}\right)\left(\frac{-12}{13}\right) - \left(\frac{3}{5}\right)\left(\frac{-5}{13}\right) = \frac{-48+15}{65} = \frac{-33}{65}$$

$\therefore \quad \cos(A+B) = \dfrac{-33}{65}$

Q.3 Reduce $\sqrt{3}\sin x + \cos x$ as a single term consisting

(i) sine only.

(ii) cosine only.

Sol. We can written as

$$\sqrt{3}\sin x + \cos x = 2\left(\frac{\sqrt{3}}{2}\sin x + \frac{1}{2}\cos x\right)$$

(i) using values $\cos\dfrac{\pi}{6} = \dfrac{\sqrt{3}}{2}$ and $\sin\dfrac{\pi}{6} = \dfrac{1}{2}$

$$\sqrt{3}\sin x + \cos x = 2\left(\frac{\sqrt{3}}{2}\sin x + \frac{1}{2}\cos x\right)$$

$$= 2\left(\cos\frac{\pi}{6}\sin x + \sin\frac{\pi}{6}\cos x\right) = 2\left(\sin\left(x + \frac{\pi}{6}\right)\right)$$

$[\because \sin(A+B) = \sin A \cos B + \sin B \cos A]$

$$= 2\sin\left(x + \frac{\pi}{6}\right)$$

For

(ii) using values $\sin\dfrac{\pi}{3} = \dfrac{\sqrt{3}}{2}$ and $\cos\dfrac{\pi}{3} = \dfrac{1}{2}$

$$\sqrt{3}\sin x + \cos x = 2\left(\frac{\sqrt{3}}{2}\sin x + \frac{1}{2}\cos x\right)$$

$$= 2\left(\sin\frac{\pi}{3}\sin x + \cos\frac{\pi}{3}\cos x\right)$$

$$= 2\left(\cos\left(x - \frac{\pi}{3}\right)\right)$$

$[\because \cos(A-B) = \cos A \cos B + \sin A \sin B]$

$$= 2\cos\left(x - \frac{\pi}{3}\right)$$

Complex Numbers and Quadratic Equations

CHAPTER 04

Important Points

01 Complex number A number of the form $a + ib$, where a and b are real numbers is defined to be a complex number. It is usually denoted by z.

i.e., $z = a + ib$

Real part Re (z) — Imaginary part Im (z)

If $z = 2 + i5$

Then, $\text{Re}(z) = 2$ and $\text{Im}(z) = 5$

Here, $i = \sqrt{-1}$ is a greek word known as 'iota'.

02 Power of i Since, $i = \sqrt{-1}$

$$\Rightarrow \quad i^2 = -1$$

$$\Rightarrow \quad i^3 = i \cdot i^2 = i(-1) = -i$$

$$\Rightarrow \quad i^4 = (i^2)^2 = (-1)^2 = 1$$

$$\Rightarrow \quad i^5 = i^4 i = 1 \times i = i$$

$$\Rightarrow \quad i^6 = i^4 i^2 = 1 \times (-1) = -1, \text{ and so on.}$$

Also, $$i^{-1} = \frac{1}{i} = \frac{1}{i} \times \frac{i}{i} = \frac{i}{i^2} = \frac{i}{-1} = -i$$

$$i^{-2} = \frac{1}{i^2} = \frac{1}{-1} = -1, \text{ etc.}$$

In general, for any integer k, $i^{4k} = 1, i^{4k+1} = i, i^{4k+2} = -1, i^{4k+3} = -i$

03 (i) $\sqrt{a} \times \sqrt{b} = \sqrt{ab}$, when $a > 0, b > 0$

(ii) $\sqrt{-a} \times \sqrt{-b} \neq \sqrt{ab}$ when $a > 0, b > 0$

Note If $a + ib = c + id$ if and only if $a = c$ and $b = d$.

04 Addition, difference, multiplication and Division of two complex number.

Let $z_1 = a + ib$ and $z_2 = c + id$

(i) $z_1 + z_2 = (a + ib) + (c + id) = (a + c) + i(b + d)$

(ii) $z_1 - z_2 = (a + ib) - (c + id) = (a - c) + i(b - d)$

(iii) $z_1 z_2 = (a + ib)(c + id) = (ac - bd) + i(ad + bc)$

(iv) $\dfrac{z_1}{z_2} = \dfrac{(a + ib)}{(c + id)} = \dfrac{(a + ib)}{c + id} \times \dfrac{c - id}{c - id} = \left(\dfrac{ac + bd}{c^2 + d^2}\right) + i\left(\dfrac{bc - ad}{c^2 + d^2}\right)$

Where $z_2 \neq 0$.

Note For every non-zero complex number $z = a + ib$, we have the complex number $\dfrac{a}{a^2 + b^2} + i\dfrac{-b}{a^2 + b^2}$ $\left(\text{denoted by } \dfrac{1}{z} \text{ or } z^{-1}\right)$, called the multiplicative inverse of z such that

$$z \cdot \frac{1}{z} = 1 \text{ i.e., } z^{-1} = \frac{\bar{z}}{|z|^2}$$

05 The Modulus and Conjugate of a Complex Number

Let $z = a + ib$ be a complex number. Then, modulus of z is denoted by $|z|$ and is defined as $|z| = \sqrt{a^2 + b^2}$ e.g. if $z = 3 + 4i$

$\Rightarrow |z| = \sqrt{3^2 + 4^2} = \sqrt{9 + 16} = \sqrt{25} = 5$ and conjugate of z is denoted by $\bar{z}$ and defined as $\bar{z} = a - ib$ e.g. if $z = 2 + 3i$, then $\bar{z} = 2 - 3i$.

Properties

(i) $|z_1 + z_2| \leq |z_1| + |z_2|$

(ii) $\overline{z_1 + z_2} = \overline{z_1} + \overline{z_2}$

(iii) $|z_1 - z_2| \geq |z_1| - |z_2|$

(iv) $\overline{z_1 - z_2} = \overline{z_1} - \overline{z_2}$

(v) $|z_1 z_2| = |z_1||z_2|$

(vi) $\overline{z_1 z_2} = \overline{z_1}\,\overline{z_2}$

(vii) $\left|\dfrac{z_1}{z_2}\right| = \dfrac{|z_1|}{|z_2|}$, provided $z_2 \neq 0$

(viii) $\overline{\left(\dfrac{z_1}{z_2}\right)} = \dfrac{\overline{z_1}}{\overline{z_2}}$, provided $z_2 \neq 0$

(ix) $z\bar{z} = |z|^2$

(x) $|z| = |\bar{z}|$

(xi) $|z|^n = |z^n|$

06 **Argand Plane and Polar Representation** The plane having a complex number assigned to each of its point is called the complex plane or the argand plane.

Some complex numbers such as (1, 2), (–2, 1), (2, –1), (–2, –1) represented geometrically by the points A, B, C and D, respectively shown in the figure.

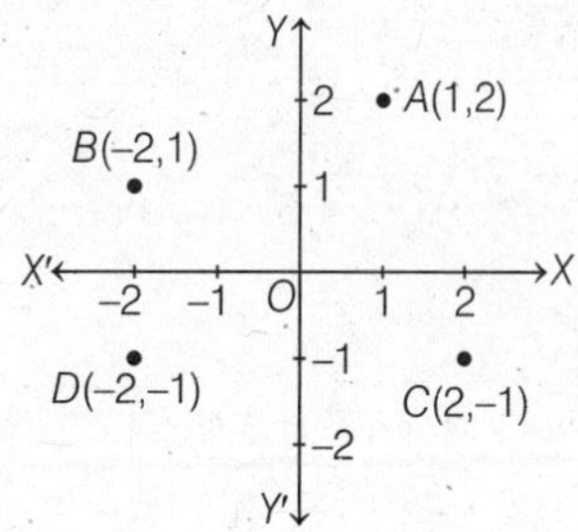

07 The representation of a complex number $z = x + iy$ and its conjugate $z = x - iy$ in the Argand plane are respectively, the points $P(x,y)$ and $Q(x,-y)$

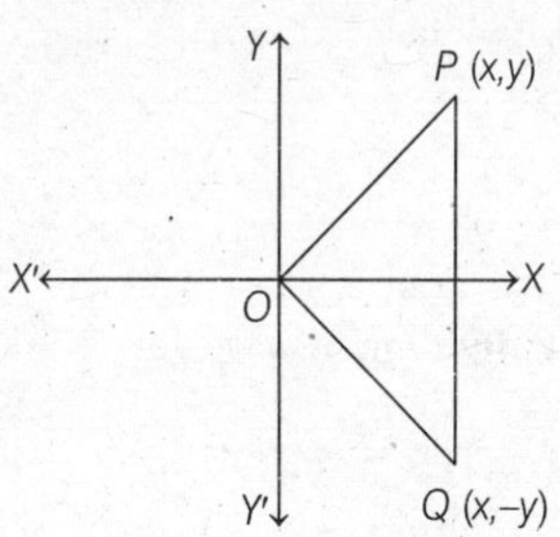

Exercises

Direction (Q. No. 1 to 10) *Express each of the complex number given in the form a + ib.*

◎ **Thinking Process** (Q. No. 1 to 3) Use $i^2 = -1, i^3 = i^2 \cdot i = -i$, $i^4 = (i^2)^2 = (-1)^2 = 1$. If any higher power of i then try to convert the power in multiple of 4 plus a remainder. The remainder will determine the value of the power as follows:

$$i^{4k} = 1 \Rightarrow i^{4k+1} = i$$
$$i^{4k+2} = -1 \Rightarrow i^{4k+3} = -i$$

Where k is integer.

Question 1 $(5i)\left(-\frac{3}{5}i\right)$.

Sol. We have, $5\left(-\frac{3}{5}\right)i^2 = (-3)(-1) = 3 = 3 + 0i$ $\quad (\because i^2 = -1)$

Question 2 $i^9 + i^{19}$.

Sol. We have, $i^9 + i^{19} = i^9 (1 + i^{10}) = i^9 [1 + (i^2)^5]$ $\quad$ (Taking i^9 common)

$$= i^9 [(1 + (-1)^5] = i^9 [1 - 1] = 0 = 0 + 0i$$

Quick Solution

$$i^9 + i^{19} = (i^{4(2)+1}) + (i^{4(4)+3})$$
$$= i + (-i) \quad (\because i^{4k+1} = i \text{ and } i^{4k+3} = -i)$$
$$= 0 = 0 + i0$$

Question 3 i^{-39}.

Sol. We have, $i^{-39} = \frac{1}{i^{39}}$

On multiplying and dividing by i, we get

$$= \frac{i}{i^{40}} = \frac{i}{(i^4)^{10}} = \frac{i}{(1)^{10}} = \frac{i}{1} = i \quad (\because i^4 = 1)$$

(as denominator is a multiple of 4) = 0 + i

Quick Solution

$$i^{-39} = i^{4(-10)+1} \quad [\because -39 = 4(-10) + 1]$$
$$= i \quad [\because i^{4k+1} = i \text{ if } k \text{ is integer}]$$
$$= 0 + i$$

Question 4 $3(7 + i7) + i(7 + i7)$.

◎ *Thinking Process* (Q. No. 4 to 7) Firstly separate the real and imaginary part and then simplify it.

Sol. We have, $3(7+i7)+i(7+i7)$

$$= 21 + 21i + 7i + i^2 7 = 21 + 28i - 7 \qquad (\because i^2 = -1)$$
$$= 14 + 28i$$

Note Students should remember that corresponding real or imaginary part are added or subtracted.

Question 5 $(1 - i) - (-1 + 6i)$.

Sol. We have, $(1 - i) - (-1 + 6i) = 1 - i + 1 - 6i = (1 + 1) - (i + 6i) = 2 - 7i$

Question 6 $\left(\frac{1}{5} + i\frac{2}{5}\right) - \left(4 + i\frac{5}{2}\right)$.

Sol. We have, $\left(\frac{1}{5} + i\frac{2}{5}\right) - \left(4 + i\frac{5}{2}\right) = \frac{1}{5} + i\frac{2}{5} - 4 - \frac{i5}{2}$

$$= \left(\frac{1}{5} - \frac{4}{1}\right) + i\left(\frac{2}{5} - \frac{5}{2}\right) = \left(\frac{1-20}{5}\right) + i\left(\frac{4-25}{10}\right)$$
$$= -\frac{19}{5} - \frac{21i}{10}$$

Question 7 $\left[\left(\frac{1}{3} + i\frac{7}{3}\right) + \left(4 + i\frac{1}{3}\right)\right] - \left(-\frac{4}{3} + i\right)$.

Sol. We have, $\left[\left(\frac{1}{3} + i\frac{7}{3}\right) + \left(4 + i\frac{1}{3}\right)\right] - \left(-\frac{4}{3} + i\right) = \left(\frac{1}{3} + i\frac{7}{3} + 4 + i\frac{1}{3}\right) + \frac{4}{3} - i$

$$= \left(\frac{1}{3} + 4 + \frac{4}{3}\right) + i\left(\frac{7}{3} + \frac{1}{3} - 1\right)$$
$$= \left(\frac{1}{3} + \frac{4}{1} + \frac{4}{3}\right) + i\left(\frac{7}{3} + \frac{1}{3} - \frac{1}{1}\right)$$
$$= \frac{(1 + 12 + 4)}{3} + i\left(\frac{7 + 1 - 3}{3}\right) = \frac{17}{3} + i\frac{5}{3}$$

Question 8 $(1 - i)^4$.

Sol. We have, $(1 - i)^4 = [(1 - i)^2]^2 = (1 + i^2 - 2i)^2 \quad [\text{Use } (a - b)^2 = a^2 + b^2 - 2ab]$

$$= (1 - 1 - 2i)^2 \qquad (\because i^2 = -1)$$
$$= (-2i)^2 = (-2)^2 i^2 = 4(-1)$$
$$= -4 + 0i$$

Question 9 $\left(\frac{1}{3}+3i\right)^3$.

◎ *Thinking Process* Here, we will use the formula $(a+b)^3 = a^3 + b^3 + 3ab(a+b)$ and simplify it.

Sol. We have, $\left(\frac{1}{3}+3i\right)^3 = \left(\frac{1}{3}\right)^3 + (3i)^3 + 3 \times \frac{1}{3} \times 3i\left(\frac{1}{3}+3i\right)$

$$= \frac{1}{27} + 27i^3 + 3i\left(\frac{1}{3}+3i\right)$$

$$= \frac{1}{27} - 27i + 3i \times \frac{1}{3} + 3i \times 3i \qquad (\because i^3 = -i)$$

$$= \frac{1}{27} - 27i + i + 9i^2$$

$$= \frac{1}{27} - 27i + i - 9 \qquad (\because i^2 = -1)$$

$$= \left(\frac{1}{27} - \frac{9}{1}\right) - i(27-1)$$

$$= \left(\frac{1-243}{27}\right) - 26i$$

$$= -\frac{242}{27} - 26i$$

Question 10 $\left(-2-\frac{1}{3}i\right)^3$.

Sol. We have, $(-1)^3\left(2+\frac{1}{3}i\right)^3 = -\left[(2)^3 + \left(\frac{1}{3}i\right)^3 + 3 \times 2 \times \frac{1}{3}i\left(2+\frac{1}{3}i\right)\right]$

$$= -\left[8 + \frac{1}{27}i^3 + 2i\left(2+\frac{1}{3}i\right)\right]$$

$$= -\left[8 - \frac{1}{27}i + 4i + \frac{2}{3}i^2\right] \qquad (\because i^3 = -i)$$

$$= -\left[8 - \frac{1}{27}i + 4i - \frac{2}{3}\right] \qquad (\because i^2 = -1)$$

$$= -\left[\left(\frac{8}{1} - \frac{2}{3}\right) + i\left(\frac{4}{1} - \frac{1}{27}\right)\right]$$

$$= -\left[\left(\frac{24-2}{3}\right) + i\left(\frac{108-1}{27}\right)\right]$$

$$= -\left[\frac{22}{3} + i\frac{107}{27}\right]$$

Direction (Q. No. 11 to 13) Find the multiplicative inverse of each of the complex numbers.

◎ ***Thinking Process*** (Q. No. 11 to 13.) If complex number is z, then write in the term of $\frac{1}{z}$, then multiply by conjugate complex number and solve till then you do not get the form of $a + ib$.

Question 11 $4 - 3i$.

Sol. Let $z = 4 - 3i$

Then, its multiplicative inverse is

$$\frac{1}{z} = \frac{1}{4-3i} = \frac{1}{4-3i} \times \frac{4+3i}{4+3i} = \frac{4+3i}{16-9i^2} \qquad \text{(Use } (a-b)(a+b) = a^2 - b^2)$$

$$= \frac{4+3i}{16+9} \qquad (\because i^2 = -1)$$

$$= \frac{4+3i}{25} = \frac{4}{25} + \frac{3i}{25}$$

Question 12 $\sqrt{5} + 3i$.

Sol. Let $z = \sqrt{5} + 3i$

Then, its multiplicative inverse is

$$\frac{1}{z} = \frac{1}{\sqrt{5}+3i} = \frac{1}{\sqrt{5}+3i} \times \frac{\sqrt{5}-3i}{\sqrt{5}-3i}$$

$$= \frac{\sqrt{5}-3i}{5-9i^2} \qquad \text{(Use } (a+b)(a-b) = a^2 - b^2)$$

$$= \frac{\sqrt{5}-3i}{5+9} = \frac{\sqrt{5}-3i}{14} \qquad (\because i^2 = -1)$$

$$= \frac{\sqrt{5}}{14} - \frac{3i}{14}$$

Question 13 $-i$.

Sol. Let $z = -i$

Then, its multiplicative inverse is

$$\frac{1}{z} = -\frac{1}{i}$$

$$= -\frac{1}{i} \times \frac{i}{i} = \frac{-i}{i^2} = \frac{-i}{-1} = i \qquad (\because i^2 = -1)$$

$$= 0 + i$$

Question 14 Express the following in the terms of $a + ib$

$$\frac{(3 + i\sqrt{5})(3 - i\sqrt{5})}{(\sqrt{3} + \sqrt{2}\,i) - (\sqrt{3} - i\sqrt{2})}.$$

Sol. Let $z = \dfrac{(3 + i\sqrt{5})(3 - i\sqrt{5})}{(\sqrt{3} + \sqrt{2}\,i) - (\sqrt{3} - i\sqrt{2})}$

$$= \frac{(3)^2 - (i\sqrt{5})^2}{\sqrt{3} + \sqrt{2}\,i - \sqrt{3} + i\sqrt{2}} \qquad [\because (a + b)(a - b) = a^2 - b^2]$$

$$= \frac{9 - i^2 5}{2\sqrt{2}\,i} = \frac{9 + 5}{2\sqrt{2}\,i} \qquad (\because i^2 = -1)$$

$$= \frac{14}{2\sqrt{2}i} = \frac{7}{\sqrt{2}\,i} \times \frac{i}{i} = \frac{7i}{\sqrt{2}\,i^2} = -\frac{7i}{\sqrt{2}} = 0 - i\left(\frac{7}{\sqrt{2}}\right)$$

Miscellaneous Exercise

Question 1 Evaluate $\left[i^{18} + \left(\dfrac{1}{i}\right)^{25}\right]^3$.

Thinking Process Firstly to solve it, we will convert the power of i in the multiple of 2 or 4 and solve them by using $i^2 = -1, i^3 = -i, i^4 = 1$, etc and after that we use $(a + b)^3 = a^3 + b^3 + 3ab(a + b)$.

Sol. We have, $\left[i^{18} + \left(\dfrac{1}{i}\right)^{25}\right]^3 = \left[(i^2)^9 + \dfrac{1}{i^{25}}\right]^3 = \left[(i^2)^9 + \dfrac{1}{i \cdot i^{24}}\right]^3$

$$= \left[(-1)^9 + \frac{1}{i(i^4)^6}\right]^3 \qquad (\because i^2 = -1)$$

$$= \left[-1 + \frac{1}{i}\right]^3 \qquad (\because i^4 = 1)$$

$$= \left[-1 + \frac{1}{i} \times \frac{i}{i}\right]^3 = \left[-1 + \frac{i}{i^2}\right]^3$$

$$= [-1 - i]^3 \quad (\because i^2 = -1) = (-1)^3\,[1 + i]^3$$

$$= -[(1)^3 + i^3 + 3 \times 1 \times i(1 + i)]$$

$$[\because (a + b)^3 = a^3 + b^3 + 3ab(a + b)]$$

$$= -[1 - i + 3i + 3i^2] \qquad (\because i^3 = -i)$$

$$= -[1 - i + 3i - 3] \qquad (\because i^2 = -1)$$

$$= -[-2 + 2i] = 2 - 2i$$

Mistake Alert Students are suggested not to open the cube of expression at initial stage because by doing so the expression becomes complex.

Question 2 For any two complex numbers z_1 and z_2, prove that $\text{Re}(z_1 z_2) = \text{Re}(z_1)\,\text{Re}(z_2) - \text{Im}(z_1)\,\text{Im}(z_2)$.

Sol: Let $z_1 = a + ib$

$\Rightarrow \quad \text{Re}(z_1) = a \text{ and } \text{Im}(z_1) = b \quad \ldots\text{(i)}$

and $\quad z_2 = c + id$

$\Rightarrow \quad \text{Re}(z_2) = c \text{ and } \text{Im}(z_2) = d \quad \ldots\text{(ii)}$

Now, $z_1 z_2 = (a + ib)(c + id)$

$= ac + iad + ibc + i^2 bd$

$= ac + i(ad + bc) - bd \quad (\because i^2 = -1)$

$\Rightarrow \quad z_1 z_2 = (ac - bd) + i(ad + bc)$

$\Rightarrow \quad \text{Re}(z_1 z_2) = ac - bd$

$\Rightarrow \quad \text{Re}(z_1 z_2) = \text{Re}(z_1)\,\text{Re}(z_2) - \text{Im}(z_1)\,\text{Im}(z_2)$ [Using Eqs. (i) and (ii)]

Here, Re stand for real part and Im stands for imaginary part.

Question 3 Reduce $\left(\frac{1}{1-4i} - \frac{2}{1+i}\right)\left(\frac{3-4i}{5+i}\right)$ to the standard form.

◎ ***Thinking Process*** First we take the LCM and then convert the complex number of denominator into purely real number.

Sol. We have, $\left(\frac{1}{1-4i} - \frac{2}{1+i}\right)\left(\frac{3-4i}{5+i}\right) = \frac{\{1 + i - 2(1 - 4i)\}}{(1-4i)(1+i)} \times \left(\frac{3-4i}{5+i}\right)$

$$= \frac{1 + i - 2 + 8i}{1 + i - 4i - 4i^2} \times \frac{3 - 4i}{5 + i}$$

$$= \frac{(1-2) + i(1+8)}{1 + i(1-4) - 4(-1)} \times \frac{3-4i}{5+i} \quad (\because i^2 = -1)$$

$$= \frac{-1 + 9i}{5 - 3i} \times \frac{3 - 4i}{5 + i} = \frac{-3 + 4i + 27i - 36i^2}{25 + 5i - 15i - 3i^2}$$

$$= \frac{-3 + i(4 + 27) - 36(-1)}{25 + (5 - 15)i - 3(-1)} \quad (\because i^2 = -1)$$

$$= \frac{-3 + 31i + 36}{25 - 10i + 3} = \frac{33 + 31i}{28 - 10i} \times \frac{28 + 10i}{28 + 10i}$$

$$= \frac{924 + 330i + 868i + 310i^2}{784 - 100i^2} \quad [\because (a+b)(a-b) = a^2 - b^2]$$

$$= \frac{924 + (330 + 868)i - 310}{784 + 100} \quad (\because i^2 = -1)$$

$$= \frac{614 + 1198i}{884} = \frac{307 + i599}{442} = \frac{307}{442} + i\frac{599}{442}$$

Question 4 If $x - iy = \sqrt{\frac{a-ib}{c-id}}$, then prove that $(x^2 + y^2)^2 = \frac{a^2 + b^2}{c^2 + d^2}$.

◎ *Thinking Process* To prove the required expression, first take the modulus of both sides and then use the properties

$$|z|^n = |z^n| \quad \text{and} \quad \left|\frac{z_1}{z_2}\right| = \frac{|z_1|}{|z_2|}$$

Sol. Given, $x - iy = \sqrt{\frac{a - ib}{c - id}} \Rightarrow x + i(-y) = \left(\frac{a - ib}{c - id}\right)^{1/2}$

On taking modulus both sides, we get

$$|x + i(-y)| = \left|\left(\frac{a - ib}{c - id}\right)^{\frac{1}{2}}\right|$$

$$\Rightarrow \sqrt{x^2 + (-y)^2} = \left|\frac{a - ib}{c - id}\right|^{\frac{1}{2}} \qquad \left(\because |x + iy| = \sqrt{x^2 + y^2} \text{ and } |z^n| = |z|^n\right)$$

$$\Rightarrow \sqrt{x^2 + y^2} = \left|\frac{a - ib}{c - id}\right|^{\frac{1}{2}}$$

On squaring both sides, we get

$$x^2 + y^2 = \left|\frac{a - ib}{c - id}\right|$$

$$\Rightarrow x^2 + y^2 = \frac{|a - ib|}{|c - id|} \qquad \left(\because \left|\frac{z_1}{z_2}\right| = \frac{|z_1|}{|z_2|}\right)$$

$$\Rightarrow (x^2 + y^2) = \frac{\sqrt{a^2 + b^2}}{\sqrt{c^2 + d^2}} \qquad (\because |x - iy| = \sqrt{x^2 + y^2})$$

On squaring on both sides, we get

$$(x^2 + y^2)^2 = \frac{a^2 + b^2}{c^2 + d^2}$$

Mistake Alert Please be careful while find the values of x and y separately in the given condition by squaring on both sides because this method is very complicated and time taken.

Keep in mind that $|x + iy| = \sqrt{x^2 + y^2} \neq \sqrt{x^2 + (iy)^2}$.

Question 5 If $z_1 = 2 - i, z_2 = 1 + i$, find $\left|\dfrac{z_1 + z_2 + 1}{z_1 - z_2 + 1}\right|$.

◎ *Thinking Process* Firstly, we will put the values of z_1 and z_2 in the given expression and then after converting the numerator and denominator in the form of $a + ib$, then we use the properties of modulus.

Sol. We have, $\left|\dfrac{z_1 + z_2 + 1}{z_1 - z_2 + 1}\right| = \left|\dfrac{2 - i + 1 + i + 1}{2 - i - (1 + i) + 1}\right|$ $\quad (\because z_1 = 2 - i, z_2 = 1 + i)$

$$= \left|\frac{4}{2 - i - 1 - i + 1}\right| = \left|\frac{4}{2 - 2i}\right| = \left|\frac{2}{1 - i}\right| = \frac{2}{|1 - i|} \qquad \left[\because \left|\frac{z_1}{z_2}\right| = \frac{|z_1|}{|z_2|}\right]$$

$$= \frac{2}{\sqrt{(1)^2 + (-1)^2}} \qquad (\because |z| = \sqrt{a^2 + b^2})$$

$$= \frac{2}{\sqrt{2}} = \sqrt{2}$$

Mistake Alert Keep in mind that $|z_1 + z_2| \neq |z_1| + |z_2|$

Question 6 If $a + ib = \dfrac{(x + i)^2}{2x^2 + 1}$, then prove that $a^2 + b^2 = \dfrac{(x^2 + 1)^2}{(2x^2 + 1)^2}$.

Sol. Given, $a + ib = \dfrac{(x + i)^2}{2x^2 + 1}$

On taking modulus both sides, we get

$$|a + ib| = \left|\frac{(x + i)^2}{2x^2 + 1}\right|$$

$$\Rightarrow \sqrt{a^2 + b^2} = \frac{|(x + i)^2|}{|2x^2 + 1|} = \frac{|x + i|^2}{2x^2 + 1}$$

$$\left[\because \left|\frac{z_1}{z_2}\right| = \frac{|z_1|}{|z_2|}, (|z^n| = |z|^n \text{ and} |\text{Re}(z)| = \text{Re}(z))\right]$$

$$\Rightarrow \sqrt{a^2 + b^2} = \frac{(\sqrt{x^2 + 1})^2}{2x^2 + 1}$$

On squaring both sides, we get, $a^2 + b^2 = \dfrac{(x^2 + 1)^2}{(2x^2 + 1)^2}$

Question 7 Let $z_1 = 2 - i, z_2 = -2 + i$.

Find (i) $\text{Re}\left(\dfrac{z_1 z_2}{\bar{z}_1}\right)$ and (ii) $\text{Im}\left(\dfrac{1}{z_1 \bar{z}_1}\right)$.

◎ *Thinking Process*

(i) First convert $\dfrac{z_1 z_2}{\bar{z}_1}$ in the form of $a + ib$ by putting the given values. Then, find its real part (Re).

(ii) To find the value of $z_1 \bar{z}_2$ by using the property $z\bar{z} = |z|^2$ and then find its imaginary part (Im).

Sol. (i) We have, $\dfrac{z_1 z_2}{\bar{z}_1} = \dfrac{(2 - i)(-2 + i)}{\overline{(2 - i)}} = \dfrac{-(2 - i)(2 - i)}{(2 + i)}$

$(\because z_1 = 2 - i, z_2 = -2 + i)$
$(\because z = a + ib \Rightarrow \bar{z} = a - ib)$

$$= \frac{-(2 - i)^2}{2 + i} = \frac{-(4 + i^2 - 4i)}{2 + i} = \frac{-(4 - 1 - 4i)}{2 + i} \quad (\because i^2 = -1)$$

$$= \frac{-(3 - 4i)}{2 + i} \times \frac{2 - i}{2 - i}$$

$$= \frac{-(6 - 3i - 8i + 4i^2)}{(2)^2 - (i)^2} \quad [\because (a + b)(a - b) = (a^2 - b^2)]$$

$$= \frac{-(6 - 11i - 4)}{4 - i^2} \quad (\because i^2 = -1)$$

$$= \frac{-(2 - 11i)}{4 + 1} \quad (\because i^2 = -1)$$

$$= -\left(\frac{2}{5} - \frac{11i}{5}\right)$$

$$= -\frac{2}{5} + \frac{11}{5} i$$

$$\therefore \text{Re}\left(\frac{z_1 z_2}{\bar{z}_1}\right) = -\frac{2}{5}$$

(ii) $\text{Im}\left(\dfrac{1}{z_1 \bar{z}_1}\right)$

$\because \quad z\bar{z} = |z|^2$

$\Rightarrow \quad z_1 \bar{z}_1 = |z_1|^2$

$\Rightarrow \quad z_1 \bar{z}_1 = |-2 + i|^2 = (\sqrt{4 + 1})^2 = 5 + 0i$

$\therefore \quad \dfrac{1}{z_1 \bar{z}_1} = \dfrac{1}{5} + 0i$

$\Rightarrow \quad \text{Im}\left(\dfrac{1}{z_1 \bar{z}_1}\right) = 0$

Quick Solution

Given $\quad z_1 = 2 - i,\ \bar{z}_1 = 2 = 1°$ $\quad [\because \overline{(a + bi)} = a - bi]$

$\therefore \quad \dfrac{1}{z_1\bar{z}_1} = \dfrac{1}{(2)^2 - (i)^2}$ $\quad [\because (a - b)(a + b) = a^2 - b^2]$

$$= \frac{1}{4 - (-1)} = \frac{1}{5} + 0i$$

$\therefore \quad \text{Im}\left(\dfrac{1}{z_1\bar{z}_1}\right) = 0$

Question 8 Find the real numbers x and y if $(x - iy)(3 + 5i)$ is the conjugate of $(-6 - 24i)$.

◎ ***Thinking Process*** We will find the values of x and y by comparing the real and imaginary parts of $(x - iy)(3 + 5i)$ and conjugate of $(-6 - 24i)$.

Sol. We have, $(x - iy)(3 + 5i) = 3x + 5xi - 3yi - 5yi^2$

$$= 3x + (5x - 3y)i + 5y \quad (\because i^2 = -1)$$

$$= (3x + 5y) + (5x - 3y)i \quad \ldots\text{(i)}$$

Given, $\quad (x - iy)(3 + 5i) = \overline{(-6 - 24i)}$

$\Rightarrow \quad (3x + 5y) + i(5x - 3y) = -6 + 24i$

[Using Eq. (i) and $z = (a + ib) \Rightarrow \bar{z} = (a - ib)$]

On comparing the real and imaginary parts both sides, we get

$$3x + 5y = -6$$

and $\quad 5x - 3y = 24$

Solving the above equations by substitution or elimination method, we get $x = 3,\ y = -3$.

Question 9 Find the modulus of $\dfrac{1 + i}{1 - i} - \dfrac{1 - i}{1 + i}$.

◎ ***Thinking Process*** First we will convert the given expression into standard form and then find its modulus.

Sol. Let $\quad z = \dfrac{1 + i}{1 - i} - \dfrac{1 - i}{1 + i} = \dfrac{(1 + i)^2 - (1 - i)^2}{(1 - i)(1 + i)}$

$$= \frac{(1 + i^2 + 2i) - (1 + i^2 - 2i)}{1 - i^2}$$

$$= \frac{4i}{2} = 2i = 0 + 2i \quad \left[\begin{aligned} &\because (a + b)^2 = a^2 + b^2 + 2ab \\ &\text{and } (a - b)^2 = a^2 + b^2 - 2ab \end{aligned}\right]$$

$\therefore \quad |z| = \sqrt{0^2 + 2^2} = 2 \quad [\because |x + iy| = \sqrt{x^2 + y^2}]$

Question 10 If $(x+iy)^3 = u+iv$, then show that
$$\frac{u}{x}+\frac{v}{y}=4(x^2-y^2).$$

Sol. Given, $(x+iy)^3 = u+iv$

$$\Rightarrow \quad x^3+(iy)^3+3xiy(x+iy)=u+iv$$
$$\Rightarrow \quad x^3+i^3y^3+3ix^2y+3xy^2i^2=u+iv$$
$$\Rightarrow \quad x^3-iy^3+3ix^2y-3xy^2=u+iv \qquad (\because i^3=-i, i^2=-1)$$
$$\Rightarrow \quad (x^3-3xy^2)+i(3x^2y-y^3)=u+iv$$

On comparing real and imaginary parts, we get

$$x^3-3xy^2=u \quad \text{and} \quad 3x^2y-y^3=v$$
$$\therefore \quad \frac{u}{x}+\frac{v}{y}=\frac{x^3-3xy^2}{x}+\frac{3x^2y-y^3}{y}$$
$$=x^2-3y^2+3x^2-y^2$$
$$=4x^2-4y^2=4(x^2-y^2)$$

Hence Proved.

Question 11 If α and β are different complex numbers with $|\beta|=1$, then find $\left|\frac{\beta-\alpha}{1-\bar{\alpha}\beta}\right|$.

Sol. We have, $\left|\frac{\beta-\alpha}{1-\bar{\alpha}\beta}\right|=\left|\frac{(\beta-\alpha)\bar{\beta}}{(1-\bar{\alpha}\beta)\bar{\beta}}\right|=\left|\frac{(\beta-\alpha)\bar{\beta}}{\bar{\beta}-\bar{\alpha}\beta\bar{\beta}}\right|$

(Multiply numerator and denominator by $\bar{\beta}$)

$$=\left|\frac{(\beta-\alpha)\bar{\beta}}{\bar{\beta}-\bar{\alpha}}\right| \qquad (\because \beta\bar{\beta}=|\beta|^2=|1|^2=1)$$
$$=\frac{|(\beta-\alpha)\bar{\beta}|}{|\bar{\beta}-\bar{\alpha}|} \qquad \left(\because \left|\frac{z_1}{z_2}\right|=\frac{|z_1|}{|z_2|}\right)$$
$$=\frac{|\beta-\alpha||\bar{\beta}|}{|\overline{\beta-\alpha}|} \qquad (\because |z_1z_2|=|z_1||z_2| \text{ and } |\bar{z}_1-\bar{z}_2|=|\overline{z_1-z_2}|)$$
$$=\frac{|\beta-\alpha||\beta|}{|\beta-\alpha|} \qquad (\because |\bar{z}|=|z|)$$
$$=|\beta|=1$$

Mistake Alert Advise for students that never assume the values of α and β in complex form and put in given expression because this approach is too long and time taken also.

Question 12 Find the number of non-zero integral solutions of the equation $|1-i|^x = 2^x$.

◎ *Thinking Process* First we will take the modulus of LHS of given expression and then compare the power on both sides.

Sol. Given, $|1-i|^x = 2^x$

$$\Rightarrow \quad (\sqrt{(1)^2+(-1)^2})^x = 2^x \qquad (\because |a+ib| = \sqrt{a^2+b^2})$$

$$\Rightarrow \quad (\sqrt{1+1})^x = 2^x$$

$$\Rightarrow \quad (\sqrt{2})^x = 2^x \Rightarrow 2^{\frac{x}{2}} = 2^x$$

On comparing the power of 2 both sides, we get

$$\Rightarrow \quad \frac{x}{2} = x$$

$$\Rightarrow \quad x = 2x$$

$$\Rightarrow \quad 2x - x = 0$$

$$x = 0$$

But we need the non-zero solutions.

Hence, number of non-zero solutions is zero.

Note Here, $x = 0$ represents the solution. Students understand the difference between the word solution and number of solutions.

Question 13 If $(a+ib)(c+id)(e+if)(g+ih) = A+iB$, then show that $(a^2+b^2)(c^2+d^2)(e^2+f^2)(g^2+h^2) = A^2+B^2$.

Sol. Given, $(a+ib)(c+id)(e+if)(g+ih) = A+iB$

On taking modulus both sides, we get

$$|(a+ib)(c+id)(e+if)(g+ih)| = |A+iB|$$

$$\Rightarrow \quad |a+ib||c+id||e+if||g+ih| = |A+iB|$$

$$(\because |z_1z_2 \ldots z_n| = |z_1||z_2||z_3| \ldots |z_n|)$$

$$\Rightarrow \quad \sqrt{a^2+b^2}\sqrt{c^2+d^2}\sqrt{e^2+f^2}\sqrt{g^2+h^2} = \sqrt{A^2+B^2}$$

$$(\because \text{If } z = a+ib, \text{ then } |z| = \sqrt{a^2+b^2})$$

On squaring both sides, we get

$$(a^2+b^2)(c^2+d^2)(e^2+f^2)(g^2+h^2) = A^2+B^2$$

Question 14 If $\left(\frac{1+i}{1-i}\right)^m = 1$, then find the least positive integral value of m.

Sol. Given, $$\left(\frac{1+i}{1-i}\right)^m = 1$$

$$\Rightarrow \left[\frac{1+i}{1-i} \times \frac{1+i}{1+i}\right]^m = 1 \Rightarrow \left[\frac{(1+i)^2}{1-i^2}\right]^m = 1$$

$$\Rightarrow \left[\frac{1+i^2+2i}{1+1}\right]^m = 1$$

$(\because (a+b)^2 = a^2 + b^2 + 2ab \text{ and } i^2 = -1)$

$$\Rightarrow \left[\frac{1-1+2i}{2}\right]^m = 1$$

$$\Rightarrow i^m = 1$$

$$\Rightarrow (\sqrt{-1})^m = 1 \qquad (\because i^2 = -1 \Rightarrow i = \sqrt{-1})$$

$$\Rightarrow (-1)^{\frac{m}{2}} = (-1)^2$$

On comparing the power both sides, we get

$$\frac{m}{2} = 2$$

$$\Rightarrow m = 4$$

Hence, the least positive integral value of m is 4.

Note 1 can be written as $(-1)^2, (-1)^4, (-1)^6$ .... etc. But for least positive integer value we take $(-1)^2$.

DIKSHA APP Questions

Multiple Choice Questions

Q.1 Write the real and imaginary part of $1-2i^2$.

(a) Re = 1, Im = 2
(b) Re = 1, Im = − 2
(c) Re = 3, Im = 0
(d) Re = 0, Im = 3

Sol. (c) Let $z = 1 - 2i^2$

$\Rightarrow \quad z = 1 - 2(-1)$ $[\because i^2 = -1]$

$\Rightarrow \quad z = 1 + 2 = 3 = 3 + 0i$

$\therefore$ Re = 3 and Im = 0

Q.2 Find the value of i^{102}.

(a) 1
(b) −1
(c) i
(d) $-i$

◎ ***Thinking Process*** Use $i^{4k+2} = -1$, where k is integer.

Sol. (b) We have, $i^{102} = i^{4(25)+2}$ $[\because 102 = 4(25) + 2]$

$= -1$ $[\because i^{4k+2} = -1$ if k is integer$]$

Quick Solution

$$i^{102} = i^{100+2} = (i^{100})(i^2) = (i^2)^{50}(i^2)$$
$$= (-1)^{50}(-1) = -1$$

Q.3 Evaluate $i^n + i^{n+1} + i^{n+2} + i^{n+3}$ where n is integer number.

(a) 1
(b) −1
(c) 2
(d) 0

Sol. (d) We have, $i^n + i^{n+1} + i^{n+2} + i^{n+3} = i^n + i^n i + i^n i^2 + i^n i^3$

$= i^n(1 + i + i^2 + i^3) = i^n(1 + i - 1 - i)$

$[\because i^2 = -1$ and $i^3 = -i]$

$= i^n(0) = 0$

Note The sum of four consecutive powers of 'i' is always zero.

Q.4 The real value of θ for which the expression $\dfrac{1+i\cos\theta}{1-2i\cos\theta}$ is real

(a) $n\pi \pm \dfrac{\pi}{4}$ (b) $n\pi \pm \dfrac{\pi}{2}$

(c) $2n\pi \pm \dfrac{\pi}{2}$ (d) $2n\pi \pm \dfrac{\pi}{4}$

◎ ***Thinking Process*** Firstly, we will change it into standard form $(a+ib)$ and after that, we will apply $\text{Im}\left(\dfrac{1+i\cos\theta}{1-2i\cos\theta}\right)=0.$

Sol. (c) Let $z = \dfrac{1+i\cos\theta}{1-2i\cos\theta}$

$$\Rightarrow \quad z = \frac{1+i\cos\theta}{1-2i\cos\theta} \times \frac{1+2i\cos\theta}{1+2i\cos\theta} = \frac{1+2i\cos\theta + i\cos\theta + 2i^2\cos^2\theta}{1^2-(2i\cos\theta)^2}$$

$[\because (a-b)(a+b) = a^2-b^2]$

$$= \frac{1+3i\cos\theta - 2\cos^2\theta}{1+4\cos^2\theta} \quad [\because i^2=-1]$$

$$= \frac{1-2\cos^2\theta}{1+4\cos^2\theta} + i\left[\frac{3\cos\theta}{1+4\cos^2\theta}\right]$$

Given, Im $(z) = 0$

i.e., $\dfrac{3\cos\theta}{1+4\cos^2\theta} = 0$

$\Rightarrow \quad 3\cos\theta = 0 \Rightarrow \cos\theta = 0$

$\Rightarrow \quad \cos\theta = \cos\dfrac{\pi}{2} \quad \left[\because \cos\dfrac{\pi}{2} = 0\right]$

$\Rightarrow \quad \theta = 2n\pi \pm \dfrac{\pi}{2}$

Hence, General solution is $\theta = 2n\pi \pm \dfrac{\pi}{2}$, where n is integer.

Note Remember that $\cos\theta = \cos\alpha$

$\Rightarrow \theta = 2n\pi \pm \alpha$, where n is integer number.

Q.5 If $\left(\dfrac{1+i}{1-1}\right)^x = 1$, then

(a) $x = 2n$ (b) $x = 2n+1$

(c) $x = 4n$ (d) $x = 4n+i$

◎ ***Thinking Process*** Here, we will use $i^{4n} = 1$, where n is any integer.

Sol. (c) $\left(\frac{1+i}{1-i}\right)^x = 1 \Rightarrow \left(\frac{1+i}{1-i} \times \frac{1+i}{1+i}\right)^x = 1$

$\Rightarrow \left(\frac{1+i^2+2i}{1^2-i^2}\right)^x = 1$ $[\because (a-b)(a+b) = a^2 - b^2]$

$\Rightarrow \left(\frac{1-1+2i}{1+1}\right)^x = 1$ $[\because i^2 = -1]$

$\Rightarrow \left(\frac{2i}{2}\right)^x = 1 \Rightarrow (i)^x = 1$

$\Rightarrow (i)^x = (i)^{4n}$ $[\because i^{4n} = 1$ if n is any integer$]$

$\Rightarrow x = 4n$, where n is any integer number.

Q.6 Let $z = \frac{(11-3i)}{1+i}$. If α is a real number such that $|z - i\alpha|$ is 4, then the value of α.

(a) 4 (b) –4 (c) 7 (d) –7

Sol. (d) Given, $z = \frac{11-3i}{1+i}$

$$z - i\alpha = \frac{11-3i}{1+i} - i\alpha = \frac{11-3i-i\alpha+\alpha}{1+i} = \frac{11-3i-i\alpha+\alpha}{1+i} \times \frac{1-i}{1-i}$$

$$= \frac{11-11i-3i-3-i\alpha-\alpha+\alpha-i\alpha}{1^2-i^2}$$

$$= \frac{8-14i-2i\alpha}{2} = 4 - i(7+\alpha)$$

Now, $|z - i\alpha| = |4 - i(7+\alpha)|$

$= \sqrt{(4)^2 + (-(7+\alpha))^2}$ $[\because |x+iy| = \sqrt{x^2+y^2}]$

$= \sqrt{16+49+\alpha^2+14\alpha} = \sqrt{\alpha^2+14\alpha+65}$

Since, $|z - i\alpha| = 4$, $\sqrt{\alpha^2 + 14\alpha + 65} = 4$

On squaring both side, we get

$\alpha^2 + 14\alpha + 65 = 16 \Rightarrow \alpha^2 + 14\alpha + 49 = 0$

$\Rightarrow \alpha^2 + 7\alpha + 7\alpha + 49 = 0 \Rightarrow \alpha(\alpha+7) + 7(\alpha+7) = 0$

$\Rightarrow (\alpha+7)^2 = 0$

$\Rightarrow \alpha = -7$

Mistake Alert First we have to put the value of z in $|z - i\alpha|$ and after that find its value.

☐ Subjective Type Questions

Q.1 Find the conjugate of $\dfrac{(3-2i)(2+3i)}{(1+2i)(2-i)}$

◎ *Thinking Process* Here, we will use formula, conjugate of $(a+ib) = a - ib$.

Sol. We have, $\dfrac{(3-2i)(2+3i)}{(1+2i)(2-i)} = \dfrac{6+9i-4i+6}{2-i+4i+2} = \dfrac{12+5i}{4+3i} \times \dfrac{4-3i}{4-3i}$

$$= \frac{48-36i+20i+15}{16+9} = \frac{63-16i}{25} = \frac{63}{25} - \frac{16}{25}i$$

$\therefore$ Conjugate is $\dfrac{63}{25} + \dfrac{16}{25}i$

Q.2 Find the modulus of $\dfrac{(1+i)}{(1-i)}$

◎ *Thinking Process* Here, we will use $\left|\dfrac{z_1}{z_2}\right| = \dfrac{|z_1|}{|z_2|}$ and $|x+iy| = \sqrt{x^2+y^2}$

Sol. Let $z = \dfrac{(1+i)}{(1-i)}$

$$|z| = \left|\frac{(1+i)}{(1-i)}\right| = \frac{|1+i|}{|1-i|} \qquad \left[\because \left|\frac{z_1}{z_2}\right| = \frac{|z_1|}{|z_2|}\right]$$

$$= \frac{\sqrt{1^2+1^2}}{\sqrt{1^2+(-1)^2}} \qquad [\because |x+iy| = \sqrt{x^2+y^2}]$$

$$= \frac{\sqrt{2}}{\sqrt{2}} = 1$$

$\therefore \quad |z| = 1$

Q.3 If z_1, z_2 and z_3 are any three complex numbers such that $|z_1| = |z_2| = |z_3| = \left|\dfrac{1}{z_1} + \dfrac{1}{z_2} + \dfrac{1}{z_3}\right| = 1$, then find the value of $|z_1 + z_2 + z_3|$.

◎ *Thinking Process* Here, we will use some properties $|z|^2 = z\bar{z}$, $\bar{z}_1 + \bar{z}_2 = \overline{z_1 + z_2}$ and $|\bar{z}| = |z|$.

Sol. We have, $\quad |z_1| = |z_2| = |z_3| = 1$

$\Rightarrow \quad |z_1|^2 = |z_2|^2 = |z_3|^2 = 1$

using properties $|z|^2 = z\bar{z}$, we get

$$\Rightarrow \quad z_1\bar{z}_1 = z_2\bar{z}_2 = z_3\bar{z}_3 = 1 \Rightarrow \bar{z}_1 = \frac{1}{z_1}, \bar{z}_2 = \frac{1}{z_2} \text{ and } \bar{z}_3 = \frac{1}{z_3}$$

Given, $\left|\frac{1}{z_1} + \frac{1}{z_2} + \frac{1}{z_3}\right| = 1 \Rightarrow |\bar{z}_1 + \bar{z}_2 + \bar{z}_3| = 1$

$\Rightarrow \quad |\overline{(z_1 + z_2 + z_3)}| = 1 \quad [\because \bar{z}_1 + \bar{z}_2 = \overline{z_1 + z_2}]$

$\Rightarrow \quad |z_1 + z_2 + z_3| = 1 \quad [\because |\bar{z}| = |z|]$

Mistake Alert $|z_1 + z_2 + z_3| \neq |z_1| + |z_2| + |z_3|$

Q.4 Find the value of k, if for the complex numbers z_1 and z_2,
$|1 - \bar{z}_1 z_2|^2 - |z_1 - z_2|^2 = k(1 - |z_1|^2)(1 - |z_2|^2)$

Sol. LHS $= |1 - \bar{z}_1 z_2|^2 - |z_1 - z_2|^2$

$= (1 - \bar{z}_1 z_2)\overline{(1 - \bar{z}_1 z_2)} - (z_1 - z_2)\overline{(z_1 - z_2)} \quad [\because |z|^2 = z\bar{z}]$

$= (1 - \bar{z}_1 z_2)(1 - z_1\bar{z}_2) - (z_1 - z_2)(\bar{z}_1 - \bar{z}_2)$

$[\because \overline{z_1 + z_2} = \bar{z}_1 + \bar{z}_2, \overline{z_1 z_2} = \bar{z}_1\bar{z}_2 \text{ and } \bar{\bar{z}} = z]$

$= 1 + z_1\bar{z}_1 z_2\bar{z}_2 - z_1\bar{z}_2 - \bar{z}_1 z_2 - z_1\bar{z}_1 + z_1\bar{z}_2 + z_2\bar{z}_1 - z_2\bar{z}_2$

$= 1 + |z_1|^2 |z_2|^2 - |z_1|^2 - |z_2|^2 \quad [\because z\bar{z} = |z|^2]$

$= -|z_1|^2(1 - |z_2|^2) + 1(1 - |z_2|^2)$

$= (1 - |z_1|)^2 (1 - |z_2|^2)$

given LHS $= k(1 - |z_1|^2)(1 - |z_2|^2)$

i.e., $\quad (1 - |z_1|^2)(1 - |z_2|^2) = k(1 - |z_1|^2)(1 - |z_2|^2)$

On comparing both sides, we get

$\therefore \quad k = 1$

Linear Inequalities

CHAPTER 05

Important Points

01 Two real numbers or two algebraic expressions related by the symbol <, >, ≤ or ≥ form an inequality.

For example, $2 < 5$ $7 > 5$ are the example of numerical inequality while $x < 5, y > 2, x \leq 7$ $y \geq 4$ are some examples of linear inequalities.

Now, $4 \leq x < 7$ (read as x is greater than or equal to 4 and less than 7) is an example of double inequalities.

Algebraic Solutions of Linear Inequalities in one Variable and their Graphical Representation Notations

- $a > b$ means, a is greater than b.
- $a < b$ means, a is less than b.
- $a \geq b$ means, a is greater than or equal to b.
- $a \leq b$ means, a is less than or equal to b.
- $a \neq b$ means, a is not equal to b.

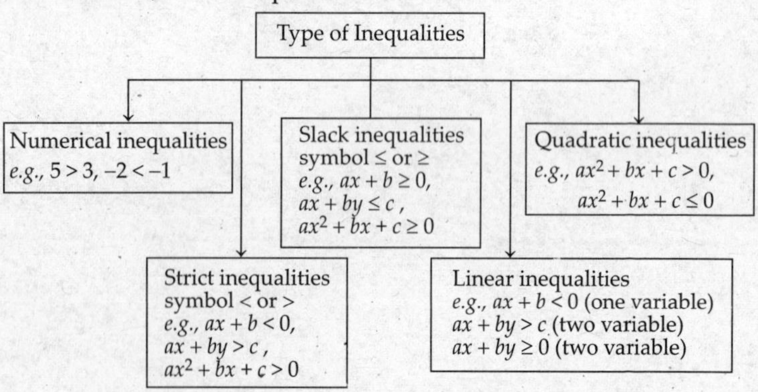

Rules to Solve Linear Inequalities

Rule 1 Equal numbers may be added to (or subtracted from) both sides of an inequality without affecting the sign of inequality.

Rule 2 Both sides of an inequality can be multiplied (or divided) by the same positive number. But, when both sides are multiplied or divided by a negative number, then the sign of an inequality is reversed.

Exercise 5.1

Question 1 Solve $24x < 100$, when

(i) x is a natural number. (ii) x is an integer.

◎ *Thinking Process* (Q. No. 1 to 4) Here, we will use rule (1) and rule (2) to simplify the Inequalities. Our aim is to solve the inequality by leaving only the variable on LHS.

Sol. We have, $24x < 100$,

On dividing both sides by 24, we get

$$\Rightarrow \quad \frac{24x}{24} < \frac{100}{24} \quad \text{(using rule 2)}$$

$$\Rightarrow \quad x < \frac{50}{12} \Rightarrow x < \frac{25}{6} \Rightarrow x < 4\frac{1}{6} \quad \left(\text{i.e., } x \text{ is less than } 4\frac{1}{6}\right)$$

(i) When x is a natural number (only positive integer) in this case, the solution set of the inequality is {1, 2, 3, 4}.

(ii) When x is an integer, the solution set of the given inequality is {......– 4, – 3, – 2, – 1, 0, 1, 2, 3, 4}.

Question 2 Solve $-12x > 30$, when

(i) x is a natural number. (ii) x is an integer.

Sol. We have, $-12x > 30$,

On dividing both sides by –12, we get

$$\frac{-12x}{-12} < \frac{30}{-12} \Rightarrow x < -\frac{5}{2} \quad \text{(using rule 2)}$$

(i) When x is a natural number, then there is no solution of given inequality. As natural numbers are positive numbers and there is no positive number which is less than negative number.

(ii) When x is an integer, the solution of given inequality is {....– 4, – 3} as there are infinite number which are less then $-\frac{5}{2}$.

Mistake Alert If we multiply or divide both sides of an inequality by a negative number, it is important to note the sign of the inequality will change.

Question 3 Solve $5x - 3 < 7$, when

(i) x is an integer. (ii) x is a real number.

Sol. We have, $5x - 3 < 7$,

On adding 3 on both sides, we get

$$\Rightarrow \quad 5x - 3 + 3 < 7 + 3 \quad \text{(using rule 1)}$$

$$5x < 10$$

On dividing both sides by 5, we get

$$\frac{5x}{5} < \frac{10}{5} \quad \text{(using rule 2)}$$

$$\Rightarrow \quad x < 2$$

(i) When x is an integer, the solution set of the given inequality is $\{\ldots, -1, 0, 1\}$.

(ii) When x is a real number, the solution set of given inequality is $(-\infty, 2)$ *i.e.*, all the numbers lying between $-\infty$ and 2 but $-\infty$ and 2 are not included as $x < 2$.

Mistake Alert If x is a real number, then use interval for solution set. Don't use numbers with commas.

Question 4 Solve $3x + 8 > 2$, when

(i) x is an integer. (ii) x is a real number.

Sol. We have, $3x + 8 > 2$

On adding -8 on both sides, we get

$$\Rightarrow \quad 3x + 8 - 8 > 2 - 8 \quad \text{(using rule 1)}$$

$$\Rightarrow \quad 3x > -6$$

On dividing both sides by 3, we get

$$\Rightarrow \quad \frac{3x}{3} > \frac{-6}{3} \quad \text{(using rule 2)}$$

$$\Rightarrow \quad x > -2$$

(i) When x is an integer, the solution set of the given inequality is $\{-1, 0, 1, 2 \ldots\}$.

(ii) When x is a real number, the solution set of the given inequality is $(-2, \infty)$. *i.e.*, all the numbers lying between -2 and ∞ but -2 and ∞ are not included as $x > -2$.

Direction (Q. No. 5 to 16) Solve the inequalities for real x.

Question 5 $4x + 3 < 5x + 7$.

Sol. We have, $4x + 3 < 5x + 7$

Transferring the term $5x$ to LHS and the term 3 to RHS, we get

$$4x - 5x < 7 - 3 \Rightarrow -x < 4$$

On multiplying both sides by -1, we get

$x > -4$ (using rule 2)

With the help of number line, we can easily look for the numbers greater than – 4.

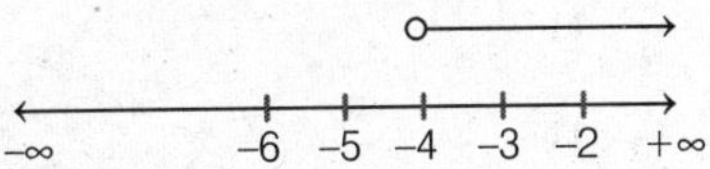

Solution set = (– 4, ∞) *i.e.*, all the numbers lying between – 4 and ∞ but – 4 and ∞ are not included as $x > -4$.

Question 6 $3x - 7 > 5x - 1$.

Sol. We have, $3x - 7 > 5x - 1$

Transferring the term $5x$ to LHS and the term – 7 to RHS, we get

$$3x - 5x > -1 + 7 \Rightarrow -2x > 6$$

On dividing both sides by 2, we get

$$\Rightarrow \quad \frac{2x}{2} < -\frac{6}{2} \quad \text{(using rule 2)}$$

$$\Rightarrow \quad x < -3$$

With the help of number line we can easily look for the real numbers less than – 3.

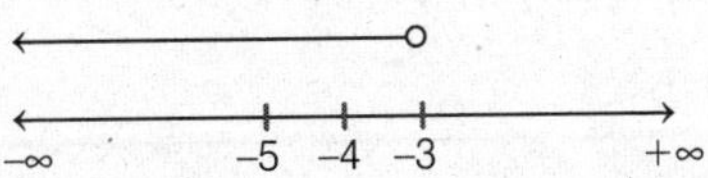

∴ Solution set = (– ∞, – 3) *i.e.*, all the numbers between – ∞ and – 3 but – ∞ and – 3 are not included as $x < -3$.

Question 7 $3(x - 1) \le 2(x - 3)$.

Sol. We have, $3x - 3 \le 2x - 6$

Transferring the term $2x$ to LHS and the term – 3 to RHS, we get

$$3x - 2x \le -6 + 3$$

$$x \le -3$$

∴ Solution set = (– ∞, – 3]

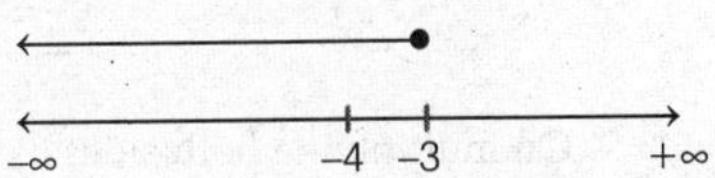

Question 8 $3(2 - x) \ge 2(1 - x)$.

Sol. We have, $3(2 - x) \ge 2(1 - x) = 6 - 3x \ge 2 - 2x$

Transferring the term 2 to LHS and the term – $3x$ to RHS,

$$6 - 2 \ge -2x + 3x$$

$$4 \ge x \Rightarrow x \le 4$$

∴ Solution set = (– ∞, 4].

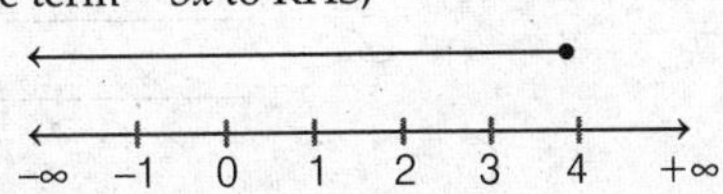

Mistake Alert Please be careful while transferring the term from one side to another side in inequality. First, check the sign of inequality, then use interval.

Question 9 $x + \frac{x}{2} + \frac{x}{3} < 11.$

Sol. We have, $x + \frac{x}{2} + \frac{x}{3} < 11$

$\Rightarrow \quad \frac{x}{1} + \frac{x}{2} + \frac{x}{3} < 11$

On taking LCM in LHS, we get

$$\frac{6x + 3x + 2x}{6} < 11$$

$$\Rightarrow \quad \frac{11x}{6} < 11$$

On multiplying both sides by $\frac{6}{11}$, we get

$$\frac{6}{11} \times \frac{11x}{6} < 11 \times \frac{6}{11} \qquad \text{(using rule 2)}$$

$$\Rightarrow \quad x < \frac{6 \times 11}{11}$$

$$\Rightarrow \quad x < 6$$

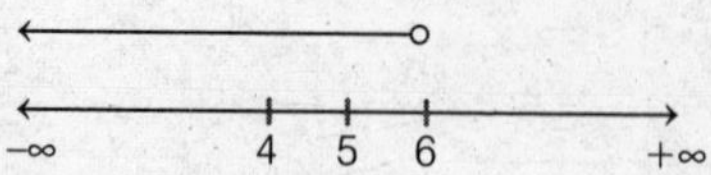

$\therefore$ Solution set = $(-\infty, 6)$.

Question 10 $\frac{x}{3} > \frac{x}{2} + 1.$

Sol. We have, $\frac{x}{3} > \frac{x}{2} + 1$

On transferring the term $\frac{x}{2}$ to LHS,

$$\frac{x}{3} - \frac{x}{2} > 1$$

On taking LCM in LHS, we get

$$\frac{2x - 3x}{6} > 1 \Rightarrow \frac{-x}{6} > 1$$

On multiplying both sides by 6, we get

$$6 \times \frac{-x}{6} > 1 \times 6 \qquad \text{(using rule 2)}$$

$$\Rightarrow \quad -x > 6 \qquad (\because \text{multiplying both sides by } -1)$$

$$\Rightarrow \quad x < -6 \qquad \text{(using rule 2)}$$

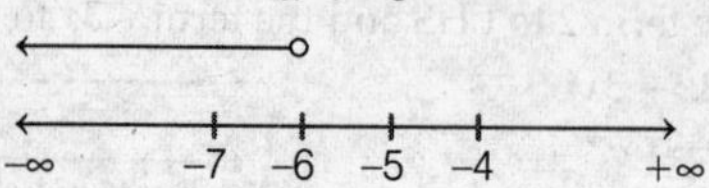

$\therefore$ Solution set = $(-\infty, -6)$

Question 11 $\dfrac{3(x-2)}{5} \leq \dfrac{5(2-x)}{3}$.

Sol. We have, $\dfrac{3(x-2)}{5} \leq \dfrac{5(2-x)}{3} \Rightarrow \dfrac{3x-6}{5} \leq \dfrac{10-5x}{3} \Rightarrow 9x - 18 \leq 50 - 25x$

($\because$ multiplying both sides by $5/3$)

On transferring the terms $(-25x)$ to LHS and the term (-18) to RHS, we get

$$9x + 25x \leq 50 + 18$$

$$\Rightarrow \quad 34x \leq 68$$

$$\Rightarrow \quad x \leq \frac{68}{34} \Rightarrow x \leq 2$$

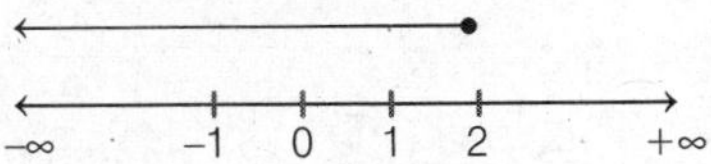

$\therefore$ Solution set = $(-\infty, 2]$

Question 12 $\dfrac{1}{2}\left(\dfrac{3x}{5}+4\right) \geq \dfrac{1}{3}(x-6)$.

Sol. We have, $\dfrac{1}{2}\left(\dfrac{3x}{5}+4\right) \geq \dfrac{1}{3}(x-6) \Rightarrow \dfrac{1}{2}\left(\dfrac{3x}{5}+\dfrac{4}{1}\right) \geq \dfrac{1}{3}(x-6)$

On taking LCM in LHS, we get

$$\frac{1}{2}\left(\frac{3x+20}{5}\right) \geq \frac{1}{3}(x-6) \Rightarrow \frac{3x+20}{10} \geq \frac{x-6}{3}$$

$\Rightarrow \quad 3(3x+20) \geq 10(x-6)$ ($\because$ multiplying both sides by $10/3$)

$\Rightarrow \quad 9x + 60 \geq 10x - 60$

Transferring the term $10x$ to LHS and the term 60 to RHS,

$$9x - 10x \geq -60 - 60 \Rightarrow -x \geq -120$$

On multiplying both sides by -1, we get

$x \leq 120$ (using rule 2)

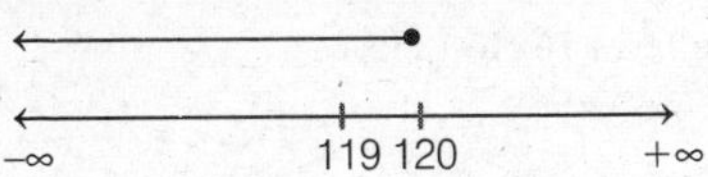

$\therefore$ Solution set = $(-\infty, 120]$.

Question 13 $2(2x+3)-10<6(x-2)$.

Sol. We have, $2(2x+3) - 10 < 6(x-2)$

$$\Rightarrow \quad 4x + 6 - 10 < 6x - 12 \Rightarrow 4x - 4 < 6x - 12$$

Transferring the term $6x$ to LHS and (-4) to RHS,

$$4x - 6x < -12 + 4 \Rightarrow -2x < -8$$

On dividing both sides by -2, we get

$\Rightarrow \quad \dfrac{-2x}{-2} > \dfrac{-8}{-2}$ (using rule 2)

$$\Rightarrow \quad x > 4$$

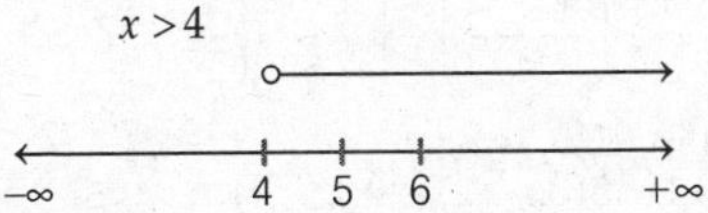

$\therefore$ Solution set = $(4, \infty)$.

Question 14 $37-(3x+5) \geq 9x-8(x-3)$.

Sol. We have, $37-(3x+5) \geq 9x-8(x-3)$

$$(37-3x-5) \geq 9x-8x+24 \Rightarrow 32-3x \geq x+24$$

Transferring the term 24 to LHS and the term $(-3x)$ to RHS,

$$32-24 \geq x+3x \Rightarrow 8 \geq 4x \Rightarrow 4x \leq 8$$

On dividing both sides by 4, we get

$$\Rightarrow \quad \frac{4x}{4} \leq \frac{8}{4} \qquad \text{(using rule 2)}$$

$$\Rightarrow \quad x \leq 2$$

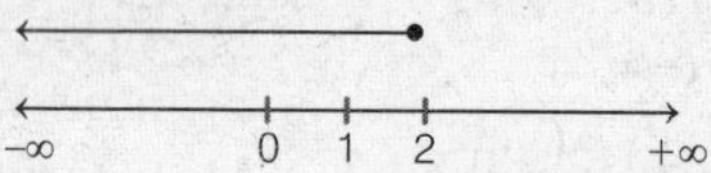

$\therefore$ Solution set $= (-\infty, 2]$.

Question 15 $\frac{x}{4} < \frac{(5x-2)}{3} - \frac{(7x-3)}{5}$.

◎ ***Thinking Process*** First take LCM of denominators of inequality to make it a simpler form.

Sol. We have, $\frac{x}{4} < \frac{(5x-2)}{3} - \frac{(7x-3)}{5}$

$$\frac{x}{4} < \frac{5(5x-2)-3(7x-3)}{15}$$

$$\Rightarrow \quad 15x < 4[(25x-10)-(21x-9)] \Rightarrow 15x < 4[(25x-10-21x+9]$$

$$\Rightarrow \quad 15x < 4[4x-1] \Rightarrow 15x < 16x-4$$

Transferring the term $16x$ to LHS,

$$15x-16x < -4$$

$$-x < -4$$

On multiplying by -1 both sides, we get

$$x > 4 \qquad \text{(using rule 2)}$$

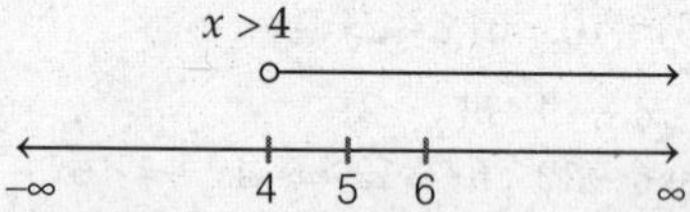

$\therefore$ Solution set $= (4, \infty)$.

Question 16 $\frac{2x-1}{3} \geq \left(\frac{3x-2}{4}\right) - \left(\frac{2-x}{5}\right)$.

Sol. We have, $\frac{2x-1}{3} \geq \left(\frac{3x-2}{4}\right) - \left(\frac{2-x}{5}\right)$

On taking LCM in RHS, we get

$$\frac{2x-1}{3} \geq \frac{5(3x-2)-4(2-x)}{20}$$

$$\Rightarrow \quad \frac{2x-1}{3} \geq \frac{(15x-10)-(8-4x)}{20}$$

$$\Rightarrow \quad \frac{2x-1}{3} \geq \frac{15x-10-8+4x}{20}$$

$$\Rightarrow \quad \frac{2x-1}{3} \geq \frac{19x-18}{20}$$

$$\Rightarrow \quad 20(2x-1) \geq 3(19x-18)$$ [$\because$ multiplying both sides by 60]

$$\Rightarrow \quad 40x-20 \geq 57x-54$$

Transferring the term $57x$ to LHS and the term -20 to RHS,

$$40x-57x \geq -54+20 \Rightarrow -17x \geq -34$$

On divide both sides by -17, we get

$$\frac{-17x}{-17} \leq \frac{-34}{-17}$$ (using rule 2)

$$\Rightarrow \quad x \leq \frac{-34}{-17} \Rightarrow x \leq 2$$

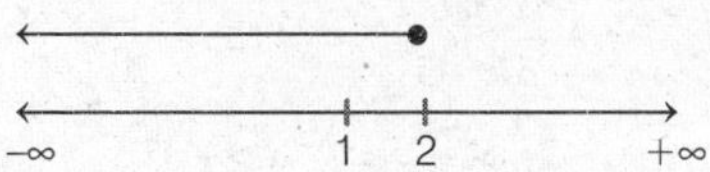

Solution set $= (-\infty, 2]$.

Direction (Q. No. 17 to 20) Solve the inequalities and show the graph of the solution in each case on the number line.

◎ ***Thinking Process*** (For Q. No. 17 to 20) All the numbers on left side of a given number are less than it and all numbers on the right side will be greater than it on the number line.

Question 17 $3x-2<2x+1$.

Sol. We have, $3x-2<2x+1$

Transferring the term $2x$ to LHS and the term (-2) to RHS,

$$3x-2x<1+2 \Rightarrow x<3$$

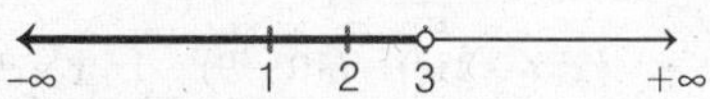

All the numbers on the left side of 3 will be less than it.

$\therefore$ Solution set $= (-\infty, 3)$

Question 18 $5x-3 \geq 3x-5$.

Sol. We have, $5x-3 \geq 3x-5$

Transferring the term $3x$ to LHS and the term (-3) to RHS,

$$5x-3x \geq -5+3 \Rightarrow 2x \geq -2$$

$$\Rightarrow \quad \frac{2x}{2} \geq -\frac{2}{2}$$ (using rule 2)

$$\Rightarrow \qquad x \geq \frac{-2}{2}$$

$$x \geq -1$$

All the numbers on the right side of – 1 will be greater than it.

$\therefore$ Solution set = $[-1, \infty)$.

Question 19 $3(1-x) < 2(x+4)$.

Sol. We have, $3(1-x) < 2(x+4)$

$$\Rightarrow \qquad 3 - 3x < 2x + 8$$

Transferring the term $2x$ to the LHS and the term 3 to RHS,

$$-3x - 2x < 8 - 3$$

$$\Rightarrow \qquad -5x < 5$$

$$\Rightarrow \qquad \frac{-5x}{-5} > \frac{5}{-5} \qquad \text{(using rule 2)}$$

$$\Rightarrow \qquad x > \frac{-5}{5} \Rightarrow x > -1$$

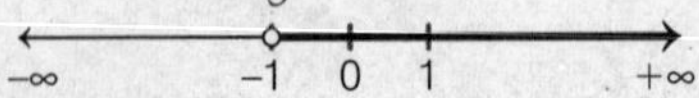

$\therefore$ Solution set = $(-1, \infty)$.

Question 20 $\frac{x}{2} \geq \frac{(5x-2)}{3} - \frac{(7x-3)}{5}$.

Sol. We have, $\frac{x}{2} \geq \frac{(5x-2)}{3} - \frac{(7x-3)}{5}$

On taking LCM in RHS, we get

$$\frac{x}{2} \geq \frac{5(5x-2) - 3(7x-3)}{15}$$

$$\Rightarrow \qquad \frac{x}{2} \geq \frac{25x - 10 - 21x + 9}{15}$$

$$\Rightarrow \qquad \frac{x}{2} \geq \frac{(25x - 21x) - (10 - 9)}{15} \Rightarrow \frac{x}{2} \geq \frac{4x - 1}{15}$$

$$\Rightarrow \qquad 15x \geq 2(4x - 1)$$

$$\Rightarrow \qquad 15x \geq 8x - 2$$

Transferring the term $8x$ to LHS, we get

$$15x - 8x \geq -2 \Rightarrow 7x \geq -2$$

$$\Rightarrow \qquad \frac{7x}{7} \geq \frac{-2}{7} \qquad \text{(using rule 2)}$$

$$\Rightarrow \qquad x \geq -\frac{2}{7}$$

$\therefore$ Solution set = $\left[\frac{-2}{7}, \infty\right)$.

Note Whenever we solve a linear inequality as in Q. Nos. 1 to 20 we should always remember how to use the brackets *i.e.*, intervals (open or closed). The following table will help you.

If	$a \le x \le b$	$[a, b]$
	$a \le x < b$	$[a, b)$ or $[a, b[$
	$a < x \le b$	$(a, b]$ or $]a, b]$
	$a < x < b$	$]a, b[$ or (a, b)
	$-\infty < x < a$	$(-\infty, a)$ or $]-\infty, a[$
	$-\infty < x \le a$	$(-\infty, a]$ or $]-\infty, a]$
	$a < x < \infty$	(a, ∞) or $]a, \infty[$
	$a \le x < \infty$	$[a, \infty)$ or $[a, \infty[$

In case of $-\infty$ and $+\infty$, closed interval are never used only use open interval.

Question 21 Ravi obtained 70 and 75 marks in first two unit tests. Find the minimum marks he should get in the third test to have an average of atleast 60 marks.

◎ ***Thinking Process*** First we will get the average of all three unit tests and then apply the given condition.

Sol. Given, Ravi obtained 70 and 75 marks in first two unit tests.

Let Ravi got x marks in third unit test.

$\therefore$ Average marks obtained by Ravi $= \dfrac{\text{Sum of marks in all tests}}{\text{Number of tests}}$

$$= \frac{70 + 75 + x}{3}$$

$$= \frac{145 + x}{3}$$

Now, it is given that he wants to obtain an average of atleast 60 marks.

Atleast 60 marks means that the marks should be greater than or equal to 60.

i.e., $$\frac{145 + x}{3} \ge 60$$

$\Rightarrow$ $145 + x \ge 60 \times 3$ [$\because$ multiplying both sides by 3]

$\Rightarrow$ $145 + x \ge 180$

Now, transferring the term 145 to RHS,

$$x \ge 180 - 145$$

$\Rightarrow$ $x \ge 35$

$\therefore$ Ravi should get atleast 35 marks in third unit test.

Question 22 To receive grade 'A' in a course, one must obtain an average of 90 marks or more in five examinations (each of 100 marks). If Sunita's marks in first four examinations are 87, 92, 94 and 95, find minimum marks that Sunita must obtain in fifth examination to get grade 'A' in the course.

Sol. Let Sunita got x marks in the fifth exam.

$$\therefore \text{ Average marks obtained by Sunita} = \frac{\text{Sum of marks in all exams}}{\text{Number of exams}}$$

$$= \frac{87 + 92 + 94 + 95 + x}{5} = \frac{368 + x}{5}$$

Now, it is given that Sunita wants to obtain grade A for that her average marks should be greater than or equal to 90.

i.e., $$\frac{368 + x}{5} \geq 90 \Rightarrow 368 + x \geq 450$$

Transferring the term 368 to RHS, $x \geq 450 - 368 \Rightarrow x \geq 82$

$\therefore$ Sunita must obtain atleast 82 marks in fifth exam to get grade 'A'.

Question 23 Find all pairs of consecutive odd positive integers both of which are smaller than 10 such that their sum is more than 11.

◎ *Thinking Process* First we will assume the two consecutive odd positive integers and apply the given condition to get the common interval and find the integer value of x in that interval and put these values in assuming consecutive term and get required pair.

Sol. Let the numbers are $2x + 1$ and $2x + 3$. Then, according to the question,

$$2x + 1 < 10 \quad \text{and} \quad 2x + 3 < 10$$

$$\Rightarrow \quad 2x < 9 \quad \text{and} \quad 2x < 7$$

$$\Rightarrow \quad x < \frac{9}{2} \quad \text{and} \quad x < \frac{7}{2}$$

Also, $\quad 2x + 3 + 2x + 1 > 11 \Rightarrow 4x + 4 > 11 \Rightarrow 4x > 11 - 4 \Rightarrow x > \frac{7}{4}$

Now, plotting all the values of x on line.

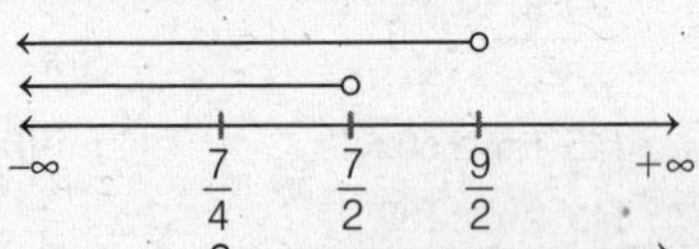

From the graph, it is clear that $x \in \left(\frac{7}{4}, \frac{7}{2}\right)$ in which integer values are $x = 2$ and 3.

When $x = 3$, the number are $(2 \times 3 + 1, 2 \times 3 + 3) = (7, 9)$

When $x = 2$, the number are $(2 \times 2 + 1, 2 \times 2 + 3) = (5, 7)$

$\therefore$ Required pairs are $(5, 7)$ and $(7, 9)$.

Note It several inequalities hold simultaneously, then their intersection region will represent the solution set.

Quick Solution

Let x be the smaller of the two consecutive odd + ve integers.
Then the other odd integer is $x+2$.

Given $\quad x<10$ and $x+2<10$

$\Rightarrow \quad x<10$ and $x<8 \quad$ ... (i) [$\because$ common solution set]

Also, given their sum is more than 11

i.e., $\quad x+x+2>11$

$\Rightarrow \quad 2x>9$

$\Rightarrow \quad x>\frac{9}{2} \quad$ ... (ii)

From inequalities (i) and (ii), we get

$\frac{9}{2}<x<8 \Rightarrow 4.5<x<8 \quad$ [$\because$ common solution]

$\Rightarrow \quad x=5, 7 \quad$ [$\because x$ is an odd integer]

$\therefore$ Required pairs are (5, 7) and (7, 9).

Question 24 Find all pairs of consecutive even positive integers, both of which are larger than 5 such that their sum is less than 23.

◎ ***Thinking Process*** First we will assume the two consecutive even positive integers and apply the given condition to get the common interval and find the integer value of x in that interval and put these values in assuming consecutive term and get required pairs.

Sol. Let the two consecutive even positive integers be $2x$ and $2x+2$.

Then, according to the question $2x>5 \Rightarrow x>\frac{5}{2}$

and $\quad 2x+2>5 \Rightarrow 2x>5-2 \Rightarrow 2x>3 \Rightarrow x>\frac{3}{2}$

and $\quad 2x+2x+2<23 \Rightarrow 4x<23-2 \Rightarrow 4x<21 \Rightarrow x<\frac{21}{4}$

Now, plotting all these values on number line.

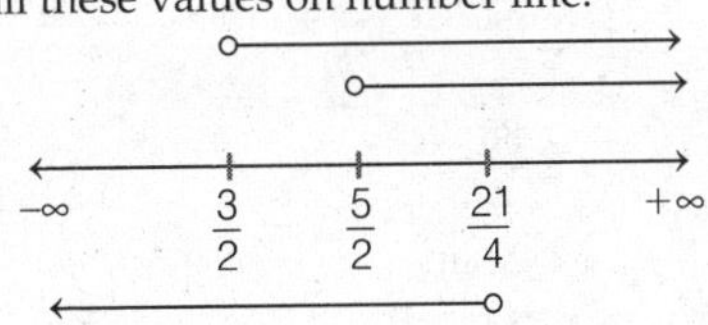

From the above graph, it is clear that $x \in \left(\frac{5}{2}, \frac{21}{4}\right)$ in which integer values are $x=3, 4, 5$.

When $x=3$, pair is $(2\times 3, 2\times 3+2)=(6, 8)$

When $x=4$, pair is $(2\times 4, 2\times 4+2)=(8, 10)$

When $x=5$, pair is $(2\times 5, 2\times 5+2)=(10, 12)$

$\therefore$ Required pairs are (6, 8), (8, 10), (10, 12).

Question 25 The longest side of a triangle is 3 times the shortest side and the third side is 2 cm shorter than the longest side. If the perimeter of the triangle is atleast 61 cm, find the minimum length of the shortest side.

◎ *Thinking Process* First we will assume the shortest side, then remaining side will be calculated easily. Then, further use the concept of perimeter to get the required results.

Sol. Let the shortest side be x cm.

Then, according to the given condition,

Longest side = $3x$ cm and third side = $(3x - 2)$ cm

Now, perimeter of triangle ≥ 61 *i.e.*, sum of all sides ≥ 61

$\Rightarrow \quad x + 3x + 3x - 2 \geq 61 \Rightarrow 2 + 7x - 2 \geq 61 + 2$ (using rule 1)

$\Rightarrow \quad 7x \geq 63 \Rightarrow \frac{7x}{7} \geq \frac{63}{7}$ (using rule 2)

$\Rightarrow \quad x \geq 9$

$\therefore$ Minimum length of the shortest side = 9 cm.

Question 26 A man wants to cut three lengths from a single piece of board of length 91 cm. The second length is to be 3 cm longer than the shortest and third length is to be twice as long as the shortest. What are the possible lengths of the shortest board if the third piece is to be atleast 5 cm longer than the second?

Sol. Given, the total length of board = 9 km

Let the shortest side be x cm.

Then, by given condition, second length = $x + 3$ cm

Third length = $2x$ cm,

$x + x + 3 + 2x \leq 91 \Rightarrow 4x + 3 \leq 91$

$\Rightarrow \quad -3 + 4x + 3 \leq 91 - 3$ (using rule 1)

$\Rightarrow \quad 4x \leq 88$

$\Rightarrow \quad \frac{4x}{4} \leq \frac{88}{4}$ (using rule 2)

$\Rightarrow \quad x \leq \frac{88}{4}$

$\Rightarrow \quad x \leq 22$ cm ...(i)

Again, given that $\quad 2x \geq (x + 3) + 5$

$2x \geq x + (3 + 5)$

Transferring the term x to LHS,

$2x - x \geq 8 \Rightarrow x \geq 8$ ...(ii)

From Eqs. (i) and (ii), length of shortest board should be greater than or equal to 8 but less than or equal to 22 *i.e.*, $8 \leq x \leq 22$.

Miscellaneous Exercise

Direction (Q. No. 1 to 6) *Solve the inequalities.*

Question 1 $2 \leq 3x - 4 \leq 5$.

Sol. We have, $2 \leq 3x - 4 \leq 5$

Adding 4 to each term $2 + 4 \leq 3x \leq 5 + 4$ (using rule 1)

$\Rightarrow \quad 6 \leq 3x \leq 9$

On dividing by 3 in each term, we get

$$\frac{6}{3} \leq \frac{3x}{3} \leq \frac{9}{3} \quad \text{(using rule 2)}$$

$\Rightarrow \quad 2 \leq x \leq 3$

$\therefore$ Solution set = [2, 3].

Question 2 $6 \leq -3(2x - 4) < 12$.

Sol. We have, $6 \leq -3(2x - 4) < 12$

$\Rightarrow \quad 6 \leq -6x + 12 < 12$

On adding (– 12) to each term, we get

$$6 - 12 \leq -6x + 12 - 12 < 12 - 12 \quad \text{(using rule 1)}$$

$\Rightarrow \quad -6 \leq -6x < 0$

On dividing by (– 6) to each term, we get (using rule 2)

$$\frac{-6}{-6} \geq \frac{-6x}{-6} > \frac{0}{-6}$$

$$1 \geq x > 0 \quad \textit{i.e.,} \quad 0 < x \leq 1$$

$\therefore$ Solution set = (0, 1] or]0, 1].

Note When we multiply the inequality by negative quantity, the sign of inequality will be change.

Question 3 $-3 \leq 4 - \frac{7x}{2} \leq 18$.

Sol. We have, $-3 \leq 4 - \frac{7x}{2} \leq 18$

On adding (– 4) to each term, we get

$$-3 - 4 \leq 4 - \frac{7x}{2} - 4 \leq 18 - 4 \quad \text{(using rule 1)}$$

$$-7 \leq \frac{-7x}{2} \leq 14$$

On multiplying by $\left(\frac{-2}{7}\right)$ to each term, we get

$$-7 \times \left(-\frac{2}{7}\right) \geq -\frac{7}{2} x \times \left(-\frac{2}{7}\right) \geq 14 \times \left(-\frac{2}{7}\right) \quad \text{(using rule 2)}$$

$\Rightarrow \quad 2 \geq x \geq -4 \quad$ *i.e.,* $\quad -4 \leq x \leq 2$

$\therefore$ Solution set = [– 4, 2].

Question 4 $-15 < \dfrac{3(x-2)}{5} \leq 0.$

Sol. We have, $-15 < \dfrac{3(x-2)}{5} \leq 0$

On multiplying by 5 to each term, we get

$$-15 \times 5 < \frac{3(x-2)}{5} \times 5 \leq 0 \times 5 \quad \text{(using rule 2)}$$

$\Rightarrow \quad -75 < 3x - 6 \leq 0$

On adding 6 to each term, we get

$$-75 + 6 < 3x - 6 + 6 \leq 0 + 6 \quad \text{(using rule 1)}$$

$\Rightarrow \quad -69 < 3x \leq 6$

On dividing by 3 in each term, we get

$$\frac{-69}{3} < \left(\frac{3x}{3}\right) \leq \frac{6}{3} \quad \text{(using rule 2)}$$

$\Rightarrow \quad -23 < x \leq 2$

$\therefore$ Solution set = (– 23, 2] or]– 23, 2].

Question 5 $-12 < 4 - \dfrac{3x}{-5} \leq 2.$

Sol. We have, $-12 < 4 - \dfrac{3x}{-5} \leq 2$

$\Rightarrow -12 < 4 + \dfrac{3x}{5} \leq 2$

On adding (– 4) to each term,

$$-12 - 4 < 4 + \frac{3x}{5} - 4 \leq 2 - 4 \quad \text{(using rule 1)}$$

$\Rightarrow \quad -16 < \dfrac{3x}{5} \leq -2$

On multiplying by $\dfrac{5}{3}$ to each term, we get

$$-16 \times \frac{5}{3} < \frac{3x}{5} \times \frac{5}{3} \leq -2 \times \frac{5}{3} \quad \text{(using rule 2)}$$

$\Rightarrow \quad -\dfrac{80}{3} < x \leq -\dfrac{10}{3}$

$\therefore$ Solution set = $\left(-\dfrac{80}{3}, -\dfrac{10}{3}\right]$ or $\left]-\dfrac{80}{3}, \dfrac{-10}{3}\right]$.

Question 6 $7 \le \frac{3x+11}{2} \le 11.$

Sol. We have, $7 \le \frac{3x + 11}{2} \le 11$

On multiplying by 2 to each term, we get

$$7 \times 2 \le \frac{(3x + 11)}{2} \times 2 \le 11 \times 2 \quad \text{(using rule 2)}$$

$$\Rightarrow \quad 14 \le 3x + 11 \le 22$$

On adding (− 11) to each term, we get

$$14 - 11 \le 3x + 11 - 11 \le 22 - 11 \quad \text{(using rule 1)}$$

$$\Rightarrow \quad 3 \le 3x \le 11$$

On dividing by 3 in each term, we get

$$\frac{3}{3} \le \frac{3x}{3} \le \frac{11}{3} \quad \text{(using rule 2)}$$

$$\Rightarrow \quad 1 \le x \le \frac{11}{3}$$

$\therefore$ Solution set $= \left[1, \frac{11}{3}\right]$.

Direction (Q. No. 7 to 10) Solve the inequalities and represent the solution graphically on the number line.

◎ ***Thinking Process*** We will solve both the inequalities and draw the graph on the number line, then the values of x which are common to both will be the required solution set.

Question 7 $5x+1>-24, 5x-1<24.$

Sol. We have, $5x + 1 > -24$

On adding (−1) on both sides,

$$-1 + 5x + 1 > -24 - 1 \quad \text{(using rule 1)}$$

$$\Rightarrow \quad 5x > -25$$

On dividing both sides by 5, we get

$$x > \frac{-25}{5} \quad \text{(using rule 2)}$$

$$\Rightarrow \quad x > -5 \quad \text{...(i)}$$

And $\quad 5x - 1 < 24$

On adding 1 on both sides, we get

$$1 + 5x - 1 < 24 + 1 \quad \text{(using rule 1)}$$

$\Rightarrow \quad 5x < 25$ On dividing both side by 5, we get

$$\frac{5x}{5} < \frac{25}{5} \quad \text{(using rule 2)}$$

$$\Rightarrow \quad x < 5 \quad \text{...(ii)}$$

Draw the graph of inequalities (i) and (ii) on the number line.

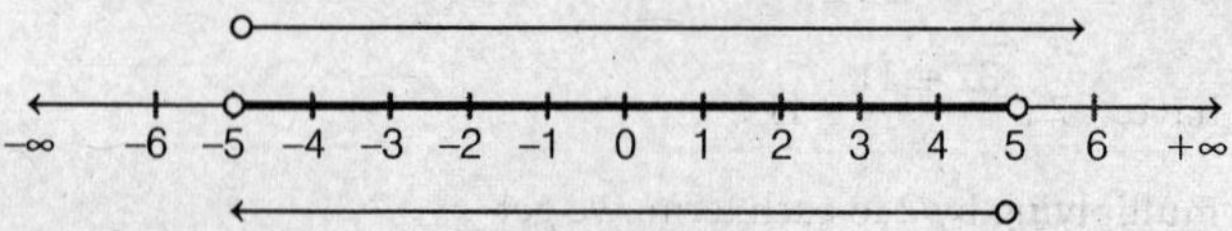

Hence, solutions of the system are real numbers x lying between -5 and 5 excluding -5 and 5 *i.e.*, $-5 < x < 5$.

$\therefore$ Solution set = $(-5, 5)$ or $]-5, 5[$.

Mistake Alert It $x > -5$ and $x < 5$, then our solution will not be $(-5, \infty) \cup (-\infty, 5)$. The solution will be $(-5, \infty) \cap (-\infty, 5)$ *i.e.*, $(-5, 5)$ Be careful for this type of mistake.

Question 8 $2(x-1) < x+5,\ 3(x+2) > 2-x$.

Sol. We have,

$$2(x-1) < x+5 \quad \text{and} \quad 3(x+2) > 2-x$$

Now, $$2x-2 < x+5$$

Transferring the term x to LHS and the term -2 to RHS,

$$2x - x < 5 + 2 \qquad \text{...(i)}$$

$$\Rightarrow \quad x < 7$$

and $$3(x+2) > 2-x$$

$$\Rightarrow \quad 3x + 6 > 2 - x$$

Transferring the term $(-x)$ to LHS and the term 6 to RHS,

$$3x + x > 2 - 6$$

$$\Rightarrow \quad 4x > -4$$

On dividing both side by 4, we get

$$x > \frac{-4}{4} \qquad \text{(using rule 2)}$$

$$\Rightarrow \quad x > -1 \qquad \text{...(ii)}$$

Draw the graph of inequalities (i) and (ii) on the number line.

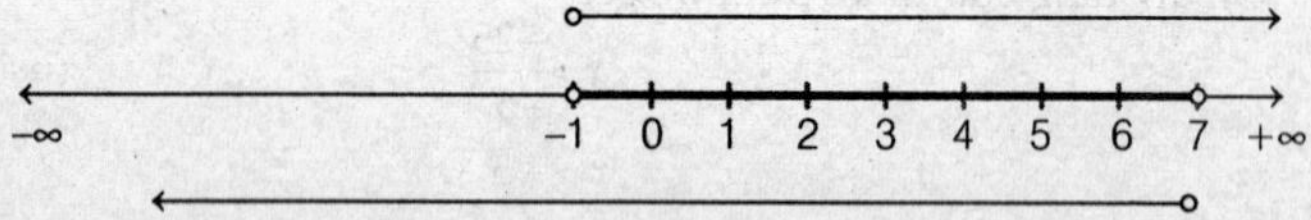

Hence, solution set of the equalities are real numbers, x lying between -1 and 7 excluding -1 and 7.

i.e., $$-1 < x < 7$$

$\therefore$ Solution set = $(-1, 7)$ or $]-1, 7[$.

Question 9 $3x-7>2(x-6), 6-x>11-2x$.

Sol. We have, $3x-7>2(x-6)$

$\Rightarrow \quad 3x-7>2x-12$

Transferring the term $2x$ to LHS and the terrm (-7) to RHS,

$$3x-2x>-12+7 \Rightarrow x>-5 \quad \text{...(i)}$$

and $\quad 6-x>11-2x$

Transferring the term $(-2x)$ to LHS and the term 6 to RHS,

$$-x+2x>11-6$$

$\Rightarrow \quad x>5 \quad$ ...(ii)

Draw the graph of inequalities (i) and (ii) on the number line,

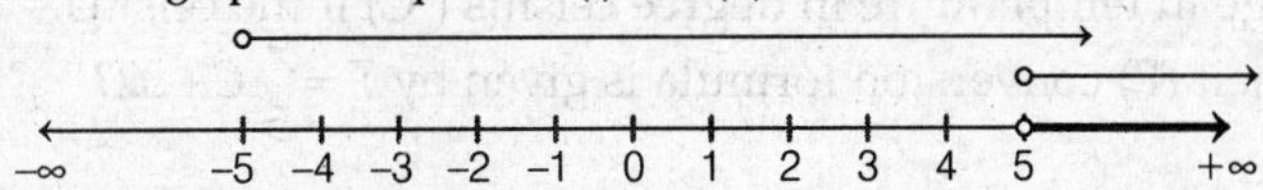

Hence, solution set of the equalities are real numbers, x lying on greater than 5 excluding 5 .

i.e., $\quad x>5$

$\therefore$ Solution set = $(5, \infty)$ or $]5, \infty[$.

Question 10 $5(2x-7)-3(2x+3) \le 0, 2x+19 \le 6x+47$.

Sol. We have, $5(2x-7)-3(2x+3) \le 0$,

$\Rightarrow \quad 10x-35-6x-9 \le 0$

$\Rightarrow \quad (10x-6x)-(35+9) \le 0$

$\Rightarrow \quad 4x-44 \le 0$

On adding 44 on both sides, we get

$$4x-44+44 \le 0+44 \quad \text{(using rule 1)}$$

$\Rightarrow \quad 4x \le 44$

$\Rightarrow \quad x \le \frac{44}{4} \quad$ (using rule 2)

$$x \le 11 \quad \text{...(i)}$$

Now, $\quad 2x+19 \le 6x+47$

Transferring the term $6x$ to LHS and the term 19 to RHS,

$$2x-6x \le 47-19$$

$\Rightarrow \quad -4x \le 28$

On dividing both sides by 4, we get

$$\frac{-4x}{4} \le \frac{28}{4} \quad \text{(using rule 2)}$$

$\Rightarrow \quad -x \le 7 \Rightarrow x \ge -7 \quad$ ...(ii)

Draw the graph of inequalities (i) and (ii) on the number line,

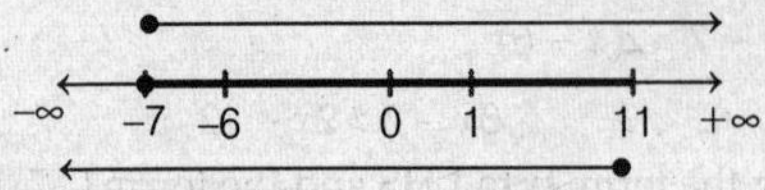

Hence, solution set of the inequalities are real numbers x lying between -7 and 11, including -7 and 11.

i.e., $$-7 \le x \le 11$$

$\therefore$ Solutions set $= [-7, 11]$.

Question 11 A solution is to be kept between 68° F and 77° F. What is the range in temperature in degree celsius (°C) if the celsius, fahrenheit (F) conversion formula is given by $F = \frac{9}{5}C + 32$?

◎ *Thinking Process* Here, we will put the given formula in the range of fahrenheit and get the range of celsius.

Sol. Given, $$68° < F < 77° \quad \ldots(i)$$

On putting $F = \frac{9}{5}C + 32$ in Eq. (i),

$$\Rightarrow \quad 68° < \frac{9}{5}C + 32 < 77°$$

On adding (-32) in each term, we get

$$68° - 32 < \frac{9}{5}C + 32 - 32 < 77° - 32 \quad \text{(using rule 1)}$$

$$\Rightarrow \quad 36° < \frac{9}{5}C < 45°$$

On multiplying by $\left(\frac{5}{9}\right)$ in each term,

$$36° \times \frac{5}{9} < \frac{9}{5}C \times \frac{5}{9} < 45° \times \frac{5}{9} \quad \text{(using rule 2)}$$

$$\Rightarrow \quad 4° \times 5 < C < 5° \times 5$$

$$\Rightarrow \quad 20° < C < 25°$$

i.e., $C \in (20, 25)$

Hence, temperature in degree celsius lies between 20°C and 25°C.

Question 12 A solution of 8% boric acid is to be diluted by adding a 2% boric acid solution to it. The resulting mixture is to be more than 4% but less than 6% boric acid. If we have 640 L of the 8% solution, how many litres of the 2% solution will have to be added?

Sol. Let the 2% boric acid solution be x litre.

$\therefore$ Mixture $= (640 + x)$ L

Now, according to the question, two conditions arise

I. 2% of x + 8% of 640 > 4% of $(640 + x)$

II. 2% of x + 8% of 640 < 6% of $(640 + x)$

From condition I,

$$\frac{2}{100} \times x + \frac{8}{100} \times 640 > \frac{4}{100} \times (640 + x)$$

$$\Rightarrow \quad 100 \times \left[\frac{2x}{100} + \frac{8}{100} \times 640\right] > \frac{4}{100} \times (640 + x) \times 100 \quad \text{(using rule 2)}$$

$$\Rightarrow \quad 2x + 8 \times 640 > 4 \times 640 + 4x$$

Transferring the term 4x to LHS and the term (8×640) to RHS,

$$\Rightarrow \quad 2x - 4x > 4 \times 640 - 8 \times 640$$

$$\Rightarrow \quad -2x > 640(4 - 8) \Rightarrow -2x > -4 \times 640$$

On dividing both sides by -2, we get

$$\frac{-2x}{-2} < \frac{-4 \times 640}{-2} \quad \text{(using rule 2)}$$

$$\Rightarrow \quad x < 2 \times 640$$

$$\Rightarrow \quad x < 1280 \quad \text{...(i)}$$

From condition II,

$$\frac{2}{100} \times x + \frac{8}{100} \times 640 < \frac{6}{100} \times (640 + x)$$

$$\Rightarrow \quad 100 \times \left[\frac{2x}{100} + \frac{8}{100} \times 640\right] < [6 \times 640 + 6x] \times \frac{100}{100} \quad \text{(using rule 2)}$$

$$\Rightarrow \quad 2x + 8 \times 640 < 6 \times 640 + 6x$$

Transferring the term $6x$ to LHS and the term (8×640) to RHS,

$$2x - 6x < 6 \times 640 - 8 \times 640$$

$$\Rightarrow \quad -4x < 640(6 - 8) \Rightarrow -4x < -2 \times 640$$

On dividing both sides by -4, we get

$$\frac{-4x}{-4} > \frac{-2 \times 640}{-4} \quad \text{(using rule 2)}$$

$$\Rightarrow \quad x > 320 \quad \text{...(ii)}$$

Hence, from Eqs. (i) and (ii), $320 < x < 1280$

i.e., $x \in (320, 1280)$

The number of litres to be added should be greater than 320 L and less than 1280 L.

Note Remember that $x\%$ of $y = \frac{x}{100} \times y$

Question 13 How many litres of water will have to be added to 1125 L of the 45% solution of acid so that the resulting mixture will contain more than 25% but less than 30% acid content?

Sol. Let x litres water be added in 1125 L of the 45% solution of acid.

Now, according to the question,

25% of $(1125 + x) <$ 45% of $1125 <$ 30% of $(1125 + x)$

$\Rightarrow \quad \frac{25}{100} \times (1125 + x) < \frac{45}{100} \times 1125 < \frac{30}{100} \times (1125 + x)$

$\Rightarrow \quad 25 \times 1125 + 25x < 45 \times 1125 < 30 \times 1125 + 30x$ (using rule 2)

Taking first two parts of above inequality,

$$25 \times 1125 + 25x < 45 \times 1125$$

Transferring the term 25×1125 to the RHS,

$$25x < 45 \times 1125 - 25 \times 1125$$

$\Rightarrow \quad 25x < 1125(45 - 25)$

$\Rightarrow \quad 25x < 1125 \times 20$

On dividing both sides by 25, we get

$$\frac{25}{25}x < \frac{1125 \times 20}{25}$$ (using rule 2)

$\Rightarrow \quad x < 45 \times 20$

$\Rightarrow \quad x < 900$ ...(i)

Now, taking last two parts of the above inequality,

$$45 \times 1125 < 30 \times 1125 + 30x$$

Transferring the term (30×1125) to LHS,

$$45 \times 1125 - 30 \times 1125 < 30x$$

$\Rightarrow \quad 1125(45 - 30) < 30x$

$\Rightarrow \quad 1125 \times 15 < 30x$

$\Rightarrow \quad 30x > 1125 \times 15$

On dividing both sides by 30, we get

$$\frac{30x}{30} > \frac{1125 \times 15}{30}$$ (using rule 2)

$\Rightarrow \quad x > \frac{1125}{2} \Rightarrow x > 562.5$ ...(ii)

Hence, from Eqs. (i) and (ii), $562.5 < x < 900$ *i.e.*, $x \in (562.5, 900)$.

The number of litres of water to be added should be greater than 562.5 L and less than 900 L.

Question 14 IQ of a person is given by the formula $IQ = \frac{MA}{CA} \times 100$ where, MA is the mental age and CA is chronological age. If $80 \le IQ \le 140$ for a group of 12 years old children, find the range of their mental age.

Sol. Given, $$80 \le IQ \le 140 \quad \ldots(i)$$

On putting $IQ = \frac{MA}{CA} \times 100$ in Eq. (i), we get

$$80 \le \frac{MA}{CA} \times 100 \le 140$$

$$\Rightarrow \quad 80 \le \frac{MA}{12} \times 100 \le 140 \quad (\because \text{given CA} = 12 \text{ years})$$

On multiplying by 12 in each term, we get

$$80 \times 12 \le \frac{MA}{12} \times 100 \times 12 \le 140 \times 12 \quad \text{(using rule 2)}$$

$$\Rightarrow \quad 960 \le MA \times 100 \le 1680$$

On dividing by 100 in each term, we get

$$\frac{960}{100} \le \frac{MA \times 100}{100} \le \frac{1680}{100} \quad \text{(using rule 2)}$$

$$\Rightarrow \quad 9.6 \le MA \le 16.8$$

$$\Rightarrow \quad MA \in [9.6, 16.8]$$

Hence, mental age should be greater than equal to 9.6 but less than equal to 16.8.

DIKSHA APP Questions

☐ Multiple Choice Questions

Q.1 If x is a real number and $|x|<3$, then x lies between?

(a) $x \geq 3$ (b) $x \leq -3$ (c) $-3 \leq x \leq 3$ (d) $-3 < x < 3$

Sol. (d) Given, $|x|< 3$

For real values of x. It lies between -3 and 3.

$\Rightarrow$ $-3 < x < 3$

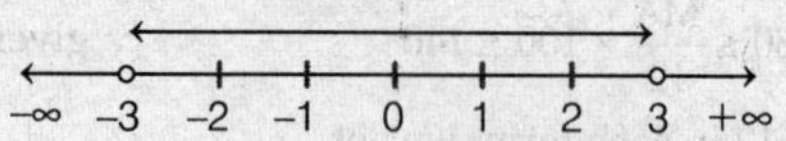

i.e., $(-3,3)$

Q.2 What is the solution set of $\left|\dfrac{2}{x-6}\right| \geq 1$, where $x \neq 6$ is

(a) $[4,6) \cup (6,8]$ (b) $(6, 8)$ (c) $(-\infty,4)$ (d) $(6,\infty)$

Sol. (a) Given, $\left|\dfrac{2}{x-6}\right| \geq 1$, where $x \neq 6$.

$\Rightarrow$ $\left(\dfrac{2}{x-6}\right) \leq -1$ or $\left(\dfrac{2}{x-6}\right) \geq 1$ [if $|x| \geq a$, then $x \leq -a$ or $x \geq a$]

$\Rightarrow$ $\dfrac{x-6}{2} \geq -1$ or $\dfrac{x-6}{2} \leq 1$

[taking reciprocal of both inequality.]

$\Rightarrow$ $x-6 \geq -2$ or $x-6 \leq 2$ [adding 6 in both inequality.]

$\Rightarrow$ $x \geq 4$ or $x \leq 8$

$\therefore$ Solution set $= [4,6) \cup (6,8]$.

Q.3 If $x^2 + 4ax + 4 > 0$ for all x, then

(a) $0 < a < 1$ (b) $-1 < a < 1$ (c) $-1 < a < 0$ (d) $-4 < a < 4$

Sol. (b) Given, $1x^2 + 4ax + 4 > 0$

We know that if $ax^2 + bx + c > 0$, then $b^2 - 4ac < 0$.

Here, $a = 1, b = 4a, c = 4$

Put in $b^2 - 4ac < 0$

$$(4a)^2 - 4 \times 1 \times 4 < 0 \Rightarrow 16a^2 - 16 < 0$$

$$\Rightarrow \quad a^2 - 1 < 0 \Rightarrow a^2 < 1$$

Hence, $-1 < a < 1$.

Permutations and Combinations

CHAPTER 06

Important Points

01 **Fundamental Principle of Counting (FPC)** If there are m different ways of occurrence of an event and n different ways of occurrence of another event, then the total the number of ways of occurrence of the event is $m \times n$.

02 **Factorial Notation** The notation '$n!$' represents the product of first n natural numbers.

i.e., $n! = 1 \cdot 2 \cdot 3 \cdot 4 \ldots (n-1)n$ ($n!$ is read as factorial n)

$$n! = n(n-1)! = n(n-1)(n-2)!$$
$$= n(n-1)(n-2)(n-3)! \text{ and so on.}$$

We define $0! = 1$

03 **Permutations** A permutation is an arrangement in a definite order of a number of distinct objects taken some or all at a time.

The number of permutations of n different objects taken r at a time, when $0 < r \le n$ and the objects do not repeat is ^nP_r or $P(n, r)$.

where, $$^nP_r = P(n, r) = \frac{n!}{(n-r)!}, 0 \le r \le n$$

Remember

(i) The number of permutations of n different objects taken r at a time, where repetition is allowed, is n^r.

(ii) The number of permutations of n objects, where p objects are of the same kind and rest are all different $= \frac{n!}{p!}$

(iii) The number of permutations of n objects, where p_1 objects are of one kind, p_2 are of second kind, ..., p_k are of the kth kind and the rest, if any, are of different kind is $\frac{n!}{p_1!\, p_2! \ldots p_k!}$

04 Key properties of permutation

(i) ${}^nP_n = n(n-1)(n-2)...3 \times 2 \times 1 = n!$

(ii) ${}^nP_0 = \dfrac{n!}{n!} = 1$

(iii) ${}^nP_1 = n$

(iv) ${}^nP_{n-1} = n!$

(v) ${}^{n-1}P_r + r({}^{n-1}P_{r-1}) = {}^nP_r$

(vi) $\dfrac{{}^nP_r}{{}^nP_{r-1}} = n - r + 1$

05 Combinations Each of different selections made by taking some or all of a number of objects, irrespective of their arrangements is called a combination.

The number of all combinations of n distinct objects taken r at a time is given by

$${}^nC_r = \frac{n!}{(n-r)!\, r!}, 0 \le r \le n$$

Understanding between permutations and combinations

- Let (A), (B) and (C) are three different objects, then the collection of permutations of 3 different objects taken 2 at a time. (Order is important)

  Number of permutations $= {}^3P_2 = 6$

Ⓐ	Ⓑ
Ⓑ	Ⓐ
Ⓑ	Ⓒ
Ⓒ	Ⓑ
Ⓒ	Ⓐ
Ⓐ	Ⓒ

The collection of combinations of 3 different objects taken 2 at a time. (Order is not important)

Number of combinations $= {}^3C_2 = 3$

Ⓐ	Ⓑ
Ⓑ	Ⓒ
Ⓒ	Ⓐ

Note (A), (B) and (B), (A) are same in combination because the order of objects does not matter, but (A), (B) and (B), (A) are different permutations.

Remember

(i) In a combination, only selection is made whereas in a permutation not only a selection is made but also an arrangement in a definite order is considered.

(ii) Generally, the word 'arrangements' used for permutations and the word 'selections' is used for combinations.

(iii) If all (some) things are identical, then we do not apply ${}^nC_r$ or ${}^nP_r$.

(iv) The number of ways of selecting one or more than one in n different objects is ${}^nC_1 + {}^nC_2 + \ldots\ldots + {}^nC_n = 2^n - 1$.

06 Shortcut tricks for solving ${}^nC_r$

1. ${}^nC_1 = n, {}^nC_n = 1 = {}^nC_0$

   ${}^nC_2 = \dfrac{n(n-1)}{2}, {}^nC_3 = \dfrac{n(n-1)(n-2)}{6},$

   ${}^nC_4 = \dfrac{n(n-1)(n-2)(n-3)}{24}$

2. ${}^nC_r = {}^nC_{n-r}$ (e.g., ${}^{10}C_8 = {}^{10}C_2 = \dfrac{10 \times 9}{2} = 45$)

3. ${}^nC_r + {}^nC_{r-1} = {}^{n+1}C_r$

4. ${}^nC_x = {}^nC_y \Rightarrow x + y = n$ or $x = y$

5. ${}^nP_r = {}^nC_r\ r!$

Exercise 6.1

Question 1 How many 3-digit numbers can be formed from the digits 1, 2, 3, 4 and 5 assuming that

(i) repetition of the digits is allowed?

(ii) repetition of the digits is not allowed?

Sol. (i) When repetition of digits is allowed,

Since, there are 5 digits.

Therefore, number of ways to fill each place is 5.

Hence, by the Fundamental Principles of Counting (FPC), total number of ways = $5 \times 5 \times 5 = 125$

(ii) When repetition is not allowed,

Since, there are 5 digits *i.e.*, 1, 2, 3, 4, 5.

Therefore, number of ways to fill the unit's place = 5,

number of ways to fill the ten's place = 4,

and number of ways to fill the hundred's place = 3

Hence, by FPC, total number of ways = $5 \times 4 \times 3 = 60$

Question 2 How many 3-digits even numbers can be formed from the digits 1, 2, 3, 4, 5, 6 if the digits can be repeated?

◎ ***Thinking Process*** We know that a number is even, if its unit's place is even. First we select an even number for units place and after that two numbers are selected.

Sol. Even digits = 2, 4, 6

∴ Number of ways to fill the unit's place = 3,

Number of ways to fill the ten's place = 6,

Number of ways of fill the hundred's place = 6

Hence, by FPC total number of ways = $3 \times 6 \times 6 = 108$

Question 3 How many 4-letters code can be formed using the first 10 letters of the English alphabet, if no letter can be repeated?

Sol. Number of ways to fill the I place = 10,

number of ways to fill the II place = 9,

number of ways to fill III place = 8

and number of ways to fill IV place = 7

Hence, by FPC total number of ways = $10 \times 9 \times 8 \times 7 = 630 \times 8 = 5040$

Question 4 How many 5-digit telephone numbers can be constructed using the digits 0 to 9 if each number starts with 67 and no digit appears more than once?

◎ ***Thinking Process*** Take the choice only for last three digits with keeping in mind that repetition is not allowed.

Sol. Out of the ten digits 0 to 9, two are fixed. Also no digit appears more than once. Therefore, the remaining digits = 10 − 2 = 8

Now, number of ways to fill the III place = 8,

number of ways to fill the IV place = 7

and number of ways to fill the V place = 6

6	7			
I	II	III	IV	V

Hence, by FPC total number of ways $= 8 \times 7 \times 6 = 56 \times 6 = 336$

Question 5 A coin is tossed 3 times and the outcomes are recorded. How many possible outcomes are there?

Sol. In tossing a coin, there are 2 possible outcomes (head and tail). In tossing the coin second time, again there are 2 possible outcomes and in third time, there are again 2 possible outcomes.

Hence, by FPC total number of outcomes $= 2 \times 2 \times 2 = 2^3 = 8$

Question 6 Given 5 flags of different colours, how many different signals can be generated, if each signal requires the use of 2 flags, one below the other?

Sol. Number of ways choose the first flag = 5

and number of ways to choose the second flag from the rest of four flags = 4

Hence, by FPC total number of ways $= 5 \times 4 = 20$

Exercise 6.2

Question 1 Evaluate

(i) 8! (ii) 4! − 3!

(**Hint** Here, we will use the formula $n! = n(n-1)(n-2)\ldots 3 \times 2 \times 1$.)

Sol. (i) We have, $8! = 8 \times 7 \times 6 \times 5 \times 4 \times 3 \times 2 \times 1 = 40320$

(ii) We have, $4! - 3! = (4 \times 3 \times 2 \times 1) - (3 \times 2 \times 1) = 24 - 6 = 18$

Mistake Alert The two factorial numbers can not be add, subtract, divide and multiply directly. Example, $3! + 3! \neq 6!$, $3! - 2! \neq 1!$, $3! \times 3! \neq 9!$ and $\frac{4!}{2!} \neq 2!$

Question 2 Is $3!+4!=7!$?

Sol. No, because

LHS $= 3! + 4! = (3 \times 2 \times 1) + (4 \times 3 \times 2 \times 1) = 6 + 24 = 30$ ...(i)

RHS $= 7! = 7 \times 6 \times 5 \times 4 \times 3 \times 2 \times 1 = 5040$ ...(ii)

From Eqs. (i) and (ii), LHS $\neq$ RHS

Question 3 Compute $\frac{8!}{6! \times 2!}$.

◎ *Thinking Process* Open the factorial number of numerator until it same as the larger factorial number of denominator to make the calculation easier. Use $n! = n(n-1)!$

Sol. We have, $\frac{8!}{6! \times 2!} = \frac{8 \times 7 \times 6!}{6! \times 2 \times 1} = \frac{56}{2} = 28$

Question 4 Solve $\frac{1}{6!} + \frac{1}{7!} = \frac{x}{8!}$

Sol. Given, $\frac{1}{6!} + \frac{1}{7!} = \frac{x}{8!}$

$$\frac{1}{6!} + \frac{1}{7 \times 6!} = \frac{x}{8 \times 7 \times 6!}$$

Take $\frac{1}{6!}$ common from LHS,

$$\frac{1}{6!}\left[1 + \frac{1}{7}\right] = \frac{x}{8 \times 7 \times 6!} \Rightarrow \frac{1}{1} + \frac{1}{7} = \frac{x}{8 \times 7} \Rightarrow \frac{7+1}{7} = \frac{x}{8 \times 7}$$

$$\Rightarrow \qquad x = 8 \times 8 = 64$$

Question 5 Evaluate $\frac{n!}{(n-r)!}$, when

(i) $n=6, r=2$ (ii) $n=9, r=5$

Sol. (i) $\frac{n!}{(n-r)!}$

On putting $n = 6$ and $r = 2$ in the given expression, we get

$$\frac{6!}{(6-2)!} = \frac{6!}{4!} = \frac{6 \times 5 \times 4!}{4!} = 30$$

(ii) $\frac{n!}{(n-r)!}$

On putting $n = 9$ $r = 5$ in the given expression, we get

$$\frac{9!}{(9-5)!} = \frac{9!}{4!} = \frac{9 \times 8 \times 7 \times 6 \times 5 \times 4!}{4!}$$

$$= 72 \times 42 \times 5 = 72 \times 210 = 15120$$

Note We have to open the factorial of the numerator to the extent that it is present in the denominator.

Exercise 6.3

Question 1 How many 3-digit numbers can be formed by using the digits 1 to 9 if no digit is repeated?

◎ *Thinking Process* Here, we can use either ^nP_r or FPC.

Sol. Number of three-digit numbers made by taking 3 different numbers out of 9 numbers,

$$^9P_3 = \frac{9!}{(9-3)!} = \frac{9!}{6!}$$

$$= \frac{9 \times 8 \times 7 \times 6!}{6!} = 504 \qquad \left[\because {}^nP_r = \frac{n!}{(n-r)!}\right]$$

Question 2 How many 4 digit numbers are there with no digit repeated?

◎ *Thinking Process* We have ten digits from 0 to 9 but first place can't be filled with 0, as by doing so, the number will be of 3 digit only.

Sol. Here, the first place can be filled in 9 ways.
The second place can be filled in 9 ways.
The third place can be filled in 8 ways.
The fourth place can be filled in 7 ways.
Hence, by FPC total number of ways $= 9 \times 9 \times 8 \times 7$
$= 4536$ ways

I II III IV

Note Four digit numbers *i.e.*, unit's, ten's and hundred's place can be filled by using the digits '0 to 9' but in a thousand's place 0 digit never occur because it form the three digit number.

Question 3 How many 3-digit even numbers can be made using the digits 1, 2, 3, 4, 6, 7, if no digit is repeated ?

◎ *Thinking Process* A number is even, if its unit place is even. Then, first we select the even number for the unit place and select other two numbers.

Sol. For 3-digit even numbers, the unit's place can be occupied by one of the 3 digits 2, 4 or 6 (out of the given digits)

H T U

∴ Number of ways to fill the units place = 3
Number of ways to fill the tens place (in rest of 5 digits) = 5
Number of ways to fill the hundreds place (in rest of 4 digits) = 4
Hence, by FPC total number of ways $= 3 \times 5 \times 4 = 60$

Question 4 Find the number of 4-digit numbers that can be formed using the digits 1, 2, 3, 4, 5, if no digit is repeated. How many of these will be even?

Sol. Given, total number of digits = 5 (given 1, 2, 3, 4, 5)

$\therefore$ Number of ways to fill the unit's place = 5,

Th H T U

number of ways to fill the ten's place = 4,

number of ways to fill the hundred's place = 3

and number of ways to fill the thousand's place = 2

Hence, total number of ways by FPC = $5 \times 4 \times 3 \times 2 = 120$

Again,

Th H T U

number of ways to fill the unit's place = 2 (out of 2 and 4)

number of ways to fill the ten's place = 4,

number of ways to fill the hundred's place = 3

and number of ways to fill the thousand's place = 2

Hence, by FPC total number of ways = $2 \times 4 \times 3 \times 2 = 48$

Question 5 From a committee of 8 persons, in how many ways can we choose a chairman and a vice chairman assuming one person can not hold more than one position?

Sol. Out of 8 persons, one person can be chosen for chairman in 8 ways. Now, a person cannot hold more than one position *i.e.*, out of 7 persons, one person can be chosen for vice chairman in 7 ways.

Hence, by FPC total number of ways = $8 \times 7 = 56$

Question 6 Find n if ${}^{n-1}P_3 : {}^nP_4 = 1:9$.

◎ ***Thinking Process*** We will use the formula ${}^nP_r = \dfrac{n!}{(n-r)!}$ to simplify it.

Sol. Given, ${}^{n-1}P_3 : {}^nP_4 = 1:9$

$$\therefore \quad \frac{(n-1)!}{(n-1-3)!} : \frac{n!}{(n-4)!} = 1:9 \qquad \left[\because {}^nP_r = \frac{n!}{(n-r)!}\right]$$

$$\Rightarrow \quad \frac{(n-1)!}{(n-4)!} : \frac{n(n-1)!}{(n-4)!} = 1:9 \qquad [\because n! = n(n-1)!]$$

$$\Rightarrow \quad \frac{(n-1)!}{(n-4)!} \times \frac{(n-4)!}{n(n-1)!} = \frac{1}{9}$$

$$\Rightarrow \quad \frac{1}{n} = \frac{1}{9}$$

$$\Rightarrow \quad n = 9$$

Question 7 Find r if (i) ${}^5P_r = 2\ {}^6P_{r-1}$ (ii) ${}^5P_r = {}^6P_{r-1}$.

Sol. (i) Given, ${}^5P_r = 2\ {}^6P_{r-1}$

$$\frac{5!}{(5-r)!} = 2 \times \frac{6!}{(6-r+1)!} \qquad \left[\because {}^nP_r = \frac{n!}{(n-r)!}\right]$$

$$\Rightarrow \quad \frac{5!}{(5-r)!} = 2 \times \frac{6 \times 5!}{(7-r)!} \Rightarrow \frac{1}{(5-r)!} = \frac{12}{(7-r)(6-r)(5-r)!}$$

$\Rightarrow \quad (7-r)(6-r) = 12$

$\Rightarrow \quad 42 - 7r - 6r + r^2 = 12$

$\Rightarrow \quad r^2 - 13r + 30 = 0$

$\Rightarrow \quad r^2 - 10r - 3r + 30 = 0$

$\Rightarrow \quad r(r-10) - 3(r-10) = 0$

$\Rightarrow \quad (r-10)(r-3) = 0$

Hence, $r = 10, 3$ but we will take only $r = 3$ as $0 \le r \le 5$.

(ii) Given, ${}^5P_r = {}^6P_{r-1}$

$$\therefore \quad \frac{5!}{(5-r)!} = \frac{6!}{\{6-(r-1)\}!} \qquad \left(\because {}^nP_r = \frac{n!}{(n-r)!}\right)$$

$$\Rightarrow \quad \frac{5!}{(5-r)!} = \frac{6 \times 5!}{(6-r+1)!} \Rightarrow \frac{5!}{(5-r)!} = \frac{6 \times 5!}{(7-r)!}$$

$$\Rightarrow \quad \frac{1}{(5-r)!} = \frac{6}{(7-r)(6-r)(5-r)!}$$

$\Rightarrow \quad (7-r)(6-r) = 6 \Rightarrow 42 - 7r - 6r + r^2 = 6$

$\Rightarrow \quad 42 - 13r + r^2 = 6$

$\Rightarrow \quad r^2 - 13r + 42 - 6 = 0$

$\Rightarrow \quad r^2 - 13r + 36 = 0$

Now, factorizing it by splitting the middle term,

$\Rightarrow \quad r^2 - (9+4)r + 36 = 0$

$\Rightarrow \quad r^2 - 9r - 4r + 36 = 0$

$\Rightarrow \quad r(r-9) - 4(r-9) = 0$

$\Rightarrow \quad (r-4)(r-9) = 0 \Rightarrow r = 4, 9$

But we will only take $r = 4$ as $0 \le r \le 5$.

Question 8 How many words, with or without meaning, can be formed using all the letters of the word EQUATION, using each letter exactly once?

Sol. The word EQUATION has 8 different letters.

$\therefore$ Number of ways taken 8 letters at a time $= {}^8P_8 = \dfrac{8!}{(8-8)!} = \dfrac{8!}{0!}$

$$= \frac{8 \times 7 \times 6 \times 5 \times 4 \times 3 \times 2 \times 1}{1} = 40320 \qquad (\because 0! = 1)$$

Question 9 How many words, with or without meaning can be made from the letters of the word MONDAY, assuming that no letter is repeated, if.

(i) 4 letters are used at a time,

(ii) all letters are used at a time,

(iii) all letters are used but first letter is a vowel?

◎ *Thinking Process* The number of different words means the number of permutation of a letter of the given word *i.e.*, use the concept ${}^nP_r$ for each part.

Sol. In the word MONDAY, all letters are different.

(i) Out of 6 different letters 4 letters can be selected in ${}^6P_4$ ways.

$\therefore$ Required number of words $= {}^6P_4$

$$= \frac{6!}{(6-4)!} = \frac{6!}{2!} = \frac{6 \times 5 \times 4 \times 3 \times 2!}{2!} = 360$$

(ii) The word 'MONDAY' has 6 different letters.

Number of ways taking 6 letters at a time $= {}^6P_6$

$\therefore$ Required number of words $= {}^6P_6$

$$= \frac{6!}{(6-6)!} = \frac{6 \times 5 \times 4 \times 3 \times 2 \times 1}{0!} = 720$$

(iii) First, we will fix the vowel.

In the word MONDAY, there are two vowels O and A.

$\therefore$ First letter can be chosen by 2 ways.

Number of ways taking 5 different letters from remaining 5 letters $= {}^5P_5$

$\therefore$ Required number of words $= {}^5P_5 = \frac{5!}{(5-5)!} = \frac{5!}{0!}$

$$= 5 \times 4 \times 3 \times 2 \times 1 = 120$$

Hence, by FPC, total number of ways $= 2 \times 120 = 240$

Question 10 In how many of the distinct permutations of the letters in the MISSISSIPPI do the four I's not come together ?

Sol. The word MISSISSIPPI has 11 letters in which

$M \rightarrow 1$ time

$I \rightarrow 4$ times

$S \rightarrow 4$ times

$P \rightarrow 2$ times

The number of permutations of the word 'MISSISSIPPI' in which 4 I's and 4 S's are alike

$$= \frac{11!}{4!\,4!\,2!} \quad \ldots(i)$$

If all the I's are together, then they will be considered as one letter and remaining 7 letters and 1 I's letter (including 4 I's) will be considered as 8 letters. So, the number of permutation is $\frac{8!}{4!\,2!}$.

Hence, total number of arrangements $= \frac{11!}{4!\,4!\,2!} - \frac{8!}{4!\,2!}$

$$= \frac{11 \times 10 \times 9 \times 8 \times 7 \times 6 \times 5 \times 4!}{4! \times 4 \times 3 \times 2 \times 1 \times 2 \times 1} - \frac{8 \times 7 \times 6 \times 5 \times 4!}{4! \times 2 \times 1} = 34650 - 840 = 33810$$

Question 11 In how many ways can the letters of the word PERMUTATIONS be arranged, if the

(i) words start with P and end with S

(ii) vowels are all together

(iii) there are always 4 letters between P and S ?

Sol. The word 'PERMUTATIONS' has 12 letters i.e.

P — 1 time
E — 1 time
R — 1 time
M — 1 time
U — 1 time
T — 2 times
A — 1 time
I — 1 time
O — 1 time
N — 1 time
S — 1 time

(i) Word start with P and end with S *i.e.*,

P □ □ □ □ □ □ □ □ □ □ S

First and last position are already filled by P and S, respectively.

Hence, remaining 10 positions can be filled in $= \frac{10!}{2!}$ ways

$$= \frac{10 \times 9 \times 8 \times 7 \times 6 \times 5 \times 4 \times 3 \times 2!}{2!}$$

$$= 720 \times 7 \times 6 \times 5 \times 4 \times 3 = 720 \times 2520 = 1814400$$

(ii) If all the vowels are together, then they will be considered as one letter, *i.e.*, (A, E, I, O, U) and remaining 7 letters and 1 vowel (including 5 vowels) will be considered as 8 letters and 5 vowels can be arranged in 5! ways.

$\therefore$ Required number of permutations $= \frac{5! \times 8!}{2!}$

$$= \frac{5 \times 4 \times 3 \times 2 \times 1 \times 8 \times 7 \times 6 \times 5 \times 4 \times 3 \times 2 \times 1}{2 \times 1} = 2419200$$

(iii) Total number of letters to be arranged = 12

There are always 4 letters between P and S *i.e.*,

	1	2	3	4	5	6	7	8	9	10	11	12
Ist ways	P					S						
IInd ways		P					S					
IIIrd ways			P					S				
IVth ways				P					S			
Vth ways					P					S		
VIth ways						P					S	
VIIth ways							P					S

So, P and S having 4 places between them can be filled in 7 ways.

So, P and S or S and P can be filled in 7 + 7 = 14 ways

Remaining 10 letters (in which T repeated twice) can be filled in

$= \frac{10!}{2!}$ ways

Hence, by FPC total number of ways

$$= 14 \times \frac{10!}{2!} = \frac{14 \times 10 \times 9 \times 8 \times 7 \times 6 \times 5 \times 4 \times 3 \times 2 \times 1}{2}$$

$$= \frac{14 \times 3628800}{2} = 25401600$$

Mistake Alert Students may get confuse to arrange the letters *P* and *S*. So, be careful in this arrangement.

Exercise 6.4

Question 1 If $^nC_8 = {}^nC_2$, find $^nC_2$.

Thinking Process We will use the result $^nC_x = {}^nC_y \Rightarrow x + y = n$ and simplify the given expression easily.

Sol. Given, $^nC_8 = {}^nC_2 \quad \Rightarrow \quad n = 8 + 2 = 10$

Now, $^nC_2 = {}^{10}C_2 = \frac{10 \times 9}{2} = 5 \times 9 = 45 \qquad \left(\because {}^nC_2 = \frac{n(n-1)}{2}\right)$

Question 2 Determine n if

(i) ${}^{2n}C_3 : {}^{n}C_2 = 12:1$ (ii) ${}^{2n}C_3 : {}^{n}C_3 = 11:1$

◎ *Thinking Process* In (i) and (ii) part, we will use ${}^{n}C_3 = \dfrac{n(n-1)(n-2)}{6}$ and ${}^{n}C_2 = \dfrac{n(n-1)}{2}$ and then simplify.

Sol. (i) Give, ${}^{2n}C_3 : {}^{n}C_2 = 12:1$

$$\therefore \quad \frac{2n(2n-1)(2n-2)}{6} : \frac{n(n-1)}{2} = 12:1$$

$$\Rightarrow \quad \frac{2n(2n-1)\,2(n-1)}{6} \times \frac{2}{n(n-1)} = \frac{12}{1}$$

$$\Rightarrow \quad \frac{4(2n-1)}{3} = \frac{12}{1} \Rightarrow \frac{2n-1}{3} = 3$$

$$\Rightarrow \quad 2n-1 = 9 \quad \Rightarrow \quad 2n = 9+1 \Rightarrow 2n = 10 \quad \Rightarrow \quad n = 5$$

(ii) Given, ${}^{2n}C_3 : {}^{n}C_3 = 11:1$

$$\therefore \quad \frac{2n(2n-1)(2n-2)}{6} : \frac{n(n-1)(n-2)}{6} = 11:1$$

$$\Rightarrow \quad 2n(2n-1)\,2(n-1) : n(n-1)(n-2) = 11:1$$

$$\Rightarrow \quad 2n(2n-1)\,2(n-1) \times \frac{1}{n(n-1)(n-2)} = \frac{11}{1} \Rightarrow \frac{4(2n-1)}{n-2} = \frac{11}{1}$$

$$\Rightarrow \quad 8n - 4 = 11n - 22 \Rightarrow 11n - 8n = -4 + 22 \quad \Rightarrow 3n = 18 \Rightarrow n = 6$$

Question 3 How many chords can be drawn through 21 points on a circle?

◎ *Thinking Process* We can get a chord by joining any two points on the circle. So, if there are n points then total number of chords (or lines) is ${}^{n}C_2$.

Sol. Here, $n = 21$ then total number of chords $= {}^{21}C_2 = \dfrac{21 \times 20}{2} \quad \left(\because {}^{n}C_2 = \dfrac{n(n-1)}{2}\right)$

$$= 210 \text{ ways}$$

Question 4 In how many ways can a team of 3 boys and 3 girls be selected from 5 boys and 4 girls?

Sol. 3 boys out of 5 boys can be selected in ${}^{5}C_3$ ways and 3 girls out of 4 girls can be selected in ${}^{4}C_3$ ways.

Hence, by FPC total number of ways

$$= {}^{5}C_3 \times {}^{4}C_3 = {}^{5}C_2 \times {}^{4}C_1 \qquad (\because {}^{n}C_r = {}^{n}C_{n-r})$$

$$= \frac{5 \times 4}{2} \times 4 \qquad \left(\because {}^{n}C_2 = \frac{n(n-1)}{2}, {}^{n}C_1 = n\right)$$

$$= 40$$

Mistake Alert Please be careful while using either ${}^{n}C_r$ or ${}^{n}P_r$. If the things are to be only selected, then use ${}^{n}C_r$ and if the things are to be selected and arranged then use ${}^{n}P_r$.

Question 5 Find the number of ways of selecting 9 balls from 6 red balls, 5 white balls and 5 blue balls if each selection consists of 3 balls of each colour.

Sol. Since, 3 red balls out of 6 red balls can be selected in ${}^6C_3$ ways, 3 white balls out of 5 white balls can be selected in ${}^5C_3$ ways and 3 blue balls out of 5 blue balls can be selected in ${}^5C_3$ ways.

Hence, by FPC total number of ways selecting 9 balls (3 balls of each colour) is

$$= {}^6C_3 \times {}^5C_3 \times {}^5C_3 = {}^6C_3 \times {}^5C_2 \times {}^5C_2 \qquad (\because {}^nC_r = {}^nC_{n-r})$$

$$= \frac{6 \times 5 \times 4}{6} \times \frac{5 \times 4}{2} \times \frac{5 \times 4}{2} \qquad \left(\because {}^nC_3 = \frac{n(n-1)(n-2)}{6},\ {}^nC_2 = \frac{n(n-1)}{2} \right)$$

$$= 20 \times 10 \times 10 = 2000 \text{ ways}$$

Question 6 Determine the number of 5 card combinations out of a deck of 52 cards if there is exactly one ace in each combination.

◎ ***Thinking Process*** In a pack of 52 cards, there are four aces *i.e.*, one ace will be selected from 4 cards and remaining 4 cards will be selected from rest of 48 (*i.e.*, $52 - 4 = 48$) cards.

Sol. Number of ways selecting one ace from 4 aces $= {}^4C_1$

Number of ways selecting 4 cards out of 48 cards $= {}^{48}C_4$

Hence, by FPC, 5 cards out of 52 cards with exactly one ace can be selected in ${}^4C_1 \times {}^{48}C_4$ ways

$$= 4 \times \frac{48 \times 47 \times 46 \times 45}{24} \qquad \left(\because {}^nC_1 = n \text{ and } {}^nC_4 = \frac{n(n-1)(n-2)(n-3)}{24} \right)$$

$$= \frac{48 \times 47 \times 46 \times 45}{6} = 8 \times 47 \times 46 \times 45 = 778320 \text{ ways}$$

Question 7 In how many ways can one select a cricket team of eleven from 17 players in which only 5 players can bowl if each cricket team of 11 must include exactly 4 bowlers?

Sol. Out of 17 players, 5 are bowlers, therefore, there are $17 - 5 = 12$ other players i.e.

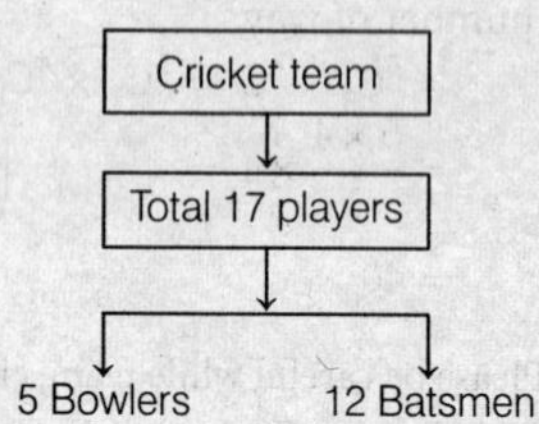

We are to select 11 players including exactly 4 bowlers.

Hence, 4 bowlers will be selected from 5 bowlers and remaining 7 players will be selected from 12 batsmen.

Now, 4 bowlers out of 5 bowlers can be selected in ${}^5C_4$ ways.

7 players out of 12 players can be selected in ${}^{12}C_7$ ways.

Hence, by FPC, total number of ways selecting the eleven players

$= {}^5C_4 \times {}^{12}C_7 = {}^5C_1 \times {}^{12}C_5 \qquad (\because {}^nC_r = {}^nC_{n-r})$

$= \dfrac{5 \times 12 \times 11 \times 10 \times 9 \times 8}{120} \qquad \left(\because {}^nC_5 = \dfrac{n(n-1)(n-2)(n-3)(n-4)}{120}\right)$

$= 5 \times 11 \times 9 \times 8 = 55 \times 72 = 3960$ ways

Question 8 A bag contains 5 black and 6 red balls. Determine the number of ways in which 2 black and 3 red balls can be selected.

Sol. Out of 5 black balls, 2 black balls can be selected in ${}^5C_2$ ways.

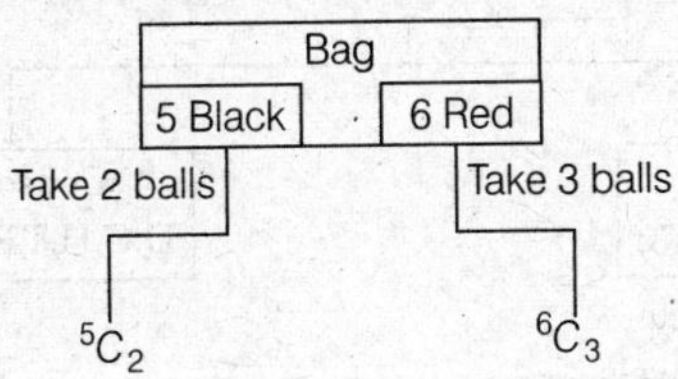

Out of 6 red balls, 3 red balls can be selected in ${}^6C_3$ ways.

Hence, by FPC, total number of ways

$$= {}^5C_2 \times {}^6C_3 \qquad \left(\because {}^nC_2 = \frac{n(n-1)}{2} \text{ and } {}^nC_3 = \frac{n(n-1)(n-2)}{6}\right)$$

$$= \frac{5 \times 4}{2} \times \frac{6 \times 5 \times 4}{6} = 10 \times 20 = 200 \text{ ways}$$

Question 9 In how many ways can a student choose a programme of 5 courses if 9 courses are available and 2 specific courses are compulsory for every student?

Sol. Given, total number of available courses = 9

Out of these 5 courses have to be chosen. But it is given that 2 courses are compulsory for every student *i.e.*, you have to choose only 3 courses instead of 5, out of 7 instead of 9.

It can be done in ${}^7C_3$ ways

$$= \frac{7 \times 6 \times 5}{6} = 35 \text{ ways} \qquad \left(\because {}^nC_3 = \frac{n(n-1)(n-2)}{6}\right)$$

Miscellaneous Exercise

Question 1 How many words, with or without meaning, each of 2 vowels and 3 consonants can be formed from the letters of the word DAUGHTER?

◎ ***Thinking Process*** First find number of vowels and consonants in the given word and select 2 vowels and 3 consonants between them and arrange these five letters in 5! ways.

Sol. In the word DAUGHTER, there are 3 vowels, namely, A, U, E and 5 consonants, namely D, G, H, T, R.

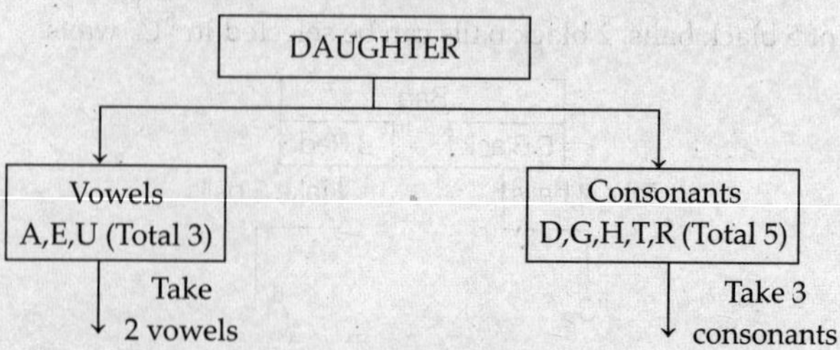

2 vowels out of 3 vowels can be selected = ${}^3C_2$ ways

3 consonants out of 5 consonants can be selected = ${}^5C_3$ ways

And these 5 letters (2 vowels and 3 consonants) can be arranged in 5! ways.

Hence, by FPC, total number of ways

$$= {}^3C_2 \times {}^5C_3 \times 5! = {}^3C_1 \times {}^5C_2 \times 5!$$

$$= \frac{3 \times 5 \times 4 \times 5 \times 4 \times 3 \times 2 \times 1}{2} = 3600 \text{ ways}$$

🔔 ***Mistake Alert*** Students should not forget to take the all possible ways of arrangement.

Question 2 How many words, with or without meaning, can be formed using all the letters of the word 'EQUATION' at a time so that the vowels and consonants occur together?

◎ ***Thinking Process*** Firstly, we will separate the consonants and vowels and consider each time the set of vowels and consonants as a single letter.

Sol. Given word is EQUAT ION

Vowels → EUAIO

Consonants → TQN

The vowels can be arranged in 5! ways.

The consonants can be arranged in 3! ways.

These vowels and consonants (both are as a single letter) can be arranged in 2! ways *i.e.*, Either all vowels first and then all consonants or all consonants first and then all vowels.

Hence, by FPC, total number of ways

$$= 5! \times 3! \times 2! = 5 \times 4 \times 3 \times 2 \times 1 \times 3 \times 2 \times 1 \times 2 \times 1$$
$$= 120 \times 6 \times 2 = 120 \times 12 = 1440$$

Question 3 A committee of 7 has to be formed from 9 boys and 4 girls. In how many ways can this be done when the committee consists of

(i) exactly 3 girls? (ii) atleast 3 girls? (iii) atmost 3 girls?

Sol. (i) Out of 7 persons, we want to select exactly 3 girls *i.e.*, remaining 4 person will be boys.

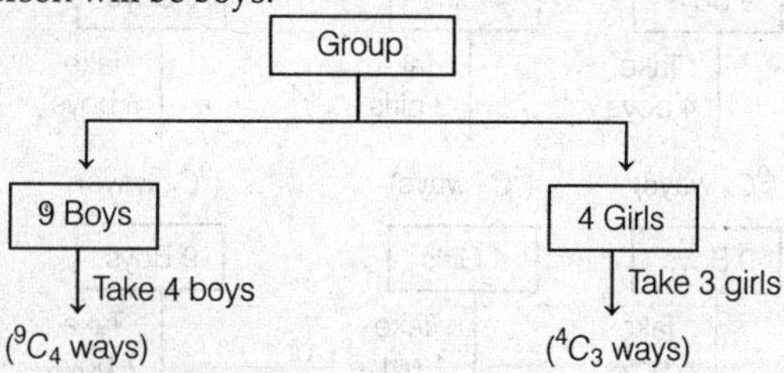

4 boys out of 9 boys can be selected in $^9C_4$ ways.
3 girls out of 4 girls can be selected in $^4C_3$ ways.
Hence, by FPC, total number of ways for making the committee

$$= {}^9C_4 \times {}^4C_3$$
$$= \frac{9 \times 8 \times 7 \times 6}{24} \times {}^4C_1 \qquad (\because {}^nC_r = {}^nC_{n-r})$$
$$= \frac{9 \times 8 \times 7 \times 6 \times 4}{24} \qquad (\because {}^nC_1 = n)$$
$$= 9 \times 8 \times 7 \qquad \left(\because {}^nC_4 = \frac{n(n-1)(n-2)(n-3)}{24}\right)$$
$$= 72 \times 7 = 504 \text{ ways}$$

(ii) Here, we have to select atleast 3 girls.
i.e., There are following two possibilities

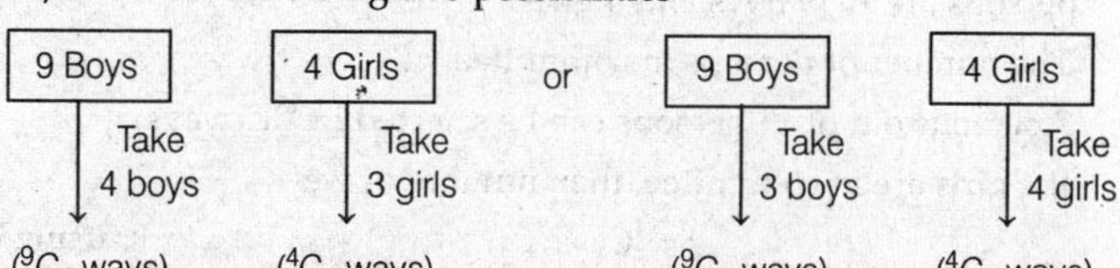

In first case, 4 boys out of 9 boys can be selected in $^9C_4$ ways and 3 girls out of 4 girls can be selected in $^4C_3$ ways.

Hence, by FPC, total number of ways in this case

$$= {}^9C_4 \times {}^4C_3 = \frac{9 \times 8 \times 7 \times 6}{4 \times 3 \times 2 \times 1} \times 4 = 504 \text{ ways}$$

In second case, 3 boys out of 9 boys can be select in ${}^9C_3$ ways.

And, 4 girls out of 4 girls can be select in ${}^4C_4$ ways.

Hence, by FPC, total number of ways in this case $= {}^9C_3 \times {}^4C_4$

$$= \frac{9 \times 8 \times 7}{6} \times 1 = 84 \text{ ways} \qquad \left(\because {}^nC_3 = \frac{n(n-1)(n-2)}{6}\right)$$

Hence, by fundamental principle of addition, total number of ways

$$= 504 + 84 = 588$$

(iii) Here, we have to select atmost 3 girls *i.e.*, there are following four possibilities

9 Boys	4 Girls		9 Boys	4 Girls
Take 4 boys	Take 3 girls	or	Take 5 boys	Take 2 girls
(${}^9C_4$ ways)	(${}^4C_3$ ways)		(${}^9C_5$ ways)	(${}^4C_2$ ways)

or

9 Boys	4 Girls		9 Boys	4 Girls
Take 6 boys	Take 1 girl	or	Take 7 boys	Take 0 girls
(${}^9C_6$ ways)	(${}^4C_1$ ways)		(${}^9C_7$ ways)	(${}^4C_0$ ways)

Hence, total number of ways (as these events are dependent to each other)

$$= ({}^9C_4 \times {}^4C_3) + ({}^9C_5 \times {}^4C_2) + ({}^9C_6 \times {}^4C_1) + ({}^9C_7 \times {}^4C_0)$$

$$= ({}^9C_5 \times {}^4C_1) + ({}^9C_4 \times {}^4C_2) + ({}^9C_3 \times {}^4C_1) + ({}^9C_2 \times {}^4C_0)$$

$$(\because {}^nC_r = {}^nC_{n-r})$$

$$= \left(\frac{9 \times 8 \times 7 \times 6}{120} \times 4\right) + \left(\frac{9 \times 8 \times 7 \times 6}{24} \times \frac{4 \times 3}{2}\right) + \left(\frac{9 \times 8 \times 7}{6} \times 4\right) + \left(\frac{9 \times 8}{2} \times 1\right)$$

$$= 504 + 756 + 336 + 36 = 1632 \text{ ways}$$

Quick Solution

Here, we have to select atmost 3 girls given, the total number of persons are 13 (9 boys and 4 girls).

The number of persons in committee = 7

7 persons out of 13 persons can be selected in ${}^{13}C_7$ ways

If 4 girls are in committee, then number of ways

$$= {}^4C_4 \times {}^9C_3 \qquad [\because \text{using by FPC}]$$

So, the required number of ways

$$= {}^{13}C_7 - {}^4C_4 \times {}^9C_3 = 1716 - 84 = 1632$$

Question 4 If the different permutations of all the letters of the word EXAMINATION are listed as in a dictionary, how many words are there in this list before the first word starting with E?

Sol. The letters of given word are A, A, E, I, I, M, N, N, O, T, X *i.e.*, Word starting with A are formed with the letters 2I's, 2N's, A, E, X, M, T, O (total 10 letters).

Hence, number of words formed by these letters

$$= \frac{10!}{2!\,2!} = \frac{10 \times 9 \times 8 \times 7 \times 6 \times 5 \times 4 \times 3 \times 2 \times 1}{2 \times 1 \times 2 \times 1}$$

$$= \frac{10 \times 9 \times 8 \times 7 \times 6 \times 5 \times 4 \times 3 \times 2 \times 1}{4}$$

$$= 10 \times 9 \times 8 \times 7 \times 6 \times 5 \times 3 \times 2 \times 1 = 907200 \text{ ways}$$

Mistake Alert Students make error while choosing the letter *A*. So, be careful for this step.

Question 5 How many 6-digit numbers can be formed from the digits 0, 1, 3, 5, 7 and 9 which are divisible by 10 and no digit is repeated?

Thinking Process A number is divisible by 10, if zero occurs at the unit's place and rest digits come in rest of the places.

Sol. Number of ways to fill the unit place = 1 (*i.e.*, 0 in units place) and remaining 5 numbers (1, 3, 5, 7, 9) can be arranged in 5! ways.

Hence, by FPC, total number of ways = $5! \times 1 = 5 \times 4 \times 3 \times 2 \times 1 = 120$ ways

Question 6 The English alphabet has 5 vowels and 21 consonants. How many words with two different vowels and two different consonants can be formed from the alphabet?

Sol.

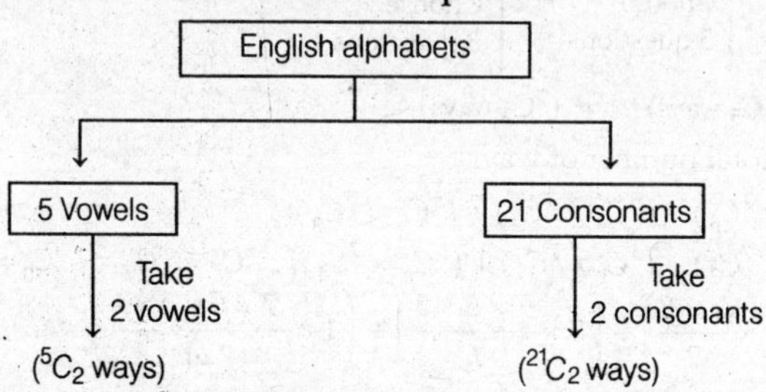

2 vowels out of 5 vowels can be selected in ${}^5C_2$ ways.
2 consonants out of 21 consonants can be selected in ${}^{21}C_2$ ways.
And, these 4 alphabets (2 vowels and 2 consonants) can be arranged in 4! ways.
Hence, by FPC, total number of ways

$$= {}^5C_2 \times {}^{21}C_2 \times 4! = \frac{5 \times 4}{2} \times \frac{21 \times 20}{2} \times 4 \times 3 \times 2 \times 1$$

$$= 10 \times 210 \times 24 = 240 \times 210 = 50400 \qquad \left(\because {}^nC_2 = \frac{n(n-1)}{2}\right)$$

Question 7 In an examination, a question paper consists of 12 questions divided into two parts *i.e.*, part I and part II, containing 5 and 7 questions, respectively. A student is required to attempt 8 questions in all, selecting atleast 3 from each part. In how many ways can a student select the questions?

Sol. According to given information

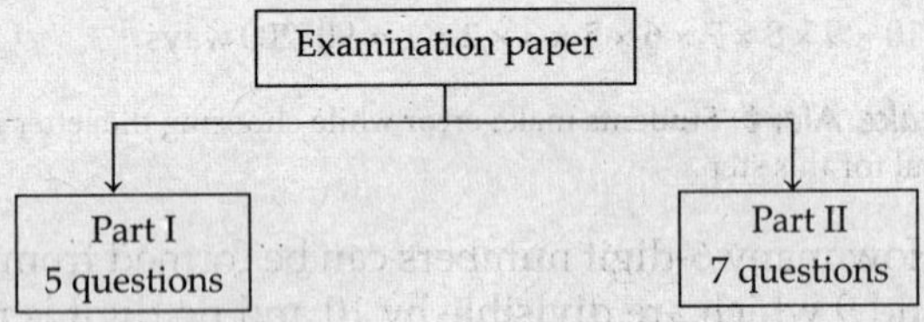

Here, we have to attempt 8 questions keeping in mind that atleast 3 from each part, then following possibility arises

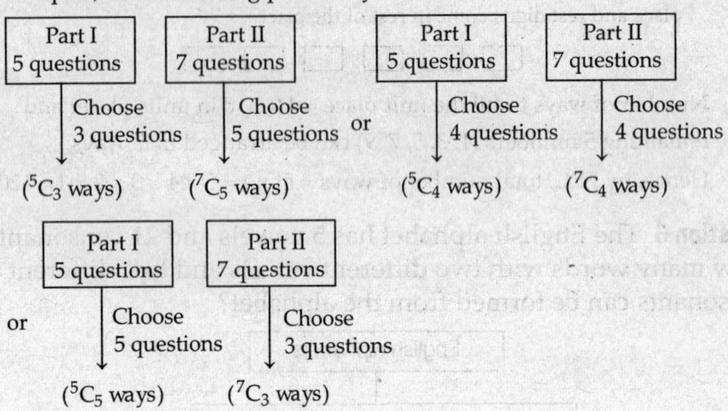

Hence, total number of ways

$$= ({}^5C_3 \times {}^7C_5) + ({}^5C_4 \times {}^7C_4) + ({}^5C_5 \times {}^7C_3)$$

$$= ({}^5C_2 \times {}^7C_2) + ({}^5C_1 \times {}^7C_3) + ({}^5C_0 \times {}^7C_4) [\because {}^nC_r = {}^nC_{n-r},\ {}^nC_0 = 1,\ {}^nC_1 = n]$$

$$= \left(\frac{5 \times 4}{2} \times \frac{7 \times 6}{2}\right) + \left(5 \times \frac{7 \times 6 \times 5}{6}\right) + \left(1 \times \frac{7 \times 6 \times 5 \times 4}{24}\right)$$

$$= (10 \times 21) + 175 + 35$$

$$\left[\because {}^nC_2 = \frac{n(n-1)}{2},\ {}^nC_3 = \frac{n(n-1)(n-2)}{6},\ {}^nC_4 = \frac{n(n-1)(n-2)(n-3)}{2}\right]$$

$$= 210 + 210 = 420 \text{ ways}$$

Question 8 Determine the number of 5-card combinations out of a deck of 52 cards if each selection of 5 cards has exactly one king.

Sol. 1 king out of 4 kings can be selected in ${}^4C_1$ ways.

Remaining 4 cards out of remaining 48 cards can be selected in ${}^{48}C_4$ ways.

Hence, by FPC, total number of ways = ${}^4C_1 \times {}^{48}C_4$

Question 9 It is required to seat 5 men and 4 women in a row so that the women occupy the even places. How many such arrangements are possible?

Sol. Total number of persons = 9

$$\boxed{1} \overset{2}{\times} \boxed{3} \overset{4}{\times} \boxed{5} \overset{6}{\times} \boxed{7} \overset{8}{\times} \boxed{9}$$

There are 4 even numbers and 4 women want to sit, this can be done in 4! ways.

Remaining 5 seats can be filled by 5 men in 5! ways.

Hence, by FPC, total number of ways = 5! × 4!

$$= 5 \times 4 \times 3 \times 2 \times 1 \times 4 \times 3 \times 2 \times 1$$
$$= 120 \times 24$$
$$= 2880 \text{ ways}$$

Mistake Alert Students should choose first those places which are given in question to avoid making any error.

Question 10 From a class of 25 students, 10 are to be chosen for an excursion party. There are 3 students who decide that either all of them will join or none of them will join. In how many ways can the excursion party be chosen?

Sol. There are two possibilities

(a) If all the three students will go in party then, we have to select 7 students out of 22 students.

(b) If all of three students will not go for party then, we have to select 10 students out of 22 students.

Now, 7 students out of 22 students can be selected in ${}^{22}C_7$ ways.

or 10 students out of 22 students can be selected in ${}^{22}C_{10}$ ways.

∴ Total number of ways = ${}^{22}C_7 + {}^{22}C_{10}$

Question 11 In how many ways can the letters of the word ASSASSINATION be arranged so that all the S's are together?

◎ *Thinking Process* We will consider all S as one letter and then arrange remaining letters with S.

Sol. Given word in A S S A S S I N A T I O N

A → 3 times

S → 4 times

I → 2 times

T → 1 time

O → 1 time

N → 2 times

If all the S's are together, then it will be considered as 1 letter and remaining 9 letters (3A's, 2I's, T, O, 2N's) and 1 S (including 4S's) will be considered as

10 letters.

Hence, total number of ways

$$= \frac{10!}{3!\,2!\,2!} \quad \text{(four S)}$$

$$= \frac{10 \times 9 \times 8 \times 7 \times 6 \times 5 \times 4 \times 3!}{3! \times 2 \times 1 \times 2 \times 1}$$

$$= 10 \times 9 \times 8 \times 7 \times 6 \times 5$$

$$= 151200 \text{ ways}$$

Mistake Alert Please be careful while making a different words, if some letters are repeated.

DIKSHA APP Questions

☐ Multiple Choice Questions

Q.1 If $\frac{1}{7!}+\frac{1}{8!}=\frac{x}{9!}$ then x is

(a) 9 (b) 18
(c) 27 (d) 81

Sol. (d) Given, $\frac{1}{7!}+\frac{1}{8!}=\frac{x}{9!}$

$$\Rightarrow \frac{1}{7!}+\frac{1}{8\times 7!}=\frac{x}{9\times 8\times 7!} \quad [\because n! = n(n-1)!]$$

$$\Rightarrow \frac{1}{7!}\left[1+\frac{1}{8}\right]=\frac{x}{9\times 8\times 7!}$$

$$\Rightarrow 1+\frac{1}{8}=\frac{x}{9\times 8}\Rightarrow\frac{8+1}{8}=\frac{x}{9\times 8}$$

$$\Rightarrow \frac{x}{9}=9\Rightarrow x=81$$

Q.2 The difference between LCM and HCF of 4!, 5! and 6! is

(a) 24 (b) 120
(c) 696 (d) 500

◎ ***Thinking Process*** If $a<b<c$, then LCM of $a!, b!$, and $c!$ is $c!$ and HCF of $a!, b!$ and $c!$ is $a!$.

Sol. (c) Given, 4!, 5! and 6! such that $4<5<6$

So, LCM of 4!, 5! and 6! is 6! and HCF is 4!

∴ The difference between them $= 6! - 4!$

$$= 6\times 5\times 4! - 4! \quad [\because n! = n(n-1)!]$$
$$= 4!(30-1)$$
$$= 4\times 3\times 2\times 1(29) = 696$$

Q.3 If ${}^{2n}P_3 = 2\times {}^{n}P_4$, then n is

(a) 10 (b) 2
(c) 4 (d) 8

◎ ***Thinking Process*** Here, we will use ${}^{n}P_r=\frac{n!}{(n-r)!}$

Sol. (d) We have, $^{2n}P_3 = 2 \times {}^nP_4$

$\Rightarrow \dfrac{(2n)!}{(2n-3)!} = 2\dfrac{(n!)}{(n-4)!}$ $\left[\because {}^nP_r = \dfrac{n!}{(n-r)!}\right]$

$\Rightarrow \dfrac{2n(2n-1)(2n-2)(2n-3)!}{(2n-3)!} = \dfrac{2(n)(n-1)(n-2)(n-3)(n-4)!}{(n-4)!}$

$[\because n! = n(n-1)!]$

$\Rightarrow 2n(2n-1)\,2(n-1) = 2n(n-1)(n-2)(n-3)$

$\Rightarrow 2(2n-1) = (n-2)(n-3)$

$\Rightarrow 4n - 2 = n^2 - 5n + 6$

$\Rightarrow n^2 - 9n + 8 = 0$

$\Rightarrow n^2 - 8n - n + 8 = 0$

$\Rightarrow n(n-8) - 1(n-8) = 0 \Rightarrow (n-1)(n-8) = 0$

$\Rightarrow n = 1 \text{ or } 8$

Clearly, by the given expression $n \geq 4$

So, $n = 8$

Q.4 If $^{n+2}C_8 \div {}^{n-2}P_4 = \dfrac{57}{16}$, then n is equal to

(a) 11 (b) 19
(c) 12 (d) 7

Sol. (b) Given, $^{n+2}C_8 \div {}^{n-2}P_4 = \dfrac{57}{16}$ $\left[\because {}^nC_r = \dfrac{n!}{r!(n-r)!}\right]$

$\Rightarrow \dfrac{(n+2)!}{(n+2-8)!\,8!} \div \dfrac{(n-2)!}{(n-2-4)!} = \dfrac{57}{16}$

$\Rightarrow \dfrac{(n+2)!}{(n-6)!\,8!} \div \dfrac{(n-2)!}{(n-6)!} = \dfrac{57}{16}$

$\Rightarrow \dfrac{(n+2)!}{(n-6)!\,8!} \times \dfrac{(n-6)!}{(n-2)!} = \dfrac{57}{16}$

$\Rightarrow \dfrac{(n+2)(n+1)(n)(n-1)(n-2)!}{8!} \times \dfrac{1}{(n-2)!} = \dfrac{57}{16}$ $[\because n! = n(n-1)!]$

$\Rightarrow \dfrac{(n+2)(n+1)(n)(n-1)}{8!} = \dfrac{57}{16}$

$\Rightarrow (n+2)(n+1)(n)(n-1) = \dfrac{57}{16} \times 8!$

$\Rightarrow (n+2)(n+1)(n)(n-1) = \dfrac{57 \times 8 \times 7 \times 6 \times 5 \times 4 \times 3 \times 2 \times 1}{16}$

$\Rightarrow (n+2)(n+1)(n)(n-1) = 19 \times 3 \times 7 \times 6 \times 5 \times 4 \times 3$

$\Rightarrow (n+2)(n+1)(n)(n-1) = 18 \times 19 \times 20 \times 21$

$\because (n-1), n, (n+1)$ and $(n+2)$ are consecutive positive integer numbers.

So, by comparison of both side

$$n-1=18,\ n=19,\ n+1=20 \text{ and } n+2=21$$

$$\therefore \qquad n=19$$

Mistake Alert We should not multiply $(n+2)(n+1)(n)(n-1)$ otherwise, it will become a 4th degree polynomial equation which will be more difficult to solve.

Q.5 Find the value of ${}^nC_r + 2\cdot {}^nC_{r-1} + {}^nC_{r-2}$

(a) ${}^{n+1}C_{r+1}$ (b) ${}^{n+2}C_r$

(c) ${}^{n+2}C_{r+1}$ (d) ${}^{n+1}C_r$

Thinking Process Here, we will use ${}^nC_r + {}^nC_{r-1} = {}^{n+1}C_r$

Sol. (b) We have, ${}^nC_r + 2\cdot {}^nC_{r-1} + {}^nC_{r-2} = {}^nC_r + ({}^nC_{r-1} + {}^nC_{r-1}) + {}^nC_{r-2}$

$$= ({}^nC_r + {}^nC_{r-1}) + {}^nC_{r-1} + {}^nC_{r-2})$$

$$= {}^{n+1}C_r + {}^{n+1}C_{r-1} \qquad [\because {}^nC_r + {}^nC_{r-1} = {}^{n+1}C_r]$$

$$= {}^{n+2}C_r \qquad [\because {}^nC_r + {}^nC_{r-1} = {}^{n+1}C_r]$$

Mistake Alert In this type of problem, we should not open ${}^nC_r$ because doing so will make the solution complicated.

Q.6 From 4 officers and 8 Jawans, the number of ways in which 6 can be chosen to include atleast one officer?

(a) 686 (b) 896

(c) 968 (d) 698

Sol. (b) Selection of 6 from 12 (4 officers and 8 Jawans) = ${}^{12}C_6$

Selection of 6 in which no officer = ${}^8C_6$

Therefore, selection of 6 with at least one officer

$$= {}^{12}C_6 - {}^8C_6$$

$$= \frac{12!}{6!\times 6!} - \frac{8!}{6!\times 2!} \qquad \left[\because {}^nC_r = \frac{n!}{r!(n-r)!}\right]$$

$$= \frac{12\times 11\times 10\times 9\times 8\times 7\times 6!}{6\times 5\times 4\times 3\times 2\times 1\times 6!} - \frac{8\times 7\times 6!}{6!\times 2}$$

$$= 11\times 2\times 3\times 2\times 7 - 4\times 7$$

$$= 924 - 28 = 896 \text{ ways}$$

Q.7 If $n = {}^mC_2$, then the value of ${}^nC_2$

(a) ${}^{m+1}C_4$ (b) $2\,{}^{m+1}C_4$
(c) $3\,{}^{m+1}C_4$ (d) $4\,{}^{m+1}C_4$

Sol. (c) Given $n = {}^mC_2$

$$\Rightarrow \quad n = \frac{m!}{(m-2)!\,2!} \qquad \left[\because {}^nC_r = \frac{n!}{(n-r)!\,r!}\right]$$

$$\Rightarrow \quad n = \frac{m(m-1)}{2}$$

Now $${}^nC_2 = \frac{n!}{(n-2)!2!} = \frac{n(n-1)}{2} \qquad \text{...(i)}$$

On putting the value of $n = \dfrac{m(m-1)}{2}$ in equation (i), we get

$$\Rightarrow \quad {}^nC_2 = \frac{\frac{m(m-1)}{2}\left(\frac{m(m-1)}{2} - 1\right)}{2} \qquad \left[\because n = \frac{m(m-1)}{2}\right]$$

$$= \frac{1}{8} m(m-1)\,(m(m-1) - 2)$$

$$= \frac{1}{8}[m(m-1)\,(m^2 - m - 2)$$

$$= \frac{1}{8}[m(m-1)\,(m^2 - 2m + m - 2)]$$

$$= \frac{1}{8}[m(m-1)\,((m-2)\,(m+1)]$$

$$= \frac{1}{8}[(m+1)\,(m)\,(m-1)\,(m-2)]$$

Since $${}^{m+1}C_4 = \frac{(m+1)!}{(m+1-4)!\,4!} = \frac{(m+1)!}{(m-3)!4!}$$

$$= \frac{(m+1)\,(m)\,(m-1)\,(m-2)}{24} \qquad \text{...(ii)}$$

So, $${}^nC_2 = \frac{1}{8}(24 \cdot {}^{m+1}C_4) \qquad [\because \text{by equation (ii)}]$$

$$\therefore \quad {}^nC_2 = 3 \cdot {}^{m+1}C_4$$

Note We have to keep the value of ${}^nC_2$ within the product of linear factors because we need to convert it into the form ${}^{m+1}C_4$.

Q.8 If ${}^{k+5}P_{k+1} = \dfrac{11(k-1)}{2} \times {}^{k+3}P_k$, then the value of k are

(a) 5, 6 (b) 6, 7
(c) 7, 8 (d) 8, 9

Sol. (b) We have, ${}^{k+5}P_{k+1} = \dfrac{11(k-1)}{2} \times {}^{k+3}P_k$

$$\Rightarrow \quad \frac{(k+5)!}{[(k+5)-(k+1)]!} = \frac{11(k-1)}{2} \times \frac{(k+3)!}{(k+3-k)!} \qquad \left[\because {}^nP_r = \frac{n!}{(n-r)!}\right]$$

$$\Rightarrow \quad \frac{(k+5)!}{(4)!} = \frac{11(k-1)}{2} \times \frac{(k+3)!}{(3)!}$$

$$\Rightarrow \quad \frac{(k+5)(k+4)(k+3)!}{4 \times 3!} = \frac{11(k-1)}{2} \times \frac{(k+3)!}{3!} \qquad [\because n! = n(n-1)!]$$

$$\Rightarrow \quad (k+5)(k+4) = 22(k-1)$$

$$\Rightarrow \quad k^2 + 9k + 20 = 22k - 22$$

$$\Rightarrow \quad k^2 - 13k + 42 = 0$$

$$\Rightarrow \quad k^2 - 6k - 7k + 42 = 0$$

$$\Rightarrow \quad k(k-6) - 7(k-6) = 0 \Rightarrow (k-7)(k-6) = 0 \Rightarrow k = 6, 7$$

$$\therefore \quad k = 6 \text{ and } 7$$

Note We need to expand the factorial in the numerator to the same extent as it is in the denominator.

□ Subjective Type Questions

Q.1 How many 4-digit numbers can be formed by using the digits 1 to 9 if repetition of digits is not allowed?

Sol. The given digits are 1, 2, 3, 4, 5, 6, 7, 8, 9

I	II	III	IV

The first place can be filled in 9 ways given repetition of digits is not allowed.
So, the second place can be filled in 8 ways
The III place can be filled in 7 ways similar, the IV place can be filled in 6 ways.
Hence, by the FPC total number of ways = $9 \times 8 \times 7 \times 6 = 3024$

Q.2 How many number of ways we can post 5 letters in 10 letter boxes?

◎ ***Thinking Process*** We use repetation is allowed concept in such type of questions.

Sol. We can post the first letter in 10 ways, second letter in 10 ways and so on.

Thus, the number of ways of posting 5 letters in 10 letter boxes are

$10 \times 10 \times 10 \times 10 \times 10$ *i.e* 10^5.

Note Here, we will use ${}^nP_r = \dfrac{n!}{(n-r)!}$

Binomial Theorem

CHAPTER 07

Important Points

01 Binomial theorem of expansion for any positive integer n

$$(x+y)^n = {}^nC_0x^n + {}^nC_1x^{n-1}y + {}^nC_2\,x^{n-2}y^2 + \ldots + {}^nC_ny^n$$

Pascal's triangle

Index	Coefficients
0	1 $({}^0C_0)$
1	1 $({}^1C_0)$, 1 $({}^1C_1)$
2	1 $({}^2C_0)$, 2 $({}^2C_1)$, 1 $({}^2C_2)$
3	1 $({}^3C_0)$, 3 $({}^3C_1)$, 3 $({}^3C_2)$, 1 $({}^3C_3)$
4	1 $({}^4C_0)$, 4 $({}^4C_1)$, 6 $({}^4C_2)$, 4 $({}^4C_3)$, 1 $({}^4C_4)$

Remember

(i) The notation $(x+y)^n = \sum_{k=0}^{n} {}^nC_k\, x^{n-k}y^k$ also stands for binomial expansion.

(ii) The coefficients ${}^nC_0, {}^nC_1, {}^nC_2, \ldots, {}^nC_n$ are called binomial coefficients.

(iii) There are $(n+1)$ terms in the expansion of $(x+y)^n$ *i.e.*, one more than the index number.

(iv) In the successive terms of the expansion, the index of x goes on decreasing by unity. At the same time the index of y increases by unity.

(v) In the expansion of $(x+y)^n$, in each term the sum of powers of x and y is n.

(vi) $(x-y)^n = {}^nC_0x^n - {}^nC_1x^{n-1}y + {}^nC_2x^{n-2}y^2 \ldots (-1)^n\ {}^nC_ny^n$

02 Some special cases in the expansion of $(x + y)^n$

(i) Taking $y = 1$, we obtain $(1 + x)^n = {}^nC_0 + {}^nC_1x^1 + \ldots + {}^nC_nx^n$

(ii) Taking $x = 1$ and $y = 1$, we obtain $2^n = {}^nC_0 + {}^nC_1 + {}^nC_2 + \ldots + {}^nC_n$

(iii) Taking $x = 1$ and $y = -1$, we obtain

$$0 = {}^nC_0 - {}^nC_1 + {}^nC_2 - {}^nC_3 + \ldots + (-1)^n\, {}^nC_n$$

(iv) ${}^nC_0 + {}^nC_2 + {}^nC_4 + \ldots = {}^nC_1 + {}^nC_3 + {}^nC_5 + \ldots = 2^{n-1}$

Remember

(i) ${}^nC_r = \dfrac{n!}{(n-r)!\, r!}$

(ii) ${}^nC_{r_1} = {}^nC_{r_2} \Rightarrow r_1 = r_2$ or $r_1 + r_2 = n$

(iii) ${}^nC_r + {}^nC_{r-1} = {}^{n+1}C_r$

(iv) ${}^nC_n = {}^nC_0 = 1$

(v) ${}^nC_r = {}^nC_{n-r}$

(vi) ${}^nC_1 = {}^nC_{n-1} = n$

Exercise 7.1

Direction (Q. No. 1 to 5) Expand each of the expressions.

◎ *Thinking Process* (For Q. Nos. 1 to 5) To expand the binomial theorem, use

$$(x+y)^n = {}^nC_0x^n + {}^nC_1x^{n-1}y + {}^nC_2x^{n-2}y^2 + \ldots + {}^nC_ny^n$$

and $$(x-y)^n = {}^nC_0x^n - {}^nC_1x^{n-1}y + {}^nC_2\,x^{n-2}y^2 - \ldots + (-1)^n\,{}^nC_ny^n$$

and using the results

$${}^nC_0 = {}^nC_n = 1,\ {}^nC_1 = n,\ {}^nC_2 = \frac{n(n-1)}{2},\ {}^nC_3 = \frac{n(n-1)(n-2)}{6} \text{ etc.}$$

Question 1 $(1-2x)^5$.

Sol. We have, $(1-2x)^5 = {}^5C_0\,(1)^5 - {}^5C_1(1)^4\,2x + {}^5C_2(1)^3\,(2x)^2$

$$- {}^5C_3(1)^2\,(2x)^3 + {}^5C_4(1)(2x)^4 - {}^5C_5(2x)^5$$

$$= {}^5C_0 - {}^5C_1\,2x + {}^5C_2\,4x^2 - {}^5C_2\,8x^3 + {}^5C_1\,16x^4 - {}^5C_0\,32x^5 \quad (\because {}^nC_r = {}^nC_{n-r})$$

$$= 1 - 5\times 2x + \frac{5\times 4}{2}\times 4x^2 - \frac{5\times 4}{2}\times 8x^3 + 5\times 16\times x^4 - 32x^5$$

$$= 1 - 10x + 40x^2 - 80x^3 + 80x^4 - 32x^5$$

Question 2 $\left(\frac{2}{x}-\frac{x}{2}\right)^5$.

Sol. We have, $\left(\frac{2}{x}-\frac{x}{2}\right)^5 = {}^5C_0\left(\frac{2}{x}\right)^5 - {}^5C_1\left(\frac{2}{x}\right)^4\frac{x}{2} + {}^5C_2\left(\frac{2}{x}\right)^3\left(\frac{x}{2}\right)^2$

$$- {}^5C_3\left(\frac{2}{x}\right)^2\left(\frac{x}{2}\right)^3 + {}^5C_4\left(\frac{2}{x}\right)\left(\frac{x}{2}\right)^4 - {}^5C_5\left(\frac{x}{2}\right)^5$$

$$= {}^5C_0\,\frac{32}{x^5} - {}^5C_1\,\frac{16}{x^4}\times\frac{x}{2} + {}^5C_2\,\frac{8}{x^3}\times\frac{x^2}{4} - {}^5C_2\,\frac{4}{x^2}\times\frac{x^3}{8}$$

$$+ {}^5C_1\,\frac{2}{x}\times\frac{x^4}{16} - {}^5C_0\,\frac{x^5}{32} \quad (\because {}^nC_r = {}^nC_{n-r})$$

$$= \frac{32}{x^5} - \frac{5\times 16\times x}{2x^4} + \frac{5\times 4}{2}\times\frac{8}{x^3}\times\frac{x^2}{4} - \frac{5\times 4}{2}\times\frac{4}{x^2}\times\frac{x^3}{8}$$

$$+ 5\times\frac{2}{x}\times\frac{x^4}{16} - \frac{x^5}{32}$$

$$= \frac{32}{x^5} - \frac{40}{x^3} + \frac{20}{x} - 5x + \frac{5x^3}{8} - \frac{x^5}{32}$$

Question 3 $(2x-3)^6$.

Sol. We have, $(2x-3)^6 = {}^6C_0\,(2x)^6 - {}^6C_1(2x)^5 \times 3 + {}^6C_2\,(2x)^4\,(3)^2 - {}^6C_3\,(2x)^3\,(3)^3$

$$+ {}^6C_4\,(2x)^2\,(3)^4 - {}^6C_5\,(2x)\,3^5 + {}^6C_6\,3^6$$

$$= {}^6C_0\,64x^6 - {}^6C_1\,32x^5 \times 3 + {}^6C_2\,16x^4 \times 9 - {}^6C_3\,8x^3 \times 27$$

$$+ {}^6C_2\,4x^2 \times 81 - {}^6C_1\,2x \times 243 + {}^6C_0\,729 \quad (\because {}^nC_r = {}^nC_{n-r})$$

$$= 64x^6 - 6 \times 32 \times 3 \times x^5 + \frac{6 \times 5}{2} \times 16x^4 \times 9 - \frac{6 \times 5 \times 4 \times 8x^3 \times 27}{6}$$

$$+ \frac{6 \times 5}{2} \times 4x^2 \times 81 - 6 \times 2x \times 243 + 729$$

$$= 64x^6 - 576x^5 + 2160x^4 - 4320x^3 + 4860x^2 - 2916x + 729$$

Question 4 $\left(\frac{x}{3}+\frac{1}{x}\right)^5$.

Sol. We have, $\left(\frac{x}{3}+\frac{1}{x}\right)^5 = {}^5C_0\left(\frac{x}{3}\right)^5 + {}^5C_1\left(\frac{x}{3}\right)^4\frac{1}{x} + {}^5C_2\left(\frac{x}{3}\right)^3\left(\frac{1}{x}\right)^2$

$$+ {}^5C_3\left(\frac{x}{3}\right)^2\left(\frac{1}{x}\right)^3 + {}^5C_4\left(\frac{x}{3}\right)\left(\frac{1}{x}\right)^4 + {}^5C_5\left(\frac{1}{x}\right)^5$$

$$= {}^5C_0\,\frac{x^5}{243} + {}^5C_1\,\frac{x^4}{81} \times \frac{1}{x} + {}^5C_2 \times \frac{x^3}{27} \times \frac{1}{x^2} + {}^5C_2\,\frac{x^2}{9} \times \frac{1}{x^3}$$

$$+ {}^5C_1\,\frac{x}{3} \times \frac{1}{x^4} + {}^5C_0 \times \frac{1}{x^5} \quad (\because {}^nC_r = {}^nC_{n-r})$$

$$= \frac{x^5}{243} + \frac{5}{81} \times x^3 + \frac{5 \times 4}{2} \times \frac{1}{27} \times x$$

$$+ \frac{5 \times 4}{2} \times \frac{1}{9} \times \frac{1}{x} + 5 \times \frac{x}{3} \times \frac{1}{x^4} + \frac{1}{x^5}$$

$$= \frac{x^5}{243} + \frac{5x^3}{81} + \frac{10x}{27} + \frac{10}{9x} + \frac{5}{3x^3} + \frac{1}{x^5}$$

Question 5 $\left(x+\frac{1}{x}\right)^6$.

Sol. We have, $\left(x+\frac{1}{x}\right)^6 = {}^6C_0\,x^6 + {}^6C_1\,x^5\left(\frac{1}{x}\right) + {}^6C_2x^4\left(\frac{1}{x}\right)^2 + {}^6C_3x^3\left(\frac{1}{x}\right)^3$

$$+ {}^6C_4x^2\left(\frac{1}{x}\right)^4 + {}^6C_5\,(x)\left(\frac{1}{x}\right)^5 + {}^6C_6\left(\frac{1}{x}\right)^6$$

$$= {}^6C_0\,x^6 + {}^6C_1x^4 + {}^6C_2\,\frac{x^4}{x^2} + {}^6C_3\,x^3 \times \frac{1}{x^3}$$

$$+ {}^6C_2\,x^2 \times \frac{1}{x^4} + {}^6C_1\,x \times \frac{1}{x^5} + {}^6C_0\,\frac{1}{x^6} \quad (\because {}^nC_r = {}^nC_{n-r})$$

$$= x^6 + 6x^4 + \frac{6 \times 5}{2}\,x^2 + \frac{6 \times 5 \times 4}{6} \times 1 + \frac{6 \times 5}{2}\,\frac{1}{x^2} + 6 \times \frac{1}{x^4} + \frac{1}{x^6}$$

$$= x^6 + 6x^4 + 15x^2 + 20 + \frac{15}{x^2} + \frac{6}{x^4} + \frac{1}{x^6}$$

Direction (Q. No. 6 to 9) Using Binomial theorem, evaluate each of the following.

◎ *Thinking Process* To find the value of some power of a function using binomial theorem we have to split that number in two parts so that we can apply binomial theorem like as $96 = 100 - 4, 102 = 100 + 2, 101 = 100 + 1$ and $99 = 100 - 1$, then use the expression of $(x + y)^n$ and $(x - y)^n$.

Question 6 $(96)^3$.

Sol. We have, $(96)^3 = (100-4)^3 = {}^3C_0\,(100)^3 - {}^3C_1(100)^2\,4 + {}^3C_2(100)(4)^2 - {}^3C_3\,(4)^3$

$$= {}^3C_0(10^6) - {}^3C_1(10)^4 \times 4 + {}^3C_1\,10^2 \times 16 - {}^3C_0\,64 \quad (\because {}^nC_r = {}^nC_{n-r})$$

$$= 10^6 - 3 \times 10^4 \times 4 + 3 \times 10^2 \times 16 - 64$$

$$= 10^6 - 12 \times 10^4 + 48 \times 10^2 - 64 = (10^6 + 48 \times 10^2) - (12 \times 10^4 + 64)$$

$$= (10^6 + 4800) - (120000 + 64) = 1004800 - 120064 = 884736$$

Note While applying the binomial theorem to solve the given number, we break number into two parts such a way that one is a multiple of 10 so that it is easy to calculate.

Question 7 $(102)^5$

Sol. We have, $(102)^5 = (100+2)^5$.

$$= {}^5C_0\,(100)^5 + {}^5C_1\,(100)^4(2)^1 + {}^5C_2\,(100)^3\,(2)^2 + {}^5C_3\,(100)^2\,(2)^3 + {}^5C_4\,(100)\,(2)^4 + {}^5C_5\,(2)^5$$

$$= {}^5C_0(10)^{10} + {}^5C_1(10^8)2 + {}^5C_2(10^6) \times 4 + {}^5C_2\,(10^4) \times 8 + {}^5C_1\,100 \times 16 + {}^5C_0 \times 32 \quad (\because {}^nC_r = {}^nC_{n-r})$$

$$= 1 \times 10^{10} + 5 \times 10^8 \times 2 + \frac{5 \times 4}{2} \times 10^6 \times 4 + \frac{5 \times 4}{2} \times 10^4 \times 8 + 5 \times 100 \times 16 + 32$$

$$= 10000000000 + 1000000000 + 40000000 + 800000 + 8000 + 32$$

$$= 11040808032$$

Question 8 $(101)^4$.

Sol. We have, $(100+1)^4 = {}^4C_0\,(100)^4 + {}^4C_1(100)^3\,(1) + {}^4C_2(100)^2 \cdot (1)^2 + {}^4C_3\,100 \cdot (1)^3 + {}^4C_4 \cdot (1)^4$

$$= {}^4C_0\,10^8 + {}^4C_1 10^6 + {}^4C_2\,10^4 + {}^4C_1\,(100) + {}^4C_0$$

$$= 10^8 + 4 \times 10^6 + \frac{4 \times 3}{2} \times 10^4 + 4 \times 10^2 + 1 \quad (\because {}^nC_r = {}^nC_{n-r})$$

$$= 100000000 + 4000000 + 60000 + 400 + 1 = 104060401$$

Question 9 $(99)^5$.

Sol. We have, $(99)^5 = (100-1)^5 = {}^5C_0\,(100)^5 - {}^5C_1\,(100)^4 \times 1 + {}^5C_2\,(100)^3 \times (1)^2$

$$- {}^5C_3\,(100)^2 \times 1^3 + {}^5C_4\, 100 \times 1^4 - {}^5C_5 \times 1^5$$

$$= {}^5C_0(10)^{10} - {}^5C_1(10)^8 + {}^5C_2(10)^6 - {}^5C_2(10)^4 + {}^5C_1 \times (10)^2 - {}^5C_0 \quad (\because {}^nC_r = {}^nC_{n-r})$$

$$= 10000000000 - 5 \times 100000000 + \frac{5 \times 4}{2} \times 1000000 - \frac{5 \times 4}{2} \times 10000 + 5 \times 100 - 1$$

$$= (10000000000 + 10000000 + 500) - (500000000 + 100000 + 1)$$

$$= 10010000500 - 500100001 = 9509900499$$

Question 10 Using binomial theorem, indicate which number is larger $(1\cdot1)^{10000}$ or 1000?

◎ ***Thinking Process*** Use binomial theorem in $(1\cdot1)^{10000}$ *i.e.*, break $(1\cdot1)$ as $(1+0\cdot1)$.

Sol. We have, $(1\cdot1)^{10000} = (1+0\cdot1)^{10000}$

$$= {}^{10000}C_0\,(1)^{10000} + {}^{10000}C_1\,(1)^{9999}(0\cdot1) + \text{.... other terms}$$

$$= 1 \times 1 + 10000 \times 0\cdot1 + \text{...other terms} \quad (\because {}^nC_0 = 1,\ {}^nC_1 = n)$$

$$= 1 + 1000 + \text{other terms}$$

$$= (1001 + \text{other terms}) > 1000 \Rightarrow (1\cdot1)^{10000} > 1000$$

Question 11 Find $(a+b)^4 - (a-b)^4$.

Hence, evaluate $(\sqrt{3}+\sqrt{2})^4 - (\sqrt{3}-\sqrt{2})^4$.

Sol. Now, $(a+b)^4 = {}^4C_0\,a^4 + {}^4C_1\,a^3b + {}^4C_2\,a^2b^2 + {}^4C_3\,ab^3 + {}^4C_4\,b^4$

$$= {}^4C_0a^4 + {}^4C_1\,a^3b + {}^4C_2a^2b^2 + {}^4C_1ab^3 + {}^4C_0\,b^4 \quad (\because {}^nC_r = {}^nC_{n-r})$$

$$= 1 \times a^4 + 4\,a^3b + \frac{4 \times 3}{2}\,a^2b^2 + 4ab^3 + 1 \times b^4$$

$$\Rightarrow \quad (a+b)^4 = a^4 + 4a^3b + 6a^2b^2 + 4ab^3 + b^4 \quad \text{...(i)}$$

Similarly, $(a-b)^4 = a^4 - 4a^3b + 6a^2b^2 - 4ab^3 + b^4$ ...(ii)

On subtracting Eq. (ii) from Eq. (i), we get

$$(a+b)^4 - (a-b)^4 = 8a^3b + 8ab^3 = 8\,ab\,(a^2+b^2)$$

Now, putting $a = \sqrt{3}$ and $b = \sqrt{2}$

$$(\sqrt{3}+\sqrt{2})^4 - (\sqrt{3}-\sqrt{2})^4 = 8\sqrt{3}\sqrt{2}\,[(\sqrt{3})^2 + (\sqrt{2})^2]$$

$$= 8\sqrt{6}\,(3+2) = 8\sqrt{6} \times 5 = 40\sqrt{6}$$

Mistake Alert Sometimes students make error while putting the value. They expand the second part of question without putting the value of *a* and *b*.

Question 12 Find $(x+1)^6+(x-1)^6$.
Hence or otherwise evaluate $(\sqrt{2}+1)^6+(\sqrt{2}-1)^6$.

Sol. Now, $(x+1)^6 = {}^6C_0\,x^6 + {}^6C_1x^5 \times 1 + {}^6C_2x^4 \times (1)^2$

$$+ {}^6C_3\,x^3 \times (1)^3 + {}^6C_4x^2 \times (1)^4 + {}^6C_5\,x \times (1)^5 + {}^6C_6(1)^6$$

$$\Rightarrow \quad (x+1)^6 = {}^6C_0\,x^6 + {}^6C_1x^5 + {}^6C_2x^4 + {}^6C_3\,x^3 + {}^6C_2x^2 + {}^6C_1x + {}^6C_0 \quad (\because {}^nC_r = {}^nC_{n-r})$$

$$\Rightarrow \quad (x+1)^6 = x^6 + 6x^5 + \frac{6\times 5}{2}x^4 + \frac{6\times 5\times 4}{6}x^3 + \frac{6\times 5}{2}x^2 + 6x + 1$$

$$\Rightarrow \quad (x+1)^6 = x^6 + 6x^5 + 15x^4 + 20x^3 + 15x^2 + 6x + 1 \quad \ldots\text{(i)}$$

Similarly, $\quad (x-1)^6 = x^6 - 6x^5 + 15x^4 - 20x^3 + 15x^2 - 6x + 1 \quad \ldots$(ii)

Now, addition Eq. (i) and Eq. (ii), we get

$$(x+1)^6 + (x-1)^6 = 2[x^6 + 15x^4 + 15x^2 + 1]$$

Now, put $x = \sqrt{2}$

$$\Rightarrow \quad (\sqrt{2}+1)^6 + (\sqrt{2}-1)^6 = 2[(\sqrt{2})^6 + 15(\sqrt{2})^4 + 15(\sqrt{2})^2 + 1]$$

$$= 2\,[2^3 + 15 \times 2^2 + 15 \times 2 + 1]$$

$$= 2\,[8 + 15 \times 4 + 30 + 1]$$

$$= 2\,[8 + 60 + 30 + 1] = 2\,[99] = 198$$

Question 13 Show that $9^{n+1}-8n-9$ is divisible by 64, whenever n is a positive integer.

◎ ***Thinking Process*** Here, 9^{n+1} can be written as $9^n \times 9$ and 9^n can be written as $(1+8)^n$ and use the expansion of $(x+y)^n$.

Sol. Now, $9^{n+1} - 8n - 9 = 9^n \times 9 - 8n - 9 = (1+8)^n \times 9 - 8n - 9$

$$= ({}^nC_0 + {}^nC_1 8 + {}^nC_2 8^2 + {}^nC_3 8^3 + \ldots\ldots + {}^nC_n 8^n)\,9 - 8n - 9$$

$$= (1 + 8n + {}^nC_2 8^2 + {}^nC_3 8^3 + \ldots. + {}^nC_n 8^n)\,9 - 8n - 9$$

$$= 9 + 72n + ({}^nC_2 8^2 + {}^nC_3 8^3 + \ldots + {}^nC_n 8^n)\,9 - 8n - 9$$

$$= (72n - 8n) + 8^2\,({}^nC_2 + {}^nC_3 8 + \ldots + {}^nC_n 8^{n-2})\,9$$

$$= 64n + 64\,({}^nC_2 + {}^nC_3 8 + \ldots + {}^nC_n\, 8^{n-2})9$$

$$= 64\,[n + ({}^nC_2 + {}^nC_3 8 + \ldots + {}^nC_n\, 8^{n-2})\,9]$$

$$= 64 \times \text{Some constant numbers} = \text{Divisible by } 64$$

Question 14 Prove that $\sum\limits_{r=0}^{n} 3^r\ {}^nC_r = 4^n$.

◎ ***Thinking Process***

Use $(1+x)^n = {}^nC_0 + {}^nC_1x + {}^nC_2x^2 + {}^nC_3x^3 + \ldots. + {}^nC_nx^n \quad \ldots$(i)

Sol. Now, $\sum\limits_{r=0}^{n} {}^nC_r \times 3^r = {}^nC_0 3^0 + {}^nC_1 3 + {}^nC_2 3^2 + {}^nC_3 3^3 + \ldots. + {}^nC_n 3^n$

$$= {}^nC_0 + {}^nC_1 3 + {}^nC_2\, 3^2 + {}^nC_3\, 3^3 + \ldots + {}^nC_n 3^n$$

$$= (1+3)^n \quad = 4^n \quad \text{[Using Eq. (i)]}$$

Miscellaneous Exercise

Question 1 If a and b are distinct integers, prove that $(a-b)$ is a factor of $a^n - b^n$, whenever n is a positive integer.

Sol. If we take $a^n = (a-b+b)^n$

$$= {}^nC_0 (a-b)^n + {}^nC_1(a-b)^{n-1} b + {}^nC_2 (a-b)^{n-2} b^2 + \ldots\ldots + {}^nC_n b^n$$

$$\Rightarrow \quad a^n = (a-b)[{}^nC_0 (a-b)^{n-1} + {}^nC_1 (a-b)^{n-2} b + {}^nC_2 (a-b)^{n-3} b^2 + \ldots] + b^n$$

$$\Rightarrow \quad a^n - b^n = (a-b)[{}^nC_0 (a-b)^{n-1} + {}^nC_1 (a-b)^{n-2} b + \ldots]$$

$\Rightarrow$ $(a-b)$ is a factor of $a^n - b^n$

Mistake Alert Some students get confuse in this step $a^n = (a-b+b)^n$ is taken, then a^n will remain as it is.

Question 2 Evaluate $(\sqrt{3}+\sqrt{2})^6 - (\sqrt{3}-\sqrt{2})^6$.

Thinking Process Use the expansions

$$(x+y)^n = {}^nC_0 x^n + {}^nC_1 x^{n-1} y + {}^nC_2 x^{n-2} y^2 + \ldots + {}^nC_n y^n$$

and $(x-y)^n = {}^nC_0 x^n - {}^nC_1 x^{n-1} y + {}^nC_2 x^{n-2} y^2 - \ldots + (-1)^n\, {}^nC_n y^n$

Sol. Use, $(x+y)^6 = {}^6C_0 x^6 + {}^6C_1 x^5 y + {}^6C_2 x^4 y^2 + {}^6C_3 x^3 y^3 + {}^6C_4 x^2 y^4 + {}^6C_5 xy^5 + {}^6C_6 y^6$

$$= {}^6C_0 x^6 + {}^6C_1 x^5 y + {}^6C_2 x^4 y^2 + {}^6C_3 x^3 y^3 + {}^6C_2 x^2 y^4 + {}^6C_1 xy^5 + {}^6C_0 y^6 \quad (\because {}^nC_r = {}^nC_{n-r})$$

$$= x^6 + 6x^5 y + \frac{6\times 5}{2} x^4 y^2 + \frac{6\times 5\times 4}{6} x^3 y^3 + \frac{6\times 5}{2} x^2 y^4 + 6xy^5 + y^6$$

$$\Rightarrow \quad (x+y)^6 = x^6 + 6x^5 y + 15x^4 y^2 + 20x^3 y^3 + 15x^2 y^4 + 6xy^5 + y^6 \quad \ldots(\text{i})$$

Similarly, $(x-y)^6 = x^6 - 6x^5 y + 15x^4 y^2 - 20x^3 y^3 + 15x^2 y^4 - 6xy^5 + y^6 \quad \ldots(\text{ii})$

Subtracting Eq. (ii) from Eq. (i), we get

$$(x+y)^6 - (x-y)^6 = 12x^5 y + 40x^3 y^3 + 12xy^5 = 4xy[3x^4 + 10x^2 y^2 + 3y^4]$$

Putting $x = \sqrt{3}$ and $y = \sqrt{2}$, we get

$$(\sqrt{3}+\sqrt{2})^6 - (\sqrt{3}-\sqrt{2})^6$$

$$= 4\sqrt{3}\sqrt{2}[3(\sqrt{3})^4 + 10(\sqrt{3})^2(\sqrt{2})^2 + 3(\sqrt{2})^4]$$

$$= 4\sqrt{6}[3\times 3^2 + 10\times 3\times 2 + 3\times 2^2]$$

$$= 4\sqrt{6}[3\times 9 + 60 + 3\times 4] = 4\sqrt{6}\times(39+60)$$

$$= 4\sqrt{6}\times 99 = 396\sqrt{6}$$

Question 3 Find the value of $(a^2 + \sqrt{a^2 - 1})^4 + (a^2 - \sqrt{a^2 - 1})^4$.

◎ *Thinking Process* Here, we will construct $x = a^2$ and $y = \sqrt{a^2 - 1}$ to make the calculation easier and after calculation, we will put back the value of x and y.

Sol. Let $a^2 = x$ and $\sqrt{a^2 - 1} = y$

Now, $(x + y)^4 = {}^4C_0 x^4 + {}^4C_1 x^3 y + {}^4C_2 x^2 y^2 + {}^4C_3\, xy^3 + {}^4C_4 y^4$

$= {}^4C_0 x^4 + {}^4C_1\, x^3 y + {}^4C_2\, x^2 y^2 + {}^4C_1 xy^3 + {}^4C_0 y^4 \quad (\because {}^nC_r = {}^nC_{n-r})$

$= x^4 + 4x^3 y + \dfrac{4 \times 3}{2} x^2 y^2 + 4xy^3 + y^4$

$\Rightarrow \quad (x + y)^4 = x^4 + 4x^3 y + 6x^2 y^2 + 4xy^3 + y^4 \quad$ ...(i)

Similarly, $(x - y)^4 = x^4 - 4x^3 y + 6x^2 y^2 - 4xy^3 + y^4 \quad$ ...(ii)

Adding Eqs. (i) and (ii), we get

$$(x + y)^4 + (x - y)^4 = 2x^4 + 12x^2 y^2 + 2y^4$$
$$= 2[x^4 + 6x^2 y^2 + y^4]$$

On putting the values of x and y *i.e.*, $x = a^2$ and $y = \sqrt{a^2 - 1}$

$\therefore \quad (a^2 + \sqrt{a^2 - 1})^4 + (a^2 - \sqrt{a^2 - 1})^4$

$$= 2[(a^2)^4 + 6(a^2)^2 (\sqrt{a^2 - 1})^2 + (\sqrt{a^2 - 1})^4]$$
$$= 2[a^8 + 6a^4 (a^2 - 1) + (a^2 - 1)^2]$$
$$= 2[a^8 + 6a^6 - 6a^4 + a^4 + 1 - 2a^2]$$
$$= 2[a^8 + 6a^6 - 5a^4 - 2a^2 + 1]$$
$$= 2a^8 + 12a^6 - 10a^4 - 4a^2 + 2$$

Question 4 Find an approximation of $(0.99)^5$ using the first three terms of its expansion.

◎ *Thinking Process* Write $0.99 = (1 - 0.01)$, then in the expansion of $(0 \cdot 99)^5$, there will be six terms but you have to take only first three terms.

Sol. We have, $(0.99)^5 = (1 - 0.01)^5$

$= {}^5C_0 (1)^5 - {}^5C_1 (1)^4 (0.01) + {}^5C_2 (1)^3 (0.01)^2 \quad$ (ignore the other terms)

$= 1 - 5 \times 1 \times 0.01 + \dfrac{5 \times 4}{2} \times 1 \times 0.01 \times 0.01$

$= 1 - 0.05 + 10 \times 0.0001$

$= 1 - 0.05 + 0.001$

$= 1.001 - 0.05$

$= 0.951$

Question 5 Expand using binomial theorem $\left(1+\frac{x}{2}-\frac{2}{x}\right)^4, x \neq 0.$

◎ *Thinking Process* Consider first two terms as x and last term as y and use the expansion of $(x-y)^n$.

Sol. We have, $\left[\left(1+\frac{x}{2}\right)-\frac{2}{x}\right]^4 = {}^4C_0\left(1+\frac{x}{2}\right)^4 - {}^4C_1\left(1+\frac{x}{2}\right)^3\left(\frac{2}{x}\right)$

$$+ {}^4C_2\left(1+\frac{x}{2}\right)^2\left(\frac{2}{x}\right)^2 - {}^4C_3\left(1+\frac{x}{2}\right)\left(\frac{2}{x}\right)^3 + {}^4C_4\left(\frac{2}{x}\right)^4$$

$$= \left(1+\frac{x}{2}\right)^4 - 4\left(1+\frac{x}{2}\right)^3\frac{2}{x} + \frac{4\times 3}{2}\left(1+\frac{x}{2}\right)^2\frac{4}{x^2} - 4\left(1+\frac{x}{2}\right)\times\frac{8}{x^3} + \frac{16}{x^4}$$

$$= \left(1+\frac{x}{2}\right)^4 - \frac{8}{x}\left(1+\frac{x}{2}\right)^3 + \frac{24}{x^2}\left(1+\frac{x}{2}\right)^2 - \frac{32}{x^3}\left(1+\frac{x}{2}\right) + \frac{16}{x^4}$$

Now, open the expansion of $\left(1+\frac{x}{2}\right)^4, \left(1+\frac{x}{2}\right)^3, \left(1+\frac{x}{2}\right)^2$, then we get

$$\left(1+\frac{x}{2}-\frac{2}{x}\right)^4 = \left(1+4\cdot\frac{x}{2}+6\cdot\frac{x^2}{4}+4\cdot\frac{x^3}{8}+\frac{x^4}{16}\right) - 8\cdot\frac{1}{x}\left(1+3\cdot\frac{x}{2}+3\cdot\frac{x^2}{4}+\frac{x^3}{8}\right)$$

$$+ 24\cdot\frac{1}{x^2}\left(1+x+\frac{x^2}{4}\right) - 32\times\frac{1}{x^3}\left(1+\frac{x}{2}\right) + \frac{16}{x^4}$$

$$= \left(1+2x+\frac{3x^2}{2}+\frac{x^3}{2}+\frac{x^4}{16}\right) - \left(\frac{8}{x}+12+6x+x^2\right) + \left(\frac{24}{x^2}+\frac{24}{x}+6\right) - \left(\frac{32}{x^3}+\frac{16}{x^2}\right) + \frac{16}{x^4}$$

$$= \frac{x^4}{16}+\frac{x^3}{2}+x^2\left(\frac{3}{2}-1\right)+x(2-6)+(1-12+6) + (24-8)\frac{1}{x}+(24-16)\frac{1}{x^2}-\frac{32}{x^3}+\frac{16}{x^4}$$

$$= \frac{x^4}{16}+\frac{x^3}{2}+\frac{x^2}{2}-4x-5+\frac{16}{x}+\frac{8}{x^2}-\frac{32}{x^3}+\frac{16}{x^4}$$

Question 6 Find the expansion of $(3x^2 - 2ax + 3a^2)^3$ using binomial theorem.

Thinking Process Here, we will split $(3x^2 - 2ax + 3a^2)$ into two parts as $3(x^2 + a^2)$ and $-2ax$ for the given expansion.

Sol. $(3x^2 - 2ax + 3a^2)^3 = [3(x^2 + a^2) - 2ax]^3$

$$= {}^3C_0 \{3(x^2 + a^2)\}^3 - {}^3C_1 \{3(x^2 + a^2)\}^2 2ax + {}^3C_2 3(x^2 + a^2)(2ax)^2 - {}^3C_3 (2ax)^3$$

$$= 27(x^2 + a^2)^3 - 3 \times 9 (x^2 + a^2)^2 \times 2ax + 3 \times 3 (x^2 + a^2) 4a^2x^2 - 8a^3x^3$$

Now, open the expansion of $(x^2 + a^2)^3, (x^2 + a^2)^2$, we get

$$= 27 [{}^3C_0(x^2)^3 + {}^3C_1(x^2)^2 a^2 + {}^3C_2x^2(a^2)^2 + {}^3C_3(a^2)^3] - 27 [{}^2C_0(x^2)^2 + {}^2C_1x^2a^2 + {}^2C_2(a^2)^2] \times 2ax + 9 (x^2 + a^2) 4a^2x^2 - 8a^3x^3$$

$$= 27 [x^6 + 3x^4a^2 + 3x^2a^4 + a^6] - 27 [x^4 + 2x^2a^2 + a^4] 2ax + 36a^2x^2 (x^2 + a^2) - 8a^3x^3$$

$$= 27x^6 + 81x^4a^2 + 81x^2a^4 + 27a^6 - 54ax (x^4 + 2x^2a^2 + a^4) + 36a^2x^4 + 36a^4x^2 - 8a^3x^3$$

$$= 27x^6 + 117x^4a^2 + 117a^4x^2 + 27a^6 - 54ax^5 - 54a^5x - 8a^3x^3 - 108a^3x^3$$

$$= 27x^6 - 54ax^5 + 117a^2x^4 - 116a^3x^3 + 117a^4x^2 - 54a^5x + 27a^6$$

DIKSHA APP Questions

Multiple Choice Questions

Q.1 Total number of term in the expansion of $(x+y)^{99}$ is

(a) 98 (b) 99 (c) 101 (d) 100

◎ *Thinking Process* Total number of terms in the expansion of $(x+y)^n$ is $n+1$ *i.e.*, one more than the index number.

Sol. (d) Index of $(x+y)^{99} = 99$. So, total number of term in its expansion $= 99 + 1 = 100$

Q.2 If the three consecutive coefficients in the expansion of $(1+x)^n$ are 28, 56 and 70 then the value of n is

(a) 6 (b) 7 (c) 8 (d) 9

◎ *Thinking Process* Here, we will consider three consecutive coefficients which are as ${}^nC_{r-1}$, ${}^nC_r$ and ${}^nC_{r+1}$ and then we will use

$$\frac{{}^nC_r}{{}^nC_{r-1}} = \frac{n!}{(n-r)!r!} \times \frac{[n-[r-1]]!(r-1)!}{n!} = \frac{n-r+1}{r}$$

Sol. (c) Let the three consecutive coefficients be

$${}^nC_{r-1} = 28,\ {}^nC_r = 56 \text{ and } {}^nC_{r+1} = 70$$

$$\therefore \quad \frac{{}^nC_r}{{}^nC_{r-1}} = \frac{n-r+1}{r} = \frac{56}{28} = 2 \quad \left[\because \frac{{}^nC_r}{{}^nC_{r-1}} = \frac{n-r+1}{r}\right]$$

$$\Rightarrow \quad n-r+1 = 2r$$

$$\Rightarrow \quad n+1 = 3r \quad \text{... (i)}$$

$$\text{Again,} \quad \frac{{}^nC_{r+1}}{{}^nC_r} = \frac{n-(r+1)+1}{(r+1)} = \frac{70}{56} = \frac{5}{4}$$

$$\Rightarrow \quad \frac{n-r}{r+1} = \frac{5}{4} \Rightarrow 4n - 4r = 5r + 5$$

$$\Rightarrow \quad 4n - 5 = 9r \quad \text{... (ii)}$$

By Eq. (i) and Eq. (ii), we get

$$\frac{4n-5}{n+1} = \frac{9r}{3r} \Rightarrow \frac{4n-5}{n+1} = 3 \Rightarrow 4n - 5 = 3n + 3 \Rightarrow n = 8$$

$$\therefore \quad n = 8$$

□ Subjective Type Questions

Q.1 Find out which one is larger $99^{50}+100^{50}$ or 101^{50}.

◎ ***Thinking Process*** First of all, we will take $101^{50}-(99^{50}+100^{50})$ and after that use the binomial theorem.

Sol. Let's try to find out $101^{50}-(99^{50}+100^{50})$

i.e. $(101)^{50}-(99)^{50}-(100)^{50}$

$=(100+1)^{50}-(100-1)^{50}-(100)^{50}$

$=(100)^{50}\,[(1+0.01)^{50}-(1-0.01)^{50}-1]$

$=(100)^{50}[({}^{50}C_0+{}^{50}C_1(0.01)^1+{}^{50}C_2(0.01)^2+....)-({}^{50}C_0-{}^{50}C_1(0.01)^1+{}^{50}C_2(0.01)^2-...)-1]$

$=(100)^{50}\,[(2({}^{50}C_1(0.01)^1))+2({}^{50}C_3(0.01)^3)+2({}^{50}C_5(0.01)^5+...)-1]$

$=(100)^{50}[2({}^{50}C_3(0.01)^3)+2({}^{50}C_5(0.01)^5)+....]$ $\qquad [\because 2({}^{50}C_1(0.01)^1=1]$

$\because (100)^{50}[2({}^{50}C_3(0.01)^3)+2({}^{50}C_5(0.01)^5)+...]$ is positive value

So, $(101)^{50}-99^{50}-100^{50}>0 \Rightarrow (101)^{50}>99^{50}+100^{50}$

$\therefore (101)^{50}$ is larger than $99^{50}+100^{50}$

Note Note that we don't need to calculate the exact value of $101^{50}-(99^{50}+100^{50})$, our goal is simply to determine whether $101^{50}-(99^{50}+100^{50})$ is positive or negative.

Q.2 Using the binomial theorem, show that 6^n-5n always leaves remainder 1 when divided by 25.

◎ ***Thinking Process*** Here, 6^n can be written as $(1+5)^n$ and use the expansion of $(x+y)^n$.

Sol. We have, $6^n-5n=(1+5)^n-5n$

By using Binomial expansion

$$=[{}^nC_0+{}^nC_1(5)+{}^nC_2(5)^2+...+{}^nC_n(5)^n]-5n$$
$$=[1+5n+{}^nC_2(5)^2+...+{}^nC_n(5)^n]-5n$$
$$=1+5^2[{}^nC_2+{}^nC_3(5)+...+{}^nC_n(5)^{n-2}]=1+25(k)$$

$\therefore\ 6^n-5n=1+25k$

Where $k={}^nC_2+{}^nC_3(5)+...+{}^nC_n(5)^{n-2}$

Therefore, 6^n-5n always leave remainder 1 when divided by 25

Hence Proved.

Sequences and Series

CHAPTER 08

Important Points

01 **Sequence** A sequence is an arrangement of numbers in a definite order according to some rule.

02 **Series** A series is formed by addition or subtraction (–) in the terms of a sequence.

03 **Progression** It is a sequence in which the terms increase or decrease consistently by a constant value or ratio.

04 **Geometric Progression (GP)** A sequence of the form a, ar, ar^2, ar^3 .... is called a GP, where, $a =$ first term and $r =$ common ratio.

Its nth term from beginning is given by $T_n\ (l) = ar^{n-1}$.

If three numbers a, b, c are in GP, then $\frac{b}{a} = \frac{c}{b} \Rightarrow b^2 = ac$

Sum of the n terms of a GP

$$S_n = a + ar + ar^2 + ar^3 + ... + ar^{n-1}$$

$$S_n = \frac{a(r^n - 1)}{r - 1}, r > 1 \quad \text{or} \quad S_n = \frac{a(1 - r^n)}{1 - r}, r < 1$$

It is also written as $S_n = \frac{a - lr}{1 - r}$. $\quad (\because l = ar^{n-1} \Rightarrow rl = ar^n)$

where, l is a last term of G.P.

05 **Geometric Mean (GM)** Let there are two numbers a and b. We can insert a number G between a and b so that a, G, b are in GP, then G is called the geometric mean of a and b where, $G^2 = ab$

If n GMs $G_1, G_2, G_3, ... G_n$ are inserted between two positive numbers a and b, then the resulting sequence is GP.

And $b = ar^{n+1}$ or $r = \left(\frac{b}{a}\right)^{\frac{1}{n+1}}$, $G_K = ar^k = a\left(\frac{b}{a}\right)^{\frac{k}{n+1}}; 1 \le k \le n$

06 Properties of GP

(i) Three terms in a GP can be taken as $\frac{a}{r}, a, ar$.

(ii) If a non-zero constant is multiplied (or divided) in GP, then resulting sequence is also a GP.

(iii) If n geometric means $G_1, G_2, G_3, \ldots, G_n$ are inserted between two positive numbers a and b, then product of 's is equal to the nth root of their single GM

i.e., $$G_1 \cdot G_2 \cdot G_3 \cdot \ldots\ldots G_n = (ab)^{n/2}$$

Problem Solving Tip

The n number of terms in a GP can be taken as following.

n	**Terms**	**Common ratio**
3	$\frac{a}{r}, a, ar$	r
4	$\frac{a}{r^3}, \frac{a}{r}, ar, ar^3$	r^2
5	$\frac{a}{r^2}, \frac{a}{r}, a, ar, ar^2$	r
6	$\frac{a}{r^5}, \frac{a}{r^3}, \frac{a}{r}, ar, ar^3, ar^5$	r^2

07 Relationship between AM and GM Arithmetic mean is greater than equal to geometric mean *i.e.*, $A \geq G$.

08 Sum to *n* terms of a special series

(i) Sum of first n natural numbers,

$$S = 1 + 2 + 3 + \ldots + n \Rightarrow \Sigma n = \frac{n(n+1)}{2}$$

(ii) Sum of squares of first n natural numbers

$$S = 1^2 + 2^2 + 3^2 + \ldots\ldots + n^2 \Rightarrow \Sigma n^2 = \frac{n(n+1)(2n+1)}{6}$$

(iii) Sum of cubes of first n natural numbers

$$S = 1^3 + 2^3 + 3^3 + \ldots + n^3 \Rightarrow \Sigma n^3 = \left[\frac{n(n+1)}{2}\right]^2$$

Exercise 8.1

Direction (Q. No. 1 to 6) Write the first five terms of each of the sequence we have, whose nth terms are given in questions.

Question 1 $a_n = n(n+2)$

◎ *Thinking Process* (Q. No. 1 to 6) To find the first five terms of each of the sequence then put $n = 1, 2, 3,. 4, 5$ and simplify the sequence.

Sol. We have, $a_n = n(n + 2)$

Putting $n = 1, 2, 3, 4, 5$,

At $n = 1$, $a_1 = 1(1 + 2) = 3$

At $n = 2$, $a_2 = 2(2 + 2) = 8$

At $n = 3$, $a_3 = 3(3 + 2) = 15$

At $n = 4$, $a_4 = 4(4 + 2) = 24$

At $n = 5$, $a_5 = 5(5 + 2) = 35$

Question 2 $a_n = \dfrac{n}{n+1}$

Sol. We have, $a_n = \dfrac{n}{n + 1}$

Putting $n = 1, 2, 3, 4, 5$,

At $n = 1$, $a_1 = \dfrac{1}{1 + 1} = \dfrac{1}{2}$

At $n = 2$, $a_2 = \dfrac{2}{2 + 1} = \dfrac{2}{3}$

At $n = 3$, $a_3 = \dfrac{3}{3 + 1} = \dfrac{3}{4}$

At $n = 4$, $a_4 = \dfrac{4}{4 + 1} = \dfrac{4}{5}$

At $n = 5$, $a_5 = \dfrac{5}{5 + 1} = \dfrac{5}{6}$

Question 3 $a_n = 2^n$

Sol. We have, $a_n = 2^n$

Putting $n = 1, 2, 3, 4, 5$,

At $n = 1$, $a_1 = 2^1 = 2$

At $n = 2$, $a_2 = 2^2 = 4$

At $n = 3$, $a_3 = 2^3 = 8$

At $n = 4$, $a_4 = 2^4 = 16$

At $n = 5$, $a_5 = 2^5 = 32$

Question 4 $a_n = \dfrac{2n-3}{6}$

Sol. We have, $a_n = \dfrac{2n-3}{6}$

Putting $n = 1, 2, 3, 4, 5$,

At $n = 1$, $a_1 = \dfrac{2\times1-3}{6} = \dfrac{2-3}{6} = -\dfrac{1}{6}$

At $n = 2$, $a_2 = \dfrac{2\times2-3}{6} = \dfrac{4-3}{6} = \dfrac{1}{6}$

At $n = 3$, $a_3 = \dfrac{2\times3-3}{6} = \dfrac{6-3}{6} = \dfrac{3}{6} = \dfrac{1}{2}$

At $n = 4$, $a_4 = \dfrac{2\times4-3}{6} = \dfrac{8-3}{6} = \dfrac{5}{6}$

At $n = 5$, $a_5 = \dfrac{2\times5-3}{6} = \dfrac{10-3}{6} = \dfrac{7}{6}$

Question 5 $a_n = (-1)^{n-1}\, 5^{n+1}$

Sol. We have, $a_n = (-1)^{n-1}\, 5^{n+1}$

Putting $n = 1, 2, 3, 4, 5$,

At $n = 1$, $a_1 = (-1)^{1-1}\, 5^{1+1} = (-1)^0\, 5^2 = 25$

At $n = 2$, $a_2 = (-1)^{2-1}\, 5^{2+1} = (-1)^1\, 5^3 = -125$

At $n = 3$, $a_3 = (-1)^{3-1}\, 5^{3+1} = (-1)^2\, 5^4 = 625$

At $n = 4$, $a_4 = (-1)^{4-1}\, 5^{4+1} = (-1)^3\, 5^5 = -3125$

At $n = 5$, $a_5 = (-1)^{5-1}\, 5^{5+1} = (-1)^4\, 5^6 = 15625$

Question 6 $a_n = \dfrac{n(n^2+5)}{4}$

Sol. We have, $a_n = \dfrac{n(n^2+5)}{4}$

Putting $n = 1, 2, 3, 4, 5$,

At $n = 1$, $a_1 = \dfrac{1(1^2+5)}{4} = \dfrac{6}{4} = \dfrac{3}{2}$

At $n = 2$, $a_2 = \dfrac{2(2^2+5)}{4} = \dfrac{2(4+5)}{4} = \dfrac{9}{2}$

At $n = 3$, $a_3 = \dfrac{3(3^2+5)}{4} = \dfrac{3(9+5)}{4} = \dfrac{21}{2}$

At $n = 4$, $a_4 = \dfrac{4(4^2+5)}{4} = \dfrac{4(16+5)}{4} = 21$

At $n = 5$, $a_5 = \dfrac{5(5^2+5)}{4} = \dfrac{5(25+5)}{4} = \dfrac{75}{2}$

Direction (Q. No. 7 to 10) Find the indicated terms in each of the sequence, whose *n*th terms are given in questions.

Question 7 $a_n = 4n - 3, a_{17}, a_{24}$.

Sol. We have, $a_n = 4n - 3$

Putting $n = 17$, $a_{17} = 4 \times 17 - 3 = 68 - 3 = 65$

Putting $n = 24$, $a_{24} = 4 \times 24 - 3 = 96 - 3 = 93$

Question 8 $a_n = \frac{n^2}{2^n}, a_7$.

Sol. We have, $a_n = \frac{n^2}{2^n}$

Putting $n = 7$, $a_7 = \frac{7^2}{2^7} = \frac{49}{128}$

Question 9 $a_n = (-1)^{n-1} n^3, a_9$.

Sol. We have, $a_n = (-1)^{n-1} n^3$

Putting $n = 9$,

$$a_9 = (-1)^{9-1} 9^3 = (-1)^8 \times 9 \times 9 \times 9 = 729$$

Question 10 $a_n = \frac{n(n-2)}{n+3}, a_{20}$.

Sol. We have, $a_n = \frac{n(n-2)}{n+3}$

Putting $n = 20$, $a_{20} = \frac{20(20-2)}{20+3} = \frac{20 \times 18}{23} = \frac{360}{23}$

Direction (Q. No. 11 to 13) Write the first five terms of each of the sequences and obtain the corresponding series.

Question 11 $a_1 = 3, a_n = 3a_{n-1} + 2$ for all $n > 1$.

Sol. We have, $a_1 = 3, a_n = 3a_{n-1} + 2$, for all $n > 1$

Putting $n = 2$, $a_2 = 3a_{2-1} + 2$

$\Rightarrow$ $a_2 = 3a_1 + 2 = 3 \times (3) + 2 = 9 + 2 = 11$ $[\because a_1 = 3]$

Putting $n = 3, a_3 = 3a_{3-1} + 2 = 3a_2 + 2 = 3(11) + 2 = 33 + 2 = 35$ $[\because a_2 = 11]$

Putting $n = 4, a_4 = 3a_{4-1} + 2 = 3a_3 + 2 = 3 \times 35 + 2 = 105 + 2 = 107$ $[\because a_3 = 35]$

Putting $n = 5, a_5 = 3 \times a_{5-1} + 2 = 3a_4 + 2 = 3 \times 107 + 2 = 321 + 2 = 323$ $[\because a_4 = 107]$

$\therefore$ Series is $3 + 11 + 35 + 107 + 323 \ldots$

Question 12 $a_1 = -1, a_n = \dfrac{a_{n-1}}{n}, n \ge 2.$

Sol. We have, $a_1 = -1$, $a_n = \dfrac{a_{n-1}}{n}, n \ge 2$

Putting $n = 2$, $a_2 = \dfrac{a_{2-1}}{2} = \dfrac{a_1}{2} = -\dfrac{1}{2}$ $[\because a_1 = -1]$

Putting $n = 3$, $a_3 = \dfrac{a_{3-1}}{3} = \dfrac{a_2}{3} = \dfrac{-\frac{1}{2}}{3} = -\dfrac{1}{6}$ $\left[\because a_2 = -\dfrac{1}{2}\right]$

Puttinig $n = 4$, $a_4 = \dfrac{a_{4-1}}{4} = \dfrac{a_3}{4} = \dfrac{-\frac{1}{6}}{4} = -\dfrac{1}{24}$ $\left[\because a_3 = -\dfrac{1}{6}\right]$

Putting $n = 5$, $a_5 = \dfrac{a_{5-1}}{5} = \dfrac{a_4}{5} = \dfrac{-\frac{1}{24}}{5} = -\dfrac{1}{120}$ $\left[\because a_4 = -\dfrac{1}{24}\right]$

$\therefore$ Series is $(-1) + \left(-\dfrac{1}{2}\right) + \left(-\dfrac{1}{6}\right) + \left(-\dfrac{1}{24}\right) + \left(-\dfrac{1}{120}\right) + \ldots$

$$= -1 - \frac{1}{2} - \frac{1}{6} - \frac{1}{24} - \frac{1}{120} - \ldots$$

Question 13 $a_1 = a_2 = 2, a_n = a_{n-1} - 1, n > 2.$

Sol. We have, $a_1 = a_2 = 2$

and $a_n = a_{n-1} - 1, n > 2$

Putting $n = 3$, $a_3 = a_{3-1} - 1 = a_2 - 1 = 2 - 1 = 1$ $[\because a_2 = 2]$

Putting $n = 4$, $a_4 = a_{4-1} - 1$

$= a_3 - 1 = 1 - 1 = 0$ $[\because a_3 = 1]$

Putting $n = 5$, $a_5 = a_{5-1} - 1 = a_4 - 1 = 0 - 1 = -1$ $[\because a_4 = 0]$

$\therefore$ Series is $2 + 2 + 1 + 0 + (-1) + \ldots$

Question 14 The Fibonacci sequence is defined by $1 = a_1 = a_2$ and $a_n = a_{n-1} + a_{n-2}, n > 2$. Find $\dfrac{a_{n+1}}{a_n}$, for $n = 1, 2, 3, 4, 5$.

Sol. Here, $1 = a_1 = a_2$

$$a_n = a_{n-1} + a_{n-2}, n > 2$$

Putting $n = 3, 4, 5, 6$

At $n = 3$, $a_3 = a_{3-1} + a_{3-2}$ $[\because a_1 = a_2 = 1]$

$= a_2 + a_1$

$= 1 + 1 = 2$

At $n = 4$, $a_4 = a_{4-1} + a_{4-2} = a_3 + a_2 = 2 + 1 = 3$ $[\because a_3 = 2, a_2 = 1]$

At $n = 5$, $a_5 = a_{5-1} + a_{5-2} = a_4 + a_3 = 3 + 2 = 5$ $[\because a_4 = 3, a_3 = 2]$

At $n = 6$, $a_6 = a_{6-1} + a_{6-2} = a_5 + a_4 = 5 + 3 = 8$ $[\because a_5 = 5, a_4 = 3]$

Now, $\frac{a_{n+1}}{a_n}$, for $n = 1, 2, 3, 4, 5$.

At $n = 1$, $\quad \frac{a_2}{a_1} = \frac{1}{1} = 1$

At $n = 2$, $\quad \frac{a_3}{a_2} = \frac{2}{1} = 2$

At $n = 3$, $\quad \frac{a_4}{a_3} = \frac{3}{2}$

At $n = 4$, $\quad \frac{a_5}{a_4} = \frac{5}{3}$

At $n = 5$, $\quad \frac{a_6}{a_5} = \frac{8}{5}$

Hence, the terms are $1, 2, \frac{3}{2}, \frac{5}{3}$ and $\frac{8}{5}$.

Mistake Alert Students sometime put $n = 1, 2$ in fibonacci sequence *i.e.*, a_1 and a_2, but this is already given in question that $a_1 = a_2 = 1$, so start by putting $n = 3$ in fibonacci sequence.

Exercise 8.2

Question 1 Find the 20th and nth terms of the GP; $\frac{5}{2}, \frac{5}{4}, \frac{5}{8}, \ldots$

Thinking Process (Q. No. 1 to 4) The nth term of a GP is $T_n = ar^{n-1}$.

Sol. The given series is $\frac{5}{2}, \frac{5}{4}, \frac{5}{8}, \ldots$

Here, a = first term = $\frac{5}{2}$ and common ratio $(r) = \frac{\frac{5}{4}}{\frac{5}{2}} = \frac{2}{4} = \frac{1}{2}$

Now, $\quad T_n = ar^{n-1}$

$\Rightarrow \quad T_{20} = ar^{20-1} = \left(\frac{5}{2}\right) \times \left(\frac{1}{2}\right)^{20-1} = \frac{5}{2} \times \left(\frac{1}{2}\right)^{19}$

$= \frac{5}{2} \times \frac{1}{2^{19}} = \frac{5}{2^{20}}$

Again, $\quad T_n = ar^{n-1} = \left(\frac{5}{2}\right) \times \left(\frac{1}{2}\right)^{n-1} = \frac{5}{2} \times \frac{1}{2^{n-1}}$

$= \frac{5}{2^{1+n-1}} = \frac{5}{2^n}$

Question 2 Find the 12th term of a GP whose 8th term is 192 and the common ratio is 2.

Sol. Given, 8th term, $T_8 = 192$

and common ratio $r = 2$

$\therefore \quad ar^{8-1} = 192 \qquad (\because T_n = ar^{n-1})$

$\Rightarrow \quad a \times (2)^7 = 192 \Rightarrow a \times 128 = 192$

$\Rightarrow \quad a = \dfrac{192}{128} \Rightarrow a = \dfrac{48}{32} = \dfrac{3}{2}$

Now, $T_{12} = ar^{12-1} = \dfrac{3}{2} \times (2)^{11}$

$= \dfrac{3}{2} \times 2^{11} = 3 \times 2^{10}$

$= 3 \times 1024 = 3072$

Question 3 The 5th, 8th and 11th terms of a GP are p, q and s, respectively. Show that $q^2 = ps$.

Sol. Let a and r be the first term and common ratio of the GP.

Given, $T_5 = p \Rightarrow ar^4 = p \qquad \ldots\text{(i)}$

$T_8 = q \Rightarrow ar^7 = q \qquad \ldots\text{(ii)}$

and $T_{11} = s \Rightarrow ar^{10} = s \qquad \ldots\text{(iii)}$

Now, multiplying Eqs. (i) and (iii), we get

$ar^4 \times ar^{10} = ps \Rightarrow a^2 r^{14} = ps$

$\Rightarrow \quad [ar^7]^2 = ps$

$\Rightarrow \quad q^2 = ps$ [from Eq. (ii)

Hence Proved.

Question 4 The 4th term of a GP is square of its second term and the first term is -3. Determine its 7th term.

Sol. Let a and r be the first term and common ratio of the GP.

Given, $T_4 = (T_2)^2 \qquad (\because T_n = ar^{n-1})$

$\Rightarrow \quad ar^3 = (ar)^2$

$\Rightarrow \quad ar^3 = a^2 r^2$

$\Rightarrow \quad r = a$

But given, $a = -3$

$\Rightarrow \quad r = -3$

Now, $T_7 = ar^6 = (-3)(-3)^6 = (-3)^7$

$= -2187$

Question 5 Which term of the following sequences

(i) $2, 2\sqrt{2}, 4....$ is 128? (ii) $\sqrt{3}, 3, 3\sqrt{3}$ ... is 729?

(iii) $\frac{1}{3}, \frac{1}{9}, \frac{1}{27}$ ... is $\frac{1}{19683}$?

◎ ***Thinking Process*** The nth term of a GP is $T_n = ar^{n-1}$ and with the help of this relation we will determine the value of n.

Sol. (i) The series is $2, 2\sqrt{2}, 4, ... 128$

Here, $a = 2, r = \frac{2\sqrt{2}}{2} = \sqrt{2}$

and $T_n = 128$

Now, $T_n = ar^{n-1}$

$$\Rightarrow \quad 128 = 2(\sqrt{2})^{n-1} \Rightarrow 2^{\frac{n-1}{2}} = \frac{128}{2}$$

$$\Rightarrow \quad 2^{\frac{n-1}{2}} = 64 \Rightarrow 2^{\frac{n-1}{2}} = 2^6$$

On comparing the power of 2 both sides, we get

$$\Rightarrow \quad \frac{n-1}{2} = 6 \quad \Rightarrow \quad n = 12 + 1$$

$$\Rightarrow \quad n = 13$$

(ii) $\sqrt{3}, 3, 3\sqrt{3}, ..., 729$

Here, $a = \sqrt{3}, r = \frac{3}{\sqrt{3}} = \sqrt{3}, T_n = 729$

Now, $T_n = ar^{n-1}$

$$\Rightarrow \quad 729 = \sqrt{3}(\sqrt{3})^{n-1} \Rightarrow 729 = (\sqrt{3})^n \quad \Rightarrow \quad 3^{\frac{n}{2}} = 3^6$$

On comparing the power of 3 both sides, we get

$$\Rightarrow \quad \frac{n}{2} = 6 \quad \Rightarrow \quad n = 12$$

(iii) $\frac{1}{3}, \frac{1}{9}, \frac{1}{27}, ..., \frac{1}{19683}$

Here, $a = \frac{1}{3}, r = \frac{\frac{1}{9}}{\frac{1}{3}} = \frac{3}{9} = \frac{1}{3} \Rightarrow T_n = \frac{1}{19683}$

Now, $T_n = ar^{n-1}$

$$\frac{1}{19683} = \frac{1}{3} \times \left(\frac{1}{3}\right)^{n-1} \Rightarrow \frac{1}{6561} = \left(\frac{1}{3}\right)^{n-1} \Rightarrow \left(\frac{1}{3}\right)^{n-1} = \left(\frac{1}{3}\right)^8$$

On comparing the power of (1/3) both sides, we get

$$\Rightarrow \quad n - 1 = 8 \Rightarrow n = 8 + 1 \Rightarrow n = 9$$

Note r is a common ratio such that $r = \frac{a_{n+1}}{a_n}; n \geq 1$

Question 6 For what values of x, the numbers $-\frac{2}{7}, x, -\frac{7}{2}$ are in GP?.

◎ *Thinking Process* We know that if three numbers a, b, c are in GP, then $b^2 = ac$.

Sol. Since, $-\frac{2}{7}, x, -\frac{7}{2}$ are in GP, then

$$\Rightarrow \quad x^2 = \left(-\frac{2}{7}\right) \times \left(-\frac{7}{2}\right)$$

$$\Rightarrow \quad x^2 = \frac{2}{7} \times \frac{7}{2}$$

$$\Rightarrow \quad x^2 = 1$$

$$\Rightarrow \quad x = \pm 1$$

Direction (Q. No. 7 to 10) Find the sum to indicated number of terms in each of the following geometric progression.

Question 7 0.15, 0.015, 0.0015 .... 20 terms.

◎ *Thinking Process* (Q.No. 7 to 10) Here, we will use the formula,

$$S_n = \frac{a(r^n - 1)}{r - 1}, r > 1 \text{ or } S_n = \frac{a(1 - r^n)}{1 - r}, r < 1 \text{ and simplify it.}$$

Sol. Here, $a = 0.15$, $r = \frac{0.015}{0.15} = \frac{15}{1000} \times \frac{100}{15}$

$$r = \frac{1}{10} < 1 \quad \text{and} \quad n = 20$$

As we know, $S_n = \frac{a(1 - r^n)}{1 - r}$

$$\therefore \quad S_{20} = \frac{0.15\left[1 - \left(\frac{1}{10}\right)^{20}\right]}{1 - \frac{1}{10}}$$

$$= \frac{0.15\left[1 - \frac{1}{10^{20}}\right]}{\frac{10 - 1}{10}} = \frac{0.15 \times 10}{9}\left[1 - \frac{1}{10^{20}}\right]$$

$$= \frac{15 \times 10}{900}\left[1 - \left(\frac{1}{10}\right)^{20}\right]$$

$$= \frac{1}{6}[1 - (0.1)^{20}]$$

Question 8 $\sqrt{7}, \sqrt{21}, 3\sqrt{7}$ .... n terms.

Sol. Here, $a = \sqrt{7}$, $r = \dfrac{\sqrt{21}}{\sqrt{7}} = \dfrac{\sqrt{7 \times 3}}{\sqrt{7}} = \sqrt{3} > 1$

As we know, $S_n = \dfrac{a(r^n - 1)}{r - 1}$ $(\because r > 1)$

$$\therefore \quad S_n = \frac{\sqrt{7}\,[(\sqrt{3})^n - 1]}{\sqrt{3} - 1} = \frac{\sqrt{7}\,[(3^{1/2})^n - 1]}{\sqrt{3} - 1} \times \frac{\sqrt{3} + 1}{\sqrt{3} + 1}$$

$$= \frac{\sqrt{7}\,(\sqrt{3} + 1)\,(3^{n/2} - 1)}{3 - 1} \quad [\because a^2 - b^2 = (a + b)(a - b)]$$

$$= \frac{\sqrt{7}}{2}(\sqrt{3} + 1)(3^{n/2} - 1)$$

Question 9 $1, -a, a^2, -a^3, \ldots, n$ terms (if $a \neq -1$).

Sol. Here, $a = 1$, $r = -\dfrac{a}{1} = -a < 1$

As we know, $S_n = \dfrac{a(1 - r^n)}{1 - r}$ $(\because r < 1)$

$$\therefore \quad S_n = \frac{1\,\{1 - (-a)^n\}}{1 - (-a)} = \frac{1 - (-a)^n}{1 + a}$$

Question 10 $x^3, x^5, x^7, \ldots, n$ terms (if $x \neq \pm 1$).

Sol. Here, $a = x^3$, $r = \dfrac{x^5}{x^3} = x^2 \because S_n = \dfrac{a(1 - r^n)}{1 - r}$ $(\because r < 1)$

$$\therefore \quad S_n = \frac{x^3\,[1 - (x^2)^n]}{1 - x^2} = \frac{x^3\,[1 - x^{2n}]}{1 - x^2}$$

Question 11 Evaluate $\sum\limits_{k=1}^{11} (2 + 3^K)$.

◎ *Thinking Process* $\sum\limits_{i=1}^{n}(x_i \pm y_i) = \sum\limits_{i=1}^{n} x_i \pm \sum\limits_{i=1}^{n} y_i$ and $\sum\limits_{i=1}^{n} a = an$

Sol. We have, $\sum\limits_{k=1}^{11}(2 + 3)^k$

$$\sum_{k=1}^{11} 2 + \sum_{k=1}^{11} 3^k = 2 \times 11 + (3^1 + 3^2 + 3^3 + \ldots + 3^{11})$$

$$\left[\because S_n = \frac{a\,(r^n - 1)}{r - 1}, r > 1\right]$$

$$= 22 + \frac{3(3^{11} - 1)}{3 - 1} = 22 + \frac{3(3^{11} - 1)}{2}$$

Question 12 The sum of first three terms of a GP is $\frac{39}{10}$ and their product is 1. Find the common ratio and the terms.

◎ *Thinking Process* Here, we will take three consecutive terms in GP as $\frac{a}{r}$, a, ar and apply the given conditions.

Sol. Let the first three number of GP be $\frac{a}{r}$, a and ar.

∴ According to the question,

$$\frac{a}{r} + a + ar = \frac{39}{10} \quad \text{...(i)}$$

and

$$\left(\frac{a}{r}\right) \times (a) \times (ar) = 1 \quad \text{...(ii)}$$

$$\Rightarrow \quad a^3 = 1 \Rightarrow a = 1$$

On putting the value of $a = 1$ in Eq. (i), we get

$$\frac{1}{r} + 1 + r = \frac{39}{10} \Rightarrow \frac{1}{r} + \frac{1}{1} + \frac{r}{1} = \frac{39}{10} \Rightarrow \frac{1 + r + r^2}{r} = \frac{39}{10}$$

$$\Rightarrow \quad 10 + 10r + 10r^2 = 39r$$

$$\Rightarrow \quad 10r^2 + 10r - 39r + 10 = 0$$

$$\Rightarrow \quad 10r^2 - 29r + 10 = 0$$

Now, factorising it by splitting the middle term, we get

$$\Rightarrow \quad 10r^2 - 25r - 4r + 10 = 0$$

$$\Rightarrow \quad 5r(2r - 5) - 2(2r - 5) = 0$$

$$\Rightarrow \quad (5r - 2)(2r - 5) = 0$$

$$\Rightarrow \quad 5r - 2 = 0 \text{ and } 2r - 5 = 0 \Rightarrow r = \frac{2}{5} \text{ and } r = \frac{5}{2}$$

When $a = 1$ and $r = \frac{2}{5}$, then numbers are

$$\frac{a}{r} = \frac{1}{\frac{2}{5}} = \frac{5}{2}; \; a = 1 \text{ and } ar = 1 \times \frac{2}{5} = \frac{2}{5}$$

Therefore, three terms are $\frac{5}{2}, 1, \frac{2}{5}$

When $a = 1$ and $r = \frac{5}{2}$, then numbers are

$$\frac{a}{r} = \frac{1}{\frac{5}{2}} = \frac{2}{5}; \; a = 1$$

$$ar = 1 \times \frac{5}{2} = \frac{5}{2}$$

Therefore, three terms are $\frac{2}{5}, 1, \frac{5}{2}$

Question 13 How many terms of a GP $3, 3^2, 3^3, \ldots$ are needed to give the sum 120?

◎ *Thinking Process* Here, we will use the formula $S_n = \frac{a(r^n - 1)}{r-1}, r > 1$ to determine the value of n.

Sol. Here, $a = 3, r = 3, S_n = 120$ $\left[\because r = \frac{3^2}{3} = 3\right]$

As we know that $$S_n = \frac{a(r^n - 1)}{r - 1}, r > 1$$

$$\therefore \quad 120 = \frac{3(3^n - 1)}{3 - 1} \Rightarrow 120 = \frac{3(3^n - 1)}{2}$$

$$\Rightarrow \quad 120 \times 2 = 3(3^n - 1) \Rightarrow \frac{240}{3} = 3^n - 1$$

$$\Rightarrow \quad 3^n - 1 = 80 \Rightarrow 3^n = 80 + 1$$

$$\Rightarrow \quad 3^n = 81 \Rightarrow \quad 3^n = 3^4$$

On comparing the power of 3 both sides, we get

$$\Rightarrow \quad n = 4$$

Question 14 The sum of the first three terms of a GP is 16 and the sum of next three terms is 128. Determine the first term, the common ratio and the sum to n terms of the GP.

Sol. Let the GP is $a, ar, ar^2, ar^3, \ldots\ldots$

Given, $$a + ar + ar^2 = 16 \quad \ldots(i)$$

and $$ar^3 + ar^4 + ar^5 = 128 \quad \ldots(ii)$$

Dividing Eq. (i) by Eq. (ii), $$\frac{a + ar + ar^2}{ar^3 + ar^4 + ar^5} = \frac{16}{128}$$

$$\Rightarrow \quad \frac{a(1 + r + r^2)}{ar^3(1 + r + r^2)} = \frac{1}{8} \Rightarrow \frac{1}{r^3} = \left(\frac{1}{2}\right)^3$$

On comparing the base of the power 3 both sides, we get

$$\Rightarrow \quad r = 2$$

On putting $r = 2$ in Eq. (i), we get

$$\Rightarrow \quad a + 2a + 4a = 16 \Rightarrow 7a = 16 \Rightarrow a = \frac{16}{7}$$

Now, $$S_n = \frac{a(r^n - 1)}{r - 1} \quad (\because r = 2 > 1)$$

$$= \frac{\frac{16}{7}(2^n - 1)}{2 - 1} = \frac{16}{7}(2^n - 1) \quad (\because r > 1)$$

Hence, $$a = \frac{16}{7}, r = 2 \text{ and } S_n = \frac{16}{7}(2^n - 1)$$

Question 15 Given a GP with $a = 729$ and 7th term 64, determine S_7.

Sol. Given, $a = 729$, $T_7 = 64$

$$\therefore \quad ar^{7-1} = 64$$

$$\Rightarrow \quad 729r^6 = 64 \Rightarrow r^6 = \frac{64}{729} = \left(\frac{2}{3}\right)^6$$

On comparing base of the power 6 both sides, we get

$$\Rightarrow \quad r = \frac{2}{3} < 1$$

Now, $$S_n = \frac{a(1-r^n)}{1-r} \quad [\because r < 1]$$

$$\therefore \quad S_7 = \frac{729\left[1-\left(\frac{2}{3}\right)^7\right]}{1-\frac{2}{3}}$$

$$= \frac{729\left[\frac{1}{1}-\frac{128}{2187}\right]}{\frac{3-2}{3}} = \frac{729 \times 3}{1} \times \frac{2187-128}{2187}$$

$$= \frac{1}{1} \times 2059 = 2059$$

Question 16 Find a GP for which sum of the first two terms is -4 and fifth term is 4 times the third term.

Sol. Let the GP is $a, ar, ar^2, ar^3, \ldots$.

Given, $$a + ar = -4 \quad \ldots(\text{i})$$

and $$T_5 = 4T_3$$

$$\Rightarrow \quad ar^{5-1} = 4ar^{3-1} \Rightarrow r^4 = 4r^2 \quad [\text{Given}]$$

$$\Rightarrow \quad r^2 = 4 \quad \Rightarrow \quad r = \pm 2$$

If $r = 2$, then from Eq. (i), $a + a(2) = -4$

$$3a = -4$$

$$\Rightarrow \quad a = -\frac{4}{3}$$

Hence, GP is $-\frac{4}{3}, \left(-\frac{4}{3}\right)(2), \left(-\frac{4}{3}\right)(2)^2 \ldots = -\frac{4}{3}, -\frac{8}{3}, -\frac{16}{3}, \ldots$

If $r = -2$, then from Eq. (i),

$$a + a(-2) = -4$$

$$\Rightarrow \quad -a = -4$$

$$\Rightarrow \quad a = 4$$

Hence, GP is $4, 4(-2), 4(-2)^2, \ldots = 4, -8, 16, \ldots$

Question 17 If the 4th, 10th and 16th terms of a GP are x, y and z, respectively, prove that x, y, z are in GP.

◎ *Thinking Process* x, y, z are in GP if and only if $y^2 = xz$.

Sol. Given,

$$T_4 = x \Rightarrow ar^{4-1} = x \Rightarrow ar^3 = x \quad \text{...(i)}$$
$$T_{10} = y \Rightarrow ar^{10-1} = y \Rightarrow ar^9 = y \quad \text{...(ii)}$$
$$T_{16} = z \Rightarrow ar^{16-1} = z \Rightarrow ar^{15} = z \quad \text{...(iii)}$$

Now, multiplying Eq. (i) by Eq. (iii),

$$\Rightarrow ar^3 \times ar^{15} = x \times z$$
$$\Rightarrow a^2 r^{3+15} = xz$$
$$\Rightarrow a^2 r^{18} = xz$$
$$\Rightarrow (ar^9)^2 = xz$$
$$\Rightarrow y^2 = xz \quad \text{[from Eq. (ii)]}$$

Therefore, x, y, z are in GP.

Question 18 Find the sum of n terms of the sequence 8, 88, 888, 8888.....

◎ *Thinking Process* In such type of question (like as 5, 55, 555, ... and 7, 77, 777 ......), we take out the common factor and then multiply and divide each term by 9 to make the GP.

Sol. Let $S = 8 + 88 + 888 + 8888 + ... + n$ terms

$$\Rightarrow S = 8(1 + 11 + 111 + 1111 + ... + n \text{ terms})$$
$$= \frac{8}{9}[9 + 99 + 999 + 9999 + ... + n \text{ terms}]$$
$$= \frac{8}{9}[(10-1) + (100-1) + (1000-1) + ... + n \text{ terms}]$$
$$= \frac{8}{9}[(10 + 100 + 1000 + ... + n \text{ terms}) - (1 + 1 + 1 + ... + n \text{ terms})]$$
$$= \frac{8}{9}\left[10\frac{(10^n - 1)}{10 - 1} - n\right] \quad \left[\because S_n = \frac{a(r^n - 1)}{r - 1} \text{ as } r > 1\right]$$
$$= \frac{8}{9}\left[\frac{10(10^n - 1)}{9} - n\right]$$
$$= \frac{8}{9} \times \frac{10}{9} \times (10^n - 1) - \frac{8}{9} \times n$$
$$= \frac{80}{81}(10^n - 1) - \frac{8n}{9}$$

Question 19 Find the sum of the products of the corresponding terms of the sequence 2, 4, 8, 16, 32 and 128, 32, 8, 2, $\frac{1}{2}$.

Sol. Given, sequences are 2, 4, 8, 16, 32 ...(i)

and $128, 32, 8, 2, \frac{1}{2}$ ...(ii)

Multiplying the corresponding terms of sequence (i) and (ii) to obtain a new sequence, we get

$$256, 128, 64, 32, 16$$

Let $S = 256 + 128 + 64 + 32 + 16$

Here, $a = 256, r = \frac{1}{2}$

$$\therefore \text{ Required sum } S = \frac{256\left[1-\left(\frac{1}{2}\right)^5\right]}{1-\frac{1}{2}} = 256 \times 2\left(1-\frac{1}{2^5}\right)$$

$$\left[\because S_n = \frac{a(1-r^n)}{1-r}, r<1\right]$$

$$= 512 \times \left(1-\frac{1}{32}\right) = 512\left(\frac{32-1}{32}\right) = 16 \times 31 = 496$$

Note The product of two GP is again a GP.

Question 20 Show that the products of the corresponding terms of the sequences $a, ar, ar^2, \dots ar^{n-1}$ and $A, AR, AR^2, \dots\dots, AR^{n-1}$ form a GP and find the common ratio.

Sol. Given, sequences are $a, ar, ar^2, \dots\dots, ar^{n-1}$ ...(i)

and $A, AR, AR^2, \dots, AR^{n-1}$ ...(ii)

Now, multiplying the corresponding terms of Eqs. (i) and (ii), we get

$$aA, ar\,AR, ar^2\,AR^2, \dots, ar^{n-1}\,AR^{n-1}$$

$$\frac{\text{second term}}{\text{first term}} = \frac{arAR}{aA} = rR$$

$$\frac{\text{third term}}{\text{second term}} = \frac{ar^2 AR^2}{arAR} = rR$$

Thus, the above sequence forms a as p and the common ratio is rR.

Question 21 Find four numbers forming a GP in which the third term is greater than the first term by 9 and the second term is greater than 4th by 18.

Sol. Let the GP is $a, ar, ar^2, ar^3 \dots$

Given, third term = first term + 9

$$T_3 = a + 9 \Rightarrow ar^2 = a + 9$$

$$ar^2 - a = 9 \quad \text{...(i)}$$

Again, second term = fourth term + 18

$$T_2 = T_4 + 18 \Rightarrow ar = ar^3 + 18$$

$$\Rightarrow \quad ar - ar^3 = 18 \quad \text{...(ii)}$$

On dividing Eq. (i) by Eq. (ii), we get

$$\frac{ar^2 - a}{ar - ar^3} = \frac{9}{18}$$

$$\Rightarrow \quad \frac{a(r^2 - 1)}{ar(1 - r^2)} = \frac{1}{2}$$

$$\Rightarrow \quad \frac{-1}{r}\frac{(1 - r^2)}{(1 - r^2)} = \frac{1}{2}$$

$$\Rightarrow \quad -\frac{1}{r} = \frac{1}{2} \Rightarrow r = -2$$

On putting $r = -2$ in Eq. (ii), we get

$$a(-2) - a(-2)^3 = 18$$

$$\Rightarrow \quad -2a + 8a = 18 \Rightarrow 6a = 18 \Rightarrow a = 3$$

Therefore, GP is $3, 3(-2), 3(-2)^2, 3(-2)^3$ ......

$\Rightarrow$ $3, -6, 12, -24, \ldots\ldots$

Note Here, greater than word stands for excess in term.

Question 22 If the pth, qth, and rth terms of a GP are a, b and c, respectively, prove that $a^{q-r}\, b^{r-p} c^{p-q} = 1$.

Sol. Let the first term of GP is A and common ratio is R.

Given, pth term $= T_p = a \Rightarrow AR^{p-1} = a$ ...(i)

qth term $= T_q = b \Rightarrow AR^{q-1} = b$ ...(ii)

rth term $= T_r = c \Rightarrow AR^{r-1} = c$ ...(iii)

Now, we are to prove $a^{q-r}\, b^{r-p}\, c^{p-q} = 1$

$\text{LHS} = a^{q-r}\, b^{r-p}\, c^{p-q}$

On putting the values of a, b and c from Eqs. (i), (ii) and (iii), we get

$$\begin{aligned}\text{LHS} &= (AR^{p-1})^{q-r}\,(AR^{q-1})^{r-p}\,(AR^{r-1})^{p-q}\\ &= A^{q-r}\,R^{(p-1)(q-r)}\,A^{r-p}\,R^{(q-1)(r-p)}\,A^{p-q}\,R^{(r-1)(p-q)}\\ &= A^{q-r+r-p+p-q}\,R^{(p-1)(q-r)+(q-1)(r-p)+(r-1)(p-q)}\\ &= A^0\,R^{pq-pr-q+r+qr-pq-r+p+rp-rq-p+q}\\ &= A^0\,R^0 = 1 \times 1 = 1 = \text{RHS}\end{aligned}$$

Hence Proved.

Note Take first term and common ratio of a GP as A and R because a and r are already given in the question.

Question 23 If the first and nth term of a GP are a and b, respectively and if P is the product of n terms, prove that $P^2 = (ab)^n$.

Sol. Let the GP is A, AR, AR^2, AR^3 ....

Given, first term $A = a$ ...(i)

nth term $AR^{n-1} = b$ ...(ii)

Now, $P=$ product of n terms

$\Rightarrow$ $P = A \times AR^1 \times AR^2 \times AR^3 \times ... \times n$ terms

$P = A^{1+1+1+...+n \text{ terms}} R^{1+2+3+...+(n-1)}$

$P = A^n R^{\frac{n(n-1)}{2}}$ $\left[\because \text{Sum of first } n \text{ natural numbers } = \frac{n(n+1)}{2}\right]$

On squaring both sides, we get

$P^2 = A^{2n} R^{n(n-1)}$

$\Rightarrow$ $P^2 = A^n A^n R^{n(n-1)} = A^n (AR^{n-1})^n$

$\Rightarrow$ $P^2 = a^n b^n$ [using Eqs. (i) and (ii)]

$\Rightarrow$ $P^2 = (ab)^n$

Hence Proved.

Question 24 Show that the ratio of the sum of the first n terms of a GP to the sum of terms from $(n+1)$ th to $(2n)$ th term is $\frac{1}{r^n}$.

◎ *Thinking Process* Here, we will take the GP up to ($2n$) terms.

Sol. Let a be the first term and r be the common ratio of the GP.

Sum of first n terms $= \frac{a(1-r^n)}{(1-r)}$

Since, there are r terms from $(n+1)$th to $(2n)$th term $= \frac{a^{n+1}(1-r^n)}{(1-r)}$

Sum of terms from $(n+1)$th to $(2n)$th term is $= a^{n+1} = ar^{n+1-1} = ar^n$

Thus, required ratio $= \frac{a(1-r^n)}{(1-r)} \times \frac{(1-r)}{ar^n(1-r^n)}$

Thus, the ratio of the sum of first n terms of a GP to the sum of terms from $(n+1)$ th to $(2n)$th term is $\frac{1}{r^n}$.

Question 25 If a, b, c and d are in GP show that

$$(a^2 + b^2 + c^2)(b^2 + c^2 + d^2) = (ab + bc + cd)^2$$

Sol. Given, a, b, c, d are in GP.

$\therefore$ $\frac{b}{a} = \frac{c}{b} = \frac{d}{c} = r$ (say)

$\Rightarrow$ $b = ar, c = br, d = cr \Rightarrow b = ar, c = (ar)r, d = (br)r$

$\Rightarrow \quad b = ar,\ c = ar^2,\ d = br^2$

$\Rightarrow \quad b = ar,\ c = ar^2,\ d = (ar)r^2 = ar^3$ ...(i)

Now, we have to prove that

$$(a^2 + b^2 + c^2)(b^2 + c^2 + d^2) = (ab + bc + cd)^2$$

Taking LHS $= (a^2 + b^2 + c^2)(b^2 + c^2 + d^2)$

$= (a^2 + a^2r^2 + a^2r^4)(a^2r^2 + a^2r^4 + a^2r^6)$

$= a^2(1 + r^2 + r^4)\, a^2 r^2 (1 + r^2 + r^4)$

$= a^4r^2(1 + r^2 + r^4)^2 = [a^2r(1 + r^2 + r^4)]^2$

$= [a^2r + a^2r^3 + a^2r^5]^2 = [a \cdot ar + ar \cdot ar^2 + ar^2 \cdot ar^3]^2$

$= [ab + bc + cd]^2$ [from Eq. (i)]

$=$ RHS

Question 26 Insert two numbers between 3 and 81 so that resulting sequence is GP.

◎ **Thinking Process** After inserting the numbers, first we will find the common ratio using T_n.

Sol. Let the two numbers are a and b, then 3, a, b, 81 are in GP.

Let A be the first terms and R be the common ratio of the GP.

$\because$ nth term $T_n = AR^{n-1}$

$\therefore$ $81 = 3R^{4-1}$

$\Rightarrow$ $R^3 = \dfrac{81}{3} \Rightarrow R^3 = 27 \Rightarrow R^3 = 3^3 \Rightarrow R = 3$

Now, $a = AR = 3 \times 3 = 9, \quad b = AR^2 = 3 \times 3^2 = 27$

Thus, the required two numbers are 9 and 27.

Question 27 Find the value of n so that $\dfrac{a^{n+1} + b^{n+1}}{a^n + b^n}$ may be the geometric mean between a and b.

◎ **Thinking Process** We know that the geometric mean between two numbers a and b is $\sqrt{ab}$, we will put it equal to the given geometric mean and solve it for n. Use this relation and simplify it.

Sol. Given, $\dfrac{a^{n+1} + b^{n+1}}{a^n + b^n} = \sqrt{ab}$

$\Rightarrow$ $\dfrac{a^{n+1} + b^{n+1}}{a^n + b^n} = \dfrac{a^{\frac{1}{2}} b^{\frac{1}{2}}}{1} \Rightarrow a^{n+1} + b^{n+1} = (a^n + b^n)(a^{\frac{1}{2}} b^{\frac{1}{2}})$

$\Rightarrow$ $a^{n+1} + b^{n+1} = a^{n+\frac{1}{2}} b^{\frac{1}{2}} + a^{\frac{1}{2}} b^{n+\frac{1}{2}}$

$\Rightarrow$ $a^{n+1} + b^{n+1} - a^{n+\frac{1}{2}} b^{\frac{1}{2}} - a^{\frac{1}{2}} b^{n+\frac{1}{2}} = 0$

$$\Rightarrow \quad (a^{n+1} - a^{n+\frac{1}{2}} b^{\frac{1}{2}}) + (b^{n+1} - a^{\frac{1}{2}} b^{n+\frac{1}{2}}) = 0$$

$$\Rightarrow \quad a^{n+\frac{1}{2}} [a^{\frac{1}{2}} - b^{\frac{1}{2}}] - b^{n+\frac{1}{2}} [a^{\frac{1}{2}} - b^{\frac{1}{2}}] = 0$$

$$\Rightarrow \quad (a^{n+\frac{1}{2}} - b^{n+\frac{1}{2}})(a^{\frac{1}{2}} - b^{\frac{1}{2}}) = 0$$

$$\Rightarrow \quad a^{n+\frac{1}{2}} - b^{n+\frac{1}{2}} = 0 \qquad (\text{as } a^{\frac{1}{2}} - b^{\frac{1}{2}} \neq 0)$$

$$\Rightarrow \quad a^{n+\frac{1}{2}} = b^{n+\frac{1}{2}} \Rightarrow \left(\frac{a}{b}\right)^{n+\frac{1}{2}} = 1 \Rightarrow \left(\frac{a}{b}\right)^{n+\frac{1}{2}} = \left(\frac{a}{b}\right)^{0}$$

On comparing the power of base (a/b) both sides, we get

$$\Rightarrow \quad n + \frac{1}{2} = 0 \Rightarrow n = -\frac{1}{2}$$

Question 28 The sum of two numbers is 6 times their geometric mean, show that the numbers are in the ratio $(3 + 2\sqrt{2}) : (3 - 2\sqrt{2})$.

◎ *Thinking Process* After taking the given condition, we will use componendo and dividendo.

$$\text{i.e.,} \quad \frac{a}{b} = \frac{c}{d} \Rightarrow \frac{a+b}{a-b} = \frac{c+d}{c-d}$$

Sol. Let the numbers are a and b.

Given, $$a + b = 6\sqrt{ab} \Rightarrow \frac{a+b}{2\sqrt{ab}} = \frac{3}{1}$$

Now, applying componendo and dividendo, we get

$$\Rightarrow \quad \frac{a + b + 2\sqrt{ab}}{a + b - 2\sqrt{ab}} = \frac{3+1}{3-1} \Rightarrow \frac{(\sqrt{a})^2 + (\sqrt{b})^2 + 2\sqrt{ab}}{(\sqrt{a})^2 + (\sqrt{b})^2 - 2\sqrt{ab}} = \frac{4}{2}$$

$$\Rightarrow \quad \frac{(\sqrt{a} + \sqrt{b})^2}{(\sqrt{a} - \sqrt{b})^2} = \frac{2}{1} \Rightarrow \frac{\sqrt{a} + \sqrt{b}}{\sqrt{a} - \sqrt{b}} = \frac{\sqrt{2}}{1}$$

Again, applying componendo and dividendo, we get

$$\Rightarrow \quad \frac{\sqrt{a} + \sqrt{b} + \sqrt{a} - \sqrt{b}}{\sqrt{a} + \sqrt{b} - (\sqrt{a} - \sqrt{b})} = \frac{\sqrt{2} + 1}{\sqrt{2} - 1} \Rightarrow \frac{2\sqrt{a}}{2\sqrt{b}} = \frac{\sqrt{2}+1}{\sqrt{2}-1} \Rightarrow \frac{\sqrt{a}}{\sqrt{b}} = \frac{\sqrt{2}+1}{\sqrt{2}-1}$$

On squaring both sides, we get

$$\Rightarrow \quad \frac{a}{b} = \frac{(\sqrt{2}+1)^2}{(\sqrt{2}-1)^2}$$

$$\Rightarrow \quad \frac{a}{b} = \frac{2 + 1 + 2\sqrt{2}}{2 + 1 - 2\sqrt{2}} \qquad \left[\because (a+b)^2 = a^2 + b^2 + 2ab \text{ and } (a-b)^2 = a^2 + b^2 - 2ab\right]$$

$$\Rightarrow \quad \frac{a}{b} = \frac{3 + 2\sqrt{2}}{3 - 2\sqrt{2}} \Rightarrow a : b = (3 + 2\sqrt{2}) : (3 - 2\sqrt{2})$$

Question 29 If A and G be AM and GM respectively, between two positive numbers prove that the numbers are $A \pm \sqrt{(A+G)(A-G)}$.

◎ *Thinking Process* We know that if roots of a quadratic equation are given, then quadratic equation is x^2 − (Sum of roots) x + Product of roots = 0

Sol. Let the numbers are α and β.

Given, sum of the roots, $\dfrac{\alpha+\beta}{2} = A$ (Arithmetic mean)

$\Rightarrow \quad \alpha + \beta = 2A$

and product of the roots,

$$\sqrt{\alpha\beta} = G \text{ (Geometric mean)} \Rightarrow \alpha\beta = G^2$$

Let quadratic equation having roots α and β is

$$x^2 - (\alpha+\beta)x + \alpha\beta = 0$$

$$\Rightarrow \quad x^2 - 2Ax + G^2 = 0$$

$$\Rightarrow \quad x = \frac{2A \pm \sqrt{4A^2 - 4 \times 1 \times G^2}}{2 \times 1} \quad \left[\because x = \frac{-b \pm \sqrt{b^2 - 4ac}}{2a}\right]$$

$$= \frac{2A \pm 2\sqrt{A^2 - G^2}}{2} = A \pm \sqrt{(A+G)(A-G)}$$

$[\because a^2 - b^2 = (a+b)(a-b)]$ **Hence Proved.**

Quick Solution

Let the numbers are α and β

Given $\dfrac{\alpha+\beta}{2} = A$ (Arithmetic mean)

$\Rightarrow \quad \alpha + \beta = 2A \quad$ ...(i)

and, $\quad \sqrt{\alpha\beta} = G$ (Geometric mean)

$\Rightarrow \quad G^2 = \alpha\beta \quad$ ...(ii)

Now, $\quad (\alpha-\beta)^2 = (\alpha+\beta)^2 - 4\alpha\beta = 4A^2 - 4G^2$

$[\because \alpha + \beta = 2A \text{ and } \alpha\beta = G^2]$

$= 4(A^2 - G^2) \Rightarrow \alpha - \beta = \pm 2\sqrt{A^2 - G^2}$

If $\quad \alpha - \beta = 2\sqrt{A^2 - G^2} \quad$ ... (iii)

By Eqs. (i) and (iii), we get

$$\alpha = A + \sqrt{A^2 - G^2} \text{ and } \beta = A - \sqrt{A^2 - G^2}$$

similarly, for $\alpha - \beta = -2\sqrt{A^2 - G^2}$

we get $\quad \alpha = A - \sqrt{A^2 - G^2}$ and $\beta = A + \sqrt{A^2 - G^2}$

$\therefore$ Numbers are $A \pm \sqrt{(A+G)(A-G)}$

Question 30 The number of bacteria in a certain culture doubles every hour. If there were 30 bacteria present in the culture originally, how many bacteria will be present at the end of 2nd hour, 4th hour and nth hour?

◎ *Thinking Process* Here, we use the formula of GP because the bacteria increases in every hour on a multiple.

Sol. Number of bacteria present in the culture, form a GP whose first term $a = 30$ and common ratio $r = 2$

Bacteria present after 2nd hour $= ar^2 = 30 \times (2)^2 = 120$ $\quad (\because T_n = ar^{n-1})$

Bacteria present after 4th hour $= ar^4 = 30 \times (2)^4 = 30 \times 16 = 480$

Bacteria present after nth hour $= ar^n = 30 \times 2^n = (30) \cdot (2^n)$

Question 31 What will ₹ 500 amounts to in 10 yr after its deposit in a bank which pays annual interest rate of 10% compounded annually?

Sol. Let A be the amount, P be principal, r be the rate of interest and t be the time period in years. Then, amount A is given by

$$A = P\left(1 + \frac{r}{100}\right)^t = 500\left[1 + \frac{10}{100}\right]^{10}$$

$$= 500\left[1 + \frac{1}{10}\right]^{10}$$

$$= 500\,[1 + 0 \cdot 1]^{10}$$

$$= 500 \times (1 \cdot 1)^{10}$$

Question 32 If AM and GM of roots of a quadratic equation are 8 and 5, respectively, then obtain the quadratic equation.

Sol. Let the roots of the quadratic equation are α and β, then

(Arithmetic mean) $\dfrac{\alpha + \beta}{2} = 8$ and (Geometric mean) $\sqrt{\alpha\beta} = 5$

$$\Rightarrow \qquad \alpha + \beta = 16$$

and $$\alpha\beta = 25$$

Now, if roots are α and β, then quadratic equation is

$$x^2 - (\text{Sum of roots})x + \text{Product of roots} = 0$$

$$\Rightarrow \qquad x^2 - (\alpha + \beta)x + \alpha\beta = 0$$

$$\Rightarrow \qquad x^2 - 16x + 25 = 0$$

Miscellaneous Exercise

Question 1 If f is a function satisfying $f(x+y)=f(x)f(y)$ for all $x, y \in N$ such that $f(1)=3$ and $\sum_{x=1}^{n} f(x)=120$, find the value of n.

◎ ***Thinking Process*** From given functional relation, first we will find the values of $f(1)$, $f(2)$, $f(3)$, $f(4)$ ...... and so on then put the value of their sum *i.e.,* 120.

Sol. Given, $$f(x+y)=f(x)\,f(y) \quad \text{...(i)}$$

On putting $x=y=1$ in Eq. (i), we get

$$f(1+1)=f(1)f(1)$$
$$\Rightarrow f(2)=3\times 3 \quad [\because f(1)=3]$$
$$\Rightarrow f(2)=9$$

On putting $x=2$, $y=1$ in Eq. (i), we get

$$f(2+1)=f(2)f(1)$$
$$\Rightarrow f(3)=9\times 3 \quad [\because f(2)=9,\ f(1)=3]$$
$$\Rightarrow f(3)=27$$

On putting $x=3$, $y=1$ in Eq. (i), we get

$$f(3+1)=f(3)f(1)$$
$$\Rightarrow f(4)=27\times 3 \quad [\because f(3)=27]$$
$$\Rightarrow f(4)=81$$

Now, $$\sum_{x=1}^{n} f(x)=120$$
$$\Rightarrow f(1)+f(2)+f(3)+\ldots+f(n)=120$$
$$\Rightarrow 3+9+27+\ldots+n\text{ terms}=120$$

Here, $$a=3,\ r=\frac{9}{3}=3$$

$$\because \frac{a(r^n-1)}{r-1}=\frac{3(3^n-1)}{3-1}=120 \quad (\therefore r>1)$$
$$\Rightarrow 3(3^n-1)=120\times 2$$
$$\Rightarrow 3(3^n-1)=240$$
$$\Rightarrow 3^n-1=\frac{240}{3}$$
$$\Rightarrow 3^n-1=80$$
$$\Rightarrow 3^n=80+1$$
$$\Rightarrow 3^n=81 \Rightarrow 3^n=3^4$$

On comparing the power of 3 both sides, we get

$$\Rightarrow n=4$$

Question 2 The sum of the some terms of a GP is 315 whose first term and the common ratio are 5 and 2 respectively. Find the last term and the number of terms.

◎ *Thinking Process* Here, we will use formula $S_n = \frac{a(r^n - 1)}{r - 1}, r > 1$

Sol. Let GP of n terms is $a, ar, ar^2, ar^3, \ldots\ldots, ar^{n-1}$

Given, $a = 5, r = 2$ and $S_n = 315$

Therefore, $315 = \frac{5(2^n - 1)}{2 - 1} \Rightarrow \frac{315}{5} = 2^n - 1$ $\left[\because S_n = \frac{a(r^n - 1)}{r - 1}, r > 1\right]$

$\Rightarrow \quad 2^n - 1 = 63 \Rightarrow 2^n = 63 + 1$

$\Rightarrow \quad 2^n = 64$

$\Rightarrow \quad 2^n = 2^6$

On comparing the power of 2 both sides, we get

$\Rightarrow \quad n = 6$

Again, for last term use

$$T_n = ar^{n-1} = 5 \times (2)^{6-1}$$
$$= 5 \times 2^5 = 5 \times 32 = 160$$

Question 3 The first term of a GP is 1. The sum of the third term and fifth term is 90. Find the common ratio of the GP.

Sol. Let the GP is $a, ar, ar^2, ar^3 \ldots\ldots\ldots$

Given, $a = 1$ and $T_3 + T_5 = 90$

$\therefore \quad ar^2 + ar^4 = 90$ $(\because T_n = ar^{n-1})$

$\Rightarrow \quad r^2 + r^4 = 90$ (as $a = 1$)

$\Rightarrow \quad r^4 + r^2 - 90 = 0$

Now, factorizing it by splitting the middle term, we get

$\Rightarrow \quad r^4 + 10r^2 - 9r^2 - 90 = 0$

$\Rightarrow \quad r^2(r^2 + 10) - 9(r^2 + 10) = 0$

$\Rightarrow \quad (r^2 + 10)(r^2 - 9) = 0$

$\because \quad r^2 + 10 \neq 0 \Rightarrow r^2 - 9 = 0$

$\Rightarrow \quad r^2 = 9 \Rightarrow r = \pm 3$

Hence, the common ratio (r) is 3, –3.

Note $r^2 = -10$ is not possible because square of any real number is always non-negative number.

Question 4 The sum of three numbers in GP is 56. If we subtract the 1, 7, 21 from these numbers in that order, we obtain an Arithmetic Progression (AP). Find the numbers.

◎ *Thinking Process* x, y and z are in AP if and only if $2y = x + z$

Sol. Let three numbers in GP are a, ar, ar^2.

Given, $a + ar + ar^2 = 56$ ...(i)

Again, $a - 1, ar - 7, ar^2 - 21$ are in AP.

$\Rightarrow \quad 2(ar - 7) = (a - 1) + (ar^2 - 21)$ ($\because$ If a, b, c are in AP, then $2b = a + c$)

$\Rightarrow \quad 2ar - 14 = a + ar^2 - 22$

$\Rightarrow \quad a + ar^2 - 2ar = -14 + 22$

$\Rightarrow \quad a + ar^2 - 2ar = 8$ ...(ii)

On dividing Eq. (i) by Eq. (ii), we get

$$\frac{a + ar + ar^2}{a + ar^2 - 2ar} = \frac{56}{8} \Rightarrow \frac{1 + r + r^2}{1 + r^2 - 2r} = \frac{7}{1}$$

$\Rightarrow \quad 1 + r + r^2 = 7 + 7r^2 - 14r \Rightarrow 6r^2 - 15r + 6 = 0$

$2r^2 - 5r + 2 = 0$ [$\because$ On dividing by 3]

Factorizing it by splitting the middle term,

$$2r^2 - (4 + 1)r + 2 = 0 \Rightarrow 2r^2 - 4r - r + 2 = 0$$

$\Rightarrow \quad 2r(r - 2) - (r - 2) = 0 \Rightarrow (r - 2)(2r - 1) = 0$

$\Rightarrow \quad r = 2, \frac{1}{2}$

If $r = 2$, then from Eq. (i),

$$a + 2a + 4a = 56 \Rightarrow 7a = 56$$

$$a = 8$$

Then, numbers are

$$a = 8$$

$$ar = 8 \times 2 = 16 \Rightarrow ar^2 = 8 \times 4 = 32$$

$$8, 16, 32$$

If $r = \frac{1}{2}$, then from Eq. (i),

$$\frac{a}{1} + \frac{a}{2} + \frac{a}{4} = 56 \Rightarrow \frac{4a + 2a + 1}{4} = 56 \Rightarrow \frac{7a}{4} = 56 \Rightarrow a = 32$$

Then, numbers are

$$a = 32$$

$$ar = 32 \times \frac{1}{2} = 16 \text{ or } ar^2 = 32 \times \frac{1}{4} = 8$$

$\Rightarrow \quad 32, 16, 8$

Hence, required numbers are 8, 16, 32 or 32, 16, 8.

Question 5 A GP consists of an even number of terms. If the sum of all the terms is 5 times the sum of terms occupying odd places, then find its common ratio.

Sol. Let the GP is $a, ar, ar^2, ar^3, ar^4, \ldots, ar^{2n-2}, ar^{2n-1}$

where a, ar^2, ar^4, ar^6 ......occupy odd places and ar, ar^3, ar^5, ar^7 ... occupy even places.

Given, sum of all terms = 5 × Sum of terms occupying odd places

i.e., $a + ar + ar^2 + \dots + ar^{2n-1} = 5 \times (a + ar^2 + ar^4 + \dots + ar^{2n-2})$

$$\Rightarrow \frac{a(r^{2n} - 1)}{r - 1} = \frac{5a[(r^2)^n - 1]}{r^2 - 1} \qquad \left(\because S_n = \frac{a(r^n - 1)}{r - 1}, r > 1\right)$$

$$\Rightarrow \frac{r^{2n} - 1}{r - 1} = \frac{5(r^{2n} - 1)}{(r - 1)(r + 1)}$$

$$\Rightarrow 1 = \frac{5}{r + 1}$$

$$\Rightarrow r + 1 = 5$$

$$\Rightarrow r = 4$$

Mistake Alert Students should remember that if a GP has $2n$ (even terms) then there are n even and n odd terms.

Question 6 If $\dfrac{a+bx}{a-bx} = \dfrac{b+cx}{b-cx} = \dfrac{c+dx}{c-dx}$ $(x \neq 0)$, then show that a, b, c and d are in GP.

Sol. Given, $$\frac{a + bx}{a - bx} = \frac{b + cx}{b - cx} = \frac{c + dx}{c - dx}$$

On applying componendo and dividendo, we get

$$\Rightarrow \frac{a + bx + a - bx}{a + bx - (a - bx)} = \frac{b + cx + b - cx}{b + cx - (b - cx)} = \frac{c + dx + c - dx}{c + dx - (c - dx)}$$

$$\Rightarrow \frac{2a}{2bx} = \frac{2b}{2cx} = \frac{2c}{2dx}$$

$$\Rightarrow \frac{a}{bx} = \frac{b}{cx} = \frac{c}{dx}$$

On multiplying each term by x, we get

$$\Rightarrow \frac{a}{b} = \frac{b}{c} = \frac{c}{d}$$

Therefore, a, b, c, d are in GP.

Question 7 Let S be the sum, P be the product and R be the sum of reciprocals of n terms in a GP. Prove that $P^2 R^n = S^n$.

Sol. Let the GP is $a, ar, ar^2, ar^3 \dots ar^{n-1}$.

Given, S = Sum of n terms $= a + ar + ar^2 + ar^3 + \dots + ar^{n-1}$

$$= \frac{a(r^n - 1)}{r - 1} \quad (\text{let } r > 1) \qquad \dots(\text{i})$$

and R = Sum of the reciprocals of n terms

$$= \frac{1}{a} + \frac{1}{ar} + \frac{1}{ar^2} + \dots + \frac{1}{ar^{n-1}} \quad \left(\frac{1}{r} < 1\right)$$

$$= \frac{\frac{1}{a}\left[1-\left(\frac{1}{r}\right)^n\right]}{1-\frac{1}{r}} = \frac{1}{a}\left[\frac{1}{1}-\frac{1}{r^n}\right] \times \frac{1}{\frac{r-1}{r}} = \frac{1}{a}\left[\frac{r^n-1}{r^n}\right] \times \frac{r}{r-1}$$

$$\Rightarrow \quad R = \frac{(r^n-1)r}{ar^n(r-1)} \qquad \text{...(ii)}$$

and $P =$ Product of n terms $= a \times ar \times ar^2 \times ar^3 \times \ldots \times ar^{n-1}$

$$= a^{1+1+1+\ldots+n} \; r^{1+2+3+\ldots+(n-1)}$$

$$= a^n r^{\frac{(n-1)(n-1+1)}{2}} = a^n r^{\frac{n(n-1)}{2}} \qquad \left[\because \Sigma n = \frac{n(n+1)}{2}\right]$$

$$\Rightarrow P^2 = a^{2n} r^{n(n-1)} \qquad \text{...(iii)}$$

Now, we have to prove $P^2 R^n = S^n$

or $\quad P^2 = \frac{S^n}{R^n} \Rightarrow P^2 = \left(\frac{S}{R}\right)^n$

Taking $\text{RHS} = \left(\frac{S}{R}\right)^n = \left[\frac{a(r^n-1)}{r-1} \times \frac{ar^n(r-1)}{(r^n-1)r}\right]^n$ [using Eqs. (i) and (ii)]

$$= [a^2 r^n r^{-1}]^n = (a^2 r^{n-1})^n = [a^{2n} r^{n(n-1)}]$$

$= P^2 =$ LHS [from Eq. (iii)]

Hence Proved.

Mistake Alert Students should remember that if you are taking $r<1$ in S then you have to take $r>1$ in R.

Question 8 If a, b, c, d are in GP, prove that

$$a^n + b^n, b^n + c^n, c^n + d^n \text{ are in GP.}$$

Thinking Process We know that three numbers a, b, c are in GP, if $b^2 = ac$.

Sol. Given, a, b, c, d are in GP.

$$\Rightarrow \quad b = ar, c = ar^2, d = ar^3 \qquad \text{...(i)}$$

Now, we have to prove, $a^n + b^n, b^n + c^n, c^n + d^n$ are in GP.

$$\Rightarrow \quad (b^n + c^n)^2 = (a^n + b^n)(c^n + d^n) \qquad [\because b^2 = ac]$$

Now, $\quad \text{RHS} = (a^n + b^n)(c^n + d^n)$

$= [a^n + a^n r^n] \times [a^n r^{2n} + a^n r^{3n}]$ [from Eq. (i)]

$= a^n(1 + r^n) a^n r^{2n}(1 + r^n)$

$= a^{2n} r^{2n}(1 + r^n)^2 = [a^n r^n(1 + r^n)]^2 = [a^n r^n + a^n r^{2n}]^2$

$= [(ar)^n + (ar^2)^n]^2 = [b^n + c^n]^2$ [from Eq. (i)]

$=$ LHS

$\therefore \quad$ LHS $=$ RHS **Hence Proved.**

Question 9 If a and b are the roots of $x^2 - 3x + p = 0$ and c and d are roots of $x^2 - 12x + q = 0$, where a, b, c, d form a GP prove that $(q + p) : (q - p) = 17 : 15$.

Thinking Process If a quadratic equation, $ax^2 + bx + c = 0$ has roots α and β, then sum of roots $= \alpha + \beta = -\frac{b}{a}$ and product of roots $= \alpha\beta = \frac{c}{a}$.

Sol. Given, a and b are roots of $x^2 - 3x + p = 0$.

$\therefore$ Sum of roots, $a + b = -\frac{(-3)}{1} = 3$

$\Rightarrow \quad a + b = 3 \quad$ ...(i)

and product of roots, $ab = p \quad$ ...(ii)

Again, given that c and d are roots of $x^2 - 12x + q = 0$

$\Rightarrow$ Sum of roots, $c + d = -\frac{(-12)}{1} = 12$

$\Rightarrow \quad c + d = 12 \quad$ ...(iii)

and product of roots, $\quad cd = q \quad$ ...(iv)

Again, it is given that a, b, c, d are in GP.

$\Rightarrow \quad b = ar, c = ar^2, d = ar^3$

On putting these values in Eqs. (i) and (iii), then dividing Eq. (i) by Eq. (iii), we get

$$\frac{a + ar}{ar^2 + ar^3} = \frac{3}{12} \Rightarrow \frac{a(1 + r)}{ar^2(1 + r)} = \frac{1}{4}$$

$$\Rightarrow \quad \frac{1}{r^2} = \frac{1}{4} \Rightarrow r^2 = 4 \Rightarrow r = \pm 2$$

Again, from Eq. (i),

$$a + ar = 3 \Rightarrow a + 2a = 3 \quad (\because r = 2)$$

$$\Rightarrow \quad 3a = 3 \Rightarrow a = 1$$

So, the GP is

$$a = 1,\ b = ar = 1 \times 2 = 2,\ c = ar^2 = 1 \times 2^2 = 4,\ d = ar^3 = 1 \times 2^3 = 8$$

From Eq. (ii), $\quad p = ab = 1 \times 2 = 2$

From Eq. (iv), $\quad q = cd = 4 \times 8 = 32$

$$\therefore \quad \frac{q + p}{q - p} = \frac{32 + 2}{32 - 2} = \frac{34}{30} = \frac{17}{15}$$

Hence, $(q + p) : (q - p) = 17 : 15$

Again, from Eq. (i) $\quad a + ar = 3 \quad (\because r = -2)$

$\Rightarrow \quad a - 2a = 3 \Rightarrow a = -3$

So, the GP is $\quad a = -3, \quad b = ar = (-3)(-2) = 6$

$$c = ar^2 = (-3)(-2)^2 = -12$$

$$d = ar^3 = (-3)(-2)^3 = 24$$

From Eq. (ii), $P = ab = (-3)\cdot(+6) = -18$

From Eq. (iv), $q = cd = (-12)(24) = -288$

$$\therefore \quad \frac{q+P}{q-P} = \frac{-288-18}{-288+18} = \frac{-306}{-270} = \frac{17}{15}$$

$(q+P):(q-P) = 17:15$ **Hence Proved.**

Question 10 The ratio of the AM and GM of two positive numbers a and b is $m:n$. Show that $a:b = (m+\sqrt{m^2-n^2}):(m-\sqrt{m^2-n^2})$.

Sol. Let the AM of the number a and b is A and GM of a and b is G then,

$$A = \frac{a+b}{2} \text{ and } G = \sqrt{ab}$$

Given, $A:G = m:n$

i.e.,
$$\frac{A}{G} = \frac{m}{n} \Rightarrow \frac{a+b}{2\sqrt{ab}} = \frac{m}{n}$$

On applying componendo and dividendo rule, we get

$$\Rightarrow \frac{a+b+2\sqrt{ab}}{a+b-2\sqrt{ab}} = \frac{m+n}{m-n} \Rightarrow \frac{(\sqrt{a})^2+(\sqrt{b})^2+2\sqrt{ab}}{(\sqrt{a})^2+(\sqrt{b})^2-2\sqrt{ab}} = \frac{m+n}{m-n}$$

$$\Rightarrow \frac{(\sqrt{a}+\sqrt{b})^2}{(\sqrt{a}-\sqrt{b})^2} = \frac{m+n}{m-n} \Rightarrow \frac{\sqrt{a}+\sqrt{b}}{\sqrt{a}-\sqrt{b}} = \frac{\sqrt{m+n}}{\sqrt{m-n}}$$

Again, applying componendo and dividendo rule

$$\Rightarrow \frac{(\sqrt{a}+\sqrt{b})+(\sqrt{a}-\sqrt{b})}{(\sqrt{a}+\sqrt{b})-(\sqrt{a}-\sqrt{b})} = \frac{\sqrt{m+n}+\sqrt{m-n}}{\sqrt{m+n}-\sqrt{m-n}}$$

$$\Rightarrow \frac{2\sqrt{a}}{2\sqrt{b}} = \frac{\sqrt{m+n}+\sqrt{m-n}}{\sqrt{m+n}-\sqrt{m-n}}$$

$$\Rightarrow \frac{\sqrt{a}}{\sqrt{b}} = \frac{\sqrt{m+n}+\sqrt{m-n}}{\sqrt{m+n}-\sqrt{m-n}}$$

Now, squaring both sides,

$$\Rightarrow \frac{a}{b} = \frac{(\sqrt{m+n}+\sqrt{m-n})^2}{(\sqrt{m+n}-\sqrt{m-n})^2}$$

$$\Rightarrow \frac{a}{b} = \frac{m+n+m-n+2\sqrt{m+n}\sqrt{m-n}}{m+n+m-n-2\sqrt{m+n}\sqrt{m-n}} \quad \left[\begin{array}{l}\because (a+b)^2 = a^2+b^2+2ab \\ (a-b)^2 = a^2+b^2-2ab\end{array}\right]$$

$$\Rightarrow \frac{a}{b} = \frac{2m+2\sqrt{m^2-n^2}}{2m-2\sqrt{m^2-n^2}} \quad [\because (a+b)(a-b) = a^2-b^2]$$

$$\Rightarrow \frac{a}{b} = \frac{m+\sqrt{m^2-n^2}}{m-\sqrt{m^2-n^2}}$$

$\Rightarrow a:b = (m+\sqrt{m^2-n^2}):(m-\sqrt{m^2-n^2})$ **Hence Proved.**

Question 11 Find the sum of the following series upto n terms

(i) $5 + 5 + 555 + \dots$ (ii) $0.6 + 0.66 + 0.666 + \dots$

◎ *Thinking Process* In such type of question (like as a, aa, aaa, ...)

Always take out the common factor, then multiply and divide by 9 to each term to make the GP.

Sol. (i) Let $S = 5 + 55 + 555 + \dots + n$ terms

$$= 5(1 + 11 + 111 + \dots + n \text{ terms})$$

$$= \frac{5}{9}(9 + 99 + 999 + \dots + n \text{ terms})$$

$$= \frac{5}{9}[(10 - 1) + (100 - 1) + (1000 - 1) + \dots + n \text{ terms}]$$

$$= \frac{5}{9}[(10 + 100 + 1000 + \dots + n \text{ terms}) - (1 + 1 + 1 + \dots + n \text{ terms})]$$

$$= \frac{5}{9}\left[\frac{10(10^n - 1)}{10 - 1} - n\right] \qquad \left(\because \text{Sum of GP} = \frac{a(r^n - 1)}{r - 1}, r > 1\right)$$

$$= \frac{5}{9}\left[\frac{10(10^n - 1)}{9} - n\right] \qquad (\because \Sigma 1 = n)$$

(ii) Let $S = 0.6 + 0.66 + 0.666 + \dots + n$ terms

$$S = 6(0.1 + 0.11 + 0.111 + \dots + n \text{ terms})$$

$$= \frac{6}{9}(0.9 + 0.99 + 0.999 + \dots + n \text{ terms})$$

$$= \frac{2}{3}\left[\frac{9}{10} + \frac{99}{100} + \frac{999}{1000} + \dots + n \text{ terms}\right]$$

$$= \frac{2}{3}\left[\left(1 - \frac{1}{10}\right) + \left(1 - \frac{1}{100}\right) + \left(1 - \frac{1}{1000}\right) + \dots + n \text{ terms}\right]$$

$$= \frac{2}{3}\left[(1 + 1 + 1 + \dots + n \qquad - \left(\frac{1}{10} + \frac{1}{100} + \frac{1}{1000} + \dots + n \qquad \right)\right]$$

$$= \frac{2}{3}\left[n - \frac{\frac{1}{10}\left\{1 - \left(\frac{1}{10}\right)^n\right\}}{1 - \frac{1}{10}}\right] \qquad \left(\because \qquad = \frac{a(1 - r^n)}{1 - r}, r < 1\right)$$

$$= \frac{2}{3}\left[n - \frac{\frac{1}{10}\left\{1 - \left(\frac{1}{10}\right)^n\right\}}{\frac{9}{10}}\right] = \frac{2}{3}\left[n - \frac{1}{9}\left\{1 - \left(\frac{1}{10}\right)^n\right\}\right]$$

Question 12 Find the 20th term of the series

$$2 \times 4 + 4 \times 6 + 6 \times 8 + \ldots + n \text{ terms}.$$

Hint The nth term for AP $a, a+d, a+2d, \ldots$ is $a+(n-1)d$ *i.e.*, $T_n = a+(n-1)d$

Sol. Given series is $2 \times 4 + 4 \times 6 + 6 \times 8 + \ldots + n$ terms here, we will split the series into two parts which are 2, 4, 6, ... and 4, 6, 8, ... and then find nth term of each part separately to find the nth term of the given series. *i.e.*,

$$T_n = (n\text{th term of } 2, 4, 6 \ldots) \times (n\text{th term of } 4, 6, 8, \ldots)$$
$$= [2 + (n-1)2]\,[4 + (n-1)\,2] \qquad [\because T_n = a + (n-1)\,d]$$
$$= (2 + 2n - 2)(4 + 2n - 2) = 2n(2n + 2)$$

Putting $n = 20$,

$$T_{20} = 2 \times 20\,(2 \times 20 + 2) = 40\,(40 + 2) = 40 \times 42 = 1680$$

Question 13 A farmer buys a used tractor of ₹ 12000. He pays ₹ 6000 cash and agrees to pay the balance in annual instalment of ₹ 500 plus 12% interest on the unpaid amount. How much will the tractor cost him?

◎ ***Thinking Process*** Here, will find the value of simple interest for each year repeatedly by using the formula

$$\text{Simple interest} = \frac{\text{Principal} \times \text{Rate} \times \text{Time}}{100}$$ and then we can find the total cost of the tractor by adding all of them.

Sol. Given, tractor cost = ₹ 12000

Down payment = ₹ 6000

Balance amount = ₹ 6000

$$\therefore \text{Interest on Ist instalment} = \frac{6000 \times 12 \times 1}{100} = ₹720 \qquad \left(\because I = \frac{P \times R \times T}{100}\right)$$

Now, unpaid amount = 6000 − 500 = ₹ 5500

$$\text{Interest on IInd instalment} = \frac{5500 \times 12 \times 1}{100} = ₹\,660$$

Again, unpaid amount = 5500 − 500

= ₹ 5000

$$\text{Interest on IIIrd instalment} = \frac{5000 \times 12 \times 1}{100} = ₹\,600$$

Total interest paid by him = 720 + 660 + 600 + ...+ 12 terms

which is an AP with $a = 720, d = 660 - 720 = -60$

$$\text{Therefore, total interest} = \frac{12}{2}[2 \times 720 + (12-1)(-60)]$$

$$\left[\because \text{Sum of first } n \text{ term in AP } S_n = \frac{n}{2}[2a + (n-1)d]\right]$$

$= 6 [1440 - 11 \times 60] = 6 [1440 - 660] = 6 \times 780 =$ ₹ 4680

Hence, total amount or actual cost = 12000 + 4680 = ₹ 16680

Note Keep in mind that interest will be charged only on the unpaid amount.

Question 14 Shamshad Ali buys a scooter for ₹ 22000. He pays ₹ 4000 cash and agrees to pay the balance in annual instalments of ₹ 1000 plus 10% interest on the unpaid amount. How much will scooter cost him?

Sol. Given, Scooter cost = ₹ 22000

Down payment = ₹ 4000. Balance payment = ₹ 18000

Now, interest on Ist instalment $= \frac{18000 \times 10 \times 1}{100} =$ ₹ 1800 $\left(\because I = \frac{P \times R \times T}{100}\right)$

Unpaid amount = 18000 − 1000 = 17000

Interest on IInd instalment $= \frac{17000 \times 10 \times 1}{100} =$ ₹ 1700

Unpaid amount = 17000 − 1000 = 16000

Interest on IInd instalment $= \frac{16000 \times 10 \times 1}{100} =$ ₹ 1600

....

....

∴ Total interest paid by him = 1800 + 1700 + 1600 + ...+ 18 terms

which is an AP with $a = 1800, d = 1700 - 1800 = -100$

Therefore, total interest $= \frac{18}{2} [2 \times 1800 + (18 - 1)(-100)]$

$\left(\because \text{Sum of AP} = S_n = \frac{n}{2}[2a + (n-1)d]\right)$

$= 9 (3600 - 1700) = 9 \times 1900 =$ ₹ 17100

Hence, total amount or actual cost = 22000 + 17100 = ₹ 39100

Question 15 A person writes a letter to four of his friends. He asks each one of them, to copy the letter and mail to four different persons with instructions that they move the chain similarly. Assuming that the chain is not broken and that it costs 50 paise to mail one letter. Find the amount spent on postage when 8th set of letter is mailed.

Sol. Firsty, one person post four letters to four of his friends. Then those four persons post 4-4 letters *i.e.,* a total $4 \times 4 = 16$ letters. Similary, in next step $4 \times 4 \times 4 = 64$ letters are posted.

Thus, there will be a GP of series

i.e., 4, 16, 64, 256,...

where, $a = 4$ and $r = 4$

Now, total number of letters till 8th set

$$S_n = \frac{a(r^n - 1)}{r - 1} \Rightarrow S_8 = \frac{4(4^8 - 1)}{4 - 1} \Rightarrow S_8 = \frac{4}{3}(4^8 - 1)$$

$$\left[\because S_n = \frac{a(r^n - 1)}{(r - 1)}, r > 1\right]$$

$\because$ Cost for one letter = ₹ 0.50

Hence, total cost $= \frac{4}{3}(4^8 - 1) \times 0.50 = \frac{4}{3} \times (65536 - 1) \times 0.50$

$= \frac{4}{3} \times 65535 \times 0.50 =$ ₹ 43690

Question 16 A man deposited ₹ 10000 in a bank at the rate of 5% simple interest to annually. Find the amount in 15th yr, since he deposited the amount and also calculate the amount after 20 yr.

Sol. Since, interest on ₹ 10000 after 1 yr.

$= \frac{10000 \times 5 \times 1}{100} =$ ₹ 500 $\quad \left(\because I = \frac{P \times R \times T}{100}\right)$

Therefore, amount after 1 yr $= 10000 + 500 = 10500$

Now, interest on ₹ 10000 after 2 yr

$= \frac{10000 \times 5 \times 2}{100} =$ ₹ 1000

$\therefore$ Amount after 2 yr $= 10000 + 1000 =$ ₹ 11000

Similarly, interest on ₹ 10000 after 3 yr

$= \frac{10000 \times 5 \times 3}{100} = 1500$

$\therefore$ Amount after 3 yr $= 10000 + 1500 =$ ₹ 11500

Hence, the amount in the account of man in first, second and third year are ₹ 10000, 10500, 11000, ...

It is an AP, where $a = 10000$ and $d = 500$

Amount in 15th yr $= T_{15}$

$= a + 14d \quad [\because T_n = a + (n - 1)d$ in $AP]$

$= 10000 + 14 \times 500$

$= 10000 + 7000 =$ ₹ 17000

$\therefore$ Amount after 20 yr $= 10000 + 20 \times 500$

$= 10000 + 10000 =$ ₹ 20000

Question 17 A manufacturer reckons that the value of a machine, which costs him ₹ 15625 will depreciate each year by 20%. Find the estimated value at the end of 5 yr.

◎ ***Thinking Process*** If the value of a machine is P which depreciate every year at the rate of $r\%$, then value of the machine after n year is given by

$$A = P\left(1 - \frac{r}{100}\right)^n$$

Sol. Here, series is $15625\left(1-\frac{20}{100}\right), 15625\left(1-\frac{20}{100}\right)^2,$

$$15625\left(1-\frac{20}{100}\right)^3, \ldots\ldots$$

Estimated values at the end of 5 yr = T_5

$$= 15625\left(1-\frac{20}{100}\right)^5 = 15625 \times \left(1-\frac{1}{5}\right)^5$$

$$= 15625 \times \left(\frac{5-1}{5}\right)^5 = 15625 \times \left(\frac{4}{5}\right)^5$$

$$= \frac{15625 \times 1024}{625 \times 5}$$

$$= \frac{25 \times 1024}{5} = 5 \times 1024 = ₹5120$$

Note In depreciation, the cost value decrease every year.

Question 18 150 workers were engaged to finish a job in a certain number of days. 4 workers dropped out on second day, 4 more workers dropped out on third day and so on. It took 8 more days to finish the work. Find the number of days in which the work was completed.

Sol. 150 workers were engaged to finish a job in a certain number of days say k days.

$\therefore$ Number of workers who would have worked for k days

$$= 150 + 150 + 150 + \ldots + k \text{ terms}$$

$$= 150k \quad \ldots(\text{i})$$

But workers present on first day are 150, on second day $150 - 4 = 146$

($\because$ 4 workers dropped on second day)

On third day = $146 - 4 = 142$ and so on.

Since, the dropping out of workers, it took 8 more days to finish the work.

$\therefore$ Number of days taken to finish the work

$$= k + 8 = nl \text{ (let)} \quad \ldots(\text{ii})$$

$\therefore 150 + 146 + 142 + \ldots$ to n terms = $150k$ [from Eq. (i)]

The left hand series is a A.P with $a = 150$ and $d = 146 - 150 = -4$.

$$\Rightarrow \quad \frac{n}{2}[2a + (n-1)]d = 15k$$

On putting $k = n - 8$ from Eq. (ii), we get

$$\Rightarrow \quad \frac{n}{2}[150 \times 2 + (n-1)(-4)] = 150(n-8)$$

$$\Rightarrow \quad \frac{n}{2}[300 - 4n + 4] = 150n - 1200$$

$$\Rightarrow \quad n[304 - 4n] = 300(n-8)$$

$$\Rightarrow \quad n^2 - n - 600 = 0 \quad \text{[dividing by} - 4]$$
$$\Rightarrow \quad n^2 - 25n + 24n - 600 = 0$$
$$\Rightarrow \quad n(n-25) + 24(n-25) = 0$$
$$\Rightarrow \quad (n-25)(n+24) = 0$$
$$\Rightarrow \quad n - 25 = 0 \text{ or } n + 24 = 0$$
$$\Rightarrow \quad n = 25 \text{ or } n = -24$$

$\because n = -24$ is impossible because number of days can not be negative.

$\therefore$ The number of days = 25

DIKSHA APP Questions

Multiple Choice Questions

Q.1 Two sequence cannot be in both AP and GP together.

(a) False (b) True (c) May be (d) None of these

Thinking Process If a sequence is an AP then common difference between any two consecutive terms is constant.

Sol. (a) Let GP $a, ar, ar^2, \ldots$

we know that $a, ar, ar^2, \ldots$ is an AP

then $ar - a = ar^2 - ar = d$ (constant)

$$\Rightarrow \quad ar^2 - 2ar + a = 0 \quad \Rightarrow \quad a(r^2 - 2r + 1) = 0$$
$$\Rightarrow \quad a(r-1)^2 = 0 \quad \Rightarrow \quad a = 0 \text{ or } r = 1$$

That means GP a, ar, ar^2 is an AP if $a = 0$ or $r = 1$

$\therefore$ A constant sequence like $a, a, a, \ldots$ is both AP and GP together.

Q.2 The sum or difference of two GPs is again a GP.

(a) False (b) True (c) May be (d) None of these

Thinking Process A sequence is a GP if common ratio of any two consecutive terms is constant.

Sol. (a) Let two GP

$$2, 4, 8, \ldots \quad \ldots \text{(i)}$$
$$3, 9, 27, \ldots \quad \ldots \text{(ii)}$$

Sum of sequence (i) and (ii), we get

$$2+3, 4+9, 8+27, \ldots$$

i.e., $\quad 5, 13, 35, \ldots$

Common ratio $(r) = \dfrac{13}{5} \neq \dfrac{35}{13}$

$\therefore$ Sum of two GPs is not a GP.

again, Difference of GPs (i) and (ii), we get

$$2-3, 4-9, 8-27, \ldots$$

i.e., $\quad -1, -5, -19, \ldots$

Common ratio $(r) = \dfrac{-5}{-1} \neq \dfrac{-19}{-5}$

$\therefore$ Difference of two GPs is not a GP.

Note We can prove the statement wrong with an example but cannot prove it right.

Q.3 If the third term of G.P. is 4, then the product of its first 5 terms is

(a) 4^3 (b) 4^4 (c) 4^5 (d) 4^6

◎ **Thinking Process** 5 consecutive terms can be taken as $\dfrac{a}{r^2}, \dfrac{a}{r}, a, ar, ar^2$ in GP.

Sol. (c) Given third term = 4 *i.e.,* $a = 4$

Let 5 first terms in a GP $\dfrac{a}{r^2}, \dfrac{a}{r}, a, ar, ar^2$

Now, product of first 5 terms $= \left(\dfrac{a}{r^2}\right)\left(\dfrac{a}{r}\right)(a)(ar)(ar^2) = a^5 = 4^5 \quad [\because a = 4]$

Q.4 If $x, 2y$ and $3z$ are in AP, where the distinct number x, y and z are in GP then the common ratio of the GP is

(a) $\dfrac{1}{3}$ (b) $\dfrac{1}{4}$ (c) $\dfrac{1}{5}$ (d) $\dfrac{2}{5}$

◎ **Thinking Process** If a, b and c are in AP then $2b = a + c$ and a, b and c are in GP the $b^2 = ac$.

Sol. (a) Given x, $2y$ and $3z$ are in AP. then $2(2y) = x + 3z$

$\Rightarrow \quad 4y = x + 3z \quad \ldots\text{(i)}$

And, x, y and z are in GP

then $\quad y^2 = xz \quad \ldots\text{(ii)}$

By Eqs. (i) and (ii), we get $y^2 = (4y - 3z)z \Rightarrow y^2 = 4zy - 3z^2$

$\Rightarrow \quad 3z^2 - 4yz + y^2 = 0 \Rightarrow 3z^2 - 3yz - yz + y^2 = 0$

$\Rightarrow 3z(z-y) - y(z-y) = 0 \Rightarrow (3z - y)(z - y) = 0$

$z \neq y \quad$ [$\because$ given x, y and z are distinct numbers]

$\Rightarrow \quad 3z - y = 0 \Rightarrow \dfrac{z}{y} = \dfrac{1}{3}$

$\therefore$ Common ratio of GP $= \dfrac{1}{3}$

Q.5 The lengths of three unequal edges of a rectangular solid block are in GP. If the volume of the block is 216 cm^3 and the total surface area is 252 cm^3, then the length of the longest edge is

(a) 12 cm (b) 6 cm (c) 18 cm (d) 3 cm

◎ ***Thinking Process*** Here, we will use formulas Volume $= 1 \times b \times h$, and Surface area $= 2[lb + bh + lh]$ for rectangular solid block where l, b and h are length of edges of block.

Sol. (a) Given, volume = 216 cm^3

Let $\frac{a}{r}$, a, ar are the lengths of edges of a block which are in GP.

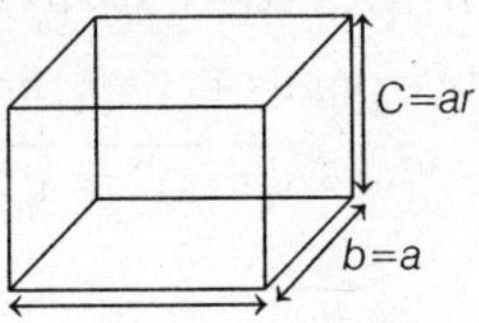

$$l \times b \times h = 216 \quad [\because \text{volume} = l \times b \times h]$$

$$\left(\frac{a}{r}\right) \times (a) \times (ar) = 216 \Rightarrow a^3 = 216 \Rightarrow a = 6$$

and, surface area = 252 cm^2

$$= 2[lb + bh + lh] = 252 \quad [\because \text{surface area} = 2[lb + bh + lh]]$$

$$2\left[\left(\frac{a}{r} \times a\right) + (a \times ar) + \left(\frac{a}{r} \times ar\right)\right] = 252$$

$$\Rightarrow \quad 2\left[\frac{a^2}{r} + a^2r + a^2\right] = 252 \Rightarrow \frac{36}{r} + 36r + 36 = 126 \quad [\because a = 6]$$

$$\Rightarrow \quad \frac{1}{r} + r + 1 = \frac{7}{2}$$

$$\Rightarrow \quad 2(r^2 + r + 1) = 7r \Rightarrow 2r^2 - 5r + 2 = 0$$

$$\Rightarrow \quad 2r^2 - 4r - r + 2 = 0 \Rightarrow 2r(r-2) - 1(r-2) = 0$$

$$\Rightarrow \quad (2r-1)(r-2) = 0 \Rightarrow r = \frac{1}{2} \text{ or } r = 2$$

If $r = \frac{1}{2}$, then lengths of edges of block

$$\frac{a}{r} = \frac{6}{\frac{1}{2}} = 12, \; a = 6 \text{ and } ar = 6 \times \frac{1}{2} = 3$$

∴ Length of edges are 3, 6 and 12 cm.

If $r = 2$, then $\frac{a}{r} = \frac{6}{2} = 3$, $a = 6$ and $ar = 6 \times 2 = 12$

∴ Length of edges are 3, 6 and 12 cm

Thus, length of longest edge is 12 cm.

Straight Lines

CHAPTER 09

Important Points

01 Distance between two points $P(x_1, y_1)$ and $Q(x_2, y_2)$ is

$$PQ = \sqrt{(x_2 - x_1)^2 + (y_2 - y_1)^2}$$

02 The coordinates of a point dividing the line segment joining the points (x_1, y_1) and (x_2, y_2) internally, in the ratio $m:n$ are $\left(\frac{mx_2 + nx_1}{m+n}, \frac{my_2 + ny_1}{m+n}\right)$ and in externally in the ratio $m:n$ are $\left(\frac{mx_2 - nx_1}{m-n}, \frac{my_2 - ny_1}{m-n}\right)$.

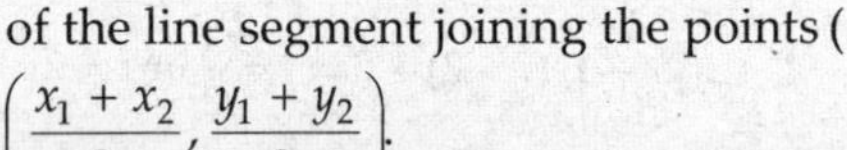

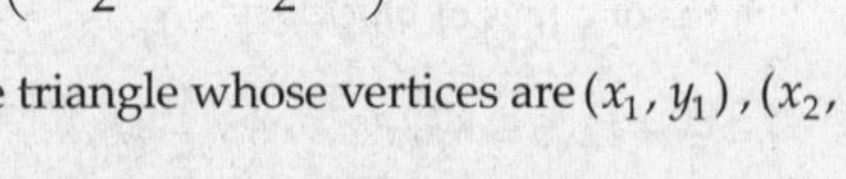

03 Mid-point of the line segment joining the points (x_1, y_1) and (x_2, y_2) are $\left(\frac{x_1 + x_2}{2}, \frac{y_1 + y_2}{2}\right)$.

04 Area of the triangle whose vertices are (x_1, y_1), (x_2, y_2) and (x_3, y_3) is

$$\frac{1}{2} |x_1 (y_2 - y_3) + x_2 (y_3 - y_1) + x_3 (y_1 - y_2)|$$

Note If the area of the $\Delta\, ABC$ is zero, then three points A, B and C lie on a line *i.e.,* they are collinear.

05 **Slope of a Line** A line in a coordinate plane forms two angles with the X-axis which are supplementary. The angle θ (say) made by the line l with positive direction of X-axis and measured anticlockwise is called the inclination of the line, where $0 \le \theta \le 180°$. If the line parallel to X-axis or coinciding with X-axis, have inclination of 0°. The inclination of a vertical line (parallel or coinciding with Y-axis) is 90°.

If angle θ is the inclination of a line l, then $\tan\theta$ is called the slope or gradient of the line l. The slope of a line whose inclination is 90° is not defined. The slope of a line is denoted by m.

Hence, $m = \tan\theta, \theta \ne 90°$

$\therefore$ Slope of X-axis is zero and slope of Y-axis is not defined.

06 Slope of a line when coordinates of any two points on the line are given. Let any two points on the line be $P(x_1, y_1)$ and $Q(x_2, y_2)$.

Slope of line $= m = \tan\theta = \dfrac{y_2 - y_1}{x_2 - x_1}$

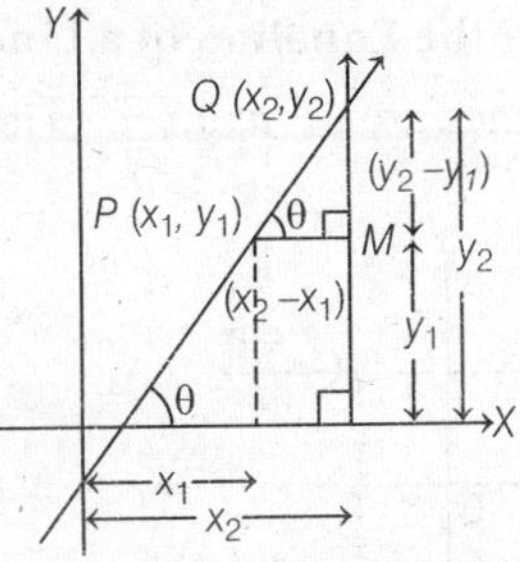

07 **Angle between Two Lines** The acute angle say (θ) between two lines L_1 and L_2 with slopes m_1 and m_2 respectively, is given by

$$\tan\theta = \left|\frac{m_2 - m_1}{1 + m_1 m_2}\right| \quad \ldots(i)$$

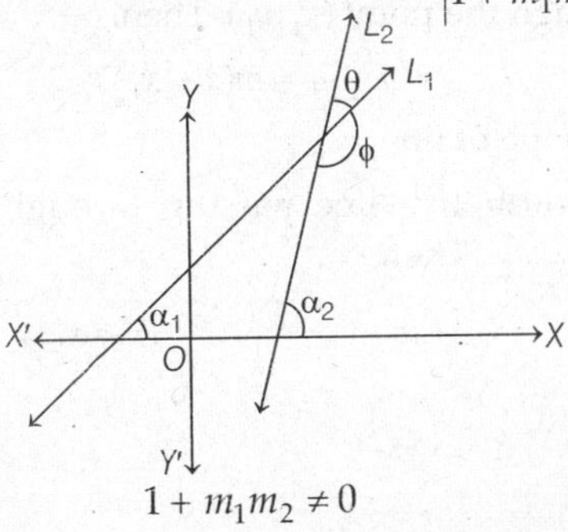

as $1 + m_1 m_2 \ne 0$

Note
- If lines $l_1 \perp l_2 \Rightarrow m_1 \times m_2 = -1$ or $m_2 = -\frac{1}{m_1}$
- If lines $l_1 \parallel l_2$ *i.e.*, $m_1 = m_2$, *i.e.*, their slopes are equal.
- The obtuse angle (say ϕ) can be found by using $\phi = 180° - \theta$.

08 Collinearity of Three Points If A, B and C are three points in the X-Y plane, then they will lie on a line, *i.e.*, three points are collinear if and only if slope of AB = slope of BC.

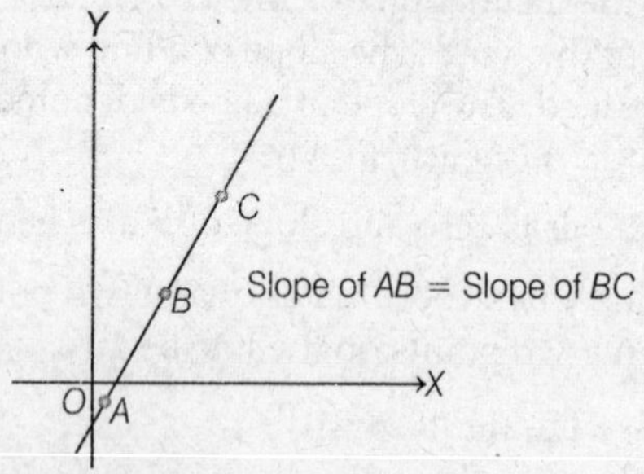

09 Various Forms of the Equation of a Line

(i) Horizontal lines are $y = a$ or $y = -a$ and vertical lines are $x = -b$ or $x = b$.

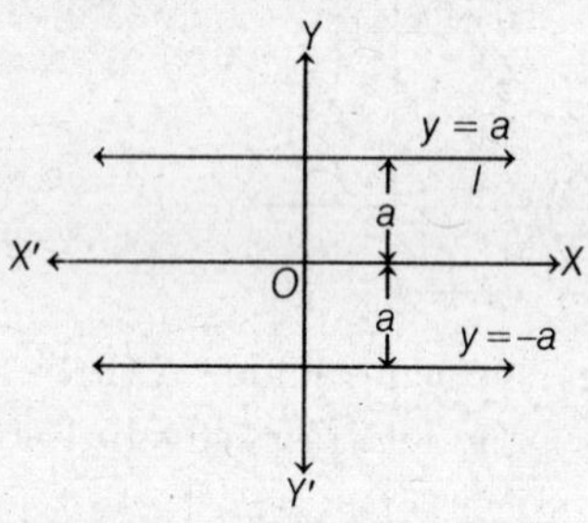

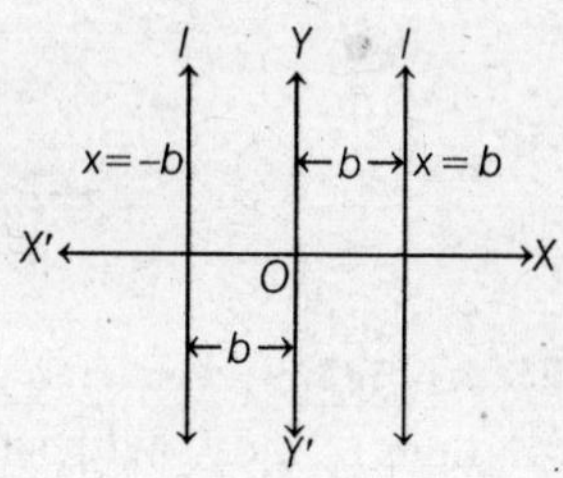

(ii) **Point Slope Form or One-point Form** If a line with slope m passing through the point (x_1, y_1). Then,

$$y - y_1 = m(x - x_1)$$

where, m is slope of line.

(iii) **Two-points form** If a line passing through the two points (x_1, y_1) and (x_2, y_2). Then,

$$y - y_1 = \frac{y_2 - y_1}{x_2 - x_1}(x - x_1)$$

(iv) **Slope-intercept Form**

$$y = mx + c$$

where, c is the distance from origin to the point of intercept on Y-axis.

Note If line l with slope m makes x-intercept d. Then, $y = m(x - d)$

(v) **Intercept Form** $\frac{x}{a} + \frac{y}{b} = 1$

where, a and b are intercepts on X-axis and Y-axis.

(vi) **General equation of a Line** Any equation of the form $Ax + By + C = 0$, where A and B are not zero simultaneously is called general linear equation or general equation of a line.

10 Distance of a Point (x_1, y_1) from a Line ax+ by+ c **is**

$$Ax + By + C = 0$$

$$d = \left| \frac{Ax_1 + By_1 + C}{\sqrt{A^2 + B^2}} \right|$$

11 Distance between two parallel lines

Then, distance d between two parallel lines $y = mx + c_1$ and $y = mx + c_2$ is given by $d = \frac{|c_1 - c_2|}{\sqrt{1 + m^2}}$.

If lines are given in general form *i.e.*, $Ax + By + C = 0$ and $Ax + By + C_2 = 0$, then $d = \frac{|C_1 - C_2|}{\sqrt{A^2 + B^2}}$

12 Concurrent lines

If three or more lines meet at same point, they are concurrent.

Exercise 9.1

Question 1 Draw a quadrilateral in the cartesian plane, whose vertices are $(-4, 5), (0, 7), (5, -5)$ and $(-4, -2)$. Also, find its area.

Thinking Process

(i) If $A(x_1, y_1), B(x_2, y_2)$ and $C(x_3, y_3)$ are the vertices of a triangle, then

Area of $\Delta ABC = \frac{1}{2}|[x_1(y_2 - y_3) + x_2(y_3 - y_1) + x_3(y_1 - y_2)]|$

(ii) Area of quadrilateral = Area of ΔABC + Area of ΔADC

Sol. Given vertices $A(-4, 5)$, $B(0, 7)$, $C(5, -5)$ and $D(-4, -2)$ are shown below in the X-Y plane. Joining all the vertices a quadrilateral $ABCD$ is formed.

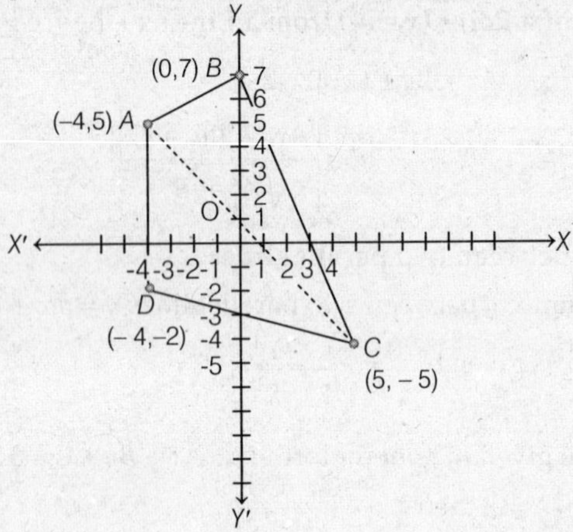

Area of quadrilateral $ABCD$ = Area of ΔADC + Area of ΔABC ...(i)

Now, area of $\Delta ADC = \frac{1}{2}|[-4(-2+5) - 4(-5-5) + 5(5+2)]|$

$$\left[\begin{array}{l} \because \text{Area} = \frac{1}{2}[x_1(y_2 - y_3) + x_2(y_3 - y_1) + x_3(y_1 - y_2)] \\ \text{Here}, (x_1, y_1) = (-4, 5), (x_2, y_2) = (-4, -2) \text{ and } (x_3, y_3) = (5, -5) \end{array}\right]$$

$$= \frac{1}{2}|[-4 \times 3 - 4(-10) + 5 \times 7]|$$

$$= \frac{1}{2}|[-12 + 40 + 35]|$$

$$= \frac{1}{2}|[75 - 12]| = \frac{63}{2}$$

Area of $\Delta ABC = \frac{1}{2}\left|[-4(7+5)+0(-5-5)+5(5-7)]\right|$

[Here, $(x_1, y_1) = (-4, 5)$, $(x_2, y_2) = (0, 7)$ and $(x_3, y_3) = (5, -5)$]

$= \frac{1}{2}\left|[-4 \times 12 + 0 \times (-10) + 5(-2)]\right|$

$= \frac{1}{2}|-48-10| = \frac{|-58|}{2} = 29$

$\therefore$ From Eq. (i),

area of quadrilateral $ABCD = \frac{63}{2} + 29 = \frac{63+58}{2}$

$= \frac{121}{2}$ sq. unit

Question 2 The base of an equilateral triangle with side $2a$ lies along the Y-axis such that the mid-point of the base is at the origin. Find vertices of the triangle.

◎ ***Thinking Process*** As one side of a triangle is on Y-axis, so third vertex be either left or right of Y-axis.

Sol. Let BC be the base of a triangle which lies on Y-axis and third vertex may be $A(h, 0)$ or A'.

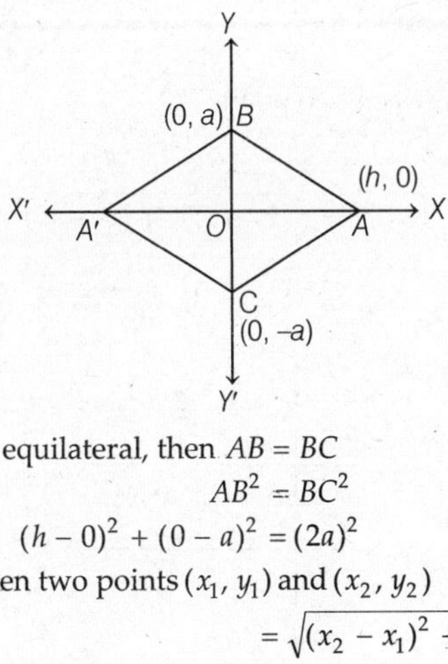

Since, ΔABC is an equilateral, then $AB = BC$

$$AB^2 = BC^2$$

$$\Rightarrow \quad (h-0)^2 + (0-a)^2 = (2a)^2$$

[$\because$ Distance between two points (x_1, y_1) and (x_2, y_2)

$= \sqrt{(x_2-x_1)^2 + (y_2-y_1)^2}$]

$$\Rightarrow \quad h^2 + a^2 = 4a^2$$

$$\Rightarrow \quad h^2 = 3a^2$$

$$\Rightarrow \quad h = \pm\sqrt{3}a \qquad (\because \text{taking square root})$$

Hence, the vertices of triangle are $(\sqrt{3}a, 0), (0, a), (0, -a)$

or $(-\sqrt{3}a, 0), (0, a), (0, -a)$

Question 3 Find the distance between $P(x_1, y_1)$ and $Q(x_2, y_2)$ when

(i) PQ is parallel to the Y-axis.

(ii) PQ is parallel to the X-axis.

Sol. (i) When PQ is parallel to the Y-axis it means the x-coordinates of P and Q are same *i.e.*, $x_1 = x_2$.

$\therefore$ Distance between two points PQ

$$= \sqrt{(x_2 - x_1)^2 + (y_2 - y_1)^2}$$

$$= \sqrt{(x_1 - x_1)^2 + (y_2 - y_1)^2} \qquad (\because x_1 = x_2)$$

$$= \sqrt{(y_2 - y_1)^2} = |y_2 - y_1|$$

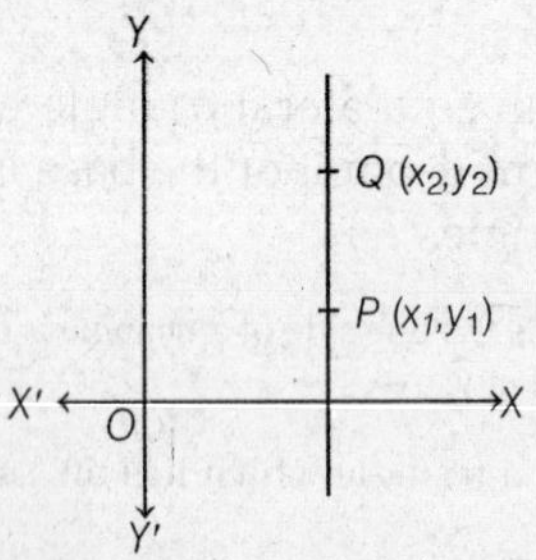

(ii) When PQ is parallel to X-axis, it means y-coordinates of P and Q are same *i.e.*, $y_2 = y_1$

$\therefore$ Distance between two points PQ

$$= \sqrt{(x_2 - x_1)^2 + (y_2 - y_1)^2}$$

$$= \sqrt{(x_2 - x_1)^2 + (y_1 - y_1)^2} \qquad (\because y_1 = y_2)$$

$$= \sqrt{(x_2 - x_1)^2} = |x_2 - x_1|$$

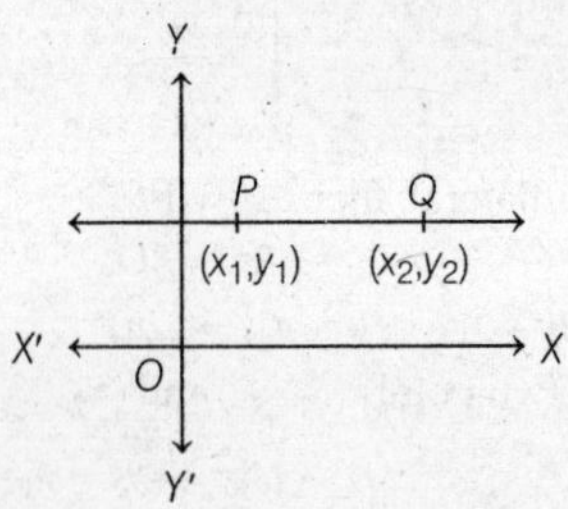

Question 4 Find a point on the X-axis, which is equidistant from the points (7,6) and (3,4).

Sol. Let any point P on the X-axis is $(x, 0)$ as for a point on X-axis y-coordinate is zero and the given points are $A(7, 6)$ and $B(3, 4)$.

Given, $PA = PB \Rightarrow PA^2 = PB^2$

$$\Rightarrow (x_1 - x_2)^2 + (y_1 - y_2)^2 = (x_1 - x_3)^2 + (y_1 - y_3)^2$$

where, $x_1 = x,\ x_2 = 7,\ y_1 = 0,\ y_2 = 6,\ x_3 = 3,\ y_3 = 4$

$$\Rightarrow (x - 7)^2 + (0 - 6)^2 = (x - 3)^2 + (0 - 4)^2$$

[$\because$ distance between two points $= \sqrt{(x_1 - x_2)^2 + (y_1 - y_2)^2}$]

$$\Rightarrow x^2 + 49 - 14x + 36 = x^2 + 9 - 6x + 16 \Rightarrow -14x + 6x = 25 - 36 - 49$$

$$\Rightarrow -8x = 25 - 85 \Rightarrow -8x = -60 \Rightarrow x = \frac{60}{8} \Rightarrow x = \frac{15}{2}$$

$\therefore$ Point P on X-axis $= \left(\frac{15}{2}, 0\right)$

Question 5 Find the slope of a line, which passes through the origin, and mid-point of the line segment joining the points $P(0, -4)$ and $B(8, 0)$.

◎ *Thinking Process* If two points are given, then slope $m = \frac{y_2 - y_1}{x_2 - x_1}$ and mid-point of the line segment joining the points (x_1, y_1) and (x_2, y_2) is $\left(\frac{x_1 + x_2}{2}, \frac{y_1 + y_2}{2}\right)$.

Sol. Given points are $P(0, -4)$ and $Q(8, 0)$.

$$\therefore \quad x_1 = 0,\ y_1 = -4,\ x_2 = 8,\ y_2 = 0$$

These points are plotted in X-Y plane given below.

Mid-point of PQ is

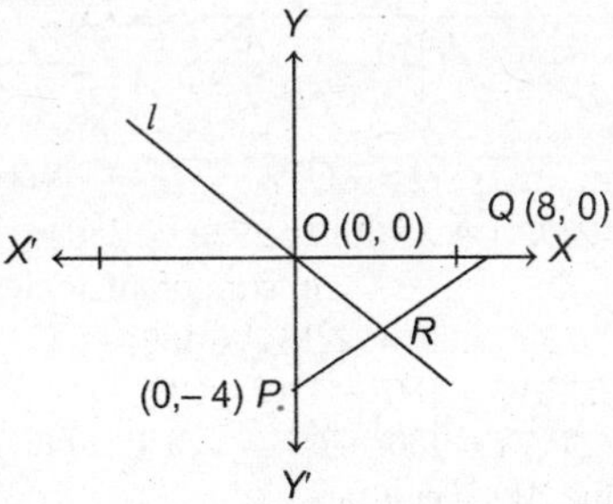

$$R = \left(\frac{x_1 + x_2}{2}, \frac{y_1 + y_2}{2}\right) = \left(\frac{0 + 8}{2}, \frac{-4 + 0}{2}\right) = (4, -2)$$

$$\therefore \quad \text{Slope of } OR = \frac{y_2 - y_1}{x_2 - x_1} = \frac{-2 - 0}{4 - 0} = \frac{-2}{4} = -\frac{1}{2} \quad \left(\begin{array}{l}\because x_1 = 0, y_1 = 0,\\ x_2 = 4, y_2 = -2\end{array}\right)$$

Question 6 Without using the Pythagoras theorem, show that the points (4, 4), (3, 5) and (−1, −1) are the vertices of a right angled triangle.

◎ *Thinking Process*

(i) When two points are given, then slope of line $m = \dfrac{y_2 - y_1}{x_2 - x_1}$.

(ii) Two lines are perpendicular if $m_1 \times m_2 = -1$.

Sol. Let the given points are $A(4, 4)$, $B(3, 5)$ and $C(-1, -1)$.

Here, $(x_1, y_1) \to A(4, 4), (x_2, y_2) \to B(3, 5), (x_3, y_3) \to C(-1, -1)$

$$\text{Slope of } AB,\ m_1 = \frac{y_2 - y_1}{x_2 - x_1} = \frac{5-4}{3-4} = \frac{1}{-1} = -1 \qquad \left(\because \text{Slope} = \frac{y_2 - y_1}{x_2 - x_1}\right)$$

$$\text{Slope of } BC,\ m_2 = \frac{y_3 - y_2}{x_3 - x_2} = \frac{-1-5}{-1-3} = \frac{-6}{-4} = \frac{3}{2}$$

$$\text{Slope of } CA,\ m_3 = \frac{y_3 - y_1}{x_3 - x_1} = \frac{-1-4}{-1-4} = \frac{-5}{-5} = 1$$

$\because$ Slope of $AB \times$ Slope of $CA = (-1) \times 1 = -1$

$\therefore$ ΔABC is a right angled triangle at A.

Question 7 Find the slope of a line, which makes an angle of 30° with the positive direction of Y-axis measured anticlockwise.

Sol. Given, $\angle YPQ = 30°$

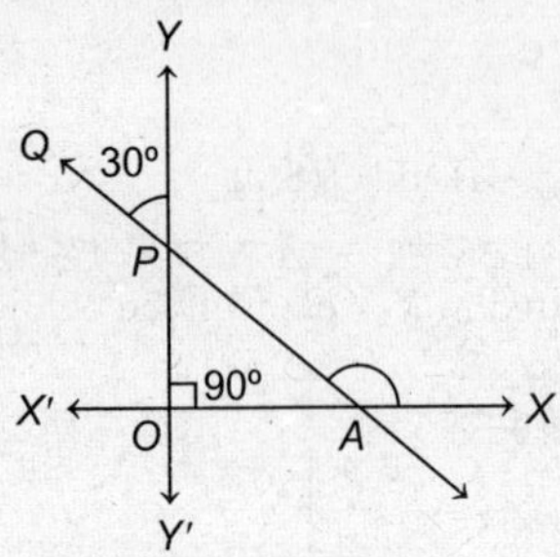

Here, $\angle YPQ = \angle OPA$ (vertically opposite angles)

$\because$ $\angle OPA + \angle POA + \angle PAO = 180°$

($\because$ sum of all angles of a triangle is 180°)

$\Rightarrow$ $30° + 90° + \angle PAO = 180°$

$\Rightarrow$ $\angle PAO = 180° - 120° = 60°$

$\Rightarrow$ $\angle PAX = 180° - 60° = 120°$ [$\because \angle OPA + \angle PAX = 180°$]

$\therefore$ Slope of line $AQ = m = \tan 120°$ ($\because m = \tan\theta$)

$= \tan(180° - 60°)$ [$\because \tan(180° - \theta) = -\tan\theta$]

$= -\tan 60° = -\sqrt{3}$

Mistake Alert Many students assumed the given angle with the positive direction of X-axis and make error in this type of question.

Question 8 Without using distance formula, show that the points $(-2,-1), (4,0), (3,3)$ and $(-3,2)$ are the vertices of a parallelogram.

Thinking Process Use the concept, the diagonals of a parallelogram bisect each other.

Sol. Let $ABCD$ be a parallelogram, where vertices are

$$(x_1, y_1) \rightarrow A(-2,-1), (x_2, y_2) \rightarrow B(4, 0), (x_3, y_3) \rightarrow C(3, 3)$$

and $(x_4, y_4) \rightarrow (-3, 2)$

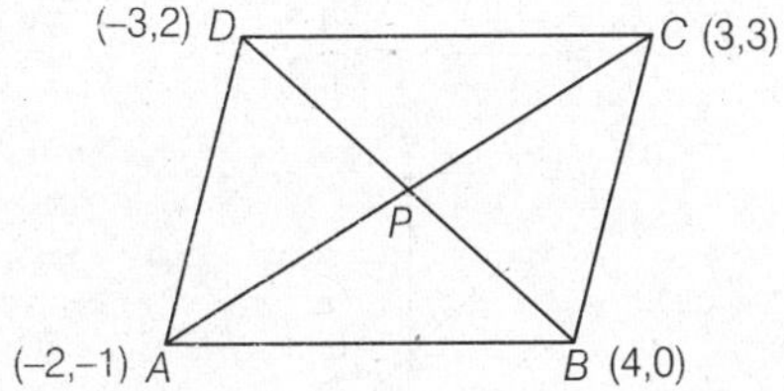

Mid-point of

$$AC = \left(\frac{x_1 + x_3}{2}, \frac{y_1 + y_3}{2}\right)$$

$$\left[\because \text{Mid-point of two points} = \left(\frac{x_1 + x_2}{2}, \frac{y_1 + y_2}{2}\right)\right]$$

$$= \left(\frac{-2+3}{2}, \frac{-1+3}{2}\right) = \left(\frac{1}{2}, \frac{2}{2}\right) = \left(\frac{1}{2}, 1\right)$$

$$\text{Mid-point of } BD = \left(\frac{x_2 + x_4}{2}, \frac{y_2 + y_4}{2}\right) = \left(\frac{4-3}{2}, \frac{0+2}{2}\right) = \left(\frac{1}{2}, 1\right)$$

$\because$ Mid-point of AC = Mid-point of BD

$\therefore$ $ABCD$ be a parallelogram.

Quick Solution

$$\text{Slope of side, } AB = \frac{0-(-1)}{4-(-2)} = \frac{1}{6}$$

$$\text{and Slope of side, } BC = \frac{3-0}{3-4} = \frac{3}{-1} = -3$$

$$\text{and Slope of side } CD = \frac{2-3}{-3-3} = \frac{1}{6}$$

$$\text{Similarly, Slope of } AD = \frac{2-(-1)}{-3-(-2)} = \frac{3}{-1} = -3$$

$\because$ Slope of AB = Slope of CD and slope of BC = Slope of AD.

$\therefore$ $AB \parallel CD$ and $BC \parallel AD$, Then, given points are vertices of parallelogram.

Question 9 Find the angle between the X-axis and the line joining the points (3, –1) and (4, –2).

◎ ***Thinking Process*** When two points are given, to determine angle use

$$\theta = \tan^{-1}\left(\frac{y_2 - y_1}{x_2 - x_1}\right).$$

Sol. Given, $(x_1, y_1) = (3, -1)$ and $(x_2, y_2) = (4, -2)$

Slope of line $m = \frac{y_2 - y_1}{x_2 - x_1} = \frac{-2+1}{4-3} = \frac{-1}{1}$

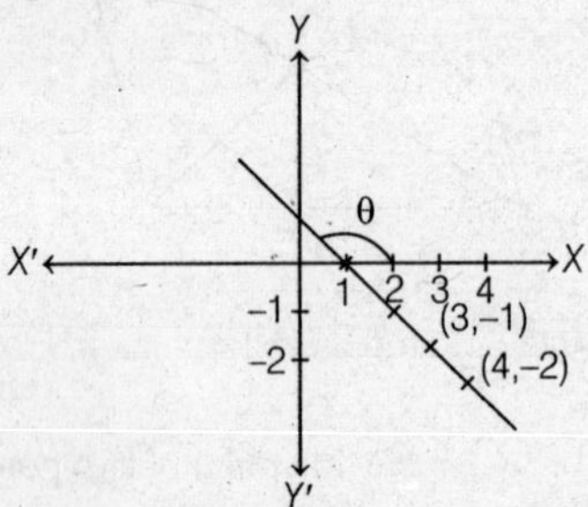

$$\tan\theta = \frac{-1}{1} \Rightarrow \tan\theta = -1 \qquad [\because m = \tan\theta]$$

$$\Rightarrow \tan\theta = -\tan 45° \qquad [\because 1 = \tan 45°]$$

$$\Rightarrow \tan\theta = \tan(180° - 45°) \qquad [\because \tan(180° - \theta) = -\tan\theta]$$

$$\Rightarrow \tan\theta = \tan 135° \Rightarrow \theta = 135°$$

Question 10 The slope of a line is double the slope of another line. If tangent of the angle between them is $\frac{1}{3}$, find the slope of the lines.

◎ ***Thinking Process*** If m_1 and m_2 are the slopes of a line, then tangent of angle between the lines

$$\tan\theta = \left|\frac{m_1 - m_2}{1 + m_1 m_2}\right|$$

Sol. Let slope of one line is m, then slope of another line is $2m$.

Given, the tangent of the angle between them is $\tan\theta = \frac{1}{3}$

$$\therefore \left|\frac{m_1 - m_2}{1 + m_1 m_2}\right| = \frac{1}{3}$$

$$\Rightarrow \frac{1}{3} = \left|\frac{m - 2m}{1 + m \times 2m}\right| \Rightarrow \frac{1}{3} = \left|\frac{-m}{1 + 2m^2}\right|$$

$$\Rightarrow \quad \frac{1}{3}=\frac{|m|}{|1+2m^2|}$$

$$\Rightarrow \quad \frac{1}{3}=\frac{|m|}{1+2m^2} \qquad [\because 1+2m^2>0]$$

$$\Rightarrow \quad 2m^2-3|m|+1=0$$

Case I If $m=-1$, then

$$2m^2+3m+1=0$$

$$\Rightarrow \quad 2m^2+2m+m+1=0$$

$$\Rightarrow \quad (2m+1)(m+1)=0 \Rightarrow m=-\frac{1}{2} \text{ or } m=-1$$

Case II If $m=1$, then

$$2m^2-3m+1=0$$

$$\Rightarrow \quad 2m^2-2m-m+1=0$$

$$\Rightarrow \quad (2m-1)(m-1)=0 \Rightarrow m=\frac{1}{2} \text{ or } 1$$

$$\therefore \quad m=-1, \frac{-1}{2}, \frac{1}{2} \text{ and } 1 \Rightarrow 2m=-2, -1, 1 \text{ and } 2$$

$\therefore$ Slope of the two lines are $(m, 2m)=(-1,-2), \left(-\frac{1}{2},-1\right), \left(\frac{1}{2}, 1\right)$ and $(1, 2)$

Question 11 A line passes through (x_1, y_1) and (h, k). If slope of the line is m, show that

$$k-y_1=m(h-x_1)$$

◎ ***Thinking Process*** If two points are given, then use slope $m=\frac{y_2-y_1}{x_2-x_1}$ and simplify it.

Sol. Let the given points are $P(x_1, y_1)$ and $Q(h, k)$.

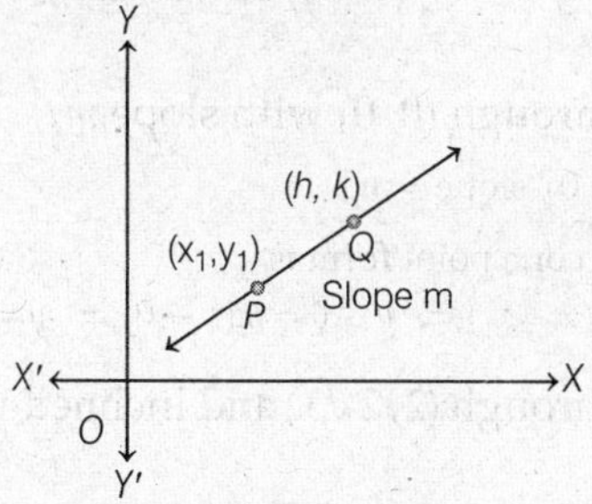

Then, slope $\quad m=\frac{k-y_1}{h-x_1} \qquad \left(\because m=\frac{y_2-y_1}{x_2-x_1}\right)$

$$\Rightarrow \quad k-y_1=m(h-x_1)$$

Hence Proved.

Exercise 9.2

Direction (Q. No. 1 to 8) Find the equation of the line which satisfy the given conditions.

Thinking Process A straight line is uniquely determined, if

(i) it passes through a given point with a given slope *i.e.*,

$$y - y_1 = m(x - x_1)$$

(ii) it passes through two points *i.e.*, $y - y_1 = \frac{y_2 - y_1}{x_2 - x_1}(x - x_1)$

Question 1 Write the equation for the *X*-axis and *Y*-axis.

Sol. Any point on *X*-axis is $(x, 0)$, as *y*-coordinate on *X*-axis is zero.

Also slope on *X*-axis is $m = 0$

$\because$ Equation of line is $y - y_1 = m(x - x_1)$

$\therefore \quad y - 0 = 0(x - x) \qquad (\because x_1 = x, y_1 = 0)$

$\Rightarrow \quad y = 0$

Hence, equation of *X*-axis, $y = 0$

Similarly, we can determine the equation of *Y*-axis,

$$x = 0$$

Question 2 Passing through the point $(-4, 3)$ with slope $\frac{1}{2}$.

Sol. Equation of line in one point form is

$$y - y_1 = m(x - x_1)$$

Here, $(x_1, y_1) = (-4, 3)$ and $m = \frac{1}{2}$

$\therefore \quad y - 3 = \frac{1}{2}(x + 4) \Rightarrow 2y - 6 = x + 4 \Rightarrow x - 2y + 10 = 0$

Question 3 Passing through (0, 0) with slope *m*.

Sol. Here, $(x_1, y_1) = (0, 0)$, slope $= m$

Equation of line in one point form is

$$y - y_1 = m(x - x_1) \Rightarrow y - 0 = m(x - 0) \Rightarrow y = mx$$

Question 4 Passing through $(2, 2\sqrt{3})$ and inclined with the *X*-axis at an angle of 75°.

Sol. Here, $(x_1, y_1) = (2, 2\sqrt{3})$, $\Rightarrow m = \tan 75° = \tan(45° + 30°)$

$$= \frac{\tan 45° + \tan 30°}{1 - \tan 45° \tan 30°} \qquad \left(\because \tan(A + B) = \frac{\tan A + \tan B}{1 - \tan A \tan B}\right)$$

$$\Rightarrow \quad m = \frac{1 + \frac{1}{\sqrt{3}}}{1 - \frac{1}{\sqrt{3}}} = \frac{\sqrt{3} + 1}{\sqrt{3} - 1}$$

$$\Rightarrow \quad m = \frac{\sqrt{3} + 1}{\sqrt{3} - 1} \times \frac{\sqrt{3} + 1}{\sqrt{3} + 1} = \frac{(\sqrt{3} + 1)^2}{3 - 1}$$

(multiply numerator and denominator by $\sqrt{3} + 1$)

$$\Rightarrow \quad m = \frac{3 + 1 + 2\sqrt{3}}{2} = \frac{4 + 2\sqrt{3}}{2} = 2 + \sqrt{3}$$

Equation of line in one point form is

$$y - y_1 = m(x - x_1)$$

$$\Rightarrow \quad y - 2\sqrt{3} = (2 + \sqrt{3})(x - 2)$$

$$\Rightarrow \quad y - 2\sqrt{3} = (2 + \sqrt{3})x - 2(2 + \sqrt{3})$$

$$\Rightarrow \quad y - 2\sqrt{3} = (2 + \sqrt{3})x - 4 - 2\sqrt{3}$$

$$\Rightarrow \quad (2 + \sqrt{3})x - y - 4 = 0$$

Question 5 Intersecting the X-axis at a distance of 3 units to the left of origin with slope -2.

Sol. Since, the line intersect the X-axis to the left of origin. It means it intersect the negative X-axis. Clearly, line AB passes through the point $(-3, 0)$ and $m = -2$.

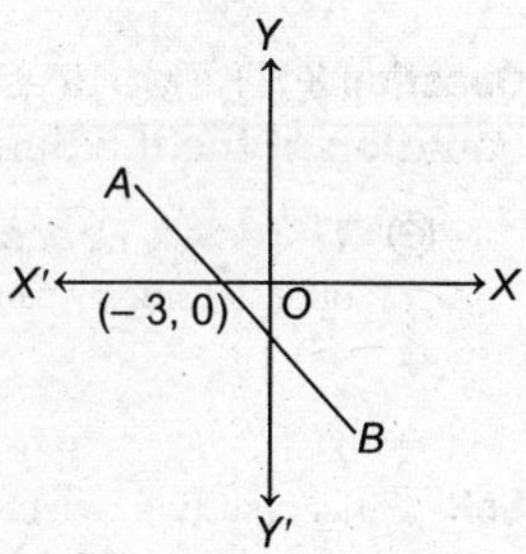

Equation of line in one point form is

$$y - y_1 = m(x - x_1)$$

$$\Rightarrow \quad y - 0 = -2(x + 3)$$

$$\Rightarrow \quad y = -2x - 6$$

$$\Rightarrow \quad 2x + y + 6 = 0$$

Question 6 Intersecting the Y-axis at a distance of 2 units above the origin and making an angle of 30° with positive direction of the X-axis.

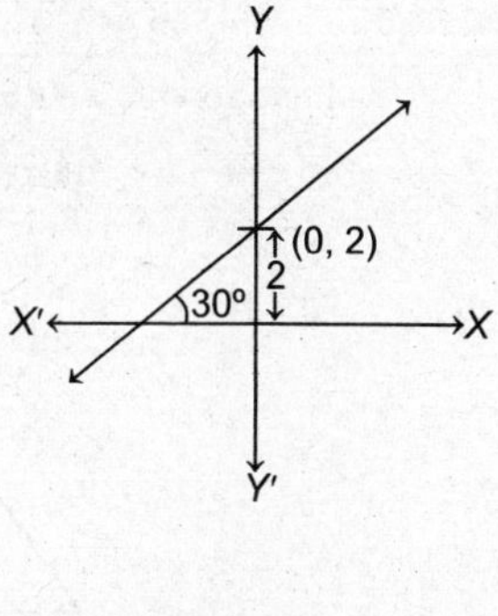

◎ ***Thinking Process*** If the slope of the line is m and the y-intercept is c, then equation of the line is $y = mx + c$

Sol. Since, the line intersect the Y-axis, above the origin. It means it intersects the positive Y-axis. Here, $c = 2$

$$m = \tan 30° \Rightarrow m = \frac{1}{\sqrt{3}}$$

$\therefore$ Equation of line is $\qquad y = mx + c$

$$\Rightarrow \qquad y = \frac{1}{\sqrt{3}} x + 2$$

$$\Rightarrow \qquad \sqrt{3}y = x + 2\sqrt{3}$$

$$\Rightarrow \qquad x - \sqrt{3}y + 2\sqrt{3} = 0$$

Question 7 Passing through the points $(-1, 1)$ and $(2, -4)$.

Sol. Given points are $A(-1, 1)$ and $B(2, -4)$, then equation of line AB is

$$y - y_1 = \frac{y_2 - y_1}{x_2 - x_1}(x - x_1)$$

$$\Rightarrow \qquad y - 1 = \frac{-4-1}{2+1}(x+1) \quad (\because x_1 = -1, y_1 = 1, x_2 = 2, y_2 = -4)$$

$$\Rightarrow \qquad y - 1 = \frac{-5}{3}(x+1)$$

$$\Rightarrow \qquad 3y - 3 = -5x - 5 \Rightarrow 5x + 3y + 2 = 0$$

Note We can also write the equation of the line as $y - y_2 = \dfrac{y_2 - y_1}{x_2 - x_1}(x - x_2)$, so don't be confused.

Question 8 The vertices of ΔPQR are $P(2, 1)$, $Q(-2, 3)$ and $R(4, 5)$. Find equation of the median through the vertex R.

◎ *Thinking Process* Firstly we find the coordinates of median R on opposite side by using mid-point formula and then use the equation of line

$$y - y_1 = \frac{y_2 - y_1}{x_2 - x_1}(x - x_1)$$

Sol. Since, median bisects the opposite side *i.e.*, S is the mid-point of PQ.

$$S = \left(\frac{x_1 + x_2}{2}, \frac{y_1 + y_2}{2}\right)$$

$$= \left(\frac{2-2}{2}, \frac{1+3}{2}\right) = \left(0, \frac{4}{2}\right) = (0, 2) \quad (\because x_1 = 2, y_1 = 1, x_2 = -2, y_1 = 3)$$

$\therefore$ Equation of line RS by using

$$y - y_1 = \frac{y_2 - y_1}{x_2 - x_1}(x - x_1)$$

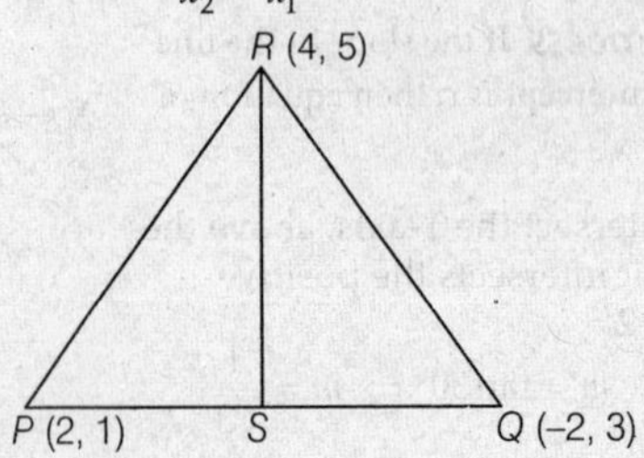

$$\Rightarrow \quad y - 5 = \frac{2-5}{0-4}(x-4) \quad (\because x_1 = 4, y_1 = 5, x_2 = 0, y_2 = 2)$$

$$\Rightarrow \quad y - 5 = \frac{-3}{-4}(x-4)$$

$$\Rightarrow \quad 4y - 20 = 3x - 12$$

$$\Rightarrow \quad 3x - 4y + 8 = 0$$

Question 9 Find the equation of the line passing through $(-3, 5)$ and perpendicular to the line through the points $(2, 5)$ and $(-3, 6)$.

◎ ***Thinking Process*** First we find the slope 'm' of required line using the concept that two lines are perpendicular it and only if $m_1 \times m_2 = -1$ and then we use the equation of line $y - y_1 = m(x - x_1)$

Sol. Let the points P and Q are $(2, 5)$ and $(-3, 6)$. We have to find equation of AB.

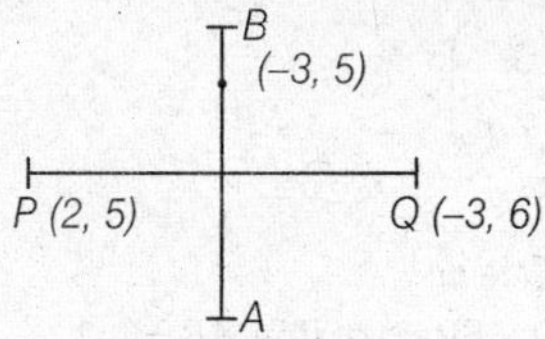

Let slope of AB be m.

Since, $AB \perp PQ$

$\therefore$ Slope of $AB \times$ Slope of $PQ = -1$ $\quad (\because m_1 \times m_2 = -1)$

$$\Rightarrow \quad m \times \frac{y_2 - y_1}{x_2 - x_1} = -1$$

$$\Rightarrow \quad m \times \frac{6-5}{-3-2} = -1 \quad \left(\because \text{Slope of } PQ = \frac{6-5}{-3-2}\right)$$

$$\Rightarrow \quad m \times \frac{1}{-5} = -1 \Rightarrow m = 5$$

$\therefore$ Equation of line AB is given by

$$y - y_1 = m(x - x_1)$$

$$y - 5 = 5(x + 3) \quad (\because x_1 = -3, y_1 = 5)$$

$$\Rightarrow \quad y - 5 = 5x + 15 \Rightarrow 5x - y + 20 = 0$$

Question 10 A line perpendicular to the line segment joining the points $(1, 0)$ and $(2, 3)$ divides it in the ratio $1 : n$. Find the equation of the line.

◎ ***Thinking Process*** The coordinates of a point dividing the line segment joining the points (x_1, y_1) and (x_2, y_2) internally in the ratio $m : n$ are $\left(\frac{mx_2 + nx_1}{m+n}, \frac{my_2 + ny_1}{m+n}\right)$

Sol. Let the given points are $A(1, 0)$ and $B(2, 3)$. Let the line PQ divide AB in the ratio $1 : n$ at R.

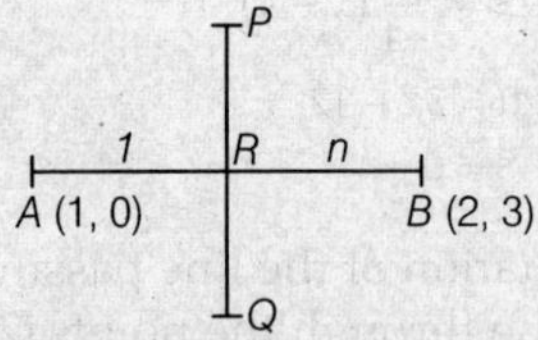

Using internally ratio, coordinates of point

$$R = \left(\frac{1 \times x_2 + n \times x_1}{1+n}, \frac{1 \times y_2 + n \times y_1}{1+n}\right)$$

$$= \left(\frac{1 \times 2 + n \times 1}{1+n}, \frac{1 \times 3 + n \times 0}{1+n}\right) \quad (\because x_1 = 1, y_1 = 0, x_2 = 2, y_2 = 3)$$

$$= \left(\frac{n+2}{n+1}, \frac{3}{1+n}\right)$$

Also, $PQ \perp AB$

Let slope of line PQ is m.

$\therefore$ Slope of line PQ × Slope of line $AB = -1$ $\quad (\because m_1 m_2 = -1)$

$$\Rightarrow \quad m \times \frac{y_2 - y_1}{x_2 - x_1} = -1$$

$$\Rightarrow \quad m \times \frac{3-0}{2-1} = -1 \quad (\because x_1 = 1, y_1 = 0, x_2 = 2, y_2 = 3)$$

$$\Rightarrow \quad m \times 3 = -1$$

$$\Rightarrow \quad m = -\frac{1}{3}$$

Now, equation of line PQ is given by

$$y - y_1 = m(x - x_1)$$

$$\Rightarrow \quad y - \frac{3}{1+n} = \frac{-1}{3}\left(x - \frac{n+2}{n+1}\right) \quad \left[\because R\left(\frac{n+2}{n+1}, \frac{3}{1+n}\right) = (x_1, y_1)\right]$$

$$\Rightarrow \quad \frac{3(n+1)y - 9}{1+n} = \frac{-x(n+1) + (n+2)}{n+1}$$

$$\Rightarrow \quad 3(n+1)y - 9 = -x(n+1) + (n+2)$$

$$\Rightarrow \quad x(n+1) + 3(n+1)y = n + 2 + 9$$

$$\Rightarrow \quad x(n+1) + 3(n+1)y = n + 11$$

Question 11 Find the equation of the line that cuts off equal intercepts on the coordinate axes and passes through the point (2,3).

◎ *Thinking Process* The intercept form of a line is $\frac{x}{a}+\frac{y}{b}=1$

Sol. Equation of line in intercept form is

$$\frac{x}{a}+\frac{y}{b}=1 \quad \text{...(i)}$$

Since, the line makes equal intercepts on the axes *i.e.*,

$$a=b$$

$\therefore$ From Eq. (i), $\frac{x}{a}+\frac{y}{a}=1$

$\Rightarrow$ $x+y=a$ ...(ii)

Line (ii) passes through the point (2, 3) *i.e.*, it will satisfy the line (ii).

$\Rightarrow$ $2+3=a \Rightarrow a=5$

On putting the value of a in Eq. (ii), we get $x+y=5$

Question 12 Find equation of the line passing through the point (2,2) and cutting off intercepts the axes whose sum is 9.

Sol. Equation of line in intercept form is

$$\frac{x}{a}+\frac{y}{b}=1 \quad \text{...(i)}$$

Given, $a+b=9$ ...(ii)

And line (i) passes through the point (2, 2) *i.e.*, it will satisfy the line (i) *i.e.*, put $x=2$, $y=2$ in Eq. (i)

$\Rightarrow$ $\frac{2}{a}+\frac{2}{b}=1$ ...(iii)

Solve Eqs. (ii) and (iii), to find the values of a and b.

From Eq. (ii), $b=9-a$ put in Eq. (iii), we get

$$\frac{2}{a}+\frac{2}{9-a}=1 \Rightarrow 2(9-a)+2a=a(9-a)$$

$\Rightarrow$ $18-2a+2a=9a-a^2 \Rightarrow a^2-9a+18=0$

On factorize it by splitting the middle term,

$\Rightarrow$ $a^2-6a-3a+18=0 \Rightarrow a(a-6)-3(a-6)=0$

$\Rightarrow$ $(a-6)(a-3)=0 \Rightarrow a=6 \text{ or } 3$

On putting the value of a in Eq. (ii), to find the values of b.

$\Rightarrow$ $b=3 \text{ or } 6$

Hence, Eq. (i) becomes

$$\frac{x}{6}+\frac{y}{3}=1 \quad \text{or} \quad \frac{x}{3}+\frac{y}{6}=1$$

$\Rightarrow$ $3x+6y=18$ or $6x+3y=18$

$\Rightarrow$ $x+2y=6$

or $2x+y=6$ (divide by 3)

Question 13 Find equation of the line through the point (0, 2) making an angle $\frac{2\pi}{3}$ with the positive X-axis. Also, find the equation of the line parallel to it and crossing the Y-axis at a distance of 2 units below the origin.

◎ *Thinking Process* If lines $l_1 || l_2$ iff their slopes are equal *i.e.*, $m_1 = m_2$

Sol. $\because m = \tan\theta = \tan\frac{2\pi}{3}$

$$= \tan\left(\pi - \frac{\pi}{3}\right) = -\tan\frac{\pi}{3} \quad [\because \tan(\pi - \theta) = -\tan\theta]$$

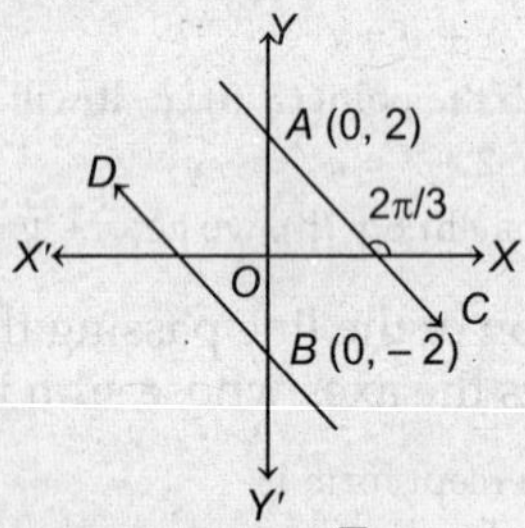

$$m = -\sqrt{3}$$

Hence, equation of line AC through the point $A(0, 2)$ by using $y - y_1 = m(x - x_1)$

$\Rightarrow \quad y - 2 = -\sqrt{3}(x - 0) \quad (\because x_1 = 0, y_1 = 2)$

$\Rightarrow \quad y - 2 = -\sqrt{3}x \Rightarrow \sqrt{3}x + y - 2 = 0$

Also, the line BD intersect below Y-axis. It means the coordinate of y is negative and x-coordinate is 0. *i.e.*, point is (0, – 2).

Hence, equation of line through the point B (0, – 2) is

$$y + 2 = -\sqrt{3}(x - 0) \quad (\because y - y_1 = m(x - x_1))$$

$\Rightarrow \quad \sqrt{3}x + y + 2 = 0$

Question 14 The perpendicular from the origin to a line meets it at the point $(-2, 9)$. Find the equation of the line.

◎ *Thinking Process* We have to find out the equation of the line PQ, for which we find the slope of PQ.

Sol. Since, $PQ \perp OR$

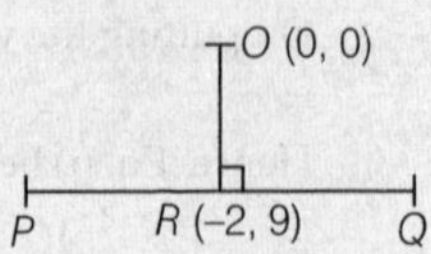

Let the slope of line PQ is m.

$\therefore$ Slope of $PQ \times$ Slope of $OR = -1 \quad (\because m_1 \times m_2 = -1)$

$\Rightarrow \quad m \times \frac{y_2 - y_1}{x_2 - x_1} = -1$

$\Rightarrow \quad m \times \frac{9 - 0}{-2 - 0} = -1 \quad (\because x_1 = 0, y_1 = 0, x_2 = -2, y_2 = 9)$

$$\Rightarrow \quad m \times \frac{9}{-2} = -1 \Rightarrow m = \frac{2}{9}$$

Now, equation of PQ is given by

$$y - y_1 = m(x - x_1)$$

$$y - 9 = \frac{2}{9}(x + 2) \qquad (\because x_1 = -2, y = 9)$$

$$\Rightarrow \quad 9y - 81 = 2x + 4$$

$$\Rightarrow \quad 2x - 9y + 85 = 0$$

Question 15 The length L (in centimetres) of a copper rod is a linear function of its celsius temperature C. In an experiment, if $L = 124.942$ when $C = 20$ and $L = 125.134$ when $C = 110$, express L in terms of C.

Sol. Given, $L = 124.942$ when $C = 20$ and $L = 125.134$ when $C = 110$

$\therefore$ In coordinate form (20, 124.942) and (110, 125.134) are two points.

Equation of linear function *i.e.*, line can be taken as

$$L - L_1 = \frac{L_2 - L_1}{C_2 - C_1}(C - C_1) \qquad \left[\because y - y_1 = \frac{y_2 - y_1}{x_2 - x_1}(x - x_1)\right]$$

$$\Rightarrow \quad L - 124.942 = \frac{125.134 - 124.942}{110 - 20}(C - 20)$$

$$\Rightarrow \quad L - 124.942 = \frac{0.192}{90}(C - 20)$$

$$\Rightarrow \quad L = \frac{0.192}{90}(C - 20) + 124.942$$

Quick Solution

Given, L is a linear function of C *i.e.*, $L = a + bC$, where a and b are constant.

Given, $L = 124.942$ when $C = 20$

$$124.942 = a + b(20) \qquad \ldots(i)$$

and $L = 125.134$ when $C = 110$,

$$125.135 = a + b(110) \qquad \ldots(ii)$$

By Eqs. (i) and (ii), we get

$$b = \frac{0.192}{90} \text{ and } a = 124.8994$$

$$\therefore \quad L = 124.8994 + 0.00213C$$

Question 16 The owner of a milk store finds that, he can sell 980 litres of milk each week at ₹ 14/ litre and 1220 litre of milk each week at ₹ 16/litre. Assuming a linear relationship between selling price and demand, how many litres could he sell weekly at ₹ 17 litre?

Sol. Let price and litre be denoted in ordered pair (x, y) where x denotes the ₹ per litre and y denotes the quantity of milk in litre.

Given, (14, 980) and (16, 1220) are two points.

Let linear relations *i.e.*, linear equation is

$$y - y_1 = \frac{y_2 - y_1}{x_2 - x_1}(x - x_1)$$

$$\Rightarrow \quad y - 980 = \frac{1220 - 980}{16 - 14}(x - 14)$$

$$(\because x_1 = 14, y_1 = 980, x_2 = 16, y_2 = 1220)$$

$$\Rightarrow \quad y - 980 = \frac{240}{2}(x - 14)$$

$$\Rightarrow \quad y - 980 = 120(x - 14)$$

$$\Rightarrow \quad y - 980 = 120x - 120 \times 14$$

$\Rightarrow 120x - y = 1680 - 980 \Rightarrow 120x - y = 700$

When price $x = 17$,

$$\Rightarrow \quad 120 \times 17 - y = 700 \Rightarrow y = 2040 - 700$$

$$y = 1340$$

He will sell weekly 1340 litres milk at the rate of ₹ 17 litres.

Question 17 $P(a, b)$ is the mid-point of a line segment between axes. Show that the equation of the line is $\frac{x}{a} + \frac{y}{b} = 2$.

Sol. Let equation of line AB is

$$\frac{x}{h} + \frac{y}{k} = 1 \quad \text{...(i)}$$

where, h and k are the intercepts made by the line on X-axis and Y-axis, respectively.

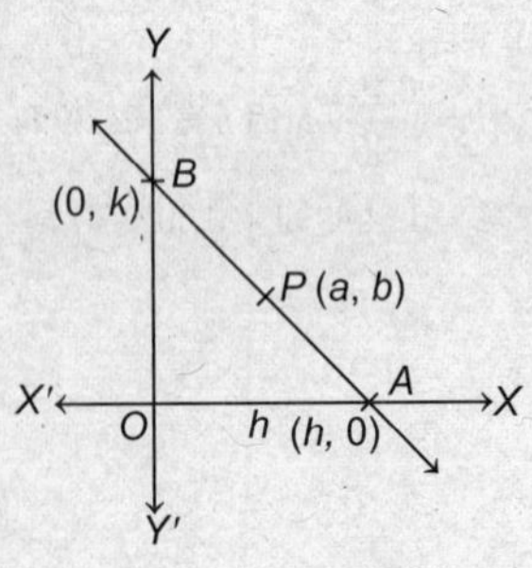

Mid-point of $AB = \left(\frac{x_1 + x_2}{2}, \frac{y_1 + y_2}{2}\right) = \left(\frac{h + 0}{2}, \frac{0 + k}{2}\right)$

$(\because x_1 = h, y_1 = 0, x_2 = 0, y_2 = k)$

$\because P(a, b)$ is the mid-point of AB *i.e.*,

$$\frac{h + 0}{2} = a \quad \text{and} \quad \frac{0 + k}{2} = b \Rightarrow h = 2a \text{ and } k = 2b$$

On putting the values of h and k in Eq. (i), we get

$$\frac{x}{2a} + \frac{y}{2b} = 1 \Rightarrow \frac{x}{a} + \frac{y}{b} = 2$$

Hence Proved.

Question 18 Point $R(h, k)$ divides a line segment between the axes in the ratio 1 : 2. Find equation of the line.

Sol. Let equation of line AB is

$$\frac{x}{a} + \frac{y}{b} = 1 \qquad \text{...(i)}$$

Let a point $R(h, k)$ divide line AB in the ratio 1 : 2.

By using internally ratio

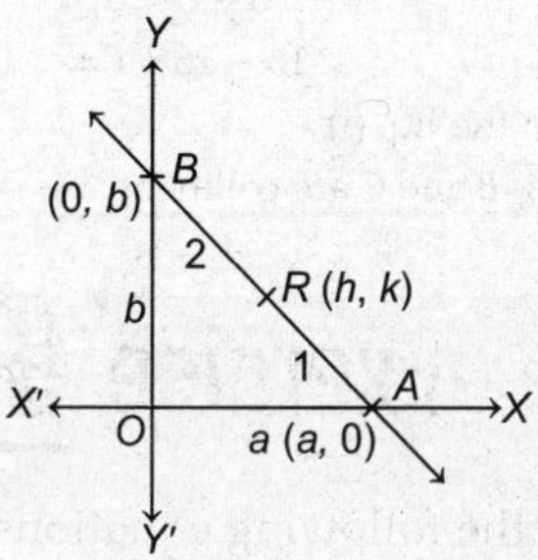

$$R(h, k) = \left(\frac{1x_2 + 2x_1}{1+2}, \frac{1y_2 + 2y_1}{1+2}\right) \Rightarrow h = \frac{1 \times 0 + 2 \times a}{1+2}, k = \frac{1 \times b + 2 \times 0}{1+2}$$

[$\because P(x, y)$ divide the line $A(x_1, y_1)$ and $B(x_2, y_2)$ in the ratio $m : n$ internally

$$\therefore P(x, y) = \left(\frac{mx_2 + nx_1}{m+n}, \frac{my_2 + ny_1}{m+n}\right)\Bigg]$$

$$\Rightarrow \qquad h = \frac{2a}{3}, k = \frac{b}{3} \Rightarrow a = \frac{3h}{2}, b = 3k$$

On putting the values of a and b in Eq. (i), we get

$$\frac{x}{\frac{3h}{2}} + \frac{y}{3k} = 1 \Rightarrow \frac{2x}{3h} + \frac{y}{3k} = 1$$

$$\Rightarrow \qquad \frac{2kx + hy}{3hk} = 1 \Rightarrow 2kx + hy = 3hk$$

Question 19 By using the concept of equation of a line, prove that the three points (3, 0) (−2, −2) and (8, 2) are collinear.

◎ *Thinking Process* Find the equation of a line by taking any two points, if third point satisfy the equation of line, then points are collinear.

Sol. Let the given points are $A(3, 0)$, $B(-2, -2)$, and $C(8, 2)$.

Equation of line AB is

$$y - y_1 = \frac{y_2 - y_1}{x_2 - x_1}(x - x_1)$$

$$y - 0 = \frac{-2-0}{-2-3}(x-3) \quad (\because x_1 = 3, y_1 = 0, x_2 = -2, y_2 = -2)$$

$$\Rightarrow \quad y = \frac{-2}{-5}(x-3) \Rightarrow 5y = 2x - 6$$

$$\Rightarrow \quad 2x - 5y - 6 = 0 \qquad \text{...(i)}$$

On putting the point $C(8, 2)$ in Eq. (i), we get

$$2 \times 8 - 5 \times 2 - 6 = 0$$

$$\Rightarrow \quad 16 - 10 - 6 = 0$$

$$\Rightarrow \quad 16 - 16 = 0 \Rightarrow \quad 0 = 0$$

$\therefore$ $C(8, 2)$ lies on the Eq. (i)

Hence, points A, B and C are collinear.

Exercise 9.3

Question 1 Reduce the following equations into slope-intercept form and find their slopes and the y-intercepts.

(a) $x + 7y = 0$. (b) $6x + 3y - 5 = 0$. (c) $y = 0$.

◎ *Thinking Process* Use slope intercept form of line $y = mx + c$ and determine the value of m and c.

Sol. (a) Given, $x + 7y = 0$

$$\Rightarrow \quad 7y = -x \Rightarrow y = -\frac{1}{7}x + 0$$

On comparing with $y = mx + c$, we get

$$m = -\frac{1}{7}, \quad c = 0$$

(b) Given, $6x + 3y - 5 = 0$

$$\Rightarrow \quad 3y = -6x + 5 \Rightarrow y = \frac{-6}{3}x + \frac{5}{3}$$

$$\Rightarrow \quad y = -2x + \frac{5}{3}$$

On comparing with $y = mx + c$, we get

$$m = -2, c = \frac{5}{3}$$

(c) Given, $y = 0$

$\Rightarrow$ $y = 0x + 0$

On comparing with $y = mx + c$, we get

$\Rightarrow$ $m = 0, c = 0$

Question 2 Reduce the following equations into intercept form and find their intercepts on the axes.

(a) $3x + 2y - 12 = 0$. (b) $4x - 3y = 6$. (c) $3y + 2 = 0$.

◎ *Thinking Process* Convert the given equation into intercept form $\frac{x}{a} + \frac{y}{b} = 1$, where a and b are intercepts on the axes.

Sol. (a) Given, $3x + 2y = 12$

$\Rightarrow$ $\frac{3x}{12} + \frac{2y}{12} = 1$ [dividing by 12 both sides]

$\Rightarrow$ $\frac{x}{4} + \frac{y}{6} = 1$

On comparing with $\frac{x}{a} + \frac{y}{b} = 1 \Rightarrow a = 4, b = 6$

$\therefore$ X-intercept = 4, Y-intercept = 6

(b) Given, $4x - 3y = 6$

$\Rightarrow$ $\frac{4x}{6} - \frac{3y}{6} = 1$ [dividing by 6 both sides]

$\Rightarrow$ $\frac{x}{\frac{6}{4}} - \frac{y}{2} = 1$

$\Rightarrow$ $\frac{x}{\frac{3}{2}} + \frac{y}{(-2)} = 1$

On comparing with $\frac{x}{a} + \frac{y}{b} = 1$, we get

X-intercept = $\frac{3}{2}$ and Y-intercept = -2

(c) Given, $3y + 2 = 0$

$\Rightarrow 3y = -2 \Rightarrow y = -\frac{2}{3}$ or $0x + \frac{y}{(-2/3)} = 1$

On comparing with $\frac{x}{a} + \frac{y}{b} = 1$, we get

Intercept with Y-axis = $-\frac{2}{3}$ and no intercept on X-axis.

Question 3 Find the distance of the point $(-1, 1)$ from the line $12(x+6)=5(y-2)$.

◎ *Thinking Process* (Q. No. 3 to 4) The distance of the point (h, k) from the line $ax+by+c=0$ is $d=\dfrac{|ah+bk+c|}{\sqrt{a^2+b^2}}$

Sol. Given, equation of line is

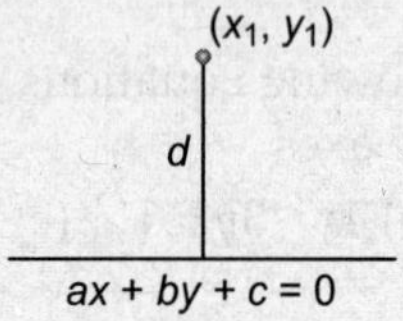

$$12(x+6)=5(y-2) \Rightarrow 12x+72=5y-10 \Rightarrow 12x-5y+82=0$$

Hence, distance from the point $(-1, 1)$ is

$$d=\left|\frac{12\times(-1)-5\times1+82}{\sqrt{(12)^2+(-5)^2}}\right|$$

$$\left[\because d=\left|\frac{ax_1+by_1+c}{\sqrt{a^2+b^2}}\right|; x_1=-1, y_1=1; a=12, b=-5, c=82\right]$$

$$=\left|\frac{-12-5+82}{\sqrt{144+25}}\right|=\left|\frac{82-17}{\sqrt{169}}\right|=\frac{65}{13}=5$$

Question 4 Find the points on the X-axis, whose distance from the line $\dfrac{x}{3}+\dfrac{y}{4}=1$ are 4 units.

Sol. Let any point on the X-axis is $(h, 0)$, as on X-axis is y-coordinate will be zero.

Given, equation of line is

$$\frac{x}{3}+\frac{y}{4}=1 \Rightarrow 4x+3y=12 \Rightarrow 4x+3y-12=0 \qquad \text{...(i)}$$

Now, distance of $(h, 0)$ from the line (i) is $d=\left|\dfrac{ax_1+by_1+c}{\sqrt{a^2+b^2}}\right|$

$$\Rightarrow \quad 4=\left|\frac{4\times h+3\times0-12}{\sqrt{4^2+3^2}}\right| \qquad (\because a=4, b=3, c=12, x_1=h, y_1=0)$$

$$\Rightarrow \quad \left|\frac{4h-12}{5}\right|=4 \Rightarrow |4h-12|=20 \Rightarrow 4h-12=\pm 20$$

On taking positive sign, $4h-12=20 \Rightarrow 4h=32 \Rightarrow h=8$

On taking negative sign, $4h-12=-20 \Rightarrow 4h=-8 \Rightarrow h=-2$

Hence, points on the X-axis are $(8, 0)$ and $(-2, 0)$.

Question 5 Find the distance between parallel lines

(a) $15x+8y-34=0$ and $15x+8y+31=0$

(b) $l(x+y)+p=0$ and $l(x+y)-r=0$

◎ *Thinking Process* Distance between two parallel lines $ax+by+c=0$ and $ax+by+d=0$ is

$$\left|\frac{c-d}{\sqrt{a^2+b^2}}\right|$$

Sol. (i) Given, lines $15x+8y-34=0$ and $15x+8y+31=0$ are parallel.

$\therefore$ Distance between two parallel lines $=\left|\frac{c-d}{\sqrt{a^2+b^2}}\right|$

$$=\left|\frac{-34-31}{\sqrt{15^2+8^2}}\right| \qquad (\because c=-34,\ d=31,\ a=15,\ b=8)$$

$$=\frac{|-65|}{\sqrt{225+64}}=\frac{65}{\sqrt{289}}$$

$$=\frac{65}{17}\text{ units}$$

(ii) Given, lines $lx+ly+p=0$ and $lx+ly-r=0$ are parallel.

$\therefore$ Required distance $=\left|\frac{c-d}{\sqrt{a^2+b^2}}\right|$

$$=\left|\frac{p+r}{\sqrt{l^2+l^2}}\right|=\left|\frac{p+r}{\sqrt{2}l}\right| \qquad (\because a=l,\ b=l,\ c=p,\ d=-r)$$

Question 6 Find equation of the line parallel to the line $3x-4y+2=0$ and passing through the point $(-2,3)$.

Sol. Given equation of a line is

$$3x-4y+2=0 \qquad \ldots(i)$$

Equation of line parallel to Eq. (i) is

$$3x-4y+k=0 \qquad \ldots(ii)$$

$\because$ Line (ii) passes through the point $(-2, 3)$

i.e., put $x=-2$, $y=3$ in Eq. (ii).

$\therefore \quad 3(-2)-4\times3+k=0$

$\Rightarrow \quad -6-12+k=0$

$\Rightarrow \quad k=18$

Put $k=18$ in Eq. (ii), we get

$$3x-4y+18=0$$

Question 7 Find the equation of the line perpendicular to the line $x - 7y + 5 = 0$ and having X-intercept 3.

Sol. Given equation $x - 7y + 5 = 0 \Rightarrow -7y = -x - 5 \Rightarrow 7y = x + 5$

i.e. $$y = \frac{1}{7}x + \frac{5}{7} \quad \ldots\text{(i)}$$

$\therefore$ $$m_1 = \frac{1}{7} \text{ and } c = \frac{5}{7} \quad \text{[by comparison of } y = mx + c\text{]}$$

We know that two lines are perpendicular each other iff the product of their slopes $(m_1 \times m_2)$ is -1

i.e., $$m_1 \times m_2 = -1$$

So, slope of line perpendicular to the given line $= -\frac{1}{m_1} = -\frac{-1}{1/7} = -7$

$\therefore$ $$m_2 = -7$$

Now, equation of line having slope $m_2 = -7$ which cuts x – intercept 3 (i.e passing through the point (3, 0) will be given by

$$y - 0 = -7(x - 3)$$

$$y = -7x + 21$$

$$7x + y - 21 = 0$$

Question 8 Find angles between the lines $\sqrt{3}x + y = 1$ and $x + \sqrt{3}y = 1$.

◎ **Thinking Process** Use angle between the lines $y = m_1x + c_1$ and $y = m_2x + c_2$ is $\tan\theta = \left|\frac{m_1 - m_2}{1 + m_1m_2}\right|$

Sol. Given, equation of lines are

$$\sqrt{3}x + y = 1 \Rightarrow y = -\sqrt{3}x + 1$$

and $$x + \sqrt{3}y = 1$$

$\Rightarrow$ $$\sqrt{3}y = -x + 1 \Rightarrow y = \frac{-1}{\sqrt{3}}x + \frac{1}{\sqrt{3}}$$

On comparing with $y = m_1x + c_1$ and $y = m_2x + c_2$, we get

$$m_1 = -\sqrt{3} \text{ and } m_2 = -\frac{1}{\sqrt{3}}$$

$\therefore$ $$\tan\theta = \left|\frac{-\sqrt{3} - \left(-\frac{1}{\sqrt{3}}\right)}{1 + (-\sqrt{3})\left(-\frac{1}{\sqrt{3}}\right)}\right| \quad \left[\because \tan\theta = \left|\frac{m_1 - m_2}{1 + m_1m_2}\right|\right]$$

$$\Rightarrow \tan\theta = \left|\frac{-\sqrt{3} + \frac{1}{\sqrt{3}}}{1 + 1}\right| = \left|\frac{\frac{-3+1}{\sqrt{3}}}{2}\right| \Rightarrow \tan\theta = \frac{1}{\sqrt{3}} \Rightarrow \tan\theta = \tan 30^\circ \Rightarrow \theta = 30^\circ$$

$\therefore$ The acute angle between the given two lines is 30° and the other obtuse angle is 180°–30°= 150°

Question 9 The line through the points $(h, 3)$ and $(4, 1)$ intersects the line $7x - 9y - 19 = 0$ at right angle. Find the value of h.

Sol. Equation of line through $(h, 3)$ and $(4, 1)$ is given by

$$y - y_1 = \frac{y_2 - y_1}{x_2 - x_1}(x - x_1)$$

$$\Rightarrow \quad y - 3 = \frac{1-3}{4-h}(x - h) \qquad (\because x_1 = h, y_1 = 3, x_2 = 4, y_2 = 1)$$

$$\Rightarrow \quad y - 3 = \frac{-2}{4-h}(x - h) \Rightarrow y - 3 = -\frac{2x}{4-h} + \frac{2h}{4-h}$$

$$\Rightarrow \quad y = -\frac{2x}{4-h} + \left(3 + \frac{2h}{4-h}\right) = 0 \qquad \ldots\text{(i)}$$

Given equation of line is

$$7x - 9y - 19 = 0$$

$$\Rightarrow \quad y = \frac{7}{9}x - \frac{19}{9} \qquad \ldots\text{(ii)}$$

On comparing lines Eq. (i) and (ii) are with $y = mx + c$

$$\therefore \quad m_1 = -\frac{2}{4-h} \text{ and } m_2 = \frac{7}{9}$$

$\because$ Lines (i) and (ii) are perpendicular to each other, *i.e.*,

Slope of line (i) $\times$ Slope of line (ii) $= -1$

$$\therefore \quad m_1 \times m_2 = -1 \Rightarrow -\frac{2}{4-h} \times \frac{7}{9} = -1$$

$$\Rightarrow \quad 14 = 9(4 - h) \Rightarrow 14 = 36 - 9h$$

$$\Rightarrow \quad 9h = 22 \Rightarrow h = \frac{22}{9}$$

Question 10 Prove that the line through the point (x_1, y_1) and parallel to the line $Ax + By + C = 0$ is

$$A(x - x_1) + B(y - y_1) = 0$$

Sol. Given equation of line is

$$Ax + By + C = 0 \qquad \ldots\text{(i)}$$

Equation of line parallel to Eq. (i) is

$$Ax + By + K = 0 \qquad \ldots\text{(ii)}$$

Line (ii) passes through the point (x_1, y_1) *i.e., it* will satisfy the line (ii)

$$\therefore \quad Ax_1 + By_1 + K = 0$$

$$\Rightarrow \quad K = -(Ax_1 + By_1)$$

On putting the value of K in Eq. (ii),

$$\Rightarrow \quad Ax + By - (Ax_1 + By_1) = 0$$

$$\Rightarrow \quad Ax + By - Ax_1 - By_1 = 0$$

$$\Rightarrow \quad A(x - x_1) + B(y - y_1) = 0$$

Hence Proved.

Question 11 Two lines passing through the point (2, 3) intersect each other at an angle of 60°. If slope of one line is 2, find the equation of the other line.

Sol. Equation of line l_1 by using $y - y_1 = m(x - x_1)$

where, $(x_1, y_1) = (2, 3)$ and $m = 2$ is

$$y - 3 = 2(x - 2) \Rightarrow y - 3 = 2x - 4 \Rightarrow 2x - y - 1 = 0$$

$$\Rightarrow \quad y = 2x - 1 \quad \text{...(i)}$$

Here, slope of line l_1 is $m_1 = 2$.

Let slope of line l_2 is m.

Given, $\theta = 60°$

Angle between two lines is

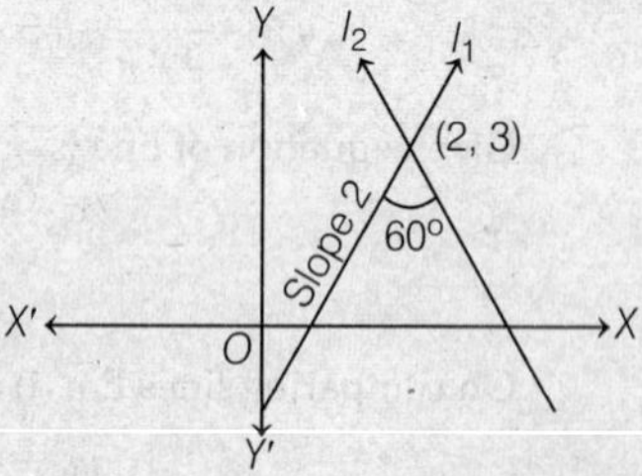

$$\tan\theta = \left|\frac{m_1 - m_2}{1 + m_1 m_2}\right|$$

$$\Rightarrow \quad \tan 60° = \left|\frac{2 - m}{1 + 2m}\right|$$

$$\Rightarrow \quad \sqrt{3} = \left|\frac{2 - m}{1 + 2m}\right|$$

$$\Rightarrow \quad \frac{2 - m}{1 + 2m} = \pm\sqrt{3}$$

On taking positive sign, we get

$$\frac{2 - m}{1 + 2m} = \frac{\sqrt{3}}{1}$$

$$\Rightarrow \quad 2 - m = \sqrt{3}(1 + 2m) \Rightarrow 2 - m = \sqrt{3} + 2\sqrt{3}m$$

$$\Rightarrow \quad 2 - \sqrt{3} = m(1 + 2\sqrt{3}) \Rightarrow m = \frac{2 - \sqrt{3}}{1 + 2\sqrt{3}}$$

On again taking negative sign, we get

$$\frac{2 - m}{1 + 2m} = -\sqrt{3} \Rightarrow 2 - m = -\sqrt{3}(1 + 2m)$$

$$\Rightarrow 2 - m = -\sqrt{3} - 2\sqrt{3}m \Rightarrow m - 2\sqrt{3}m = \sqrt{3} + 2$$

$$\Rightarrow \quad -m(2\sqrt{3} - 1) = (\sqrt{3} + 2) \Rightarrow m = -\left(\frac{\sqrt{3} + 2}{2\sqrt{3} - 1}\right)$$

Now, equation of line l_2 by using

$$y - y_1 = m(x - x_1) \text{ is}$$

$$y - 3 = \frac{2 - \sqrt{3}}{1 + 2\sqrt{3}}(x - 2) \quad \left(m = \frac{2 - \sqrt{3}}{1 + 2\sqrt{3}} \text{ and } x_1 = 2, y_1 = 3\right)$$

$$\Rightarrow \quad y(1 + 2\sqrt{3}) - 3 - 6\sqrt{3} = x(2 - \sqrt{3}) - 4 + 2\sqrt{3}$$

$$\Rightarrow \quad x(2 - \sqrt{3}) - y(1 + 2\sqrt{3}) + 8\sqrt{3} - 1 = 0$$

Again, $y - 3 = -\left(\dfrac{\sqrt{3}+2}{2\sqrt{3}-1}\right)(x-2)$ $\left[\text{when } m = -\left(\dfrac{\sqrt{3}+2}{2\sqrt{3}-1}\right) \text{ and } x_1 = 2, y_1 = 3\right]$

$\Rightarrow y(2\sqrt{3}-1) - 6\sqrt{3} + 3 = -(\sqrt{3}+2)x + 2\sqrt{3} + 4$

$\Rightarrow (2+\sqrt{3})x + (2\sqrt{3}-1)y - 8\sqrt{3} - 1 = 0$

Mistake Alert If we take only $\left|\dfrac{2-m}{1+2m}\right| = \left(\dfrac{2-m}{1+2m}\right)$, here we are forgetting the $-\left(\dfrac{2-m}{1+2m}\right)$ *i.e.*, $\left|\dfrac{2-m}{1+2m}\right| = \pm\left(\dfrac{2-m}{1+2m}\right)$, so careful in these types of questions.

Question 12 Find the equation of the right bisector of the line segment joining the points (3, 4) and (– 1, 2).

Sol. Let the given points are $P(3, 4)$ and $Q(-1, 2)$, then B is the mid-point of PQ.

i.e., $B = \left(\dfrac{x_1+x_2}{2}, \dfrac{y_1+y_2}{2}\right) = \left(\dfrac{3-1}{2}, \dfrac{4+2}{2}\right) = (1, 3)$

$(\because x_1 = 3, y_1 = 4, x_2 = -1, y_2 = 2)$

Now, $AB \perp PQ$

Let the slope of AB be m.

i.e., Slope of $AB \times$ Slope of $PQ = -1$

$\Rightarrow \quad m \times \dfrac{y_2-y_1}{x_2-x_1} = -1 \Rightarrow m \times \dfrac{2-4}{-1-3} = -1$

$\Rightarrow \quad m \times \dfrac{-2}{-4} = -1$

$\Rightarrow \quad m \times \dfrac{1}{2} = -1$

$\Rightarrow \quad m = -2$

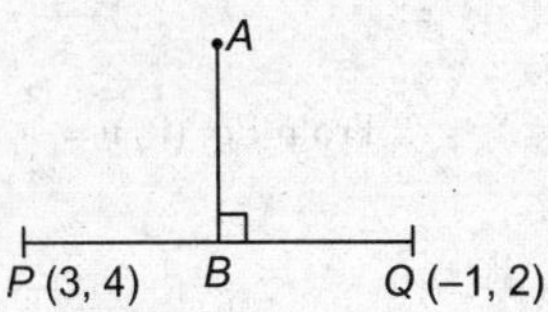

Now, equation of line AB by using

$y - y_1 = m(x - x_1)$ where $(x_1, y_1) = (1, 3)$ and $m = -2$, is

$y - 3 = -2(x-1) \Rightarrow y - 3 = -2x + 2$

$\Rightarrow \quad 2x + y - 5 = 0$

Question 13 Find the coordinates of the foot of perpendicular from the point $(-1, 3)$ to the line $3x - 4y - 16 = 0$

Thinking Process The foot is the point of intersection of given line and perpendicular to it.

Sol. Given equation of line AB is

$3x - 4y - 16 = 0 \Rightarrow y = \dfrac{3}{4}x - 4$ ...(i)

Slope of line (i) is $m_1 = \dfrac{3}{4}$

Let slope of line PQ is m.

Since, $PQ \perp AB$

$\therefore$ Slope of $PQ \times$ Slope of $AB = -1$

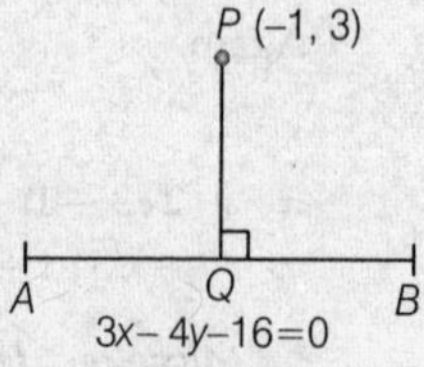

$\Rightarrow \quad m \times \left(\frac{3}{4}\right) = -1 \quad (\because m_1 \times m_2 = -1)$

$\Rightarrow \quad m = -\frac{4}{3}$

Hence, equation of line PQ by using

$$y - y_1 = m(x - x_1)$$

where $(x_1, y_1) = (-1, 3)$ and $m = -\frac{4}{3}$ is

$$y - 3 = -\frac{4}{3}(x + 1) \Rightarrow 3y - 9 = -4x - 4$$

$\Rightarrow \quad 4x + 3y - 5 = 0$ ...(ii)

Now, solving Eqs. (i) and (ii), to find the coordinates of Q.

From Eq. (i),

$$y = \frac{3}{4}x - 4$$

On putting the value of y in Eq. (ii), we get

$$4x + 3\left(\frac{3}{4}x - 4\right) - 5 = 0$$

$\Rightarrow \quad 4x + \frac{9x}{4} - 12 - 5 = 0$

$\Rightarrow \quad \frac{25x}{4} = 17 \Rightarrow x = \frac{68}{25}$

$\therefore$ From Eq. (i), $y = \frac{3}{4} \times \frac{68}{25} - 4 = \frac{3 \times 17}{25} - \frac{4}{1}$

$$= \frac{51}{25} - \frac{4}{1} = \frac{51 - 100}{25} = -\frac{49}{25}$$

Hence, required point of intersection is

$$\left(\frac{68}{25}, -\frac{49}{25}\right)$$

Question 14 The perpendicular from the origin to the line $y = mx + c$ meets at the point $(-1, 2)$. Find the values of m and c.

Sol. $\because$ line $OP \perp$ line AB

Let the slope of line AB is m.

$\therefore$ Slope of $OP \times$ Slope of $AB = -1$

$\because$ Slope of $OP = \frac{y_2 - y_1}{x_2 - x_1}$

$\Rightarrow \quad \frac{2 - 0}{-1 - 0} \times m = -1 \quad (\because x, = o, y, 0, x_2 = -1, y^2 = 2)$

$\Rightarrow \quad -2m = -1 \Rightarrow m = \frac{1}{2}$

Also, point $(-1, 2)$ satisfies the line

$y = mx + c$ i.e., $2 = m(-1) + c$ (putting $x = -1$, $y = 2$ and $m = \frac{1}{2}$)

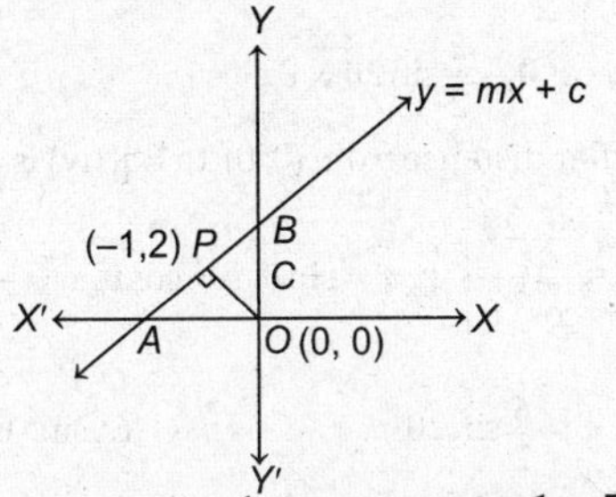

$$\Rightarrow \quad 2 = -\frac{1}{2} + c \Rightarrow c = 2 + \frac{1}{2} = \frac{5}{2}$$

Hence, $$m = \frac{1}{2}, \quad c = \frac{5}{2}$$

Question 15 If p and q are lengths of perpendiculars from origin to the lines $x\cos\theta - y\sin\theta = k\cos 2\theta$ and $x\sec\theta + y\operatorname{cosec}\theta = k$ respectively, prove that $p^2 + 4q^2 = k^2$

◎ ***Thinking Process*** The perpendicular distance from (x_1, y_1) to the line $ax + by + c = 0$ is $p = \left|\frac{ax_1 + by_1 + c}{\sqrt{a^2 + b^2}}\right|$

Sol.

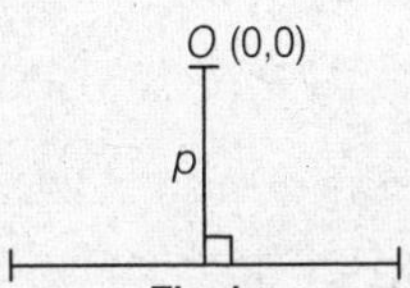

Fig. I

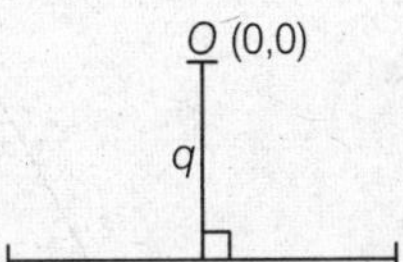

Fig. II

For Fig. I, $x\cos\theta - y\sin\theta = k\cos 2\theta$ ...(i)

For Fig. II, $x\sec\theta + y\operatorname{cosec}\theta = k$

...(ii)

$\therefore$ Perpendicular distance from (0, 0) to the Eq. (i) is

$(\because a = \cos\theta,\ b = \sin\theta,\ c = -(\cos 2\theta))$

$(\because \cos^2\theta + \sin^2\theta = 1)$

$$p = \left|\frac{0 - 0 - k\cos 2\theta}{\sqrt{\cos^2\theta + \sin^2\theta}}\right| = k\cos 2\theta \quad \text{...(iii)}$$

$$\left[\because d = \left|\frac{ax_1 + by_1 + c}{\sqrt{a^2 + b^2}}\right|\right]$$

Again, Eq. (ii) can be written as

$$\frac{x}{\cos\theta} + \frac{y}{\sin\theta} = k \Rightarrow x\sin\theta + y\cos\theta = k\cos\theta\sin\theta$$

$$\Rightarrow x\sin\theta + y\cos\theta = \frac{k}{2}(2\cos\theta\sin\theta)$$

$$\Rightarrow x\sin\theta + y\cos\theta = \frac{k}{2}\sin 2\theta \qquad (\because 2\sin\theta\cdot\cos\theta = \sin 2\theta)$$

$$\Rightarrow \quad x\sin\theta + y\cos\theta - \frac{k}{2}\sin 2\theta = 0 \qquad \text{...(iv)}$$

Now, perpendicular distance from (0, 0) to Eq. (iv) is

$$q = \left|\frac{0+0-\frac{k}{2}\sin 2\theta}{\sqrt{\sin^2\theta + \cos^2\theta}}\right| \qquad \left(\because a = \sin\theta, b = \cos\theta, c = -\frac{k}{2}\sin 2\theta, x_1 = 0, y_1 = 0\right)$$

$$\Rightarrow \quad q = \frac{k}{2}\sin 2\theta \qquad (\therefore \sin^2\theta + \cos^2\theta = 1) \qquad \text{...(v)}$$

$$\Rightarrow \quad 2q = k\sin 2\theta$$

On squaring and adding Eqs. (iii) and (v),

$$p^2 + 4q^2 = k^2\cos^2 2\theta + k^2\sin^2 2\theta = k^2(\cos^2 2\theta + \sin^2 2\theta)$$

$$\therefore \quad p^2 + 4q^2 = k^2 \qquad (\because \sin^2\theta + \cos^2\theta = 1)$$ **Hence Proved.**

Question 16 In the ΔABC with vertices $A(2,3)$, $B(4,-1)$ and $C(1,2)$, find the equation and length of altitude from the vertex A.

Thinking Process First use $m_1 \times m_2 = -1$, then determine the equation of line by using $y - y_1 = m(x - x_1)$

Sol. Given, vertices of a ΔABC are $A(2, 3)$, $B(4, -1)$ and $C(1, 2)$

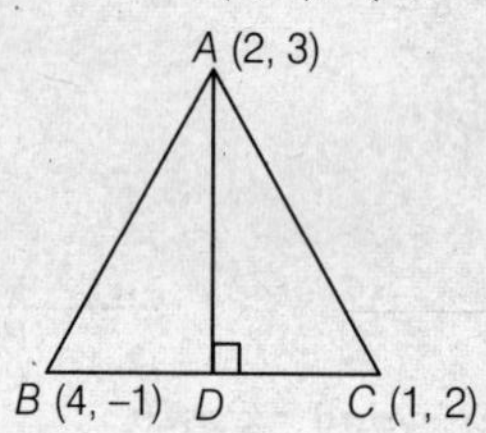

$\because$ Line $AD \perp$ line BC

Let the slope of line AD is m.

$\therefore$ Slope of $AD \times$ Slope of $BC = -1 \Rightarrow m \times \frac{y_2 - y_1}{x_2 - x_1} = -1$

$$\Rightarrow \quad m \times \frac{2+1}{1-4} = -1 \qquad (\because x_1 = 4, y_1 = -1, x_2 = 1, y_2 = 2)$$

$$\Rightarrow \quad m \times \frac{3}{-3} = -1 \;\Rightarrow\; m = 1$$

Hence, equation of AD, by using $y - y_1 = m(x - x_1)$ where $(x_1, y_1) = (2, 3)$ and $m = 1$ is

$$y - 3 = 1(x-2) \Rightarrow x - y - 2 + 3 = 0 \;\Rightarrow\; x - y + 1 = 0$$

Now, equation of BC by using $y - y_1 = \frac{y_2 - y_1}{x_2 - x_1}(x - x_1)$ is

$$y+1=\frac{2+1}{1-4}(x-4) \qquad (\because x_1=4, y_1=-1, x_2=1, y_2=2)$$

$$\Rightarrow \quad y+1=\frac{3}{-3}(x-4) \Rightarrow y+1=-x+4 \Rightarrow x+y-3=0$$

$\therefore$ Length of AD = Perpendicular distance from (2, 3) to the line BC

i.e., $\quad x+y-3=0$

$$=\left|\frac{2+3-3}{\sqrt{1^2+1^2}}\right|=\frac{2}{\sqrt{2}}=\sqrt{2} \qquad \left[\because p=\left|\frac{ax_1+by_1+c}{\sqrt{a^2+b^2}}\right|\right]$$

$$(\because x_1=2, y_1=3, a=1, b=1)$$

Hence, length of AD is $\sqrt{2}$.

Question 17 If p is the length of perpendicular from origin to the line whose intercepts on the axes are a and b, then show that

$$\frac{1}{p^2}=\frac{1}{a^2}+\frac{1}{b^2}$$

◎ **Thinking Process** Use intercept form of line $\frac{x}{a}+\frac{y}{b}=1$ and perpendicular distance from (x_1, y_1) to the line $ax+by+c=0$ is $p=\left|\frac{ax_1+by_1+c}{\sqrt{a^2+b^2}}\right|$

Sol. Equation of line in intercept form is

$$\frac{x}{a}+\frac{y}{b}=1$$

$$\Rightarrow \quad \frac{x}{a}+\frac{y}{b}-1=0$$

Its distance from origin is

$$\left|\frac{0+0-1}{\sqrt{\frac{1}{a^2}+\frac{1}{b^2}}}\right|=p \qquad \left(\because d=\left|\frac{ax_1+by_1+c}{\sqrt{a^2+b^2}}\right|\right)$$

$$\left(\because a=\frac{1}{a}, b=\frac{1}{b}, x_1=0, y_1=0\right)$$

$$\Rightarrow \quad p=\frac{1}{\sqrt{\frac{1}{a^2}+\frac{1}{b^2}}}$$

$$\Rightarrow \quad \frac{1}{p}=\sqrt{\frac{1}{a^2}+\frac{1}{b^2}}$$

On squaring both sides, we get $\frac{1}{p^2}=\frac{1}{a^2}+\frac{1}{b^2}$

Miscellaneous Exercise

Question 1 Find the values of k for which the line $(k-3)x-(4-k^2)y+k^2-7k+6=0$ is

(a) Parallel to the X-axis. (b) Parallel to the Y-axis,

(c) Passing through the origin.

Sol. Equation of given line is

$$(k-3)x-(4-k^2)y+k^2-7k+6=0$$

$$y=\left(\frac{k-3}{4-k^2}\right)x+\left(\frac{k^2-7k+6}{4-k^2}\right) \quad \text{...(i)}$$

(a) When line (i) is parallel to X-axis, then slope = 0

i.e., $$\frac{(k-3)}{(4-k^2)}=0 \quad \left(\because \text{slope of line (i) is} \frac{k-3}{4-k^2}\right)$$

$\Rightarrow$ $$k-3=0$$

$\Rightarrow$ $$k=3$$

(b) When line (i) is parallel to Y-axis, then slope $= \tan 90° = \infty = \frac{1}{0}$

i.e., $$\frac{k-3}{4-k^2}=\frac{1}{0} \quad \left(\because \text{slope of line (i) is} \frac{k-3}{4-k^2}\right)$$

$\Rightarrow$ $$4-k^2=0$$

$\Rightarrow$ $$k=\pm 2$$

(c) When line (i) passing through origin (0, 0), then it will satisfy it

$$\left(\frac{k-3}{4-k^2}\right)0+\frac{k^2-7k+6}{4-k^2}=0 \quad (\text{put } x=0, y=0 \text{ is Eq. (i)})$$

$\Rightarrow$ $$k^2-7k+6=0$$

$\Rightarrow$ $$k^2-6k-k+6=0$$

$\Rightarrow$ $$k(k-6)-1(k-6)=0$$

$\Rightarrow$ $$(k-6)(k-1)=0$$

$\Rightarrow$ $$k=1, 6$$

Question 2 Find the equations of the lines, which cut-off intercepts on the axes whose sum and product are 1 and −6, respectivley.

Sol. Let the intercept form of a line is $\frac{x}{a}+\frac{y}{b}=1$. ...(i)

Given, $$a+b=1 \quad \text{...(ii)}$$

and $$ab=-6 \quad \text{...(iii)}$$

From Eq. (iii), $ab = -6$, $b = -\frac{6}{a}$

Put $b = \frac{-6}{a}$ in Eq. (ii),

$$a - \frac{6}{a} = 1 \Rightarrow \frac{a}{1} - \frac{6}{a} = 1 \Rightarrow a^2 - 6 = a$$

$\Rightarrow$ $$a^2 - a - 6 = 0 \Rightarrow a^2 - (3-2)a - 6 = 0$$

$\Rightarrow$ $$a^2 - 3a + 2a - 6 = 0 \Rightarrow a(a-3) + 2(a-3) = 0$$

$\Rightarrow$ $$(a+2)(a-3) = 0 \Rightarrow a = 3, -2$$

On putting $a = -2, 3$ in $b = \frac{-6}{a}$, we get $b = 3, -2$

Put $a = 3, -2$ respectively in Eq. (i), we get the required equations of lines

$$\frac{x}{3} + \frac{y}{-2} = 1 \quad \text{or} \quad \frac{x}{-2} + \frac{y}{3} = 1$$

$\Rightarrow$ $$2x - 3y = 6 \quad \text{or} \quad -3x + 2y = 6$$

$\Rightarrow$ $$2x - 3y - 6 = 0 \quad \text{or} \quad 3x - 2y + 6 = 0$$

Question 3 What are the points on the Y-axis whose distance from the line $\frac{x}{3} + \frac{y}{4} = 1$ is 4 units.

Sol. Any point on the Y-axis is $(0, h)$ as on Y-axis the x coordinate will be zero. Equation of given line is

$$\frac{x}{3} + \frac{y}{4} = 1 \text{ or } 4x + 3y = 12$$

$\Rightarrow$ $4x + 3y - 12 = 0$ its distance from $(0, h)$ is 4 units.

i.e.,
$$\left|\frac{0 + 3h - 12}{\sqrt{4^2 + 3^2}}\right| = 4$$

[$\because$ perpendicular distance, $d = \frac{ax_1 + by_1 + c}{\sqrt{a^2 + b^2}}$

and $a = 4, b = 3, c = -12, x_1 = 0, y_1 = h$]

$\Rightarrow$ $$\left|\frac{3h - 12}{5}\right| = 4 \Rightarrow |3h - 12| = 20 \Rightarrow 3h - 12 = \pm 20$$

On taking positive sign, $3h = 20 + 12 \Rightarrow 3h = 32 \Rightarrow h = \frac{32}{3}$

On taking negative sign, $3h = -20 + 12 \Rightarrow 3h = -8 \Rightarrow h = -\frac{8}{3}$

Hence, points on the Y-axis are $\left(0, -\frac{8}{3}\right)$ or $\left(0, \frac{32}{3}\right)$.

Mistake Alert In such type of questions, students make error that they don't take both $\pm$ ve signs. They take only + ve sign.

Question 4 Find the perpendicular distance from the origin of the line joining the points $(\cos\theta, \sin\theta)$ and $(\cos\phi, \sin\phi)$.

◎ *Thinking Process* It is a multiple concept problem, first find the equation of line by using two points formula $\left((y - y_1) = \frac{y_2 - y_1}{x_2 - x_1}(x - x_1)\right)$ and then find the distance from origin to the line.

Sol. Equation of line joining the points $(\cos\theta, \sin\theta)$ and $(\cos\phi, \sin\phi)$ is

$$y - \sin\theta = \frac{\sin\phi - \sin\theta}{\cos\phi - \cos\theta}(x - \cos\theta) \quad \left(\because y - y_1 = \frac{y_2 - y_1}{x_2 - x_1}(x - x_1) \text{ here } x_1 = \cos\theta, y_1 = \sin\theta,\ x_2 = \cos\phi, y_2 = \sin\phi\right)$$

$$\Rightarrow \quad y - \sin\theta = \frac{2\cos\frac{\phi+\theta}{2}\sin\frac{\phi-\theta}{2}}{-2\sin\frac{\phi+\theta}{2}\sin\frac{\phi-\theta}{2}}(x - \cos\theta)$$

$$\left[\because \cos C - \cos D = -2\sin\frac{C+D}{2}\sin\frac{C-D}{2} \text{ and } \sin C - \sin D = 2\cos\frac{C+D}{2}\sin\frac{C-D}{2}\right]$$

$$\Rightarrow \quad y - \sin\theta = \frac{\cos\frac{\phi+\theta}{2}}{-\sin\frac{\phi+\theta}{2}}(x - \cos\theta)$$

$$\Rightarrow \quad -y\sin\frac{\phi+\theta}{2} + \sin\theta\sin\frac{\phi+\theta}{2} = x\cos\frac{\phi+\theta}{2} - \cos\theta\cos\frac{\phi+\theta}{2}$$

$$\Rightarrow \quad x\cos\frac{\phi+\theta}{2} + y\sin\frac{\phi+\theta}{2} = \sin\theta\sin\frac{\phi+\theta}{2} + \cos\theta\cos\frac{\phi+\theta}{2}$$

$$\Rightarrow \quad x\cos\frac{\phi+\theta}{2} + y\sin\frac{\phi+\theta}{2} = \cos\left(\theta - \frac{\theta+\phi}{2}\right)$$

$$[\because \cos(A - B) = \cos A\cos B + \sin A\sin B]$$

$$\Rightarrow \quad x\cos\frac{\phi+\theta}{2} + y\sin\frac{\phi+\theta}{2} - \cos\left(\frac{\theta-\phi}{2}\right) = 0$$

It's distance from origin (0, 0) is

$$p = \left|\frac{0 + 0 - \cos\left(\frac{\theta-\phi}{2}\right)}{\sqrt{\cos^2\left(\frac{\phi+\theta}{2}\right) + \sin^2\left(\frac{\phi+\theta}{2}\right)}}\right| \quad \left[\because p = \left|\frac{ax_1 + by_1 + c}{\sqrt{a^2 + b^2}}\right|\right]$$

where, $a = \cos\left(\frac{\phi+\theta}{2}\right), b = \sin\left(\frac{\phi+\theta}{2}\right)$ $x_1 = 0, y_1 = 0$

$$\Rightarrow \quad p = \cos\left(\frac{\theta-\phi}{2}\right) \quad (\because \cos^2\theta + \sin^2\theta = 1)$$

Question 5 Find the equation of line parallel to Y-axis and drawn through the point of intersection of the line $x-7y+5=0$ and $3x+y=0$.

Sol. Given, equation of lines are

$$x - 7y + 5 = 0 \quad \ldots(i)$$

and $$3x + y = 0 \quad \ldots(ii)$$

On solving Eqs. (i) and (ii), to get the point of intersection, from Eq. (i)

$$x = 7y - 5$$

On putting the value of x in Eq. (ii), we get

$$3(7y - 5) + y = 0$$

$$\Rightarrow \quad 21y - 15 + y = 0$$

$$\Rightarrow \quad 22y = 15$$

$$\Rightarrow \quad y = \frac{15}{22}$$

On putting the volume of y in Eq. (i), we get

$$x = \frac{7 \times 15}{22} - 5 = \frac{105 - 110}{22} \Rightarrow x = -\frac{5}{22}$$

Hence, the point is $\left(-\frac{5}{22}, \frac{15}{22}\right)$

Hence, equation of required line by using

$$y - y_1 = m(x - x_1)$$

where $(x_1, y_1) = \left(\frac{-5}{22}, \frac{15}{22}\right)$ and tan 90° i.e. $m = \frac{1}{0}$ as line parallel to Y-axis, is

$$y - \frac{15}{22} = \frac{1}{0}\left(x + \frac{5}{22}\right)$$

$$\Rightarrow \quad 0 = x + \frac{5}{22} \Rightarrow 22x + 5 = 0$$

Question 6 Find the equation of a line drawn perpendicular to the line $\frac{x}{4} + \frac{y}{6} = 1$ through the point where it meets the Y-axis.

Sol. Given, equation of line is

$$\frac{x}{4} + \frac{y}{6} = 1$$

$$\Rightarrow \quad \frac{3x + 2y}{12} = 1 \Rightarrow 3x + 2y = 12 \quad \ldots(i)$$

$$\Rightarrow \quad 2y = -3x + 12 \Rightarrow y = -\frac{3}{2}x + 12$$

Slope of Eq. (i) $(m_1) = \frac{-3}{2}$

If line (i) meet the Y-axis put $x = 0$ in Eq. (i), we get

$$0 + 2y = 12 \Rightarrow y = 6$$

$\therefore$ Point is (0, 6).

Now, slope of line perpendicular to Eq. (i) is

$$m_1 \times m_2 = -1$$

$$\Rightarrow \quad \frac{-3}{2} m_2 = -1 \Rightarrow m_2 = \frac{2}{3}$$

Equation of the line passes through the point (0, 6) and slope is $\frac{2}{3}$

i.e., $$y - 6 = \frac{2}{3}(x - 0)$$

$$\Rightarrow \quad 3y - 18 = 2x \Rightarrow 2x - 3y + 18 = 0$$

Question 7 Find the area of the triangle formed by the lines $y - x = 0$, $x + y = 0$ and $x - k = 0$.

Thinking Process First find the vertices of the triangle by solving given lines simultaneously and then use the formula,

$$\text{Area} = \frac{1}{2}[x_1(y_2 - y_3) + x_2(y_3 - y_1) + x_3(y_1 - y_2)]$$

Sol. Let the given lines represent the sides of the triangle are

$$AB : y - x = 0 \quad \ldots(i)$$

$$BC : x + y = 0 \quad \ldots(ii)$$

and $$CA : x - k = 0 \quad \ldots(iii)$$

For point A, on solving Eqs. (i) and (iii), we get $A(k, k)$.

For point B, on solving Eqs. (i) and (ii), we get $B(0, 0)$.

For point C, on solving Eqs. (ii) and (iii), we get $C(k, -k)$.

So, the required points are

$$A(k, k), B(0, 0) \text{ and } C(k, -k)$$

Hence, area of ΔABC

$$= \frac{1}{2}[k(0 + k) + 0(-k - k) + k(k - 0)]$$

$$\left[\because \quad = \frac{1}{2}\{x_1(y_2 - y_3) + x_2(y_3 - y_1) + x_3(y_1 - y_2)\}\right]$$

$$= \frac{1}{2}[k^2 + k^2] = \frac{2k^2}{2} = k^2 \text{ sq. unit}$$

Question 8 Find the value of p so that the three lines $3x + y - 2 = 0$, $px + 2y - 3 = 0$ and $2x - y - 3 = 0$ may intersect at one point.

Thinking Process If lines meets at the same point, then they are concurrent.

Sol. Given, equation of lines are

$$3x + y - 2 = 0 \quad \ldots(i)$$

$$px + 2y - 3 = 0 \quad \text{...(ii)}$$

and $$2x - y - 3 = 0 \quad \text{...(iii)}$$

On adding Eqs. (i) and (iii), we get

$$5x - 5 = 0$$

$$\Rightarrow \quad x = 1$$

$\therefore$ From Eq. (i), $3 \times 1 + y - 2 = 0$ $\quad$ ($\because$ put $x = 1$)

$$\Rightarrow \quad y = -1$$

So, the point is (1, – 1).

Above point will satisfy Eq. (ii) *i.e.,*

$$p \times 1 + 2(-1) - 3 = 0 \Rightarrow p - 2 - 3 = 0 \quad (\text{put } x = 1, y = -1)$$

$$\Rightarrow \quad p = 5$$

Question 9 If three lines whose equations are $y = m_1x + c_1$, $y = m_2x + c_2$ and $y = m_3x + c_3$ are concurrent, then show that $m_1(c_2 - c_3) + m_2(c_3 - c_1) + m_3(c_1 - c_2) = 0$.

Sol. Given, equation of lines are

$$y = m_1x + c_1 \quad \text{...(i)}$$

$$y = m_2x + c_2 \quad \text{...(ii)}$$

$$y = m_3x + c_3 \quad \text{...(iii)}$$

On solving Eqs. (i) and (ii), we get

$$m_1x + c_1 = m_2x + c_2$$

$$\Rightarrow \quad m_1x - m_2x = c_2 - c_1 \Rightarrow x = \frac{c_2 - c_1}{m_1 - m_2}$$

From Eq. (i), $$y = m_1\left(\frac{c_2 - c_1}{m_1 - m_2}\right) + \frac{c_1}{1}$$

$$\Rightarrow \quad y = \frac{m_1c_2 - m_1c_1 + m_1c_1 - m_2c_1}{m_1 - m_2}$$

$$\Rightarrow \quad y = \frac{m_1c_2 - m_2c_1}{m_1 - m_2}$$

On putting the values of x and y in Eq. (iii), we get

$$\frac{m_1c_2 - m_2c_1}{m_1 - m_2} = m_3\left(\frac{c_2 - c_1}{m_1 - m_2}\right) + \frac{c_3}{1}$$

$$\Rightarrow \quad \frac{m_1c_2 - m_2c_1}{m_1 - m_2} = \frac{m_3c_2 - m_3c_1 + m_1c_3 - m_2c_3}{m_1 - m_2}$$

$$\Rightarrow \quad m_1c_2 - m_2c_1 = m_3c_2 - m_3c_1 + m_1c_3 - m_2c_3$$

$$\Rightarrow m_1c_2 - m_2c_1 - m_3c_2 + m_3c_1 - m_1c_3 + m_2c_3 = 0$$

$$\Rightarrow m_1(c_2 - c_3) + m_2(c_3 - c_1) + m_3(c_1 - c_2) = 0$$

Hence Proved.

Question 10 Find the equation of the lines through the point $(3, 2)$ which make an angle of $45°$ with the line $x - 2y = 3$.

Thinking Process Angle between two lines is $\tan\theta = \left|\frac{m_1 - m_2}{1 + m_1 m_2}\right|$, where m_1 and m_2 are the slopes of the lines.

Sol. Equation of line l_1 is

$$x - 2y = 3 \quad \text{...(i)}$$
$$-2y = 3 - x$$
$$y = \frac{1}{2}x - \frac{3}{2}$$

Slope of Eq. (i),

$$m_1 = \frac{1}{2}$$

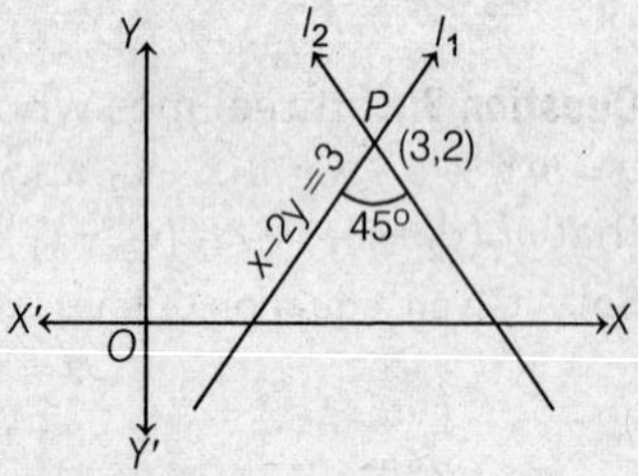

Angle between two lines is

$$\tan\theta = \left|\frac{m_1 - m_2}{1 + m_1 m_2}\right|$$

Given, $\theta = 45°$, $m_1 = \frac{1}{2}$, $m_2 = m$ (let)

$$\therefore \quad \tan 45° = \left|\frac{\frac{1}{2} - m}{1 + \frac{1}{2}m}\right| \Rightarrow 1 = \left|\frac{1 - 2m}{2 + m}\right| \Rightarrow \frac{1 - 2m}{2 + m} = \pm 1$$

Taking positive sign,

$$\frac{1 - 2m}{2 + m} = 1$$
$$\Rightarrow \quad 1 - 2m = 2 + m \Rightarrow 1 - 2 = 3m$$
$$\Rightarrow \quad m = -\frac{1}{3}$$

Taking negative sign,

$$\frac{1 - 2m}{2 + m} = -1 \Rightarrow 1 - 2m = -2 - m$$
$$\Rightarrow \quad 1 + 2 = 2m - m$$
$$\Rightarrow \quad m = 3$$

Now, equation of line l_2 by using

$$y - y_1 = m(x - x_1)$$
$$\Rightarrow \quad y - 2 = -\frac{1}{3}(x - 3) \quad \left(\text{when } m = -\frac{1}{3}, x_1 = 3, y_1 = 2\right)$$
$$\Rightarrow \quad 3y - 6 = -x + 3$$
$$\Rightarrow \quad x + 3y - 9 = 0$$

Again, $y - 2 = 3(x - 3)$ $\left(\begin{matrix}\text{when } m = 3,\\ x_1 = 3, y_1 = 2\end{matrix}\right)$

$\Rightarrow$ $y - 2 = 3x - 9$

$\Rightarrow$ $3x - y - 9 + 2 = 0$

$\Rightarrow$ $3x - y - 7 = 0$

$\therefore$ The required equation of lines are $3x - y - 7 = 0$ and $x + 3y - 9 = 0$

Question 11 Find the equation of the line passing through the point of intersection of the lines $4x + 7y - 3 = 0$ and $2x - 3y + 1 = 0$ that has equal intercepts on the axes.

◎ ***Thinking Process*** First find point of intersection of given line, then use intercept form of line is $\frac{x}{a} + \frac{y}{b} = 1$.

Sol. Given equation of lines are

$$4x + 7y - 3 = 0 \quad \ldots(i)$$

and

$$2x - 3y + 1 = 0 \quad \ldots(ii)$$

On solving Eqs. (i) and (ii), we get

From Eq. (ii), $3y = 2x + 1$

$\Rightarrow$ $y = \frac{2}{3}x + \frac{1}{3}$

On putting $y = \frac{2}{3}x + \frac{1}{3}$ in Eq. (i), we get

$$4x + 7\left(\frac{2}{3}x + \frac{1}{3}\right) - 3 = 0$$

$\Rightarrow$ $4x + \frac{14}{3}x + \frac{7}{3} - 3 = 0$

$\Rightarrow$ $\frac{12x + 14x}{3} + \frac{7 - 9}{3} = 0$

$\Rightarrow$ $\frac{26x - 2}{3} = 0$

$\Rightarrow$ $x = \frac{2}{26}$

$\Rightarrow$ $x = \frac{1}{13}$

On putting the value of x in Eq. (i), we get

$$\frac{4}{13} + 7y - 3 = 0$$

$\Rightarrow$ $7y = 3 - \frac{4}{13}$ $\Rightarrow$ $7y = \frac{39 - 4}{13}$ $\Rightarrow$ $7y = \frac{35}{13}$ $\Rightarrow$ $y = \frac{5}{13}$

Point is $\left(\frac{1}{13}, \frac{5}{13}\right)$.

Now, equation of line in intercept form is

$$\frac{x}{a}+\frac{y}{b}=1 \qquad \text{...(iii)}$$

Since, line (iii) has equal intercepts on the axes *i.e.*, $a = b$

$$\Rightarrow \qquad \frac{x}{a}+\frac{y}{a}=1 \Rightarrow \quad x+y=a \qquad \text{...(iv)}$$

Above line passes through the point $\left(\frac{1}{13}, \frac{5}{13}\right)$ *i.e.*, point will satisfy it

$$\frac{1}{13}+\frac{5}{13}=a \Rightarrow \quad a=\frac{6}{13}$$

Hence, required equation of line (iv) becomes

$$x+y=\frac{6}{13} \Rightarrow \ 13x+13y=6$$

Question 12 Show that the equation of the line passing through the origin and making an angle θ with the line $y = mx + c$ is

$$\frac{y}{x}=\frac{m \pm \tan\theta}{1 \mp m\tan\theta}$$

Thinking Process Angle between two lines is $\tan\theta=\left|\frac{m_1-m_2}{1+m_1m_2}\right|$.

Sol. Slope of given line is m and slope of another line is m_2. Angle between two lines is

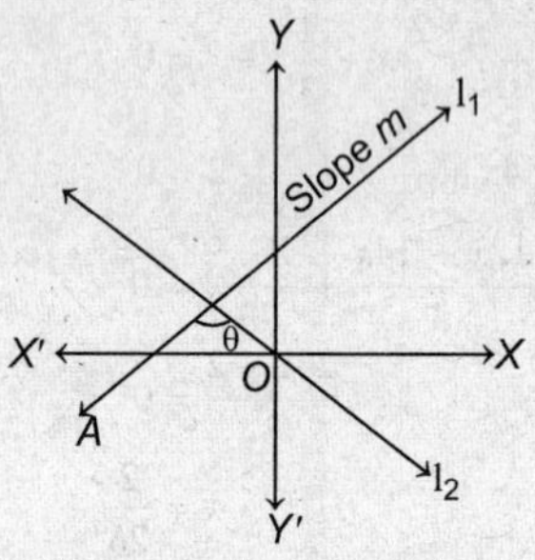

$$\tan\theta=\left|\frac{m_1-m_2}{1+m_1m_2}\right| \Rightarrow \tan\theta=\left|\frac{m-m_2}{1+mm_2}\right| \qquad (\because m_1=m)$$

$$\Rightarrow \qquad \frac{m-m_2}{1+mm_2}=\pm\tan\theta$$

Taking positive sign, $\quad \dfrac{m-m_2}{1+mm_2}=\dfrac{\tan\theta}{1}$

$$\Rightarrow \qquad m-m_2=\tan\theta+mm_2\tan\theta \Rightarrow m-\tan\theta=m_2+mm_2\tan\theta$$

$$\Rightarrow \qquad m_2(1+m\tan\theta)=m-\tan\theta$$

$$\Rightarrow \qquad m_2=\frac{m-\tan\theta}{1+m\tan\theta} \qquad \text{...(i)}$$

Taking negative sign,

$$\frac{m - m_2}{1 + mm_2} = \frac{-\tan\theta}{1} \Rightarrow m - m_2 = -\tan\theta - mm_2 \tan\theta$$

$\Rightarrow$ $$m + \tan\theta = m_2 - mm_2 \tan\theta$$

$\Rightarrow$ $$m + \tan\theta = m_2(1 - m\tan\theta)$$

$\Rightarrow$ $$m_2 = \frac{m + \tan\theta}{1 - m\tan\theta} \quad \text{...(ii)}$$

$\therefore$ From Eqs. (i) and (ii) $m_2 = \dfrac{m \pm \tan\theta}{1 \mp m\tan\theta}$

Equation of line through (0, 0) by using

$$y - y_1 = m(x - x_1)$$

where $m = m_2$ is $y - 0 = \dfrac{m \pm \tan\theta}{1 \mp m\tan\theta}(x - 0) \Rightarrow \dfrac{y}{x} = \dfrac{m \pm \tan\theta}{1 \mp m\tan\theta}$

Question 13 In what ratio, the line joining $(-1, 1)$ and $(5, 7)$ is divided by the line $x + y = 4$?

◎ *Thinking Process* Use section formula for internally $P(x, y) = \left(\dfrac{mx_2 + nx_1}{m + n}, \dfrac{my_2 + ny_1}{m + n}\right)$ and solve it.

Sol. Let the point P divides the line joining the points $A(-1, 1)$ and $B(5, 7)$ in the ratio is $K : 1$.

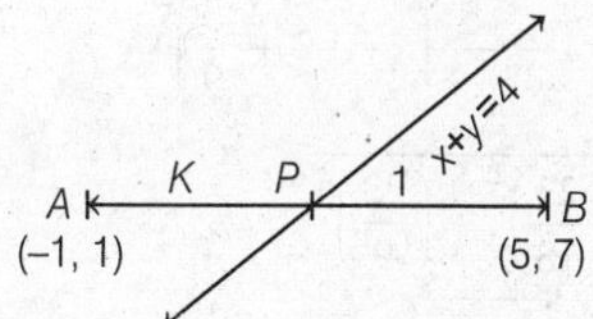

Then, $$P = \left(\frac{K \times x_2 + 1 \times x_1}{K + 1}, \frac{K \times y_2 + 1 \times y_1}{K + 1}\right)$$

$$= \left(\frac{K \times 5 + 1 \times (-1)}{K + 1}, \frac{K \times 7 + 1 \times 1}{K + 1}\right) = \left(\frac{5K - 1}{K + 1}, \frac{7K + 1}{K + 1}\right)$$

$[\because x_1 = -1, y_1 = 1, x_2 = 5, y_2 = 7]$

Point P will satisfy the line $x + y = 4$

i.e., $$\frac{5K - 1}{K + 1} + \frac{7K + 1}{K + 1} = \frac{4}{1} \Rightarrow \frac{5K - 1 + 7K + 1}{K + 1} = 4$$

$\Rightarrow$ $$12K = 4K + 4$$

$\Rightarrow$ $$8K = 4 \Rightarrow K = \frac{4}{8} = \frac{1}{2}$$

Hence, the required ratio is $K : 1 = 1 : 2$ (internally).

Question 14 Find the distance of the line $4x+7y+5=0$ from the point $(1,2)$ along the line $2x-y=0$.

Sol. The equation of line AB is

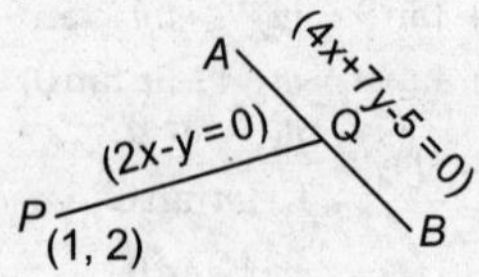

$$4x + 7y + 5 = 0 \quad \ldots(i)$$

and equation of PQ is $2x - y = 0$ ...(ii)

On solving Eqs. (i) and (ii), to obtain the coordinate of Q,

From Eq. (ii) put $y = 2x$ in Eq. (i)

$$4x + 7(2x) + 5 = 0$$

$$\Rightarrow \quad 18x + 5 = 0 \Rightarrow x = -\frac{5}{18}$$

On putting $x = -\frac{5}{18}$ in Eq. (ii), we get

$$2\left(-\frac{5}{18}\right) - y = 0 \Rightarrow y = -\frac{5}{9}$$

$$\therefore \text{ Coordinate of } Q = \left(-\frac{5}{18}, -\frac{5}{9}\right)$$

$$\text{Length of } QP = \sqrt{(x_2 - x_1)^2 + (y_2 - y_1)^2}$$

$$= \sqrt{\left(1 + \frac{5}{18}\right)^2 + \left(2 + \frac{5}{9}\right)^2} \quad \left(\because x_1 = -\frac{5}{18}, y_1 = -\frac{5}{9}, \; x_2 = 1, \; y_2 = 2\right)$$

$$= \sqrt{\left(\frac{23}{18}\right)^2 + \left(\frac{23}{9}\right)^2}$$

$$= \frac{23}{9}\sqrt{\frac{1}{4} + 1}$$

$$= \frac{23}{9} \times \frac{\sqrt{5}}{2}$$

$$= \frac{23}{18}\sqrt{5} \text{ sq. unit}$$

Question 15 Find the direction in which a straight line must be drawn through the point $(-1, 2)$, so that its point of intersection with the line $x + y = 4$ may be at a distance of 3 units from this point.

Sol. A line passing through point $P(-1, 2)$ and having slope m is

$$y - 2 = m(x + 1) \quad \left(\because y - y_1 = m(x - x_1), \; x_1 = -1, y_1 = 2\right)$$

$$y = mx + m + 2 \quad \ldots(i)$$

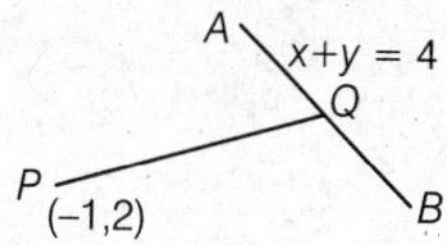

Now, determine the point of intersection of line AB and line PQ.

On putting the value of y from Eq. (i) in $x + y = 4$, we get

$$x + mx + m + 2 = 4$$

$$\Rightarrow \quad x(1+m) = 2 - m \Rightarrow x = \frac{2-m}{1+m}$$

$\therefore$ From Eq. (i),
$$y = m\left(\frac{2-m}{1+m}\right) + m + 2$$
$$= \frac{2m - m^2 + m + m^2 + 2 + 2m}{1+m} = \frac{2+5m}{1+m}$$

$$\therefore \text{ Coordinate of } Q = \left(\frac{2-m}{1+m}, \frac{2+5m}{1+m}\right)$$

$\because$ Distance between $PQ = 3$ (given)

$$\Rightarrow \quad (PQ)^2 = 9$$

$$\Rightarrow \quad (x_2 - x_1)^2 + (y_2 - y_1)^2 = 9$$

$$\Rightarrow \quad \left(\frac{2-m}{1+m} + 1\right)^2 + \left(\frac{2+5m}{1+m} - 2\right)^2 = 9 \qquad \left[\because x_1 = -1, \; y_1 = 2, \; x_2 = \frac{2-m}{1+m}, \; y_2 = \frac{2-5m}{1+m}\right]$$

$$\Rightarrow \quad \left(\frac{3}{1+m}\right)^2 + \left(\frac{3m}{1+m}\right)^2 = 9$$

$$\Rightarrow \quad 9 + 9m^2 = 9(1+m)^2$$

$$\Rightarrow \quad 1 + m^2 = 1 + 2m + m^2$$

$$\Rightarrow \quad 2m = 0 \Rightarrow m = 0$$

$\therefore$ Slope of PQ is zero, *i.e.*, it is parallel to X-axis.

Question 16 The hypotenuse of a right-angled triangle has its ends at the points (1, 3) and (– 4, 1). Find an equation of the legs (perpendicular sides) of the triangle. Which are parallel to the axes.

Sol. Given the hypotenuse of a right angled triangle has its ends at the points (1, 3) and (–4, 1)

Let ABC and ABC′ be the right angled triangles, where $\angle C = \angle C' = 90°$

For ΔABC

$$\therefore \quad AC \parallel y\text{-axis}$$

So, equation of $AC: y - 3 = \frac{1}{0}(x-1) \Rightarrow x = 1$ $\left[\because \tan 90 = \frac{1}{0}\right]$

and equation of BC is

$$y-1=0[x-(-4)] \quad [\because BC \parallel x-\text{axis}]$$

$$\Rightarrow \quad y=1$$

Now, For $\Delta ABC'$

$$\therefore \quad AC' \parallel x-\text{axis}$$

So, equation of line AC' is $y-3=0(x-1) \Rightarrow y=3$

$\therefore BC' \parallel y-$ axis, so equation of line BC' is

$$y-1=\frac{1}{0}[x-(-4)] \Rightarrow x=-4$$

$\therefore$ Equation of legs (perpendicular sides) of the triangle which are parallel to the axes are

$$x=1, y=1, y=3 \text{ and } x=-4$$

Question 17 Find the image of the point (3, 8) with respect to the line $x+3y=7$ assuming the line to be plane mirror.

Thinking Process It is a multiple concept question. So, first find the equation of line perpendicular to given line, then find their point of intersection. Finally use mid-point concept.

Sol. Let equation of line AB is

$$x+3y=7 \quad \ldots(i)$$

$$\Rightarrow 3y=-x+7 \Rightarrow y=\frac{-1}{3}x+\frac{7}{3}$$

Here, slope of a line AB is $m_1=-\frac{1}{3}$

Let $P(3, 8)$ be the given point for which image to be found.

Here, $\quad PQ \perp AB$

Slope of $PQ \times$ Slope of $AB=-1$

Let slope of PQ is m.

$$\therefore \quad m \times \left(\frac{-1}{3}\right)=-1 \quad (\because m_1 \times m_2=-1)$$

$$\Rightarrow \quad m=3$$

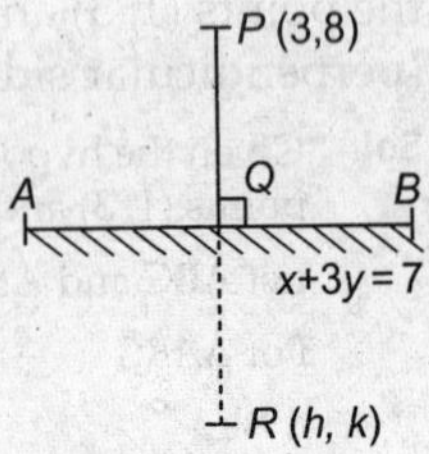

Now, equation of line PQ by using

$$y-y_1=m(x-x_1)$$

where, $\quad (x_1, y_1)=(3, 8)$ and $m=3$ is

$$y-8=3(x-3)$$

$$\Rightarrow \quad y-8=3x-9$$

$$\Rightarrow \quad 3x-y-1=0 \quad \ldots(ii)$$

To determine point Q, solving Eqs. (i) and (ii).

From Eq. (i) $x=7-3y$ put in Eq. (ii), we get

$$\Rightarrow \quad 3(7-3y)-y-1=0$$

$$\Rightarrow \quad 21 - 9y - y - 1 = 0 \Rightarrow 20 - 10y = 0$$

$$\Rightarrow \quad y = \frac{20}{10} \Rightarrow y = 2$$

$\therefore$ From Eq. (i), $x = 7 - 3 \times 2 = 7 - 6 = 1$

$\therefore$ Coordinate of $Q = (1, 2)$.

Let the image of point P be $R(h, k)$, since the line is a plane mirror, so point Q will be

the mid-point *i.e.*, $Q(1, 2)$.

Now, mid-point of $P(3, 8)$ and $R(h, k)$ is

$$= \left(\frac{x_1 + x_2}{2}, \frac{y_1 + y_2}{2}\right) = \left(\frac{3 + h}{2}, \frac{8 + k}{2}\right)$$

On comparing with coordinate $Q(1, 2)$, we get

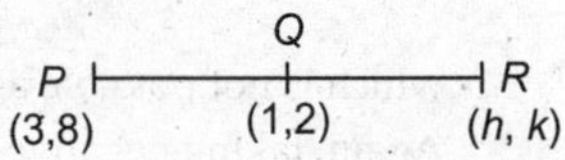

$$\therefore \quad \frac{3 + h}{2} = 1 \text{ and } \frac{8 + k}{2} = 2$$

$$\Rightarrow \quad 3 + h = 2 \text{ and } 8 + k = 4$$

$$\Rightarrow \quad h = 2 - 3 \text{ and } k = 4 - 8$$

$$\Rightarrow \quad h = -1 \text{ and } k = -4$$

Hence, image of a point P is $R(-1, -4)$.

Question 18 If the lines $y = 3x + 1$ and $2y = x + 3$ are equally inclined to the line $y = mx + 4$, find the value of m.

Thinking Process The angle between two lines is using by

$$\tan\theta = \left|\frac{m_1 - m_2}{1 + m_1 m_2}\right|$$

Sol. Let the angle between the lines $y = 3x + 1$ and $y = mx + 4$ is θ.

Here, slopes of the lines are $m_1 = 3, m_2 = m$

$$\tan\theta = \left|\frac{3 - m}{1 + 3m}\right| \quad \text{...(i)}$$

$$\left(\because \tan\theta = \left|\frac{m_1 - m_2}{1 + m_1 m_2}\right|\right)$$

Again, it is given that angle between the lines

$2y = x + 3$ and $y = mx + 4$ is also θ.

Here, slopes are $m_1 = \frac{1}{2}$ and $m_2 = m$.

$$\therefore \quad \tan\theta = \left|\frac{\frac{1}{2} - m}{1 + \frac{1}{2} \times m}\right| \quad \text{...(ii)}$$

From Eqs. (i) and (ii), we get

$$\left|\frac{3-m}{1+3m}\right| = \left|\frac{\frac{1}{2}-m}{1+\frac{m}{2}}\right|$$

$$\Rightarrow \quad \frac{3-m}{1+3m} = \pm\left(\frac{1-2m}{2+m}\right)$$

Taking positive sign,

$$\Rightarrow \quad (3-m)(2+m) = (1-2m)(1+3m)$$

$$\Rightarrow \quad 6+3m-2m-m^2 = 1+3m-2m-6m^2$$

$$\Rightarrow \quad 6 = 1-5m^2 \Rightarrow 5m^2 = 1-6$$

$$m^2 = \frac{-5}{5}$$

which is not possible as $m^2 \geq 0$.

Again, taking negative sign, we get

$$\frac{3-m}{1+3m} = -\frac{1-2m}{2+m}$$

$$\Rightarrow \quad (3-m)(2+m) = (2m-1)(1+3m)$$

$$\Rightarrow \quad 6+3m-2m-m^2 = 2m+6m^2-1-3m$$

$$\Rightarrow \quad 6+m-m^2 = 6m^2-m-1$$

$$\Rightarrow \quad 6m^2-m-1-6-m+m^2 = 0$$

$$\Rightarrow \quad 7m^2-2m-7 = 0$$

$$\Rightarrow \quad m = \frac{2 \pm \sqrt{4+4\times7\times7}}{2\times7} \qquad \left[\because x = \frac{-b \pm \sqrt{b^2-4ac}}{2a}\right]$$

$$\Rightarrow \quad = \frac{2 \pm 2\sqrt{1+49}}{2\times7}$$

$$\Rightarrow \quad m = \frac{1 \pm \sqrt{50}}{7}$$

$$m = \frac{1 \pm 5\sqrt{2}}{7}$$

Mistake Alert When we remove the mode sign, then use both $\pm$ signs. Sometimes students forget this step.

Question 19 If sum of perpendicular distances of a variable point $P(x, y)$ from the lines $x+y-5=0$ and $3x-2y+7=0$ is always 10. Show that P must move on a line.

Thinking Process Use the distance of point (x_1, y_1) from the line $ax+by+c=0$ is

$\left|\frac{ax_1+by_1+c}{\sqrt{a^2+b^2}}\right|$ and simplify it.

Sol. Given equations of lines are

$$x + y - 5 = 0 \quad \ldots(i)$$

and
$$3x - 2y + 7 = 0 \quad \ldots(ii)$$

Since, the sum of perpendicular distances of a variable point $P(x, y)$ from lines $x + y - 5 = 0$ and $3x - 2y + 7 = 0$ is 10.

$$\therefore \left|\frac{x + y - 5}{\sqrt{(1)^2 + (1)^2}}\right| + \left|\frac{3x - 2y + 7}{\sqrt{3^2 + (-2)^2}}\right| = 10$$

$$\left(\because \text{perpendicular distance } d = \left|\frac{ax_1 + by_1 + c}{\sqrt{a^2 + b^2}}\right|\right)$$

$$\Rightarrow \frac{x + y - 5}{\sqrt{2}} + \frac{3x - 2y + 7}{\sqrt{13}} = 10 \quad [\because \text{if we take + sign for both}]$$

$$\Rightarrow \sqrt{13}(x + y - 5) + \sqrt{2}(3x - 2y + 7) = 10\sqrt{2}\sqrt{13}$$

$$\Rightarrow x(\sqrt{13} + 3\sqrt{2}) + y(\sqrt{13} - 2\sqrt{2}) - 5\sqrt{13} + 7\sqrt{2} = 10\sqrt{26}$$

$$\Rightarrow x(\sqrt{13} + 3\sqrt{2}) + y(\sqrt{13} - 2\sqrt{2}) + 7\sqrt{2} - 5\sqrt{13} - 10\sqrt{26} = 0$$

Similarly, we can obtain the equation of line for any sign of $|x + y - 5|$ and $|3x - 2y + 7|$

which is of the form $ax + by + c = 0$

Hence, it represents a line. This means that P is moving along the line.

Mistake Alert Here, point (x_1, y_1) is given as (x, y), so students should not create any confusion.

Question 20 Find the equation of the line which is equidistant from parallel lines $9x + 6y - 7 = 0$ and $3x + 2y + 6 = 0$.

Thinking Process Use any line parallel to $ax + by + c = 0$ is $ax + by + k = 0$ and distance between these lines is $\left|\frac{c - k}{\sqrt{a^2 + b^2}}\right|$.

Sol. Given, the equations of lines are

$$9x + 6y - 7 = 0$$

or
$$3x + 2y - \frac{7}{3} = 0 \quad \text{[dividing by 3]} \ldots(i)$$

and
$$3x + 2y + 6 = 0 \quad \ldots(ii)$$

Equation of line parallel to either Eq. (i) or Eq. (ii) is

$$3x + 2y + k = 0 \quad \ldots(iii)$$

Now, given line (iii) is equidistant from lines (i) and (ii).

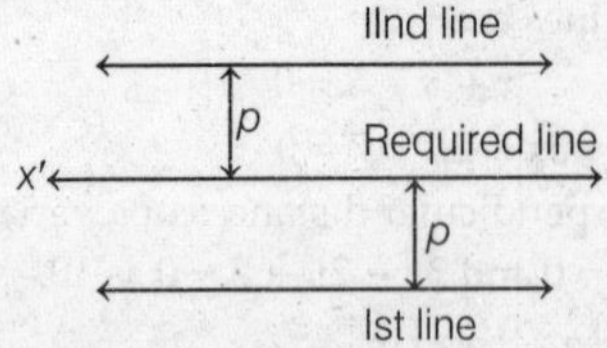

i.e., Distance between lines (i) and (iii) = Distance between lines (ii) and (iii)

$$\therefore \quad \left|\frac{k+\frac{7}{3}}{\sqrt{3^2+2^2}}\right| = \left|\frac{k-6}{\sqrt{3^2+2^2}}\right|$$

$$\left(\because \text{distance between parallel lines is } \left|\frac{c-d}{\sqrt{a^2+b^2}}\right|\right)$$

$$\Rightarrow \quad \left|k+\frac{7}{3}\right| = |k-6| \Rightarrow k+\frac{7}{3} = \pm(k-6)$$

Taking negative sign,

$$\Rightarrow \quad k+\frac{7}{3} = -k+6$$

$$\Rightarrow \quad 2k = 6-\frac{7}{3}$$

$$\Rightarrow \quad 2k = \frac{11}{3}$$

$$\Rightarrow \quad k = \frac{11}{6}$$

If we take positive sign, then we are getting wrong result.
i.e., k will be ommitted both sides

Hence, Eq. (iii) becomes

$$3x+2y+\frac{11}{6} = 0 \qquad \left(\text{Put } k = \frac{11}{6}\right)$$

$\therefore$ $18x + 12y + 11 = 0$ is the required line.

Question 21 A ray of light passing through the point (1, 2) reflects on the X-axis at point A and the reflected ray passes through the point (5, 3). Find the coordinates of A.

Sol. In a figure PA is the incident ray and AR is the reflected ray, which makes an angle θ from the X-axis.

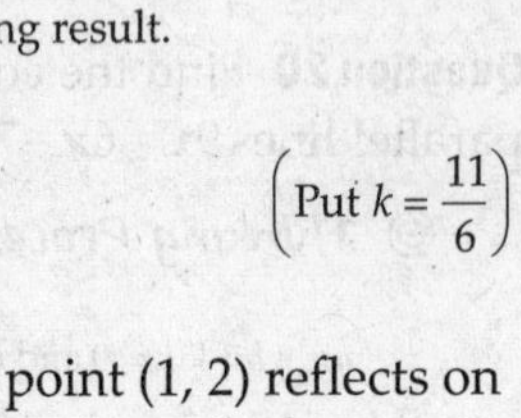

It is clear from the figure that $AS \perp OX$

It means AS bisect the angle PAR.

Then, $\angle PAS = \angle RAS$

$$\Rightarrow \quad \angle RAX = \angle PAO = \theta \text{ (Let)} \Rightarrow \angle XAP = 180 - \theta$$

$$\text{Slope of } AR = \tan\theta = \frac{y_2-y_1}{x_2-x_1} = \frac{3-0}{5-k} \qquad \dots(i)$$

[where point A is $(k, 0)$]

Slope of $AP = \tan(180° - \theta) = -\tan\theta = \dfrac{y_2 - y_1}{x_2 - x_1} = \dfrac{2-0}{1-k}$ ...(ii)

$\therefore$ From Eqs. (i) and (ii), $\dfrac{3}{5-k} = -\dfrac{2}{1-k} \Rightarrow 3 - 3k = -10 + 2k$

[$\because$ Slope of AR $(\tan\theta) = -$ slope of AP $(-\tan\theta)$]

$$\Rightarrow \quad 5k = 13 \Rightarrow k = \frac{13}{5}$$

Hence, the coordinate of A is $\left(\dfrac{13}{5}, 0\right)$.

Question 22 Prove that the product of the lengths of the perpendiculars drawn from the points $(\sqrt{a^2 - b^2}, 0)$ and $(-\sqrt{a^2 - b^2}, 0)$ to the line $\dfrac{x}{a}\cos\theta + \dfrac{y}{b}\sin\theta = 1$ is b^2.

◎ ***Thinking Process*** Use the distance of point (x_1, y_1) from the line $ax + by + c = 0$ is $\left|\dfrac{ax_1 + by_1 + c}{\sqrt{a^2 + b^2}}\right|$

Sol. Given, equation of line is $\dfrac{x}{a}\cos\theta + \dfrac{y}{b}\sin\theta = 1 \Rightarrow \dfrac{bx\cos\theta + ay\sin\theta}{ab} = 1$

$$\Rightarrow \quad bx\cos\theta + ay\sin\theta = ab$$

$$\Rightarrow \quad bx\cos\theta + ay\sin\theta - ab = 0 \quad \text{...(i)}$$

At point $(\sqrt{a^2 - b^2}, 0)$ the perpendicular distance from line (i)

$$p_1 = \left|\frac{Ax_1 + By_1 + C}{\sqrt{A^2 + B^2}}\right| = \left|\frac{b\sqrt{a^2 - b^2}\cos\theta - 0 - ab}{\sqrt{b^2\cos^2\theta + a^2\sin^2\theta}}\right|$$

$(\because A = b\cos\theta, B = a\sin\theta, C = -ab; x_1 = \sqrt{a^2 - b^2}, y_1 = 0)$

and at point $(-\sqrt{a^2 - b^2}, 0)$ the perpendicular distance from line (i),

$$p_2 = \left|\frac{-b\sqrt{a^2 - b^2}\cos\theta - ab}{\sqrt{b^2\cos^2\theta + a^2\sin^2\theta}}\right| \quad \left(\because A = b\cos\theta, B = a\sin\theta, C = -ab, x_1 = -\sqrt{a^2 - b^2}, y_1 = 0\right)$$

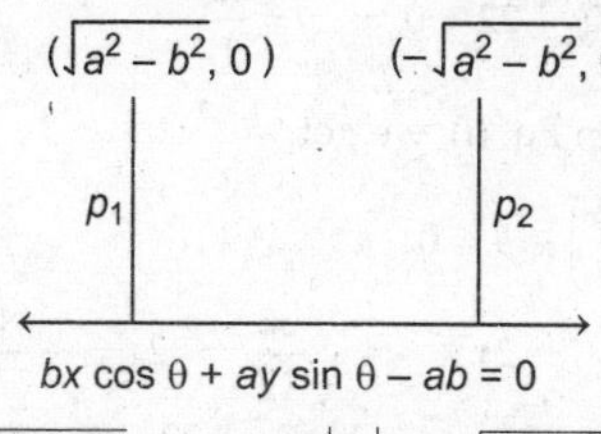

$$\therefore \quad p_1 p_2 = \left|\frac{b\sqrt{a^2 - b^2}\cos\theta - ab}{\sqrt{b^2\cos^2\theta + a^2\sin^2\theta}}\right| \times \left|\frac{-b\sqrt{a^2 - b^2}\cos\theta - ab}{\sqrt{b^2\cos^2\theta + a^2\sin^2\theta}}\right|$$

$$= \frac{b\,|\sqrt{a^2 - b^2}\cos\theta - a| \times b\,|\sqrt{a^2 - b^2}\cos\theta + a|}{(b^2\cos^2\theta + a^2\sin^2\theta)}$$

$$= \frac{b^2\,|(a^2 - b^2)\cos^2\theta - a^2|}{(b^2\cos^2\theta + a^2\sin^2\theta)} \quad [\because (A+B)(A-B) = A^2 - B^2]$$

$$= \frac{b^2\,|a^2\cos^2\theta - b^2\cos^2\theta - a^2|}{(b^2\cos^2\theta + a^2\sin^2\theta)}$$

$$= \frac{b^2\,|a^2(\cos^2\theta - 1) - b^2\cos^2\theta|}{(b^2\cos^2\theta + a^2\sin^2\theta)}$$

$$\Rightarrow \quad p_1p_2 = \frac{b^2\,|-a^2\sin^2\theta - b^2\cos^2\theta|}{(b^2\cos^2\theta + a^2\sin^2\theta)}$$

$(\because \sin^2\theta + \cos^2\theta = 1)$

$$= \frac{b^2\,|a^2\sin^2\theta + b^2\cos^2\theta|}{(b^2\cos^2\theta + a^2\sin^2\theta)} \quad (\because |-A| = |A|)$$

$\therefore \quad p_1p_2 = b^2$ **Hence Proved.**

Question 23 A person standing at the junction (crossing) of two straight paths represented by the equations $2x - 3y + 4 = 0$ and $3x + 4y - 5 = 0$ wants to reach the path whose equation is $6x - 7y + 8 = 0$ in the least time. Find equation of the path that he should follow.

Sol. Given equation of straight path is

$$2x - 3y + 4 = 0 \quad \text{...(i)}$$

and $$3x + 4y - 5 = 0 \quad \text{...(ii)}$$

On solving Eqs. (i) and (ii) for crossing point.

From Eq. (i), $2x = -4 + 3y \Rightarrow x = \dfrac{-4 + 3y}{2}$

On putting the value of x in Eq. (ii), $3\left(\dfrac{-4 + 3y}{2}\right) + 4y - 5 = 0$

$\Rightarrow \quad -12 + 9y + 8y - 10 = 0$

$\Rightarrow \quad 17y - 22 = 0 \Rightarrow y = \dfrac{22}{17}$

On putting $y = \dfrac{22}{17}$ in Eq. (i), we get

$$2x - 3\left(\frac{22}{17}\right) + 4 = 0$$

$\Rightarrow \quad 2x = -4 + \dfrac{66}{17} \Rightarrow 2x = \dfrac{-68 + 66}{17} \Rightarrow x = -\dfrac{1}{17}$

$\therefore \quad x = -\dfrac{1}{17},\ y = \dfrac{22}{17}$

Suppose the person is standing at point P, then he can reach the path AB in least time if he goes straight to it *i.e.,* perpendicular to it. It means we have to find the equation of PQ.

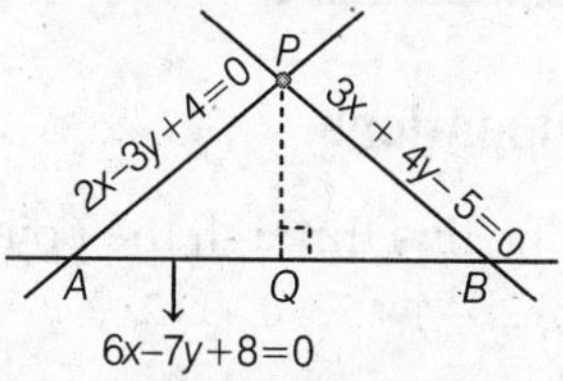

$\because$ Line $PQ \perp$ line AB

$\therefore$ Slope of PQ $\times$ Slope of $AB = -1$

$\Rightarrow \quad m \times \left(\frac{6}{7}\right) = -1 \qquad \left[\because \text{Slope of line } 6x - 7y + 8 = 0 \text{ is } \left(\frac{6}{7}\right)\right]$

$\Rightarrow \quad m \times \frac{6}{7} = -1 \Rightarrow m = -\frac{7}{6}$

Equation of line PQ by using

$$y - y_1 = m(x - x_1)$$

where $(x_1, y_1) = \left(-\frac{1}{17}, \frac{22}{17}\right)$ and $m = -\frac{7}{6}$ is

$$y - \frac{22}{17} = -\frac{7}{6}\left(x + \frac{1}{17}\right)$$

$$\Rightarrow \quad \frac{17y - 22}{17} = -\frac{7}{6}\left(\frac{17x + 1}{17}\right)$$

$$\Rightarrow \quad 6 \times 17y - 22 \times 6 = -7 \times 17x - 7$$

$$\Rightarrow \quad 102y - 132 = -119x - 7$$

$$\Rightarrow \quad 119x + 102y - 132 + 7 = 0$$

$$\Rightarrow \quad 119x + 102y - 125 = 0$$

DIKSHA APP Questions

☐ Multiple Choice Questions

Q.1 The equations of the line through the points (1, 5) and (2, 3) is

(a) $2x-y-2=0$ (b) $2x+y+7=0$ (c) $2x+y-7=0$ (d) $x+2y-7=0$

◎ *Thinking Process* The equation of the line which passes through the two point (x_1, y_1) and (x_2, y_2) is $y-y_1=\frac{y_2-y_1}{x_2-x_1}(x-x_1)$

Sol. (c) Let $(x_1, y_1)=(1,5)$ and $(x_2, y_2)=(2,3)$

Equation of line is given by

$$\Rightarrow \quad y-5=\frac{3-5}{2-1}(x-1) \quad \left[\because y-y_1=\frac{y_2-y_1}{x_2-x_1}(x-x_1)\right]$$

$$\Rightarrow \quad y-5=-2(x-1)$$

$$\Rightarrow \quad y-5=-2x+2$$

$$\Rightarrow \quad 2x+y-7=0$$

Q.2 The distance between the line $3x+4y=9$ and $6x+8y=15$ is

(a) $\frac{3}{10}$ (b) $\frac{2}{3}$ (c) $\frac{3}{2}$ (d) $\frac{7}{10}$

◎ *Thinking Process* Distance between two parallel lines $ax+by+c_1=0$ and $ax+by+c_2=0$ is $\frac{|c_1-c_2|}{\sqrt{a^2+b^2}}$

Sol. (a) Given, the equations of lines are $3x+4y=9$

$$\Rightarrow \quad 3x+4y-9=0 \quad \ldots\text{(i)}$$

and $\quad 6x+8y=15$

$$\Rightarrow \quad 3x+4y-\frac{15}{2}=0 \quad \ldots\text{(ii)}$$

Distance between lines (i) and (ii)

$$=\frac{\left|-9-\left(-\frac{15}{2}\right)\right|}{\sqrt{3^2+4^2}} \quad \left[\because d=\frac{|c_1-c_2|}{\sqrt{a^2+b^2}}\right]$$

$$=\frac{\left|-9+\frac{15}{2}\right|}{\sqrt{9+16}}=\frac{\left|\frac{-3}{2}\right|}{5}=\frac{3}{10}$$

Q.3 A point equidistant from the lines $4x+3y+10=0$, $5x-12y+26=0$ and $7x+24y-50=0$ is

(a) $(1,-1)$ (b) $(1,1)$

(c) $(0,0)$ (d) $(0,1)$

Thinking Process Distance of a point (x_1, y_1) from a line $ax+by+c$ is $\left|\dfrac{ax_1+by_1+c}{\sqrt{a^2+b^2}}\right|$

Sol. (c) Let (α,β) be the point equidistant from given lines

$$\frac{|4\alpha+3\beta+10|}{\sqrt{4^2+3^2}}=\frac{|5\alpha-12\beta+26|}{\sqrt{5^2+(-12)^2}}=\frac{|7\alpha+24\beta-50|}{\sqrt{7^2+(24)^2}} \quad \text{...(i)}$$

Out of 4 options, the choice (0, 0) satisfies the Eq. (i)

$$\frac{10}{5}=\frac{26}{13}=\frac{50}{25}=2, \text{ it makes each distance 2 units}$$

Q.4 The ratio in which the line $3x+4y+2=0$ divides the distance between the lines $3x+4y+5=0$ and $3x+4y-5=0$ is

(a) 1 : 2 (b) 3 : 7

(c) 2 : 3 (d) 2 : 5

Sol. (b) Given $3x+4y+2=0$ divides the distance between the lines

$$3x+4y+5=0$$

and $$3x+4y-5=0$$

Since, given lines are parallel to each other.

$\therefore$ distance between l_1 and l_2

$$d_1=\frac{|5-2|}{\sqrt{3^2+4^4}}=\frac{3}{5}$$

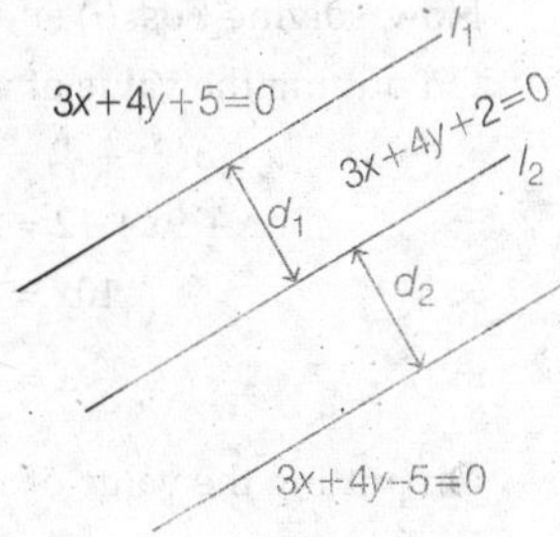

And, distance between l_2 and l_3

$$d_2=\frac{|2-(-5)|}{\sqrt{3^2+4^2}}=\frac{7}{5}$$

$$\therefore \quad \frac{d_1}{d_2}=\frac{3}{5}\times\frac{5}{7}=\frac{3}{7} \text{ i.e}$$

$d_1 : d_2 = 3 : 7$

Q.5 The coordinates of the foot of perpendicular from the point (2, 3) on the line $y = 3x + 4$ is given by

(a) $\left(\frac{37}{10}, \frac{-1}{10}\right)$ (b) $\left(\frac{-1}{10}, \frac{37}{10}\right)$

(c) $\left(\frac{10}{37}, -10\right)$ (d) $\left(\frac{2}{3}, \frac{-1}{3}\right)$

◎ ***Thinking Process*** The foot of the perpendicular is the intersection between the given line and the line perpendicular to it

Sol. (b) Given equation of line AB is

$$y = 3x + 4 \quad \ldots(i)$$

Now, comparing with $y = mx + C$, then

slope of line is $m_1 = 3$

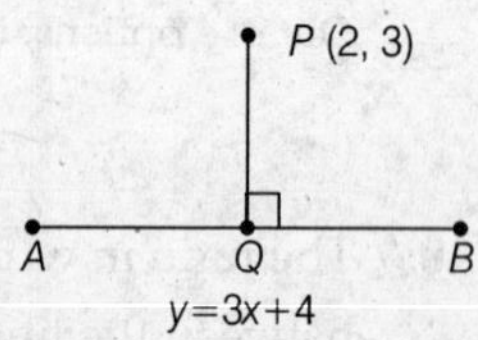

Let slope of line PQ is m_2.

$\therefore \quad PQ \perp AB \Rightarrow m_2 \times m_1 = -1$

$\Rightarrow \quad m_2 \times (3) = -1 \quad [\because m_1 = 3]$

$\Rightarrow \quad m_2 = -\frac{1}{3}$

Now, equation of a line (PQ) whose passing through the point $P(2,3)$ with slope m_2 is

$$y - 3 = m_2(x - 2)$$

$\Rightarrow \quad y - 3 = \left(\frac{-1}{3}\right)(x - 2)$

$\Rightarrow \quad 3y - 9 = -x + 2$

$\Rightarrow \quad x + 3y = 11 \quad \ldots(ii)$

Now, solving Eqs. (i) and (ii), to find the coordinates of Q.

On putting the value of y by Eq .(i) in Eq. (ii) we get

$$x + 3(3x + 4) = 11$$

$\Rightarrow \quad x + 9x + 12 = 11$

$\Rightarrow \quad 10x = -1$

$\Rightarrow \quad x = \frac{-1}{10}$

On putting the value of x in Eq. (i), we get

$$y = 3\left(\frac{-1}{10}\right) + 4$$

$\Rightarrow \quad y = \frac{-3}{10} + 4 \Rightarrow y = \frac{37}{10}$

Hence, required point of intersection is $\left(\frac{-1}{10}, \frac{37}{10}\right)$

Q.6 The line if the slope is zero is

(a) Y-axis

(b) angle is an obtuse angle

(c) X-axis or parallel to X-axis

(d) angle is acute angle

Sol. (c) Given, slope of line, $m = 0$

Let line makes an angle θ from $+ve$ direction of X-axis, then

$$\Rightarrow \quad \tan\theta = 0 \Rightarrow \theta = 0° \text{ or } 180°$$

$\Rightarrow$ Hence, given line will be X-axis or parallel to X-axis.

Q.7 The equation of the locus of a point equidistant from the point $A(1, 3)$ and $B(-2, 1)$ is

(a) $6x - 4y = 5$ (b) $6x + 4y = 5$

(c) $6x + 4y = 7$ (d) $6x - 4y = 7$

Thinking Process Distance between two points (x_1, y_1) and (x_2, y_2)

$$d = \sqrt{(x_2 - x_1)^2 + (y_2 - y_1)^2}$$

Sol. (b) Let the point $P(x, y)$ which is equidistant from the point $A(1, 3)$ and $B(-2, 1)$.

$$\therefore \quad AP = BP$$

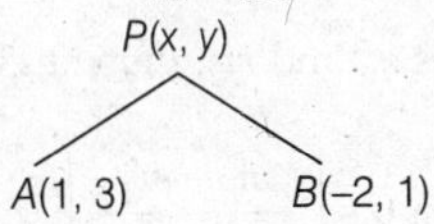

$$\Rightarrow \quad \sqrt{(x-1)^2 + (y-3)^2} = \sqrt{(x+2)^2 + (y-1)^2}$$

On squaring both side, we get

$$(x-1)^2 + (y-3)^2 = (x+2)^2 + (y-1)^2$$

$$\Rightarrow \quad x^2 + 1 - 2x + y^2 + 9 - 6y = x^2 + 4 + 4x + y^2 + 1 - 2y$$

$$\Rightarrow \quad -2x - 4x - 6y + 2y + 10 - 5 = 0$$

$$\Rightarrow \quad -6x - 4y + 5 = 0$$

$$\Rightarrow \quad 6x + 4y - 5 = 0$$

$$\Rightarrow \quad 6x + 4y = 5$$

Q.8 The line which cuts off equal intercept from the axes and passess through the point $(1, -2)$ is

(a) $x + y + 1 = 0$ (b) $x - y + 1 = 0$

(c) $x - y - 1 = 0$ (d) $-x - y + 1 = 0$

Sol. (a) We know that, equation of the line is intercept form is

$$\frac{x}{a} + \frac{y}{b} = 1 \quad \text{...(i)}$$

Since, the line makes equal intercepts with the axes *i.e*, $a = b$

$\therefore$ From Eq. (i) $\quad \frac{x}{a} + \frac{y}{a} = 1$

$\Rightarrow \quad x + y = a \quad$ ...(ii)

The line passess through the point $(1, -2)$ *i.e*, it will satisfy the Eq. (ii)

$$1 + (-2) = a \Rightarrow a = -1$$

On putting the value of a in Eq. (ii), we get

$$x + y = -1 \Rightarrow x + y + 1 = 0$$

Q.9 Angle between the lines $x - 2y = 5$ and $y - 2x = 5$ is

(a) $\tan^{-1}\left(\frac{1}{4}\right)$ (b) $\tan^{-1}\left(\frac{3}{5}\right)$

(c) $\tan^{-1}\left(\frac{3}{4}\right)$ (d) $\tan^{-1}\left(\frac{2}{3}\right)$

Sol. (c) Given equations of lines $x - 2y = 5$ and $y - 2x = 5$.

Now, comparing with $y = mx + C$

Then the slope of lines $m_1 = -\left(\frac{1}{-2}\right) = \frac{1}{2}$ and $m_2 = -\left(\frac{-2}{1}\right) = 2$

If slopes of two lines m_1 and m_2, then angle between them. By using the formula

$$\tan\theta = \left|\frac{m_1 - m_2}{1 + m_1 \cdot m_2}\right|$$

$$\Rightarrow \quad \tan\theta = \left|\frac{\frac{1}{2} - 2}{1 + \frac{1}{2} \times 2}\right| \quad \left[\because m_1 = \frac{1}{2}, m_2 = 2\right]$$

$$\tan\theta = \left|\frac{\frac{-3}{2}}{2}\right| \Rightarrow \theta = \tan^{-1}\left(\frac{3}{4}\right)$$

Q.10 The inclination of the line $x - y + 3 = 0$ with the positive direction of X-axis is

(a) 45° (b) 135°

(c) – 45° (d) – 135°

Sol. (a) Given, line $x - y + 3 = 0$

$$\because \text{ Slope of the line } (m) = \frac{-\text{ Coefficient of } x}{\text{Coefficient of } y} \Rightarrow m = \frac{-1}{-1} = 1$$

$\Rightarrow$ Let θ is the inclination of the given line with the positive direction of X-axis, then

$$m = \tan\theta$$

$$\Rightarrow \quad \tan\theta = 1 \Rightarrow \quad \theta = 45^\circ$$

Q.11 Equation of the line passing through $(1, 2)$ and perpendicular to $x + y + 7 = 0$.

(a) $y - x + 1 = 0$ (b) $y - x - 1 = 0$
(c) $y - x + 2 = 0$ (d) $y - x - 2 = 0$

Sol. (b) Given, equation of the line $x + y + 7 = 0$, then slope of given line,

$$m_1 = \frac{-\text{ coefficient of } x}{\text{coefficient of } y} = \frac{-1}{1} = -1.$$

Two lines are perpendicular to each other, if $m_1 \times m_2 = -1$, then slope of other line $m_2 = -\dfrac{1}{m_1}$

$$\Rightarrow \quad m_2 = \frac{-1}{-1} = 1$$

Equation of the line which passes through (1, 2) and slope 1.

$$y - y_1 = m(x - x_1)$$

$$\Rightarrow \quad y - 2 = 1(x - 1) \Rightarrow y - 2 = x - 1 \Rightarrow y - x - 1 = 0$$

Q.12 The distance of the point $P(1, -3)$ from the line $2y - 3x = 4$ is

(a) 13 (b) $\dfrac{7\sqrt{13}}{13}$ (c) $\sqrt{13}$ (d) None of these

Sol. (c) By using distance of point (x_1, y_1) from the line $ax + by + c = 0$.

$$d = \left| \frac{ax_1 + by_1 + c}{\sqrt{a^2 + b^2}} \right|$$

Here, $x_1 = 1$, $y_1 = -3$ and line $-3x + 2y - 4 = 0$, then

$$d = \left| \frac{-3 \times 1 + 2 \times -3 - 4}{\sqrt{(-3)^2 + (2)^2}} \right|$$

$$= \left| \frac{-3 - 6 - 4}{\sqrt{9 + 4}} \right| \Rightarrow \left| \frac{-13}{\sqrt{13}} \right| = \sqrt{13}$$

Q.13 A line cutting, if intercept −3 from the Y-axis and the tangent at angle to the X-axis is $\frac{3}{5}$, its equation.

(a) $5y - 3x + 15 = 0$ (b) $3y - 5x + 15 = 0$
(c) $5y - 3x - 15 = 0$ (d) None of these

Sol. (a) Given line cuts off intercept − 3 on Y-axis, then point on Y-axis is $(0, -3)$ and tangent at angle to the X-axis is $\frac{3}{5}$ i.e, slope of line $m = \frac{3}{5}$.

Now, equation of the line,

$$y - (-3) = \frac{3}{5}(x - 0) \qquad [\because y - y_1 = m(x - x_1)]$$

$$5y + 15 = 3x - 0$$

$$5y - 3x + 15 = 0$$

☐ Subjective Type Questions

Q.1 Find the slope of the line which makes angle $\frac{\pi}{4}$ with positive direction of Y – axis?

Sol. Given line make an angle $\frac{\pi}{4}$ with positive direction of Y – axis

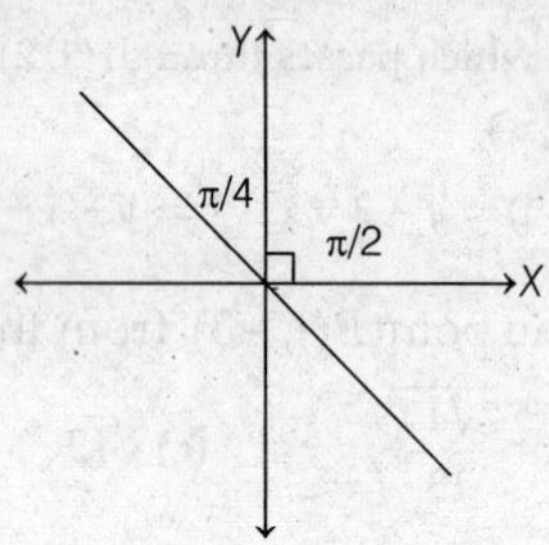

Since, inclination of line with positive directions of X-axis $= \frac{\pi}{2} + \frac{\pi}{4}$

$$\therefore \text{Slope of given line} = \tan\left(\frac{\pi}{2} + \frac{\pi}{4}\right) \qquad [\because \text{slope } m = \tan\theta]$$

$$= -\cot\left(\frac{\pi}{4}\right) = -(1) = -1 \qquad \left[\therefore \tan\left(\frac{\pi}{2} + \theta\right) = -\cot\theta\right]$$

Q.2 Acute angle between two line is 40°. Find the obtuse angle between the same lines?

◎ ***Thinking Process*** Acute angle between two lines + obtuse angle between two line = 180°

Sol. Given acute angle between two lines is 40°.

Now, acute angle + obtuse angle = 180° [between two lines]

40°+ obtuse angle = 180°

∴ Obtuse angle = 180°–40°= 140°

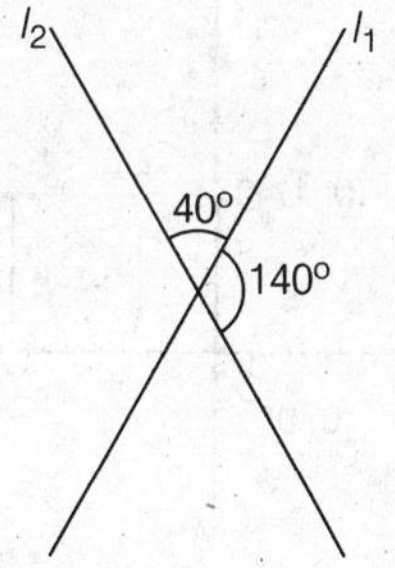

Note Two non-parallel lines make two angle with each other.

Q.3 Find the slope of the line perpendicular to the line passing through the points (6, 3) and (4, 8).

◎ ***Thinking Process*** It two lines are perpendicular, then $m_1 \times m_2 = -1$

Sol. Given a line passing through the points (6, 3) and (4, 8).

Let $(x_1, y_1) = (6, 3)$ and $(x_2, y_2) = (4,8)$

Now, slope of line

$$m_1 = \frac{y_2 - y_1}{x_2 - x_1} = \frac{8-3}{4-6} = \frac{5}{-2} = -\frac{5}{2}$$

And slope of perpendicular line

$$m_2 = -\frac{1}{m_1} \quad [\because l_1 \perp l_2 \Leftrightarrow m_1 \times m_2 = -1]$$

$$m_2 = -\frac{1}{\left(\frac{-5}{2}\right)} = \frac{2}{5}$$

∴ Slope for perpendicular line $= \frac{2}{5}$

Q.4 Equation of the diagonals of the square formed by the lines $x=0, y=0\; x=1$ and $y=1$ are

◎ *Thinking Process* Equation of the line which passess through the point (x_1, y_1) and (x_2, y_2) is $y - y_1 = \frac{y_2 - y_1}{x_2 - x_1}(x - x_1)$

Sol. Given lines $x = 0, y = 0, x = 1$ and $y = 1$

Let a square be $OABC$

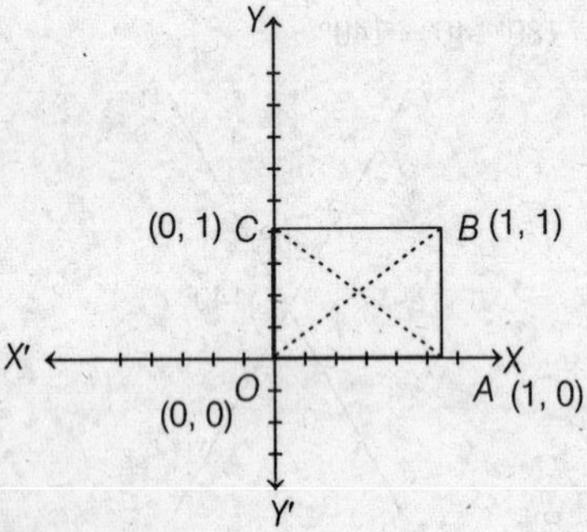

Clearly, coordinates of $A = (1,0)$, $B = (1, 1)$,

$C = (0, 1)$ and $O = (0,0)$

Now, equation of diagonal OB

$$y - y_1 = \frac{y_2 - y_1}{x_2 - x_1}(x - x_1)$$

$$y - 0 = \frac{1-0}{1-0}(x - 0) \qquad [\because (x_1, y_1) = (0,0) \text{ and } (x_2, y_2) = (1, 1)]$$

$$\Rightarrow \qquad y = x \Rightarrow x - y = 0$$

and, equation of diagonal AC

$$y - 0 = \frac{1-0}{0-1}(x - 1) \qquad [\because (x_1, y_1) = (1,0) \text{ and } (x_2, y_2) = (0, 1)]$$

$$\Rightarrow \qquad y = -1(x - 1)$$

$$\Rightarrow \qquad y = -x + 1$$

$$\Rightarrow \qquad x + y = 1$$

Hence, equations of diagonals of square are $x - y = 0$ and $x + y = 1$

Q.5 The intercept cut off by a line form Y-axis is twice than from X-axis and then line passes through the point $(1,2)$. Find the equation of the line?

◎ *Thinking Process* Use the intercept form of equation of line i.e.,

$$\frac{x}{a} + \frac{y}{b} = 1$$

Sol. Let line make intercept 'a' on X-axis and '2a' on Y-axis

The equation of the line is given by

$$\frac{x}{a} + \frac{y}{2a} = 1$$

It is passes through (1, 2), we get

$$\frac{1}{a} + \frac{2}{2a} = 1 \Rightarrow \frac{2+2}{2a} = 1 \Rightarrow 4 = 2a \Rightarrow a = 2$$

$\therefore$ The required equation of line is given by

$$\frac{x}{2} + \frac{y}{4} = 1 \Rightarrow 2x + y = 4$$

Q.6 Line through the points $(-2, 6)$ and $(4, 8)$ is perpendicular to the line through the points $(8, 12)$ and $(x, 24)$. Find the value of x.

Sol. Let line l_1 passing through the points $A(-2, 6)$ and $B(4, 8)$ then slope of line, $m_1 = \frac{8-6}{4-(-2)}$ $\left[\because m = \frac{y_2 - y_1}{x_2 - x_1}\right]$

$$= \frac{2}{6} = \frac{1}{3}$$

and line l_2 passing through the points $C(8, 12)$ and $D(x, 24)$, then slope of line,

$$m_2 = \frac{24-12}{x-8} = \frac{12}{x-8}$$

Since, line $l_1 \perp$ line l_2, then $m_1 \times m_2 = -1$

$$\Rightarrow \quad \frac{1}{3} \times \frac{12}{x-8} = -1 \Rightarrow \quad 4 = -x + 8$$

$$\Rightarrow \quad x = 8 - 4 \Rightarrow x = 4$$

Q.7 Find the tangent of the angle between the lines $2x + 3y - 8 = 0$ and $5x - y + 7 = 0$.

Sol. Given, lines $2x + 3y - 8 = 0$ and $5x - y + 7 = 0$, let the slope of first line, $m_1 = -\frac{2}{3}$

and slope of second line, $m_2 = \frac{-5}{-1} = 5$ $\left[m = \frac{-\text{coefficient of } x}{\text{coefficient of } y}\right]$

The tangent of the angle between given lines $\tan\theta = \left|\frac{m_1 - m_2}{1 + m_1 m_2}\right|$

$$= \left|\frac{\frac{-2}{3} - 5}{1 + \left(\frac{-2}{3}\right)\cdot 5}\right| = \left|\frac{\frac{-17}{3}}{\frac{-7}{3}}\right| \Rightarrow \tan\theta = \frac{17}{7}$$

Q.8 Find the equation of the line intersecting X-axis at distance 3 units to the left of origin with slope -2.

Sol. Given, slope of the line, $m = -2$ and line cuts the X-axis to the left of origin at a distance 3 units, then point on X-axis let $A(-3, 0)$, then equation of the line,

$$y - 0 = -2(x - (-3)) \quad [\because y - y_1 = m(x - x_1)]$$

$$\Rightarrow \quad y = -2x - 6 \Rightarrow 2x + y + 6 = 0$$

Q.9 Find the equation of the line for which $\tan\theta = \frac{1}{2}$, where θ is the inclination of the line and y-intercept $\frac{-3}{2}$.

Sol. By slope intercept form, $y = mx + c$.

where, $m = \tan\theta \Rightarrow m = \frac{1}{2}$ and y-intercept, $c = \frac{-3}{2}$

Then, equation of the line, $y = \frac{1}{2}x + \left(-\frac{3}{2}\right)$ [equation of line $y = mx + c$]

$$\Rightarrow \quad 2y = x - 3 \Rightarrow x - 2y - 3 = 0$$

Q.10 Find the equation of the median of the triangle PQR through the vertex R whose vertices are given by $P(2,1)$, $Q(-2,3)$, $R(4,5)$.

◎ ***Thinking Process*** Mid points (X, Y) of the line whose end points are (x_1, y_1) and (x_2, y_2)

$$X = \frac{x_1 + x_2}{2} \text{ and } Y = \frac{y_1 + y_2}{2}$$

Sol. Let the median through the vertex R bisects the side PQ at point M. Then, M is the mid-point of PQ. The coordinates of point

$$M = \left(\frac{2 + (-2)}{2}, \frac{1 + 3}{2}\right) = (0, 2)$$

$$\left[\because \text{mid-point} = \frac{x_1 + x_2}{2}, \frac{y_1 + y_2}{2}\right]$$

Now, Median RM, passes through the points $R(4, 5)$ and $M(0, 2)$.

Equation of the median RM,

$$\Rightarrow \quad y - 5 = \frac{2 - 5}{0 - 4}(x - 4)$$

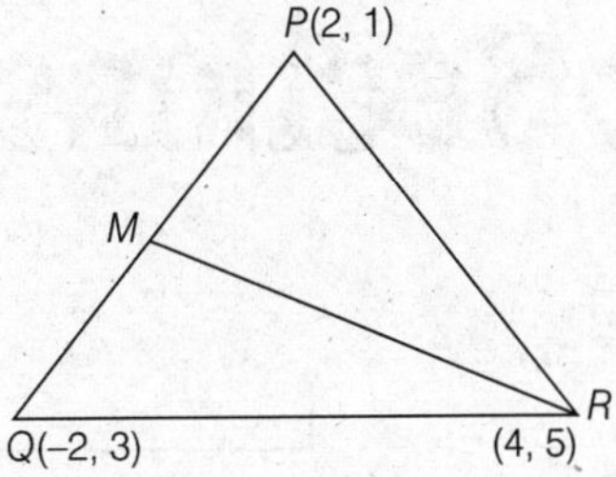

$$\Rightarrow \quad y - 5 = \frac{-3}{-4}(x - 4)$$

$$\Rightarrow \quad 4y - 20 = 3x - 12 \Rightarrow 3x - 4y + 8 = 0$$

Q.11 Find the equation of right bisector of the line segment joining the point $(3, 4)$ and $(-1, 2)$.

Sol. Firstly, we find the slope of the line segment joining the point $A(3, 4)$ and $B(-1, 2)$.

$$\text{Slope of } AB = \frac{2-4}{-1-3} = \frac{-2}{-4} = \frac{1}{2}$$

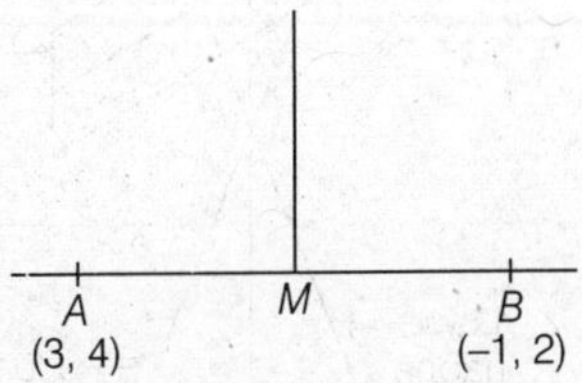

Now, mid-point of AB, $M = \left(\frac{3+(-1)}{2}, \frac{4+2}{2}\right) = (1, 3)$

and slope of right bisector $= \dfrac{-1}{\text{Slope of line segment } AB} = \dfrac{-1}{\frac{1}{2}} = -2$

Now, Equation of right bisector with slope -2 and passing through point $M(1, 3)$.

$$\Rightarrow \quad y - 3 = -2(x - 1)$$

$$\Rightarrow \quad y - 3 = -2x + 2$$

$$\Rightarrow \quad 2x + y = 5$$

Conic Sections

CHAPTER 10

Important Points

01 Conic Section A conic section is a curve obtained by intersecting a cone with a plane. The type of curve formed depends on the angle at which the plane intersects the cone.

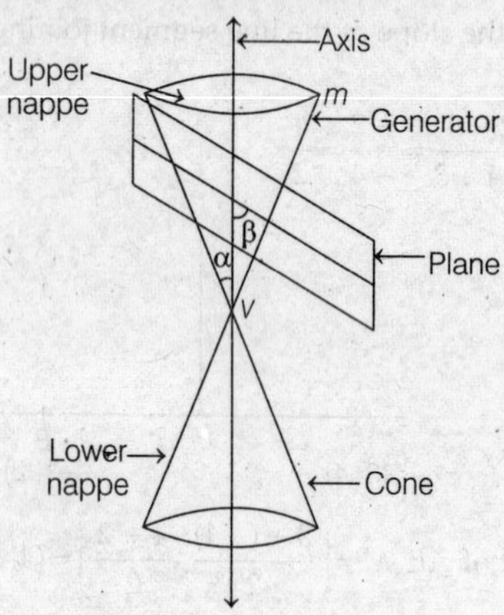

Circles, ellipses, parabolas and hyperbolas are known as conic sections because they can be obtained as intersections of plane with a double napped right circular cone. From the given figure

(i) When $\beta = 90°$, the section is a circle.

(ii) When $\alpha < \beta < 90°$, the section is an ellipse.

(iii) When $\beta = \alpha$, the section is a parabola.

(iv) When $0 \le \beta < \alpha$, the plane cuts through both the nappes and the curves of intersection is a hyperbola.

All the above conditions will hold if the plane cuts other than the vertex.

When the plane cuts at the vertex (V) of the cone than

(i) When $\alpha < \beta \le 90°$, the section is a point.

(ii) When $\beta = \alpha$, the plane contains a generator of the cone and the section is a straight line.

(iii) When $0 \le \beta < \alpha$, the section is a pair of intersecting straight lines. It is the degenerated case of a hyperbola.

02 **Circle** A circle is the set of all points in a plane that are equidistant from a fixed point in the plane, where fixed point is called the centre and fixed distance is called the radius of the circle.

03 Equation of circle when centre (h, k) and radius r is

$$(x-h)^2+(y-k)^2=r^2$$

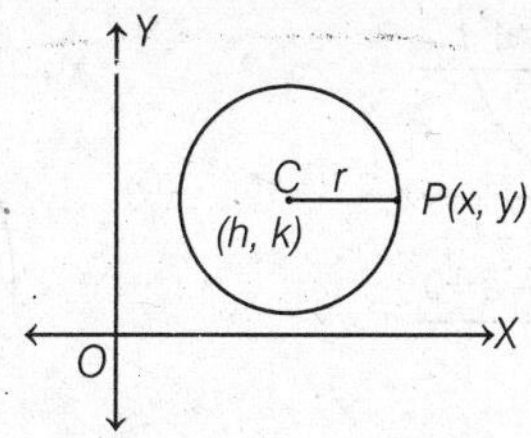

when centre is at origin

i.e., $(h, k) \to (0,0)$

Then, equation is $x^2+y^2=r^2$

04 General equation of circle is $x^2+y^2+2gx+2fy+c=0$

where centre $=(-g,-f)$ and radius $=\sqrt{g^2+f^2-c}$

05 **Parabola** A parabola is the set of all points in a plane that are equidistant from a fixed line and a fixed point S (not on the line) in the plane. Here fixed line is called the directrix and fixed point is called the focus.

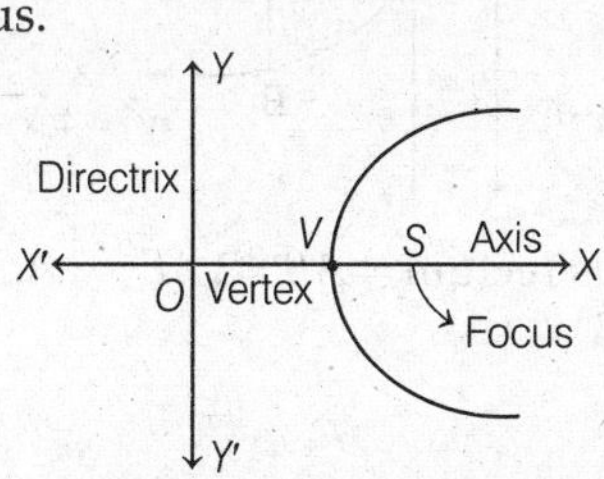

The point of intersection of parabola with the axis is called the vertex V of the parabola.

06 Standard forms of parabola

Length of latus rectum in each case is $4a$.

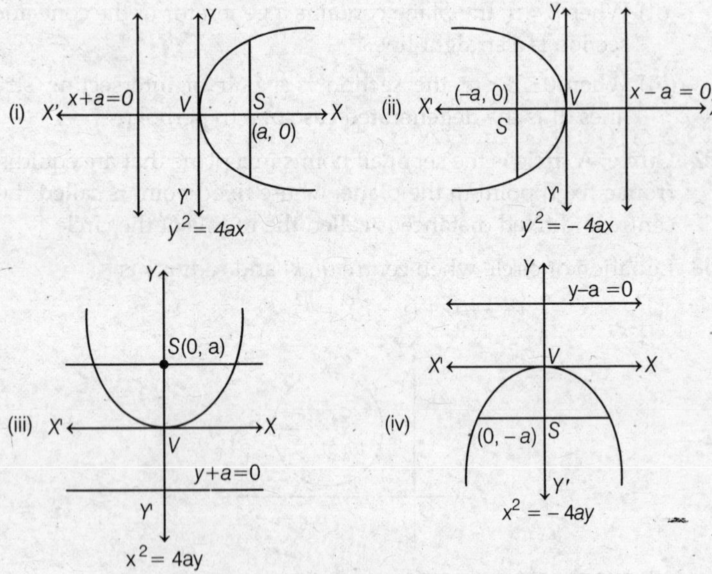

Note Parabola is symmetric w.r.t. the axis of the parabola.

latus rectum latus rectum of a parabola is a line segment perpendicular to the axis of the parabola, through the focus and whose end points lie on the parabola.

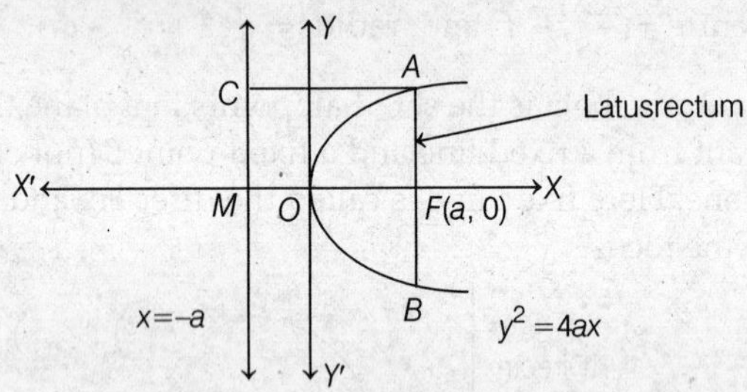

Length of the latus rectum = $AB = 2\,AF = 2\,AC = 4a$

Key facts for standard parabolas

Parabola	Vertex	Focus	Directrix	Equation of Axis	Equation of latus rectum and length	Symmetry
$y^2 = 4ax$	(0, 0)	$(a, 0)$	$x = -a$	$y = 0$	$x = a$ and $4a$	X-axis
$y^2 = -4ax$	(0, 0)	$(-a, 0)$	$x = a$	$y = 0$	$x = -a$ and $4a$	X-axis
$x^2 = 4ay$	(0, 0)	$(0, a)$	$y = -a$	$x = 0$	$y = a$ and $4a$	Y-axis
$x^2 = -4ay$	(0, 0)	$(0, -a)$	$y = a$	$x = 0$	$y = -a$ and $4a$	Y-axis

07 Ellipse An ellipse is the set of all points in a plane, the sum of whose distances from two fixed points in the plane is constant. These fixed points are called foci (S, S') and constant length is known as the length of major axis.

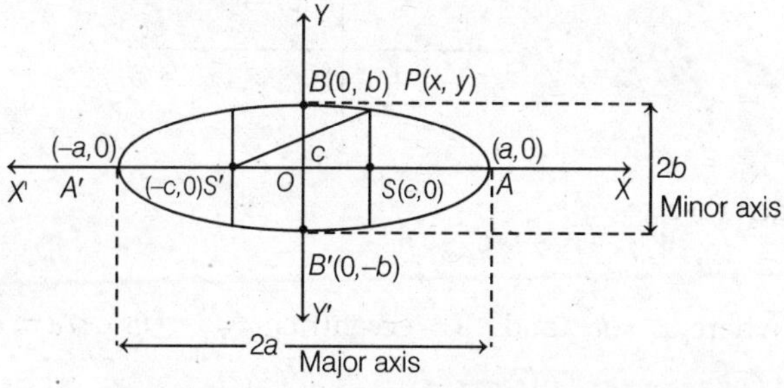

Note The constant which is the sum of the distances of a point on the ellipse from the two fixed points is always greater than the distance between the two fixed points.

08 Standard Forms of an Ellipse

(i) $\dfrac{x^2}{a^2} + \dfrac{y^2}{b^2} = 1$, where $a > b$.

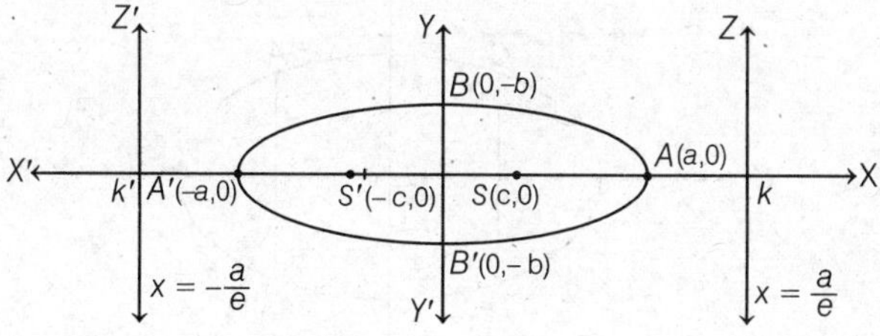

(ii) $\frac{x^2}{b^2}+\frac{y^2}{a^2}=1$, where $a>b$.

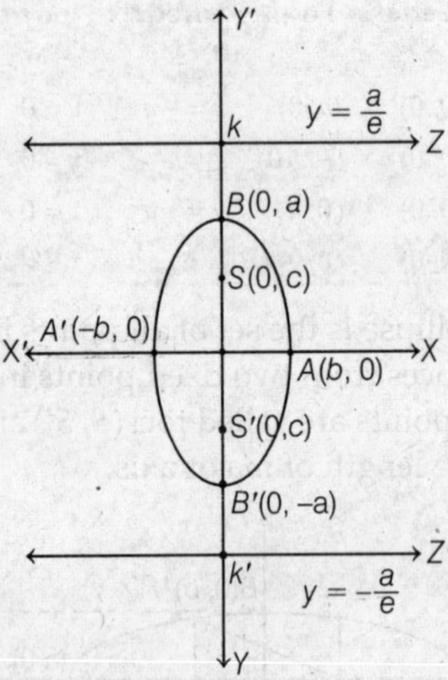

In each case,

(i) $c^2=a^2-b^2$

where, $c=ae$ and $e=$ eccentricity $=\frac{c}{a}$ $(\because c<a \Rightarrow 0<e<1)$

(ii) **latus rectum** latus rectum of an ellipse is a line segment perpendicular to the major axis through any of the foci and whose end points lie on the ellipse.

Length of the latus rectum is $\frac{2b^2}{a}$

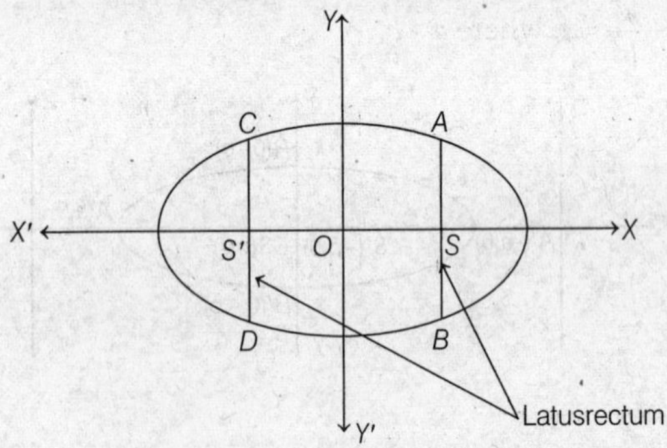

(iii) Length of major axis $=2a$ and length of minor axis is $=2b$

Key facts for standard Ellipse

Ellipse	$\frac{x^2}{a^2}+\frac{y^2}{b^2}=1, a>b$	$\frac{x^2}{b^2}+\frac{y^2}{a^2}=1, a\ b$
Centre	(0, 0)	(0, 0)
Vertices	$(\pm a, 0)$	$(0, \pm a)$
Foci	$(\pm c, 0)$ or $\pm (ae, 0)$	$(0, \pm c)$ or $(0, \pm ae)$
Major axis	$y=0$ and length $=2a$	$x=0$ and length $=2a$
Minor axis	$x=0$ and length $=2b$	$y=0$ and length $=2b$
Value of c	$\sqrt{a^2-b^2}$	$\sqrt{a^2-b^2}$
Directrix	$x=\pm\frac{a}{e}$ or $\frac{a^2}{c}$	$y=\pm\frac{a}{e}$ or $\frac{a^2}{c}$
Length of latus rectum	$\frac{2b^2}{a}$	$\frac{2b^2}{a}$
Eccentricity	$e=\frac{c}{a}$	$e=\frac{c}{a}$

09 Hyperbola A hyperbola is the set of all points in a plane, the difference of whose distances from two fixed points in the plane is a constant. These fixed points are called foci (S, S') and constant length is known as the length of transverse axis.

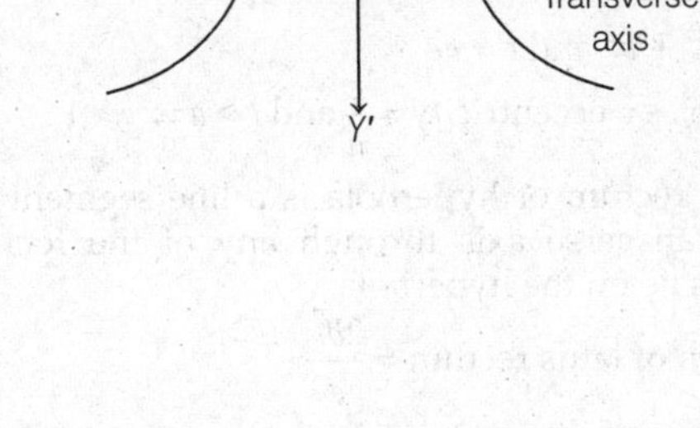

10 Standard Form of Hyperbola

(i) $\dfrac{x^2}{a^2}-\dfrac{y^2}{b^2}=1$

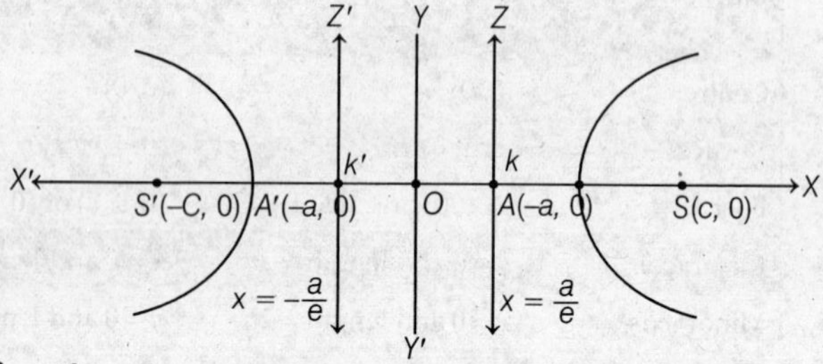

(ii) $\dfrac{y^2}{a^2}-\dfrac{x^2}{b^2}=1$

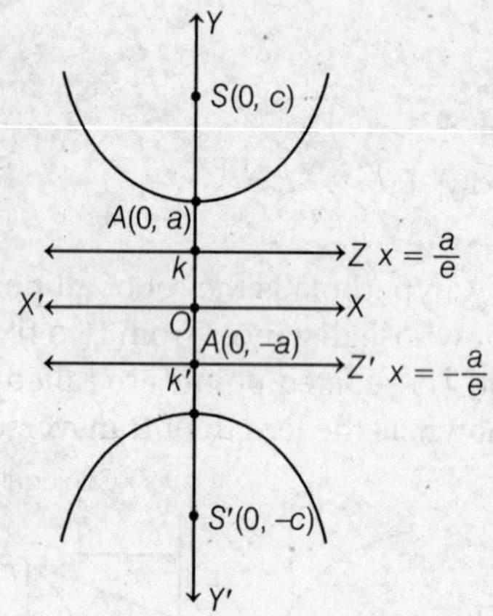

Note A hyperbola in which $a=b$ is called an equilateral hyperbola.

In each case,

(i) $c^2=a^2+b^2$ and $c=ae$

where, $e=\text{eccentricity}=\dfrac{c}{a}$ and $c>a\Rightarrow e>1$

(ii) Latus rectum of hyperbola is a line segment perpendicular to the transverse axis through any of the foci and whose end points lie on the hyperbola.

Length of latus rectum $=\dfrac{2b^2}{a}$

(iii) Length of transverse axis $=2a$, Length of conjugate axis $=2b$.

Key Facts for Standard Hyperbola

	Hyperbola	Conjugate Hyperbola
Equation	$\frac{x^2}{a^2}-\frac{y^2}{b^2}=1$	$\frac{y^2}{a^2}-\frac{x^2}{b^2}=1$
Centre	(0, 0)	(0, 0)
Vertices	$(\pm a, 0)$	$(0, \pm a)$
Foci	$(\pm ae, 0)$ or $(\pm c, 0)$	$(0, \pm ae)$ or $(0, \pm c)$
Value of c	$\sqrt{a^2+b^2}$	$\sqrt{a^2+b^2}$
Transverse axis	$y = 0$, length $= 2a$	$x = 0$, length $= 2a$
Conjugate axis	$x = 0$, length $= 2b$	$y = 0$, length $= 2b$
Directrices	$x = \pm \frac{a^2}{c}$ or $\frac{a}{e}$	$y = \pm \frac{a^2}{c}$ or $\frac{a}{e}$
length of latus rectum	$\frac{2b^2}{a}$	$\frac{2b^2}{a}$
Eccentricity	$e=\frac{c}{a}=\sqrt{1+\frac{b^2}{a^2}}$	$e=\frac{c}{a}=\sqrt{1+\frac{b^2}{a^2}}$

Observations for standard ellipse and hyperbola

(i) Ellipse hyperbola are symmetric w.r.t. both the axes. Since if (x, y) is a point on the ellipse and hyperbola, then $(-x, y)$, $(x, -y)$ and $(-x, -y)$ are also points lie on the ellipse and hyperbola.

(ii) (a) The foci always lie on the major axis.

(b) If x^2 has a larger denominator then the major axis will be along the X-axis

(c) If y^2 has a larger denominator then the major axis will be along the Y-axis.

(iii) The foci always on the transverse axis. It is the positive term in the equation of hyperbola whose denominator gives the transverse axis.

Exercise 10.1

Directions (Q. No. 1 to 5) In each of the following find the equation of the circle with

1. centre (0, 2) and radius 2.
2. centre $(-2, 3)$ and radius 4.
3. centre $\left(\frac{1}{2}, \frac{1}{4}\right)$ and radius $\frac{1}{12}$.
4. centre (1, 1) and radius $\sqrt{2}$.
5. centre $(-a, -b)$ and radius $\sqrt{a^2 - b^2}$.

◎ ***Thinking Process*** If (h, k) be the centre and r be the radius of circle, then equation of circle is $(x-h)^2 + (y-k)^2 = r^2$

Sol. (Q. No. 1 to 5)

1. Given, centre $= (h, k) = (0, 2)$ and radius $r = 2$

$\therefore$ Equation of the circle by using $(x-h)^2 + (y-k)^2 = r^2$ is given by

$$(x-0)^2 + (y-2)^2 = 2^2$$

$$\Rightarrow \quad x^2 + y^2 + 4 - 4y = 4 \qquad [\because (a-b)^2 = a^2 + b^2 - 2ab]$$

$$\Rightarrow \quad x^2 + y^2 - 4y = 0$$

2. Given, centre $= (h, k) = (-2, 3)$ and radius $r = 4$

$\therefore$ Equation of the circle by using $(x-h)^2 + (y-k)^2 = r^2$ is given by

$$(x+2)^2 + (y-3)^2 = 4^2$$

$$\Rightarrow \quad x^2 + 4 + 4x + y^2 + 9 - 6y = 16$$

$$[\because (a+b)^2 = a^2 + b^2 + 2ab \text{ and } (a-b)^2 = a^2 + b^2 - 2ab]$$

$$\Rightarrow \quad x^2 + y^2 + 4x - 6y + 13 - 16 = 0$$

$$\Rightarrow \quad x^2 + y^2 + 4x - 6y - 3 = 0$$

3. Given, centre $= (h, k) = \left(\frac{1}{2}, \frac{1}{4}\right)$ and radius $r = \frac{1}{12}$

$\therefore$ Equation of the circle by using $(x-h)^2 + (y-k)^2 = r^2$ is given by

$$\left(x - \frac{1}{2}\right)^2 + \left(y - \frac{1}{4}\right)^2 = \left(\frac{1}{12}\right)^2$$

$$\Rightarrow \quad x^2 + \frac{1}{4} - 2\cdot\frac{1}{2}x + y^2 + \frac{1}{16} - 2\cdot\frac{y}{4} = \frac{1}{144} \quad [\because (a-b)^2 = a^2 + b^2 - 2ab]$$

$$\Rightarrow \quad x^2 + y^2 - x - \frac{y}{2} + \frac{1}{4} + \frac{1}{16} - \frac{1}{144} = 0$$

$$\Rightarrow \quad x^2 + y^2 - x - \frac{y}{2} + \frac{36 + 9 - 1}{144} = 0$$

$$\Rightarrow \quad x^2 + y^2 - x - \frac{y}{2} + \frac{44}{144} = 0 \Rightarrow x^2 + y^2 - x - \frac{y}{2} + \frac{11}{36} = 0$$

$$\Rightarrow \quad 36x^2 + 36y^2 - 36x - 18y + 11 = 0$$

4. Given, centre $= (h, k) = (1, 1)$ and radius $= r = \sqrt{2}$

$\therefore$ Equation of the circle by using $(x-h)^2 + (y-k)^2 = r^2$ is given by

$$(x-1)^2 + (y-1)^2 = (\sqrt{2})^2$$

$$\Rightarrow \quad x^2 + 1 - 2x + y^2 + 1 - 2y = 2 \qquad [\because (a-b)^2 = a^2 + b^2 - 2ab]$$

$$\Rightarrow \quad x^2 + y^2 - 2x - 2y = 0$$

5. Given, centre $= (h, k) = (-a, -b)$ and radius $r = \sqrt{a^2 - b^2}$

$\therefore$ Equation of the circle by using $(x-h)^2 + (y-k)^2 = r^2$ is given by

$$(x+a)^2 + (y+b)^2 = (\sqrt{a^2 - b^2})^2$$

$$\Rightarrow x^2 + a^2 + 2ax + y^2 + b^2 + 2by = a^2 - b^2 \quad [\because (a+b)^2 = a^2 + b^2 + 2ab]$$

$$\Rightarrow \quad x^2 + y^2 + 2ax + 2by + 2b^2 = 0$$

Directions (Q. No. 6 to 9) In each of the following, find the centre and radius of the circles

6. $(x+5)^2 + (y-3)^2 = 36$

7. $x^2 + y^2 - 4x - 8y - 45 = 0$

8. $x^2 + y^2 - 8x + 10y - 12 = 0$

9. $2x^2 + 2y^2 - x = 0$

Sol. (Q. No. 6 to 9)

6. Given equation of the circle is

$$(x+5)^2 + (y-3)^2 = 36$$

i.e. $\quad (x-(-5))^2 + (y-3)^2 = (6)^2 \qquad \ldots(\text{i})$

On comparing Eq. (i) with $(x-h)^2 + (y-k)^2 = r^2$, we get

$$h = -5, k = 3 \text{ and } r = 6$$

Hence, centre $= (h, k) = (-5, 3)$ and radius $r = 6$

7. Given equation of the circle is $x^2 + y^2 - 4x - 8y - 45 = 0 \qquad \ldots(\text{i})$

On comparing Eq. (i) with $x^2 + y^2 + 2gx + 2fy + c = 0$, we get

$$2g = -4,\ 2f = -8,\ c = -45 \Rightarrow g = -2,\quad f = -4,\ c = -45$$

$\because$ Centre and radius of the circle $x^2 + y^2 + 2gx + 2fy + c = 0$ is

$$C(-g, -f) \quad \text{and} \quad r = \sqrt{g^2 + f^2 - c}$$

$\therefore \quad$ Centre $= (-g, -f) = (2, 4)$

and radius $= \sqrt{g^2 + f^2 - c}$

$$= \sqrt{(2)^2 + (4)^2 - (-45)}$$

$$= \sqrt{4 + 16 + 45} = \sqrt{65}$$

8. Given equation of the circle is $x^2 + y^2 - 8x + 10y - 12 = 0$ ...(i)

On comparing Eq. (i) with $x^2 + y^2 + 2gx + 2fy + c = 0$, we get

$2g = -8, 2f = 10, c = -12 \Rightarrow g = -4, f = 5, c = -12$

$\therefore$ Centre $= (-g, -f) = (4, -5)$

and radius $= \sqrt{g^2 + f^2 - c} = \sqrt{(4)^2 + (-5)^2 - (-12)}$

$= \sqrt{16 + 25 + 12} = \sqrt{53}$

9. Given equation of the circle is

$$2x^2 + 2y^2 - x = 0 \quad \text{...(i)}$$

On dividing Eq. (ii) by 2, we get $x^2 + y^2 - \frac{x}{2} = 0$ ...(ii)

On comparing Eq. (ii) with $x^2 + y^2 + 2gx + 2fy + c = 0$, we get

$$2g = -\frac{1}{2}, 2f = 0, c = 0 \Rightarrow g = -\frac{1}{4}, f = 0, c = 0$$

$\therefore$ Centre $= (-g, -f) = (1/4, 0)$

and radius $= \sqrt{g^2 + f^2 - c} = \sqrt{\left(\frac{1}{4}\right)^2 + 0 - 0} = \sqrt{\frac{1}{16}} = \frac{1}{4}$

Note In general equation of the circle firstly make the coefficients of x^2 and y^2 non-negative with unity. Otherwise, it may be error on taking centre and radius.

Question 10 Find the equation of the circle passing through (4, 1) and (6, 5) and whose centre is on the line $4x + y = 16$.

Sol. Let equation of circle be

$$x^2 + y^2 + 2gx + 2fy + c = 0 \quad \text{...(i)}$$

Eq. (i), passes through the points (4, 1) and (6, 5) *i.e.*, they will satisfy it.

When circle passes through point (4, 1) then

$$(4)^2 + (1)^2 + 2g(4) + 2f(1) + c = 0$$

$\Rightarrow$ $17 + 8g + 2f + c = 0$

$\Rightarrow$ $8g + 2f + c + 17 = 0$ ...(ii)

When circle passes through point (6, 5), then

$$(6)^2 + (5)^2 + 2g(6) + 2f(5) + c = 0$$

$\Rightarrow$ $36 + 25 + 12g + 10f + c = 0$

$\Rightarrow$ $12g + 10f + c + 61 = 0$ ...(iii)

Since centre $(-g, -f)$ of Eq. (i), lies on the line

$$4x + y = 16$$

$\therefore$ $4(-g) + (-f) = 16$

$\Rightarrow$ $4g + f + 16 = 0$ ...(iv)

On substracting Eq. (ii) from Eq. (iii), we get

$$4g + 8f + 44 = 0 \quad \text{...(v)}$$

On substracting Eq. (iv) from Eq. (v), we get

$$7f + 28 = 0$$

$$\Rightarrow \quad 7f = -28$$
$$\Rightarrow \quad f = -4$$

On putting the value of $f = -u$ in Eq. (iv), we get

$$4g - 4 + 16 = 0$$
$$\Rightarrow \quad 4g + 12 = 0$$
$$\Rightarrow \quad 4g = -12 \Rightarrow g = -3$$

On putting the values of $g = -3$ and $f = -4$ in Eq. (ii), we get

$$8(-3) + 2(-4) + c + 17 = 0$$
$$\Rightarrow \quad -24 - 8 + c + 17 = 0$$
$$\Rightarrow \quad c - 32 + 17 = 0 \Rightarrow c - 15 = 0$$
$$\Rightarrow \quad c = 15$$

On putting the values of g, f and c in Eq. (i), we get required equation of circle

$$x^2 + y^2 + 2(-3)x + 2(-4)y + 15 = 0$$
$$\Rightarrow \quad x^2 + y^2 - 6x - 8y + 15 = 0$$

Question 11 Find the equation of the circle passing through the points $(2, 3)$ and $(-1, 1)$ and whose centre is on the line $x - 3y - 11 = 0$.

Sol. Let equation of circle be

$$x^2 + y^2 + 2gx + 2fy + c = 0 \quad \text{...(i)}$$

Eq. (i) passes through the points (2, 3) and (– 1, 1) *i.e.*, they will satisfy it.

When circle passes through point (2, 3), then

$$(2)^2 + (3)^2 + 2g(2) + 2f(3) + c = 0$$
$$\Rightarrow \quad 4g + 6f + c + 13 = 0 \quad \text{...(ii)}$$

and when circle passes through point (–1, 1), then

$$(-1)^2 + (1)^2 + 2g(-1) + 2f(1) + c = 0$$
$$\Rightarrow \quad -2g + 2f + c + 2 = 0 \quad \text{...(iii)}$$

Since centre $(-g, -f)$ lies on the line $x - 3y - 11 = 0$

$$\therefore \quad (-g) - 3(-f) - 11 = 0$$
$$\Rightarrow \quad -g + 3f - 11 = 0 \quad \text{...(iv)}$$

On subtracting Eq. (iii) from Eq. (ii), we get

$$6g + 4f + 11 = 0 \quad \text{...(v)}$$

On putting value of $g = 3f - 11$ from Eq. (iv), in Eq. (v)

$$6(3f - 11) + 4f + 11 = 0$$
$$\Rightarrow \quad 18f - 66 + 4f + 11 = 0$$
$$\Rightarrow \quad 22f - 55 = 0$$
$$\Rightarrow \quad f = \frac{55}{22} \Rightarrow f = \frac{5}{2}$$

On putting the value of $f = \frac{5}{2}$ in Eq. (iv), we get

$$g = 3 \times \frac{5}{2} - 11 = \frac{15 - 22}{2} = \frac{-7}{2}$$

On putting the value of $g = \frac{-7}{2}$ and $f = \frac{5}{2}$ in Eq. (ii), we get

$$4 \times \left(-\frac{7}{2}\right) + 6\left(\frac{5}{2}\right) + c + 13 = 0$$

$$\Rightarrow \quad -14 + 15 + c + 13 = 0 \Rightarrow c + 14 = 0$$

$$\Rightarrow \quad c = -14$$

On putting the values of g, f and c in Eq. (i) to get the required equation of circle

$$\therefore \quad x^2 + y^2 + 2x\left(-\frac{7}{2}\right) + 2y\left(\frac{5}{2}\right) - 14 = 0$$

$$\Rightarrow \quad x^2 + y^2 - 7x + 5y - 14 = 0$$

Question 12 Find the equation of the circle with radius 5 whose centre lies on X-axis and passing through the point (2, 3).

Sol. Let centre of circle be $(h, 0)$, as centre of circle lies on X-axis, so y-coordinate will be zero.

The distance between any point on the circle to the centre = Radius

$$\therefore \quad \sqrt{(x_2 - x_1)^2 + (y_2 - y_1)^2} = r$$

$$\therefore \quad \sqrt{(h-2)^2 + (0-3)^2} = 5 \qquad (\because x_1 = 2, y_1 = 3, x_2 = h, y_2 = 0)$$

$$\Rightarrow \quad h^2 + 4 - 4h + 9 = 25 \qquad \text{(squaring both sides)}$$

$$\Rightarrow \quad h^2 - 4h + 13 - 25 = 0$$

$$\Rightarrow \quad h^2 - 4h - 12 = 0$$

$$\Rightarrow \quad h^2 - 6h + 2h - 12 = 0$$

$$\Rightarrow \quad h(h-6) + 2(h-6) = 0$$

$$\Rightarrow \quad (h-6)(h+2) = 0$$

$$\Rightarrow \quad h - 6 = 0 \text{ or } h + 2 = 0 \Rightarrow h = 6 \text{ or } -2$$

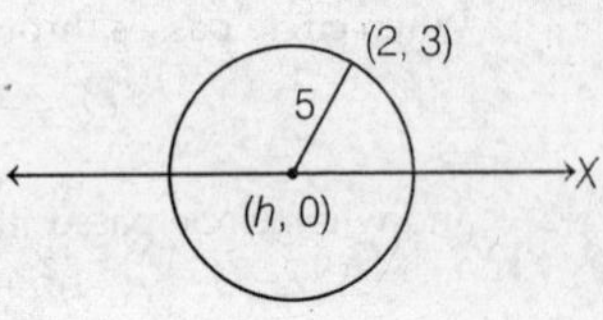

$\therefore$ Centre is (6, 0) or (− 2, 0).

So, equation of circle by using

$$(x-h)^2 + (y-k)^2 = r^2$$

when $(h, k) = (6, 0)$ and $r = 5$ is

$$(x-6)^2 + (y-0)^2 = 5^2 \Rightarrow x^2 + 36 - 12x + y^2 = 25$$

$$\Rightarrow \quad x^2 + y^2 - 12x + 11 = 0$$

And when $(h, k) = (-2, 0)$ and $r = 5$

$$\Rightarrow \quad (x+2)^2 + (y-0)^2 = 5^2 \qquad [\because (x-h)^2 + (y-k)^2 = r^2]$$

$$\Rightarrow \quad x^2 + 4 + 4x + y^2 = 25$$

$$\Rightarrow \quad x^2 + y^2 + 4x - 21 = 0$$

Question 13 Find the equation of the circle passing through (0, 0) and making intercepts a and b on the coordinate axes.

Sol. Since, the circle intersects the coordinate axis at a and b. It means circle intersects the X-axis at $(a, 0)$ and it intersects the Y-axis at $(0, b)$.

Hence, the circle passes through the points $O(0, 0)$, $A(a, 0)$ and $B(0, b)$.
Let general equation of circle be

$$x^2 + y^2 + 2gx + 2fy + c = 0 \quad \text{...(i)}$$

Circle passes through the points $O(0, 0)$, $A(a, 0)$ and $B(0, b)$ *i.e.*, they will satisfy it.

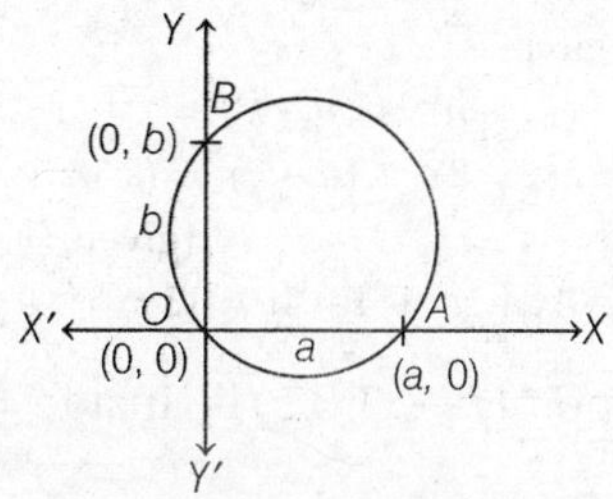

When circle passes through point $(0,0)$, then

$$0 + 0 + 0 + 0 + c = 0 \Rightarrow c = 0 \quad \text{...(ii)}$$

When circle passes through point $(a, 0)$, then

$$a^2 + 0 + 2ag + 0 + 0 = 0 \quad [\because \text{from Eq. (ii)}, c = 0]$$

$$\Rightarrow a^2 + 2ag = 0$$

$$\Rightarrow g = -\frac{a}{2} \quad \text{...(iii)}$$

and when circle passes through point $(0, b)$, then

$$0 + b^2 + 0 + 2bf + 0 = 0 \quad [\because \text{from Eq. (ii)}, c = 0]$$

$$\Rightarrow b^2 + 2bf = 0$$

$$\Rightarrow f = -\frac{b}{2} \quad \text{...(iv)}$$

On putting the values of g, f and c in Eq. (i) to get the required equation of circle.

$$x^2 + y^2 + 2x\left(-\frac{a}{2}\right) + 2y\left(-\frac{b}{2}\right) + 0 = 0$$

$$\Rightarrow x^2 + y^2 - ax - by = 0$$

Question 14 Find the equation of a circle with centre $(2,2)$ and passes through the point $(4, 5)$.

Thinking Process If $P(x, y)$ is any point on the circle and (h, k) be the centre of circle, then radius

$$r = \sqrt{(x-h)^2 + (y-k)^2}$$

Sol. Here, centre $(h, k) = (2, 2)$ and point on the circle $P(x, y) = (4, 5)$

$$\therefore \quad r = \sqrt{(2-4)^2 + (2-5)^2} = \sqrt{4+9} = \sqrt{13} \quad [\because r = \sqrt{(x-h)^2 + (y-k)^2}]$$

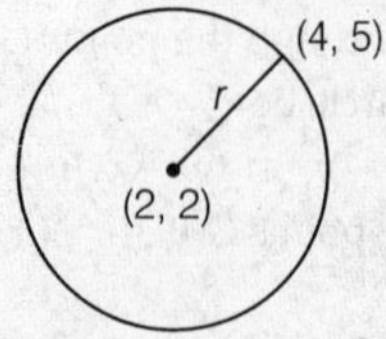

Hence, equation of circle is

$$(x-h)^2+(y-k)^2=r^2$$

$$\Rightarrow \quad (x-2)^2+(y-2)^2=(\sqrt{13})^2$$

[given, $(h, k) = (2, 2)$ and $r=\sqrt{13}$]

$$\Rightarrow \quad x^2+4-4x+y^2+4-4y=13 \Rightarrow x^2+y^2-4x-4y-5=0$$

Question 15 Does the point $(-2.5, 3.5)$ lie inside, outside or on the circle $x^2+y^2=25$?

◎ ***Thinking Process*** A point (x_1, y_1) lies outside, on or inside a circle $S=x^2+y^2+2gx+2fy+c=0$ according as $S_1=x_1^2+y_1^2+2gx_1+2fy_1+c$ is positive, zero or negatives *i.e.*, if, $S_1>0 \Rightarrow$ Point lies outside the circle.

$S_1=0 \Rightarrow$ Point lies on the circle.

$S_1=0 \Rightarrow$ Point lies inside the circle.

Sol. Given, equation of circle is

$$x^2+y^2=25$$

Let $\quad S=x^2+y^2-25 \quad$ ...(i)

On putting $(x, y)=(-2.5, 3.5)$ in Eq. (i), we get

$$\Rightarrow \quad S=(-2.5)^2+(3.5)^2-25=6.25+12.25-25$$

$$=18.50-25=-6.50<0$$

$\therefore$ Point lies inside the circle.

Exercise 10.2

Directions (Q. No. 1 to 6) In each of the following questions, find the coordinates of the focus, axis of the parabola, the equation of the directrix and the length of the latus rectum.

1. $y^2=12x$ **2.** $x^2=6y$ **3.** $y^2=-8x$

4. $x^2=-16y$ **5.** $y^2=10x$ **6.** $x^2=-9y$

◎ ***Thinking Process*** First convert to standard form ($y^2=\pm 4ax$ or $x^2=\pm 4ay$).

Sol. (Q. No. 1 to 6)

1. Given equation of parabola is $y^2=12x$, ...(i)

which is of the form

$y^2 = 4ax$, *i.e.*, focus lies on the positive direction of X-axis.

On comparing Eq. (i) with $y^2 = 4ax$, we get

$$4a = 12 \Rightarrow a = 3$$

Focus $= (a, 0) = (3, 0)$

Axis = X-axis

Directrix, $x = -a \Rightarrow x = -3$

Length of latus rectum $= 4a = 4 \times 3 = 12$

2. Given equation of parabola is $x^2 = 6y$, which is of the form $x^2 = 4ay$ *i.e.*, focus lies on the positive direction of Y-axis.

On comparing Eq. (i) with $x^2 = 4ay$, we get $4a = 6 \Rightarrow a = \frac{6}{4} = \frac{3}{2}$

Focus $= (0, a) = \left(0, \frac{3}{2}\right)$

Axis = Y-axis

Directrix, $y = -a \Rightarrow y = -\frac{3}{2}$

Length of latus rectum $= 4a = 4 \times \frac{3}{2} = 6$

3. Given equation of parabola is $y^2 = -8x$, which is of the form $y^2 = -4ax$ *i.e.*, focus lies on the negative direction of X-axis.

On comparing $y^2 = 8x$, with $y^2 = -4ax$, we get $4a = 8 \Rightarrow a = 2$

Focus $= (-a, 0) = (-2, 0)$

Axis = X-axis

Directrix, $x = a \Rightarrow x = 2$

Length of latus rectum $= 4a = 4 \times 2 = 8$

4. Given equation of parabola is $x^2 = -16y$, which is of the form $x^2 = -4ay$, *i.e.*, focus lies on the negative direction of Y-axis.

On comparing $x^2 = -16y$, with $x^2 = -4ay$, we get $4a = 16 \Rightarrow a = 4$

Focus $= (0, -a) = (0, -4)$

Axis = Y-axis.

Directrix, $y = a \Rightarrow y = 4$

Length of latus rectum $= 4a = 4 \times 4 = 16$

5. Given equation of parabola is $y^2 = 10x$, which is of the form $y^2 = 4ax$, *i.e.*, focus lies on the positive direction of X-axis.

On comparing $y^2 = 10x$, with $y^2 = 4ax$, we get $4a = 10 \Rightarrow a = \frac{5}{2}$

Focus $= (a, 0) = \left(\frac{5}{2}, 0\right)$

Axis = X-axis

Directrix, $x = -a \Rightarrow x = -\frac{5}{2}$

Length of latus rectum $= 4a = 4 \times \frac{5}{2} = 10$

6. Given equation of parabola is $x^2 = -9y$, which is of the form $x^2 = -4ay$, *i.e.*, focus lies on the negative direction of Y-axis.

On comparing $x^2 = -9y$, with $x^2 = -4ay$, we get

$$4a = 9 \Rightarrow a = \frac{9}{4}$$

Focus $= (0, -a) = \left(0, -\frac{9}{4}\right)$

Axis $= Y$-axis

Directrix, $y = a \Rightarrow y = \frac{9}{4}$

Length of latus rectrum $= 4a = 9$

Note Always keep $a > 0$

Direction (Q. No. 7 to 12) In each of the question find the equation of the parabola that satisfies the given conditions.

Question 7 Focus $(6, 0)$ and directrix $x = -6$.

Sol. Given, focus $(6, 0)$ and directrix $x = -6$

Since, focus lies on the positive direction of X-axis and the directrix is $x = -6$. So, equation of parabola will be of the form $y^2 = 4ax$ with $a = 6$.

Hence, required equation of parabola is $y^2 = 4 \times 6x \Rightarrow y^2 = 24x$

Question 8 Focus $(0, -3)$ and directrix, $y = 3$.

Sol. Given, focus $= (0, -3)$ and directrix, $y = 3$

Since, focus lies on the negative direction of Y-axis and directrix is $y = 3$. So, equation of parabola will be of the form $x^2 = -4ay$ with $a = 3$.

Hence, required equation of parabola is

$$x^2 = -4(3)y \Rightarrow x^2 = -12y$$

Question 9 Vertex $(0, 0)$ and focus $(3, 0)$.

Sol. Given, vertex $= (0, 0)$

Focus $= (3, 0)$

Since, vertex is $(0, 0)$ and focus lies on positive direction of X-axis.

Hence, equation of parabola will be of the form $y^2 = 4ax$ with $a = 3$.

Hence, required equation is

$$y^2 = 4 \times 3x$$

$$\Rightarrow \quad y^2 = 12x$$

Question 10 Vertex (0, 0) and focus $(-2, 0)$.

Sol. Given, vertex = (0, 0)

Focus = (– 2, 0)

Since, vertex is (0, 0) and focus lies on the negative direction of X-axis. Hence, equation of parabola will be of the form

$$y^2 = -4ax \text{ with } a = 2$$

Hence, required equation of parabola is

$$y^2 = -4(2)x = -8x$$

Question 11 Vertex (0, 0) passing through $(2, 3)$ and axis is along X-axis.

Sol. Given, vertex = (0, 0)

Point = (2, 3), Axis = X-axis

Since, point (2, 3) lies in first quadrant and axis is X-axis. So, equation of parabola will be of the form $y^2 = 4ax$, which passes through (2, 3),

On putting $x = 2, y = 3$ in $y^2 = 4ax$, we get

$$(3)^2 = 4a \times (2)$$

$$\Rightarrow \quad a = \frac{9}{8}$$

Hence, required equation of parabola is

$$y^2 = 4\left(\frac{9}{8}\right)x$$

$$\Rightarrow \quad y^2 = \frac{9}{2}x$$

Question 12 Vertex (0, 0) passing through (5, 2) and symmetric with respect to Y-axis.

Sol. Given, vertex = (0, 0), Point = (5, 2)

Since, point (5, 2) lies in first quadrant and axis is Y-axis. So, parabola is symmetric with respect to Y-axis. Hence, equation of parabola will be of the form $x^2 = 4ay$, which passes through (5, 2),

On putting $x = 5, y = 2$ in $x^2 = 4ay$, we get

$$\therefore \quad (5)^2 = 4a \times 2$$

$$\Rightarrow \quad a = \frac{25}{8}$$

Hence, required equation of parabola is $x^2 = 4 \times \frac{25}{8}y$

$$\Rightarrow \quad x^2 = \frac{25}{2}y$$

Exercise 10.3

Directions (Q. No. 1 to 9) In each of the questions find the coordinates of the foci, the vertices, the length of major axis, the minor axis, the eccentricity and the length of the latus rectum of the ellipse.

Question 1 $\frac{x^2}{36}+\frac{y^2}{16}=1$

Sol. Given, equation of ellipse $\frac{x^2}{36}+\frac{y^2}{16}=1$

$\because$ Denominator of $\frac{x^2}{36}$ is larger than the denominator of $\frac{y^2}{16}$.

$\therefore$ The major axis is along X-axis. On comparing the given equation with $\frac{x^2}{a^2}+\frac{y^2}{b^2}=1$, we get

$$a^2 = 36 \quad \text{and} \quad b^2 = 16$$

$$\Rightarrow \quad a = 6 \quad \text{and} \quad b = 4$$

Here, a and b are lengths, so we take only positive sign.

Now, $c^2 = a^2 - b^2 = 36 - 16 = 20 \Rightarrow c = 2\sqrt{5}$

Here, major axis is along X-axis.

$$\text{Foci} = (\pm\, c, 0) = (\pm\, 2\sqrt{5}, 0)$$

$$\text{Vertices} = (\pm\, a, 0) = (\pm\, 6, 0)$$

$$\text{Length of major axis} = 2a = 2 \times 6 = 12$$

$$\text{Length of minor axis} = 2b = 2 \times 4 = 8$$

$$\text{Eccentricity, } e = \frac{c}{a} = \frac{2\sqrt{5}}{6} = \frac{\sqrt{5}}{3}$$

$$\text{Length of latus rectum} = \frac{2b^2}{a} = \frac{2 \times 16}{6} = \frac{16}{3}$$

Question 2 $\frac{x^2}{4}+\frac{y^2}{25}=1$

Sol. Given, equation of ellipse is $\frac{x^2}{4}+\frac{y^2}{25}=1$

$\because$ Denominator of $\frac{x^2}{4}$ is smaller than the denominator of $\frac{y^2}{25}$.

$\therefore$ The major axis is along Y-axis.

On comparing the given equation with $\frac{x^2}{b^2}+\frac{y^2}{a^2}=1$, we get

$$b^2 = 4 \quad \text{and} \quad a^2 = 25$$

$$\Rightarrow \quad b = 2 \quad \text{and} \quad a = 5$$

Since, a and b are lengths, so we take only positive sign.

$\because$ $$c^2 = a^2 - b^2 = 25 - 4 = 21$$

$\Rightarrow$ $$c = \sqrt{21}$$

Since, major axis is along Y-axis. So,

$$\text{Foci} = (0, \pm c) = (0, \pm \sqrt{21})$$

$$\text{Vertices} = (0, \pm a) = (0, \pm 5)$$

$$\text{Length of major axis} = 2a = 2 \times 5 = 10$$

$$\text{Length of minor axis} = 2b = 2 \times 2 = 4$$

$$\text{Eccentricity, } e = \frac{c}{a} = \frac{\sqrt{21}}{5}$$

$$\text{Length of latus rectum} = \frac{2b^2}{a} = \frac{2 \times 4}{5} = \frac{8}{5}$$

Mistake Alert Always take the larger number as a^2 to avoid confusion.

Question 3 $\dfrac{x^2}{16} + \dfrac{y^2}{9} = 1.$

Sol. Given, equation of ellipse is

$$\frac{x^2}{16} + \frac{y^2}{9} = 1$$

$\because$ Denominator of $\dfrac{x^2}{16}$ is greater than the denominator of $\dfrac{y^2}{9}$.

$\therefore$ The major axis is along X-axis.

On comparing given equation with $\dfrac{x^2}{a^2} + \dfrac{y^2}{b^2} = 1$, we get

$$a^2 = 16 \quad \text{and} \quad b^2 = 9$$

$\Rightarrow$ $$a = 4 \quad \text{and} \quad b = 3$$

Since, a and b are lengths, so we take only positive sign.

Now, $$c^2 = a^2 - b^2 = 16 - 9 = 7$$

$\Rightarrow$ $$c = \sqrt{7}$$

Since, major axis is along X-axis. So,

$$\text{Foci} = (\pm c, 0) = (\pm \sqrt{7}, 0)$$

$$\text{Vertices} = (\pm a, 0) = (\pm 4, 0)$$

$$\text{Length of major axis} = 2a = 2 \times 4 = 8$$

$$\text{Length of minor axis} = 2b = 2 \times 3 = 6$$

$$\text{Eccentricity, } e = \frac{c}{a} = \frac{\sqrt{7}}{4}$$

$$\text{Length of latus rectum} = \frac{2b^2}{a} = \frac{2 \times 9}{4} = \frac{9}{2}$$

Question 4 $\dfrac{x^2}{25}+\dfrac{y^2}{100}=1$

Sol. Given equation of ellipse is $\dfrac{x^2}{25}+\dfrac{y^2}{100}=1$

$\because$ Denominator of $\dfrac{x^2}{25}$ is smaller than the denominator of $\dfrac{y^2}{100}$.

$\therefore$ The major axis is along Y-axis.

On comparing given equation with $\dfrac{x^2}{b^2}+\dfrac{y^2}{a^2}=1$, we get

$$b^2=25 \text{ and } a^2=100 \Rightarrow b=5 \quad \text{and} \quad a=10$$

Since, a and b are lengths, so we take only positive sign.

Now, $c^2=a^2-b^2=100-25=75=25\times 3 \Rightarrow c=5\sqrt{3}$

Since, major axis is along Y-axis. So, Foci $=(0,\pm c)=(0,\pm 5\sqrt{3})$

Vertices $=(0,\pm a)=(0,\pm 10)$

Length of major axis $=2a=2\times 10=20$

Length of minor axis $=2b=2\times 5=10$

$$\text{Eccentricity, } e=\frac{c}{a}=\frac{5\sqrt{3}}{10}=\frac{\sqrt{3}}{2}$$

$$\text{Length of latus rectum}=\frac{2b^2}{a}=\frac{2\times 25}{10}=5$$

Question 5 $\dfrac{x^2}{49}+\dfrac{y^2}{36}=1$

Sol. Given equation of ellipse is $\dfrac{x^2}{49}+\dfrac{y^2}{36}=1$

$\because$ Denominator of $\dfrac{x^2}{49}$ is larger than the denominator of $\dfrac{y^2}{26}$.

$\therefore$ The major axis is along X-axis.

On comparing given equation with $\dfrac{x^2}{a^2}+\dfrac{y^2}{b^2}=1$, we get

$$a^2=49,\ b^2=36 \Rightarrow a=7,\ b=6$$

Since, a and b are lengths, so we take only positive sign.

Now, $c^2=a^2-b^2=49-36=13 \Rightarrow c=\sqrt{13}$

Since, major axis is along X-axis. So, Foci $=(\pm c,0)=(\pm\sqrt{13},0)$

Vertices $=(\pm a,0)=(\pm 7,0)$

Length of major axis $=2a=2\times 7=14$

Length of minor axis $=2b=2\times 6=12$

$$\text{Eccentricity, } e=\frac{c}{a}=\frac{\sqrt{13}}{7}$$

$$\text{Length of latus rectum}=\frac{2b^2}{a}=\frac{2\times 36}{7}=\frac{72}{7}$$

Question 6 $\dfrac{x^2}{100}+\dfrac{y^2}{400}=1$

Sol. Given, equation of ellipse is

$$\frac{x^2}{100}+\frac{y^2}{400}=1$$

$\because$ Denominator of $\dfrac{x^2}{100}$ is smaller than the denominator of $\dfrac{y^2}{400}$.

$\therefore$ The major axis is along Y-axis.

On comparing given equation with $\dfrac{x^2}{b^2}+\dfrac{y^2}{a^2}=1$, we get

$$b^2=100 \quad \text{and} \quad a^2=400$$

$$\Rightarrow \qquad b=10 \text{ and } a=20$$

Since, a and b are lengths, so we take only positive sign.

Now, $$c^2=a^2-b^2=400-100=300$$

$$\Rightarrow \qquad c=10\sqrt{3}$$

Since, major axis is along Y-axis. So,

$$\text{Foci}=(0,\pm c)=(0,\pm 10\sqrt{3})$$

$$\text{Vertices}=(0,\pm a)=(0,\pm 20)$$

$$\text{Length of major axis}=2a=2\times 20=40$$

$$\text{Length of minor axis}=2b=2\times 10=20$$

$$\text{Eccentricity, } e=\frac{c}{a}=\frac{10\sqrt{3}}{20}=\frac{\sqrt{3}}{2}$$

$$\text{Length of latus rectum}=\frac{2b^2}{a}=\frac{2\times 100}{20}=10$$

Question 7 $36x^2+4y^2=144$

◎ ***Thinking Process*** First, we will convert it into the standard form of an ellipse.

Sol. Given, equation of ellipse is

$$36x^2+4y^2=144$$

$$\Rightarrow \qquad \frac{36x^2}{144}+\frac{4y^2}{144}=1 \qquad \text{(divide by 144)}$$

$$\Rightarrow \qquad \frac{x^2}{4}+\frac{y^2}{36}=1$$

$\because$ Denominator of $\dfrac{x^2}{4}$ is smaller than the denominator of $\dfrac{y^2}{36}$.

$\therefore$ The major axis is along Y-axis.

On comparing given equation with $\dfrac{x^2}{b^2}+\dfrac{y^2}{a^2}=1$, we get

$$b^2=4 \quad \text{and} \quad a^2=36$$

$$\Rightarrow \qquad b=2 \quad \text{and} \quad a=6$$

Since, a and b are lengths, so we take only positive sign.

and $$c^2 = a^2 - b^2 = 36 - 4 = 32$$

$$\Rightarrow \quad c = 4\sqrt{2}$$

Since, major axis is along Y-axis. So,

$$\text{Foci} = (0, \pm c) = (0, \pm 4\sqrt{2})$$

$$\text{Vertices} = (0, \pm a) = (0, \pm 6)$$

$$\text{Length of major axis} = 2a = 2 \times 6 = 12$$

$$\text{Length of minor axis} = 2b = 2 \times 2 = 4$$

$$\text{Eccentricity, } e = \frac{c}{a} = \frac{4\sqrt{2}}{6} = \frac{2\sqrt{2}}{3}$$

$$\text{Length of latus rectum} = \frac{2b^2}{a} = \frac{2 \times 4}{6} = \frac{4}{3}$$

Question 8 $16x^2 + y^2 = 16$

Sol. Given, equation of ellipse is

$$16x^2 + y^2 = 16$$

$$\Rightarrow \quad \frac{16x^2}{16} + \frac{y^2}{16} = 1 \quad \text{(divide by 16)}$$

$$\Rightarrow \quad \frac{x^2}{1} + \frac{y^2}{16} = 1$$

$\because$ Denominator of $\frac{x^2}{1}$ is smaller than the denominator of $\frac{y^2}{16}$.

$\therefore$ The major axis is along Y-axis.

On comparing given equation with $\frac{x^2}{b^2} + \frac{y^2}{a^2} = 1$, we get

$$b^2 = 1 \text{ and } a^2 = 16$$

$$\Rightarrow \quad b = 1 \quad \text{and} \quad a = 4$$

Since, a and b are lengths, so we take only positive sign.

Now, $$c^2 = a^2 - b^2$$

$$= 16 - 1 = 15$$

$$\Rightarrow \quad c = \sqrt{15}$$

Since, major axis is along Y-axis. So,

$$\text{Foci} = (0, \pm c) = (0, \pm \sqrt{15})$$

$$\text{Vertices} = (0, \pm a) = (0, \pm 4)$$

$$\text{Length of major axis} = 2a = 2 \times 4 = 8$$

$$\text{Length of minor axis} = 2b = 2 \times 1 = 2$$

$$\text{Eccentricity, } e = \frac{c}{a} = \frac{\sqrt{15}}{4}$$

$$\text{Length of latu srectum} = \frac{2b^2}{a} = \frac{2 \times 1}{4} = \frac{1}{2}$$

Question 9 $4x^2 + 9y^2 = 36$

Sol. Given, equation of ellipse is

$$4x^2 + 9y^2 = 36$$

On dividing the above equation by 36, we get

$$\Rightarrow \quad \frac{4x^2}{36} + \frac{9y^2}{36} = 1 \Rightarrow \frac{x^2}{9} + \frac{y^2}{4} = 1$$

$\because$ Denominator of $\frac{x^2}{9}$ is greater than denominator of $\frac{y^2}{4}$.

$\therefore$ The major axis is along X-axis. On comparing given equation with $\frac{x^2}{a^2} + \frac{y^2}{b^2} = 1$, we get

$$a^2 = 9 \quad \text{and} \quad b^2 = 4$$

$$\Rightarrow \quad a = 3 \quad \text{and} \quad b = 2$$

Since, a and b are lengths, so we take only positive sign.

Now, $$c^2 = a^2 - b^2 = 9 - 4 = 5$$

$$\Rightarrow \quad c = \sqrt{5}$$

Since, major axis is along X-axis. So,

$$\text{Foci} = (\pm c, 0) = (\pm \sqrt{5}, 0)$$

$$\text{Vertices} = (\pm a, 0) = (\pm 3, 0)$$

$$\text{Length of major axis} = 2a = 2 \times 3 = 6$$

$$\text{Length of minor axis} = 2b = 2 \times 2 = 4$$

$$\text{Eccentricity, } e = \frac{c}{a} = \frac{\sqrt{5}}{3}$$

$$\text{Length of latus rectum} = \frac{2b^2}{a} = \frac{2 \times 4}{3} = \frac{8}{3}$$

Direction (Q. No. 10 to 20) *In each of the following questions find the equation for the ellipse that satisfies the given conditions.*

Question 10 Vertices $(\pm 5, 0)$ and foci $(\pm 4, 0)$.

Sol. Since, vertices $(\pm 5, 0)$ and foci $(\pm 4, 0)$ are on X-axis, as y-coordinate of both points is zero. So, equation of ellipse will be of the form

$$\frac{x^2}{a^2} + \frac{y^2}{b^2} = 1 \quad \ldots\text{(i)}$$

where, $a = 5$ and $c = 4$ $\quad [\because (\pm a, 0) = (\pm 5, 0) \text{ and } (0, \pm c) = (\pm 4, 0)]$

Now, $$c^2 = a^2 - b^2$$

$$\therefore \quad (4)^2 = (5)^2 - b^2$$

$$\Rightarrow \quad 16 = 25 - b^2 \Rightarrow b^2 = 25 - 16 \Rightarrow b^2 = 9$$

On putting put the values of $a^2 = 25$ and $b^2 = 9$ in Eq. (i), we get

$$\frac{x^2}{25} + \frac{y^2}{9} = 1$$

which is required equation of ellipse.

Question 11 Vertices $(0, \pm 13)$ foci $(0, \pm 5)$

Sol. Since, vertices $(0, \pm 13)$ and foci $(0, \pm 5)$ are on Y-axis, as x-coordinate of both points is zero.

So, equation of ellipse will be of the form

$$\frac{x^2}{b^2} + \frac{y^2}{a^2} = 1 \quad \text{...(i)}$$

where, $a = 13$ and $c = 5$ [$\because (0, \pm a) = (0, \pm 13)$ and $(0, \pm c) = (0, \pm 5)$]

$\because \quad c^2 = a^2 - b^2$

$\Rightarrow \quad (5)^2 = (13)^2 - b^2$

$\Rightarrow \quad 25 = 169 - b^2$

$\Rightarrow \quad b^2 = 169 - 25$

$\Rightarrow \quad b^2 = 144$

On putting the values of $a^2 = 169$ and $b^2 = 144$ in Eq. (i), we get

$$\frac{x^2}{144} + \frac{y^2}{169} = 1,$$ which is required equation of ellipse.

Question 12 Vertices $(\pm 6, 0)$ and foci $(\pm 4, 0)$

Sol. Since, vertices $(\pm 6, 0)$ and foci $(\pm 4, 0)$ are on X-axis, as y-coordinate of both points is zero. So, equation of ellipse will be of the form

$$\frac{x^2}{a^2} + \frac{y^2}{b^2} = 1 \quad \text{...(i)}$$

where, $a = 6$ and $c = 4$ [$\because (\pm a, 0) = (\pm 6, 0)$ and $(\pm c, 0) = (\pm 4, 0)$]

$\because \quad c^2 = a^2 - b^2$

On putting $a = 6$, $c = 4$ in $c^2 = a^2 - b^2$, we get

$\Rightarrow \quad (4)^2 = (6)^2 - b^2$

$\Rightarrow \quad 16 = 36 - b^2$

$\Rightarrow \quad b^2 = 36 - 16 = 20$

On putting the values of $a^2 = 36$ and $b^2 = 20$ in Eq. (i), we get

$$\frac{x^2}{36} + \frac{y^2}{20} = 1,$$ which is required equation of ellipse.

Question 13 Ends of major axis $(\pm 3, 0)$ and ends of minor axis $(0, \pm 2)$.

Sol. Since, major axis $(\pm 3, 0)$ is along X-axis and minor axis $(0, \pm 2)$ is along Y-axis. So, equation of ellipse will be of the form

$$\frac{x^2}{a^2} + \frac{y^2}{b^2} = 1 \quad \text{...(i)}$$

where, $a = 3$ and $b = 2$ [$\because (\pm a, 0) = (\pm 3, 0)$ and $(0, \pm b) = (0, \pm 2)$]

On putting the values of $a^2 = 9$ and $b^2 = 4$ in Eq. (i) we get

$\Rightarrow \quad \frac{x^2}{9} + \frac{y^2}{4} = 1,$ which is required equation of ellipse.

Question 14 Ends of major axis $(0, \pm\sqrt{5})$, ends of minor axis $(\pm 1, 0)$.

Sol. Since, major axis $(0, \pm\sqrt{5})$ is along Y-axis and minor axis $(\pm 1, 0)$ is along X-axis. So, equation of ellipse will be of the form

$$\frac{x^2}{b^2} + \frac{y^2}{a^2} = 1 \quad \text{...(i)}$$

where, $a = \sqrt{5}$ and $b = 1$ $\quad [\because (0, \pm a) = (0, \pm\sqrt{5})$ and $[(\pm b, 0) = (\pm 1, 0)]$

On putting the values of $a^2 = 5$ and $b^2 = 1$ in Eq. (i) we get

$$\frac{x^2}{1} + \frac{y^2}{5} = 1,$$ which is required equation of ellipse.

Question 15 Length of major axis 26, foci $(\pm 5, 0)$.

Sol. Since, foci $(\pm 5, 0)$ lies on X-axis, as y-coordinate is zero. So, equation of ellipse will be of the form

$$\frac{x^2}{a^2} + \frac{y^2}{b^2} = 1 \quad \text{...(i)}$$

Given that length of major axis, $2a = 26$

$\Rightarrow \quad a = 13$ and $c = 5 \quad [\because (\pm c, 0) = (\pm 5, 0)]$

$\because \quad c^2 = a^2 - b^2$

On putting $a = 13$ and $c = 5$ in $c^2 = a^2 - b^2$, we get

$\Rightarrow \quad (5)^2 = (13)^2 - b^2$

$\Rightarrow \quad 25 = 169 - b^2$

$\Rightarrow \quad b^2 = 169 - 25 = 144$

On putting the values of $a^2 = 169$ and $b^2 = 144$ in Eq. (i), we get

$$\frac{x^2}{169} + \frac{y^2}{144} = 1,$$ which is required equation of ellipse.

Question 16 Length of minor axis 16, foci $(0, \pm 6)$.

Sol. Since, foci $(0, \pm 6)$ lies on Y-axis, as x-coordinate is zero. So, equation of ellipse will be of the form

$$\frac{x^2}{b^2} + \frac{y^2}{a^2} = 1 \quad \text{...(i)}$$

Given that length of minor axis $2b = 16$ and $c = 6 \quad [\because (0, \pm c) = (0, \pm 6)]$

$\Rightarrow \quad b = 8$ and $c = 6$

$\because \quad c^2 = a^2 - b^2$

On putting $a = 13$ and $c = 6$ in $c^2 = a^2 - b^2$, we get

$\Rightarrow \quad (6)^2 = a^2 - (8)^2 \Rightarrow 36 = a^2 - 64$

$\Rightarrow \quad a^2 = 36 + 64 = 100$

On putting the values of $a^2 = 100$ and $b^2 = 64$ in Eq. (i), we get

$$\frac{x^2}{64} + \frac{y^2}{100} = 1,$$ which is required equation of ellipse.

Question 17 Foci $(\pm 3, 0)$, $a = 4$.

Sol. Since, foci $(\pm 3, 0)$ lies on X-axis, as y-coordinate is zero. So, equation of ellipse will be of the form

$$\frac{x^2}{a^2} + \frac{y^2}{b^2} = 1 \quad \text{...(i)}$$

Since, foci $(\pm c, 0) = (\pm 3, 0)$

$$c = 3 \text{ and } a = 4$$

$$\because \quad c^2 = a^2 - b^2$$

On putting $a = 3$ and $a = 4$ in $c^2 = a^2 - b^2$, we get

$$\Rightarrow \quad (3)^2 = (4)^2 - b^2$$

$$\Rightarrow \quad 9 = 16 - b^2 \Rightarrow b^2 = 16 - 9 \Rightarrow b^2 = 7$$

On putting the values of $a^2 = 16$ and $b^2 = 7$ in Eq. (i), we get

$$\frac{x^2}{16} + \frac{y^2}{7} = 1, \text{ which is required equation of ellipse.}$$

Question 18 $b = 3$, $c = 4$, centre at origin, foci on the X-axis.

Sol. Since, foci lie on X-axis. So, equation of ellipse will be of the form

$$\frac{x^2}{a^2} + \frac{y^2}{b^2} = 1 \quad \text{...(i)}$$

Given, $b = 3, c = 4$

$$\because \quad c^2 = a^2 - b^2$$

On putting $b = 3$ and $c = 4$ in $c^2 = a^2 - b^2$, we get

$$\Rightarrow \quad (4)^2 = a^2 - (3)^2$$

$$\Rightarrow \quad 16 = a^2 - 9 \Rightarrow a^2 = 16 + 9$$

$$\Rightarrow \quad a^2 = 25$$

On putting the values of $a^2 = 25$ and $b^2 = 9$ in Eq. (i), we get

$$\frac{x^2}{25} + \frac{y^2}{9} = 1, \text{ which is required equation of ellipse.}$$

Question 19 Centre at (0, 0), major axis on the Y-axis passes through the points (3, 2) and (1, 6).

Sol. Since, major axis is along Y-axis.
So, equation of ellipse will be of the form

$$\frac{x^2}{b^2} + \frac{y^2}{a^2} = 1 \quad \text{...(i)}$$

Since, Eq. (i) passes through the points (3, 2) and (1, 6)
i.e., they will satisfy it.

$$\therefore \quad \frac{3^2}{b^2} + \frac{2^2}{a^2} = 1 \Rightarrow \frac{9}{b^2} + \frac{4}{a^2} = 1 \quad \text{...(ii)}$$

$$\text{and} \quad \frac{1^2}{b^2} + \frac{6^2}{a^2} = 1 \Rightarrow \frac{1}{b^2} + \frac{36}{a^2} = 1 \quad \text{...(iii)}$$

On multiplying Eq. (ii) by 9 and then subtracting the Eq. (iii) from it, we get

$$\frac{80}{b^2} = 8 \Rightarrow b^2 = \frac{80}{8}$$

$$\Rightarrow \quad b^2 = 10$$

On putting the values of $b^2 = 10$ in Eq. (ii), we get $\frac{9}{10} + \frac{4}{a^2} = 1$

$$\Rightarrow \quad \frac{4}{a^2} = 1 - \frac{9}{10} \Rightarrow \frac{4}{a^2} = \frac{1}{10} \Rightarrow a^2 = 40$$

On putting the values of $a^2 = 40$ and $b^2 = 10$ in Eq. (i), we get

$$\frac{x^2}{10} + \frac{y^2}{40} = 1, \text{ which is required equation of ellipse.}$$

Question 20 Major axis on the X-axis and passes through the points (4, 3) and (6, 2).

Sol. Since, major axis is along X-axis. So, equation of ellipse will be of the form

$$\frac{x^2}{a^2} + \frac{y^2}{b^2} = 1 \quad \text{...(i)}$$

Since, that Eq. (i) passes through the points (4, 3) and (6, 2) *i.e.,* they will satisfy it

$$\therefore \quad \frac{(4)^2}{a^2} + \frac{(3)^2}{b^2} = 1 \Rightarrow \frac{16}{a^2} + \frac{9}{b^2} = 1 \quad \text{...(ii)}$$

$$\text{and} \quad \frac{(6)^2}{a^2} + \frac{(2)^2}{b^2} = 1 \Rightarrow \frac{36}{a^2} + \frac{4}{b^2} = 1 \quad \text{...(iii)}$$

On multiplying Eq. (ii) by 4 and Eq. (iii) by 9, then subtracting Eq. (iii) from Eq. (ii), we get

$$\frac{64}{a^2} - \frac{324}{a^2} = 4 - 9 \Rightarrow -\frac{260}{a^2} = -5$$

$$\Rightarrow \quad a^2 = \frac{260}{5}$$

$$\Rightarrow \quad a^2 = 52$$

On putting the values of $a^2 = 52$ in Eq. (ii), we get

$$\frac{9}{b^2} = 1 - \frac{16}{52}$$

$$\Rightarrow \quad \frac{9}{b^2} = \frac{52 - 16}{52}$$

$$\Rightarrow \quad \frac{9}{b^2} = \frac{36}{52}$$

$$\Rightarrow \quad b^2 = \frac{9 \times 52}{36} = 13$$

On putting the values of $a^2 = 52$ and $b^2 = 13$ in Eq. (i), we get

$$\frac{x^2}{52} + \frac{y^2}{13} = 1, \text{ which is required equation of ellipse.}$$

Exercise 10.4

Direction (Q. Nos. 1 to 6) In each of the questions, find the coordinates of the foci and the vertices, the eccentricity and the length of the latus rectum of the hyperbolas.

Question 1 $\frac{x^2}{16}-\frac{y^2}{9}=1$

◎ *Thinking Process* If in the given equation of hyperbola, coefficient of x^2 is positive then its transverse axis will be along X-axis and coefficient of y^2 is positive then its transverse axis will be along Y-axis.

Sol. On comparing the given equation $\frac{x^2}{16}-\frac{y^2}{9}=1$ with $\frac{x^2}{a^2}-\frac{y^2}{b^2}=1$, we get

$$a^2 = 16 \text{ and } b^2 = 9 \Rightarrow a = 4 \text{ and } b = 3$$

Now, $$c^2 = a^2 + b^2 = 16 + 9 = 25$$

$\Rightarrow$ $$c = 5 \qquad (\because c \text{ must be positive})$$

Since, in given hyperbolic equation, coefficient of x^2 is positive, so transverse axis is along X-axis.

$\therefore$ $$\text{Foci} = (\pm c, 0) = (\pm 5, 0), \text{ Vertices} = (\pm a, 0) = (\pm 4, 0)$$

$$\text{Eccentricity, } e = \frac{c}{a} = \frac{5}{4}, \text{ latus rectum} = \frac{2b^2}{a} = \frac{2\times 9}{4} = \frac{9}{2}$$

🔔 *Mistake Alert* Some students can make an error to find the value of c. They can use the formula ($c^2 = a^2 - b^2$) which is used for ellipse problems.

Question 2 $\frac{y^2}{9}-\frac{x^2}{27}=1$

Sol. On comparing the given equation $\frac{y^2}{9}-\frac{x^2}{27}=1$ with $\frac{y^2}{a^2}-\frac{x^2}{b^2}=1$.

we get, $$a^2 = 9 \text{ and } b^2 = 27$$

$\Rightarrow$ $$a = 3 \text{ and } b = 3\sqrt{3} \qquad (\because a, b > 0)$$

On putting $a = 3, b = 3\sqrt{3}$ in $c^2 = a^2 + b^2$, we get

$\because$ $$c^2 = a^2 + b^2 = 9 + 27 = 36$$

$\Rightarrow$ $$c = 6 \qquad (\because c \text{ must be positive})$$

Since, in the given hyperbolic equation, coefficient of y^2 is positive, so transverse axis is along Y-axis.

$$\text{Foci} = (0, \pm c) = (0, \pm 6)$$

$$\text{Vertices} = (0, \pm a) = (0, \pm 3)$$

$$\text{Eccentricity, } e = \frac{c}{a} = \frac{6}{3} = 2, \text{ length of latus rectum} = \frac{2b^2}{a} = \frac{2\times 27}{3} = 18$$

Question 3 $9y^2 - 4x^2 = 36.$

◎ *Thinking Process* First we will convert it into the standard form of a hyperbola.

Sol. Given, equationof hyperbola is $9y^2 - 4x^2 = 36$,

On dividing $9y^2 - 4x^2 = 36$ by 36, we get

$$\frac{9y^2}{36} - \frac{4x^2}{36} = \frac{36}{36} \Rightarrow \frac{y^2}{4} - \frac{x^2}{9} = 1$$

Now, on comparing $\frac{y^2}{4} - \frac{x^2}{9} = 1$ with $\frac{y^2}{a^2} - \frac{x^2}{b^2} = 1$, we get

$$a^2 = 4 \text{ and } b^2 = 9 \Rightarrow a = 2 \text{ and } b = 3$$

$\because \quad c^2 = a^2 + b^2$

On putting $a = 2$, $b = 3$ in $c^2 = a^2 + b^2$, we get

$\Rightarrow \quad c^2 = 4 + 9 = 13$

$\Rightarrow \quad c = \sqrt{13} \qquad (\because c > 0)$

Since, in the given hyperbolic equation, coefficient of y^2 is positive, so transverse axis is along Y-axis.

$$\text{Foci} = (0, \pm c) = (0, \pm \sqrt{13})$$

$$\text{Vertices} = (0, \pm a) = (0, \pm 2)$$

$$\text{Eccentricity, } e = \frac{c}{a} = \frac{\sqrt{13}}{2}$$

$$\text{Length of latus rectum} = \frac{2b^2}{a} = \frac{2 \times 9}{2} = 9$$

Question 4 $16x^2 - 9y^2 = 576$

Sol. Given equation of hyperbola is $16x^2 - 9y^2 = 576$,

On dividing $16x^2 - 9y^2 = 576$ by 576, we get

$$\frac{16x^2}{576} - \frac{9y^2}{576} = \frac{576}{576} \Rightarrow \frac{x^2}{36} - \frac{y^2}{64} = 1$$

Now, on comparing $\frac{x^2}{36} - \frac{y^2}{64} = 1$ with $\frac{x^2}{a^2} - \frac{y^2}{b^2} = 1$, we get

$$a^2 = 36 \quad \text{and} \quad b^2 = 64$$

$\Rightarrow \quad a = 6 \quad \text{and} \quad b = 8$

$\because \quad c^2 = a^2 + b^2 = 36 + 64 = 100 \Rightarrow c = 10$

Since, in the given hyperbolic equation, coefficient of x^2 is positive, so transverse axis is along X-axis.

$$\text{Foci} = (\pm c, 0) = (\pm 10, 0)$$

$$\text{Vertices} = (\pm a, 0) = (\pm 6, 0)$$

$$\text{Eccentricity, } e = \frac{c}{a} = \frac{10}{6} = \frac{5}{3}$$

$$\text{Length of latus rectum} = \frac{2b^2}{a} = \frac{2 \times 64}{6} = \frac{64}{3}$$

Question 5 $5y^2 - 9x^2 = 36.$

Sol. Given equation of hyperbola is $5y^2 - 9x^2 = 36$,

On dividing $5y^2 - 9x^2 = 36$ by 36, we get

$$\frac{5y^2}{36} - \frac{9x^2}{36} = \frac{36}{36} \Rightarrow \frac{y^2}{\frac{36}{5}} - \frac{x^2}{4} = 1$$

On comparing $\frac{y^2}{\frac{36}{5}} - \frac{x^2}{4} = 1$ with $\frac{y^2}{a^2} - \frac{x^2}{b^2} = 1$, we get

$$a^2 = \frac{36}{5} \quad \text{and} \quad b^2 = 4 \Rightarrow a = \frac{6}{\sqrt{5}} \quad \text{and} \quad b = 2$$

$$\because \quad c^2 = a^2 + b^2 = \frac{36}{5} + 4 \Rightarrow c^2 = \frac{36 + 20}{5} = \frac{56}{5} \Rightarrow c = \frac{2\sqrt{14}}{\sqrt{5}}$$

Since, in the given hyperbolic equation coefficient of y^2 is positive, so transverse axis is along Y-axis.

$$\text{Foci} = (0, \pm c) = \left(0, \pm \frac{2\sqrt{14}}{\sqrt{5}}\right), \text{Vertices} = (0, \pm a) = \left(0, \pm \frac{6}{\sqrt{5}}\right)$$

$$\text{Eccentricity, } e = \frac{c}{a} = \frac{\frac{2\sqrt{14}}{\sqrt{5}}}{\frac{6}{\sqrt{5}}} = \frac{\sqrt{14}}{3}$$

$$\text{Length of latus rectum} = \frac{2b^2}{a} = \frac{2 \times 4}{\frac{6}{\sqrt{5}}} = \frac{8\sqrt{5}}{6} = \frac{4\sqrt{5}}{3}$$

Question 6 $49y^2 - 16x^2 = 784.$

Sol. Given equation of hyperbola is $49y^2 - 16x^2 = 784$,

On dividing $49y^2 - 16x^2 = 784$ by 784, we get

$$\frac{49y^2}{784} - \frac{16x^2}{784} = \frac{784}{784} \Rightarrow \frac{y^2}{16} - \frac{x^2}{49} = 1$$

On comparing $\frac{y^2}{16} \frac{x^2}{49} = 1$ with $\frac{y^2}{a^2} - \frac{x^2}{b^2} = 1$, we get

$$a^2 = 16 \text{ and } b^2 = 49 \Rightarrow a = 4 \text{ and } b = 7$$

$$\because \quad c^2 = a^2 + b^2 = 16 + 49 = 65$$

$$\Rightarrow \quad c = \sqrt{65} \qquad (\because c > 0)$$

Since, in the given hyperbolic equation, coefficient of y^2 is positive, so transverse axis is along Y-axis.

Foci $= (0, \pm c) = (0, \pm \sqrt{65})$, Vertices $= (0, \pm a) = (0, \pm 4)$

$$\text{Eccentricity, } e = \frac{c}{a} = \frac{\sqrt{65}}{4}$$

$$\text{Length of latus rectum} = \frac{2b^2}{a} = \frac{2 \times 49}{4} = \frac{49}{2}$$

Direction (Q. No. 7 to 15) In each of the question find the equations of the hyperbola satisfying the given conditions.

Question 7 Vertices $(\pm 2, 0)$ and foci $(\pm 3, 0)$.

Sol. Since, vertices $(\pm 2, 0)$ and foci $(\pm 3, 0)$ lie on X-axis, as y-coordinate of both points is zero.

So, equation of hyperbola will be of the form

$$\frac{x^2}{a^2} - \frac{y^2}{b^2} = 1 \quad \text{...(i)}$$

where it is given that $a = 2$ and $c = 3$

$$[\because (\pm a, 0) = (\pm 2, 0) \text{ and } (\pm c, 0) = (\pm 3, 0)]$$

$\because \quad c^2 = a^2 + b^2$

On putting the values of $a = 2$ in $c = 3$ in $c^2 = a^2 + b^2$, we get

$\Rightarrow \quad 9 = 4 + b^2$

$\Rightarrow \quad b^2 = 5$

On putting the values of $a^2 = 4$ and $b^2 = 5$ in Eq. (i), we get

$$\frac{x^2}{4} - \frac{y^2}{5} = 1, \text{ which is required equation of hyperbola.}$$

Question 8 Vertices $(0, \pm 5)$, foci $(0, \pm 8)$.

Sol. Since, vertices $(0, \pm 5)$ and foci $(0, \pm 8)$ lie on Y-axis, as x-coordinate of both points is zero .

So, equation of hyperbola will be of the form

$$\frac{y^2}{a^2} - \frac{x^2}{b^2} = 1 \quad \text{...(i)}$$

where it is given that $(0, \pm a) = (0, \pm 5)$ and foci $(0, \pm c) = (0, \pm 8)$

$a = 5$ and $c = 8$

$\because \quad c^2 = a^2 + b^2 \Rightarrow 64 = 25 + b^2$

$\Rightarrow \quad b^2 = 64 - 25$

$\Rightarrow \quad b^2 = 39$

On putting the values of $a^2 = 25$ and $b^2 = 39$ in Eq. (i), we get

$$\frac{y^2}{25} - \frac{x^2}{39} = 1, \text{ which is required equation of hyperbola.}$$

Question 9 Vertices $(0, \pm 3)$ and foci $(0, \pm 5)$.

Sol. Since, vertices $(0, \pm 3)$ and foci $(0, \pm 5)$ lie on Y-axis, as x-coordinate of both points is zero.

So, equation of hyperbola will be of the form

$$\frac{y^2}{a^2} - \frac{x^2}{b^2} = 1 \quad \text{...(i)}$$

where it is given that vertices $(0, \pm 3) = (0, \pm a)$ and foci $(0, \pm 5) = (0, \pm c)$

$$a = 3 \quad \text{and} \quad c = 5$$

$$\because \quad c^2 = a^2 + b^2$$

On putting the values of $a = 3$ and $c = 5$ in $c^2 = a^2 + b^2$, we get

$$\Rightarrow \quad 25 = 9 + b^2 \Rightarrow b^2 = 16$$

On putting the values of $a^2 = 9$ and $b^2 = 16$ in Eq. (i), we get

$$\frac{y^2}{9} - \frac{x^2}{16} = 1,$$ which is required equation of hyperbola.

Question 10 Foci $(\pm 5, 0)$ and the transverse axis is of length 8.

Sol. Since, foci $(\pm 5, 0)$ lie on X-axis, as Y-coordinate is zero.

So, equation of hyperbola will be of the form

$$\frac{x^2}{a^2} - \frac{y^2}{b^2} = 1 \quad \text{...(i)}$$

where it is given that foci $(\pm 5, 0) = (\pm c, 0)$ and length of transverse axis is $2a = 8$

$$c = 5 \quad \text{and} \quad 2a = 8 \Rightarrow \quad a = 4$$

$$\because \quad c^2 = a^2 + b^2$$

On putting the values of $c = 5$ and $a = 4$ in $c^2 = a^2 + b^2$, we get

$$\Rightarrow \quad 25 = 16 + b^2 \Rightarrow b^2 = 9$$

On putting the values of $a^2 = 16$ and $b^2 = 9$ in Eq. (i), we get

$$\frac{x^2}{16} - \frac{y^2}{9} = 1,$$ which is required equation of hyperbola.

Question 11 Foci $(0, \pm 13)$, the conjugate axis is of length 24.

Sol. Since, foci $(0, \pm 13)$ lie on Y-axis, as x-coordinate is zero. So, equation of hyperbola will be of the form

$$\frac{y^2}{a^2} - \frac{x^2}{b^2} = 1 \quad \text{...(i)}$$

where it is given that foci $(0, \pm 13) = (0, \pm c)$ and conjugate length, $2b = 24$

$$c = 13 \quad \text{and } b = 12 \because c^2 = a^2 + b^2$$

On putting the values of $c = 13$ and $b = 12$ in $c^2 = a^2 + b^2$, we get

$$\therefore \quad 169 = a^2 + 144 \Rightarrow a^2 = 169 - 144 \Rightarrow a^2 = 25$$

On putting the values of $a^2 = 25$ and $b^2 = 144$ in Eq. (i), we get $\frac{y^2}{25} - \frac{x^2}{144} = 1$

Which is required equation of hyperbola.

Question 12 Foci $(\pm 3\sqrt{5}, 0)$ the latus rectum is of length 8.

Sol. Since, foci $(\pm 3\sqrt{5}, 0)$ lie on X-axis, as y-coordinate is zero.

So, equation of hyperbola will be of the form

$$\frac{x^2}{a^2} - \frac{y^2}{b^2} = 1 \quad \text{...(i)}$$

where it is given that foci $(\pm 3\sqrt{5}, 0) = (\pm c, 0)$

$$c = 3\sqrt{5}$$

and length of latus rectum

$$\frac{2b^2}{a} = 8 \Rightarrow b^2 = 4a$$

$\because$ $$c^2 = a^2 + b^2$$

On putting $b^2 = 4a$ and $c = 3\sqrt{5}$ in $c^2 = a^2 + b^2$, we get

$\therefore$ $$(3\sqrt{5})^2 = a^2 + (4a)$$

$\Rightarrow$ $$9 \times 5 = a^2 + 4a \Rightarrow a^2 + 4a - 45 = 0$$

On splitting the middle term, we get

$\Rightarrow$ $$a^2 + 9a - 5a - 45 = 0$$

$\Rightarrow$ $$a(a + 9) - 5(a + 9) = 0 \Rightarrow (a - 5)(a + 9) = 0$$

$\Rightarrow$ $$a - 5 = 0,\ a + 9 = 0 \Rightarrow a = 5, -9$$

$\because$ a can't be negative.

So, $[a = 5 \Rightarrow b^2 = 4 \times 5 = 20]$

On putting the values of $a^2 = 25$ and $b^2 = 20$ in Eq. (i), we get

$$\frac{x^2}{25} - \frac{y^2}{20} = 1,$$ which is required equation of hyperbola.

Question 13 Foci $(\pm 4, 0)$, the latus rectum is of length 12.

Sol. Since, foci $(\pm 4, 0)$ lie on X-axis. So, equation of hyperbola will be of the form

$$\frac{x^2}{a^2} - \frac{y^2}{b^2} = 1 \quad \text{...(i)}$$

where it is given that foci $(\pm 4, 0) = (\pm c, 0)$ and length of latus rectum,

$$\frac{2b^2}{a} = 12$$

$\therefore$ $$c = 4 \quad \text{and} \quad b^2 = 6a \quad \text{...(ii)}$$

$\because$ $$c^2 = a^2 + b^2$$

On putting $b^2 = 6a$ and $c = 4$ in $c^2 = a^2 + b^2$, we get

$\Rightarrow$ $$16 = a^2 + 6a \Rightarrow a^2 + 6a - 16 = 0$$

On splitting the middle term, we get

$$a^2 + 8a - 2a - 16 = 0$$

$\Rightarrow$ $$a(a + 8) - 2(a + 8) = 0$$

$\Rightarrow$ $$(a - 2)(a + 8) = 0$$

$\Rightarrow$ $$a - 2 = 0, a + 8 = 0 \Rightarrow a = 2, -8$$

$\because$ a can't be negative.

So, $[a = 2 \Rightarrow b^2 = 6a = 6 \times 2 = 12]$

On putting the values of $a^2 = 4$ and $b^2 = 12$ in Eq. (i), we get

$$\frac{x^2}{4} - \frac{y^2}{12} = 1,$$ which is required equation of hyperbola.

Question 14 Vertices $(\pm 7, 0)$ and $e = \frac{4}{3}$.

Sol. Since, vertices $(\pm\ 7,\ 0)$ lie on X-axis, as y-coordinate is zero.

So, equation of hyperbola will be of the form

$$\frac{x^2}{a^2} - \frac{y^2}{b^2} = 1 \quad \ldots\text{(i)}$$

Where it is given that vertices $(\pm\ 7,\ 0) = (\pm\ a,\ 0)$

$$a = 7 \text{ and } e = \frac{4}{3}$$

$$\because \quad e = \frac{c}{a} \text{ i.e., } c = ae \Rightarrow c = 7 \times \frac{4}{3} = \frac{28}{3}$$

Also, $\quad c^2 = a^2 + b^2$

On putting the values of $c = \frac{28}{3}$ and $a = 7$ in $c^2 = a^2 + b^2$, we get

$$\frac{784}{9} = 49 + b^2 \Rightarrow b^2 = \frac{784}{9} - \frac{49}{1} \Rightarrow b^2 = \frac{784 - 441}{9} \Rightarrow b^2 = \frac{343}{9}$$

On putting the values of $a^2 = 49$ and $b^2 = \frac{343}{9}$ in Eq. (i), we get

$$\frac{x^2}{49} - \frac{y^2}{\frac{343}{9}} = 1 \text{ or } \frac{x^2}{49} - \frac{9y^2}{343} = 1,$$

Which is required equation of hyperbola.

Question 15 Foci $(0, \pm\sqrt{10})$ passing through the point $(2, 3)$.

Sol. Since, foci $(0, \pm\ \sqrt{10})$ lie on Y-axis, as x-coordinate is zero.

So, equation of hyperbola will be of the form

$$\frac{y^2}{a^2} - \frac{x^2}{b^2} = 1 \quad \ldots\text{(i)}$$

where it is given that foci $(0, \pm\ \sqrt{10}) = (0, \pm\ c) \Rightarrow c = \sqrt{10}$.

Also hyperbola passes through the point $(2,3)$ *i.e.*, point will satisfy Eq. (i).

$$\therefore \quad \frac{(3)^2}{a^2} - \frac{(2)^2}{b^2} = 1$$

$$\Rightarrow \quad \frac{9}{a^2} - \frac{4}{b^2} = 1 \quad \ldots\text{(ii)}$$

$$\because \quad c = \sqrt{10} \Rightarrow c^2 = 10$$

$$\Rightarrow \quad a^2 + b^2 = 10 \quad (\because c^2 = a^2 + b^2)$$

$$\Rightarrow \quad b^2 = 10 - a^2 \quad \ldots\text{(iii)}$$

On putting $b^2 = 10 - a^2$ in Eq. (ii), we get $\frac{9}{a^2} - \frac{4}{10 - a^2} = 1$

$$\Rightarrow \quad \frac{90 - 9a^2 - 4a^2}{a^2(10 - a^2)} = 1$$

$$\Rightarrow \quad 90 - 13a^2 = 10a^2 - a^4$$
$$\Rightarrow \quad a^4 - 23a^2 + 90 = 0$$
$$\Rightarrow \quad a^4 - 18a^2 - 5a^2 + 90 = 0$$
$$\Rightarrow \quad a^2(a^2 - 18) - 5(a^2 - 18) = 0$$
$$\Rightarrow \quad (a^2 - 5)(a^2 - 18) = 0$$
$$\Rightarrow \quad a^2 = 5 \quad \text{or} \quad a^2 = 18$$

From Eq. (iii), if $a^2 = 5$

$$\Rightarrow \quad b^2 = 10 - 5 = 5$$

If $\quad a^2 = 18$

$$\Rightarrow \quad b^2 = 10 - 18 = -8$$

Which is not possible as $b^2 > 0$

So, $a^2 = b^2 = 5$

On putting the values of $a^2 = b^2 = 5$ in Eq. (i), we get

$$\Rightarrow \quad \frac{y^2}{5} - \frac{x^2}{5} = 1 \Rightarrow y^2 - x^2 = 5,$$

Which is required equation of hyperbola.

Miscellaneous Exercise

Question 1 If a parabolic reflector is 20 cm in diameter and 5 cm deep, find the focus.

Sol. Given depth is 5 cm, diameter is 20 cm.

Taking vertex of the parabolic reflector at origin, X-axis along the axis of parabola. The equation of the parabola is $y^2 = 4ax$.

$\because$ Point $P(5,10)$ lies on parabola.

$\therefore (10)^2 = 4a(5) \Rightarrow a = 5$

Clearly focus is at the mid-point of given diameter.

i.e., $\quad S = (5, 0)$

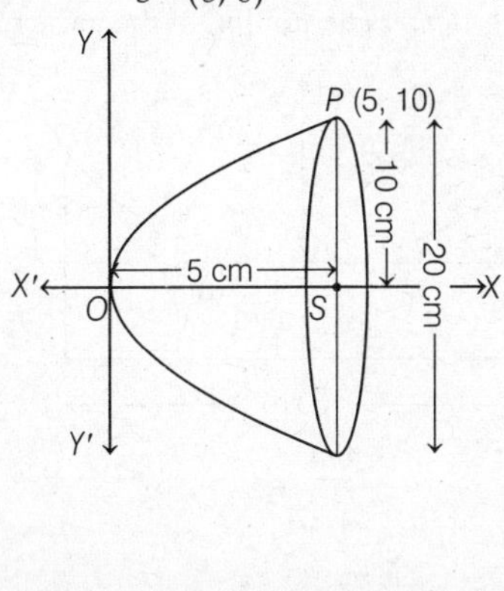

Question 2 An arch is in the form of a parabola with its axis vertical. The arch is 10 m high and 5 m wide at the base. How wide it is 2 m from the vertex of the parabola.

Sol. Since, axis is vertical, so let arch of parabola is in the form

$$x^2 = -4ay \quad \text{...(i)}$$

Given, $OB = 10$ m

and $AC = 5$ m $\Rightarrow \quad AB = \frac{5}{2}$ m $\quad (\because AC = 5)$

Hence, coordinates of $A = \left(\frac{5}{2}, -10\right)$ lies on orch will satisfy Eq. (i).

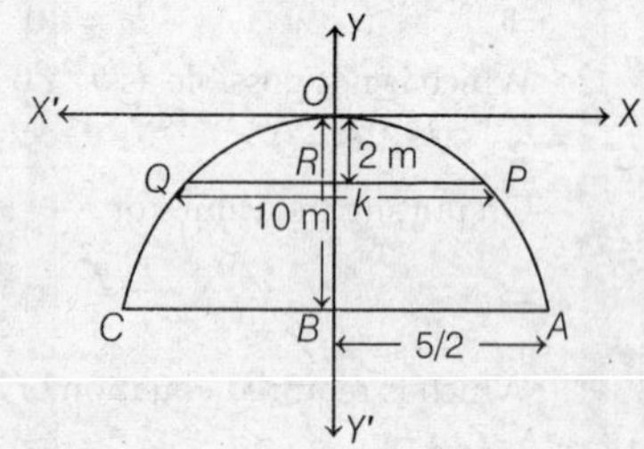

i.e., $\left(\frac{5}{2}\right)^2 = -4a \times (-10)$

$\Rightarrow \quad \frac{25}{4} = -40a \Rightarrow a = -\frac{5}{32}$

On putting the values of $a = \frac{5}{32}$ in Eq. (i),

$$x^2 = -4 \times \frac{5}{32} y \Rightarrow x^2 = -\frac{5}{8} y$$

Now, let $OR = 2$ and $PQ = k \Rightarrow RP = \frac{k}{2}$

Therefore, $P = \left(\frac{k}{2}, -2\right)$ will lies on parabola.

$\therefore \quad \left(\frac{k}{2}\right)^2 = -\frac{5}{8} \times (-2) \quad \left(\because x^2 = -\frac{5}{8} y\right)$

$\Rightarrow \quad \frac{k^2}{4} = \frac{5}{4} \Rightarrow k = \sqrt{5} = 2.23$ m (approx).

Question 3 The cable of a uniformly loaded suspension bridge hangs in the form of a parabola. The roadway which is horizontal and 100 m long is supported by vertical wires attached to the cable, the longest wire being 30 m and the shortest being 6 m. Find the length of a supporting wire attached to the roadway 18 m from the middle.

Sol. Since, wires are vertical. Let equation of the parabola is in the form

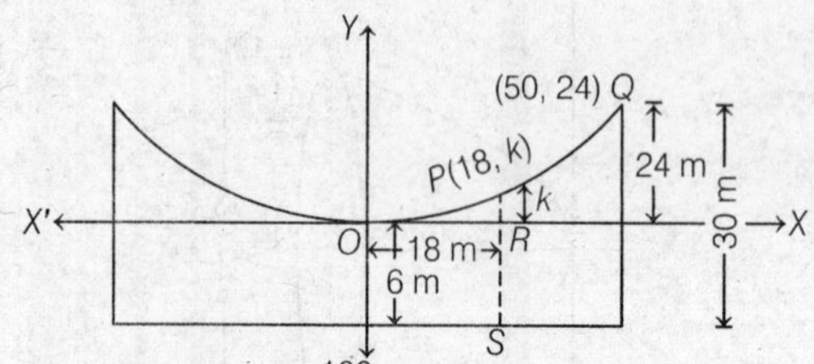

$$x^2 = 4ay \quad \text{...(i)}$$

Focus is at the middle of the cable and shortest and longest vertical supports are 6 m and 30 m and roadway is 100 m long.

Clearly, coordinate of $Q(50, 24)$ will satisfy Eq. (i)

$$\therefore \quad (50)^2 = 4a \times 24$$

$$\Rightarrow \quad 2500 = 96a \Rightarrow a = \frac{2500}{96}$$

On putting the value of $a = \frac{2500}{96}$ in Eq. (i), we get

$$x^2 = 4 \times \frac{2500}{96} y \Rightarrow x^2 = \frac{2500}{24} y$$

Let $\quad PR = k$ m

$\therefore$ Point $P(18, k)$ will satisfy the equation of parabola *i.e.*,

From Eq. (i), $(18)^2 = \frac{2500}{24} \times k$ $\quad$ [$\because OR = 18$m]

$$\Rightarrow \quad 324 = \frac{2500}{24} k \Rightarrow k = \frac{324 \times 24}{2500} = \frac{324 \times 6}{625} = \frac{1944}{625}$$

$$k = 3.11$$

$\therefore$ Required length $= 6 + k = 6 + 3.11 = 9.11$ m (approx)

Question 4 An arch is the form of a semi ellipse. It is 8 m wide and 2 m high at the centre. Find the height of the arch at a point 1.5 m from one end.

Sol. Let ABA' be the semi-elliptical arch.

Given, $AA' = 2a = 8$, $OB = b = 2$

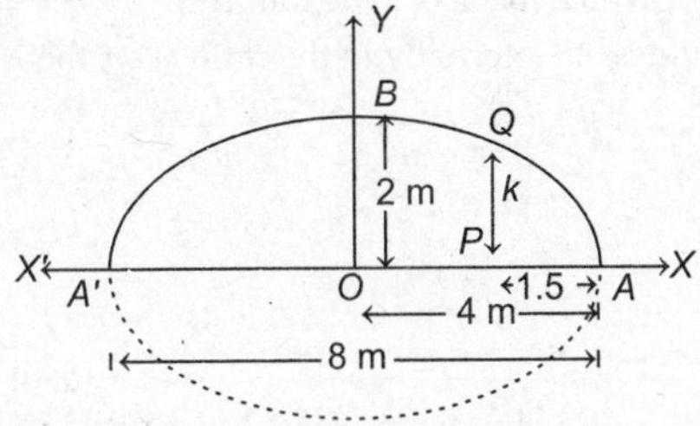

Clearly, equation of ellipse takes the form

$$\frac{x^2}{a^2} + \frac{y^2}{b^2} = 1 \quad \text{...(i)}$$

Here, it is given $\quad 2a = 8$ and $b = 2 \Rightarrow a = 4, \quad b = 2$

On putting the values of a and b in Eq. (i), we get

$$\frac{x^2}{16} + \frac{y^2}{4} = 1 \quad \text{...(ii)}$$

Given, $AP = 1.5$ m

$$\Rightarrow \quad OP = OA - AP = 4 - 1.5 \Rightarrow OP = 2.5 \text{ m}$$

Let $PQ = k$

since, point $Q(2.5, k)$ lies on elliptical arch

$\therefore Q(2.5, k)$ will satisfy the Eq. (ii)

i.e., $$\frac{(2.5)^2}{16} + \frac{k^2}{4} = 1$$

$$\Rightarrow \frac{6.25}{16} + \frac{k^2}{4} = 1 \Rightarrow \frac{k^2}{4} = \frac{1}{1} - \frac{6.25}{16} = \frac{16 - 6.25}{16}$$

$$\Rightarrow \frac{k^2}{4} = \frac{9.75}{16} \Rightarrow k^2 = \frac{9.75}{4} \Rightarrow k^2 = 2.4375$$

$$\Rightarrow k = 1.56 \text{ m (approx.)}$$

Question 5 A rod of length 12 cm moves with its ends always touching the coordinate axes. Determine the equation of the locus of a point P on the rod, which is 3 cm from the end in contact with the X-axis.

Sol. Let AB be the rod of length 12 cm.

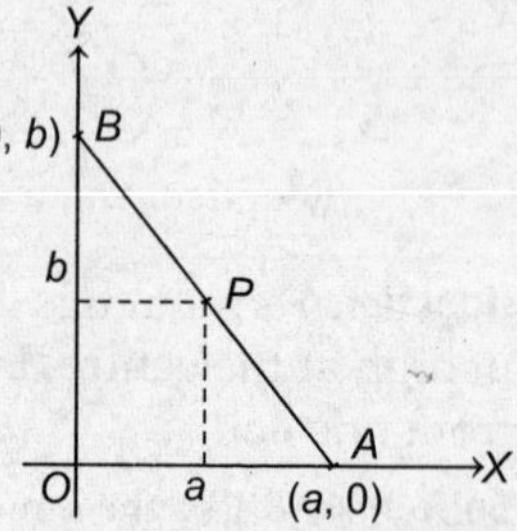

Let $OA = a$ and $OB = b$

On using Pythagoras theorem in ΔOAB, we get

$(\text{Base})^2 + (\text{Perpendicular})^2 = (\text{Hypotenuse})^2$

$$\Rightarrow a^2 + b^2 = (12)^2$$

$$\Rightarrow a^2 + b^2 = 144 \quad \ldots\text{(i)}$$

Let $AP = 3$ cm

$\Rightarrow PB = AB - AP = 12 - 3 = 9$ cm

$$\Rightarrow AP : PB = 3 : 9 = 1 : 3$$

Let $P = (h, k)$ for which locus is to be found.

$\therefore$ If $P(h, k)$ divides AB internally in the ratio $m : n$, then

$$h = \frac{mx_2 + nx_1}{m + n}, k = \frac{my_2 + ny_1}{m + n}$$

$$\therefore \quad h = \frac{1 \times 0 + 3 \times a}{1 + 3} \quad [\because m : n = 1 : 3]$$

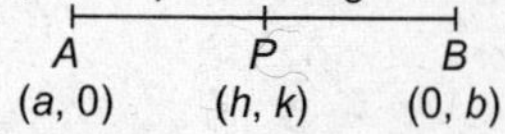

$$h = \frac{3a}{4}$$

$$a = \frac{4h}{3} \text{ and } k = \frac{1 \times b + 3 \times 0}{1 + 3} \Rightarrow k = \frac{b}{4} \Rightarrow b = 4k$$

On putting the values of $a = \frac{4h}{3}$ and $b = 4k$ in Eq. (i), we get

$$\left(\frac{4h}{3}\right)^2 + (4k)^2 = 144 \Rightarrow \frac{16h^2}{9} + 16k^2 = 144 \Rightarrow \frac{h^2}{9} + k^2 = 9 \Rightarrow \frac{h^2}{81} + \frac{k^2}{9} = 1$$

Hence, locus of a point $P(h, k)$ is $\frac{x^2}{81} + \frac{y^2}{9} = 1$

Note In locus of a point (h, k), we make a relation in h and k as per the given condition and finally, we replace h by x and k by y, we get the required result.

Question 6 Find the area of the triangle formed by the lines joining the vertex of the parabola $x^2 = 12y$ to the ends of its latus rectum.

Sol. Given, $x^2 = 12y$, which is of the form $x^2 = 4ay \Rightarrow 4a = 12 =$ Length of AB

$\therefore$ Focus $C = (0, 3)$

Clearly, latus rectum is a line perpendicular to the axes and passing through focus whose length is $4a$.

$\Rightarrow \quad OC = 3$

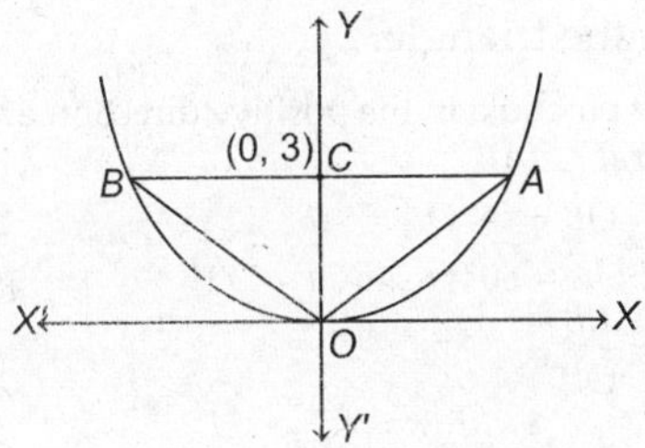

$\therefore$ Area of $\Delta OAB = \frac{1}{2} \times AB \times OC = \frac{1}{2} \times 12 \times 3 = 6 \times 3 = 18$ sq. units

$\left[\because \text{Area of triangle} = \frac{1}{2} \times \text{base} \times \text{height}\right]$

Question 7 A man running a racecourse notes that the sum of the distances from the two flag posts from him is always 10 m and the distance between the flag posts is 8 m. Find the equation of the posts traced by the man.

Sol. Clearly path traced by the man will be an ellipse.

Given, $\quad SP + S'P = 10$

i.e., $\quad 2a = 10 \Rightarrow a = 5$

The equation of the elliptical path,

$$\frac{x^2}{a^2} + \frac{y^2}{b^2} = 1$$

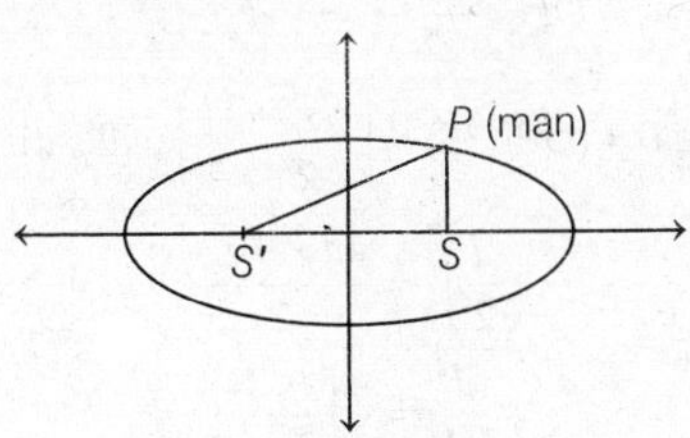

Flag posts

Since, the coordinates of S and S' are $(c, 0)$ and $(-c, 0)$. Therefore, distance between S and S', is

$$2c = 8 \Rightarrow c = 4$$

$\because \quad c^2 = a^2 - b^2$

On putting the values of $a = 5, c = 4$ in $c^2 = a^2 + b^2$, we get

$\Rightarrow \quad 16 = 25 - b^2 \Rightarrow b^2 = 25 - 16 \Rightarrow b^2 = 9 \Rightarrow b = 3$

Hence, equation of path (ellipse) is

$$\frac{x^2}{a^2} + \frac{y^2}{b^2} = 1 \Rightarrow \frac{x^2}{25} + \frac{y^2}{9} = 1 \qquad (\because a = 5, b = 3)$$

Question 8 An equilateral triangle is inscribed in the parabola $y^2 = 4ax$, where one vertex is at the vertex of the parabola. Find the length of the side of the triangle.

Sol. First, we draw the parabola in the positive direction of X-axis and inside that draw an equilateral ΔOAB.

Let $\quad OB = l = OA = AB$

$\therefore \quad \angle BOA = 60° \Rightarrow \angle BOP = 30° \qquad [\because \Delta\, AOB$ is equitateral$]$

In ΔBOP, $\sin 30° = \dfrac{PB}{OB}$

$$\Rightarrow \quad \frac{1}{2} = \frac{PB}{l} \Rightarrow PB = \frac{l}{2}$$

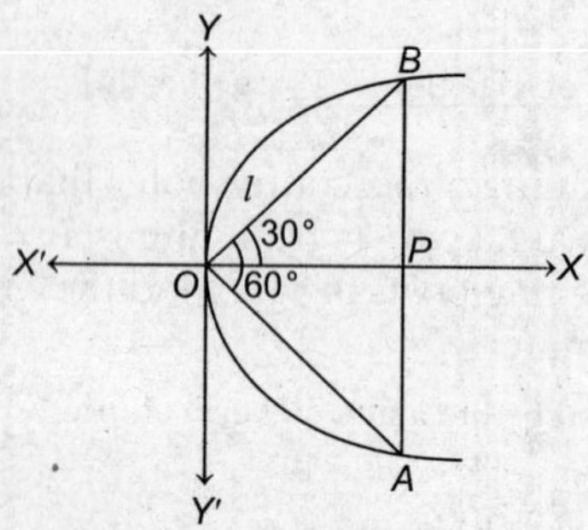

and $\cos 30° = \dfrac{OP}{OB} \Rightarrow \dfrac{\sqrt{3}}{2} = \dfrac{OP}{l}$

$$\Rightarrow \quad OP = \frac{l\sqrt{3}}{2}$$

$\therefore$ Coordinates of $B = (OP, PB) = \left(\dfrac{l\sqrt{3}}{2}, \dfrac{l}{2}\right)$ will satisfy $y^2 = 4ax$

$$\therefore \quad \left(\frac{l}{2}\right)^2 = \frac{4a \times l\sqrt{3}}{2}$$

$$\Rightarrow \quad \frac{l^2}{4} = \frac{4a\, l\sqrt{3}}{2}$$

$$\Rightarrow \quad l = 8\sqrt{3}a$$

Hence, length of side of the equilateral triangle is $8\sqrt{3}a$.

DIKSHA APP Questions

☐ Multiple Choice Questions

Q.1 The equation of directrix of the parabola $x^2 = -4ay$ is

(a) $x = a$ (b) $x = -a$
(c) $y = a$ (d) $y = -a$

Sol. (c) The equation of directrix of the parabola $x^2 = -4ay$ is $y = a$.

Q.2 The equation of the circle with center $(2, -3)$ and radius 8 is

(a) $x^2 + y^2 - 4x + 6y - 51 = 0$ (b) $x^2 + y^2 - 4x - 6y + 51 = 0$
(c) $^2 + 4x - 6y - 51 = 0$ (d) $x^2 + y^2 - 4x + 6y + 51 = 0$

Thinking Process If centre $= (h, k)$ and radius $= r$ then equation of the circle $(x - h)^2 + (y - k)^2 = r^2$

Sol. (a) Given, centre $(h, k) = (2, -3)$ and radius $(r) = 8$

$\therefore$ Equation of circle by using $(x - h)^2 + (y - k)^2 = r^2$ is

$$(x - 2)^2 + (y - (-3))^2 = (8)^2$$

$$\Rightarrow \quad (x^2 - 4x + 4) + (y^2 + 6y + 9) = 64$$

$$\Rightarrow \quad x^2 + y^2 - 4x + 6y - 51 = 0$$

Q.3 The value of eccentricity for the parabola is

(a) 1 (b) less than 1 (c) more than 1 (d) Don't have

Sol. (a) Eccentricity is defined as the ratio of the distance of the moving point P from the fixed points to its distance from a fixed line l. Draw PM perpendicular to l. Then,

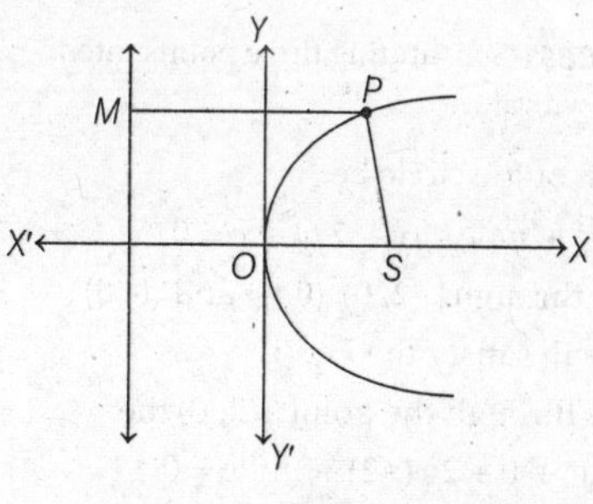

$$\text{eccentricity } (e) = \frac{PS}{PM}$$

$$\because \quad PS = PM \Rightarrow e = 1$$

Q.4 The eccentricity of $9x^2 - 16y^2 = 144$ is

(a) $\frac{2}{3}$ (b) $\frac{3}{4}$ (c) $\frac{4}{5}$ (d) $\frac{5}{4}$

◎ ***Thinking Process*** Eccentricity of a hyperbola $(e) = \frac{c}{a}$ or

$$e = \frac{\sqrt{a^2 + b^2}}{a} = \sqrt{1 + \left(\frac{b}{a}\right)^2}$$

Sol. (d) Given, $9x^2 - 16y^2 = 144$ ...(i)

On dividing Eq. (i) by 144, we get

$$\frac{9x^2}{144} - \frac{16y^2}{144} = 1$$

$$\Rightarrow \frac{x^2}{16} - \frac{y^2}{9} = 1$$

$$\Rightarrow \frac{x^2}{4^2} - \frac{y^2}{3^2} = 1 \quad \text{...(ii)}$$

On comparing Eq. (ii), with $\frac{x^2}{a^2} - \frac{y^2}{b^2} = 1$, we get

$$a^2 = 16, b^2 = 9$$

$$\because \quad e = \sqrt{1 + \frac{b^2}{a^2}} \Rightarrow e = \sqrt{1 + \frac{3^2}{4^2}} \Rightarrow e = \sqrt{1 + \frac{9}{16}} = \sqrt{\frac{25}{16}} = \frac{5}{4}$$

$$\therefore \quad e = \frac{5}{4}$$

Q.5 The centre of the circle which passes through the points (–2, 0), (0, 4) and origin is

(a) (–6, 0) (b) (–1, 3) (c) $\left(\frac{3}{2}, 5\right)$ (d) (–1, 2)

◎ ***Thinking Process*** Substituting these points into the circle's equation will give us the unknown value.

Sol. (d) Let the equation of the circle be

$$x^2 + y^2 + 2gx + 2fy + c = 0 \quad \text{... (i)}$$

∵ The circle passes through (–2, 0), (0, 4) and (0, 0)

∴ All these points will satisfy the Eq. (i)

When circle passes through the point (–2, 0) then

$$(-2)^2 + 0 + 2g(-2) + 0 + c = 0$$

$$\Rightarrow \quad -4g + c = -4 \quad \text{... (ii)}$$

When circle passes through the point (0, 4) then

$$(0)^2 + (4)^2 + 0 + 2f(4) + c = 0$$

$\Rightarrow \quad 8f + c = -16 \quad \text{... (iii)}$

When circle passes through the point (0, 0) then $0 + 0 + 0 + 0 + c = 0$

$\Rightarrow \quad c = 0$

On putting $c = 0$ in Eqs. (ii) and (iii), we get $\Rightarrow g = 1$ and $f = -2$

$\because$ centre of Eqs. (i) is $(-g, -f)$

$\therefore \quad (-g, -f) = (-1, 2)$

Hence, centre of equation (i) is $(-1, 2)$.

☐ Subjective Type Questions

Q.1 Find the vertex of the parabola $4x^2 + y = 0$

◎ *Thinking Process* First, we will convert it into standard form of parabola.

Sol. Given equation of the parabola

$$4x^2 + y = 0 \text{ i.e., } 4x^2 = -y$$

$$\Rightarrow \quad x^2 = -\frac{1}{4}y$$

Which is the form of $x^2 = -4ay$

$\because$ Vertex of $x^2 = -4ay$ is (0, 0)

$\therefore$ Vertex of given parabola is (0, 0)

Q.2 Find the equation of the circle which passes through the origin and cut off intercepts 3 and 4 on positive axes.

Sol. Let general equation of circle be

$$x^2 + y^2 + 2gx + 2fy + c = 0 \quad \text{... (i)}$$

Since, circle passes through the origin,

So, $\quad 0^2 + 0^2 + 2g(0) + 2f(0) + c = 0 \Rightarrow c = 0$

We get, $\quad x^2 + y^2 + 2gx + 2fy = 0 \quad \text{... (ii)}$

And, circle cut off the intercepts 3 and 4 on positive axes it means intersect with X-axis at (3, 0) and it intersect with Y-axis at (0, 4).

$\therefore$ Circle passes through points (3, 0) and (0, 4)

When circle passes through (3, 0), we get

$$(3)^2 + (0)^2 + 2g(3) + 2f(0) = 0 \quad [\because \text{by Eq. (ii)}]$$

$$\Rightarrow \quad 9 + 0 + 6g + 0 = 0$$

$$\Rightarrow \quad g = \frac{-9}{6} = \frac{-3}{2}$$

When circle passes through (0, 4), we get

$$(0)^2 + (4)^2 + 2g(0) + 2f(4) = 0 \quad [\because \text{by Eq. (ii)}]$$

$$\Rightarrow \quad 16 + 8f = 0 \Rightarrow f = \frac{-16}{8} = -2$$

On putting the value of g and f in Eq. (ii), we get

$$x^2 + y^2 + 2\left(\frac{-3}{2}\right)x + 2(-2)y = 0$$

$$\Rightarrow \quad x^2 + y^2 - 3x - 4y = 0$$

Note The equation of the circle passing through the origin is $x^2 + y^2 + 2gx + 2fy = 0$.

Q.3 If the eccentricity of an ellipse is $\frac{5}{8}$ and the distance between its foci is 10. Then find the length of latus rectum of the ellipse.

Sol. Given the eccentricity of an ellipse is $\frac{5}{8}$ and the distance between it's foci is 10

i.e. $e = \frac{5}{8}$ and $2c = 10 \Rightarrow c = 5$

$$\Rightarrow \frac{c}{a} = \frac{5}{8} \qquad \left[\because e = \frac{c}{a}\right]$$

$$\Rightarrow \frac{5}{a} = \frac{5}{8} \Rightarrow a = 8 \qquad [\because c = 5]$$

$$\because c^2 = a^2 - b^2, \Rightarrow 25 = 64 - b^2$$

$$\Rightarrow b^2 = 39$$

$\because$ The length of latus rectum of the ellipse $= \frac{2b^2}{a}$

$\therefore$ Length of latus rectum $= \frac{2(39)}{8} = \frac{39}{4}$

Q.4 The tower of a bridge, hung in the form of a parabola have their tops 30 m above the roadway and are 200 m apart. If the cable is 5 m above the roadway at the centre of the bridge, find the length of the vertical supporting cable 30 m from the centre.

Sol.

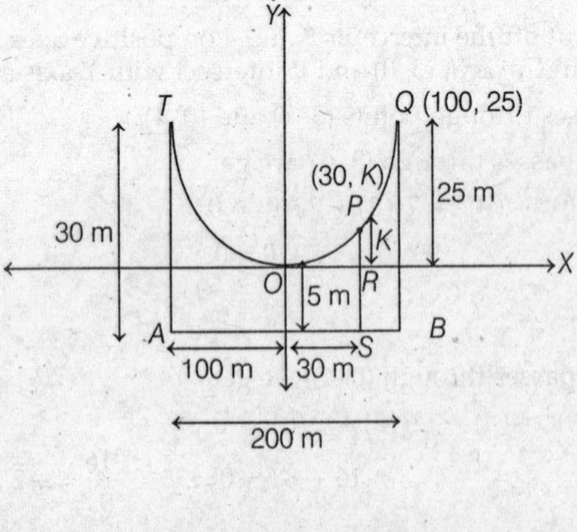

Let TOQ be the cable of the bridge and AB be the roadway.

Let O be the centre of the bridge.

From the figure, vertex of parabola is at $O(0, 0)$

Let the equation of parabola be

$$x^2 = 4ay \qquad \dots \text{(i)}$$

Since, the parabola passes through $Q(100, 25)$

So, $Q(100, 25)$ will satisfy Eq. (i)

$$(100)^2 = 4a(25) \qquad [\because x = 100, y = 25]$$

$$\Rightarrow \quad (100)^2 = 100a$$

$$\Rightarrow \quad a = 100$$

$\therefore$ from Eq. (i),

$$x^2 = 4(100)y$$

$$\Rightarrow \quad x^2 = 400y \qquad \dots \text{(ii)}$$

$\therefore$ Point $P(30, k)$ will satisfy the equation of parabola *i.e.,* from Eq. (ii)

$$(30)^2 = 400k$$

$$\Rightarrow \quad 900 = 400k \Rightarrow k = \frac{9}{4} = 2.25$$

Therefore, the required length $= PS = PR + RS = K + 5 = 2.25 + 5$

$$= 7.25 \text{ m}$$

Introduction to Three Dimensional Geometry

CHAPTER 11

Important Points

01 Coordinates of a Point in Space The coordinates of a point are the distances from the origin of the feet of the perpendiculars from the point on the respective coordinate axes.

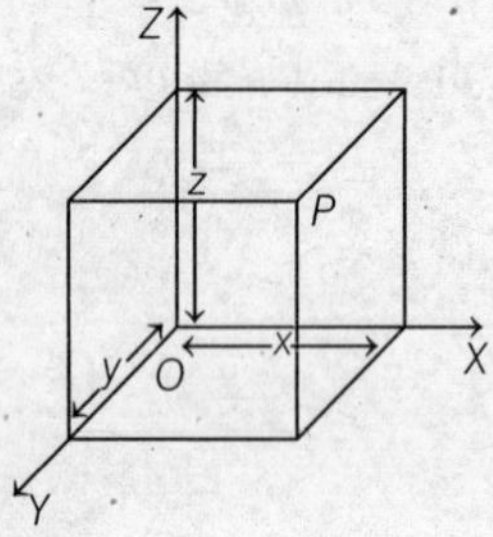

The coordinates of the origin O are (0, 0, 0). The coordinates of any point on the X-axis will be as $(x, 0, 0)$ and the coordinates of any point will be as (x, y, z). The three coordinate planes divide the space into eight parts known as octants. These octants could be named as $XOYZ$, $X'OYZ$, $X'OY'Z$, $XOY'Z$, $XOYZ'$, $X'OYZ'$, $X'OY'Z'$ and $XOY'Z'$ and denoted by I, II, III, ..., VIII, respectively. The sign of the coordinates of the point determines the octant in which the point lies.

The following table shows the signs of the coordinates in eight octants.

Coordinates \ Octants	I	II	III	IV	V	VI	VII	VIII
x	+	−	−	+	+	−	−	+
y	+	+	−	−	+	+	−	−
z	+	+	+	+	−	−	−	−

Note The coordinates of a point

- In the XY - plane : $(x, y, 0)$
- In the YZ - plane : $(0, y, z)$
- In the ZX - plane : $(x, 0, z)$

02 Distance between two Points Let $P(x_1, y_1, z_1)$ and $Q(x_2, y_2, z_2)$ be two points, then the distance between P and Q is

$$PQ = \sqrt{(x_2 - x_1)^2 + (y_2 - y_1)^2 + (z_2 - z_1)^2}$$

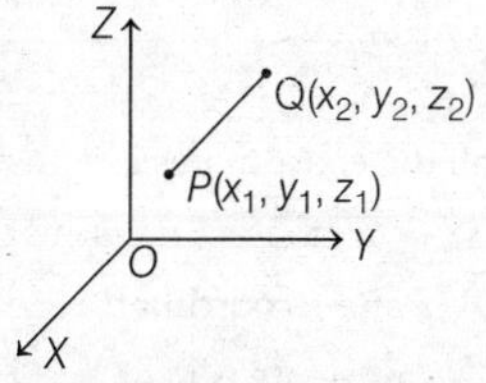

Note Points A, B and C are considered collinear if $AC = AB + BC$ or $AB = BC + CA$ or $BC = AB + CA$

03 Mid-point

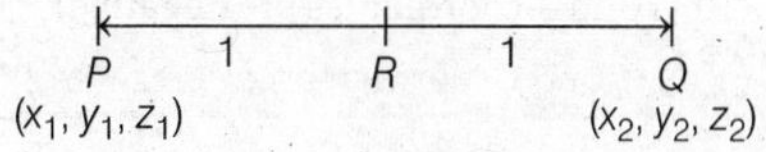

$$R = \left(\frac{x_1 + x_2}{2}, \frac{y_1 + y_2}{2}, \frac{z_1 + z_2}{2}\right)$$

04 Centroid of a Triangle The coordinates of the centroid of the triangle, whose vertices are $A(x_1, y_1, z_1)$, $B(x_2, y_2, z_2)$ and $C(x_3, y_3, z_3)$ are $\left(\frac{x_1 + x_2 + x_3}{3}, \frac{y_1 + y_2 + y_3}{3}, \frac{z_1 + z_2 + z_3}{3}\right)$.

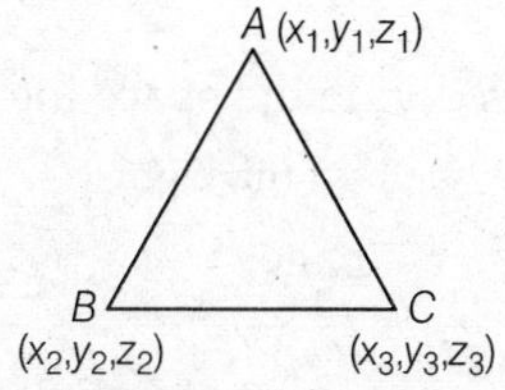

Exercise 11.1

Question 1 A point is on the X-axis. What are its y-coordinate and z-coordinate?

Sol. Coordinate of any point on the X-axis is $(x, 0, 0)$ (Because at X-axis both y and z-coordinates are zero) so its y and z-coordinates are 0.

Question 2 A point is in the XZ-plane. What can you say about its y-coordinate?

Sol. Any point on the XZ-plane will have the coordinate $(x, 0, z)$, then its y-coordinate is 0.

Question 3 Name the octants in which the following points lie;

$(1,2,3), (4,-2,3), (4,-2,-5), (4,2,-5), (-4,2,-5),$
$(-4,2,5), (-3,-1,6), (-2,-4,-7)$

Sol.

Point	Qctant	Name
$(1, 2, 3)$	I (all the coordinates are positive)	$XOYZ$
$(4, -2, 3)$	IV (y-coordinate is negative)	$XOY'Z$
$(4, -2, -5)$	VIII (y and z-coordinates are negative)	$XOY'Z'$
$(4, 2, -5)$	V (z-coordinate is negative)	$XOYZ'$
$(-4, 2, -5)$	VI (x and z-coordinates are negative)	$X'OYZ'$
$(-4, 2, 5)$	II (x-coordiante is negative)	$X'OYZ$
$(-3, -1, 6)$	III (x and y-coordinates are negative)	$X'OY'Z$
$(-2, -4, -7)$	VII (xy and z-coordiantes are negative)	$X'OY'Z'$

Mistake Alert Usually, students make error to select the right octant. So, be careful.

Question 4 Fill in the blanks.

(i) The X-axis and Y-axis taken together determine a plane known as......... .

(ii) The coordinates of a points in the XY-plane are of the form......... .

(iii) Coordinate planes divide the space into.........octants.

Sol. (i) XY-plane (ii) $(x, y, 0)$ (iii) eight

Exercise 11.2

Question 1 Find the distance between the following pairs of points

(i) $(2,3,5)$ and $(4,3,1)$ (ii) $(-3,7,2)$ and $(2,4,-1)$

(iii) $(-1,3,-4)$ and $(1,-3,4)$ (iv) $(2,-1,3)$ and $(-2,1,3)$

◎ ***Thinking Process*** The distance between two points (x_1, y_1, z_1) and (x_2, y_2, z_2) is

$$\sqrt{(x_2 - x_1)^2 + (y_2 - y_1)^2 + (z_2 - z_1)^2}$$

Sol. (i) Let the given points are $A(2, 3, 5)$ and $B(4, 3, 1)$.

$$\therefore \quad x_1 = 2,\ y_1 = 3,\ z_1 = 5$$
$$x_2 = 4,\ y_2 = 3,\ z_2 = 1$$

$\therefore$ Required distance $AB = \sqrt{(x_2 - x_1)^2 + (y_2 - y_1)^2 + (z_2 - z_1)^2}$

$$\Rightarrow \quad AB = \sqrt{(4-2)^2 + (3-3)^2 + (1-5)^2}$$
$$= \sqrt{4 + 0 + 16} = \sqrt{20} = 2\sqrt{5} \text{ units}$$

(ii) Let the given points are $A(-3, 7, 2)$ and $B(2, 4, -1)$.

Here, $x_1 = -3,\ y_1 = 7,\ z_1 = 2$

$x_2 = 2,\ y_2 = 4,\ z_2 = -1$

$\therefore$ Required distance $AB = \sqrt{(x_2 - x_1)^2 + (y_2 - y_1)^2 + (z_2 - z_1)^2}$

$$= \sqrt{[2-(-3)]^2 + (4-7)^2 + (-1-2)^2}$$
$$= \sqrt{(2+3)^2 + (4-7)^2 + (-1-2)^2}$$
$$= \sqrt{25 + 9 + 9} = \sqrt{43} \text{ units}$$

(iii) Let the given points are $A(-1, 3, -4)$ and $B(1, -3, 4)$.

$\therefore$ Required distance $AB = \sqrt{(1+1)^2 + (-3-3)^2 + (4+4)^2}$

$$= \sqrt{4 + 36 + 64} = \sqrt{104} = 2\sqrt{26} \text{ units}$$

(iv) Let the given points are $A(2, -1, 3)$ and $B(-2, 1, 3)$.

$\therefore$ Required distance

$$AB = \sqrt{(-2-2)^2 + (1+1)^2 + (3-3)^2} = \sqrt{4^2 + 2^2 + 0}$$
$$= \sqrt{16 + 4} = \sqrt{20} = 2\sqrt{5} \text{ units}$$

Question 2 Show that the points $(-2, 3, 5), (1, 2, 3)$ and $(7, 0, -1)$ are collinear.

◎ ***Thinking Process*** Three points A, B, C are said to be collinear, if $AB + BC = AC$

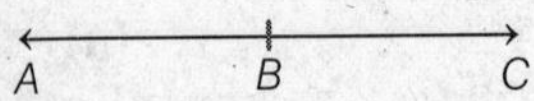

Sol. Let the given points are

$$A(-2, 3, 5), B(1, 2, 3) \text{ and } C(7, 0, -1)$$

Distance between A and B *i.e.*, $BA = \sqrt{(-2-1)^2 + (3-2)^2 + (5-3)^2}$

$$= \sqrt{(-3)^2 + (1)^2 + (2)^2}$$

$$= \sqrt{9 + 1 + 4} = \sqrt{14} \text{ units}$$

distance between B and C *i.e.*, $CB = \sqrt{(1-7)^2 + (2-0)^2 + (3+1)^2}$

$$= \sqrt{(-6)^2 + (2)^2 + (4)^2}$$

$$= \sqrt{36 + 4 + 16} = \sqrt{56} = 2\sqrt{14}$$

and distance between A and C *i.e.*, $CA = \sqrt{(-2-7)^2 + (3-0)^2 + (5+1)^2}$

$$= \sqrt{(-9)^2 + (3)^2 + (6)^2}$$

$$= \sqrt{81 + 9 + 36} = \sqrt{126} = 3\sqrt{14}$$

Clearly, $AB + BC = AC$

Hence, the given points are collinear.

Note We can consider any of the given points as A, B or C, there is no need to be confused about this.

Question 3 Verify the following.

(i) $(0, 7, -10), (1, 6, -6)$ and $(4, 9, -6)$ are the vertices of an isosceles triangle.

(ii) $(0, 7, 10), (-1, 6, 6)$ and $(-4, 9, 6)$ are the vertices of a right angled triangle.

(iii) $(-1, 2, 1), (1, -2, 5), (4, -7, 8)$ and $(2, -3, 4)$ are the vertices of a parallelogram.

◎ ***Thinking Process***

- A triangle is isosceles, if its any two sides are equal. So to prove a triangle isoceles we have to prove its two sides are equal.
- To prove a triangle a right angled triangle we have to prove that the sum of square of any two sides is equal to the square of third side.
- To prove quadrilateral, a parallelogram we have to prove that its opposite sides are equal to each other.

Sol. (i) Let $A(0, 7, -10)$, $B(1, 6, -6)$ and $C(4, 9, -6)$ are the vertices of a triangle. Then,

Side AB = distance between points A and B

$$= \sqrt{(-1-0)^2 + (6-7)^2 + (-6+10)^2}$$

$$= \sqrt{1+1+16} = \sqrt{18} = 3\sqrt{2} \text{ units}$$

and side BC = distance between points B and C

$$= \sqrt{(4-1)^2 + (9-6)^2 + (-6+6)^2}$$

$$= \sqrt{9+9+0} = \sqrt{18} = 3\sqrt{2} \text{ units}$$

Clearly, $AB = BC$. Hence, triangle is an isosceles triangle.

(ii) Let $A(0, 7, 10)$, $B(-1, 6, 6)$ and $C(-4, 9, 6)$ are the vertices of a triangle. Then,

Side $AB = \sqrt{(-1-0)^2 + (6-7)^2 + (6-10)^2}$

$\Rightarrow \quad AB = \sqrt{1+1+16} = \sqrt{18} = 3\sqrt{2}$ units

Side $BC = \sqrt{(-4+1)^2 + (9-6)^2 + (6-6)^2}$

$\Rightarrow \quad BC = \sqrt{9+9+0} = \sqrt{18} = 3\sqrt{2}$ units

and side $CA = \sqrt{(0-4)^2 + (7-9)^2 + (10-6)^2}$

$\Rightarrow \quad CA = \sqrt{16+4+16} = \sqrt{36} = 6$

Now, $AB^2 + BC^2 = (3\sqrt{2})^2 + (3\sqrt{2})^2 = 6^2 = CA^2$

$\therefore$ ΔABC is a right angled triangle at B.

(iii) Let $A(-1, 2, 1)$, $B(1, -2, 5)$, $C(4, -7, 8)$ and $D(2, -3, 4)$ are the vertices of a quadrilateral $ABCD$.

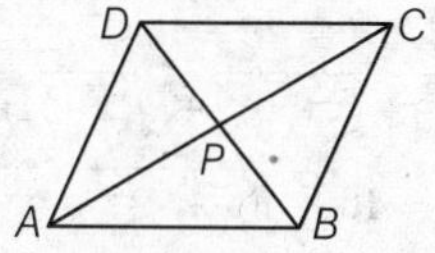

Given, let the vertices of quadrilateral $ABCD$ are $A(-1, 2, 1)$, $B(1, -2, 5)$, $C(4, -7, 8)$ and $D(2, -3, 4)$, then

Side $AB = \sqrt{(1+1)^2 + (-2-2)^2 + (5-1)^2} = \sqrt{(2)^2 + (-4)^2 + (4)^2}$

$= \sqrt{4+16+16} \Rightarrow AB = \sqrt{36} = 6$ units

Side $BC = \sqrt{(4-1)^2 + (-7+2)^2 + (8-5)^2}$

$= \sqrt{(3)^2 + (-5)^2 + (3)^2} = \sqrt{9+25+9} \Rightarrow BC = \sqrt{43}$ units

Side $CD = \sqrt{(2-4)^2 + (-3+7)^2 + (4-8)^2} = \sqrt{(-2)^2 + (4)^2 + (-4)^2}$

$= \sqrt{4+16+16} = \sqrt{36} = 6$ units

and Side $DA = \sqrt{(2+1)^2 + (-3-2)^2 + (4-1)^2} = \sqrt{(3)^2 + (-5)^2 + (3)^2}$

$= \sqrt{9+25+9} = \sqrt{43}$ units

Here, we see that $AB = CD$ and $BC = DA$.

Hence, given vertices makes a parallelogram.

Question 4 Find the equation of the set of points which are equidistant from the points $(1, 2, 3)$ and $(3, 2, -1)$.

◎ ***Thinking Process*** If P is any point in the plane which is equidistant from both the given points, then we can use the relation for equidistant of two points. $AP = BP$.

Sol. Let the given points are $A(1,2,3)$ and $B(3,2,-1)$. Let $P(x, y, z)$ be any point equidistant from A and B

$\therefore$ $PA = PB$,

i.e., distance between P and A = distance between P and B

$$\Rightarrow \sqrt{(x-1)^2 + (y-2)^2 + (z-3)^2} = \sqrt{(x-3)^2 + (y-2)^2 + (z+1)^2}$$

On squaring both sides, we get

$$\Rightarrow (x-1)^2 + (y-2)^2 + (z-3)^2 = (x-3)^2 + (y-2)^2 + (z+1)^2$$

$$\Rightarrow x^2 + 1 - 2x + y^2 + 4 - 4y + z^2 + 9 - 6z$$
$$= x^2 + 9 - 6x + y^2 + 4 - 4y + z^2 + 1 + 2z$$

$$\Rightarrow 4x - 8z = 0$$

$$\Rightarrow x - 2z = 0$$

which is the required equation.

Question 5 Find the equation of the set of points P, the sum of whose distances from $A(4, 0, 0)$ and $B(-4, 0, 0)$ and $B(-4, 0, 0)$ and is equal to 10.

Sol. Given, the two points are $A(4, 0, 0)$ and $B(-4, 0, 0)$ and let the point be $P(x, y, z)$, then it is given $PA + PB = 10$.

$$\Rightarrow \sqrt{(x-4)^2 + (y-0)^2 + (z-0)^2} + \sqrt{(x+4)^2 + (y-0)^2 + (z-0)^2} = 10$$

$$\Rightarrow \sqrt{(x-4)^2 + y^2 + z^2} = 10 - \sqrt{(x+4)^2 + y^2 + z^2}$$

On squaring both sides, we get

$$(x-4)^2 + y^2 + z^2 = 100 + (x+4)^2 + y^2 + z^2 - 20\sqrt{(x+4)^2 + y^2 + z^2}$$
$$[\because (a-b)^2 = a^2 + b^2 - 2ab]$$

$$\Rightarrow x^2 + 16 - 8x = 100 + x^2 + 16 + 8x - 20\sqrt{(x+4)^2 + y^2 + z^2}$$

$$\Rightarrow -8x - 8x - 100 = -20\sqrt{(x+4)^2 + y^2 + z^2}$$

$$\Rightarrow -16x - 100 = -20\sqrt{(x+4)^2 + y^2 + z^2} \quad \text{(dividing both sides by } -4\text{)}$$

$$\Rightarrow 4x + 25 = 5\sqrt{(x+4)^2 + y^2 + z^2}$$

Again on squaring both sides, we get

$$(4x + 25)^2 = 25[(x+4)^2 + y^2 + z^2]$$

$$\Rightarrow 16x^2 + 625 + 200x = 25[(x+4)^2 + y^2 + z^2]$$

$\Rightarrow \quad 16x^2 + 625 + 200x = 25[x^2 + 16 + 8x + y^2 + z^2]$

$\Rightarrow \quad 16x^2 + 625 + 200x = 25x^2 + 400 + 200x + 25y^2 + 25z^2$

$\Rightarrow \quad 9x^2 + 25y^2 + 25z^2 - 225 = 0$

Which is the required equation.

Miscellaneous Exercise

Question 1 Three vertices of a parallelogram *ABCD* are $A(3, -1, 2)$, $B(1, 2, -4)$ and $C(-1, 1, 2)$. Find the coordinates of the fourth vertex.

Thinking Process We can find the coordinates of the fourth vertex of the parallelogram by using the property that the diagonals of a parallelogram bisect each other.

Sol. Given, the three vertices of parallelogram *ABCD* are $A(3, -1, 2)$, $B(1, 2, -4)$ and $C(-1, 1, 2)$

Let *ABCD* be a parallelogram and coordinates of point $D(\alpha, \beta, \gamma)$ and the diagonals *AC* and *BD* intersect at *P*.

In a parallelogram, diagonals bisect each other.

$\therefore$ Coordinates of mid-point of *BD* = Coordinates of mid-point of *AC*

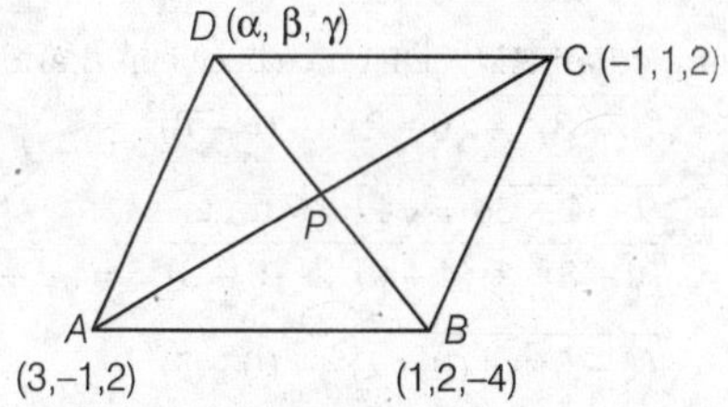

$$\Rightarrow \quad \left(\frac{\alpha+1}{2}, \frac{\beta+2}{2}, \frac{\gamma-4}{2}\right) = \left(\frac{3-1}{2}, \frac{-1+1}{2}, \frac{2+2}{2}\right)$$

$$\Rightarrow \quad \left(\frac{\alpha+1}{2}, \frac{\beta+2}{2}, \frac{\gamma-4}{2}\right) = \left(\frac{2}{2}, 0, \frac{4}{2}\right) \Rightarrow \left(\frac{\alpha+1}{2}, \frac{\beta+2}{2}, \frac{\gamma-4}{2}\right) = (1, 0, 2)$$

On comparing the corresponding coordinates, we get

$$\frac{\alpha+1}{2} = 1, \quad \frac{\beta+2}{2} = 0, \quad \frac{\gamma-4}{2} = 2$$

$$\Rightarrow \quad \alpha + 1 = 2, \quad \beta + 2 = 0, \quad \gamma - 4 = 4$$

$$\Rightarrow \quad \alpha = 1, \quad \beta = -2, \quad \gamma = 8$$

$\therefore$ Coordinates of point *D* are $(1, -2, 8)$.

Question 2 Find the length of the medians of the triangle with vertices $A(0,0,6)$, $B(0,4,0)$ and $C(6,0,0)$.

◎ *Thinking Process* We can find the length of the medians by using the property that the medians of triangle bisect the opposite sides.

Sol. Given, ABC is a triangle with vertices $A(0, 0, 6)$, $B(0, 4, 0)$ and $C(6, 0, 0)$.

Let Points D, E and F are the mid-points of BC, AC and AB, respectively. So, AD, BE and CF will be the medians of the triangle.

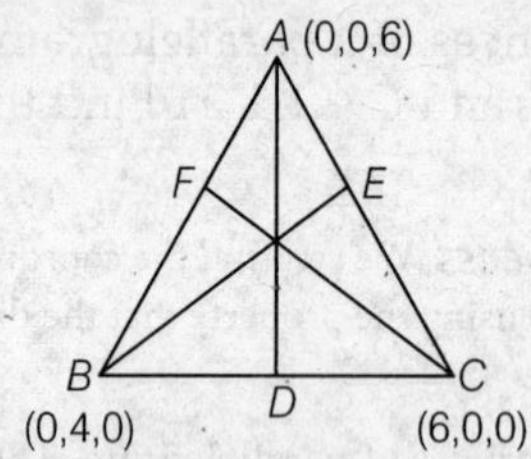

Coordinates of point $D = \left(\frac{0+6}{2}, \frac{4+0}{2}, \frac{0+0}{2}\right) = (3, 2, 0)$

Coordinates of point $E = \left(\frac{0+6}{2}, \frac{0+0}{2}, \frac{6+0}{2}\right) = (3, 0, 3)$

and coordinates of point $F = \left(\frac{0+0}{2}, \frac{0+4}{2}, \frac{6+0}{2}\right) = (0, 2, 3)$

Now, Length of median AD = Distance between A and D

$$AD = \sqrt{(0-3)^2 + (0-2)^2 + (6-0)^2}$$

$$= \sqrt{9 + 4 + 36} = \sqrt{49} = 7 \text{ units}$$

Similarly, $BE = \sqrt{(0-3)^2 + (4-0)^2 + (0-3)^2} = \sqrt{9 + 16 + 9} = \sqrt{34}$ units

and $CF = \sqrt{(6-0)^2 + (0-2)^2 + (0-3)^2}$

$$= \sqrt{36 + 4 + 9} = \sqrt{49} = 7 \text{ units}$$

Question 3 If the origin is the centroid of the triangle PQR with vertices $P(2a, 2, 6)$, $Q(-4, 3b, -10)$ and $R(8, 14, 2c)$, then find the values of a, b and c.

Sol. Given, PQR is a triangle with vertices $A(2a, 2, 6)$, $Q(-4, 3b, -10)$ and $R(8, 14, 2c)$.

Centroid of the ΔPQR is $\left(\frac{x_1 + x_2 + x_3}{3}, \frac{y_1 + y_2 + y_3}{3}, \frac{z_1 + z_2 + z_3}{3}\right)$

i.e., $\left(\frac{2a - 4 + 8}{3}, \frac{2 + 3b + 14}{3}, \frac{6 - 10 + 2c}{3}\right)$

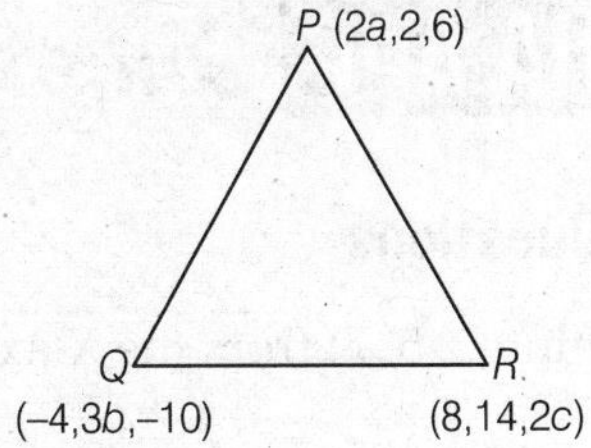

Since, origin is the centroid *i.e.*, the coordinates of the centroid are (0, 0, 0), then

$$\frac{2a-4+8}{3}=0$$

$\Rightarrow \quad 2a+4=0 \Rightarrow a=-2$

Also, $$\frac{2+3b+14}{3}=0$$

$\Rightarrow \quad 3b+16=0$

$\Rightarrow \quad b=-\frac{16}{3}$

And $$\frac{6-10+2c}{3}=0$$

$\Rightarrow \quad 2c-4=0$

$\Rightarrow \quad c=2$

$\therefore \quad a=-2,\ b=\frac{-16}{3},\ c=2$

Question 4 If A and B be the points (3, 4, 5) and (–1, 3, –7), respectively, find the equation of the set of points P such that $(PA)^2+(PB)^2=K^2$, where K is a constant.

Sol. Given, the two points $A(3, 4, 5)$ and $B(-1, 3, -7)$

Let the point P is (x, y, z).

We have, $(PA)^2+(PB)^2=K^2$

$\Rightarrow \quad (x-3)^2+(y-4)^2+(z-5)^2+(x+1)^2+(y-3)^2+(z+7)^2=K^2$

$\Rightarrow \quad x^2+9-6x+y^2+16-8y+z^2+25-10z+x^2+1+2x+y^2+9$
$-6y+z^2+49+14z=K^2$

$\Rightarrow \quad 2x^2+2y^2+2z^2-4x-14y+4z+109-K^2=0$

$\Rightarrow \quad 2(x^2+y^2+z^2)-4x-14y+4z+109-K^2=0$

Which is the required equation.

DIKSHA APP Questions

☐ Multiple Choice Questions

Q.1 The distance of point (2, 5, 7) from the X-axis is

(a) 2 (b) $\sqrt{74}$
(c) $\sqrt{29}$ (d) $\sqrt{53}$

◎ ***Thinking Process*** The foot of perpendicular from (x_1, y_1, z_1) on x-axis is $(x_1, 0, 0)$

Sol. (b) The foot of perpendicular from (2, 5, 7) on X-axis is (2, 0, 0)

∵ Minimum distance between (2, 5, 7) and X-axis is equal to distance between (2, 5, 7) and (2, 0, 0).

$$\text{So, distance } = \sqrt{(2-2)^2 + (5-0)^2 + (7-0)^2}$$
$$= \sqrt{0^2 + 5^2 + 7^2} = \sqrt{25 + 49}$$
$$= \sqrt{74} \text{ units}$$

Note The distance between (x_1, y_1, z_1) and the X-axis is $\sqrt{y_1^2 + z_1^2}$.

Q.2 The perpendicular distance of $A(6, 7, 8)$ from xy-plane is

(a) 6 (b) 7
(c) 8 (d) 9

Sol. (c) The foot of perpendicular from $A(6, 7, 8)$ on xy-plane is (6, 7, 0)

∵ The minimum distance between (6, 7, 8) and xy-plane is equal to the distance between (6, 7, 8) and (6, 7, 0)

$$\text{So, required distance} = \sqrt{(6-6)^2 + (7-7)^2 + (8-0)^2}$$
$$= \sqrt{0 + 0 + 64} = 8 \text{ units}$$

Note The distance between (x_1, y_1, z_1) and xy-plane is $|z_1|$.

☐ Subjective Type Questions

Q.1 What are the coordinates of any point on Z-axis?

Sol. $(0, 0, z)$

Q.2 What are the coordinates of any point in the yz-plane?

Sol. $(0, y, z)$

Q.3 Find the distance of the point (3, 4, 5) from the origin.

Sol. The distance between (0, 0, 0) and (3, 4, 5)

$$= \sqrt{(3-0)^2 + (4-0)^2 + (5-0)^2)}$$

$$[\because \sqrt{(x_2 - x_1)^2 + (y_2 - y_1)^2 + (z_2 - z_1)^2}]$$

$$= \sqrt{(3^2 + 4^2 + 5^2)} = \sqrt{9 + 16 + 25}$$

$$= \sqrt{50}$$

$$= 5\sqrt{2} \text{ units}$$

Q.4 If the distance of the point (2, 1, k) from the origin is 3, then find k.

Sol. The distance between (2, 1 k) and (0, 0, 0) is 3.

i.e., $\sqrt{(2-0)^2 + (1-0)^2 + (k-0)^2} = 3$

$$[\because \sqrt{(x_2 - x_1)^2 + (y_2 - y_1)^2 + (z_2 - z_1)^2}]$$

On squaring both sides, we get

$$2^2 + 1^2 + k^2 = 3^2$$

$$\Rightarrow \quad 4 + 1 + k^2 = 9$$

$$\Rightarrow \quad k^2 = 4$$

$$\Rightarrow \quad k = \pm 2$$

Q.5 Find the coordinates of the mid-point of the line joining the points (1, −2,1) and (−3, 8, 3).

◎ **Thinking Process** The mid-point of (x_1, y_1, z_1) and (x_2, y_2, z_2) is $\left(\frac{x_1 + x_2}{2}, \frac{y_1 + y_2}{2}, \frac{z_1 + z_2}{2}\right)$

Sol. Given, the two points are (1, − 2, 1) and (−3, 8, 3)

The mid-point of (1, − 2, 1) and (−3, 8, 3)

$$= \left(\frac{1 + (-3)}{2}, \frac{-2 + 8}{2}, \frac{1 + 3}{2}\right) = (-1, 3, 2)$$

Limits and Derivatives

CHAPTER 12

Important Points

01 Limit

Left Hand Limit (LHL)

$\lim_{x \to a^-} f(x)$ is the expected value of $f(x)$ at $x = a$, given the values of $f(x)$ near x to the left of a. This value is called the left hand limit of $f(x)$ at a.

Right Hand Limit (RHL)

$\lim_{x \to a^+} f(x)$ is the expected value of $f(x)$ at $x = a$, given the values of $f(x)$ near x to the right of a. This value is called the right hand limit of $f(x)$ at a.

Note If the right and left hand limits coincide, we call that common value as the limit of $f(x)$ at $x = a$ and denote it by $\lim_{x \to a} f(x)$.

or

If the value of RHL and LHL are equal, then we says that limit exists.

02 **Algebra of Limits** Let f and g be two functions such that both $\lim_{x \to a} f(x)$ and $\lim_{x \to a} g(x)$ exist. Then,

(i) Limit of sum of two functions is sum of limits of the functions, *i.e.*,

$$\lim_{x \to a} [f(x) + g(x)] = \lim_{x \to a} f(x) + \lim_{x \to a} g(x)$$

(ii) Limit of difference of two functions is difference of the limits of the functions *i.e.*,

$$\lim_{x \to a} [f(x) - g(x)] = \lim_{x \to a} f(x) - \lim_{x \to a} g(x)$$

(iii) Limit of product of two functions is product of the limits of the functions,

i.e., $\lim_{x \to a} [f(x) \cdot g(x)] = \lim_{x \to a} f(x) \cdot \lim_{x \to a} g(x)$

(iv) Limit of a quotient of two functions is quotient of the limits of the functions (whenever denominator is non-zero)

i.e., $$\lim_{x \to a} \frac{f(x)}{g(x)} = \frac{\lim_{x \to a} f(x)}{\lim_{x \to a} g(x)}$$

Note $\lim_{x\to a}[(\lambda . f)(x)] = \lambda \lim_{x\to a} f(x)$, where λ is a constant.

- **Limit of polynomial** Let $f(x) = a_0 + a_1x + a_2x^2 + \ldots + a_nx^n$ be a polynomial function then, $\lim_{x \to a} f(x) = \lim_{x \to a} [a_0 + a_1x + a_2x^2 + \ldots + a_nx^n] = f(a)$

- **Limit of Rational function** A function f is said to be a rational function, if $f(x) = \frac{g(x)}{h(x)}$, where $g(x)$ and $h(x)$ are polynomials such that $h(x) \neq 0$.

  Then, $\lim_{x \to a} f(x) = \lim_{x \to a} \frac{g(x)}{h(x)} = \frac{\lim_{x \to a} g(x)}{\lim_{x \to a} h(x)} = \frac{g(a)}{h(a)}$

  If $h(a) = 0$, then there are two cases
  (i) When $g(a) \neq 0$ then we can say that limit does not exist.
  (ii) When $g(a) = 0$, then
  We can write as

  $$g(x) = (x - a)^k p(x) \text{ and } h(x) = (x - a)^l q(x)$$
  $$\lim_{x \to a} f(x) = \frac{\lim_{x \to a} (x - a)^k p(x)}{\lim_{x \to a} (x - a)^l q(x)} = \frac{\lim_{x \to a} (x - a)^{k - l} p(x)}{\lim_{x \to a} q(x)}$$

  (a) If $k > l$, then $\lim_{x \to a} f(x) = 0$
  (b) If $k = l$, then $\lim_{x \to a} f(x) = \frac{p(a)}{q(a)}$
  (c) If $k < l$, then the limit is not defined

03 (i) For any positive integer n, $\lim_{x \to a} \frac{x^n - a^n}{x - a} = na^{n-1}$

Note The limit is true even if n is any rational number and a is positive.

(ii) $\lim_{x \to 0} \frac{\sin x}{x} = 1$ or $\lim_{x \to 0} \frac{x}{\sin x} = 1$

(iii) $\lim_{x \to 0} \frac{\tan x}{x} = 1$

(iv) $\lim_{x \to 0} \frac{1 - \cos x}{x} = 0$

(v) Let f and g be two real valued functions with the same domain such that $f(x) \le g(x)$ for all x in the domain of definition. For some a, if both $\lim_{x \to a} f(x)$ and $\lim_{x \to a} g(x)$ exist, then

$$\lim_{x \to a} f(x) \le \lim_{x \to a} g(x)$$

(vi) Sandwich theorem: Let f, g and h be real functions such that $f(x) \le g(x) \le h(x)$ for all x in the common domain of definition. For same real number a, if $\lim_{x \to a} f(x) = l = \lim_{x \to a} h(x)$, then $\lim_{x \to a} g(x) = l$.

04 Derivatives Suppose f is a real valued function, the function defined by $\lim_{h \to 0} \dfrac{f(x+h) - f(x)}{h}$, wherever the limit exists is defined to be the derivative of f at x and is denoted by $f'(x)$. This definition of derivative is also called the first principle of derivative.

Thus, $f'(x) = \lim_{h \to 0} \dfrac{f(x+h) - f(x)}{h}$.

Sometimes $f'(x)$ is denoted by $\dfrac{d}{dx}[f(x)]$ or if $y = f(x)$, it is denoted by $\dfrac{dy}{dx}$. This is referred to as derivative of $f(x)$ or y w.r.t. x. It is also denoted by $D[f(x)]$. Further the derivative of f at $x = a$ is also denoted by $\dfrac{d}{dx} f(x)\Big|_a$

or $\dfrac{df}{dx}\Big|_a$ or $\left(\dfrac{df}{dx}\right)_{x=a}$

05 Algebra of Derivative of Functions Let f and g be two functions such that their derivatives are defined in a common domain. Then,

(i) Derivative of sum of two functions is sum of the derivatives of the functions.

i.e., $$\frac{d}{dx}[f(x) + g(x)] = \frac{d}{dx} f(x) + \frac{d}{dx} g(x)$$

(ii) Derivative of difference of two functions is the difference of the derivatives of two functions.

i.e., $$\frac{d}{dx}[f(x) - g(x)] = \frac{d}{dx} f(x) - \frac{d}{dx} g(x)$$

(iii) Derivative of product of two functions is given by the following product rule:

$$\frac{d}{dx}[f(x)\cdot g(x)] = f(x)\cdot\frac{d}{dx}g(x) + g(x)\cdot\frac{d}{dx}f(x)$$

or $$(uv)' = uv' + vu'$$

(iv) Derivative of quotient of two functions is given by the following quotient rule (whenever the denominator is non-zero.)

$$\frac{d}{dx}\left[\frac{f(x)}{g(x)}\right] = \frac{g(x)\cdot\frac{d}{dx}f(x) - f(x)\cdot\frac{d}{dx}g(x)}{[g(x)]^2}$$

or $$\left(\frac{u}{v}\right)' = \frac{vu' - uv'}{v^2}$$

06 Standard Derivatives

(i) $y = x^n$, $\frac{dy}{dx} = nx^{n-1}$

(ii) $y = \text{constant}$, $\frac{dy}{dx} = 0$

(iii) $y = e^x$, $\frac{dy}{dx} = e^x$

(iv) $y = a^x$, $\frac{dy}{dx} = a^x \log_e a$

(v) $y = \log_e x$, $\frac{dy}{dx} = \frac{1}{x}$

(vi) $y = \sin x$, $\frac{dy}{dx} = \cos x$

(vii) $y = \cos x$, $\frac{dy}{dx} = -\sin x$

(viii) $y = \tan x$, $\frac{dy}{dx} = \sec^2 x$

(ix) $y = \sec x$, $\frac{dy}{dx} = \sec x \tan x$

(x) $y = \operatorname{cosec} x$, $\frac{dy}{dx} = -\operatorname{cosec} x \cot x$

(xi) $y = \cot x$, $\frac{dy}{dx} = -\operatorname{cosec}^2 x$

Derivative of Polynomials

Let $f(x) = a_n x^n + a_{n-1}x^{n-1} + ... + a_1 x + a_0$ be a polynomial function where a_i' s are *all* real numbers and $a_n \neq 0$. Then, the derivatives function is given by

$$\frac{df(x)}{dx} = na_n x^{n-1} + (n-1)a_{n-1}x^{n-2} + ... + 2a_2 x + a_1$$

Exercise 12.1

Direction (Q. No. 1 to 22) Evaluate the following limits.

◎ ***Thinking Process*** (For Q. No. 1 to 5) We will put the limit directly in the given function.

Question 1 $\lim_{x \to 3} x+3$

Sol. We have, $\lim_{x \to 3} x + 3 = 3 + 3 = 6$

Question 2 $\lim_{x \to \pi} \left(x - \frac{22}{7}\right)$

Sol. We have, $\lim_{x \to \pi} \left(x - \frac{22}{7}\right) = \pi - \frac{22}{7}$

Question 3 $\lim_{r \to 1} \pi r^2$

Sol. We have, $\lim_{r \to 1} \pi r^2 = \pi \times (1)^2 = \pi$

Question 4 $\lim_{x \to 4} \frac{4x+3}{x-2}$

Sol. We have, $\lim_{x \to 4} \frac{4x + 3}{x - 2} = \frac{4 \times 4 + 3}{4 - 2} = \frac{19}{2}$

Question 5 $\lim_{x \to -1} \frac{x^{10} + x^5 + 1}{x-1}$

Sol. We have, $\lim_{x \to -1} \frac{x^{10} + x^5 + 1}{x - 1} = \frac{(-1)^{10} + (-1)^5 + 1}{-1-1} = \frac{1-1+1}{-2} = \frac{-1}{2}$

Question 6 $\lim_{x \to 0} \frac{(x+1)^5 - 1}{x}$

◎ ***Thinking Process*** Here, we cannot put the limit directly in the given function as it is of the term $\left(\frac{0}{0}\right)$. Here, we will use $\lim_{x \to 0} \frac{x^n - a^n}{x - a} = na^{n-1}$

Sol. We have, $\lim_{x \to 0} \frac{(x + 1)^5 - 1}{x} \left(\frac{0}{0} \text{ form}\right)$

Let $x + 1 = h$, When $x \to 0$, then $h \to 1$

$$\therefore \quad \lim_{h \to 1} \frac{h^5 - 1}{h - 1} = \lim_{h \to 1} \frac{h^5 - 1^5}{h - 1} = \lim_{h \to 1} 5(h)^{5-1} = 5 \times 1^4 = 5$$

Mistake Alert Students should not forget to change the limit.

Quick Solution

$$\lim_{x\to 0}\frac{(x+1)^5-1}{x}=\lim_{x\to 0}\frac{(1+x)^5-1}{x}$$

$$=\lim_{x\to 0}\frac{[(1+5x+10x^2+10x^3+5x^4+x^5)-1]}{x}$$

$[\because (1+x)^n = {}^nC_0x^0 + {}^nC_1x^1 + {}^nC_2x^2 + \ldots + {}^nC_nx^n$, where n is an integer$]$

$$=\lim_{x\to 0}\frac{(5x+10x^2+10x^3+5x^4+x^5)}{x}$$

$$=\lim_{x\to 0}\frac{x[5+10x+10x^2+5x^3+x^4]}{x}$$

$$=\lim_{x\to 0}[5+10x+10x^2+5x^3+x^4]$$

$$=5+10(0)+10(0)^2+5(0)^3+(0)^4=5$$

Question 7 $\lim_{x\to 2}\dfrac{3x^2-x-10}{x^2-4}$

◎ ***Thinking Process*** It is not directly solvable by putting the value of $x = 2$. Firstly, factorize the numerator and denominator by splitting the middle term and cancel the common factor and put the value of x.

Sol. We have, $\lim_{x\to 2}\dfrac{3x^2-x-10}{x^2-4}\left(\dfrac{0}{0}\text{ form}\right)$

$$\lim_{x\to 2}\frac{3x^2-(6-5)x-10}{(x-2)(x+2)}=\lim_{x\to 2}\frac{3x^2-6x+5x-10}{(x-2)(x+2)}$$

$$=\lim_{x\to 2}\frac{3x(x-2)+5(x-2)}{(x-2)(x+2)}$$

$$=\lim_{x\to 2}\frac{(x-2)(3x+5)}{(x-2)(x+2)}=\lim_{x\to 2}\frac{3x+5}{x+2}$$

$$=\frac{3\times 2+5}{2+2}=\frac{6+5}{4}=\frac{11}{4}$$

Note The common factors will be cancelled only in the limit. But in a function, we do not cancel directly until it is in an indeterminate form.

Question 8 $\lim\limits_{x \to 3} \dfrac{x^4 - 81}{2x^2 - 5x - 3}$.

Sol. We have, $\lim\limits_{x \to 3} \dfrac{x^4 - 81}{2x^2 - 5x - 3}$ $\left(\dfrac{0}{0} \text{ form}\right)$

$$= \lim_{x \to 3} \frac{(x^2 - 9)(x^2 + 9)}{2x^2 - 6x + x - 3} \quad [\because a^2 - b^2 = (a + b)(a - b)]$$

$$= \lim_{x \to 3} \frac{(x - 3)(x + 3)(x^2 + 9)}{2x(x - 3) + 1(x - 3)} = \lim_{x \to 3} \frac{(x - 3)(x + 3)(x^2 + 9)}{(x - 3)(2x + 1)}$$

$$= \lim_{x \to 3} \frac{(x + 3)(x^2 + 9)}{2x + 1} = \frac{(3 + 3)(3^2 + 9)}{2 \times 3 + 1} = \frac{6 \times 18}{7} = \frac{108}{7}$$

Question 9 $\lim\limits_{x \to 0} \dfrac{ax + b}{cx + 1}$

Sol. We have, $\lim\limits_{x \to 0} \dfrac{ax + b}{cx + 1} = \dfrac{a \times 0 + b}{c \times 0 + 1} = \dfrac{b}{1} = b$

Question 10 $\lim\limits_{z \to 1} \dfrac{z^{1/3} - 1}{z^{1/6} - 1}$

◎ ***Thinking Process*** It is easy to solve by using the result.

$$\lim_{x \to a} \frac{x^n - a^n}{x - a} = na^{n-1}$$

Sol. We have, $\lim\limits_{z \to 1} \dfrac{z^{1/3} - 1}{z^{1/6} - 1} = \lim\limits_{z \to 1} \dfrac{z^{1/3} - 1}{z - 1} \times \dfrac{z - 1}{z^{1/6} - 1} = \lim\limits_{z \to 1} \dfrac{\left(\dfrac{z^{1/3} - 1}{z - 1}\right)}{\left(\dfrac{z^{1/6} - 1}{z - 1}\right)}$

$$= \frac{\lim\limits_{z \to 1}\left(\dfrac{z^{1/3} - 1}{z - 1}\right)}{\lim\limits_{z \to 1}\left(\dfrac{z^{1/6} - 1}{z - 1}\right)} = \frac{\left(\dfrac{1}{3}\right)(1)^{\frac{1}{3} - 1}}{\left(\dfrac{1}{6}\right)(1)^{\frac{1}{6} - 1}} = \frac{6}{3} \times 1 = 2 \left[\because \lim_{z \to 1} \frac{x^n - a^n}{x - a} = na^{n-1}\right]$$

Question 11 $\lim\limits_{x \to 1} \dfrac{ax^2 + bx + c}{cx^2 + bx + a}$, $a + b + c \neq 0$

Sol. We have, $\lim\limits_{x \to 1} \dfrac{ax^2 + bx + c}{cx^2 + bx + a} = \dfrac{a \times (1)^2 + b \times 1 + c}{c \times (1)^2 + b \times 1 + a} = \dfrac{a + b + c}{c + b + a} = 1$

Mistake Alert If $a + b + c = 0$, then given limit is of form 0/0, which is not determined.

Question 12 $\lim\limits_{x \to -2} \dfrac{\frac{1}{x} + \frac{1}{2}}{x+2}$.

Sol. We have, $\lim\limits_{x \to -2} \dfrac{\frac{1}{x} + \frac{1}{2}}{x+2}$

$$\Rightarrow \lim_{x \to -2} \frac{(2+x)}{2x\,(x+2)} = \lim_{x \to -2} \frac{1}{2x} = \frac{1}{2(-2)} = -\frac{1}{4}$$

Question 13 $\lim\limits_{x \to 0} \dfrac{\sin ax}{bx}$.

◎ *Thinking Process* (For Q. 13 to 15) Here, we will convert given limit into a standard form and use the result $\lim\limits_{x \to 0} \dfrac{\sin x}{x}$ or $\lim\limits_{x \to 0} \dfrac{x}{\sin x} = 1$.

Sol. We have, $\lim\limits_{x \to 0} \dfrac{\sin ax}{bx} = \lim\limits_{x \to 0} \dfrac{(a) \sin ax}{b\,(ax)}$ (On dividing and multiplying by a)

$$= \frac{a}{b} \times 1 = \frac{a}{b} \qquad \left(\because \lim_{x \to 0} \frac{\sin ax}{ax} = 1\right)$$

Mistake Alert Don't make this type of mistake $\lim\limits_{x \to 0} \dfrac{a \sin ax}{ax} = 1$, correct limit is $\lim\limits_{x \to 0} \dfrac{\sin ax}{x} = a$

Question 14 $\lim\limits_{x \to 0} \dfrac{(a) \sin ax}{\sin bx}$, $a, b \neq 0$

Sol. We have, $\lim\limits_{x \to 0} \dfrac{\sin ax}{\sin bx}$

On multiplying and dividing by $(ax)\,(bx)$, we get

$$= \lim_{x \to 0} \frac{\sin ax}{ax} \times \frac{bx}{\sin bx} \times \frac{ax}{bx} = 1 \times 1 \times \frac{a}{b} = \frac{a}{b} \qquad \left(\because \lim_{x \to 0} \frac{\sin x}{x} = \lim_{x \to 0} \frac{x}{\sin x} = 1\right)$$

Question 15 $\lim\limits_{x \to \pi} \dfrac{\sin(\pi - x)}{\pi\,(\pi - x)}$.

Sol. We have, $\lim\limits_{x \to \pi} \dfrac{\sin(\pi - x)}{\pi\,(\pi - x)}$

Let $\pi - x = h$

when $x \to \pi$, then $h \to 0$

$$\Rightarrow \lim_{h \to 0} \frac{\sin h}{\pi h} = \lim_{h \to 0} \frac{1}{\pi} \times \frac{\sin h}{h} = \frac{1}{\pi} \times 1 = \frac{1}{\pi} \qquad \left(\because \lim_{h \to 0} \frac{\sin h}{h} = 1\right)$$

Question 16 $\lim\limits_{x \to 0} \dfrac{\cos x}{\pi - x}$.

Sol. We have, $\lim\limits_{x \to 0} \dfrac{\cos x}{\pi - x}$

On putting the value of limit, we get

$$\frac{\cos 0}{\pi - 0} = \frac{1}{\pi} \qquad (\because \cos 0 = 1)$$

Question 17 $\lim\limits_{x \to 0} \dfrac{\cos 2x - 1}{\cos x - 1}$.

◎ ***Thinking Process*** When we put the limit, it is an indeterminate form. Firstly, we will use the formula $1 - \cos 2x = 2\sin^2 x$ and simplify it and put the limit.

Sol. We have, $\lim\limits_{x \to 0} \dfrac{\cos 2x - 1}{\cos x - 1} = \lim\limits_{x \to 0} \dfrac{1 - \cos 2x}{1 - \cos x}$

$$= \lim_{x \to 0} \frac{2\sin^2 x}{2\sin^2 \frac{x}{2}} \quad \left(\because 1 - \cos 2x = 2\sin^2 x \text{ and } 1 - \cos x = 2\sin^2 \frac{x}{2}\right)$$

On multiplying and dividing by x^2 and then multiplying by $\frac{4}{4}$ in the numerator.

$$= \lim_{x \to 0} \frac{\sin^2 x}{x^2} \times \frac{4 \times \frac{x^2}{4}}{\sin^2 \frac{x}{2}} = \lim_{x \to 0} \left(\frac{\sin x}{x}\right)^2 \times \left(\frac{\frac{x}{2}}{\sin \frac{x}{2}}\right)^2 \times 4 = 1 \times 1 \times 4 = 4$$

$$\left[\because \lim_{x \to 0} (f(x))^n = \left(\lim_{x \to a} f(x)\right)^n\right]$$

Question 18 $\lim\limits_{x \to 0} \dfrac{ax + x\cos x}{b \sin x}$.

Sol. We have, $\lim\limits_{x \to 0} \dfrac{ax + x\cos x}{b \sin x}$

On dividing each term by x, we get

$$= \lim_{x \to 0} \frac{\frac{ax}{x} + \frac{x\cos x}{x}}{\frac{b \sin x}{x}} = \lim_{x \to 0} \frac{a + \cos x}{b\left(\frac{\sin x}{x}\right)} = \lim_{x \to 0} (a + \cos x)$$

$$= \frac{a + \cos 0}{b \times 1} = \frac{a+1}{b} \qquad \left(\because \lim_{x \to 0} \frac{\sin x}{x} = 1\right)$$

Mistake Alert In most of the times, when we put the limit, it becomes an indeterminate form. Firstly, simplify the function by expanding or x using the formula and remove the causes which make the function indeterminate.

Question 19 $\lim_{x \to 0} x \sec x$.

Sol. We have, $\lim_{x \to 0} x \sec x = 0 \times \sec 0 = 0 \times 1 = 0$

Question 20 $\lim_{x \to 0} \frac{\sin ax + bx}{ax + \sin bx}$, a, b and $a + b \neq 0$.

Sol. $\lim_{x \to 0} \frac{\sin ax + bx}{ax + \sin bx}$

On dividing each term by x, we get

$$= \lim_{x \to 0} \frac{\frac{\sin ax}{x} + \frac{bx}{x}}{\frac{ax}{x} + \frac{\sin bx}{x}} = \lim_{x \to 0} \frac{\frac{a \sin ax}{ax} + b}{a + \frac{b \sin bx}{bx}} = \frac{\lim_{x \to 0}\left(\frac{a \sin ax}{ax} + b\right)}{\lim_{x \to 0}\left(a + \frac{b \sin bx}{bx}\right)}$$

$$\left(\because \lim_{x \to 0} \frac{\sin x}{x} = 1\right)$$

$$= \frac{a \times 1 + b}{a + b \times 1} = \frac{a + b}{a + b} = 1.$$

Question 21 $\lim_{x \to 0} (\operatorname{cosec} x - \cot x)$.

Sol. We have, $\lim_{x \to 0} (\operatorname{cosec} x - \cot x) = \lim_{x \to 0} \left(\frac{1}{\sin x} - \frac{\cos x}{\sin x}\right) = \lim_{x \to 0} \frac{1 - \cos x}{\sin x}$

$$= \lim_{x \to 0} \frac{2 \sin^2 \frac{x}{2}}{2 \sin \frac{x}{2} \cos \frac{x}{2}} = \lim_{x \to 0} \frac{\sin \frac{x}{2}}{\cos \frac{x}{2}} = \lim_{x \to 0} \tan \frac{x}{2} = \tan 0 = 0$$

$$[\because 1 - \cos 2x = 2\sin^2 x \text{ and } \sin 2x = 2 \sin x \cos x]$$

Question 22 $\lim_{x \to \frac{\pi}{2}} \frac{\tan 2x}{x - \frac{\pi}{2}}$.

Sol. We have, $\lim_{x \to \frac{\pi}{2}} \frac{\tan 2x}{x - \frac{\pi}{2}}$, Let $x - \frac{\pi}{2} = h$, when $x \to \frac{\pi}{2}$, then $h \to 0$

Therefore, $\lim_{h \to 0} \frac{\tan 2\left(\frac{\pi}{2} + h\right)}{h} = \lim_{h \to 0} \frac{\tan(\pi + 2h)}{h}$

$$= \lim_{h \to 0} \frac{\tan 2h}{h} \qquad (\because \tan(\pi + \theta) = \tan \theta)$$

$$= \lim_{h \to 0} \frac{2 \tan 2h}{2h} = 2 \times 1 = 2 \left(\because \lim_{x \to 0} \frac{\tan x}{x} = 1\right)$$

Question 23 Find $\lim_{x \to 0} f(x)$ and $\lim_{x \to 1} f(x)$,

where $f(x) = \begin{cases} 2x+3, & x \le 0 \\ 3(x+1), & x > 0 \end{cases}$.

◎ ***Thinking Process*** (For Q. No. 23 to 28) Since, $f(x)$ is given in the piecewise form. Therefore , we have to check the existence of limit. For it, we will find RHL and LHL at particular value of x.

Sol. Given, $f(x) = \begin{cases} 2x+3, & x \le 0 \\ 3(x+1), & x > 0 \end{cases}$

At $x = 0$,

$$\text{RHL} = \lim_{x \to 0^+} f(x) = \lim_{h \to 0} f(0+h) \quad [\because \text{RHL} = \text{Right hand limit}]$$

$$= \lim_{h \to 0} 3(0+h+1) = 3(0+0+1) = 3 \times 1 = 3$$

$$\text{LHL} = \lim_{h \to 0^-} f(x) = \lim_{h \to 0} f(0-h) \quad [\because \text{LHL} = \text{Left hand limit}]$$

$$= \lim_{h \to 0} 2(0-h)+3 = 2(0-0)+3 = 3 \Rightarrow \text{RHL} = \text{LHL} = 3$$

Here, at $x = 0$ limit exists and $\lim_{x \to 0} f(x) = 3$.

At $x = 1$, $\text{RHL} = \lim_{x \to 1^+} f(x) = \lim_{h \to 0} f(1+h)$

$$= \lim_{h \to 0} 3(1+h+1) \quad (\text{On putting } x = 1+h)$$

$$= 3(1+0+1) = 6$$

$$\text{LHL} = \lim_{x \to 1^-} f(x) = \lim_{h \to 0} f(1-h) \quad (\text{On putting } x = 1-h)$$

$$= \lim_{h \to 0} 3(1-h+1) = 6$$

$\Rightarrow$ RHL= LHL = 6 and hence, limit exists.

$\therefore \lim_{x \to 1} f(x) = 6$

Question 24 Find $\lim_{x \to 1} f(x)$, where $f(x) = \begin{cases} x^2-1, & x \le 1 \\ -x^2-1, & x > 1 \end{cases}$.

Sol. Given, $f(x) = \begin{cases} x^2-1, & x \le 1 \\ -x^2-1, & x > 1 \end{cases}$

At $x = 1$,

$$\text{RHL} = \lim_{x \to 1^+} f(x) = \lim_{h \to 0} f(1+h) = \lim_{h \to 0} [-(1+h)^2 - 1] \quad (\because \text{Put } x = 1+h)$$

$$= -(1+0)^2 - 1 = -1 - 1 = -2$$

$$\text{LHL} = \lim_{x \to 1^-} f(x) = \lim_{h \to 0} f(1-h) = \lim_{h \to 0} (1-h)^2 - 1 \quad (\quad x = 1-h)$$

$$= (1-0)^2 - 1 = 1 - 1 = 0$$

$\Rightarrow$ RHL $\ne$ LHL

Hence, at $x = 1$, limit doesn't exist.

Question 25 Evaluate $\lim_{x \to 0} f(x)$, where $f(x) = \begin{cases} \dfrac{|x|}{x}, & x \neq 0 \\ 0, & x = 0 \end{cases}$.

Thinking Process Here, we will use the definition of absolute function of x

i.e., $|x| = \begin{cases} x, & x \geq 0 \\ -x, & x < 0 \end{cases}$

Sol. Given, $f(x) = \begin{cases} \dfrac{|x|}{x}, & x \neq 0 \\ 0, & x = 0 \end{cases}$

At $x = 0$,

$$\text{RHL} = \lim_{x \to 0^+} f(x) = \lim_{h \to 0} f(0 + h)$$

$$= \lim_{h \to 0} \frac{|0 + h|}{(0 + h)} = \lim_{h \to 0} \frac{(0 + h)}{(0 + h)} = 1$$

$$\text{LHL} = \lim_{x \to 0^-} f(x) = \lim_{h \to 0} f(0 - h)$$

$$= \lim_{h \to 0} \frac{|0 - h|}{(0 - h)} = \lim_{h \to 0} \frac{-(0 - h)}{(0 - h)} = -1$$

$\Rightarrow$ RHL $\neq$ LHL

Hence, at $x = 0$, limit does not exist.

Note You should be careful while putting the limits, sometimes LHL $\neq$ RHL. So, check both LHL and RHL.

Question 26 $\lim_{x \to 0} f(x)$, where $f(x) = \begin{cases} \dfrac{x}{|x|}, & x \neq 0 \\ 0, & x = 0 \end{cases}$.

Sol. Given, $f(x) = \begin{cases} \dfrac{x}{|x|}, & x \neq 0 \\ 0, & x = 0 \end{cases}$

At $x = 0$,

$$\text{RHL} = \lim_{x \to 0^+} f(x) = \lim_{h \to 0} f(0 + h)$$

$$= \lim_{h \to 0} \frac{0 + h}{|0 + h|} = \lim_{h \to 0} \frac{0 + h}{(0 + h)} = 1$$

$$\text{LHL} = \lim_{x \to 0^-} f(x) = \lim_{h \to 0} f(0 - h)$$

$$= \lim_{h \to 0} \frac{(0 - h)}{|0 - h|} = \lim_{h \to 0} \frac{(0 - h)}{-(0 - h)} = -1$$

$\Rightarrow$ RHL $\neq$ LHL

Hence, at $x = 0$ limit does not exist.

Question 27 Find $\lim_{x \to 5} f(x)$, where $f(x) = |x| - 5$.

Sol. Given, $f(x) = |x| - 5$

We know that $|x| = \begin{cases} x, & x \ge 0 \\ -x, & x < 0 \end{cases}$

At $x = 5$, RHL $= \lim_{x \to 5} f(x) = \lim_{h \to 0} f(5+h) = \lim_{h \to 0} |5+h| - 5$

$= \lim_{h \to 0} (5 + h - 5) = \lim_{h \to 0} h = 0$

LHL $= \lim_{x \to 5} f(x) = \lim_{h \to 0} f(5-h) = \lim_{h \to 0} |5-h| - 5$

$= \lim_{h \to 0} (5 - h - 5) = \lim_{h \to 0} (-h) = 0$

Since, LHL = RHL = 0,

Hence, $\lim_{x \to 5} f(x) = 0$

Question 28 Suppose $f(x) = \begin{cases} a + bx, & x < 1 \\ 4, & x = 1 \\ b - ax, & x > 1 \end{cases}$ and if $\lim_{x \to 1} f(x) = f(1)$ what are possible values of a and b?

Sol. We have, $f(x) = \begin{cases} a + bx, & x < 1 \\ 4, & x = 1 \\ b - ax, & x > 1 \end{cases}$

At $x = 1$,

Since, $\lim_{x \to 1} f(x) = f(1)$ *i.e.*, RHL = LHL = $f(1)$

$\Rightarrow \lim_{x \to 1^+} f(x) = \lim_{x \to 1^-} f(x) = 4 \Rightarrow \lim_{h \to 0} f(1+h) = \lim_{h \to 0} f(1-h) = 4$

$\Rightarrow \lim_{h \to 0} b - a(1+h) = \lim_{h \to 0} a + b(1-h) = 4$

$\Rightarrow b - a(1+0) = a + b(1-0) = 4 \Rightarrow b - a = a + b = 4 \Rightarrow b - a = 4$ and $b + a = 4$

On solving, we get $b = 4$, $a = 0$.

Question 29 Let $a_1, a_2, a_3, \dots, a_n$ be fixed real numbers and define a function

$$f(x) = (x - a_1)(x - a_2) \dots (x - a_n)$$

What is $\lim_{x \to a_1} f(x)$? For some $a \ne a_1, a_2, \dots, a_n$, compute $\lim_{x \to a} f(x)$.

Sol. Given, $f(x) = (x - a_1)(x - a_2) \dots (x - a_n)$

$\therefore \lim_{x \to a_1} f(x) = \lim_{x \to a_1} (x - a_1)(x - a_2) \dots (x - a_n)$

$= (a_1 - a_1)(a_1 - a_2) \dots (a_1 - a_n) = 0 \times (a_1 - a_2) \dots (a_1 - a_n) = 0$

Again, $\lim_{x \to a} f(x) = \lim_{x \to a} (x - a_1)(x - a_2) \dots (x - a_n)$

$= (a - a_1)(a - a_2) \dots (a - a_n)$

Question 30 If $f(x)=\begin{cases} |x|+1, & x<0 \\ 0, & x=0, \\ |x|-1, & x>0 \end{cases}$ for what value(s) of a does $\lim_{x \to a} f(x)$ exist?

Sol. We have, $f(x)=\begin{cases} |x|+1, & x<0 \\ 0, & x=0 \\ |x|-1, & x>0 \end{cases}$

There are three cases become for value of 'a'.

Case I. when, $a>0$, we have

$$\lim_{x \to a} f(x) = \lim_{x \to a} |x| - 1 = \lim_{x \to a} (x-1) \qquad [\because a>0]$$
$$= a-1$$

Case II. when, $a<0$, we have

$$\lim_{x \to a} f(x) = \lim_{x \to a} |x| + 1 = \lim_{x \to a} (-x+1) \qquad [\because a<0]$$
$$= -a+1$$

Case III. when, $a=0$, we have

$$\text{RHL} = \lim_{x \to 0^+} f(x) = \lim_{h \to 0} f(0+h)$$
$$= \lim_{h \to 0} |0+h| - 1$$
$$= \lim_{h \to 0} h - 1 = 0 - 1 = -1$$
$$\text{LHL} = \lim_{x \to 0} f(x) = \lim_{h \to 0} f(0-h) = \lim_{h \to 0} |0-h| + 1$$
$$= \lim_{h \to 0} -(0-h) + 1 = \lim_{h \to 0} h + 1 = 0 + 1 = 1$$

$\Rightarrow$ RHL $\neq$ LHL

$\therefore \lim_{x \to 0} f(x)$ does not exist.

Hence, $\lim_{x \to a} f(x)$ exists for all $a \neq 0$.

Question 31 If the function $f(x)$ satisfies $\lim_{x \to 1} \dfrac{f(x)-2}{x^2-1} = \pi$, evaluate $\lim_{x \to 1} f(x)$.

◎ ***Thinking Process*** Here, we will use the property $\lim_{x \to a} \dfrac{f(x)}{g(x)} = \dfrac{\lim_{x \to a} f(x)}{\lim_{x \to a} g(x)}$ and simplify it.

Sol. Given, $\lim\limits_{x \to 1} \dfrac{f(x) - 2}{x^2 - 1} = \pi$

$$\Rightarrow \quad \frac{\lim\limits_{x \to 1} [f(x) - 2]}{\lim\limits_{x \to 1} (x^2 - 1)} = \pi \Rightarrow \lim_{x \to 1} [f(x) - 2] = \pi \lim_{x \to 1} (x^2 - 1)$$

$$\Rightarrow \quad \lim_{x \to 1} [f(x) - 2] = \pi (1^2 - 1)$$

$$\Rightarrow \quad \lim_{x \to 1} [f(x) - 2] = \pi \times 0$$

$$\Rightarrow \quad \lim_{x \to 1} [f(x) - 2] = 0 \Rightarrow \lim_{x \to 1} f(x) = 2$$

Question 32 If $f(x) = \begin{cases} mx^2 + n, & x < 0 \\ nx + m, & 0 \le x \le 1 \\ nx^3 + m, & x > 1 \end{cases}$. For what integers m and n does both $\lim\limits_{x \to 0} f(x)$ and $\lim\limits_{x \to 1} f(x)$ exist?

Sol. Given, $f(x) = \begin{cases} mx^2 + n, & x < 0 \\ nx + m, & 0 \le x \le 1 \\ nx^3 + m, & x > 1 \end{cases}$

$\because$ At $x = 0$, limit exists

Then, RHL = LHL

$$\lim_{x \to 0^+} f(x) = \lim_{x \to 0^-} f(x)$$

$$\Rightarrow \quad \lim_{h \to 0} f(0 + h) = \lim_{h \to 0} f(0 - h)$$

$$\Rightarrow \quad \lim_{h \to 0} n(0 + h) + m = \lim_{h \to 0} m(0 - h)^2 + n$$

$$\Rightarrow \quad n(0 + 0) + m = m(0 - 0)^2 + n$$

$$\Rightarrow \quad m = n \qquad \ldots\text{(i)}$$

Again, at $x = 1$ limit exists

RHL = LHL

$$\Rightarrow \quad \lim_{x \to 1^+} f(x) = \lim_{x \to 1^-} f(x)$$

$$\Rightarrow \quad \lim_{h \to 0} f(1 + h) = \lim_{h \to 0} f(1 - h)$$

$$\Rightarrow \quad \lim_{h \to 0} n(1 + h)^3 + m = \lim_{h \to 0} n(1 - h) + m$$

$$\Rightarrow \quad n(1 + 0)^3 + m = n(1 - 0) + m$$

$$\Rightarrow \quad n + m = m + n \qquad \ldots\text{(ii)}$$

Hence, from Eqs. (i) and (ii) for $\lim\limits_{x \to 0} f(x)$ to be existed, we need $m = n$ and $\lim\limits_{x \to 1} f(x)$ exists for any integral value of m and n.

Exercise 12.2

Question 1 Find the derivative of $x^2 - 2$ at $x = 10$.

◎ *Thinking Process* (For Q. No. 1 to 4) We can find the derivative of $f(x)$ is given by $f'(x) = \lim_{h \to 0} \frac{f(x+h) - f(x)}{h}$ and then simplify it.

Sol. Let $f(x) = x^2 - 2$,

As we know that $f'(x) = \lim_{h \to 0} \frac{f(x+h) - f(x)}{h}$

$$\Rightarrow f'(x) = \lim_{h \to 0} \frac{[(x+h)^2 - 2)] - (x^2 - 2)}{h} = \lim_{h \to 0} \frac{x^2 + h^2 + 2xh - 2 - x^2 + 2}{h}$$

$$= \lim_{h \to 0} \frac{h(h + 2x)}{h} = 0 + 2x = 2x$$

At $x = 10$, $f'(10) = 2 \times 10 = 20$

Quick Solution

Let $f(x) = x^2 - 2$

On differentiating both side, w.r.t x, we get

$$\frac{d}{dx}(f(x)) = f'(x) = \frac{d}{dx}(x^2 - 2)$$

$$f'(x) = \frac{d}{dx}(x^2) - \frac{d}{dx}(2) \quad \left[\because \frac{d}{dx}[f(x) \pm g(x)] = \frac{d}{dx}(f(x)) \pm \frac{d}{dx}(g(x))\right]$$

$$\Rightarrow \quad f'(x) = 2x^{2-1} - 0 \quad \left[\because \frac{d}{dx}(x^n) = nx^{n-1} \text{ and } \frac{d}{dx}(c) = 0, \text{ where } c \text{ is constant.}\right]$$

$$\Rightarrow \quad f'(x) = 2x$$

At $x = 10$,

$$\therefore \quad f'(10) = 2(10) = 20$$

Question 2 Find the derivative of x at $x = 1$.

Sol. Let $f(x) = x$

We know, $f'(x) = \lim_{h \to 0} \frac{f(x+h) - f(x)}{h} \Rightarrow f'(x) = \lim_{h \to 0} \frac{x + h - x}{h}$

$$\Rightarrow \quad f'(x) = \lim_{h \to 0} \frac{h}{h} = 1$$

At $x = 1$, $f'(1) = 1$

Question 3 Find the derivative of $99x$ at $x = 100$.

Sol. Let $f(x) = 99x$

We know, $f'(x) = \lim_{h \to 0} \frac{f(x+h) - f(x)}{h}$

$\Rightarrow \quad f'(x) = \lim_{h \to 0} \frac{99(x+h) - 99x}{h} = \lim_{h \to 0} \frac{99x + 99h - 99x}{h} = \lim_{h \to 0} \frac{99h}{h} = 99$

At $\quad x = 100, f'(100) = 99$

Question 4 Find the derivative of the following functions from first principle

(i) $x^3 - 27$ (ii) $(x-1)(x-2)$ (iii) $\frac{1}{x^3}$ (iv) $\frac{x+1}{x-1}$

Thinking Process Using the method of first principle
$f'(x) = \lim_{h \to 0} \frac{f(x+h) - f(x)}{h}$

Sol. (i) Let $f(x) = x^3 - 27$

$\Rightarrow f'(x) = \lim_{h \to 0} \frac{[(x+h)^3 - 27] - (x^3 - 27)}{h}$

$\left[\because f'(x) = \lim_{h \to 0} \frac{f(x+h) - f(x)}{h}\right]$

$= \lim_{h \to 0} \frac{(x+h)^3 - x^3}{h} = \lim_{h \to 0} \frac{x^3 + h^3 + 3xh(x+h) - x^3}{h}$

$[\because (a+b)^3 = a^3 + b^3 + 3ab(a+b)]$

$= \lim_{h \to 0} \frac{h^3 + 3xh(x+h)}{h}$

$= \lim_{h \to 0} \frac{h[h^2 + 3x(x+h)]}{h} = 0 + 3x(x+0) = 3x^2$

$\therefore \quad f'(x) = 3x^2$

(ii) Let $f(x) = (x-1)(x-2) = x^2 - 2x - x + 2 \Rightarrow f(x) = x^2 - 3x + 2$

We know that $f'(x) = \lim_{h \to 0} \frac{f(x+h) - f(x)}{h}$

$\Rightarrow \quad f'(x) = \lim_{h \to 0} \frac{[(x+h)^2 - 3(x+h) + 2] - (x^2 - 3x + 2)}{h}$

$= \lim_{h \to 0} \frac{x^2 + h^2 + 2xh - 3x - 3h + 2 - x^2 + 3x - 2}{h}$

$= \lim_{h \to 0} \frac{h^2 + 2xh - 3h}{h} = \lim_{h \to 0} \frac{h(h + 2x - 3)}{h}$

$= \lim_{h \to 0} h + 2x - 3 = 0 + 2x - 3 = 2x - 3$

$\therefore \qquad f'(x) = 2x - 3$

(iii) Let $f(x) = \dfrac{1}{x^3}$

$$\Rightarrow \quad f'(x) = \lim_{h \to 0} \frac{\dfrac{1}{(x+h)^3} - \dfrac{1}{x^3}}{h} \qquad \left[\because f'(x) = \lim_{h \to 0} \frac{f(x+h) - f(x)}{h}\right]$$

$$= \lim_{h \to 0} \frac{x^3 - (x+h)^3}{(x+h)^3\, x^3\, h}$$

$$= \lim_{h \to 0} \frac{x^3 - [x^3 + h^3 + 3xh(x+h)]}{(x+h)^3\, x^3 h}$$

$$= \lim_{h \to 0} \frac{-h^3 - 3xh(x+h)}{(x+h)^3 x^3 h}$$

$$= \lim_{h \to 0} \frac{-h[h^2 + 3x(x+h)]}{(x+h)^3 x^3 h}$$

$$= \lim_{h \to 0} \frac{-[0 + 3x(x+0)]}{(x+0)^3 x^3} = \frac{-3x^2}{x^3 x^3} = \frac{-3}{x^4}$$

$$\therefore \quad f'(x) = \frac{-3}{x^4}$$

(iv) Let $f(x) = \dfrac{x+1}{x-1}$

$$\Rightarrow \quad f'(x) = \lim_{h \to 0} \frac{\dfrac{x+h+1}{x+h-1} - \dfrac{x+1}{x-1}}{h}$$

$$f'(x) = \lim_{h \to 0} \frac{f(x+h) - f(x)}{h}$$

$$= \lim_{h \to 0} \frac{(x+h+1)(x-1) - (x+1)(x+h-1)}{(x+h-1)(x-1)h}$$

$$= \lim_{h \to 0} \frac{(x^2 - x + hx - h + x - 1) - (x^2 + hx - x + x + h - 1)}{(x+h-1)(x-1)h}$$

$$= \lim_{h \to 0} \frac{x^2 + hx - h - 1 - x^2 - hx - h + 1}{(x+h-1)(x-1)h}$$

$$= \lim_{h \to 0} \frac{-2h}{(x+h-1)(x-1)h}$$

$$= \frac{-2}{(x+0-1)(x-1)} = \frac{-2}{(x-1)^2}$$

$$\therefore \quad f'(x) = \frac{-2}{(x-1)^2}$$

Question 5 For the function

$$f(x)=\frac{x^{100}}{100}+\frac{x^{99}}{99}+\ldots+\frac{x^2}{2}+x+1. \text{ Prove that } f'(1)=100f'(0).$$

◎ **Thinking Process** (For Q No. 5 to 7) Here, we will use the relation, $f(x)=x^n \Rightarrow f'(x)=nx^{n-1}$ and simplify it.

Sol. Given, $f(x)=\frac{x^{100}}{100}+\frac{x^{99}}{99}+\ldots+\frac{x^2}{2}+x+1$

$$\Rightarrow \quad f'(x)=\frac{100x^{99}}{100}+\frac{99x^{98}}{99}+\ldots+\frac{2x}{2}+1+0$$

$$(\because f(x)=x^n \Rightarrow f'(x)=nx^{n-1})$$

$$\Rightarrow \quad f'(x)=x^{99}+x^{98}+\ldots+x+1 \quad \ldots(i)$$

On putting $x=1$, we get

$$f'(1)=\underbrace{(1)^{99}+1^{98}+\ldots+1+1}_{100 \text{ times}}=\underbrace{1+1+1\ldots+1+1}_{100 \text{ times}}$$

$$\Rightarrow \quad f'(1)=100 \quad \ldots(ii)$$

Again, putting $x=0$, we get $f'(0)=0+0+\ldots+0+1$

$$\Rightarrow \quad f'(0)=1 \quad \ldots(iii)$$

From Eqs. (ii) and (iii), $f'(1)=100f'(0)$ **Hence Proved.**

Note $f(x)=1=x^0 \Rightarrow f'(x)=0x^{0-1}=0$

Question 6 Find the derivative of $x^n+ax^{n-1}+a^2x^{n-2}+\ldots+a^{n-1}x+a^n$ for some fixed real number a.

Sol. Let $f(x)=x^n+ax^{n-1}+a^2x^{n-2}+\ldots+a^{n-1}x+a^n$

On differentiating both sides w.r.t. x, we get

$$f'(x)=nx^{n-1}+a(n-1)x^{n-1-1}+a^2(n-2)x^{n-2-1}+\ldots+a^{n-1}(1)+0$$

$$[\because f(x)=ax^n \Rightarrow f'(x)=anx^{n-1})]$$

$$\Rightarrow f'(x)=nx^{n-1}+a(n-1)x^{n-2}+a^2(n-2)x^{n-3}+\ldots+a^{n-1}$$

Question 7 For some constants a and b, find the derivative of

(i) $(x-a)(x-b)$ (ii) $(ax^2+b)^2$ (iii) $\frac{x-a}{x-b}$.

Sol. (i) Let $f(x)=(x-a)(x-b)=x^2-ax-bx+ab=x^2-(a+b)x+ab$

On differentiating both sides w.r.t. x, we get

$$f'(x)=2x-(a+b)1+0=2x-a-b \quad [\because f(x)=ax^n \Rightarrow f'(x)=anx^{n-1}]$$

(ii) Let $f(x)=(ax^2+b)^2$

$$\Rightarrow \quad f(x)=a^2x^4+b^2+2abx^2$$

On differentiating both sides w.r.t. x, we get

$$f'(x)=4a^2x^3+0+2ab(2x)=4a^2x^3+4abx=4ax(ax^2+b)$$

(iii) Let $$f(x) = \frac{x-a}{x-b}$$

On differentiating both sides w.r.t. x, we get

$$f'(x) = \frac{(x-b)\frac{d}{dx}(x-a) - (x-a)\frac{d}{dx}(x-b)}{(x-b)^2}$$

$$= \frac{(x-b)(1-0) - (x-a)(1-0)}{(x-b)^2} = \frac{(x-b)-(x-a)}{(x-b)^2}$$

$$\left(\because f(x) = \frac{f_1(x)}{f_2(x)} \quad \therefore f'(x) = \frac{f_2(x)\frac{d}{dx}f_1(x) - f_1(x)\frac{d}{dx}f_2(x)}{\{f_2(x)\}^2} \right)$$

$$= \frac{x-b-x+a}{(x-b)^2} = \frac{a-b}{(x-b)^2}$$

Mistake Alert Sometime students do this mistake $\frac{d}{dx}\left(\frac{f(x)}{g(x)}\right) = \frac{f'(x)}{g'(x)}$.

Which is completely wrong.

Question 8 Find the deriative of $\frac{x^n - a^n}{x-a}$ for some constant a.

Thinking Process Here, we will use the quotient formula for derivative *i.e.*,

$$\frac{d}{dx}\left\{\frac{f(x)}{g(x)}\right\} = \frac{g(x)\frac{d}{dx}f(x) - f(x)\frac{d}{dx}g(x)}{\{g(x)\}^2}$$

Sol. Let $$y = \frac{x^n - a^n}{x-a}$$

On differentiating both sides w.r.t. x, we get

$$\frac{dy}{dx} = \frac{(x-a)\frac{d}{dx}(x^n - a^n) - (x^n - a^n)\frac{d}{dx}(x-a)}{(x-a)^2}$$

$$= \frac{(x-a)[nx^{n-1} - 0] - (x^n - a^n)(1-0)}{(x-a)^2} \qquad \left[\because \frac{d}{dx}(x^n) = nx^{n-1}\right]$$

$$= \frac{(x-a)\,nx^{n-1} - x^n + a^n}{(x-a)^2} = \frac{x \times nx^{n-1} - anx^{n-1} - x^n + a^n}{(x-a)^2}$$

$$= \frac{nx^n - anx^{n-1} - x^n + a^n}{(x-a)^2}$$

Note The derivative of the constant function is always zero.

Question 9 Find the derivative of

(i) $2x - \frac{3}{4}$ (ii) $(5x^3 + 3x - 1)(x - 1)$ (iii) $x^{-3}(5 + 3x)$

(iv) $x^5(3 - 6x^{-9})$ (v) $x^{-4}(3 - 4x^{-5})$ (vi) $\frac{2}{x+1} - \frac{x^2}{3x-1}$.

◎ ***Thinking Process*** Here, we will use different derivative formulae which are given below

(i) $\frac{d}{dx} x^n = nx^{n-1}$

(ii) $\frac{d}{dx}\{f(x)\, g(x)\} = f(x)\left\{\frac{d}{dx} g(x)\right\} + g(x)\left\{\frac{d}{dx} f(x)\right\}$ (product formula)

(iii) $\frac{d}{dx}\left\{\frac{f(x)}{g(x)}\right\} = \frac{g(x)\left\{\frac{d}{dx} f(x)\right\} - f(x)\left\{\frac{d}{dx} g(x)\right\}}{\{g(x)\}^2}$ (quotient formula)

Sol.

(i) Let $y = 2x - \frac{3}{4}$

On differentiating y w.r.t. x, we get

$$\frac{dy}{dx} = 2 \times 1 - 0 = 2$$

(ii) Let $y = (5x^3 + 3x - 1)(x - 1)$

On differentiating y w.r.t. x, we get

$$\frac{dy}{dx} = (5x^3 + 3x - 1)\frac{d}{dx}(x - 1) + (x - 1)\frac{d}{dx}(5x^3 + 3x - 1)$$

$[\because (uv)' = uv' + vu']$

$$= (5x^3 + 3x - 1)(1 - 0) + (x - 1)(5 \times 3x^2 + 3 \times 1 - 0)$$
$$= (5x^3 + 3x - 1) + (x - 1)(15x^2 + 3)$$
$$= 5x^3 + 3x - 1 + 15x^3 + 3x - 15x^2 - 3$$
$$= 20x^3 - 15x^2 + 6x - 4$$

(iii) Let $y = x^{-3}(5 + 3x) \Rightarrow y = 5x^{-3} + 3x^{-2}$

On differentiating y w.r.t. x, we get

$$\frac{dy}{dx} = 5(-3)x^{-3-1} + 3(-2)x^{-2-1} \quad \left[\because \frac{d}{dx}(x^n) = nx^{n-1}\right]$$
$$= -15x^{-4} - 6x^{-3}$$

(iv) Let $y = x^5(3 - 6x^{-9}) = 3x^5 - 6x^{5-9} = 3x^5 - 6x^{-4}$

On differentiating y w.r.t. x, we get

$$\frac{dy}{dx} = 3 \times 5x^{5-1} - 6(-4)x^{-4-1} = 15x^4 + 24x^{-5}$$

$\left[\because \frac{d}{dx}(x^n) = nx^{n-1}\right]$

(v) Let $y = x^{-4}(3 - 4x^{-5}) \Rightarrow y = 3x^{-4} - 4x^{-4-5} \Rightarrow y = 3x^{-4} - 4x^{-9}$

On differentiating y w.r.t. x, we get

$$\frac{dy}{dx} = 3(-4)x^{-4-1} - 4(-9)x^{-9-1} = -12x^{-5} + 36x^{-10} \quad \left[\because \frac{d}{dx}(x^n) = nx^{n-1}\right]$$

(vi) Let $y = \dfrac{2}{x+1} - \dfrac{x^2}{3x-1}$

On differentiating y w.r.t. x, we get

$$\frac{dy}{dx} = \frac{(x+1)\frac{d}{dx}(2) - 2\frac{d}{dx}(x+1)}{(x+1)^2} - \frac{(3x-1)\frac{d}{dx}(x^2) - x^2\frac{d}{dx}(3x-1)}{(3x-1)^2}$$

$$\left[\because (u-v)' = u' - v' \text{ and } \left(\frac{u}{v}\right)' = \frac{vu' - uv'}{v^2}\right]$$

$$\Rightarrow \frac{dy}{dx} = \frac{(x+1)\times 0 - 2\times 1}{(x+1)^2} - \frac{(3x-1)2x - x^2(3)}{(3x-1)^2}$$

$$= -\frac{2}{(x+1)^2} - \frac{(6x^2 - 2x - 3x^2)}{(3x-1)^2} = -\frac{2}{(x+1)^2} - \frac{(3x^2 - 2x)}{(3x-1)^2}$$

$$\Rightarrow \frac{dy}{dx} = \frac{-2}{(x+1)^2} - \frac{x(3x-2)}{(3x-1)^2}.$$

Question 10 Find the derivative of $\cos x$ from first principle.

◎ ***Thinking Process*** Using the method of first principle $f'(x) = \lim\limits_{h\to 0}\dfrac{f(x+h) - f(x)}{h}$.

Sol. Let $f(x) = \cos x$

$$\because \quad f'(x) = \lim_{h\to 0}\frac{f(x+h) - f(x)}{h} \quad \text{(by first principle)}$$

$$\Rightarrow f'(x) = \lim_{h\to 0}\frac{\cos(x+h) - \cos x}{h} = \lim_{h\to 0}\frac{-2\sin\frac{x+h+x}{2}\sin\frac{x+h-x}{2}}{h}$$

$$\left(\because \cos C - \cos D = -2\sin\frac{(C+D)}{2}\sin\frac{(C-D)}{2}\right)$$

$$= \lim_{h\to 0}\frac{-2\sin\frac{2x+h}{2}\sin\frac{h}{2}}{2\times\frac{h}{2}}$$

$$= \lim_{h\to 0}\left\{-\sin\left(\frac{2x+h}{2}\right)\right\}\left\{\frac{\sin\frac{h}{2}}{\frac{h}{2}}\right\} = -\sin\frac{2x}{2}\times 1 \quad \left(\because \lim_{h\to 0}\frac{\sin\frac{h}{2}}{\frac{h}{2}} = 1\right)$$

$$\Rightarrow f'(x) = -\sin x$$

Question 11 Find the derivative of the following functions :

(i) $\sin x \cos x$ (ii) $\sec x$ (iii) $5 \sec x + 4 \cos x$

(iv) cosec x (v) $3 \cot x + 4 \text{ cosec } x$ (vi) $5 \sin x - 6 \cos x + 7$

(vii) $2 \tan x - 7 \sec x$

Sol. (i) Let $y = \sin x \cos x$

On differentiating y w.r.t. x, we get

$$\frac{dy}{dx} = \sin x \frac{d}{dx} \cos x + \cos x \frac{d}{dx} \sin x \quad \text{(by product formula)}$$

$$= \sin x(-\sin x) + \cos x \cos x = -\sin^2 x + \cos^2 x = \cos 2x$$

$$[\because \cos 2x = \cos^2 x - \sin^2 x]$$

(ii) Let $y = \sec x$

$$\Rightarrow \quad y = \frac{1}{\cos x}$$

On differentiating y w.r.t. x, we get

$$\frac{dy}{dx} = \frac{\cos x \frac{d}{dx}(1) - 1 \times \frac{d}{dx} \cos x}{\cos^2 x} \quad \text{(by quotient formula)}$$

$$= \frac{\cos x \times 0 - 1 \times (-\sin x)}{\cos^2 x} = \frac{\sin x}{\cos x} \times \frac{1}{\cos x}$$

$$\frac{dy}{dx} = \tan x \sec x$$

Quick Solution

$$y = \sec x$$

On differentiating on both sides w.r.t. to x

$$\frac{dy}{dx} = \frac{d}{dx}(\sec x)$$

$$\frac{dy}{dx} = \sec x \tan x \quad \text{[by formula]}$$

(iii) Let $y = 5 \quad x + 4\cos x$

On differentiating y w.r.t. x, we get

$$\frac{dy}{dx} = 5 \sec x \tan x - 4\sin x \quad \left[\because \frac{d}{dx}(\sec x) = \sec x \tan x\right]$$

(iv) Let $y = \quad x = \frac{1}{\sin x}$

On differentiating y w.r.t. x, we get

$$\frac{dy}{dx} = \frac{\sin x \frac{d}{dx}(1) - (1) \frac{d}{dx}(\sin x)}{\sin^2 x} = \frac{\sin x \times 0 - 1 \times \cos x}{\sin^2 x}$$

(by quotient formula)

$$= \frac{0 - \cos x}{\sin^2 x} = \frac{-\cos x}{\sin x} \times \frac{1}{\sin x} \Rightarrow \frac{dy}{dx} = -\cot x \text{ cosec} x$$

Quick Solution

$$y = \text{cosec}x$$

On differentiating on both sides w.r.t x

$$\frac{dy}{dx} = \frac{d}{dx}(\text{cosec}x)$$

$$\frac{dy}{dx} = -\cot x \,\text{cosec}\, x \qquad \text{[By formula]}$$

(v) Let $y = 3\cot x + 5 \quad x$

Differentiating y w.r.t. x, we get

$$\frac{dy}{dx} = -3\,\text{cosec}^2 x - 5\,\text{cosec}\,x\cot x$$

$$\left[\because \frac{d}{dx}(\cot x) = -\text{cosec}^2 x \text{ and } \frac{d}{dx}(\text{cosec}x) = -\text{cosec}x \cdot \cot x\right]$$

(vi) Let $y = 5\sin x - 6\cos x + 7$

On differentiating y w.r.t. x, we get

$$\frac{dy}{dx} = 5\cos x - 6(-\sin x) + 0 = 5\cos x + 6\sin x$$

(vii) Let $y = 2\tan x - 7\sec x$

On differentiating y w.r.t. x, we get

$$\frac{dy}{dx} = 2\sec^2 x - 7\sec x \tan x$$

$$\left[\because \frac{d}{dx}(\tan x) = \sec^2 x \text{ and } \frac{d}{dx}(\sec x) = \sec x \tan x\right]$$

Miscellaneous Exercise

Question 1 Find the derivative of the following functions from the first principle

(i) $-x$ (ii) $(-x)^{-1}$ (iii) $\sin(x+1)$ (iv) $\cos\left(x - \frac{\pi}{8}\right)$

◎ *Thinking Process* First principle $f'(x) = \lim_{h\to 0} \frac{f(x+h) - f(x)}{h}$

Sol.

(i) Let $f(x) = -x$

$$\because f'(x) = \lim_{h\to 0} \frac{f(x+h) - f(x)}{h} = \lim_{h\to 0} \frac{-(x+h) - (-x)}{h} \quad \text{(By first principle)}$$

$$= \lim_{h\to 0} \frac{-x - h + x}{h} \qquad [\because f(x) = -x]$$

$$\Rightarrow f'(x) = \lim_{h\to 0} \frac{-h}{h} = -1$$

(ii) Let $f(x) = (-x)^{-1} \Rightarrow f(x) = -\frac{1}{x}$

$\because \quad f'(x) = \lim_{h \to 0} \frac{f(x+h) - f(x)}{h}$ (by first principle)

$\Rightarrow \quad f'(x) = \lim_{h \to 0} \frac{-\frac{1}{x+h} + \frac{1}{x}}{h}$ $\left(\because f(x) = \frac{-1}{x}\right)$

$\Rightarrow \quad f'(x) = \lim_{h \to 0} \frac{\frac{1}{x} - \frac{1}{x+h}}{h} = \lim_{h \to 0} \frac{x+h-x}{x(x+h)h}$

$= \lim_{h \to 0} \frac{h}{x(x+h)h} = \frac{1}{x(x+0)} = \frac{1}{x^2}$

(iii) Let $f(x) = \sin(x+1)$

$\because \; f'(x) = \lim_{h \to 0} \frac{f(x+h) - f(x)}{h}$ (by first principle)

$\Rightarrow f'(x) = \lim_{h \to 0} \frac{\sin(x+h+1) - \sin(x+1)}{h}$ $[\because f(x) = \sin(x+1)]$

$\Rightarrow f'(x) = \lim_{h \to 0} \frac{2\cos\frac{x+h+1+x+1}{2}\sin\frac{x+h+1-x-1}{2}}{h}$

$\left[\because \sin C - \sin D = 2\cos\frac{C+D}{2}\sin\frac{C-D}{2}\right]$

$= \lim_{h \to 0} \frac{2\cos\frac{2x+h+2}{2}\sin\frac{h}{2}}{2 \times \frac{h}{2}} = \cos\frac{2x+0+2}{2} \times 1$ $\left(\because \lim_{h \to 0} \frac{\sin\frac{h}{2}}{\frac{h}{2}} = 1\right)$

$\Rightarrow f'(x) = \cos(x+1)$

(iv) Let $f(x) = \cos\left(x - \frac{\pi}{8}\right)$

$\because \; f'(x) = \lim_{h \to 0} \frac{f(x+h) - f(x)}{h}$ (by first principle)

$\Rightarrow f'(x) = \lim_{h \to 0} \frac{\cos\left(x+h-\frac{\pi}{8}\right) - \cos\left(x - \frac{\pi}{8}\right)}{h}$ $\left(\because f(x) = \cos\left(x - \frac{\pi}{8}\right)\right)$

$= \lim_{h \to 0} \frac{-2\sin\frac{x+h-\frac{\pi}{8}+x-\frac{\pi}{8}}{2}\sin\frac{x+h-\frac{\pi}{8}-x+\frac{\pi}{8}}{2}}{h}$

$\left[\because \cos C - \cos D = -2\sin\frac{C+D}{2}\sin\frac{C-D}{2}\right]$

$$= \lim_{h \to 0} \frac{-2\sin \dfrac{2x - 2\left(\dfrac{\pi}{8}\right) + h}{2} \sin \dfrac{h}{2}}{2 \times \dfrac{h}{2}}$$

$$= -\sin \frac{2x - 2\left(\dfrac{\pi}{8}\right) + 0}{2} \times 1 \qquad \left(\because \lim_{x \to 0} \frac{\sin \dfrac{h}{2}}{\dfrac{h}{2}} = 1\right)$$

$$= -\sin \frac{2\left(x - \dfrac{\pi}{8}\right)}{2} \Rightarrow f'(x) = -\sin\left(x - \frac{\pi}{8}\right)$$

Mistake Alert We need to keep in mind that we should not put zero in place of x in the limit as $h \to 0$.

Directions (Q. No. 2 to 30) Find the derivative of the following functions (it is to be understood that a, b, c, d, p, q, r and s are fixed non-zero constants and m and n are integers).:

Question 2 $x + a$.

Sol. Let $y = x + a$

On differentiating y w.r.t. x, $\dfrac{dy}{dx} = 1 + 0 = 1$

Question 3 $(px + q)\left(\dfrac{r}{x} + s\right)$.

Sol. Let $y = (px + q)\left(\dfrac{r}{x} + s\right)$

On differentiating y w.r.t. x, we get

$$\frac{dy}{dx} = (px + q)\frac{d}{dx}\left(\frac{r}{x} + s\right) + \left(\frac{r}{x} + s\right)\frac{d}{dx}(px + q) \qquad \text{(by product rule)}$$

$$= (px + q)\left[-\frac{r}{x^2} + 0\right] + \left(\frac{r}{x} + s\right)(p \times 1 + 0)$$

$$\left(\because \frac{d}{dx}\left(\frac{1}{x}\right) = \frac{d}{dx}(x^{-1}) = (-1)\,x^{-1-1} = -\frac{1}{x^2}\right)$$

$$= (px + q)\left(-\frac{r}{x^2}\right) + \left(\frac{r}{x} + s\right)p = -\frac{pxr}{x^2} - \frac{qr}{x^2} + \frac{pr}{x} + ps$$

$$= -\frac{pr}{x} - \frac{qr}{x^2} + \frac{pr}{x} + ps$$

$$\Rightarrow \frac{dy}{dx} = ps - \frac{qr}{x^2}$$

Quick Solution

$$y = (px + q)\left(\frac{r}{x} + s\right)$$

we can write it

$$y = \frac{rpx}{x} + \frac{qr}{x} + psx + qs$$

$$y = rp + \frac{pr}{x} + px + qs$$

Now, on differentiating. w.r.t. to x

$$\frac{dy}{dx} = 0 - \frac{qr}{x^2} + ps + 0 \qquad \left[\because \frac{d}{dx}\left(\frac{1}{x}\right) = \frac{d}{dx}(x^{-1}) = \frac{-1}{x^2}\right]$$

$$\frac{dy}{dx} = ps - \frac{qr}{x^2} \qquad \left[\frac{d}{dx}(c) = 0\right]$$

Question 4 $(ax + b)(cx + d)^2$.

◎ ***Thinking Process*** Product rule for derivative $(uv)' = uv' + vu'$

Sol. Let $y = (ax + b)(cx + d)^2$

On differentiating y w.r.t. x, we get

$$\frac{dy}{dx} = (ax + b)\frac{d}{dx}(cx + d)^2 + (cx + d)^2 \frac{d}{dx}(ax + b) \qquad \text{(by product rule)}$$

$$= (ax + b)\frac{d}{dx}(c^2x^2 + d^2 + 2cxd) + (cx + d)^2 (a \times 1 + 0)$$

$$(\because (a + b)^2 = a^2 + 2ab + b^2)$$

$$= (ax + b)(c^2(2x) + 0 + 2c \times 1 \times d) + (cx + d)^2 \times a$$

$$= (ax + b)(2c^2x + 2cd) + a(cx + d)^2$$

$$= (ax + b)\,2c(cx + d) + a(cx + d)^2 = (cx + d)[2c(ax + b) + a(cx + d)]$$

$$= (cx + d)(2acx + 2bc + acx + ad) = (cx + d)(3acx + 2bc + ad)$$

Question 5 $\dfrac{ax + b}{cx + d}$

◎ ***Thinking Process*** Quotient rule for derivative $\left(\frac{u}{v}\right)' = \frac{vu' - uv'}{v'}$

Sol. Let $y = \dfrac{ax + b}{cx + d}$

On differentiating y w.r.t. x, we get

$$\frac{dy}{dx} = \frac{(cx + d)\frac{d}{dx}(ax + b) - (ax + b)\frac{d}{dx}(cx + d)}{(cx + d)^2} \qquad \text{(by quotient formula)}$$

$$= \frac{(cx + d)(a \times 1 + 0) - (ax + b)(c \times 1 + 0)}{(cx + d)^2}$$

$$= \frac{a(cx + d) - (ax + b)c}{(cx + d)^2} = \frac{acx + ad - acx - bc}{(cx + d)^2} \Rightarrow \frac{dy}{dx} = \frac{ad - bc}{(cx + d)^2}$$

Question 6 $\dfrac{1+\dfrac{1}{x}}{1-\dfrac{1}{x}}$

Sol. Let $y = \dfrac{1+\dfrac{1}{x}}{1-\dfrac{1}{x}} \Rightarrow y = \dfrac{x+1}{x-1}$

On differentiating y w.r.t. x, we get

$$\frac{dy}{dx} = \frac{(x-1)\dfrac{d}{dx}(x+1) - (x+1)\dfrac{d}{dx}(x-1)}{(x-1)^2} \text{ (by quotient formula)}$$

$$= \frac{(x-1)(1+0)-(x+1)(1-0)}{(x-1)^2} = \frac{x-1-x-1}{(x-1)^2}$$

$$\Rightarrow \quad \frac{dy}{dx} = \frac{-2}{(x-1)^2}$$

Question 7 $\dfrac{1}{(ax^2+bx+c)}$

Sol. Let $y = \dfrac{1}{ax^2+bx+c}$

On differentiating y w.r.t. x, we get

$$\frac{dy}{dx} = \frac{(ax^2+bx+c)\dfrac{d}{dx}(1) - 1 \times \dfrac{d}{dx}(ax^2+bx+c)}{(ax^2+bx+c)^2} \text{ (by quotient formula)}$$

$$= \frac{(ax^2+bx+c)\times 0 - 1 \times (2ax+b)}{(ax^2+bx+c)^2}$$

$$\Rightarrow \frac{dy}{dx} = -\frac{(2ax+b)}{(ax^2+bx+c)^2}$$

Question 8 $\dfrac{ax+b}{px^2+qx+r}$

Sol. Let $y = \dfrac{ax+b}{px^2+qx+r}$

On differentiating y w.r.t. x, we get

$$\frac{dy}{dx}=\frac{(px^2+qx+r)\frac{d}{dx}(ax+b)-(ax+b)\frac{d}{dx}(px^2+qx+r)}{(px^2+qx+r)^2}$$

(by quotient formula)

$$=\frac{(px^2+qx+r)(a\times 1+0)-(ax+b)(2px+q)}{(px^2+qx+r)^2}$$

$$=\frac{(px^2+qx+r)\,a-(ax+b)(2px+q)}{(px^2+qx+r)^2}$$

$$=\frac{(apx^2+aqx+ra)-(2apx^2+aqx+2bpx+qb)}{(px^2+qx+r)^2}$$

$$=\frac{apx^2+aqx+ra-2apx^2-aqx-2bpx-bq}{(px^2+qx+r)^2}$$

$$=\frac{-apx^2-2bpx+ra-bq}{(px^2+qx+r)^2}$$

Question 9 $\dfrac{px^2+qx+r}{ax+b}$

Sol. Let $y=\dfrac{px^2+qx+r}{(ax+b)}$

On differentiating y w.r.t. x, we get

$$\frac{dy}{dx}=\frac{(ax+b)\frac{d}{dx}(px^2+qx+r)-(px^2+qx+r)\frac{d}{dx}(ax+b)}{(ax+b)^2}$$

(by quotient formula)

$$=\frac{(ax+b)(2px+q+0)-(px^2+qx+r)(a\times 1+0)}{(ax+b)^2}$$

$$=\frac{(ax+b)(2px+q)-(px^2+qx+r)\,a}{(ax+b)^2}$$

$$=\frac{(2apx^2+aqx+2bpx+bq)-(apx^2+aqx+ra)}{(ax+b)^2}$$

$$=\frac{2apx^2+aqx+2bpx+bq-apx^2-aqx-ra}{(ax+b)^2}$$

$$\Rightarrow\quad \frac{dy}{dx}=\frac{apx^2+2bpx+bq-ra}{(ax+b)^2}$$

Question 10 $\dfrac{a}{x^4} - \dfrac{b}{x^2} + \cos x.$

Sol. Let $y = \dfrac{a}{x^4} - \dfrac{b}{x^2} + \cos x \Rightarrow \; y = a\, x^{-4} - bx^{-2} + \cos x$

On differentiating y w.r.t. x, we get

$$\frac{dy}{dx} = a\frac{d}{dx}(x^{-4}) - b\frac{d}{dx}(x^{-2}) + \frac{d}{dx}(\cos x) \qquad \left(\because \frac{d}{dx}(x^n) = nx^{n-1}\right)$$

$$= a(-4)\, x^{-4-1} - b(-2)\, x^{-2-1} - \sin x = -\frac{4a}{x^5} + \frac{2b}{x^3} - \sin x$$

Question 11 $4\sqrt{x} - 2.$

Sol. Let $\quad y = 4\sqrt{x} - 2 \;\Rightarrow\; y = 4x^{1/2} - 2$

On differentiating y w.r.t. x, we get

$$\frac{dy}{dx} = 4 \times \frac{1}{2}\, x^{\frac{1}{2}-1} - 0 = 2\, x^{\frac{-1}{2}} = \frac{2}{\sqrt{x}}$$

Question 12 $(ax + b)^n.$

◎ *Thinking Process* (For Q. No. 12 and 13) We have the function of a function as $y = f\{g(x)\}$. Here, f is a function of g and g is a function of x. The derivative of such functions are given as $\dfrac{dy}{dx} = f'\{g(x)\}.\, g'(x)$..

Sol. Let $y = (ax + b)^n$

On differentiating y w.r.t. x,

$$\Rightarrow \quad \frac{dy}{dx} = n(ax + b)^{n-1}\frac{d}{dx}(ax + b) \qquad \left[\because \frac{d}{dx} f\{g(x)\} = f'\{g(x)\}g'(x)\right]$$

$$= n(ax + b)^{n-1} \times a$$

$$\Rightarrow \quad \frac{dy}{dx} = na\,(ax + b)^{n-1}$$

Mistake Alert $\dfrac{d}{dx}(ax + b)^n \neq n(ax + b)^{n-1}$

Question 13 $(ax + b)^n\,(cx + d)^m.$

Sol. Let $y = (ax + b)^n\,(cx + d)^m$

On differentiating y w.r.t. x, we get

$$\frac{dy}{dx} = (ax + b)^n \frac{d}{dx}(cx + d)^m + (cx + d)^m \frac{d}{dx}(ax + b)^n \qquad [\because \text{By Product rule}]$$

$$= (ax + b)^n\, m\,(cx + d)^{m-1}\frac{d}{dx}(cx + d) + (cx + d)^m\, n\,(ax + b)^{n-1}\frac{d}{dx}(ax + b)$$

$$\left[\because \frac{d}{dx} f\{g(x)\} = f'\{g(x)\}g'(x)\right]$$

$$= m(ax+b)^n (cx+d)^{m-1}(c \times 1 + 0) + n(cx+d)^m (ax+b)^{n-1}(a \times 1 + 0)$$

$$= m(ax+b)^n (cx+d)^{m-1} c + n(cx+d)^m (ax+b)^{n-1} a$$

$$\Rightarrow \frac{dy}{dx} = (ax+b)^{n-1}(cx+d)^{m-1}[mc(ax+b) + na(cx+d)]$$

Question 14 $\sin(x+a)$.

Sol. Let $y = \sin(x+a)$, $y = \sin x \cos a + \cos x \sin a$

On differentiating y w.r.t. x, we get

$$\frac{dy}{dx} = \sin x \frac{d}{dx}(\cos x) + \cos a \frac{d}{dx}(\sin x) + \cos x \frac{d}{dx}(\sin a) + \sin a \frac{d}{dx}(\cos x)$$

$[\because \sin(A+B) = \sin A \cos B + \cos A \sin B]$

$$= \cos a \cos x - \sin a \sin x = \cos(x+a)$$ $[\because \cos a$ and $\sin a$ are constant$]$

Quick Solution

Let $y = \sin(x+a)$

we have to solve this question with the help of chain rule. Differenting y w.r. to x

Then $\frac{dy}{dx} = \frac{d}{dx}[\sin(x+a)]$

$$\frac{dy}{dx} = \cos(x+a)\frac{d}{dx}(x+a)$$ $[\therefore dx \sin x = \cos x]$

$$\frac{dy}{dx} = \cos(x+a)\cdot 1$$

$$\frac{dy}{dx} = \cos(x+a)$$

Question 15 $\operatorname{cosec} x \cot x$.

Sol. Let $y = \quad x \cot x$

On differentiating y w.r.t. x, we get

$$\frac{dy}{dx} = \operatorname{cosec} x \frac{d}{dx}(\cot x) + \cot x \frac{d}{dx}(\operatorname{cosec} x) \text{ (By product rule)}$$

$$= -\operatorname{cosec} x \operatorname{cosec}^2 x + \cot x(-\operatorname{cosec} x \cot x)$$

$$\left[\because \frac{d}{dx}\cot x = -\operatorname{cosec}^2 x \text{ and } \frac{d}{dx}(\operatorname{cosec}) = -\operatorname{cosec} x \cot x\right]$$

$$= -\operatorname{cosec}^3 x - \cot^2 x \operatorname{cosec} x$$

Question 16 $\dfrac{\cos x}{1+\sin x}$.

Sol. Let $y = \dfrac{\cos x}{1+\sin x}$

On differentiating y w.r.t. x, we get

$$\frac{dy}{dx} = \frac{(1+\sin x)\frac{d}{dx}(\cos x) - \cos x\frac{d}{dx}(1+\sin x)}{(1+\sin x)^2} \quad \text{(by quotient formula)}$$

$$= \frac{(1+\sin x)(-\sin x) - \cos x(0+\cos x)}{(1+\sin x)^2}$$

$$= \frac{-\sin x - \sin^2 x - \cos^2 x}{(1+\sin x)^2} = \frac{-\sin x - (\cos^2 x + \sin^2 x)}{(1+\sin x)^2} [\because \cos^2\theta + \sin^2\theta = 1]$$

$$= \frac{-\sin x - 1}{(1+\sin x)^2} = \frac{-(1+\sin x)}{(1+\sin x)^2} = \frac{-1}{(1+\sin x)}$$

Question 17 $\dfrac{\sin x + \cos x}{\sin x - \cos x}$.

Sol. Let $y = \dfrac{\sin x + \cos x}{\sin x - \cos x}$

On differentiating y w.r.t. x, we get

$$\frac{dy}{dx} = \frac{(\sin x - \cos x)\frac{d}{dx}(\sin x + \cos x) - (\sin x + \cos x)\frac{d}{dx}(\sin x - \cos x)}{(\sin x - \cos x)^2}$$

(by quotient formula)

$$= \frac{(\sin x - \cos x)(\cos x - \sin x) - (\sin x + \cos x)(\cos x + \sin x)}{(\sin x - \cos x)^2}$$

$$= \frac{-(\cos x - \sin x)(\cos x - \sin x) - (\cos x + \sin x)^2}{(\sin x - \cos x)^2}$$

$$= \frac{-(\cos x - \sin x)^2 - (\cos x + \sin x)^2}{(\sin x - \cos x)^2}$$

$$= \frac{-[(\cos^2 x + \sin^2 x - 2\cos x\sin x) + (\cos^2 x + \sin^2 x + 2\cos x\sin x)]}{(\sin x - \cos x)^2}$$

$$= \frac{-[1+1]}{(\sin x - \cos x)^2} [\because \cos^2 x + \sin^2 x = 1] = \frac{-2}{(\sin x - \cos x)^2}$$

Question 18 $\dfrac{\sec x - 1}{\sec x + 1}$.

Sol. Let $y = \dfrac{x-1}{x+1}$

On differentiating y w.r.t. x, we get

$$\frac{dy}{dx}=\frac{(\sec x+1)\frac{d}{dx}(\sec x-1)-(\sec x-1)\frac{d}{dx}(\sec x+1)}{(\sec x+1)^2} \quad \text{(by quotient formula)}$$

$$=\frac{(\sec x+1)(\sec x\tan x-0)-(\sec x-1)(\sec x\tan x+0)}{(\sec x+1)^2}$$

$$=\frac{(\sec x+1)(\sec x\tan x)-(\sec x-1)(\sec x\tan x)}{(\sec x+1)^2} \quad \left[\because \frac{d}{dx}\sec x=\sec x\tan x\right]$$

$$=\frac{\sec x\tan x[\sec x+1-\sec x+1]}{(\sec x+1)^2}=\frac{2\sec x\tan x}{(\sec x+1)^2}$$

Question 19 $\sin^n x$.

◎ *Thinking Process* Here, we will use chain rule of differentiation.

Sol. Let $y=\sin^n x \Rightarrow y=(\sin x)^n$, On differentiating y w.r.t. x, we get

$$\frac{dy}{dx}=n(\sin x)^{n-1}\times\frac{d}{dx}(\sin x) \Rightarrow \frac{dy}{dx}=n\sin^{n-1}x\cos x$$

Question 20 $\dfrac{a+b\sin x}{c+d\cos x}$.

Sol. Let $y=\dfrac{a+b\sin x}{c+d\cos x}$

On differentiating y w.r.t. x, we get

$$\frac{dy}{dx}=\frac{(c+d\cos x)\frac{d}{dx}(a+b\sin x)-(a+b\sin x)\frac{d}{dx}(c+d\cos x)}{(c+d\cos x)^2}$$

[$\because$ by quotient rule

$$=\frac{(c+d\cos x)[0+b\cos x]-(a+b\sin x)(0-d\sin x)}{(c+d\cos x)^2}$$

$$=\frac{(c+d\cos x)(b\cos x)-(a+b\sin x)(-d\sin x)}{(c+d\cos x)^2}$$

$$=\frac{bc\cos x+bd\cos^2 x+ad\sin x+bd\sin^2 x}{(c+d\cos x)^2}$$

$$=\frac{bc\cos x+ad\sin x+bd(\cos^2 x+\sin^2 x)}{(c+d\cos x)^2} \quad [\because \sin^2\theta+\cos^2\theta=1]$$

$$\Rightarrow \frac{dy}{dx}=\frac{bc\cos x+ad\sin x+bd}{(c+d\cos x)^2}$$

Question 21 $\dfrac{\sin(x+a)}{\cos x}$.

Sol. Let $y=\dfrac{\sin(x+a)}{\cos x}=\dfrac{\sin x\cos a+\cos x\sin a}{\cos x}$

(using $\sin(A+B)=\sin A\cos B+\cos A\sin B$)

$$= \frac{\sin x \cos a}{\cos x} + \frac{\cos x \sin a}{\cos x} = \cos a \tan x + \sin a$$

On differentiating y w.r.t. x, we get

$$\frac{dy}{dx} = \cos a \frac{d}{dx}(\tan x) + \frac{d}{dx}(\sin a)$$

$$= \cos a \sec^2 x + 0 \qquad \left(\because \frac{d}{dx}(\text{constant}) = 0 \text{ and} \frac{d}{dx}(\tan x) = \sec^2 x\right)$$

$$= \frac{\cos a}{\cos^2 x} \qquad \left(\because \cos x = \frac{1}{\sec x}\right)$$

Quick Solution

$$y = \frac{\sin(x+a)}{\cos x}$$

We will solve this question with the help of quotient formula and then use chain rule

On differentiating both sides w.r.t. x

Then

$$\frac{dy}{dx} = \frac{\cos x \cdot \frac{d}{dx}[\sin(x+a)] - \sin(x+a)\frac{d}{dx}\cos x}{(\cos x)^2}$$

$$= \frac{\cos(x+a)\cos(x) + \sin(x+a)\sin x}{\cos^2 x}$$

we can write it

$$\frac{dy}{dx} = \frac{\cos(x+a-x)}{\cos^2 x} \qquad [\because \cos(A-B) = \cos A \cos B + \sin A \sin B]$$

$$\frac{dy}{dx} = \frac{\cos a}{\cos^2 x}$$

Question 22 $x^4(5\sin x - 3\cos x)$.

Sol. Let $y = x^4(5\sin x - 3\cos x)$

On differentiating y w.r.t. x, we get

$$\frac{dy}{dx} = x^4 \frac{d}{dx}(5\sin x - 3\cos x) + (5\sin x - 3\cos x)\frac{d}{dx}(x^4) \text{ (by product formula)}$$

$$= x^4(5\cos x + 3\sin x) + (5\sin x - 3\cos x)4x^3$$

$$= x^3[x(5\cos x + 3\sin x) + 4(5\sin x - 3\cos x)]$$

$$= x^3[5x\cos x + 3x\sin x + 20\sin x - 12\cos x]$$

Question 23 $(x^2 + 1)\cos x$.

Sol. Let $y = (x^2 + 1)\cos x$,

On differentiating y w.r.t. x, we get

$$\frac{dy}{dx} = (x^2 + 1)\frac{d}{dx}(\cos x) + \cos x \frac{d}{dx}(x^2 + 1) \qquad \text{(by product formula)}$$

$$= (x^2 + 1)(-\sin x) + \cos x(2x) = 2x\cos x - (x^2 + 1)\sin x$$

Question 24 $(ax^2 + \sin x)(p + q\cos x)$.

Sol. Let $y = (ax^2 + \sin x)(p + q\cos x)$

On differentiating y w.r.t. x, we get

$$\frac{dy}{dx} = (ax^2 + \sin x)\frac{d}{dx}(p + q\cos x) + (p + q\cos x)\frac{d}{dx}(ax^2 + \sin x)$$

(by product formula)

$$= (ax^2 + \sin x)(0 - q\sin x) + (p + q\cos x)(2ax + \cos x)$$
$$= -q\sin x(ax^2 + \sin x) + (p + q\cos x)(2ax + \cos x)$$

Question 25 $(x + \cos x)(x - \tan x)$.

Sol. Let $y = (x + \cos x)(x - \tan x)$

On differentiating y w.r.t. x, we get

$$\frac{dy}{dx} = (x + \cos x)\frac{d}{dx}(x - \tan x) + (x - \tan x)\frac{d}{dx}(x + \cos x) \text{ (by product formula)}$$
$$= (x + \cos x)(1 - \sec^2 x) + (x - \tan x)(1 - \sin x)$$
$$= -(x + \cos x)(\sec^2 x - 1) + (x - \tan x)(1 - \sin x)$$
$$= -(x + \cos x)\tan^2 x + (x - \tan x)(1 - \sin x) \qquad (\because \sec^2 x - \tan^2 x = 1)$$

Question 26 $\dfrac{4x + 5\sin x}{3x + 7\cos x}$.

Sol. Let $y = \dfrac{4x + 5\sin x}{3x + 7\cos x}$ Differentiating y w.r.t. x, we get

$$\frac{dy}{dx} = \frac{(3x + 7\cos x)\frac{d}{dx}(4x + 5\sin x) - (4x + 5\sin x)\frac{d}{dx}(3x + 7\cos x)}{(3x + 7\cos x)^2}$$

(by quotient formula)

$$= \frac{(3x + 7\cos x)(4 \times 1 + 5\cos x) - (4x + 5\sin x)(3 - 7\sin x)}{(3x + 7\cos x)^2}$$
$$= \frac{12x + 15x\cos x + 28\cos x + 35\cos^2 x - 12x + 28x\sin x - 15\sin x + 35\sin^2 x}{(3x + 7\cos x)^2}$$
$$= \frac{35(\cos^2 x + \sin^2 x) + 15x\cos x + 28\cos x + 28x\sin x - 15\sin x}{(3x + 7\cos x)^2}$$
$$= \frac{35 + 15x\cos x + 28\cos x + 28x\sin x - 15\sin x}{(3x + 7\cos x)^2} \qquad [\because \sin^2 x + \cos^2 x = 1]$$

Question 27 $\dfrac{x^2 \cos\left(\frac{\pi}{4}\right)}{\sin x}$

Sol Let $y = \dfrac{x^2 \cos\left(\frac{\pi}{4}\right)}{\sin x} \Rightarrow y = \left(\cos\frac{\pi}{4}\right) \times \dfrac{x^2}{\sin x}$

On differentiating y w.r.t. x, we get

$$\frac{dy}{dx} = \cos\frac{\pi}{4} \times \frac{d}{dx}\left(\frac{x^2}{\sin x}\right) \quad \left(\because \cos\frac{\pi}{4} \text{ is constant}\right)$$

$$\Rightarrow \frac{dy}{dx} = \left(\cos\frac{\pi}{4}\right) \times \frac{\sin x \frac{d}{dx}(x^2) - x^2\left(\frac{d}{dx}\sin x\right)}{\sin^2 x} \quad \text{(By quotient formula)}$$

$$= \cos\frac{\pi}{4} \times \frac{(\sin x)(2x) - x^2(\cos x)}{\sin^2 x} = \frac{x\cos\frac{\pi}{4}[2\sin x - x\cos x]}{\sin^2 x}$$

$$= \frac{x[2\sin x - x\cos x]}{\sqrt{2}\sin^2 x} \quad \left[\because \cos\frac{\pi}{4} = \frac{1}{\sqrt{2}}\right]$$

Question 28 $\frac{x}{1+\tan x}$.

Sol. Let $y = \frac{x}{1+\tan x}$

On differentiating y w.r.t. x, we get

$$\frac{dy}{dx} = \frac{(1+\tan x)\frac{d}{dx}(x) - x\frac{d}{dx}(1+\tan x)}{(1+\tan x)^2} \quad \text{[by quotient rule]}$$

$$= \frac{(1+\tan x)(1) - x(0+\sec^2 x)}{(1+\tan x)^2} = \frac{1+\tan x - x\sec^2 x}{(1+\tan x)^2} \left[\because \frac{d}{dx}(\tan x) = \sec^2 x\right]$$

Question 29 $(x+\sec x)(x-\tan x)$.

Sol. Let $y = (x+\sec x)(x-\tan x)$

On differentiating y w.r.t. x, we get

$$\frac{dy}{dx} = (x+\sec x)\frac{d}{dx}(x-\tan x) + (x-\tan x)\frac{d}{dx}(x+\sec x)$$

(by product formula)

$$= (x+\sec x)(1-\sec^2 x) + (x-\tan x)(1+\sec x\tan x)$$

Question 30 $\frac{x}{\sin^n x}$

Sol. Let $y = \frac{x}{\sin^n x}$

On differentiating y w.r.t. x, we get

$$\frac{d}{dx} = \frac{\sin^n x \cdot dx - x\frac{d}{dx}(\sin x)^n}{(\sin^n x)^2}$$

$$\frac{dy}{dx} = \frac{\sin^n x \cdot 1 - x \cdot n(\sin x)^{n-1} \cdot \cos x}{\sin^{2n} x} x \quad \left[\because \frac{d}{dx}\sin x = \cos x\right]$$

$$\frac{dy}{dx} = \frac{\sin^n x - nx \cdot \sin^{n-1} x \cdot \cos x}{\sin^{2n} x} \quad \left[\because \frac{d}{dx}x^n = nx^{n-1}\right]$$

DIKSHA APP Questions

Multiple Choice Questions

Q.1 $\lim_{x \to 5} \left(\frac{x^2 - 25}{x - 5} \right)$

(a) ∞ (b) 0 (c) 10 (d) 5

Sol. (c) We have, $\lim_{x \to 5} \left(\frac{x^2 - 25}{x - 5} \right) = \lim_{x \to 5} \left(\frac{(x-5)(x+5)}{(x-5)} \right)$

$[\because a^2 - b^2 = (a-b)(a+b)]$

$$= \lim_{x \to 5} (x+5) = 5 + 5 = 10$$

Q.2 $\lim_{x \to 0} \frac{(1+x)^6 - 1}{(1+x)^5 - 1}$

(a) 1 (b) $\frac{6}{5}$ (c) $\frac{5}{6}$ (d) 0

◎ ***Thinking Process*** Here, will use the formula $\lim_{x \to a} \frac{x^n - a^n}{x - a} = na^{n-1}$ So, to create this form, we will divide the numerator and denominator by $(y-1)$

Sol. (b) We have, $\lim_{x \to 0} \frac{(1+x)^6 - 1}{(1+x)^5 - 1}$

Let $1 + x = y$, so that when $x \to 0$, then $y \to 1$

$$\therefore \quad \lim_{y \to 1} \frac{(y)^6 - 1}{(y)^5 - 1} = \lim_{y \to 1} \frac{\left(\frac{y^6 - 1}{y - 1} \right)}{\frac{y^5 - 1}{y - 1}} = \frac{\lim_{y \to 1} \left(\frac{y^6 - 1^6}{y - 1} \right)}{\lim_{y \to 1} \left(\frac{y^5 - 1^5}{y - 1} \right)} \quad \left[\because \lim_{x \to a} \frac{f(x)}{y(x)} = \frac{\lim_{x \to a} f(x)}{\lim_{x \to a} g(x)} \right]$$

$$= \frac{6(1)^{6-1}}{5(1)^{5-1}} \quad \left[\therefore \lim_{x \to a} \frac{x^n - a^n}{x - a} = na^{n-1} \right]$$

$$= \frac{6}{5}$$

Q.3 $\lim_{x \to 0} \left(\frac{\sin 3x}{x} \right)$

(a) 0 (b) $\frac{1}{3}$ (c) 3 (d) ∞

Sol. (c) We have, $\lim_{x \to 0} \left(\frac{\sin 3x}{x} \right) = \lim_{x \to 0} \left(\frac{3 \sin 3x}{3x} \right) = 3 \lim_{x \to 0} \left(\frac{\sin 3x}{3x} \right) = 3(1) = 3$

$$\left[\because \lim_{x \to 0} \frac{\sin x}{x} = 1 \right]$$

Q.4 $\lim_{x\to 0}\left(\frac{\tan^2 3x}{3x^2}\right)$

(a) 0 (b) 3 (c) ∞ (d) 9

Sol. (b) $\lim_{x\to 0}\left(\frac{\tan^2 3x}{x^2}\right) = \lim_{x\to 0}\left(\frac{3\tan^2 3x}{9x^2}\right)$

$$= \lim_{x\to 0}\left[\frac{3\tan^2 3x}{(3x)^2}\right] = 3\lim_{x\to 0}\left[\frac{\tan 3x}{3x}\right]^2$$

$$= 3\left[\lim_{x\to 0}\left(\frac{\tan 3x}{3x}\right)\right]^2 \qquad [\because \lim_{x\to 0}(f(x))^2 = [\lim_{x\to 0} f(x)^2]$$

$$= 3\,[1]^2 = 3 \qquad \left[\because \lim_{x\to 0}\frac{\tan ax}{ax} = 1\right]$$

Q.5 $y = \sin x + \tan x$, find $\frac{dy}{dx}$ at $x = \frac{\pi}{3}$.

(a) $\frac{\sqrt{3}}{2} + \sqrt{3}$ (b) $\sqrt{\frac{3}{2}} + \frac{4}{3}$

(c) $\frac{\sqrt{3}}{2} + 4$ (d) $\frac{9}{2}$

Thinking Process Use formulae $\frac{d}{dx}(\sin x) = \cos x$ and $\frac{d}{dx}(\tan x) = \sec^2 x$

Sol. (d) We have, $y = \sin x + \tan x$, then

$$\frac{dy}{dx} = \frac{d}{dx}(\sin x + \tan x)$$

$$= \frac{d}{dx}(\sin x) + \frac{d}{dx}(\tan x)\left[\because \frac{d}{dx}[f(x) \pm g(x)] = \frac{d}{dx}\left(f(x) \pm \frac{d}{dx}g(x)\right)\right]$$

$$= \cos x + \sec^2 x \qquad \left[\because \frac{d}{dx}(\sin x) = \cos x \text{ and } \frac{d}{dx}(\tan x) = \sec^2 x\right]$$

$$\therefore \quad \frac{dy}{dx} = \cos x + \sec^2 x$$

$$\left(\frac{dy}{dx}\right)_{x=\frac{\pi}{3}} = \cos\left(\frac{\pi}{3}\right) + \sec^2\left(\frac{\pi}{3}\right)$$

$$= \frac{1}{2} + (2)^2 = \frac{1}{2} + 4 = \frac{9}{2}$$

Statistics

CHAPTER 13

Important Points

01 **Mean**

For ungrouped data,

If $x_1, x_2, x_3, ..., x_n$ be n observations,

then

$$\bar{x} = \frac{x_1 + x_2 + ... + x_n}{n} = \frac{\Sigma x_i}{n}$$

For discrete frequency distribution

If $x_1, x_2, x_3, ..., x_n$ be n observations with respective frequencies $f_1, f_2, f_3, ..., f_n$,

Then, $\bar{x} = \frac{\sum fixi}{\sum fi}$

where, $i = 1, 2, ... n$

For continuous frequency distribution.

Let A be the assumed mean, then

$$d_i = \frac{x_i - A}{h}$$

$$\therefore \bar{x} = A + \frac{\Sigma fidi}{\Sigma fi} xh$$

where h is the common factor.

02 **Median**

For ungrouped data

Arrange the data in ascending or descending order.

If n is odd, then

Median = $\left(\frac{n+1}{2}\right)$th observation.

If n is even, then

median = $\frac{n}{2}$ th observation + $\left(\frac{n}{2} + 1\right)$ th observation

For discrete frequency distribution

Same method as in ungrouped data

For continuous frequency distribution

Step 1 Find the Cumulative Frequency (CF).

Step 2 $(N/2)$th or next to $(N/2)$th CF corresponds to median class.

Step 3 Cumulative frequency C just before to $(N/2)$th CF is denoted by C.

Step 4 After collecting these terms use

$$\text{Median} = l + \frac{(N/2 - C)}{f} \times h$$

where, l = lower limit of median class

h = length of class interval of median class

f = frequency corresponding to median class.

Measures of central tendency A measure of central tendency is a value that aims to describe the center or typical value of a data set. Mean, median and mode are the measures of central tendency.

Measure of dispersion The measures of central tendency are not sufficient to give complete information about a given data. Variability is another factor which is required to be studied under statistics. The single number that describes the variability is called the measure of dispersion. It is the measure of scattering of the data about some central tendency.

There are following measures of dispersion

(i) Range

(ii) Quartile deviation

(iii) Mean deviation

(iv) Standard deviation

Range The difference between the maximum value and the minimum value of data is called the 'Range' of the data.

Range = maximum value − minimum value.

03 Mean Deviation from the Mean Let there are n observations $x_1, x_2, x_3, \dots, x_n$ having their mean $\bar{x}$, then mean deviation from the mean $\bar{x} = \sum_{i=1}^{n} \frac{|x_i - \bar{x}|}{n}$

where, $|x_i - \bar{x}|$ is the absolute value of the deviation of x_i from $\bar{x}$.

If the distribution is a grouped one *i.e.*, if frequency is given then,

$$\text{Mean deviation about mean} = \frac{\sum_{i=1}^{n} f_i|x_i - \bar{x}|}{\sum_{i=1}^{n} f_i} \text{ or } \frac{1}{N} \sum_{i=1}^{n} f_i\, |x_i - \bar{x}|$$

where, $N = \sum_{i=1}^{n} f_i$ is the sum of the frequencies.

04 Mean Deviation from the Median Let there are n observations $x_1, x_2, x_3, x_4, \dots\dots, x_n$ having their median M_d, then mean deviation from the median is $\frac{\sum_{i=1}^{n} |x_i - M_d|}{N}$, $N = \sum_{i=1}^{n} f_i$

where, $|x_i - M_d|$ is absolute value of the deviation of x_i from M_d.

If the distribution is a grouped one *i.e.*, if frequency is given, then

$$\text{Mean deviation about median} = \frac{\sum_{i=1}^{n} f_i |x_i - M_d|}{\sum_{i=1}^{n} f_i}$$

05 Variance and Standard Deviation For ungrouped data

$$\text{Variance } (\sigma)^2 = \frac{\Sigma(x_i - \bar{x})^2}{n} = \frac{\Sigma x_i^2}{n} - \left(\frac{\Sigma x_i}{n}\right)^2 = \frac{\Sigma x_i^2}{n} - (\bar{x})^2$$

For discrete frequency distribution *i.e.*, if frequency is given; then

$$\text{Variance } = \frac{\Sigma f_i(x_i - \bar{x})^2}{\Sigma fi} = \frac{\Sigma f_i x_i^2}{\Sigma f_i} - \left(\frac{\Sigma f_i x_i}{\Sigma f_i}\right)^2 = \frac{\Sigma f_i x_i^2}{\Sigma f_i} - (\bar{x}_i)^2$$

For continuous frequency distribution

$$\text{Variance} = h^2 \times \left[\frac{\Sigma f_i x_i^2}{\Sigma f_i} - \left(\frac{\Sigma f_i x_i}{\Sigma f_i}\right)^2\right]$$

where, h is the width of class interval.

Shortcut method to calculate variance

$$\text{Variance} = h^2 \times \left[\frac{\Sigma f_i d_i^2}{\Sigma f_i} - \left(\frac{\Sigma f_i d_i}{\Sigma f_i}\right)^2\right]$$

where, $d_i = \frac{x_i - A}{h}$

$A =$ Assumed mean

In this case,

$$\text{Mean } \bar{x} = A + \frac{\Sigma f_i d_i}{\Sigma f_i} \times h$$

In each case, standard deviation $= \sigma = \sqrt{\text{Variance}} = \sqrt{\sigma^2}$

Exercise 13.1

Direction (Q. No. 1 and 2) Find the mean deviation about the mean for the following series.

Question 1 4, 7, 8, 9, 10, 12, 13, 17.

◎ *Thinking Process* (Q. Nos. 1 and 2) Mean deviation about mean can be calculated by the formula $= \frac{\Sigma|x_i - \bar{x}|}{n}$, where $\bar{x}$ = mean of the given observations.

Sol. Mean of the given series

$$\bar{x} = \frac{\text{Sum of terms}}{\text{Number of terms}}$$

$$= \frac{\Sigma x_i}{n}$$

$$= \frac{4 + 7 + 8 + 9 + 10 + 12 + 13 + 17}{8} = \frac{80}{8} = 10$$

x_i	$\|x_i - \bar{x}\|$
4	$\|4 - 10\| = 6$
7	$\|7 - 10\| = 3$
8	$\|8 - 10\| = 2$
9	$\|9 - 10\| = 1$
10	$\|10 - 10\| = 0$
12	$\|12 - 10\| = 2$
13	$\|13 - 10\| = 3$
17	$\|17 - 10\| = 7$
$\Sigma x_i = 80$	$\Sigma\|x_i - \bar{x}\| = 24$

$\therefore$ Mean deviation about mean $= \frac{\Sigma|x_i - \bar{x}|}{n}$

$$= \frac{24}{8}$$

$$= 3$$

Question 2 38, 70, 48, 40, 42, 55, 63, 46, 54, 44.

Sol. We know that, mean of the given series $\bar{x} = \frac{\text{Sum of terms}}{\text{Number of terms}}$

$$= \frac{\Sigma x_i}{n}$$

$$= \frac{38 + 70 + 48 + 40 + 42 + 55 + 63 + 46 + 54 + 44}{10} = \frac{500}{10} = 50$$

x_i	$\lvert x_i - \bar{x} \rvert$
38	$\lvert 38 - 50 \rvert = 12$
70	$\lvert 70 - 50 \rvert = 20$
48	$\lvert 48 - 50 \rvert = 02$
40	$\lvert 40 - 50 \rvert = 10$
42	$\lvert 42 - 50 \rvert = 08$
55	$\lvert 55 - 50 \rvert = 05$
63.	$\lvert 63 - 50 \rvert = 13$
46	$\lvert 46 - 50 \rvert = 04$
54	$\lvert 54 - 50 \rvert = 04$
44	$\lvert 44 - 50 \rvert = 06$
$\Sigma x_i = 500$	$\Sigma \lvert x_i - \bar{x} \rvert = 84$

$\therefore$ Mean deviation about mean $= \frac{\Sigma \lvert x_i - \bar{x} \rvert}{n} = \frac{84}{10} = 8.4$

Mistake Alert Never forget to include the sign of the mode.

Direction (Q. No. 3 and 4) Find the mean deviation about the median for the following data.

Question 3 13, 17, 16, 14, 11, 13, 10, 16, 11, 18, 12, 17

Thinking Process (Q. No. 3 and 4) First arrange the given observations in ascending order and then calculate the median (M) after that mean deviation about the mean can be calculated by the relation $= \frac{\Sigma \lvert x_i - M \rvert}{n}$

where, n = number of terms and M = median

Sol. Given data is 13, 17, 16, 14, 11, 13, 10, 16, 11, 18, 12, 17

Arranging in ascending order

10, 11, 11, 12, 13, 13, 14, 16, 16, 17, 17, 18

Here, the total number of observations = 12 (even)

$$\text{Median } M = \frac{\frac{N\text{th}}{2} \text{ observation} + \left(\frac{N}{2}+1\right)\text{th observation}}{2}$$

$$= \frac{\left(\frac{12}{2}\right)\text{th observation} + \left(\frac{12}{2}+1\right)\text{th observation}}{2}$$

$$= \frac{6\text{th observation} + 7\text{th observation}}{2} = \frac{13+14}{2} = \frac{27}{2}$$

$\Rightarrow \quad M = 13.5$

x_i	$\lvert x_i - M \rvert$
10	$\lvert 10 - 13.5 \rvert = 3.5$
11	$\lvert 11 - 13.5 \rvert = 2.5$
11	$\lvert 11 - 13.5 \rvert = 2.5$
12	$\lvert 12 - 13.5 \rvert = 1.5$
13	$\lvert 13 - 13.5 \rvert = 0.5$
13	$\lvert 13 - 13.5 \rvert = 0.5$
14	$\lvert 14 - 13.5 \rvert = 0.5$
16	$\lvert 16 - 13.5 \rvert = 2.5$
16	$\lvert 16 - 13.5 \rvert = 2.5$
17	$\lvert 17 - 13.5 \rvert = 3.5$
17	$\lvert 17 - 13.5 \rvert = 3.5$
18	$\lvert 18 - 13.5 \rvert = 4.5$
	$\Sigma \lvert x_i - M \rvert = 28$

$\therefore$ Mean deviation about median $= \frac{\Sigma \lvert x_i - M \rvert}{n} = \frac{28}{12} =$

Questions 4 36, 72, 46, 42, 60, 45, 53, 46, 51, 49.

Sol. Given data is 36, 72, 46, 42, 60, 45, 53, 46, 51, 49.

Arranging the data in ascending order,

36, 42, 45, 46, 46, 49, 51, 53, 60, 72

Here, the total number of observations = 10 (even)

$$\text{Median } M = \frac{\frac{N}{2}\text{th observation} + \left(\frac{N}{2}+1\right)\text{th observation}}{2}$$

$$= \frac{\left(\frac{10}{2}\right)\text{th observation} + \left(\frac{10}{2}+1\right)\text{th observation}}{2}$$

$$= \frac{5\text{th observation} + 6\text{th observation}}{2} = \frac{46+49}{2} = 47.5$$

x_i	$\|x_i - M\|$
36	$\|36 - 47.5\| = 11.5$
42	$\|42 - 47.5\| = 5.5$
45	$\|45 - 47.5\| = 2.5$
46	$\|46 - 47.5\| = 1.5$
46	$\|46 - 47.5\| = 1.5$
49	$\|49 - 47.5\| = 1.5$
51	$\|51 - 47.5\| = 3.5$
53	$\|53 - 47.5\| = 5.5$
60	$\|60 - 47.5\| = 12.5$
72	$\|72 - 47.5\| = 24.5$
	$\Sigma\|x_i - M\| = 70$

$$\therefore \text{Mean deviation about median} = \frac{\Sigma|x_i - M|}{n} = \frac{70}{10} = 7$$

Direction (Q. No. 5 and 6) Find the mean deviation about the mean for the data in following tables.

◎ *Thinking Process* We have to find the mean deviation about the mean so, first of all find the mean using the formula $\bar{x} = \frac{\Sigma f_i x_i}{\Sigma f_i}$ and then calculate mean deviation about mean by $\frac{\Sigma(f_i|x_i - \bar{x}|)}{\Sigma f_i}$.

Question 5

x_i	5	10	15	20	25
f_i	7	4	6	3	5

Sol. We make the following table from the given data.

x_i	f_i	$f_i x_i$	$\|x_i - \bar{x}\|$	$f_i\|x - \bar{x}\|$
5	7	35	$\|5 - 14\| = 9$	63
10	4	40	$\|10 - 14\| = 4$	16
15	6	90	$\|15 - 14\| = 1$	06
20	3	60	$\|20 - 14\| = 6$	18
25	5	125	$\|25 - 14\| = 11$	55
Total	$\Sigma f_i = 25$	350		$\Sigma f\|x - \bar{x}\| = 158$

$$\text{Mean } \bar{x} = \frac{\Sigma f_i x_i}{\Sigma f_i} = \frac{350}{25} = 14$$

$$\therefore \text{Mean deviation about mean} = \frac{\Sigma f_i|x_i - \bar{x}|}{\Sigma f_i} = \frac{158}{25} = 6.32$$

Question 6

x_i	10	30	50	70	90
f_i	4	24	28	16	8

Sol. We make the following table from the given data.

x_i	f_i	$f_i x_i$	$\|x_i - \bar{x}\|$	$f_i\|x_i - \bar{x}\|$
10	4	40	$\|10-50\| = 40$	160
30	24	720	$\|30-50\| = 20$	480
50	28	1400	$\|50-50\| = 00$	000
70	16	1120	$\|70-50\| = 20$	320
90	8	720	$\|90-50\| = 40$	320
Total	$\Sigma f_i = 80$	$\Sigma f x = 4000$		$\Sigma f \|x - \bar{x}\| = 1280$

$$\text{Mean} = \frac{\Sigma f x}{\Sigma f} = \frac{4000}{80} = 50$$

$$\therefore \text{ Mean deviation about mean} = \frac{\Sigma f |x - \bar{x}|}{\Sigma f_i} = \frac{1280}{80} = 16$$

Note Be careful while doing the calculation and apply correct concept based formula.

Direction (Q. No. 7 and 8) *Find the mean deviation about the median for the given data.*

Question 7

x_i	5	7	9	10	12	15
f_i	8	6	2	2	2	6

◎ **Thinking Process** We have to find the mean deviation about the median, so first of all, find the median and then calculate the mean deviation about the median by using the formula $\frac{\Sigma f_i (x_i - M)}{\Sigma f_i}$.

Sol. We make the following table from the given data.

x_i	f	CF	$\|x - M\|$	$f\|x - M\|$
5	8	8	$\|5-7\| = 2$	16
7	6	14	$\|7-7\| = 0$	00
9	2	16	$\|9-7\| = 2$	04
10	2	18	$\|10-7\| = 3$	06
12	2	20	$\|12-7\| = 5$	10
15	6	26	$\|15-7\| = 8$	48
Total	$\Sigma f = 26$			$\Sigma f \|x - M\| = 84$

Here, $N = \Sigma f_i = 26$ (even)

$$\text{Median } M = \frac{\frac{N}{2}\text{th observation} + \left(\frac{N}{2}+1\right)\text{th observation}}{2}$$

$$= \frac{\frac{26}{2}\text{th observation} + \left(\frac{26}{2}+1\right)\text{th observation}}{2}$$

$$= \frac{\text{13th observation} + \text{14th observation}}{2} = \frac{7+7}{2} = \frac{14}{2} = 7$$

($\because$ 13th observation = 7,14 th observation = 7)

$\therefore$ Mean deviation about median $= \frac{\Sigma f_i |x_i - M|}{\Sigma f_i} = \frac{84}{26} = 3.23$

Question 8

x_i	15	21	27	30	35
f_i	3	5	6	7	8

Sol. We make the following table from the given data.

x	f	CF	$\|x - M\|$	$f\ \|x - M\|$
15	3	3	$\|15 - 30\| = 15$	45
21	5	8	$\|21 - 30\| = 9$	45
27	6	14	$\|27 - 30\| = 3$	18
30	7	21	$\|30 - 30\| = 0$	0
35	8	29	$\|35 - 30\| = 5$	40
Total	$\Sigma f = 29$			$\Sigma f\ \|x - M\| = 148$

Here, $N = \Sigma f_i = 29$ (odd)

$\therefore$ Median $M = \left(\frac{N+1}{2}\right)$th observation

$= \left(\frac{29+1}{2}\right)$th value = 15th observation = 30 $\Rightarrow M = 30$

$\therefore$ Mean deviation about median $= \frac{\Sigma f_i |x_i - M|}{\Sigma f_i} = \frac{148}{29} = 5.1$

Direction (Q. No. 9 and 10) Find the mean deviation about the mean for the data in following tables.

Question 9

Income per day	Number of persons
0-100	4
100-200	8
200-300	9
300-400	10
400-500	7
500-600	5
600-700	4
700-800	3

◎ *Thinking Process* We have to find the mean deviation about the mean, so first of all, we find the mean using the formula $\bar{x} = A + \frac{\Sigma fidi}{\Sigma fi} \times h$ and then calculate mean deviation about mean by $\frac{\Sigma(fi|x_i - \bar{x}|)}{\Sigma fi}$, where A = assumed mean, $di = \frac{x_i - A}{h}$ and x_i mid-value of class.

Sol. We make the following table as follow.

Class	f_i	Mid value ( )	$d_i = \frac{x_i - A}{h}$ $A = 350, h = 100$	$f_i d_i$	$\|x_i - \bar{x}\|$	$f_i\|x_i - \bar{x}\|$
0-100	4	50	–3	–12	308	1232
100-200	8	150	–2	–16	208	1664
200-300	9	250	–1	–9	108	972
300-400	10	350	0	0	8	80
400-500	7	450	1	7	92	644
500-600	5	550	2	10	192	960
600-700	4	650	3	12	292	1168
700-800	3	750	4	12	392	1176
Total	$\Sigma f = 50$			$\Sigma fidi = 4$		$\Sigma fi\|x_i - \bar{x}\| = 7896$

Let the assumed mean = 350

$$\text{Mean } \bar{x} = A + \frac{\Sigma f d}{\Sigma f} \times h = 350 + \frac{4}{50} \times 100$$

$$= 350 + 8$$

$$\bar{x} = 358$$

$\therefore$ Mean deviation about the mean $= \frac{\Sigma f_i|x_i - \bar{x}|}{\Sigma f_i}$

$$= \frac{7896}{50} = 157.92$$

Question 10

Height in cm	Number of boys
95-105	9
105-115	13
115-125	26
125-135	30
135-145	12
145-155	10

Sol. We make the following table as follows.

Class	f_i	Mid value (x_i)	$d_i = \frac{x_i - A}{h}$ $A = 130, h = 10$	$f_i d_i$	$\lvert x_i - \bar{x} \rvert$	$f_i \lvert x_i - \bar{x} \rvert$
95-105	9	100	−3	−27	25.3	227.7
105-115	13	110	−2	−26	15.3	198.9
115-125	26	120	−1	−26	5.3	137.8
125-135	30	130	0	0	4.7	141.0
135-145	12	140	1	12	14.7	176.4
145-155	10	150	2	20	24.7	247.0
Total	100			− 47		1128.8

Let the assumed mean (A) = 130

$$\text{Mean } \bar{x} = A + \frac{\Sigma f_i d_i}{\Sigma f_i} \times h = 130 + \frac{(-47)}{100} \times 10 = 130 - 4.7 = 125.3$$

$$\therefore \text{ Mean deviation about mean} = \frac{\Sigma f_i \lvert x_i - \bar{x} \rvert}{\Sigma f_i} = \frac{1128.8}{100} = 11.288 \text{ cm}$$

Question 11 Find the mean deviation about median for the following data

Marks	0-10	10-20	20-30	30-40	40-50	50-60
Number of girls	6	8	14	16	4	2

◎ ***Thinking Process*** We are to find the mean deviation about the median, so first of all median is to be calculated. It is a continuous data. So median can be calculated by using the formula Median $= l + \frac{\frac{N}{2} - C}{f} \times h$ and then mean deviation about the median is $\frac{\Sigma fi \lvert x_i - M \rvert}{\Sigma fi}$

Sol. We make the following table from the given data.

Class	f_i	CF	Mid value x_i	$\lvert x_i - M \rvert$	$f_i \lvert x_i - M \rvert$
0-10	6	6	5	$\lvert 5 - 27.86 \rvert = 22.86$	137.16
10-20	8	(14)C	15	$\lvert 15 - 27.86 \rvert = 12.86$	102.88
(20-30)	(14)	28	25	$\lvert 25 - 27.86 \rvert = 2.86$	40.04
30-40	16	44	35	$\lvert 35 - 27.86 \rvert = 7.14$	114.24
40-50	4	48	45	$\lvert 45 - 27.86 \rvert = 17.14$	68.56
50-60	2	50	55	$\lvert 55 - 27.86 \rvert = 27.14$	54.28
Total	$\Sigma f = 50$				517.16

Here, $\dfrac{N}{2} = \dfrac{50}{2} = 25$

$\therefore$ Median class is (20 – 30) $\Rightarrow$ $C = 14, f = 14, l = 20, h = 10$

$$\text{Median } M = l + \dfrac{\dfrac{N}{2} - C}{f} \times h = 20 + \dfrac{25 - 14}{14} \times 10 = 20 + \dfrac{11 \times 10}{14}$$

$$= 20 + 7.86 = 27.86$$

$\therefore$ Mean deviation about median $= \dfrac{\Sigma f_i |x_i - M|}{\Sigma f_i} = \dfrac{517.16}{50} = 10.34$ marks

Question 12 Calculate the mean deviation about median for the age distribution of 100 persons given below.

Age (in years)	16-20	21-25	26-30	31-35	36-40	41-45	46-50	51-55
Number	5	6	12	14	26	12	16	9

◎ ***Thinking Process*** Convert the given data into continous frequency distribution by subtracting 0.5 from the lower limit and adding 0.5 to the upper limit of each class interval and then use the formula $M = l + \dfrac{\dfrac{N}{2} - C}{f} \times h$ and then $\text{M.D}(M) = \dfrac{\Sigma fi|x_i - M|}{\Sigma fi}$

Sol. We make the following table from the given data

Age	Modified class	f_i	CF	Mid value x_i	$\|x_i - M\|$	$f_i\|x_i - M\|$
16-20	15.5-20.5	5	5	18	$\|18 - 3\ \| = 20$	100
21-25	20.5-25.5	6	11	23	$\|23 - 3\ \| = 15$	90
26-30	25.5-30.5	12	23	28	$\|28 - 3\ \| = 10$	120
31-35	30.5-35.5	14	37	33	$\|33 - 3\ \| = 5$	70
36-40	35.5-40.5	26	63	38	$\|38 - 38\| = 0$	0
41-45	40.5-45.5	12	75	43	$\|43 - 3\ \| = 5$	60
46-50	45.5-50.5	16	91	48	$\|48 - 3\ \| = 10$	160
51-55	50.5-55.5	9	100	53	$\|53 - 3\ \| = 15$	135
Total		100				735

Here, $N = 100 \therefore \dfrac{N}{2} = 50$

$\therefore$ Median class is 35.5 - 40.5.

$\Rightarrow$ $l = 35.5, C = 37, f = 26, h = 5$ $\quad \left[\because M = l + \dfrac{\dfrac{N}{2} - C}{f} \times h\right]$

$$\therefore \quad M = 35.5 + \dfrac{50 - 37}{26} \times 5 = 35.5 + \dfrac{13}{26} \times 5 = 35.5 + 2.5 = 38$$

$\therefore$ Mean deviation about median $= \dfrac{\Sigma f_i |x_i - M|}{\Sigma f_i} = \dfrac{735}{100} = 7.35$

Exercise 13.2

Direction (Q. Nos. 1 to 5) Find the mean and variance for the following data in following series.

Question 1 6, 7, 10, 12, 13, 4, 8, 12.

◎ ***Thinking Process*** Mean and variance can be calculated by using the formulas

$$\text{Mean} = \frac{\Sigma x_i}{n}, \text{Variance} = \frac{\Sigma x_i^2}{n} - \left(\frac{\Sigma x_i}{n}\right)^2.$$

Sol. From the given data, we form the following table

x_i	x_i^2
6	36
7	49
10	100
12	144
13	169
4	16
8	64
12	144
Total = 72	722

$$\text{Mean} = \frac{\Sigma x_i}{n} = \frac{72}{8} = 9$$

and $\text{variance} = \frac{\Sigma x_i^2}{n} - \left(\frac{\Sigma x_i}{n}\right)^2 = \frac{722}{8} - \left(\frac{72}{8}\right)^2 = 90.25 - 81 = 9.25$

Quick Solution

x_i	$x_i - \bar{x}$	$(x_i - \bar{x})^2$
6	−3	9
7	−2	4
10	−1	1
12	3	9
13	4	16
4	−5	25
8	−1	1
12	3	9
$\Sigma x_i = 72$		$\Sigma(x_i - \bar{x})^2 = 74$

$$\text{Mean } (\bar{x}) = \frac{\Sigma x_i}{n} = \frac{72}{8} = 9$$

$$\text{and variance} = \frac{\Sigma(x_i - \bar{x})^2}{n} = \frac{72}{8} = 9.25$$

Question 2 First n natural numbers.

Sol. First n natural numbers are 1, 2, 3, 4, ……, n.

x	x_i^2
1	1^2
2	2^2
3	3^2
4	4^2
⋮	⋮
⋮	⋮
⋮	⋮
n	n^2
Total $= \frac{n(n+1)}{2}$	$\frac{n(n+1)(2n+1)}{6}$

$$\therefore \quad \text{Mean} = \frac{\Sigma x_i}{n}$$

$$\therefore \quad \bar{x} = \frac{n(n+1)}{2n} \qquad \left[\because \Sigma x_i = \frac{n(n+1)}{2}\right]$$

$$= \frac{n+1}{2}$$

$$\text{Now, Variance} = \frac{\Sigma x_i^2}{n} - \left(\frac{\Sigma x_i}{n}\right)^2$$

$$= \frac{n(n+1)(2n+1)}{6n} - \left[\frac{n(n+1)}{2n}\right]^2$$

$$\left[\because \Sigma x_i^2 = \frac{n(n+1)(2n+1)}{6}\right]$$

$$= \frac{(n+1)(2n+1)}{6} - \frac{(n+1)^2}{4}$$

$$= \frac{(n+1)}{2}\left[\frac{2n+1}{3} - \frac{n+1}{2}\right]$$

$$= \frac{(n+1)}{2}\left[\frac{4n+2-3n-3}{6}\right]$$

$$= \left(\frac{n+1}{2}\right)\left[\frac{n-1}{6}\right]$$

$$= \frac{n^2-1}{12} \qquad [\because (a+b)(a-b) = a^2 - b^2]$$

Question 3 First 10 multiples of 3.

Sol. First 10 multiples of 3 are 3, 6, 9, 12, 15, 18, 21, 24, 27, 30.

x	x_i^2
3	9
6	36
9	81
12	144
15	225
18	324
21	441
24	576
27	729
30	900
Total = 165	3465

$$\therefore \quad \text{Mean } \bar{x} = \frac{\Sigma x_i}{n} = \frac{165}{10} = 16.5$$

$$\text{and variance} = \frac{\Sigma x_i^2}{n} - \left(\frac{\Sigma x_i}{n}\right)^2 = \frac{3465}{10} - \left(\frac{165}{10}\right)^2$$

$$= 346.5 - (16.5)^2 = 346.5 - 272.25 = 74.25$$

Question 4

x_i	6	10	14	18	24	28	30
f_i	2	4	7	12	8	4	3

Sol. We make the following table from the given data.

x	f	x_i^2	$f\,x$	$f\,x_i^2$
6	2	36	12	72
10	4	100	40	400
14	7	196	98	1372
18	12	324	216	3888
24	8	576	192	4608
28	4	784	112	3136
30	3	900	90	2700
Total = 130	40		760	16176

$$\text{Mean} = \frac{\Sigma f_i x_i}{\Sigma f_i} = \frac{760}{40} = 19$$

$$\text{Variance} = \frac{\Sigma f\,x_i^2}{\Sigma f} - \left(\frac{\Sigma f\,x}{\Sigma f}\right)^2 = \frac{16176}{40} - \left(\frac{760}{40}\right)^2$$

$$= 404.4 - (19)^2 = 404.4 - 361 = 43.4$$

Question 5

x_i	92	93	97	98	102	104	109
f_i	3	2	3	2	6	3	3

Sol. We make the following table from the given data.

x	f	x_i^2	$f x$	$f x_i^2$
92	3	8464	276	25392
93	2	8649	186	17298
97	3	9409	291	28227
98	2	9604	196	19208
102	6	10404	612	62424
104	3	10816	312	32448
109	3	11881	327	35643
Total = 695	22		2200	220640

Here, Mean $\overline{x} = \dfrac{\Sigma f x}{\Sigma f} = \dfrac{2200}{22} = 100$

$\therefore$ Variance $= \dfrac{\Sigma f_i x_i^2}{\Sigma f_i} - \left(\dfrac{\Sigma f_i x_i}{\Sigma f_i}\right)^2$

$= \dfrac{220640}{22} - (100)^2$

$= 10029.09 - 10000 = 29.09$

Question 6 Find the mean and standard deviation of following table using short-cut method

x_i	60	61	62	63	64	65	66	67	68
f_i	2	1	12	29	25	12	10	4	5

◎ **Thinking Process** Short-cut method for mean and SD.

Mean $= A + \dfrac{\Sigma f_i d_i}{\Sigma f_i} \times h$ and SD (σ)

$= h\sqrt{\left(\dfrac{\Sigma f_i d_i^2}{\Sigma f_i} - \left(\dfrac{\Sigma f_i d_i}{\Sigma f_i}\right)^2\right)}$ where, $d_i = \dfrac{x_i - A}{h}$

Sol. We make the following table from the given data.

cut (x_i) x_i	Frequency f	Deviation from mean $d = \frac{x - A}{h}$, $A = 64$, $h = 1$	d_i^2	$f_i d_i$	$f_i d_i^2$
60	2	−4	16	−8	32
61	1	−3	9	−3	9
62	12	−2	4	−24	48
63	29	−1	1	−29	29
64	25	0	0	00	00
65	12	1	1	12	12
66	10	2	4	20	40
67	4	3	9	12	36
68	5	4	16	20	80
Total	100			0	286

Let assumed mean $A = 64$

$$\therefore \quad \text{Mean} = A + \frac{\Sigma f_i d_i}{\Sigma f_i} \times h \Rightarrow \bar{x} = 64 + \frac{0}{100} = 64 \qquad (\because h = 1)$$

$$\therefore \text{Standard deviation } \sigma = h\sqrt{\left(\frac{\Sigma f_i d_i^2}{\Sigma f_i} - \left(\frac{\Sigma f_i d_i}{\Sigma f_i}\right)^2\right)} = \sqrt{\frac{286}{100} - \left(\frac{0}{100}\right)^2} = \sqrt{2.86} = 1.69$$

Note h is the width of class intervals.

Direction (Q. Nos. 7 and 8) Find the mean and variance for the following frequency distribution in following tables.

Question 7

Class	0-30	30-60	60-90	90-120	120-150	150-180	180-210
Frequency	2	3	5	10	3	5	2

Sol. We make the following table from the given data.

Class	Frequency (f_i)	Mid-value x_i	Deviation from mean $d_i = \frac{x_i - A}{h}$, $A = 105$	d_i^2	$f_i d_i$	$f_i d_i^2$
0-30	2	15	−3	9	−6	18
30-60	3	45	−2	4	−6	12
60-90	5	75	−1	1	−5	5
90-120	10	105	0	0	0	0
120-150	3	135	1	1	3	3
150-180	5	165	2	4	10	20
180-210	2	195	3	9	6	18
Total	30				2	76

Let assumed mean $A = 105$

$$\therefore \quad \text{Mean} = A + \frac{\Sigma f_i d_i}{\Sigma f_i} \times h = 105 + \frac{2}{30} \times 30 \qquad (\because h = 30)$$

$$= 105 + 2 = 107$$

Now,

$$\text{Variance} = \left[\frac{\Sigma f_i d_i^2}{\Sigma f_i} - \left(\frac{\Sigma f_i d_i}{\Sigma f_i}\right)^2\right] \times h^2$$

$$= \left[\frac{76}{30} - \left(\frac{2}{30}\right)^2\right] \times (30)^2 = \left[\frac{76}{30} - \frac{4}{30 \times 30}\right] \times 900$$

$$= \left[\frac{76 \times 30 - 4}{900}\right] \times 900 = \left(\frac{2280 - 4}{900}\right) \times 900$$

$$= \frac{2276}{900} \times 900 = 2276$$

Question 8

Class	0-10	10-20	20-30	30-40	40-50
Frequency	5	8	15	16	6

Sol. We make the following table from the given data.

Class	Frequency f_i	Mid-value x_i	Mid-value $d_i = \frac{x_i - 25}{10}$	d_i^2	$f_i d_i$	$f_i d_i^2$
0-10	5	5	−2	4	−10	20
10-20	8	15	−1	1	−8	8
20-30	15	25	0	0	0	0
30-40	16	35	1	1	16	16
40-50	6	45	2	4	12	24
Total	50				10	68

Let assumed mean $A = 25$

$$\therefore \quad \text{Mean}\,(\overline{x}) = A + \frac{\Sigma f_i d_i}{\Sigma f_i} \times h = 25 + \frac{10}{50} \times 10 \qquad (\because h = 0)$$

$$= 25 + \frac{100}{50} = 25 + 2 = 27$$

Now,

$$\text{Variance} = \left[\frac{\Sigma f_i d_i^2}{\Sigma f_i} - \left(\frac{\Sigma f_i d_i}{\Sigma f_i}\right)^2\right] \times h^2$$

$$= \left[\frac{68}{50} - \left(\frac{10}{50}\right)^2\right] \times (10)^2 = \frac{[68 \times 50 - 100]}{50 \times 50} \times 100$$

$$= \frac{(3400 - 100)}{50} \times 2$$

$$= \frac{3300 \times 2}{50} = \frac{6600}{50} = 132$$

Question 9 Find the mean, variance and standard deviation using short-cut method.

Height in cm	Number of children
70-75	3
75-80	4
80-85	7
85-90	7
90-95	15
95-100	9
100-105	6
105-110	6
110-115	3

◎ *Thinking Process* Short-cut method for mean variance and SD.

$$\text{Mean}\,(\bar{x}) = A + \frac{\Sigma f_i d_i}{\Sigma f_i} \times h, \text{ variance } (\sigma^2) = \left[\frac{\Sigma f_i d_i^2}{\Sigma f_i} - \left(\frac{\Sigma f_i d_i}{\Sigma f_i}\right)^2\right] h^2$$

and $\text{S.D.} = \sqrt{\sigma^2}$, where $di = \dfrac{x_i - A}{h}$.

Sol. We make the following table from the given data.

Class	Frequency f_i	Mid-value x_i	Deviation from mean $d_i = \dfrac{x_i - 92.5}{5}$	d_i^2	$f_i d_i$	$f_i d_i^2$
70-75	3	72.5	−4	16	−12	48
75-80	4	77.5	−3	9	−12	36
80-85	7	82.5	−2	4	−14	28
85-90	7	87.5	−1	1	−7	7
90-95	15	92.5	0	0	0	0
95-100	9	97.5	1	1	9	9
100-105	6	102.5	2	4	12	24
105-110	6	107.5	3	9	18	54
110-115	3	112.5	4	16	12	48
Total	60				6	254

Let assumed mean, $A = 92.5$, $h = 5$

$$\text{Mean}\,(\bar{x}) = A + \frac{\Sigma f_i d_i}{\Sigma f_i} \times h = 92.5 + \frac{6}{60} \times 5$$

$$= 92.5 + \frac{30}{60} = 92.5 + 0.5 = 93$$

and $\quad$ Variance $= \left[\dfrac{\Sigma f_i d_i^2}{\Sigma f_i} - \left(\dfrac{\Sigma f_i d_i}{\Sigma f_i}\right)^2\right] \times h^2 = \left[\dfrac{254}{60} - \left(\dfrac{6}{60}\right)^2\right] \times (5)^2$

$$= \left[\frac{254 \times 60 - 36}{60 \times 60}\right] \times 25 = \frac{(15240 - 36)}{60 \times 12} \times 5$$

$$= \frac{15204 \times 5}{720} = 105.58$$

$\therefore$ Standard deviation $\sigma = \sqrt{\text{Variance}} = \sqrt{105.58} = 10.27$

Question 10 The diameter of circles (in mm) drawn in design are given below.

Diameter in mm	33-36	37-40	41-44	45-48	49-52
Number of circles	15	17	21	22	25

Calculate the standard deviation and mean diameter of the circles.

◎ ***Thinking Process*** The given data is discontinous so first make the class intervals in continuous form and then solve it in same way as done in previous questions.

Sol.

Diameters	Modified class	f_i	Mid-value x_i	Deviation from mean $d_i = \dfrac{x_i - 42.5}{4}$, $A = 42.5, h = 4$	d_i^2	$f_i d_i$	$f_i d_i^2$
33-36	–	15	34.5	−2	4	−30	60
37-40	–	17	38.5	−1	1	−17	17
41-44	–	21	42.5	0	0	0	0
45-48	–	22	46.5	1	1	22	22
49-52	–	25	50.5	2	4	50	100
Total		100				25	199

Let assumed mean $A = 42.5$

Mean $\bar{x} = A + \dfrac{\Sigma f_i d_i}{\Sigma f_i} \times h = 42.5 + \dfrac{25}{100} \times 4 = 42.5 + 1 = 43.5 \qquad (\because h = 4)$

Standard deviation $\sigma = \sqrt{\dfrac{\Sigma f_i d_i^2}{\Sigma f_i} - \left(\dfrac{\Sigma f_i d_i}{\Sigma f_i}\right)^2} \times h = \sqrt{\dfrac{199}{100} - \left(\dfrac{25}{100}\right)^2} \times 4$

$$= \sqrt{\frac{199 \times 100 - 625}{100 \times 100}} \times 4 = \frac{4}{100}\sqrt{19900 - 625}$$

$$= \frac{1}{25} \times \sqrt{19275} = \frac{138.83}{25} = 5.55$$

Miscellaneous Exercise

Question 1 The mean and variance of eight observations are 9 and 9.25, respectively. If six of the observations are 6, 7, 10, 12, 12 and 13, find the remaining two observations.

Sol. Let the remaining two observations are a and b.

Given, Mean $\bar{x} = 9$ and variance $\sigma^2 = 9.25$

$\because \quad \bar{x} = 9 \Rightarrow \dfrac{\text{Sum of all observations}}{\text{Number of observations}} = 9$

$\Rightarrow$ Sum of all observations $= 9 \times 8$ [$\because$ number of observations = 8]

$\Rightarrow \quad 6 + 7 + 10 + 12 + 12 + 13 + a + b = 72$

$\Rightarrow \quad 60 + a + b = 72 \Rightarrow a + b = 72 - 60$

$\Rightarrow \quad a + b = 12 \qquad \text{...(i)}$

Again, $\sigma^2 = \dfrac{\Sigma x_i^2}{n} - \left(\dfrac{\Sigma x_i}{n}\right)^2$ or $\sigma^2 = \dfrac{\Sigma x_i^2}{n} - (\bar{x})^2$

$\Rightarrow \quad = \dfrac{36 + 49 + 100 + 144 + 144 + 169 + a^2 + b^2}{8} - (9)^2$

[$\because \sigma^2 = 9.25$ and $\bar{x} = 9$]

$\Rightarrow \quad 9.25 = \dfrac{642 + a^2 + b^2}{8} - 81$

$\Rightarrow \quad 9.25 + 81 = \dfrac{642 + a^2 + b^2}{8}$

$\Rightarrow \quad 90.25 \times 8 = 642 + a^2 + b^2$

$\Rightarrow \quad a^2 + b^2 = 722 - 642$

$\Rightarrow \quad a^2 + b^2 = 80 \qquad \text{...(ii)}$

Now, from Eq. (i) put $b = 12 - a$ in Eq. (ii),

$a^2 + (12 - a)^2 = 80$

$\Rightarrow \quad a^2 + 144 + a^2 - 24a = 80$

$\Rightarrow \quad 2a^2 - 24a + 144 - 80 = 0$

$2a^2 - 24a + 64 = 0$

$\Rightarrow \quad a^2 - 12a + 32 = 0$

$\Rightarrow \quad a^2 - 8a - 4a + 32 = 0$

$\Rightarrow \quad a(a - 8) - 4(a - 8) = 0$

$\Rightarrow \quad (a - 4)(a - 8) = 0$

$\Rightarrow \quad a = 4 \text{ or } a = 8$

From Eq. (i), $b = 8$ or $b = 4$

Hence, observations are 4 and 8.

Question 2 The mean and variance of 7 observations are 8 and 16, respectively. If five of them are 2, 4, 10, 12, 14. Find the remaining two observations.

Sol. Let the remaining two observations are a and b.

Given, mean $\bar{x} = 8$ and variance $\sigma^2 = 16$

$$\because \quad \bar{x} = 8 \quad \frac{\text{Sum of all observations}}{\text{Number of observations}} = 8$$

$$\Rightarrow \frac{2 + 4 + 10 + 12 + 14 + a + b}{7} = 8 \qquad [\because \text{number of observation} = 7]$$

$$\Rightarrow 42 + a + b = 56$$

$$\Rightarrow a + b = 14 \qquad \text{...(i)}$$

Again, $\sigma^2 = \frac{\Sigma x_i^2}{n} - \left(\frac{\Sigma x_i}{n}\right)^2 \Rightarrow \sigma^2 = \frac{\Sigma x_i^2}{n} - (\bar{x})^2$

$$\Rightarrow 16 = \frac{4 + 16 + 100 + 144 + 196 + a^2 + b^2}{n} - (8)^2 \qquad [\because \sigma^2 = 16 \text{ and } \bar{x} = 8]$$

$$\Rightarrow 16 + 64 = \frac{460 + a^2 + b^2}{7} \Rightarrow 7 \times (80) = 460 + a^2 + b^2$$

$$\Rightarrow a^2 + b^2 = 560 - 460$$

$$\Rightarrow a^2 + b^2 = 100 \qquad \text{...(ii)}$$

Now, from Eq. (i), putting $b = 14 - a$ in Eq. (ii), we get

$$a^2 + (14 - a)^2 = 100$$

$$\Rightarrow a^2 + 196 + a^2 - 28a = 100$$

$$\Rightarrow 2a^2 - 28a + 196 - 100 = 0$$

$$\Rightarrow 2a^2 - 28a + 96 = 0$$

$$\Rightarrow a^2 - 14a + 48 = 0$$

$$\Rightarrow a^2 - 8a - 6a + 48 = 0$$

$$\Rightarrow a(a - 8) - 6(a - 8) = 0$$

$$\Rightarrow (a - 6)(a - 8) = 0 \Rightarrow a = 6 \text{ or } 8$$

From Eq. (i),

$$b = 8 \text{ or } 6$$

Hence, the observations are 6 and 8.

Question 3 The mean and standard deviation of six observations are 8 and 4, respectively. If each observation is multiplied by 3, find the mean and new standard deviation of the resulting observations.

Sol. Given, mean $\bar{x} = 8$ and standard derivation $\sigma = 4$ and $n = 6$

Let the observation are $x_1, x_2, x_3, x_4, x_5, x_6$.

Mean $\bar{x} = 8$ (given)

$$i.e., \text{ Mean} = \frac{x_1 + x_2 + x_3 + x_4 + x_5 + x_6}{6} = 8$$

$$\Rightarrow x_1 + x_2 + x_3 + x_4 + x_5 + x_6 = 48$$

Now, if and each observation is multipled by 3, then mean is

$3x_1 + 3x_2 + 3x_3 + 3x_4 + 3x_5 + 3x_6 = 48 \times 3 \Rightarrow \Sigma x_i = 144$

Now, new mean $\bar{x} = \frac{144}{6} = 24$

Since, Variance $= 4^2$ (given)

i.e., $\frac{\Sigma x_i^2}{n} - \left(\frac{\Sigma x_i}{n}\right)^2 = 4^2$

$\Rightarrow \frac{\Sigma x_i^2}{6} - (8)^2 = 4^2 \Rightarrow \frac{\Sigma x_i^2}{6} = 16 + 64 \Rightarrow \Sigma xi^2 = 80 \times 6$

$\Rightarrow \Sigma x_i^2 = 480$ ...(i)

Now,

New $\Sigma x^2 = (3x_1)^2 + (3x_2)^2 + (3x_3)^2 + (3x_4)^2 + (3x_5)^2 + (3x_6)^2$

$= 9(x_1^2 + x_2^2 + x_3^2 + x_4^2 + x_5^2 + x_6^2)$

$= 9 \times 480$ [from Eq. (i)]

$\Sigma x^2 = 4320$

$\therefore$ New variance $= \frac{\Sigma x^2}{n} - (\bar{x})^2 = \frac{4320}{6} - (24)^2 = 720 - 576 = 144$

$\therefore$ New standard deviation $= \sqrt{\text{New variance}} = \sqrt{144} = 12$

Note Mean depends on the change of origin and scale. Standard deviation does not depend on the change of origin but it depends on change of scale.

Question 4 Given that $\bar{x}$ is the mean and σ^2 is variance of n observations $x_1, x_2, \ldots, x_n$. Prove that the mean and variance of the observations $ax_1, ax_2, ax_3, \ldots, ax_n$ are $a\bar{x}$ and $a^2\sigma^2$, respectively, $(a \neq 0)$.

Sol. Mean of $ax_1, ax_2, \ldots, ax_n = \frac{ax_1 + ax_2 + \ldots + ax_n}{n}$

$= a\left(\frac{x_1 + x_2 + x_3 + \ldots + x_n}{n}\right)$

$= a\bar{x}$ $\left(\because \bar{x} = \frac{x_1 + x_2 + \ldots + x_n}{n}\right)$

$\therefore$ Variance of $ax_1, ax_2, \ldots, ax_n$

$= \frac{\Sigma(ax_i - a\bar{x})^2}{n}$

$= \frac{(ax_1 - a\bar{x})^2 + (ax_2 - a\bar{x})^2 + \ldots + (ax_n - a\bar{x})^2}{n}$

$= \frac{[a^2 (x_1 - \bar{x})^2 + (x_2 - \bar{x})^2 + \ldots + (x_n - \bar{x})^2]}{n}$

$= a^2 \frac{\Sigma (x_i - \bar{x})^2}{n} = a^2\sigma^2$ $\left[\because \sigma^2 = \frac{\Sigma(x_i - \bar{x})^2}{n}\right]$

Hence Proved.

Question 5 The mean and standard deviation of 20 observations are found to be 10 and 2, respectively. On rechecking, it was found that an observation 8 was incorrect. Calculate the correct mean and standard deviation in each of the following cases

(i) If wrong item is omitted.

(ii) If it is replaced by 12.

Sol. (i) Given, mean $\bar{x} = 10$ and standard deviation $\sigma = 2$, $n = 20$

$$\Rightarrow \quad \frac{\sum_{i=1}^{20} x_i}{20} = 10 \Rightarrow \sum_{i=1}^{20} x_i = 20 \times 10$$

$$\Rightarrow \quad \sum_{i=1}^{20} x_i = 200$$

If observation 8 is omitted, then

$$\sum_{i=1}^{19} x_i = \sum_{i=1}^{20} x_i - 8 = 200 - 8 = 192$$

Now, remaining number of observation = 19

$$\Rightarrow \text{Correct mean} = \frac{\Sigma x_i}{n} = \frac{192}{19} = 10.10$$

Again, $\quad \sigma = 2 \Rightarrow \sigma^2 = 4$

$$\Rightarrow \quad \frac{\sum_{i=1}^{20} x_i^2}{n} - (\bar{x})^2 = 4$$

$$\Rightarrow \quad \frac{\sum_{i=1}^{20} x_i^2}{20} - (10)^2 = 4$$

$$\Rightarrow \quad \sum_{i=1}^{20} x_i^2 = (4 + 100) \times 20 = 104 \times 20 = 2080$$

If observation 8 is omitted, then

$$\sum_{i=1}^{19} x_i^2 = \sum_{i=1}^{20} x_i^2 - (8)^2 = 2080 - 64 = 2016$$

Now, correct standard deviation

$$\sigma = \sqrt{\frac{2016}{19} - \left(\frac{192}{19}\right)^2} = \sqrt{\frac{2016 \times 19 - (192)^2}{19 \times 19}}$$

$$= \frac{1}{19}\sqrt{38304 - 36864}$$

$$= \frac{1}{19}\sqrt{1440} = \frac{37.95}{19} = 1.99$$

(ii) Given, mean $\bar{x} = 10$, standard deviation $\sigma = 2$, $n = 20$

$$\Rightarrow \quad \frac{\Sigma x_i}{20} = 10 \quad \Rightarrow \quad \Sigma x_i = 200$$

If observation 8 is replaced by 12, then

$$\Sigma x_i = 200 - 8 + 12 = 192 + 12 = 204$$

$$\text{Correct mean} = \frac{204}{20} = \frac{102}{10} = 10.2$$

Again, $\sigma = 2 \Rightarrow \sigma^2 = 4$

$$\Rightarrow \quad \frac{\Sigma x_i^2}{n} - (\bar{x})^2 = 4 \quad \Rightarrow \quad \frac{\Sigma x_i^2}{20} - (10)^2 = 4$$

$$\Rightarrow \quad \Sigma x_i^2 = 2080$$

If observation 8 is replaced by 12, then

$$\begin{aligned} \Sigma xi^2 &= 2080 - (8)^2 + (12)^2 \\ &= 2080 - 64 + 144 \\ &= 2224 - 64 \\ &= 2160 \end{aligned}$$

Now, correct standard deviation

$$\begin{aligned} \sigma &= \sqrt{\frac{\Sigma x_i^2}{n} - (\bar{x})^2} \\ &= \sqrt{\frac{2160}{20} - \left(\frac{204}{20}\right)^2} \\ &= \sqrt{\frac{2160 \times 20 - (204)^2}{20 \times 20}} \\ &= \frac{1}{20}\sqrt{43200 - 41616} \\ &= \frac{1}{20}\sqrt{1584} = \frac{39.79}{20} = 1.98 \end{aligned}$$

Question 6 The mean and standard deviation of a group of 100 observations were found to be 20 and 3, respectively. Later on it was found that three observations were incorrect, which are recorded as 21, 21 and 18. Find the mean and standard deviation, if the incorrect observation are omitted.

Sol. Given, $n = 100$, mean $\bar{x} = 20$, standard deviation $\sigma = 3$

$$\because \quad \bar{x} = 20$$

$$\Rightarrow \quad \frac{\sum_{i=1}^{100} x_i}{100} = 20$$

$$\Rightarrow \quad \sum_{i=1}^{100} x_i = 100 \times 20$$

$$\Rightarrow \quad \sum_{i=1}^{100} x_i = 2000$$

Now, incorrect observations 21, 21 and 18 are omitted, then correct sum is

$$\sum_{i=1}^{97} x_i = \sum_{i=1}^{100} x_i - 21 - 21 - 18 = 2000 - 21 - 21 - 18$$

$$= 2000 - 60 = 1940$$

Now, correct mean of remaining 97 observations is

$$\bar{x} = \frac{1940}{97} = 20$$

Again, $\quad \sigma = 3 = \sqrt{\frac{\sum_{i=1}^{100} x_i^2}{n} - (\bar{x})^2} = 3$

$$\Rightarrow \quad \frac{\sum_{i=1}^{100} x_i^2}{100} - (20)^2 = 9$$

$$\Rightarrow \quad \frac{\sum_{i=1}^{100} x_i^2}{100} = 9 + 400 = 409$$

Now, correct $\sum_{i=1}^{97} x_i^2$ is

$$\Rightarrow \quad \frac{\sum_{i=1}^{100} x_i^2}{100} = 409 \times 100 = 40900$$

$$\sum_{i=1}^{97} x^2 = \sum_{i=1}^{100} x_i^2 - (21)^2 - (21)^2 - (18)^2 = 40900 - (21)^2 - (21)^2 - (18)^2$$

$$= 40900 - 441 - 441 - 324$$

$$= 40900 - 1206 = 39694$$

Now, correct SD for remaining 97 observations is

$$\sigma = \sqrt{\frac{39694}{97} - \left(\frac{1940}{97}\right)^2}$$

$$= \sqrt{409.2 - (20)^2} = \sqrt{409.2 - 400}$$

$$= \sqrt{9.2} = 3.03$$

Mistake Alert Student should remember that the problem ask for the standard deviation not the variance.

DIKSHA APP Questions

Multiple Choice Questions

Q.1 Let x is the variance and y is the standard deviation, then which of the following is correct.

(a) $x = y^2$ (b) $xy = 1$ (c) $x^2 = y$ (d) $x^2y^2 = 1$

Sol. (a) Given, SD = y and variance = x, we know that (Standard deviation)^2 = Variance

So, $y^2 = x$ *i.e.*, $x = y^2$

Q.2 The standard deviation of the first ten natural numbers.

(a) 5.5 (b) 2.97 (c) 3.87 (d) 2.87

Thinking Process Use the formula for calculating standard deviation is

$$\text{SD} = \sqrt{\frac{\Sigma x_i^2}{n} - \left(\frac{\Sigma x_i}{n}\right)^2}.$$

Sol. (d) First 10 natural numbers are 1, 2, 3, ..., 10

$$\frac{\sum_{i=1}^{10} x_i}{n} = \frac{1 + 2 + ... + 10}{10} = \frac{\left(\frac{10\,(10+1)}{10}\right)}{2}$$

$$\left[\because \text{sum of first } n \text{ natural numbers} = \frac{n(n+1)}{2}\right]$$

$$= \frac{110}{20} = 5.5$$

and
$$\frac{\sum_{i=1}^{10} x_i^2}{n} = \frac{1^2 + 2^2 + ... + 10^2}{10}$$

$$= \frac{10(10+1)\,(2(10)+1)}{6 \times 10} \left[\because 1^2 + 2^2 + ... + n^2 = \frac{n(n+1)\,(2n+1)}{6}\right]$$

$$= 38.5$$

Now, standard deviation = $\sqrt{\left(\frac{\Sigma x_i^2}{n} - \left(\frac{\Sigma x_i^2}{n}\right)^2\right)}$

$$= \sqrt{(38.5 - (5.5)^2)} = \sqrt{(38.5 - 30.25)} = \sqrt{8.25} = 2.87$$

Quick Solution

We know the direct formula of standard deviation for the first n natural numbers

$$SD = \sqrt{\frac{n^2 - 1}{12}}$$

Given $n = 10$

Then $$SD = \sqrt{\frac{(10)^2 - 1}{12}} = \sqrt{\frac{100 - 1}{12}} = \sqrt{\frac{99}{12}} = \sqrt{8.25}$$

$$SD = 2.87$$

Q.3 Find the range of the following data $-3, 5, 2, 9, 0, -5$.

(a) -2 (b) -8 (c) 4 (d) 14

◎ ***Thinking Process*** Range of data = maximum value – minimum value

Sol. (d) As we know that given data are –3, 5, 2, 9, 0, – 5

$\therefore$ Maximum value of data = 9

and Minimum value of data = – 5

As, we know that Range = Maximum value – Minimum value

$\therefore$ Range = $9 - (-5) = 9 + 5 = 14$

Q.4 Find the variance of the following data 5, 4, 8, 11, 7

(a) 35 (b) 30 (c) 18 (d) 6

◎ ***Thinking Process*** Variance $= \dfrac{\Sigma(x_i - \bar{x})^2}{n}$

Sol. (d) Mean $\bar{x} = \dfrac{\text{Sum of terms}}{\text{Number of terms}} = \dfrac{5 + 4 + 8 + 11 + 7}{5} = \dfrac{35}{5} = 7$

$$\because \text{Variance} = \frac{\Sigma(x_i - \bar{x})^2}{n} = \frac{\Sigma(x_i - 7)^2}{5} \qquad [\because \bar{x} = 7]$$

$$\therefore \text{Variance} = \frac{(5-7)^2 + (4-7)^2 + (8-7)^2 + (11-7)^2 + (7-7)^2}{5}$$

$$= \frac{4 + 9 + 1 + 16 + 0}{5} = \frac{30}{5} = 6$$

☐ Subjective Type Questions

Q.1 Calculate the mean deviation about the median form the following data. 34, 15, 21, 30, 24, 32, 31

◎ ***Thinking Process*** Mean deviation about median $= \dfrac{\Sigma|x_i - m|}{n}$, where m is median.

Sol. The given data is 34, 15, 21, 30, 24, 32, 31.

Arranging in ascending order 15, 21, 24, 30, 31, 32, 34

Since, number of terms = 7 (odd)

$\because$ Median = $\left(\frac{n+1}{2}\right)$th term

$\therefore$ Median = $\left(\frac{7+1}{2}\right)$ = 4th term = 30

$m = 30$

Mean deviation about median = $\frac{\Sigma|x_i - m|}{n} = \frac{\Sigma|x_i - 30|}{7}$

$= \frac{|15-30| + |21-30| + |24-30| + |30-30| + |31-30| + |32-30| + |34-30|}{7}$

$= \frac{15+9+6+0+1+2+4}{7} = \frac{37}{7} = 5.28$

Q.2 Find the mean and standard deviation from the following data

Class	33 – 35	36 – 38	39 – 41	42 – 44	45 – 47
Frequency	17	19	23	21	27

◎ *Thinking Process* The given data is discontinous, so first make the class intervals in continuous form and then solve it.

Sol.

Class	Modified class	f_i	Mid value x_i	$d_i = \frac{x_i - A}{h}$, $A = 40, h = 3$	d_i^2	$f_i d_i$	$f_i d_i^2$
33 – 35	32.5 – 35.5	17	34	–2	4	–34	68
36 – 38	35.5 – 38.5	19	37	–1	1	–19	19
39 – 41	38.5 – 41.5	23	40	0	0	0	0
42 – 44	41.5 – 44.5	21	43	1	1	21	21
45 – 47	44.5 – 47.5	27	46	2	4	54	108
Total		107				22	216

Let assumed mean $A = 40$

Mean $\bar{x} = A \times \frac{\Sigma f_i d_i}{\Sigma f_i} \times h = 40 + \frac{22}{107} \times 3 = 40 + 0.6168 = 40.6168$

Standard deviation $(\sigma) = \sqrt{\left[\frac{\Sigma f_i d_i^2}{\Sigma f_i} - \left(\frac{\Sigma f_i d_i}{\Sigma f_i}\right)^2\right]} \times h = \sqrt{\left(\frac{216}{107} - \left(\frac{22}{107}\right)^2\right)} \times 3$

$= \sqrt{(2.0186 - (0.2056)^2)} \times 3$

$= (\sqrt{2.0186 - 0.0422}) \times 3 = 1.4058 \times 3 = 4.21$

Probability

CHAPTER 14

Important Points

01 Random experiment An experiment is called random an experiment, if it satisfies the following two conditions

(i) It has more than one possible outcome.

(ii) It is not possible to predict the outcome in advance.

02 Outcomes and sample space A possible result of a random an experiment is called its outcome.

For example, when tossing a coin, the outcomes of this experiment are Head (H) and Tail (T) and the set of outcomes $\{H, T\}$ is called the sample space of the experiment.

Hence, the set of all possible outcomes of a random experiment is called the sample space associated with the experiment. It is denoted by S.

03 Event An event is associated with a subset of sample space. Events can be classified into various types on the basis of the elements they have.

(i) **Impossible and sure events** The emtpy set ϕ is called an impossible event. For example, getting two heads in tossing a unbiased coin one time.

The whole sample space (s) is called the sure event. For example, in tossing a die any number will come is a sure event.

(ii) **Simple event** If an event E has only one sample point of a sample space, it is called a simple (or elementary) event.

For example, in the experiment of tossing a coin twicely getting both head *i.e.*, $E = \{HH\}$ and sample space $(s) = \{HH, HT, TH, TT\}$.

Note In a sample space containing n distinct elements, there are exactly n simple events.

(iii) **Compound event** If an event has more than one sample point, it is called a compound event. For example, in the experiment of tossing a coin thrice the events.

E : Exactly one head appeared

F : Atleast one head appeared

G: Atmost one head appeared, etc., are all compound events. As
$E = \{HTT, THT, TTH\}$
$F = \{HTT, THT, TTH, HHT, THH, HTH, HHH\}$
$G = \{HTT, THT, TTH, TTT\}$

Each of the above subsets contain more than one sample point. Hence, they are all compound events.

04 Algebra of Events

(i) **The event *A* or *B*** Event A or $B = A \cup B$

(ii) **The event *A* and *B*** Event A and $B = A \cap B$

(iii) **Complementary event** For every event A, there corresponds another event A' or A^c or $\overline{A}$ called the complementary event to A. It is also called the event not A.

(iv) **The event *A* but not *B*** $A - B = A \cap B' = A - A \cap B$

05 Mutually Exclusive Events Two events A and B are called mutually exclusive events, if the occurrence of any one of them excludes the occurrence of the other event, *i.e.*, if they cannot occur simultaneously. In this case, the sets A and B are disjoint. For example, in rolling a die.

$A = \{\text{an odd number appear}\}$

$A = \{1, 3, 5\}$

and $B = \{\text{an even number appear}\}$

$B = \{2, 4, 6\}$

Here, $A \cap B = \phi =$ mutually exclusive events.

Note Simple events of a sample space are mutually exclusive.

06 Exhaustive events If $E_1, E_2, E_3, \ldots, E_n$ are events of a sample space S and if

$$E_1 \cup E_2 \cup E_3 \cup \ldots \cup E_n = \bigcup_{i=1}^{n} E_i = S$$

Then, $E_1, E_2, E_3, \ldots, E_n$ are said to be exhaustive.

For example, rolling a die, we have

$$S = \{1, 2, 3, 4, 5, 6\}$$

E_1 = A number less than 4 appears

E_2 = A number greater than 2 but less than 5 appears

E_3 = A number greater than 4 appears

$$\Rightarrow \quad E_1 = \{1, 2, 3\}, E_2 = \{3, 4\}, E_3 = \{5, 6\}$$

$$\therefore \quad E_1 \cup E_2 \cup E_3 = \{1, 2, 3\} \cup \{3, 4\} \cup \{5, 6\} = \{1, 2, 3, 4, 5, 6\} = S$$

07 **Axiomatic Approach to Probability** Let S be the sample space of a random experiment. The probability P is a real valued function whose domain is the power set of S and range is the interval [0, 1] satisfying the following axioms

(i) For any event E, $P(E) \geq 0$

(ii) $P(S) = 1$

(iii) If E and F are mutually exclusive events, then

$$P(E \cup F) = P(E) + P(F)$$

Let S be a sample space containing outcomes

$$w_1, w_2, \ldots w_n$$

i.e., $$S = \{w_1, w_2, \ldots w_n\}$$

Then, from the axiomatic definition of probability

(i) $0 \leq P(w_i) \leq 1$ for each $w_i \in S$

(ii) $P(w_1) + P(w_2) + \ldots + P(w_n) = 1$

(iii) For any event A, $P(A) = \Sigma P(w_i)$, $w_i \in A$.

08 **Probability of equally likely outcomes** Let S be a sample space and E be an event, such that $n(S) = n$ and $n(E) = m$. If each outcome is equally likely, then it follows that

$$P(E) = \frac{m}{n} = \frac{\text{Number of outcomes favourable to } E}{\text{Total possible outcomes}}$$

09 Let A, B and C are any three events, then

(i) $P(A \cup B) = P(A) + P(B) - P(A \cap B)$

(ii) $0 \leq P(A) \leq 1$ for an event A

(iii) $P(\overline{A}) = P(A') = 1 - P(A)$

(iv) $P(A \cup \overline{A}) = P(S) = 1$ and $P(\phi) = 0$

(v) $P(A \cup B \cup C) = P(A) + P(B) + P(C)$

$$- P(A \cap B) - P(B \cap C) - P(C \cap A) + P(A \cap B \cap C)$$

(vi) $P(A \cap \overline{B}) = P(A) - P(A \cap B)$ or $P(A - B) = P(A) - P(A \cap B)$

(vii) $P(B \cap \overline{A}) = P(B) - P(A \cap B)$ or $P(B - A) = P(B) - P(A \cap B)$

(viii) Odds in favour of an event

$$= \frac{\text{Number of favourable outcomes}}{\text{Number of unfavourable outcomes}}$$

(ix) Odds against of an event

$$= \frac{\text{Number of unfavourable outcomes}}{\text{Number of favourable outcomes}}$$

Note If A and B are mutually exclusive events than $P(A \cap B) = 0$ and $P(A \cup B) = P(A) + P(B)$.

(x) The total number of elements in a sample space for coin $= 2^n$, where, n is the total number of coins or tossing times

(xi) The total number of elements in a sample space for dice $= 6^n$, where, n is the total number of dice or throughing times.

Exercise 14.1

Question 1 A die is rolled. Let E be the event "die shows 4" and F be the event "die shows even number". Are E and F mutually exclusive?

◎ *Thinking Process* For mutually exclusive events, $A \cap B = \phi$.

Sol. No,

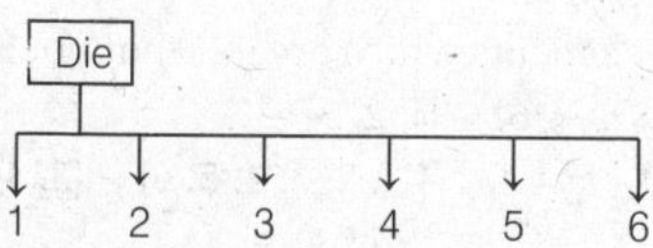

Let E = The die shows 4 = {4}

Let F = The die shows even number = {2, 4, 6}

$\therefore$ $E \cap F = \{4\} \neq \phi$

Hence, E and F are not mutually exclusive.

Question 2 A die is thrown. Describe the following events

(i) A: a number less than 7

(ii) B: a number greater than 7

(iii) C: a multiple of 3

(iv) D: a number less than 4

(v) E: an even number greater than 4

(vi) F: a number not less than 3

Also find $A \cup B$, $A \cap B$, $B \cup C$, $E \cap F$, $D \cap E$, $A - C$, $D - E$, $E \cap F'$, F'.

Sol.

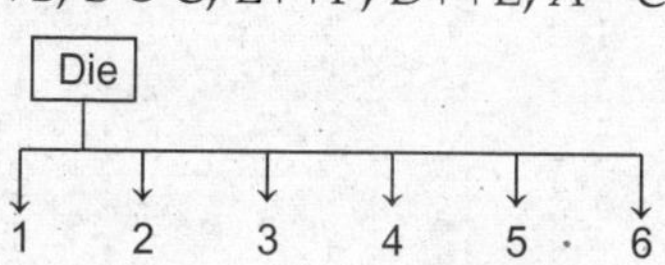

(i) A: a number less than 7 = {1, 2, 3, 4, 5, 6}

(ii) B: a number greater than 7 = { } = ϕ

($\because$ The maximum number on a die is 6, so there cannot be a number on die greater than 7)

(iii) C: a multiple of 3 = {3, 6}

(iv) D: a number less than 4 = {1, 2, 3}

(v) E: an even number greater than 4 = {6}

(vi) F: a number not less than 3 = {3, 4, 5, 6}

Now, $A \cup B$ = The elements which are in both A and B.

$= \{1, 2, 3, 4, 5, 6\} \cup \phi = \{1, 2, 3, 4, 5, 6\}$

$A \cap B$ = The elements which are common in both A and B.
$= \{1, 2, 3, 4, 5, 6\} \cap \phi = \phi$

$B \cup C$ = The elements which are in both B and C. $= \{\ \} \cup \{3, 6\} = \{3, 6\}$

$E \cap F$ = The elements which are common in both E and F.
$= \{6\} \cap \{3, 4, 5, 6\} = \{6\}$

$D \cap E$ = The elements which are common in both D and E.
$= \{1, 2, 3\} \cap \{6\} = \phi$

$A - C$ = The elements which are in A but not in C.
$= \{1, 2, 3, 4, 5, 6\} - \{3, 6\} = \{1, 2, 4, 5\}$

$D - E$ = The elements which are in D but not in E.
$= \{1, 2, 3\} - \{6\} = \{1, 2, 3\}$

$E \cap F' = E \cap (U - F) = E \cap [\{1, 2, 3, 4, 5, 6\} - \{3, 4, 5, 6\}]$

$[\because U = \{1, 2, 3, 4, 5, 6\}]$

$= \{6\} \cap \{1, 2\} = \phi$

and $F' = (U - F) = \{1, 2, 3, 4, 5, 6\} - \{3, 4, 5, 6\} = \{1, 2\}$

Note U is a sample space containing all possible outcomes.

Question 3 An experiment involves rolling a pair of dice and recording the numbers that come up. Describe the following events.

A: the sum is greater than 8.
B: 2 occurs on either die.
C: the sum is atleast 7 and a multiple of 3 .

Which pairs of these events are mutually exclusive?

Sol. When two dice are thrown, then there are 36 possible outcomes.

↓ \ →	1	2	3	4	5	6
1	1, 1	1, 2	1, 3	1, 4	1, 5	1, 6
2	2, 1	2, 2	2, 3	2, 4	2, 5	2, 6
3	3, 1	3, 2	3, 3	3, 4	3, 5	3, 6
4	4, 1	4, 2	4, 3	4, 4	4, 5	4, 6
5	5, 1	5, 2	5, 3	5, 4	5, 5	5, 6
6	6, 1	6, 2	6, 3	6, 4	6, 5	6, 6

A = The sum is greater than 8.
$= \{(3, 6), (4, 5), (5, 4), (6, 3), (4, 6), (5, 5), (6, 4), (5, 6), (6, 5), (6, 6)\}$

B = 2 occurs on the either die.
$= \{(1, 2), (2, 1), (2, 2), (2, 3), (2, 4), (2, 5), (2, 6), (3, 2), (4, 2), (5, 2), (6, 2)\}$

C = The sum is atleast 7 and a multiple of 3 *i.e.*, the sum is 9 and 12.
$= \{(3, 6), (4, 5), (5, 4), (6, 3), (6, 6)\}$

$\therefore$ $A \cap B = \phi \Rightarrow$ A and B are mutually exclusive.
$B \cap C = \phi \Rightarrow$ B and C are mutually exclusive.

Question 4 Three coins are tossed once. Let A denote the event "three heads show," B denote the event "two heads and one tail show", C denote the event "three tails show" and D denote the event "a head shows on the first toss", which events are (i) mutually exclusive?
(ii) simple? (iii) compound?

◎ *Thinking Process*

(i) For mutually exclusive event $A \cap B = \phi$.

(ii) For simple event it has only one sample point.

(iii) For compound event it has atleast two sample points.

Sol. When three coins are tossed, then there are $2^3 = 8$ possible outcomes.

i.e., $S = \{HHH, HHT, HTH, HTT, THH, THT, TTH, TTT\}$

A = Three heads shows = $\{HHH\}$

B = Two heads and one tail show = $\{HHT, HTH, THH\}$

C = Three tails show = $\{TTT\}$

D = A head shows on the first toss = $\{HHH, HHT, HTH, HTT\}$

(i) Here,

$$A \cap B = \phi$$
$$A \cap C = \phi$$
$$B \cap C = \phi$$
$$C \cap D = \phi$$
$$A \cap B \cap C = \phi$$

Here, A and B, A and C, B and C, C and D and A, B and C are mutually exclusive.

(ii) Since, events A and C have only one sample point.

Here, A and C are simple events.

(iii) Since, events B and D have two or more sample points.

Hence, B and D are compound events.

Question 5 Three coins are tossed. Describe

(i) Two events which are mutually exclusive.

(ii) Three events which are mutually exclusive and exhaustive.

(iii) Two events which are not mutually exclusive.

(iv) Two events which are mutually exclusive but not exhaustive.

(v) Three events which are mutually exclusive but not exhaustive.

◎ *Thinking Process*

(i) For mutually exclusive events $A \cap B = \phi$.

(ii) For exhaustive events $\bigcup_{i=1}^{n} E_i = S$.

Sol. If three coins are tossed, then possible number of outcomes = $2^3 = 8$

Sample space $S = \{HHH, HHT, HTH, HTT, THH, THT, TTH, TTT\}$

(i) Let A be the event 'three heads show'.

$\Rightarrow \quad A = \{HHH\}$

and B be the event 'three tails show'.

$\Rightarrow \quad B = \{TTT\} \Rightarrow A \cap B = \phi$

Hence, A and B are mutually exclusive events.

(ii) Let A be the event exactly two heads show

$\Rightarrow \quad A = \{HHT, HTH, THH\}$

Let B be the event at most one head show

$\Rightarrow \quad B = \{HTT, THT, TTH, TTT\}$

And C be the event exactly three head show

$\Rightarrow \quad C = \{HHH\}$

Then, $A \cap B \cap C = \phi$ and $A \cup B \cup C = S$

$\therefore$ A, B and C are mutually exclusive and exhaustive.

(iii) Let A be the event 'three heads show' and B be the event 'atleast two heads show'

$\Rightarrow A = \{HHH\}$ and $B = \{HHT, HTH, THH, HHH\}$

$\Rightarrow A \cap B = \{HHH\} \neq \phi$

Hence, A and B are not mutually exclusive.

(iv) Let A be the event 'three heads show and B be the event 'three tails show'.

$\Rightarrow \quad A = \{HHH\}$ and $B = \{TTT\}$

Then, $\quad A \cap B = \phi$ and $A \cup B \neq S$

$\therefore$ A and B are mutually exclusive but not exhaustive.

(v) Let A be the event 'three heads show'.

B be the event 'two heads shows', and C be the event 'three tails show'.

$\Rightarrow A = \{HHH\} \Rightarrow B = \{HHT, HTH, THH\}$ and $C = \{TTT\}$

$\Rightarrow A \cap B = B \cap C = C \cap A = \phi$ and $A \cup B \cup C \neq S$.

$\Rightarrow$ A, B and C are mutually exclusive but not exhaustive.

Note Three events A, B and C are mutually exclusive iff :
$A \cap B = B \cap C = C \cap A = \phi$.

Question 6 Two dice are thrown. The events A, B and C are as follows

A: getting an even number on the first die.

B: getting an odd number on the first die.

C: getting the sum of the numbers on the dice ≤ 5.

Describe the events.

(i) A' (ii) not B (iii) A or B (iv) A and B

(v) A but not C (vi) B or C (vii) B and C

(viii) $A \cap B' \cap C'$

Sol. If two dice are thrown then, total number of possible outcomes, $S = 6 \times 6 = 36$ which are as follows

↓ →	1	2	3	4	5	6
1	1, 1	1, 2	1, 3	1, 4	1, 5	1, 6
2	2, 1	2, 2	2, 3	2, 4	2, 5	2, 6
3	3, 1	3, 2	3, 3	3, 4	3, 5	3, 6
4	4, 1	4, 2	4, 3	4, 4	4, 5	4, 6
5	5, 1	5, 2	5, 3	5, 4	5, 5	5, 6
6	6, 1	6, 2	6, 3	6, 4	6, 5	6, 6

A = getting an even number on the first die.
$= \{(2, 1), (2, 2), (2, 3), (2, 4), (2, 5), (2, 6), (4, 1), (4, 2), (4, 3), (4, 4), (4, 5), (4, 6), (6, 1), (6, 2), (6, 3), (6, 4), (6, 5), (6, 6)\}$

B = getting an odd number on the first die.
$= \{(1, 1), (1, 2), (1, 3), (1, 4), (1, 5), (1, 6), (3, 1), (3, 2), (3, 3), (3, 4), (3, 5), (3, 6), (5, 1), (5, 2), (5, 3), (5, 4), (5, 5), (5, 6)\}$

$C = \{(1, 1), (1, 2), (1, 3), (1, 4), (2, 1), (2, 2), (2, 3), (3, 1), (3, 2), (4, 1)\}$

(i) A' = which are not in $A = B$ (If A is an event getting an even number on the first die, so A' will be the event getting an odd number on the first die *i.e.*, B)

(ii) not $B = B'$ = which are not in $B = A$ (If B is an event getting an odd number on the first, so B' will be the event getting an even number on the first die *i.e.*, A)

(iii) A or $B = A \cup B$

$A \cup B$ includes all elements of A and B *i.e.*, it will includes both the events A and B *i.e.*, event having an even number on the first die and event having an odd number on the first die *i.e.*, $A \cup B$ will include all possible event *i.e.*, S (sample space). $\therefore$ $A \cup B = S$

(iv) A and $B = A \cap B$ *i.e.*, elements which are common in both A and B. There are no element common in A and B. So, $A \cap B = \phi$ (null set).

(v) A but not $C = A - C$ = Elements which are in A but not in C.
$= \{(2, 4), (2, 5), (2, 6), (4, 2), (4, 3), (4, 4), (4, 5), (4, 6), (6, 1), (6, 2), (6, 3), (6, 4), (6, 5), (6, 6)\}$

(vi) B or $C = B \cup C$ *i.e.*, elements which are in both B or C.
$= \{(1, 1), (1, 2), (1, 3), (1, 4), (1, 5), (1, 6), (3, 1), (3, 2), (3, 3), (3, 4), (3, 5), (3, 6), (5, 1), (5, 2), (5, 3), (5, 4), (5, 5), (5, 6), (2, 1), (2, 2), (2, 3), (4, 1)\}$

(vii) B and $C = B \cap C$ *i.e.*, elements which are common in both B and C.
$= \{(1, 1), (1, 2), (1, 3), (1, 4), (3, 1), (3, 2)\}$

(viii) $A \cap B' \cap C' = \{(2, 4), (2, 5), (2, 6), (4, 2), (4, 3), (4, 4), (4, 5), (4, 6), (6, 1), (6, 2), (6, 3), (6, 4), (6, 5), (6, 6)\}$

Question 7 Refer to question 6 above, state true or false : (give reason for your answer).

(i) A and B are mutually exclusive.

(ii) A and B are mutually exclusive and exhaustive .

(iii) $A = B'$.

(iv) A and C are mutually exclusive.

(v) A and B' are mutually exclusive.

(vi) A', B' and C are mutually exclusive and exhaustive.

Sol. (i) True

$\because$ A = getting an even number on the first die.

B = getting an odd number on the first die.

$\Rightarrow$ $A \cap B = \phi$

$\therefore$ A and B are mutually exclusive events.

(ii) True

$\therefore$ $A \cup B = S$ *i.e.*, exhaustive. Also, $A \cap B = \phi$

(iii) True

$\therefore$ B = getting an odd number on the first die.

$\Rightarrow$ B' = getting an even number on first die = A

$\therefore$ $A = B'$

(iv) False

$\because A \cap C = \{(2, 1), (2, 2), (2, 3), (4, 1)\} \neq \phi$, so A and C are not mutually exclusive.

(v) False

$\because$ $B' = A$

$\therefore$ $A \cap B' = A \cap A = A \neq \phi$ $(\because B' = A)$

So, A and B' are not mutually exclusive.

(vi) False

$$A' \cup B' \cup C = B \cup A \cup C \qquad [\because A' = B \text{ and } B' = A]$$
$$= S$$

So, A', B' and C are exhaustive

But $A' \cap C = B \cap C = \{(1, 1), (1, 2), (1, 3), (1, 4), (3, 1), (3, 2)\} \neq \phi$

$(\because A' = B)$

and $B' \cap C = A \cap C = \{(2, 1), (2, 2), (2, 3), (4, 1)\} \neq \phi$ $(\because B' = A)$

$\therefore$ A', B' and C are not mutually exclusive.

Exercise 14.2

Question 1 Which of the following cannot be valid assignments of probabilities for outcomes of sample space

$$S = \{W_1, W_2, W_3, W_4, W_5, W_6, W_7\}?$$

Assignment	W_1	W_2	W_3	W_4	W_5	W_6	W_7
(a)	0.1	0.01	0.05	0.03	0.01	0.2	0.6
(b)	$\frac{1}{7}$	$\frac{1}{7}$	$\frac{1}{7}$	$\frac{1}{7}$	$\frac{1}{7}$	$\frac{1}{7}$	$\frac{1}{7}$
(c)	0.1	0.2	0.3	0.4	0.5	0.6	0.7
(d)	–0.1	0.2	0.3	0.4	–0.2	0.1	0.3
(e)	$\frac{1}{14}$	$\frac{2}{14}$	$\frac{3}{14}$	$\frac{4}{14}$	$\frac{5}{14}$	$\frac{6}{14}$	$\frac{15}{14}$

◎ ***Thinking Process*** For valid assignment sum of all probabilities of each assignment should be 1.

Sol. (a) Sum of all probabilities $= 0.1 + 0.01 + 0.05 + 0.03 + 0.01 + 0.2 + 0.6 = 1$
Hence, the assignment is valid, as sum is 1.

(b) Valid, as sum is 1 (same as part (a)).

(c) Sum of all probabilities $= 0.1 + 0.2 + 0.3 + 0.4 + 0.5 + 0.6 + 0.7 = 2.8$
Hence, assignment is not valid, as sum is $2.8 > 1$.

(d) Not valid, as probabilities of any event can't be negative.

(e) Not valid, as $\frac{15}{14} > 1$, which is not possible.

Note Probability of any event cannot be negative or cannot be greater than 1.

Question 2 A coin is tossed twice, what is the probability that atleast one tail occurs?

Sol. The sample space is $S = \{HH, HT, TH, TT\}$ i.e. $n(S) = 4$

Let E be the event of getting atleast one tail

$$\text{i.e. } E = \{HT, TH, TT\} \Rightarrow n(E) = 3$$

$$\therefore \text{Required probability } (P) = \frac{\text{Number of favourable outcomes}}{\text{Total number of outcomes}}$$

$$= \frac{n(E)}{n(S)} = \frac{3}{4}$$

Mistake Alert Student should be rememberd that first of all always verify the sample space and the favourable outcomes.

Question 3 A die is thrown, find the probability of following events.

(i) A prime number will appear.
(ii) A number greater than or equal to 3 will appear.
(iii) A number less than or equal to one will appear.
(iv) A number more than 6 will appear.
(v) A number less than 6 will appear.

Sol. When a die is thrown, then any number from 1 to 6 can be appear, so sample space of a die is $S = \{1, 2, 3, 4, 5, 6\}$

(i) Let E be the event, *a* prime number will appear.

$$\therefore \quad E = \{2, 3, 5\}$$

$\therefore$ Probability of event getting prime number

$$P = \frac{\text{Number of favourable outcomes}}{\text{Total number of outcomes}} = \frac{n(E)}{n(S)} = \frac{3}{6} = \frac{1}{2}$$

(ii) Let E be the event greater than or equal to 3 will appear.

$$\therefore \quad E = \{3, 4, 5, 6\}$$

$\therefore$ Probability of event getting a number greater than or equal to 3.

$$P = \frac{n(E)}{n(S)} = \frac{4}{6} = \frac{2}{3}$$

(iii) Let E be the event a number less than or equal to one will appear.

$$\therefore \quad E = \{1\}$$

$\therefore$ Probability of event getting a number less than or equal to 1.

$$P = \frac{n(E)}{n(S)} = \frac{1}{6}$$

(iv) Let E be the event, a number more than 6 will appear.

$E = \{\} = \phi$ ($\because$ on the die there is no number greater than 6)

$\therefore$ Probability of event getting a number greater than 6.

$$P = \frac{n(E)}{n(S)} = \frac{0}{6} = 0$$

(v) Let E be the event, the number less than 6 will appear.

$$E = \{1, 2, 3, 4, 5\}$$

$\therefore$ Probability of event getting a number less than 6.

$$P = \frac{n(E)}{n(S)} = \frac{5}{6}$$

Question 4 A card is selected from a pack of 52 cards.

(a) How many points are there in the sample space?
(b) Calculate the probability that the card is an ace of spades.
(c) Calculate the probability that the cards is
(i) an ace (ii) black card.

Sol. (a) There are 52 cards.Hence, total elements in sample space = 52

(b) There is one ace of spade

So, $n(E) = 1$

Let E be the event, the card is a ace of spade.

$\therefore$ Probability of event getting an ace of spade $P = \frac{n(E)}{n(S)} = \frac{1}{52}$

(c) (i) There are four aces in a pack of cards.

$\Rightarrow$ $n(E) = 4$

Let E be the event, the card is a ace.

$\therefore$ Probability of event getting an ace $P = \frac{n(E)}{n(S)} = \frac{4}{52} = \frac{1}{13}$

(ii) There are 26 black cards in a pack of cards.

$\Rightarrow$ $n(E) = 26$

Let E be the event, the card is black card.

$\therefore$ Probabilities of event getting a black card $P = \frac{n(E)}{n(S)}$

$$= \frac{26}{52} = \frac{1}{2}$$

Question 5 A fair coin with 1 marked on one face and 6 on the other and a fair die are both tossed. Find the probability that the sum of the numbers that turn up is

(i) 3 (ii) 12.

Sol.

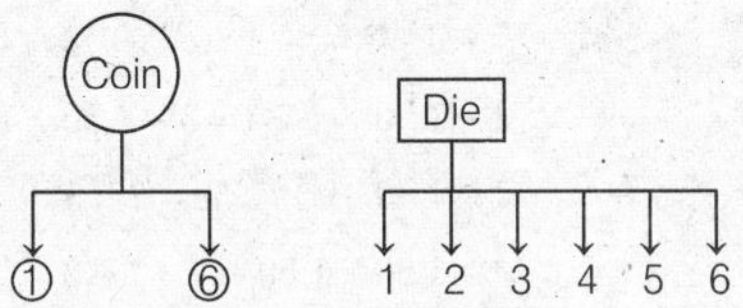

Total number of possible cases in coin = 2

Number of possible cases in die = 6

(i) The sum is 3 only if 1 turns up on coin and 2 turns up on die *i.e.*, only possibility is (1, 2).

$\therefore$ Required probability $= \frac{\text{Number of favourable outcomes}}{\text{Total number of outcomes}}$

$$= \frac{1}{2 \times 6} = \frac{1}{12}$$

(ii) The sum is 12 only if 6 turns up on coin and 6 turns up on die *i.e.*, only possibility is (6, 6).

$\therefore$ Required probability $= \frac{1}{2 \times 6} = \frac{1}{12}$

Question 6 There are four men and six women on the city council. If one council member is selected for a committee at random, how likely is it that it is a woman?

Sol. Let E be the event that woman is selected.

$$\therefore \quad n(E) = 6$$

Number of sample space $n(S)$ = Total number of persons in the council

$$= 4 + 6 = 10$$

$$\therefore \quad \text{Required probability } P(E) = \frac{n(E)}{n(S)} = \frac{6}{10} = \frac{3}{5}$$

Question 7 A fair coin is tossed four times and a person win ₹ 1 for each head and lose ₹ 1.50 for each tail that turns up. From the sample space, calculate how many different amounts of money you can have after four tosses and the probability of having each of these amounts.

Sol. If a coin is tossed four times, then total number of possible outcomes

$$2^n = 2^4 = 16 \qquad [\because n = 4]$$

For these cases, sample space can be written as

Sample space	Amount
$HHHH$	$1+1+1+1=4$
$HH\,HT$	$1+1+1-1.50=3-1.50=1.50$
$HH\,TH$	$1+1-1.50+1=3-1.50=1.50$
$HHTT$	$1+1-1.50-1.50=2-3=-1.00$
$HTHH$	$1-1.50+1+1=3-1.50=1.50$
$HTHT$	$1-1.50+1-1.50=2-3=-1.00$
$HTTH$	$1-1.50-1.50+1=2-3=-1.00$
$HTTT$	$1-1.50-1.50-1.50=1-4.50=-3.50$
$THHH$	$-1.50+1+1+1=-1.50+3=1.50$
$THHT$	$-1.50+1+1-1.50=2-3.00=-1.00$
$THTH$	$-1.50+1-1.50+1=2-3.00=-1.00$
$THTT$	$-1.50+1-1.50-1.50=1-4.50=-3.50$
$TTHH$	$-1.50-1.50+1+1=2-3.00=-1.00$
$TTHT$	$-1.50-1.50+1-1.50=1-4.50=-3.50$
$TTTH$	$-1.50-1.50-1.50+1=-4.50+1=-3.50$
$TTTT$	$-1.50-1.50-1.50-1.50=-6.00$

Hence, from above sample space, we get five types of different amounts *i.e.,* 4, 1.50, – 1.00, – 3.50, – 6. 00 *i.e.,*

Amounts	Number of times occurrence
4.00	1
1.50	4
– 1.00	6
– 3.50	4
– 6.00	1
Total	16

$$\Rightarrow \quad P(\text{Winning ₹ 4.00}) = \frac{\text{Number of favourable outcomes}}{\text{Total number of outcomes}} = \frac{1}{16}$$

$$\Rightarrow \quad P(\text{Winning ₹ 1.50}) = \frac{4}{16} = \frac{1}{4}$$

$$\Rightarrow \quad P(\text{Winning ₹} - 1.00) = \frac{6}{16} = \frac{3}{8}$$

$$\Rightarrow \quad P(\text{Winning ₹} - 3.50) = \frac{4}{16} = \frac{1}{4}$$

$$\Rightarrow \quad P(\text{Winning ₹} - 6.00) = \frac{1}{16}$$

Note Negative sign indicates the losing value of amount.

Question 8 Three coins are tossed once. Find the probability of getting

(i) 3 heads (ii) 2 heads (iii) atleast 2 heads

(iv) atmost 2 heads (v) no head (vi) 3 tails

(vii) exactly two tails (viii) no tail (ix) atmost two tails.

Sol. If three coins are tossed, then total number of possible outcomes $= 2^3 = 8$ which are

$S = \{HHH, HHT, HTH, HTT, THH, THT, TTH, TTT\}$

(i) If E be event of getting 3 heads.

$\Rightarrow \quad n(E) = 1 \quad [\because E = \{HHH\}]$

$\therefore$ Probability of getting 3 heads

$$P = \frac{\text{Number favourable outcomes}}{\text{Total number of outcomes}} = \frac{n(E)}{n(S)} = \frac{1}{8}$$

(ii) If E be event of getting 2 heads.

$\Rightarrow \quad n(E) = 3 \quad [\because E = \{HHT, THH, HTH\}]$

$\therefore$ Probability of getting 2 heads $P = \dfrac{n(E)}{n(S)} = \dfrac{3}{8}$

(iii) If E be the event of getting atleast 2 heads.

(Atleast means we can consider the cases having 2 heads and higher than 2)

$\Rightarrow \quad n(E) = 2\text{ heads} + 3\text{ heads} = 3 + 1 = 4$

$[\because E = \{HHH, HTH, THH, HHT\}]$

$\therefore$ Probability of getting atleast 2 heads $P = \dfrac{n(E)}{n(S)} = \dfrac{4}{8} = \dfrac{1}{2}$

(iv) If E be the event of getting atmost 2 heads.

$\Rightarrow \quad n(E) = 2\text{ heads} + 1\text{ head} + 0\text{ head}$

(Atmost means we cannot consider the cases of having heads higher than 2) $= 3 + 3 + 1 = 7$

$\therefore$ Probability of getting atmost 2 heads $P = \dfrac{n(E)}{n(S)} = \dfrac{7}{8}$

(v) If E be the event of getting no head.

$\Rightarrow \quad n(E) = 1 \qquad [\because E = \{TTT\}]$

$\therefore$ Probability of getting no head $P = \dfrac{n(E)}{n(S)} = \dfrac{1}{8}$

(vi) If E be the event of getting 3 tails.

$\Rightarrow \quad n(E) = 1 \Rightarrow P = \dfrac{n(E)}{n(S)} = \dfrac{1}{8} \qquad [\because E = \{TTT\}]$

(vii) If E be the event of getting exactly 2 tails. $\Rightarrow n(E) = 3$

$\therefore$ Probability of getting 2 tails $P = \dfrac{n(E)}{n(S)} = \dfrac{3}{8}$

(viii) If E be the event of getting no tail.

$\Rightarrow \quad n(E) = 1$

$\therefore$ Probability of getting no tails $P = \dfrac{n(E)}{n(S)} = \dfrac{1}{8}$

(ix) If E be the event of getting atmost 2 tails.

$\Rightarrow \quad n(E) = 2\text{ tails} + 1\text{ tail} + 0\text{ tail} = 3 + 3 + 1 = 7$

(Atmost means we cannot consider the cases of having tails higher than 2)

$\therefore$ Probability of getting atmost 2 tails $P = \dfrac{n(E)}{n(S)} = \dfrac{7}{8}$

Quick Solution

If E be the event of getting at most 2 tails then E' be the event of getting 3 tails

i.e. $\quad E' = \{TTT\}$

$\therefore$ Probability of getting exactly 3 tails $= P(E')$

$$= \frac{n(E')}{n(S)} = \frac{1}{8}$$

$\because \quad P(E) = 1 - P(E')$

$\therefore \quad P(E) = 1 - \dfrac{1}{8} = \dfrac{7}{8}$

Question 9 If $\frac{2}{11}$ is the probability of an event, what is the probability of the event 'not A'.

◎ *Thinking Process* Use the relation $P(A) + P(A') = 1$

Sol. Given, if A be any event, then $P(A) = \frac{2}{11}$

$$\therefore \quad P(\text{not } A) = P(A') = 1 - P(A) = 1 - \frac{2}{11} = \frac{9}{11}$$

[sum of an event (A) and its complementary event (A') is always 1]

Question 10 A letter is chosen at random from the word "ASSASSINATION". Find the probability that letter is (i) a vowel (ii) a consonant.

◎ *Thinking Process* In an alphabet there are 26 letters in which 5 (a, e, i, o, u) are vowels and 21 consonants, using this information and solve it.

Sol. Given word is A S S A S S I N A T I O N
Here number of vowels = $3(A) + 2(I) + 1(O) = 6$.
number of consonant = 7
and total number of letters = 13

(i) $\therefore$ Required probability P (Vowels) $= \frac{6}{13}$

(ii) $\therefore$ Required probability P (Consonant) $= \frac{7}{13}$

Question 11 In a lottery, a person choose six different natural numbers at random from 1 to 20 and if these six numbers match with the six numbers already fixed by lottery committee, he wins the prize. What is the probability of winning the prize in the game? (**Hint** Order of the numbers is not important.]

◎ *Thinking Process* From n distinct objects, r objects can be selected in $^nC_r = \frac{n!}{r!(n-r)!}$.

Sol. Since, 6 numbers out of 20 numbers can be choosed in $^{20}C_6$ ways in which only one combination of numbers is correct.
Let the probability of winning the prize be E.
i.e., $n(E) = 1$, ($\because$ if only one prize can be won)
Number of sample space $n(S) = {}^{20}C_6$

$\therefore$ Required probability $= \dfrac{1}{^{20}C_6} = \dfrac{1}{\dfrac{20!}{(20-6)!\,6!}}$ $\quad \left(\because {}^nC_r = \dfrac{n!}{(n-r)!\,r!}\right)$

$$= \frac{6 \times 5 \times 4 \times 3 \times 2 \times 1}{20 \times 19 \times 18 \times 17 \times 16 \times 15} = \frac{1}{38760}$$

Question 12 Check whether the following probabilities $P(A)$ and $P(B)$ are consistently defined

(i) $P(A) = 0.5$, $P(B) = 0.7$, $P(A \cap B) = 0.6$

(ii) $P(A) = 0.5$, $P(B) = 0.4$, $P(A \cup B) = 0.8$

◎ ***Thinking Process*** For consistent $P(A \cap B)$ must be less than or equal to $P(A)$ and $P(B)$.

Sol. (i) Here, $P(A \cap B) \not\leq P(A)$ as $0.6 \neq 0.5$

So, given data is not consistent.

(ii) Here, $P(A) = 0.5$, $P(B) = 0.4$, $P(A \cup B) = 0.8$

$\Rightarrow \quad P(A \cup B) = P(A) + P(B) - P(A \cap B)$

$\Rightarrow \quad 0.8 = 0.5 + 0.4 - P(A \cap B)$

$\Rightarrow \quad P(A \cap B) = 0.9 - 0.8 = 0.1 < P(A)$ and $P(B)$.

$\Rightarrow$ $P(A)$ and $P(B)$ are consistent.

Question 13 Fill in the blanks in the following table

	$P(A)$	$P(B)$	$P(A \cap B)$	$P(A \cup B)$
(a)	$\frac{1}{3}$	$\frac{1}{5}$	$\frac{1}{15}$	......
(b)	0.35	......	0.25	0.6
(c)	0.5	0.35	......	0.7

◎ ***Thinking Process*** Use formula $P(A \cup B) = P(A) + P(B) - P(A \cap B)$ and simplify it.

Sol. (a) $\because P(A \cup B) = P(A) + P(B) - P(A \cap B)$

$$P(A \cup B) = \frac{1}{3} + \frac{1}{5} - \frac{1}{15}$$

$$= \frac{5 + 3 - 1}{15} = \frac{8 - 1}{15} = \frac{7}{15}$$

(b) $\quad 0.6 = 0.35 + P(B) - 0.25 \quad (\because P(A \cup B) = P(A) + P(B) - P(A \cap B))$

$\Rightarrow \quad 0.6 = 0.10 + P(B)$

$\Rightarrow P(B) = 0.6 - 0.10 = 0.5$

(c) $0.7 = 0.5 + 0.35 - P(A \cap B) \quad (\because P(A \cup B) = P(A) + P(B) - P(A \cap B))$

$0.7 = 0.85 - P(A \cap B) \Rightarrow P(A \cap B) = 0.85 - 0.7 = 0.15$

Question 14 Given $P(A) = \frac{3}{5}$ and $P(B) = \frac{1}{5}$. Find $P(A \text{ or } B)$, if A and B are mutually exclusive events.

◎ *Thinking Process*

(i) If A and B are mutually exclusive then $(A \cap B) = \phi$.

(ii) Use the formula $P(A \cup B) = P(A) + P(B) - P(A \cap B)$.

Sol. Given, $P(A) = \frac{3}{5}$ and $P(B) = \frac{1}{5}$

$\because$ A and B are mutually exclusive events

$$\Rightarrow \quad A \cap B = \phi$$

$$\Rightarrow \quad P(A \cap B) = 0 \qquad [\because P(\phi) = 0]$$

$$\therefore \quad P(A \text{ or } B) = P(A \cup B) = P(A) + P(B) - P(A \cap B)$$

$$= \frac{3}{5} + \frac{1}{5} - 0 = \frac{4}{5}$$

Note $P(A \text{ or } B) = P(A \cup B)$ and $P(A \text{ and } B) = P(A \cap B)$

Question 15 If E and F are events such that $P(E) = \frac{1}{4}$, $P(F) = \frac{1}{2}$ and $P(E \text{ and } F) = \frac{1}{8}$. Find (i) $P(E \text{ or } F)$ (ii) P (not E and not F).

Sol. Given, $P(E) = \frac{1}{4}$, $P(F) = \frac{1}{2}$, $P(E \text{ and } F) = \frac{1}{8}$ *i.e.*, $P(E \cap F) = \frac{1}{8}$.

(i) $P(E \text{ or } F) = P(E \cup F) = P(E) + P(F) - P(E \cap F)$ ($\because A$ or B means $A \cup B$)

$$= \frac{1}{4} + \frac{1}{2} - \frac{1}{8} = \frac{2 + 4 - 1}{8} = \frac{5}{8}$$

(ii) $P(\text{not } E \text{ and not } F)$

$$= P(E' \cap F') \qquad (\because \text{Demorgan's law } E' \cap F' = (E \cup F)')$$

$$= P(E \cup F)' = 1 - P(E \cup F) = 1 - \frac{5}{8} = \frac{3}{8} \quad [\because P(A) + P(A') = 1]$$

Question 16 Events E and F are such that $P(\text{not } E \text{ or not } F) = 0.25$. State whether E and F are mutually exclusive.

Sol. Given, $P(\text{not } E \text{ or not } F) = 0.25$

$$\Rightarrow \quad P(E' \cup F') = P(E \cap F)' =$$

$$(\because \text{Demorgan's law } E' \cup F' = (E \cap F)')$$

$$\because \quad P(E \cap F)' = 1 - P(E \cap F)$$

$$\Rightarrow \quad P(E \cap F) = 1 - P(E \cap F)'$$

$$\therefore \quad P(E \cap F) = 1 - 0.25$$

$$= 0.75 \neq 0$$

Hence, E and F are not mutually exclusive.

Note If A and B are mutually exclusive, then $P(A \cap B) = 0$ as $A \cap B = \phi$.

Question 17 A and B are events such that

$$P(A)=0.42, P(B)=0.48, P(A \text{ and } B)=0.16$$

Determine (i) $P(\text{not } A)$, (ii) $P(\text{not } B)$ and (iii) $P(A \text{ or } B)$.

◎ **Thinking Process** Use $P(A \cup B) = P(A) + P(B) - P(A \cap B)$ and simplify it.

Sol. Given, $P(A) = 0.42, P(B) = 0.48$

$P(A \text{ and } B) = P(A \cap B) = 0.16$ $[\because P(A \cup B) = P(A) + P(B) - P(A \cap B)]$

(i) $P(\text{not } A) = P(A') = 1 - P(A)$

(Sum of an event and its complementary event is always 1

$$P(A) + P(A') = 1 = 1 - 0.42 = 0.58$$

(ii) $P(\text{not } B) = P(B') = 1 - P(B)$ $[\because P(B) + P(B') = 1]$

$$= 1 - 0.48 = 0.52$$

(iii) $P(A \text{ or } B) = P(A \cup B)$

$$= P(A) + P(B) - P(A \cap B) = 0.42 + 0.48 - 0.16$$

$$= 0.90 - 0.16 = 0.74$$

Question 18 In class XI of a school, 40% of the students study Mathematics and 30% study Biology. 10% of the class study both Mathematics and Biology. If a student is selected at random from the class, find the probability that he will be studying Mathematics or Biology.

◎ **Thinking Process** Use $P(A \cup B) = P(A) + P(B) - P(A \cap B)$ and simplify it.

Sol. Let M and B denote the students of Mathematics and Biology.

Given, $P(M) = 40\%, P(B) = 30\%, P(M \cap B) = 10\%$

($\because$ 10% of the class study both subjects *i.e.*, they are common in both subjects)

$\therefore P(M \text{ or } B) = P(M \cup B)$

$$= P(M) + P(B) - P(M \cap B) = \frac{40}{100} + \frac{30}{100} - \frac{10}{100}$$

$$= \frac{60}{100} = 60\% = 0.6$$

Question 19 In an entrance test that is graded on the basis of two examinations, the probability of a randomly chosen student passing the first examination is 0.8 and the probability of passing the second examination is 0.7. The probability of passing atleast one of them is 0.95. What is the probability of passing both?

◎ **Thinking Process** (Q.No. 19-21) Probability of passing atleast A and B,

$$P(A \cup B) = P(A) + P(B) - P(A \cap B)$$

Sol. Here, $P(\text{I}) = 0.8$, $P(\text{II}) = 0.7$

P(atleast one of I and II) $= P(\text{I} \cup \text{II}) = 0.95$

Now, $P(\text{I} \cup \text{II}) = P(\text{I}) + P(\text{II}) - P(\text{I} \cap \text{II})$

$\therefore \quad 0.95 = 0.8 + 0.7 - P(\text{I} \cap \text{II})$

$\Rightarrow \quad 0.95 = 1.5 - P(\text{I} \cap \text{II}) \Rightarrow P(\text{I} \cap \text{II}) = 1.5 - 0.95 = 0.55$

Mistake Alert Students misunderstand the probability of passing atleast one exam $P(A \cup B)$ and treating it as a simple addition of probabilities.

Question 20 The probability that a student will pass the final examination in both English and Hindi 0.5 and the probability of passing neither is 0.1. If the probability of passing the English examination is 0.75. What is the probability of passing the Hindi examination?

Sol. Let H and E denote the students passing in Hindi and English examination.

Here, $P(H \cap E) = 0.5$ (Given)

$P(H' \cap E') = P(H \cup E)' = 0.1$ [$\because$ De morgan's law $(A \cup B)' = A' \cap B'$]

(The probability of passing in both English and Hindi is $P(H \cap E)$, then probability of passing neither will be $P(H \cup E)'$ because it is complementary to 1st event)

$\therefore \quad P(H \cup E) = 1 - P(H \cup E)' = 1 - 0.1 = 0.9$ [$\because P(A) = 1 - P(A)'$]

Also, $P(E) = 0.75$

$\because \quad P(H \cup E) = P(H) + P(E) - P(H \cap E)$

$\Rightarrow \quad 0.9 = P(H) + 0.75 - 0.5 \Rightarrow 0.9 = P(H) + 0.25$

$\Rightarrow \quad P(H) = 0.9 - 0.25 = 0.65$

Question 21 In a class of 60 students, 30 opted for NCC, 32 opted for NSS and 24 opted for both NCC and NSS. If one of these students is selected at random, find the probability that

(i) The student opted for NCC or NSS.

(ii) The student has opted for neither NCC nor NSS.

(iii) The student has opted NSS but not NCC.

Sol. (i) Let A and B denote the students in NCC and NSS respectively.

Here, $n(A) = 30$, $n(B) = 32$, $n(A \cap B) = 24$

[$\because$ 24 students opted for both NCC and NSS *i.e.*, they are common in both]

$$\therefore \quad P(A) = \frac{30}{60}$$

$$P(B) = \frac{32}{60}$$

$$\text{and} \quad P(A \cap B) = \frac{24}{60}$$

P (Student opted for NCC or NSS)

$P(A \cup B) = P(A) + P(B) - P(A \cap B)$ $[\because P(A \cup B) = P(A \quad B)]$

$= \frac{30}{60} + \frac{32}{60} - \frac{24}{60}$

$= \frac{30 + 32 - 24}{60} = \frac{62 - 24}{60} = \frac{38}{60} = \frac{19}{30}$

(ii) P (Student has opted neither NCC nor NSS) *i.e.*, $P(A' \cap B')$

$P(A \cup B)' = 1 - P$ (Student opted for NCC or NSS)

$= 1 - P(A \cup B)$ $[\because A' \cap B' = (A \cup B)']$

$= 1 - \frac{19}{30} = \frac{30 - 19}{30} = \frac{11}{30}$

(iii) P (The student has opted NSS but not NCC) *i.e.*, $P(B \cap A')$

$= P(B) - P(A \cap B) = \frac{32}{60} - \frac{24}{60} = \frac{8}{60} = \frac{2}{15}$

Miscellaneous Exercise

Question 1 A box contain 10 red marbles, 20 blue marbles and 30 green marbles. 5 marbles are drawn from the box. What is the probability that

(i) all will be blue?

(ii) atleast one will be green?

Thinking Process Using the relation, from n distinct objects r objects can be related in

$${}^nC_r = \frac{n!}{r!(n-r)!} \text{ ways.}$$

Sol. Given, 10 Red marbles

20 Blue marbles

and 30 Green marbles

Total number of ways selecting 5 marbles out of 60 marbles $= {}^{60}C_5$

(i) If E be the event all marbles will be blue, then

$$n(E) = {}^{20}C_5$$

$\therefore$ Required probability $= \frac{{}^{20}C_5}{{}^{60}C_5}$

(ii) P (atleast one will be green) $= 1 - P(\text{No green}) = 1 - \frac{{}^{30}C_5}{{}^{60}C_5}$

$(\because 10R + 20B = 30)$

Question 2 4 cards are drawn from a well-shuffled deck of 52 cards. What is the probability of obtaining 3 diamonds and one spade?

Sol. In a deck of cards,

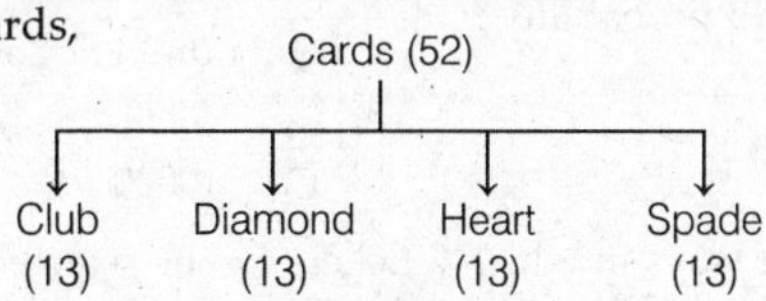

Total number of ways selecting 4 cards out of 52 cards = ${}^{52}C_4$

If E be the event obtaining 3 diamonds and one spade, thenn $(E) = {}^{13}C_3 \times {}^{13}C_1$

$$\therefore \quad \text{Required probability} = \frac{{}^{13}C_3 \times {}^{13}C_1}{{}^{52}C_4}$$

Question 3 A die has two faces each with number 1, three faces each with number 2 and one face with number 3. If die is rolled once, determine (i) $P(2)$ (ii) $P(1 \text{ or } 3)$ (iii) $P(\text{not } 3)$.

Sol. (i) If E be the event getting a number 2, then $n(E) = 3$

($\because$ There are three faces each with number 2)

$$\therefore \text{ Probability of getting } P = \frac{\text{Number of favourable outcomes}}{\text{Total number of outcomes}}$$

$$= \frac{n(E)}{n(S)} = \frac{3}{6} = \frac{1}{2}$$

(In case of die total number of outcomes is 6.)

(ii) If E be the event getting a number 1 or 3, then $n(E) = 2 + 1 = 3$

(there are two faces each with number 1 and one face with number 2)

$$\therefore \text{ Probability of getting 1 or 3} = \frac{n(E)}{n(S)} = \frac{3}{6} = \frac{1}{2}$$

(iii) If E be the event getting a number not 3, then $n(E) = 2 + 3 = 5$

(not 3 means there will be the number on die other than 3 *i.e.,* 1 and 2. There are two faces with number 1 and three faces with number 2.)

$$\therefore \text{ Probability of getting (not 3) } P = \frac{n(E)}{n(S)} = \frac{5}{6}$$

Question 4 In a certain lottery 10000 tickets are sold and ten equal prizes are awarded. What is the probability of not getting a prize if you buy (*a*) one ticket (*b*) two tickets (*c*) 10 tickets.

◎ ***Thinking Process*** (Q.No. 4-5) Using the relation, from n distinct objects r objects can be selected in ${}^nC_r$ ways.

Sol.

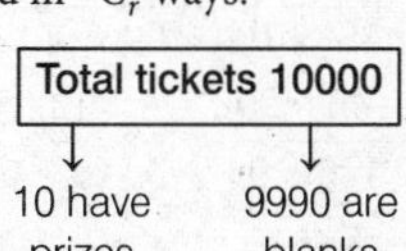

(i) 1 ticket out of 10000 ticket can be selected in = ${}^{10000}C_1$ ways.

Number of ways in which 1 ticket without prize is obtained = ${}^{9990}C_1$

$\therefore$ Required probability $P = \dfrac{\text{Number of favourable outcomes}}{\text{Total number of outcomes}}$

$$= \frac{{}^{9990}C_1}{{}^{10000}C_1} = \frac{9990}{10000} \quad (\because {}^nC_1 = n) = \frac{999}{1000}$$

(ii) Number of ways in which 2 tickets can be selected out of 10000 tickets = ${}^{10000}C_2$

Number of ways in which 2 tickets without prizes can be selected out of 9990 tickets = ${}^{9990}C_2$

$\therefore$ Required probability $= \dfrac{{}^{9990}C_2}{{}^{10000}C_2}$

(iii) Number of ways in which 10 tickets can be selected out of 10000 tickets = ${}^{10000}C_{10}$

Number of ways in which 10 tickets without prizes can be selected out of 9990 tickets = ${}^{9990}C_{10}$

$\therefore$ Required probability $= \dfrac{{}^{9990}C_{10}}{{}^{10000}C_{10}}$

Question 5 Out of 100 students, two sections of 40 and 60 are formed. If you and your friend are among the 100 students, what is the probability that

(a) you both enter the same section?

(b) you both enter the different sections?

Sol. Let the two sections have A and B are of 40 and 60 students respectively.

(a) **When both enter the same section**

There are two cases,

(I) Either both are in section A or (II) Either both are in section B.

Case I If both are in section A, then 40 students out of 100 students can be selected = ${}^{100}C_{40}$ ways

And 38 students can be selected out of 98 students = ${}^{98}C_{38}$ ways

$\therefore$ Probability

$$P = \frac{{}^{98}C_{38}}{{}^{100}C_{40}} = \frac{98!}{38!\,60!} \times \frac{40!\,60!}{100!} \quad \left(\because {}^nC_r = \frac{n!}{r!(n-r)!}\right)$$

$$= \frac{98! \times 40 \times 39 \times 38!}{38! \times 100 \times 99 \times 98!} \quad [\because n! = n\,(n-1)!]$$

$$= \frac{40 \times 39}{100 \times 99} = \frac{2}{5} \times \frac{13}{33} = \frac{26}{165} \quad \ldots\text{(i)}$$

Case II If both are in section B. Then, 60 students out of 100 students can be selected $= {}^{100}C_{60}$ ways

58 students out of 98 students can be selected $= {}^{98}C_{58}$

$$\therefore \text{Required probability} = \frac{{}^{98}C_{58}}{{}^{100}C_{60}} = \frac{98!}{58!\,40!} \times \frac{60!\,40!}{100!}$$

$$= \frac{98! \times 60 \times 59 \times 58! \times 40!}{58! \times 40! \times 100 \times 99 \times 98!}$$

$$= \frac{60 \times 59}{100 \times 99} = \frac{3}{5} \times \frac{59}{99} = \frac{59}{5 \times 33} = \frac{59}{165} \quad \text{...(ii)}$$

Hence, required probability that students are either in section A or B

$$= \frac{26}{165} + \frac{59}{165} \text{ (from Eqs. (i) and (ii))} = \frac{85}{165} = \frac{17}{33}$$

(b) The probability that both enter the different section

$$= 1 - \text{Probability that they both enter the same section} = 1 - \frac{17}{33} = \frac{16}{33}$$

Question 6 Three letters are dictated to three persons and an envelope is addressed to each of them, the letters are inserted into the envelopes at random, so that each envelope contains exactly one letter. Find the probability that at least one letter is in its proper envelope.

Sol. Let the envelope be denoted by E_1, E_2, E_3 and the corresponding letters by L_1, L_2, L_3. 1 letter in correct envelope and 2 in wrong envelope may be put as

$$(E_1L_1, E_2L_3, E_3L_2), (E_1L_3, E_2L_2, E_3L_1) \text{ and } (E_1L_2, E_2L_1, E_3L_3).$$

Two letters or consequently all the letters are in correct envelope may be put in one way *i.e.*, (E_1L_1, E_2L_2, E_3L_3)

$\therefore$ Number of cases $= 3! = 6$

Number of favourable cases $= 4$

Probability that atleast one letter in its proper envelope $= \frac{4}{6} = \frac{2}{3}$

Question 7 A and B are two events such that

$$P(A) = 0.54,\ P(B) = 0.69 \text{ and } P(A \cap B) = 0.35$$

Find (i) $P(A \cup B)$ (ii) $P(A' \cap B')$ (iii) $P(A \cap B')$ (iv) $P(B \cap A')$

Thinking Process Using the relation,

(a) $P(A \cup B) = P(A) + P(B) - P(A \cap B)$

(b) $P(A' \cap B') = P(A \cup B)' = 1 - P(A \cup B)$

(c) $P(A \cap B') = P(A) - P(A \cap B)$.

Sol. (i) $P(A \cup B) = P(A) + P(B) - P(A \cap B)$

$$= 0.54 + 0.69 - 0.35 = 1.23 - 0.35 = 0.88$$

$[\because \text{De-morgen's law } A' \cap B' = (A \cup B)']$

(ii) $P(A' \cap B') = P(A \cup B)' = 1 - P(A \cup B) = 1 - 0.88 = 0.12$

(iii) $P(A \cap B') = P(A \text{ only}) = P(A) - P(A \cap B) = 0.54 - 0.35 = 0.19$

(iv) $P(B \cap A') = P(B \text{ only})$

$$= P(B) - P(B \cap A)$$

$$= 0.69 - 0.35 = 0.34$$

Question 8 From the employees of a company, 5 persons are selected to represent them in managing committee of the company. Particulars of five persons are as follows

S.No.	Name	Sex	Age (in years)
1.	Harish	M	30
2.	Rohan	M	33
3.	Sheetal	F	46
4.	Alis	F	28
5.	Salim	M	41

A person is selected at random from this group to act as a spokes-person. What is the probability that the spokes-person will be either male or over 35 years?

◎ ***Thinking Process*** The selected person is either A or B is $P(A \cup B) = P(A) + P(B) - P(A \cap B)$ and simplify it.

Sol. Let A be the event that selected person is male or B be the event that selected person is over 35 year

$\therefore$ Required probability $P(A) = \frac{^3C_1}{^5C_1} = \frac{3}{5}$ and $P(B) = \frac{^2C_1}{^5C_1} = \frac{2}{5}$ $[\because {^nC_1} = n]$

$$\therefore \quad P(A \cup B) = P(A) + P(B) - P(A \cap B) = \frac{3}{5} + \frac{2}{5} - \frac{1}{5} = \frac{5}{5} - \frac{1}{5} = \frac{4}{5}$$

Question 9 If four digit numbers greater than 5000 are randomly formed from the digits 0, 1, 3, 5 and 7, what is the probability of forming number divisible by 5 when

(i) the digits are repeated ?

(ii) the repetition of digits is not allowed ?

◎ ***Thinking Process*** A number is divisible by 5 when unit place is zero or five.

Sol. **Case I When digits are repeated.**

Total four digit numbers which are greater than 5000 from the digits 0, 1, 3, 5, 7 *i.e.*, In thousand's place, the number will be 5 or 7 and rest of three places any five numbers will come

$$\boxed{5}\ \underline{5} \times \underline{5} \times \underline{5} = 125$$

$$\boxed{7}\ \underline{5} \times \underline{5} \times \underline{5} = 125$$

$\therefore$ Total four digit number, $n(S) = 125 + 125 = 250$

Total four digit numbers which are divisible by 5.

i.e., In unit place, number will be 0 or 5 and thousand's place, the number will be 5 to 7. And rest of the two places any five number will be come.

$\boxed{5}\ \underline{5} \times \underline{5}\ \boxed{0} = 25$

$\boxed{0}\ \underline{5} \times \underline{5}\ \boxed{5} = 25$

$\boxed{5}\ \underline{5} \times \underline{5}\ \boxed{5} = 25$

$\boxed{7}\ \underline{5} \times \underline{5}\ \boxed{5} = 25$

Number of favourable cases, $n(E) = 25 + 25 + 25 + 25 = 100$

$\therefore$ Required probability $= \dfrac{n(E)}{n(S)} = \dfrac{100}{250} = \dfrac{2}{5}$

Case II When digits are not repeated.

Total four digit numbers which are greater than 5000 from the digits 0, 1, 3, 7, 5 *i.e.*, In thousand's place, the number will be 5 or 7. Since, the digit are not repeated, then rest of the place may be filled by 4, 3, 2.

$\boxed{5}\ \underline{4} \times \underline{3} \times \underline{2} = 24$

$\boxed{7}\ \underline{4} \times \underline{3} \times \underline{2} = 24$

Total four digit number $n(S) = 24 + 24 = 48$

Total four digit numbers which are divisible by 5

$\boxed{5}\ \underline{3} \times \underline{2}\ \boxed{0} = 6$

$\boxed{7}\ \underline{3} \times \underline{2}\ \boxed{0} = 6$

$\boxed{7}\ \underline{3} \times \underline{2}\ \boxed{5} = 6$

Favourable number of cases $n(E) = 6 + 6 + 6 = 18$

$\therefore$ Required probability $= \dfrac{18}{48} = \dfrac{3}{8}$

Question 10 The number lock of a suitcase has four wheels, each labelled with 10 digits *i.e.* from 0 to 9. The lock opens with a sequence of four digits with no repeats. What is the probability of a person getting the right sequence to open the suitcase?

Sol. Since, repetition is not allowed.

So, first place can be filled in 10 ways

Second place can be filled in 9 ways

Third place can be filled in 8 ways

and fourth place can be filled in 7 ways.

Hence, by fundamental principle of counting, total number of ways

$$= 10 \times 9 \times 8 \times 7 = 5040$$

In which only 1 sequence can open the lock.

$\therefore$ Number of favourable cases = 1

$\therefore$ Required probability $= \dfrac{1}{5040}$

DIKSHA APP Questions

☐ Multiple Choice Questions

Q.1 If $P(A)$ is $\frac{3}{5}$. Find P (not A)

(a) $\frac{2}{5}$ (b) $\frac{1}{5}$ (c) $\frac{3}{5}$ (d) $\frac{4}{5}$

Sol. (a) $\because P\text{(not } A) = P(A') = 1 - P(A)$

$$\Rightarrow \quad P\text{(not } A) = 1 - \frac{3}{5} = \frac{2}{5} \qquad \left[\because P(A) = \frac{3}{5}\right]$$

Q.2 A coin is tossed twice, what is the probability that atleast one tail occurs?

(a) $\frac{1}{2}$ (b) $\frac{1}{4}$ (c) $\frac{2}{3}$ (d) $\frac{3}{4}$

Sol. (d) When a coin a tossed twice it' is the same as tossing two coins together. So, the total outcomes are {*HH, HT, TH, TT*}.

Thus, getting atleast one tail is an event which has the probability $\frac{3}{4}$.

Q.3 One card is drawn from a well-shuffled pack of 52 cards. What is the probability that a card will be a diamond?

(a) $\frac{1}{4}$ (b) $\frac{4}{13}$ (c) $\frac{1}{52}$ (d) $\frac{2}{13}$

Sol. (a) The number of possible outcome is 52. Let A be the event 'the card drawn is a diamond'.

$\therefore$ The number of events in A in 13. ($\because$ number of diamond card = 13)

$$\therefore \quad P\text{(diamond card)} = \frac{13}{52} = \frac{1}{4}$$

Q.4 A die is thrown, find the probability of following events, a prime number will appear.

(a) $\frac{1}{2}$ (b) $\frac{1}{6}$ (c) $\frac{2}{3}$ (d) $\frac{1}{5}$

Sol. (a) Sample space of a experiment in throwing a dice

$$S = \{1, 2, 3, 4, 5, 6\} \Rightarrow n(S) = 6$$

Let A be prime numbers $A = \{2, 3, 5\} \Rightarrow n(A) = 3$

Hence, probability of a prime number appearing $= \frac{n(A)}{n(S)} = \frac{3}{6} = \frac{1}{2}$